INDEX TO BRITISH
LITERARY BIBLIOGRAPHY

IX

BRITISH LITERARY BIBLIOGRAPHY, 1980-1989
A BIBLIOGRAPHY
(AUTHORS)

T.H. HOWARD-HILL

CLARENDON PRESS · OXFORD
1999

Oxford University Press, Great Clarendon Street, Oxford OX2 6DP

Oxford   New York

Athens   Auckland   Bangkok   Bogotá   Buenos Aires   Calcutta
Cape Town Chennai Dar es Salaam Delhi Florence Hong Kong Istanbul
Karachi   Kuala Lumpur   Madrid   Melbourne   Mexico City   Mumbai
Nairobi   Paris   São Paulo   Singapore   Taipei   Tokyo   Toronto   Warsaw
and associated companies in Berlin Ibadan

Oxford is a registered trade mark of Oxford University Press

Published in the United States
by Oxford University Press Inc., New York

British Library Cataloguing in Publication Data
Data available

Library of Congress Cataloguing in Publication Data
Data available
ISBN 0–19–818643–6
(2-volume set, vols. VIII–IX)

Printed in Great Britain
on acid-free paper by
Biddles Ltd.
Guildford and King's Lynn

TABLE OF ABBREVIATIONS

Aber.   Aberdeenshire
Abr.   Abroad
Abstr   Abstract/s
Acad   Academy/ia
A.D.   Anno Domini
Afric   African
Ag   August
Ala.   Alabama
Am   American
Ann   Annals; Annuals
Angl   Anglia; Anglaises
anr.   another
Antiqu   Antiquarian; Antiquities
Ap   April

Archæol   Archæology/ical
Architect   Architectural
Archiv   Archivists
archbp.   archbishop
Assn   Association/s
Asst   Assistant
attrib.   attributed
Auc   Auction
AUMLA   Australasian Universities'
   Language and Literature Association
Aust.   Australia (Index)
Austral   Australasian
Autogr   Autograph/s
Ayr   Ayrshire

b.   born
BBC   British Broadcasting Corporation
BBLB2   *Bibliography of British Literary
   Bibliographies*, 2d ed., 1987
BBTC   *British Bibliography and Textual
   Criticism*, 1979-80 (19   )
B.C.   British Columbia; Before Christ
Bd.   Bild
Beds.   Bedfordshire
Beibl   Beiblatt
Berks.   Berkshire
Bib   Bibliography/ical
Bibliogr. descr.   bibliographical description
   (Index)
bibliogr/s.   bibliographical/y/ies
Biblioph   Bibliophile/s
Biblioth   Bibliotheck
Bibs.   bibliographies (Index)
Biog   Biography/ical
Bkbndng   Bookbinding

Bkbndr   Bookbinder
Bk/s   Book/s
Bkmkr   Bookmaker
Bkmnls   Bookman/'s
Bksllng. bookselling (Index)
Bksllr Bookseller
BL British Library
BLB 1970-79 *British Literary Bibliography,
   1970-79* (1992)
B.M.   British Museum
Bndng.   bookbinding (Index)
bp.   bishop
Brecon.   Breconshire
Brit   Britain; British
Bucks.   Buckinghamshire
Bull   Bulletin/s

c.   circa (about)
Caith.   Caithness-shire
Calif.   California
Cambs.   Cambridgeshire
card.   cardinal
Cards.   Cardiganshire
Carms.   Carmarthenshire
Carnarvs.   Carnarvonshire
Cath   Catholic
CBEL   *Cambridge Bibliography of English
   Literature*
cent.   century
chapt.   chapter
Ches.   Cheshire
Chron   Chronicle
chronol.   chronological
Circ   Circular
cm.   centimetre/s
co.   County/county; Company
col/s.   coloured; column/s
Coll   Collector/'slion/; College
Collns.   collections (Index)
Coloph   Colophon
Comm   Communicationl/s
Comp   Comparée; Comparative; Com-
   puter/s
comp.   compiled/er/s
Congreg   Congregational
Conn.   Connecticut
Connoiss   Connoisseur
Contemp   Contemporary
contrib/s.   contribution/s
Cornw.   Cornwall

Crit   Criticism/ical
Cumb.   Cumberland
C.U.P.   Cambridge University Press

d.   died
D   December
Denbigh.   Denbighshire
Dept.   Department
Derbys.   Derbyshire
descr/s.   description/s
Devon.   Devonshire
diagr/s.   diagram/s

disp   dispensa
Doc   Documentation
Dumf   Dumfriesshire

Econ   Economic/s
ed.   edited; edition/s; editor/s
Educ   Education/al
Eng   English
Engl   Englishe
enl.   enlarged
Enum   Enumerative
extr.   extract/ed

F   February; folio/s
facsim/s.   facsimile/s
f/ff.   following
Fict   Fiction
Fifes.   Fifeshire
fl.   floruit (flourished)
fold.   folded
Forfars.   Forfarshire
Fortn   Fortnightly

Gaz   Gazette
Gen   General
Gent   Gentleman's
Geogr   Geography/ical
Geol   Geological
Germ   German/ic
Glam.   Glamorganshire
Glos.   Gloucestershire
Graph   Graphic
Grol   Grolier
Guildh   Guildhall

Hants.   Hampshire
Herefs.   Herefordshire
Herts.   Hertfordshire
hft   heft
Hisp   Hispanic

Hist   History/ical
H.M.S.O.   His/Her Majesty's
Stationery Office
Hndbk   Handbook
Hunts.   Huntingdonshire

ib   ibidem (in the same place)
Ill.   Illinois
illus.   illustration/s; illustrated
Illus.   illustration (Index)
Ind.   Indiana
Inst   Institute/ion
Int   International
introd.   introduced/introduction
I.O.W.   Isle of Wight
Ital   Italian

J   Journal
Ja   January
Jahrb   Jahrbuch
Je   June
Jl   July

Keats-Sh   Keats-Shelley

l.   leaf/leaves; line/s
Lanark.   Lanarkshire
Lancs.   Lancashire
Lang   Language/s; Langues
ld.   lord
Leics.   Leicestershire
Let   Letters
Libr/s   Library/ies
Librn   Librarian
Librnshp   Librarianship
Lincs.   Lincolnshire
Lit   Literary; Literature
Litt   Litterature
ltd.   limited

Mag   Magazine
Mar   Mariner's
Mass.   Massachusetts
Med   Medieval; Medicine/al
Merc   Mercury
Merion.   Merionethshire
Midloth.   Midlothian
Mirr   Mirror
Misc   Miscellany
Miss.   Mississippi
M.I.T.   Massachusetts Institute of
Technology
Mkr   Maker

Mnthly   Monthly
Mod   Modern/es
Mons.   Monmouthshire
Mr   March
ms/s.   manuscript/s
Mss.   manuscript/s (Index)
Mus   Music/al; Museum
My   May

N   Note/s; News; November
N&Q   Notes and Queries
Nat   National; Natural
N.C.   North Carolina
NCBEL   *New Cambridge Bibliography of English Literature*
n.d.   no date
Neb.   Nebraska
Neophilol   Neophilologus
Newsl   Newsletter
News-sh   News-sheet
Ninet   Nineteenth
N.J.   New Jersey
no/s.   numbers/s; numero/s, etc.
Norf   Norfolk
Northants.   Northamptonshire
Notebk   Notebook
Notts.   Nottinghamshire
n.p.   no place
nr   Nummer
NSTC   *New Short-Title Catalogue...1475–1640*
Nth   North
Nthmb   Northumberland
N.Y.   New York
N.Z.   New Zealand

Oc   October
Occas   Occasional
O.E.D.   *Oxford English Dictionary*
O.U.P.   Oxford University Press
Oxon.   Oxfordshire

p.   page/s
Pa   Paper/s; Pennsylvania
Pam/s   Pamphlet/s
Paper.   paper and papermaking (index)
Pemb.   Pembrokeshire
Perth.   Perthshire
Philobib   Philobiblon
Philol   Philology/ical
Philos   Philosophy/ical
port/s.   portrait/s
pr.   press

prep.   prepared
Print   Printer/s
Priv   Private
Proc   Proceedings
Prod   Production
pseud.   pseudonym
pt/s.   part/s
ptd.   printed
ptg.   printing
Ptg.   Printing; printing (Index)
ptr/s.   printer/s
publ.   published
Publ.   Publication (Index)
Publ/s   Public; Publication/s; Publisher/s'

Q   Quarterly; quarto/s
quasifacsim.   quasifacsimile

R   Review/s; Revue; Revista
Rec   Record/s
Recus   Recusant
refs.   references
Renaiss   Renaissance
Renfrew.   Renfrewshire
repr/s.   reprint/ed/s
Repub   Republic
Res   Research
Restor   Restoration
rev.   revised
Rev: Review/s
rf.   refer
R.I.   Rhode Island
Roxb.   Roxburghshire
Roy   Royal

S   September
Sat   Saturday
Sci   Science/s
Scot/t   Scotland; Scottish
SD   stagedirection/s
Sec   Section
ser   series
Sevent   Seventeenth
Sh   Shakespeare/'s/ian
Shrop.   Shropshire
sig/s.   signature/s
Signat   Signature
Soc   Society/ies
Som.   Somerset
SP   speechprefix/es
Staffs.   Staffordshire
Statesmn   Statesman

STC	*Short Title Catalogue*	U.P.	University Press
Sth/ly	South/erly		
Stud	Study/ies; Studien	v.	volume/s
Suff.	Suffolk	Va.	Virginia
Suppl	Supplement	Vict	Victorian
Surv	Survey		
		Warws.	Warwickshire
Tech	Technical	Westm.	Westmorland
Text.	text (Index)	Wilts.	Wiltshire
Theat	Theatre/ical	Wk	Work
Theol	Theology/ical	Wkly	Weekly
TLN	Through line number (Shakes-peare)	Worcs.	Worcestershire
TLS	*Times Literary Supplement*	Yorks.	Yorkshire
TP	title-page	Yrs	Year's
trans.	translated/ion/s		
Trans	Transactions	4o	quarto
transcr/s.	transcription/s		
Transit	Transition	8o	octavo
Typogr	Typography/ica/ical		
		12o	duodecimo
Univ	University		

AUTHORS

ABSE, DANNIE, 1923–

4553 **Curtis, Tony**. 'Bibliography [of primary and secondary sources]' *in* Dannie Abse. (Writers of Wales). Cardiff, University of Wales pr. on behalf of the Welsh arts council, 1985. p.155–19.

ACTON, SIR HAROLD MARIO MITCHELL, 1904–

4554 **Ritchie, Neil**. Harold Acton; a bibliography. Florence, 1983. 185p. port., facsims. 20cm. (Ltd. to 500 numbered copies).
Bibliogr. of books and trans. by, contribs. to books by, contribs. to periodicals by, and trans. into Italian of books and contribs. to books by.

4555 **Gretton, John R.** Harold Acton; an aesthete and his books. [Collecting]. Antiqu Bk Mnthly R 13no2:44–7 F '86. illus., port.

ADAMS, RICHARD GEORGE, 1920–

4556 **Watership** down by Richard Adams; an exhibition catalogue to celebrate the tenth anniversary of publication. London, H. Sotheran, [1982]. 41p. illus., port., facsims. 23cm. (Catalogue, 979).

ADDISON, JOSEPH, 1672–1719

4557 **Otten, Robert M.** 'Selected bibliography [of primary and secondary sources]' *in* Joseph Addison. (Twayne's English authors, 338). Boston, [Mass.], Twayne, [1982]. p.172–6.

4558 **Alsop, James D.** New light on Joseph Addison. [Material in Sunderland mss., BL]. Mod Philol 80no1:13–34 Ag '82. table.
'Appendixes. 1. Correspondence by Addison [etc.]' (p.28–34).

4559 **Edwards, Christopher**. Joseph Addison and the authorship of 'The playhouse'. [By him]. R Eng Stud new ser 34no133:21–7 F '83.

Æ, *pseud. of* GEORGE WILLIAM RUSSELL, 1867–1935

4560 **Higdon, D. Leon.** A new manuscript of Æ's 'Salutation'. Eng Lit Transit 30no2:132–9 '87. port.

AKENSIDE, MARK, 1721–70

4561 **Means, James A.** Akenside's Odes on several subjects, 1745. [Defaced device]. (Note 458). Bk Coll 33no3:375–6 '84.

4562 **Dix, Robin**. The composition of Akenside's The pleasures of the imagination, 1772. N&Q 231no4:521–3 D '86.

ALABASTER, WILLIAM, 1567–1640

4563 **Coldeway, John C.** 'William Alabaster's Roxana; some textual considerations' *in* Schoeck, Richard J., *ed.* Act conventus neo-Latini Bononiensis; proceedings of the fourth International congress of neo-Latin studies. Binghamton, N.Y., Medieval & renaissance texts & studies, 1985. p.413–19.

ALDINGTON, RICHARD, 1892–1962

4564 **Kelly, Lionel**, *ed.* 'Richard Aldington, 1892–1962; an exhibition, Department of English, University of Reading, 8–12 July' *in* Richard Aldington; papers from the Reading symposium. [Reading, Dept. of English, University of Reading], [1987]. p.137–53.

4565 **Sims, George F.** Richard Aldington and home, part two. [Publ.]. Antiqu Bk Mnthly R 10no1:4–11 Ja '83. facsims., port.
Repr. in Sims, George. The rare book game. Philadelphia, 1985. p.27–46.

4566 **Woolmer, J. Howard.** Poetry bookshop issues of Richard Aldington and F.S. Flint, and Four seas issues of Aldington and Stephen Vincent Benét. [Information sought]. (Correspondence). Pa Bib Soc Am 81no1:77 '87.

ALLINGHAM, WILLIAM, 1824–89

4567 **Husni, Samira A.** William Allingham; a bibliography. [Beirut], Lebanese establishment for publishing & printing services, [1984]. 103p. 20cm.

AMES, RICHARD, d.1692

4568 **Amory, Hugh**. 'Richard Ames, d.1692; a catalogue' *in* Essays in honor of James Edward Walsh on his sixty-fifth birthday. [Ed. by Hugh Amory and Rodney G. Dennis]. Cambridge, [Mass.], Goethe institute of Boston and the Houghton library, 1983. p.196–220. facsim.
Checklist of 48 'authentic writings', *and* 'Imitations, satires, replies, false or dubious attributions to Ames' (49–66), *with collations, locations of copies, bibliogr. refs. and notes.*

AMIS, KINGSLEY, 1922–

4569 **Gardner, Philip**. 'Selected bibliography [of primary and secondary sources]' *in* Kingsley Amis. ([Twayne's English authors, 319]). Boston, Twayne, [1981]. p.[166]–71.

ANDREWES, BP. LANCELOT, 1555–1626

4570 **McCutcheon, Elizabeth**. Recent studies in Andrewes. (Recent studies in the English renaissance). Eng Lit Renaiss 11no1:96–108 '81.

4571 **Owen, Trevor A.** 'Selected bibliography [of primary and secondary works]' *in* Lancelot Andrewes. (Twayne's English authors, 325). Boston, Twayne, [1981]. p.170–5.

ANSTEY, CHRISTOPHER, 1724–1805

4572 **Doherty, Francis**. Letter of Christopher Anstey to Robert Dodsley. [Publ.]. N&Q 230no2:237 Je '85.

ARBUTHNOT, JOHN, 1667–1835

4573 **Bruneteau, Claude**. John Arbuthnot, The history of John Bull, 1712: bibliographie sélective et commentée. Soc d'Étud Anglo-Am Bull 15:35–42 N '82.

4574 **Todd, Dennis**. New evidence for dr. Arbuthnot's authorship of The rabbit-man-midwife. [1730]. Stud Bib 41:247–67 '88.

ARDEN, JOHN, 1930–

4575 **Page, Malcolm**. 'Selected bibliography [of primary and secondary sources]' *in* John Arden. (Twayne's English authors, 378). Boston, Twayne, [1984]. p.161–8.

4576 —— '5. A select bibliography [of works and ana]' *in* Arden on file. (Writer-files). London, Methuen, [1985]. p.94–105.

ARNOLD, HENRY MALCOLM, 1921–

4577 **Poulton, Alan**. The music of Malcolm Arnold; a catalogue. London, Faber music, [1985]. 224p. illus., ports., music. 21cm.

ARNOLD, MATTHEW, 1822–88

4578 **Neiman, Fraser**. A note on Arnold scholarship.... Arnoldian 8no2:51–61 '81; 9no2:39–48 '82; 10no2:26–33 '83; 11no2:47–54 '84; 12no2:12–19 '85; 13no2:44–52 '86; 14no2:25–33 '87; 15no2:47–55 '88.

4579 **Magoon, Joseph**. A bibliography of the editions of, and writings about, Matthew Arnold's works from 1971 to 1985. [Bournemouth, J. Magoon], [1989]. vii,67p., 8l. 30cm. (Duplicated typescript).

4580 **Nadel, Ira B.** Textual criticism and non-fiction prose; the case of Matthew Arnold. Univ Toronto Q 58no2:263–74 '88/9.

4581 **Brooks, Roger L.** Matthew Arnold and female education in India; an uncollected response. [With text]. (Bibliographical notes). Pa Bib Soc Am 83no1:89–91 Mr '89.

4582 **Super, Robert H.** Matthew Arnold's Literature and dogma, the Cornhill magazine and censorship. N&Q 234no2:287–8 Je '89.

ARTHUR, LEGENDARY KING OF BRITAIN, fl.520

4583 **Reimer, Stephen R.** The Arthurian legends in contemporary English literature, 1945–1981. Bull Bib 38no3:128–38,149 Jl/S '81.

4584 **Pickford, Cedric E.** and **R. Last**, *ed.* The Arthurian bibliography. [Cambridge], D.S. Brewer, [1981–3]. 2v.(xxxiv,820; [xiv],117p.) 23cm. (Arthurian Stud, 3).
   1. Author listing. (1981).–2. Subject index [with corrs. to v.1] (1983).
   Rev: P.J.C. Field Med Ævium 53:138–9 '84; M. Lambert Mod Lang R 80:895 '85.

4585 **Boardman, Phillip C.** Recent Arthurian literature; a contribution towards a bibliography. [Works based on]. Chronica 31:15–24 '82.

4586 **Wildman, Mary**. Twentieth-century Arthurian literature; an annotated bibliography. Arthurian Lit 2:127–62 '82; A supplementary bibliography.... 3:129–36 '83; Additions... 4:172 '85.

4587 **Brewer, Elisabeth**. 'Arthurian literature since 1800; a chronological list' *in* Taylor, Beverly and Elisabeth Brewer. The return of king Arthur. [Cambridge], D.S. Brewer; [Totowa, N.J.], Barnes & Noble, [1983]. p.324–60.

4588 **Coglan, Ronan [and others]**. '6. A supplementary bibliography of twentieth century Arthurian literature' *in* Barker, Richard, *ed.* Arthurian literature III. [Woodbridge], D.S. Brewer; [Totowa, N.J. Barnes & Noble], [1983]. p.129–36.

4589 **Reiss, Edmund, Louise H. Reiss** and **Beverly Taylor**. Arthurian legend and literature; an annotated bibliography: vol. 1, The middle ages. New York, Garland, 1984. xvii,467p. 21cm. (Reference library of the humanities, 415).
Rev. Valerie M. Lagorio Speculum 61:991–2 '86; B.L. Spahr Romance Philol 40:123–6 '86.

4590 **Manchester. University. John Rylands university library.** The Arthurian legend; an exhibition 1985. [Manchester], [1985]. vii,60p. illus. 21cm. (Reprod. from typewriting).

4591 **Goodman, Jennifer**. 'Bibliography [of primary and secondary sources]' *in* The legend of Arthur in British and American literature. (Twayne's English authors, 461). Boston, [Mass.], Twayne, [1988]. p.138–44.

4592 **Hamel, Mary**. The alliterative Morte Arthure, line 3061: the crux idene. Eng Lang N 17no3:170–2 Mr '80.

4593 **The Arthurian** legend; a library exhibition. (Notes and news). John Rylands Univ Libr 68no1:1–7 '85.

ASCHAM, ROGER, 1515–68

4594 **Dees, Jerome S.** Recent studies in Ascham. (Recent studies in the English renaissance). Eng Lit Renaiss 10no2:300–10 '80.

ASHBEE, CHARLES ROBERT, 1863–1942

4595 **Crawford, Alan**. '4. A list of C.R. Ashbee's published writings' *in* C.R. Ashbee, architect, designer & romantic socialist. London; New Haven, Yale U.P., 1985. p.484–6.

ASHBEE, HENRY SPENCER, 1834–1900

4596   **Farrell, Charles.** Henry Spencer Ashbee, bibliographer of 'curious' literature. Am Bk Coll new ser 3n03:43–51 Ap/Je '82.
Classified annotated checklist of books by, pamphlets, articles in serial publs., and biogr. information about.

4597   **Farrell, Charles**. A curious and common man; Henry Spencer Ashbee reconsidered. Am Bk Coll new ser 3n04:2–18 Jl/Ag '82; 3n05:11–23 S/Oc '82. ports.
The man and the biobliographer.–The collector.

AUBREY, JOHN, 1626–97

4598 (5:8320t) **Gunther, Robert W.T.**, *comp.* 'Appendix B: Aubrey's library [donated to Ashmolean museum, Oxford]' *in* Powell, A. John Aubrey and his friends. [New rev. ed.] London, Heinemann, [1963]; New York, Barnes & Noble, [1964]. (First publ. 1948). p.295–310.

AUDEN, WYSTAN HUGH, 1907–73

4599 (7:3255) **Bloomfield, Barry C.** and **E.M. Mendelson**. W.H. Auden; a bibliography, [1972].
Bloomfield's colln. is now in Edinburgh university library.

4600 (7:3256q) **New York. Public library. Berg collection.** W.H. Auden, 1907–1973; an exhibition of manuscripts, books and photographs selected from the Henry W. and Albert A. Berg collection of English and American literature. By Edward Mendelson. [New York], New York public library & Readex books, 1976. [63]p. illus., ports., facsims. 23cm.

4601   **Bloomfield, Barry C.** and **E.M. Mendelson**. Addenda to Bloomfield and Mendelson, W.H. Auden; a bibliography. (Bibliographical notes). Library ser6 4n01:75–9 Mr '82.

4602   **Poger, Sidney**. Berlin and the two versions of W.H. Auden's 'Paid on both sides'. Ariel R Int Eng Lit 17n02:17–30 Ap '86.

4603   **Mendelson, Edward M.** The fading coal vs. the Gothic cathedral, or, what to do about an author both forgetful and deceased. [Revision of New year letter]. Text 3:409–16 '87. diagr.

4604 **Leevers, Joanna**. W.H. Auden's Poems of 1928. Brit Libr J 14n02:203–8 '88. facsims.

4605 **Stewart, James C.Q.** An Auden repudiation. [Text]. N&Q 234n02:204 Je '89.

AUSTEN, JANE, 1775–1817

4606 **Gilson, David J.** A bibliography of Jane Austen. Oxford, Clarendon pr., 1982. (Repr. with corrs. 1985). xxii,877p. facsims. 21cm. (Soho Bibs, 21).

'A note on the typographical identifications' *by* Nicolas Barker.

Bibliogr. of original ed., first Am. ed., trans. of, ed. publ. by Richard Bentley, later ed. and selections, minor works, letters, dramatizations, continuations and completions, books owned by Jane Austen, miscellaneous, and biogr. and criticism; with TP facsims. in place of transcrs., extensive notes on paper, publ., reviews of, copies examined, sale room records, etc.

Rev: J.P.W. Rogers TLS 12 N '82:1242; G.E. Bentley, jr. Library ser6 5:305–8 '83; S. Ives Bk Coll 32: 358–60 '83; B. Roth Stud Novel 15:387–9 '83; G. Watson Essays Crit 33:153–8 '83; B.C. Southam Yrbk Eng Stud 16:293–6 '86; Laura Mooneyham Mod Philol 85:209–11 '87.

4607 **Gilson, David J.** and **J.D. Grey**, *comp.* 'Jane Austen's juvenilia and Lady Susan; an annotated bibliography' *in* Grey, J. David, *ed.* Jane Austen's beginnings; the juvenilia and Lady Susan. Ann Arbor, UMI research pr., [1989]. p.[243]–62.

4608 **Morris, Eileen**. Jane Austen's hidden message to a publisher. [Richard Crosby]. Persuasions 4:16–17 D '82.

4609 **Gilson, David J.** Jane Austen's verses. [Mss. and texts]. Bk Coll 33n01:25–37 '84; Additions and a correction (Note 461) 34n03:384–5 '85.

4610 —— Jane Austen and John Murray. [Proposed reissue, 1831]. (Note 462). Bk Coll 34n04:520–1 '85.

4611 **Garside, Peter D.** Jane Austen and subscription fiction. Brit J Eight Cent Stud 10n02:175–88 '87.

4612 **Gilson, David J.** Jane Austen's handwriting. [Ms. fragments]. (Query 371). Bk Coll 36n02:269–70 '87.

4613 **Le Faye, Deirdre**. Sanditon: Jane Austen's manuscript and her niece's continuation. (Notes). R Eng Stud 38n0149:56–61 F '87.

4614 **Milligan, Ian**. A missing word in Sense and sensibility? [V.2, ch.9]. N&Q 232n04:478 D '87.

4615 **Le Faye, Deirdre**. Jane Austen's verses and lord Stanhope's disappointment. Bk Coll 37no1:86–91 '88.

4616 **Marshall, Mary G**. 'Jane Austen's manuscripts of the juvenilia and Lady Susan; a history and description' *in* Grey, J. David, *ed*. Jane Austen's beginnings; the juvenilia and Lady Susan. Ann Arbor, UMI research pr., [1989]. p.107–21. facsims.

AYCKBOURN, ALAN, 1938–

4617 **Page, Malcolm**. '5. A select bibliography [of primary and secondary sources]' *in* File on Ayckbourn. (Writer-files). [London], Methuen, [1989]. p.93–5.

BACON, FRANCIS, BARON VERULAM AND VISCOUNT ST. ALBANS, 1561–1626

4618 **Sessions, William A**. Recent studies in Francis Bacon. (Recent studies in the English renaissance). Eng Lit Renaiss 17no3:351–71 '87.

4619 **Books** by and about Bacon donated by Lambeth public library, in BL, *see* Gould, Alison, Named special collections, 1981: no.818.

4620 **Kiernan, Michael**, *ed*. 'Textual introduction [including descr. bibliogr.]' *in* The essayes or counsels, civill and morall. Oxford, Clarendon pr., 1985. p.liii–cxviii. table.
  1. The texts and their relationships.–2. The publishing rights to the Essayes.–3. This edition.

4621 **Lohf, Kenneth A**. A manuscript of sir Francis Bacon's state papers and letters. [1595–1621]. Columbia Libr Columns 38no2:30–2 F '89. facsim.

BAGE, ROBERT, 1728–1801

4622 **Moran, Michael G**. Robert Bage, 1728–1801; a bibliography. Bull Bib 38no4:173–8 Oc/D '81.

BAGEHOT, WALTER, 1826–77

4623 **Stevas, Norman St.John-**, *ed*. 'Bibliography. 1. Bagehot's writings. 2. On Bagehot. The Travelers insurance company edition' *in* Miscellany.

(The collected works of Walter Bagehot, 15). London, Economist publs., [1986]. p.387–443.

BALE, BP. JOHN, 1495–1563

4624 **Happé, Peter**. Recent studies in John Bale. (Recent studies in the English renaissance). Eng Lit Renaiss 17no1:103–13 '87.

BALLANTYNE, ROBERT MICHAEL, 1825–94

4625 **Ross, John C.** R.M. Ballantyne's revisions in Black ivory, 1873. Bib Soc Aust & N.Z. Bull 11no3:81–95 '87.

4626 **Crewdson, William H.P.** R.M. Ballantyne. [Collecting]. Antiqu Bk Mnthly R 16no5:174–81 My '89. port.
'A short-title list of the first editions of R.M. Ballantyne' (p.180–1).

BALLARD, JAMES GRAHAM, 1930–

4627 **Pringle, David**. J.G. Ballard; a primary and secondary bibliography. Boston, Mass., G.K. Hall, [1984]. xxxvi,156p. 25cm. (Masters of Sci Fict & Fantasy).
Rev. G.K. Wolfe Sci Fict Stud 12:102–3 '84; T.D. Clareson Extrapolation 25:374 '85.

BANKS, SIR JOSEPH, 1743–1820

4628 **Carter, Harold B.** Sir Joseph Banks, 1743–1820; a guide to biographical and bibliographical sources. Winchester, St. Paul's bibliographies in association with the British museum, Natural history, 1987. 328p. illus., facsims. 23cm.
A. The journals.–B. The correspondence.–C. The other papers.–D. The library.–E. The collections.–F. Personalia.
Rev. J.P.W. Rogers TLS 3 Je '88:603–4.

4629 **Printed** books mainly on natural history or printed in Iceland, formerly in Banks's library; in BL *see* Gould, Alison, Named special collections, 1981: no.818.

4630 **Meynell, Guy**. Banks papers in the Kent archives office, including notebooks by Joseph Banks and Francis Bauer. Archiv Nat Hist 10no1:77–88 Ap '81. facsims.
Bank's journal of his voyage to Scotland and Iceland, 1772.–Bauer's sketchbook of plant pathogens.

BANVILLE, JOHN, 1945–

4631   **Imhof, Rüdiger**. John Banville, a checklist. Irish Univ R 11no1:87–95 '81.
Checklist of works, reviews and interviews, and criticism on.

BARKER, GEORGE, 1913–

4632   **George** Barker b.1913: bibliography. PN R (Manchester) 9no5:65–6 '83.

BARKER, HARLEY GRANVILLE GRANVILLE-, 1877–1946

4633   **Salenius, Elmer W.** 'Selected bibliography [of primary and secondary sources]' *in* Harley Granville-Barker. (Twayne's English authors, 309). Boston, Twayne, [1982]. p.146–61.

4634   **Sims, George F.** Harley Granville Barker. [Collecting]. Antiqu Bk Mnthly R 16no8:292–301 '89. port.

BARNARD, ROBERT, 1936–

4635   **White, William**. Robert Barnard; a first bibliography and a note. Armchair Detective 17no3:295–9 '84.

BARNES, BARNABE, 1569?–1609

4636   **Bawcutt, Nigel W.** Barnabe Barnes's ownership of Machiavelli's Discorsi. N&Q 227no5:411 Oc '82.

BARNES, PETER, 1931–

4637   **Dukore, Bernard F.** The author's play; from Red noses, black death to Red noses. [Revision]. Twent Cent Lit 33no2:159–78 '87.

BARNES, WILLIAM, 1801–86

4638   **Powell, Anne**. William Barnes, 1801–1886; a short life-writ. [Collecting]. Antiqu Bk Mnthly R 13no10:376–85 Oc '86. port., illus., facsims.
'Selected bibliography' (p.385).

BARRIE, SIR JAMES MATTHEW, 1860–1937

4639 **Markgraf, Carl**. J.M. Barrie; an annotated secondary bibliography. [Greensboro, N.C., ELT pr.; Gerrards Cross, Distrib. by C. Smythe], [1989]. xxv,439p. 24cm. (1880–1920 Brit Auth ser, 4).

4640 **Ormond, Leonée**. J.M. Barrie's Mary Rose. [Mss. and typescripts]. Yale Univ Libr Gaz 58no1/2:59–63 Oc '83.

4641 **Macleod, Helen**. J.M. Barrie and Peter Pan. [Collecting]. Bk & Mag Coll 22:12–18 D '85. port., facsims.
'Collectable editions of Peter Pan' (p.18).

4642 **Johnson, Leslie**. A Barrie find. [3 letters, incl. refs. to Red Cross auction, 1918]. Antiqu Bk Mnthly R 16no9:342–4 S '89; G.F. Sims (Letters) 16no11:411 N '89. facsims.

BATES, HERBERT ERNEST, 1905–74

4643 **Vannatta, Dennis**. 'Selected bibliography [of primary and secondary sources]' *in* H.E. Bates. (Twayne's English authors, 358). Boston, Twayne, [1983]. p.139–43.

4644 **Hogg, D.C.** H.E. Bates. [Collecting]. Bk & Mag Coll 9:51–6 N '84. port., facsims.
'H.E. Bates bibliography' (p.55–6).

BATES, RALPH, 1899–

4645 **Munton, Alan** and **A. Young**, 1981: no.700.

BAXTER, RICHARD, 1615–91

4646 **Keeble, N.H.** Some erroneous, doubtful and misleading Baxterian attributions in Wing and Halkett and Laing. N&Q 230no2:187–91 Je '85.

BEARDSLEY, AUBREY VINCENT, 1872–98

4647 **Fletcher, Ian**. 'Select bibliography [of primary and secondary works]' *in* Aubrey Beardsley. (Twayne's English authors, 459). Boston, Twayne, [1987]. p.200–3.

4648   **Salerno, Nicholas A.**, *comp.* 'Part two: An annotated secondary bibliography' *in* Langenfeld, Robert, *ed.* Reconsidering Aubrey Beardsley. (Nineteenth-century studies). Ann Arbor, U.M.I. research pr., [1989]. p.[267]–493.

4649   **Benkovitz, Miriam J.** Aubrey Beardsley; an account of his life. London, H. Hamilton, [1981]. 226p. ports., facsims. 22cm.
No contents page.
Rev: P. Stansky Vict Stud 25:239–42 '82.

4650   **Hobbs, Steven.** Mr. Pollitt's book plate. Bk Coll 36no4:518–30 '87. ports., facsim.

BEAUMONT, FRANCIS, 1584–1616, AND JOHN FLETCHER, 1579–1625

4651   **Bliss, Lee.** 'Selected bibliography [of primary and secondary sources]' *in* Francis Beaumont. (Twayne's English authors, 458). Boston, Twayne, [1987]. p.161–8.

4652   **Turner, Robert K.** Another copy of The maid's tragedy, Q2. [At Univ. of Wisconsin, Milwaukee]. N&Q 225no4:322 Ag '80.

4653   **Hume, Robert D.** The Maid's tragedy and censorship in the restoration theatre. (Brief articles and notes). Philol Q 61no4:484–90 '82.

4654   **Proudfoot, G. Richard.** Francis Beaumont and the hidden princess. [Error in The knight of the burning pestle]. (Bibliographical notes). Library ser6 4no1:47–9 Mr '82.

4655   **Ringler, William A.** The 1640 and 1653 Poems: by Francis Beaumont, gent. and the canon of Beaumont's nondramatic verse. Stud Bib 40:120–40 '87.

4656   **Cronin, Lisa.** A proposed emendation in Beaumont and Fletcher's Philaster. ['once' for Q1 'wants' at 1.2.241]. N&Q 233no1:62–3 Mr '88.

4657   **Hammersmith, James P.** The proof-reading of the Beaumont and Fletcher folio of 1647: introduction. Pa Bib Soc Am 82no1:17–51 Mr '88. tables.

4658   ——— The proof-reading of the Beaumont and Fletcher folio of 1647: section 1 and b. Pa Bib Soc Am 82no2:201–27 Je '88. tables.

4659 —— The proof-reading of the Beaumont and Fletcher folio of 1647: section 2 and A, e, f; section 3 and c. Pa Bib Soc Am 82no3:287–332 S '88. tables.

4660 —— The proof-reading of the Beaumont and Fletcher folio of 1647: sections 4 and 8D–F. Pa Bib Soc Am 82no4:585–94 D '88.

4661 —— The proof-reading of the Beaumont and Fletcher folio of 1647: section 5, *8D, a, and g; section 6 and d. Pa Bib Soc Am 83no1:61–80 Mr '89. tables.

4662 —— The proof-reading of the Beaumont and Fletcher folio of 1647: sections 7 and 8A–C. Pa Bib Soc Am 83no2:187–99 Je '89. tables.

BEAZLEY, SIR JOHN DAVIDSON, 1885–1970

4663 (1:2413m) 'The published writings of sir John Beazley' *in* Oxford. University. Ashmolean museum. Dept. of antiquities. Select exhibition of sir John and lady Beazley's gifts. London, O.U.P., 1967. p.117–88.

BEBB, WILLIAM AMBROSE, 1894–1955

4664 **Griffiths, Rhidian**. Llyfryddiaeh William Ambrose Bebb / William Ambrose Bebb, a bibliography. [Aberystwyth], Cymdeithas Llyfrygell Cymru/Welsh library association, 1982. vii, 23p. 21cm. (Bib ser, 1). (Reprod. from typewriting).

BECKETT, SAMUEL BARCLAY, 1906–89

4665 **Browne, Joseph**. The 'critic' and Samuel Beckett; a bibliographic essay. College Lit 8no3:292–309 '81.

4666 **Mitchell, Breon**. A Beckett bibliography; new works, 1976–1982. Mod Fict Stud 29no1:131–52 '83.

4667 **Lake, Carlton, Linda Eichorn** and **Sally Leach**. No symbols where none intended; a catalogue of books, manuscripts, and other material relating to Samuel Beckett in the collections of the Humanities research center. Austin, Tex., Humanities research center, University of Texas, [1984]. 185p. illus., ports., facsims. 24cm.
Also publ. as Libr Chron Univ Texas new ser 28:1–185 '84.

4668 **[Bishop, Thomas** and **R. Federman]**. 'Bibliographie: seule est recensée l'édition française des œuvres de Samuel Beckett' *in* Samuel Beckett. (Le livre de poche. Biblio essais). [Paris], Cahier de l'Herne, [1985]. p.[215].

4669 **Bangert, Sharon**. The Samuel Beckett collection at Washington university libraries; a guide. [St. Louis], Washington university libraries, 1986. 22p. illus. 28cm.

4670 **Breuer, Rolf, H. Gundel** and **W. Heber**. Beckett criticism in German, a bibliography; Deutsche Beckett-Kritik, Eine Bibliographie; Samuel Beckett, Bibliographie de la critique allemande. München, W. Fink, [1986]. 85p. 22cm. (Reprod. from typewriting).
      Rev: J.C.C. Mays Irish Univ R 16:240–3 '86.

4671 **Zvi, Linda Ben-**. 'Selected bibliography [of primary and secondary sources]' *in* Samuel Beckett. (Twayne's English authors, 423). Boston, Twayne; London, Macmillan, [1986]. p.219–24.

4672 **Andonian, Cathleen C.** Samuel Beckett; a reference guide. Boston, Mass., G.K. Hall, [1989]. xxviii,754p. 23cm. (Reference guide to literature).
      Rev: J.C.C. Mays Irish Univ R 20:380–3 '90.

4673 **Gontarski, Stanley E.** Beckett's voice crying in the wilderness; from 'Kilcool' to Not I. Pa Bib Soc Am 74no1:27–47 '80.

4674 **Smith, Frederick N.** An error in Beckett's How it is. (Bibliographical notes). Pa Bib Soc Am 75no3:353 '81.

4675 **Gontarski, Stanley E.** Texts and pre-texts of Samuel Beckett's Footfalls. (Bibliographical notes). Pa Bib Soc Am 77no2:191–5 '83. table.

4676 —— The intent of undoing in Samuel Beckett's dramatic texts. [Composition and revision]. Bloomington, Ind., Indiana U.P., 1985. xviii,221p. facsims. 23cm.

BECKFORD, WILLIAM, 1759–1844

4677 **Turner, John**. William Beckford of Fonthill. Antiqu Bk Mnthly R 7no11:524–7 N '80. port., facsims.

4678 **Vaisey, David G.** Beckford, Blackwell, Bodley. [Duke of Hamilton's colln. of Beckford papers presented by Blackwells to Bodley]. TLS 14 S '84:1036.

4679 **Rabaiotto, Renato**. Beckford's A dialogue in the shades and Dibdin's The Lincolne nosegay. [And Roxburghe club]. Bk Coll 38no1:210–28 '89. illus.

BEERBOHM, SIR HENRY MAXIMILIAN, 1872–1956

4680 **Riewald, J.G.**, *comp.* 'Sir Max Beerbohm; a bibliographical checklist, 1950–1985' *in* Bakker, J. [and others], *ed.* Essays on English and American literature and a sheaf of poems offered to David Wilkinson.... (Costerus new ser 63). Amsterdam, Rodopi, 1987. p.[192]–222.

4681 **Liebert, Herman W.** Proof corrections in the first edition of Zuleika Dobson. [Bibliographical notes]. Pa Bib Soc Am 76no1:75–7 '82. table, facsim.

4682 **Burgass, John**. Special collections report; the Beerbohm collection at Merton college, Oxford. Eng Lit Transit 27no4:320–2 '84.

4683 **Hall, N. John.** A genre of his own: Max Beerbohm's title-page caricatures. Eng Lit Transit 27no4:270–88 '84. facsims.

4684 **Danson, Lawrence**. Max and mr. McCall. [Proposed The Conquest of the devil, and Ballantyne & co.]. Princeton Univ Libr Chron 47no2:172–88 '86. facsims.

4685 **Lasner, Mark S.** Max Beerbohm. [Materials sought for bibliogr.]. (Query 374). Bk Coll 36no3:410 '87; Bibliography of Max Beerbohm. (Correspondence) Pa Bib Soc Am 81no2:187 '87.

4686 **McCall, Robin H.** and **L. Danson**. Max and mr. McCall revisited; halcyon days at the Ballantyne press. Princeton Univ Libr Chron 49no1:78–86 '87. port., facsim.

BEHAN, BRENDAN, 1923–64

4687 **Mikhail, Edward H.** Brendan Behan; an annotated bibliography of criticism. [London], Macmillan, [1980]. xii,117p. 22cm.
Rev. P. Rafroidi Études irlandaises 6:259 '81; G. O'Brien Yrbk Eng Stud 14:358–60 '84.

BEHN, APHRA   (AMIS), 1640–89

4688 **Cameron, William J.** Seventeenth and eighteenth century editions of the prose works of Aphra Behn; a bibliography in short-title catalog form. [London, Ont., University of Western Ontario], 1982. 19p. 27cm. (WHSTC Bib, 8). Duplicated typescript. (Not seen: ISBN 0–7714–0385–2).

4689   **O'Donnell, Mary A.** Aphra Benn; an annotated bibliography of primary and secondary sources. New York, Garland, 1986. xix,557p. 22cm. (Reference library of the humanities, 505).
Rev: Sharon Valiant Rocky Mountain R Lang & Lit 43:235–6 '89.

BELL, ADRIAN, fl.1930–76

4690   **Musty, John.** Adrian Bell and A.G. Street. (Collecting country authors, 2). Antiqu Bk Mnthly R 11no8:350–5 Ag '84. facsims.
'Checklists of first editions' (p.355).

BELL, CLIVE, 1881–1964

4691   **Laing, Donald A.** Clive Bell; an annotated bibliography of the published writings. New York, Garland, 1983. xvi,154p. 21cm. (Reference library of the humanities, 310).
Classified bibliogr. of books and pamphlets, contribs. to books and pamphlets, with quasifacsim. TP transcrs., collations, bibliogr. notes, and contribs. to periodicals and newspapers.
Rev: Bull Bib 41:172–3 '84.

BELL, GERTRUDE MARGARET LOWTHIAN, 1868–1926

4692   **Macleod, Helen.** Gertrude Bell. [Collecting]. Bk & Mag Coll 7:42–8 S '84. port., illus.
'Complete Gertrude Bell bibliography' (p.48).

4693   **Robinson, G. Charles.** Gertrude Bell? [True to the prince, 1892 not by her]. (Letters). Antiqu Bk Mnthly R 13no1:24–5 Ja '86; Lesley Gordon 13no2:64 F '86.

BELL, VANESSA, 1879–1961

4694   **Ball, Colin F.** Vanessa Bell, 1879–1961; bibliography. [Canterbury], Canterbury college of art, 1983. [11]p. 25cm. (Duplicated typescript).

BELLOC, HILAIRE, 1870–1953

4695   **Markel, Michael H.** 'Selected bibliography [of primary and secondary sources]' *in* Hilaire Belloc. (Twayne's English authors, 347). Boston, Twayne, [1982]. p.163–9.

4696 **Coffman, Ralph J.** The Hilaire Belloc collection at Boston college. Chesterton R 12no2:209–19 My '86. illus.

The acquisition of the collection.–The manuscript archive, Belloc's publications, and the Patrick Cahill archive.–Belloc's working library.

4697 **Markel, Michael H.** The manuscript poetry of Hilaire Belloc. [At Boston college]. Chesterton R 12no2:221–9 My '86.

BENN, SIR ERNEST, 1875–1954

4698 (1:2440y) **Abel, Deryck R.E.** 'Bibliography [of primary and secondary works]' *in* Ernest Benn; counsel for liberty. London, E. Benn, [1960]. p.181–3.

BENNETT, ENOCH ARNOLD, 1867–1931

4699 (5:8514n) **Day, Alan E.** More about Arnold Bennett. [His articles on censorship in circulating and public libraries]. Libr World 68no804:337–8 Je '67.

4700 **Redman, Nicholas.** Arnold Bennett. [Collecting]. Bk & Mag Coll 5:26–35 Jl '84. port., facsims.

'Complete Arnold Bennett bibliography' (p.34–5).

BENSON, EDWARD FREDERICK, 1867–1940

4701 **Dalby, Richard.** E.F. Benson, author of Mapp and Lucia. [Collecting]. Bk & Mag Coll 18:4–13 Ag '85. illus., port., facsims.

'Complete E.F. Benson UK bibliography' (p.12–13).

BENSON, STELLA (MRS. J.C. O'G. ANDERSON), 1892–1933

4702 **Bedell, R. Meredith.** 'Selected bibliography [of primary and secondary sources]' *in* Stella Benson. (Twayne's English authors, 359). Boston, Twayne, [1983]. p.133–8.

BENTHAM, JEREMY, 1748–1832

4703 **Long, Douglas.** The manuscripts of Jeremy Bentham; a chronological index to the collection in the library of University college, London. Comp. for the Bentham committee, University college, London. London, University college library, 1981. a,90p. 29cm. (Duplicated typescript).

4704 **[Ikeda, Sadao, M. Otonashi** and **T. Shigemori].** A bibliographical catalogue of the works of Jeremy Bentham. Tokyo, Chuo university library, [1989]. xi,187p. 22cm.

BERKELEY, BP. GEORGE, 1685–1753

4705 (7:3354c) **Turbayne, Colin M.** and **R. Applebaum**. A bibliography of George Berkeley, 1963–1974. (Notes and discussions). J Hist Philos 15no1:83–95 Ja '77.

4706 **Turbayne, Colin M.**, *ed.* 'A bibliography of George Berkeley, 1963–1979' *in* Berkeley; critical and interpretive essays. Minneapolis, University of Minnesota pr., [1982]. p.313–29.

4707 **Kapstein, Matthew**. 'A bibliography of George Berkeley, 1980–1985' *in* Sosa, Ernest, *ed.* Essays on the philosophy of George Berkeley. ([Synthese historical library]). Dordrecht, D. Reidel, [1987]. p.243–60.

4708 **Benson, Charles J.** The curious case of Berkeley's Alciphron printed in 1755. [Ptg.]. Long Room 28/9:17–27 '84. table, facsims.

4709 **Berman, Jill** and **D. Berman**. Berkeley's Alciphron vignettes. Bk Coll 34no1:55–61 '85. facsims.

BERLIN, SIR ISAIAH, 1909–

4710 (7:3358*) **Hardy, Henry**. A bibliography of Isaiah Berlin. Lycidas (Wolfson college, Oxford) 3:41–5 '75; Additions and corrections 4:42 '76. *Chronological checklist, 1929–75.*

4711 (7:3358*b) ——, *ed.* 'A bibliography of Isaiah Berlin' *in* Against the current; essays on the history of ideas, [by] Isaiah Berlin. London, Hogarth pr., 1979; [New York], Viking pr., 1980. p.356–73. *Chronol. checklist, 1929–80.*

BESANT, SIR WALTER, 1836–1901

4712 **Eliot, Simon**. 'His generation read his stories'; Walter Besant, Chatto and Windus and All sorts and conditions of men. Publ Hist 21:25–67 '87.

4713 —— Unequal partnerships; Besant, Rice and Chatto, 1876–82. Publ Hist 26:73–109 '89. table.

Rice and the reprint deal of 1876.–Chatto extends his interest.–Chatto, Rice and the
later reprints.–Rice's ambivalent position.–Appendix: Chatto & Windus production
record: the main Besant and Rice novels.

BETJEMAN, SIR JOHN, 1906–84

4714 **Denton, Pennie**. An exhibition of works by sir John Betjeman from
the collection of Ray Carter in the Art gallery of St. Paul's school,
February–March MCMLXXXIII.... [Introd. by Philip Larkin]. London, Warren editions, [1983]. [19]p. facsims. 23cm. (Ltd. to 80 and
300 signed copies).

4715 **Brown, Geoffrey**. John Betjeman. [Collecting]. Bk & Mag Coll 15:4–
11 My '85. port., facsims.
'Complete UK bibliography of John Betjeman' (p.10–11).

BISHOP, MORCHARD, *pseud. of* FREDERICK FIELD STONER, 1903–87

4716 **Davis, sir Rupert Hart-**. Morchard Bishop. [Collecting]. Antiqu Bk
Mnthly R 15no2:62–3 F '88. port.
'List of books, etc.' (p.63): *1929–74*.

BLACKMORE, RICHARD DODDRIDGE, 1825–1900

4717 **Born, Anne**. The romantic market gardener. Antiqu Bk Mnthly R
11no12:474–81 D '84; E.R.S. Fifoot (Letters) 12no2:71 '85; H.F.
Janson; Anne Born 12no4:151 '85.

BLACKSTONE, SIR WILLIAM, 1723–80

4718 **Oxford. University. Bodleian library.** Blackstone and Oxford; an
exhibition held at...on the occasion of the bicentenary of sir William Blackstone, 1723–1780. Oxford, Bodleian library, 1980. 43p.
24cm. (Reprod. from typewriting).

BLAIR, HUGH, 1718–1800

4719 **Irvine, James R.** and **G.J. Gravlee**. Hugh Blair; a select bibliography
of manuscripts in Scottish archives. (Bibliographies). Rhetoric Soc
Q 13no1:75–7 '83.

4720   **Read, Dennis M.** Cromek's provincial advertisments for Blake's Grave. N&Q 225no1:73–6 F '80.

4721   **Means, James A.** Blair's The grave; the first edition, 1743. [Two states]. (Note 456). Bk Coll 33no1:99–100 '84.

4722   **Bentley, Gerald E., jr.** Thomas Sivright and the lost designs for Blair's Grave. Blake 19no3:103–6 '85/6.

BLAKE, WILLIAM, 1757–1827

4723 (7:3389) **Bentley, Gerald E., jr.** Blake books, 1977.
Rev: J.E. Grant Philol Q 61:277–304 '84; M. Gassenmaier Anglia 102:254–9 '84.

4724   **Dunbar, Pamela.** 'Appendix: A statistical list of Blake's Milton illustrations (excluding those in the Notebook)' *in* William Blake's illustrations to the poetry of Milton. Oxford, Clarendon pr., 1980. p.[195]–9.

4725   **Essick, Robert N.** 'Appendix I: Blake's political prints of 1793–1794; a catalogue of states and impressions' *in* William Blake, printmaker. Princeton, N.J., Princeton U.P., [1980]. p.[257]–8.

4726   —— Blake in the marketplace, 1978–1979. Blake 14no1:4–21 '80; with T.V. Lange, 1981–1981. 16no2:86–106 '82; 1982–1983. 18no2:68–93 '84; 19no1:24–38 '85; 20no1:12–31 '86; 21no1:4–14 '87; 22no1:4–15 '88; 23no1:4–19 '89. facsims.

4727   **Minnick, Thomas L.** and **D.W. Dörrbecker.** Blake and his circle, a checklist of recent scholarship. Blake 14no2:85–93 '80; with K. Waterai, 15no2:83–93 '81; 16no2:111–24 '82; 17no2:62–76 '83; 18no2:100–15 '84; D.W. Dörrbecker 20no3:76–100 '86/7; 21no2:52–73 '87; 22no2:36–70 '88; 23no3:120–65 '89/90. illus., facsims.
'Corrigenda to previous checklists, 1986–1988' (p.165); *titles vary.*

4728   **Easson, Roger.** 'On building a Blake library [of reference works]' *in* Bogan, James and F. Goss. Sparks of fire; Blake in a new age. Richmond, Calif., North Atlantic books, [1982]. p.426–37.

4729   **Piquet, François.** Blake, Songs of innocence, Songs of experience, The book of Thel, The marriage of heaven and hell, America, Visions of the daughters of Albion, Vala or the four Zoas (nights 2 & 3), The everlasting gospel: bibliographie sélective et critique. Soc d'Étud Anglo-Am Bull 15:43–66 N '82.

4730   **McGill university. McLennan library.** A catalogue of the Lawrence Lande William Blake collection in the Department of rare books and special collections of the McGill university libraries. Montreal, McLennan library, McGill university, 1983. xii,172p. illus., facsims. 25cm. (Ltd. to 500 copies).

4731 **Essick, Robert N.** A supplement to The separate plates of William Blake, a catalogue. [1983]. Blake 17n04:139–44 '84.

4732 **Gu, Jing-you.** Unlisted articles on Blake published in China. (Minute particulars). Blake 17n04:157–9 '84.

4733 **Essick, Robert N.** The works of William Blake in the Huntington collections; a complete catalogue. [San Marino, Calif.], Huntington library, art collections, botanical gardens, [1985]. xviii,256p. facsims. 24cm.
Rev: P. Malekin R Eng Stud new ser 40:575 '89.

4734 **Jordan, Frank,** *ed.,* 1985: no.4375.

4735 **Cambridge. University. Fitzwilliam museum.** William Blake and his contemporaries; a loan exhibition in aid of the Friends of the Fitzwilliam museum. Cambridge, Fitzwilliam enterprises, [1986]. 112p. facsims. 22cm.
Rev: D.J. McKitterick Bk Coll 36:305–6 '87.

4736 **Bryant, Barbara,** *comp.* 'The Job designs; a documentary and bibliographical record' *in* Bindman, David, *ed.* William Blake's illustrations of the Book of Job.... London, William Blake trust, 1987. p.103–47. facsim.

4737 **Essick, Robert N.** 'Blake's engravings to the Book of Job: Catalogue of states and printings' *in* Bindman, David, *ed.* William Blake's illustrations of the Book of Job.... London, William Blake trust, 1987. p.49–101. facsims.

4738 **Bentley, Gerald E., jr.** Blake records supplement; being new materials relating to the life of William Blake discovered since the publication of Blake records (1969). Oxford, Clarendon pr., 1988. xlviii,152p. port., facsims., tables. 22cm.
See BBLB2: 2488b.
Rev: L.M. Findlay N&Q 334:520–1 '89.

4739 —— Trade cards and the Blake connection. [Listed and described]. Bk Coll 37n01:127–33 '88.
William Staden Blake.–James Parker.–Blakes in the cloth trade.

4740 (5:8637s) **Bentley, Gerald E., jr.** 'William Blake's protean text' *in* Conference on editorial problems, 3d, Toronto, 1967. Editing eighteenth-century texts; papers given.... Ed. by D.I.B. Smith. [Toronto], [1968]. p.44–58.

4741 (5:8644c) **Butlin, Martin**. Blake's illustrations to Paradise lost. Blake Newsl 3no3:57 D '69.

4742 (5:8644d) ——— 'The evolution of Blake's large color prints of 1795' *in* Rosenfeld, Alvin H., *ed*. William Blake; essays for S. Foster Damon. Providence, Brown U.P., 1969. p.[109]–16.

4743 (5:8644e) **Erdman, David V.** 'A temporary report on texts of Blake' *in* Rosenfeld, Alvin H., *ed*. William Blake; essays for S. Foster Damon. Providence, Brown U.P., 1969. p.[395]–413.

4744 (5:8644f) **Keynes, sir Geoffrey L.** 'The William Blake trust' *in* Rosenfeld, Alvin H., *ed*. William Blake; essays for S. Foster Damon. Providence, Brown U.P., 1969. p.414–20.

4745 **Bentley, Gerald E., jr.** 'The great illustrated-book publishers of the 1790's and William Blake' *in* Conference on editorial problems, 15th, Toronto, 1979. Editing illustrated books; papers given.... Ed. by William Blissett. New York, 1980. p.[57]–96.

4746 **Carr, Stephen L.** William Blake's print-making process in Jerusalem. Eng Lit Hist 47no3:520–41 '80. facsims.

4747 **Deck, Raymond H.** Blake's Poetical sketches finally arrive in America. [Publ. in Harbinger]. (Notes). R Eng Stud new ser 31no122:183–92 My '80.

4748 **Essick, Robert N.** William Blake, printmaker. Princeton, N.J., Princeton U.P., [1980]. xxii,283p. + 236 facsims. [=428p.] facsims. 28cm.
Part one: Connoisseur and apprentice, 1768–1779. 1. The young collector.–2. Etching and engraving.–3. The young antiquarian.–4. Lessons from Basire.–Part two: Artist and craftsman, 1780–1800. 5. Historical ambitions.–6. Book illustration.–7. Decorative prints and portraits.–8. Original intaglio graphics.–Part three: Graphic experiments, 1788–1822. 9. Relief and white-line etching.–10. Relief and surface colouring.–11. The illuminated books and separate relief prints.–Part four: Prints, patronage, and poetry, 1800–1818. 12. Hayley and commercial plates.–13. Original intaglio graphics, new and revised.–14. The Public address.–15. The printmaker as poet.–Part five: Synthesis and mastery, 1818–182. 16. Linnell.–17. Virgil.–18. Job.–19. Dante.–Afterword.–Appendix I: Blake's political prints of 1793–1794; a catalogue of states and impressions. II. Analysis of Blake's medium in a 1795 color-printed drawing.
Rev: D. Alexander Burlington Mag 123:311–12 '81; M. Mason TLS 13 F '81:169; N. Hilton Eight Cent Stud 17:64–9 '83.

4749 **Grant, John E. [and others]**, *ed*. 'Introduction' *in* William Blake's designs for Edward Young's Night thoughts; a complete edition. Co-ordinating ed. David V. Erdman. Oxford, Clarendon pr., 1980. V.1, p.1–99.

The history of the designs.–The watercolour designs.–The engravings.–Evolution of the designs.–Copies of the engraved work.–Checklist of studies and reproductions (p.72–84).

4750 **Keynes, sir Geoffrey L.** 'Blake's own' copy of Songs of innocence and of experience. Bk Coll 29no2:202–7 '80. facsim.

4751 **Lange, Thomas V.** Blake in American almanacs. Blake 14no2:94–6 '80. facsims.

4752 **Read, Dennis M.** A new Blake engraving; Gilchrist and the Cromek connection. Blake 14:60–4 '80.

4753 **Bentley, Gerald E., jr.** William Blake's techiques of engraving and printing. Stud Bib 34:241–52 '81.

4754 **Butlin, Martin.** A newly discovered watermark and a visionary's way with his dates. [Print dated 1795 on 1804 paper]. (Minute particulars). Blake 18no2:101–3 '81. illus.

4755 **Essick, Robert N.** New information on Blake's illuminated books. Blake 15no1:4–13 '81.

4756 —— Songs copy h. [Acquired]. Blake 15no1:59–60 '81.

4757 **Essick, Robert N.** and **M.C. Young.** Blake's Canterbury print; the posthumous pilgrimage of the copperplate. Blake 15no2:78–82 '81.

4758 **Greenberg, Mark L.** Relentless quest for association copy. [William Bell Scott's annotated Songs]. Am Bkmn's Wkly 68no11:1587–96 S '81.
Repr. in AB Bkmn's Yrbk 1982pt1:105–8 '82.

4759 **Hearn, Michael P.** William Blake's illustrations for children's books. Am Bk Coll new ser 2no2:33–43 Mr/Ap '81. facsims.

4760 **Keynes, sir Geoffrey L.** To the nightingale; perhaps an unrecognised poem by William Blake. [Or G. Cumberland]. Bk Coll 30no3:335–45 '81. facsim.

4761 —— An undescribed copy of Blake's Songs of innocence and of experience. Bk Coll 30no1:39–42 '81. facsim.

4762 **Mann, Paul.** Editing The four zoas. Pacific Coast Philol 16no1:49–56 Je '81.

4763 **Paley, Morton D.** A Victorian Blake facsimile. [Works of William Blake, 1876]. Blake 15no1:24–7 '81.

4764 **Read, Dennis M.** The context of Blake's Public address; Cromek and the Chalcographic society. Philol Q 60no1:69–86 '81.

4765 **Vaughan, Frank A.** Blake's illustrations to Gray's The bard. Colby
Libr Q 17no4:211–37 D '81. facsims.

4766 **Dörrbecker, Detlef W.** Innocence lost & found; an untraced copy
traced. Blake 15no3:125–31 '81/2.

4767 **Bentley, Gerald E., jr.** Ruthven Todd's Blake papers at Leeds. Blake
16no2:72–81 '82.
Ruthven Todd's life.–Ruthven Todd's Blake work.–Catalogue.

4768 **Greenberg, Mark L.** The Rossettis' transcription of Blake's notebook.
Library ser6 4no3:249–72 S '82. facsims.
1. Description of the Rossetti's transcription.–2. Analytical list of poems transcribed
from Blake's notebook.–Rossetti's transcription and the Life of Blake.

4769 **Bentley, Gerald E., jr.** Flaxman's 'Sports of genius': The casket as an
illustrated poem. Harvard Libr Bull 31no3:256–84 '83. facsims.

4770 **De Luca, V.A.** The changing order of plates in Jerusalem, chapter II.
Blake 16no4:192–205 '83. facsims.
The early core of chapter II: a reconstruction.–The rearrangement of sequences in
copies D–E.

4771 **Erdman, David V.** Redefining the texts of Blake (another temporary
report). [List of cruxes]. Blake 17no1:4–15 '83.

4772 **Essick, Robert N.** John Linnell, William Blake, and the printmaker's
craft. Huntington Libr Q 46no1:18–32 '83.

4773 **Gourlay, Alexander S.** An emendation in 'The chimney sweeper' of
Innocence. (Minute particulars). Blake 17no1:16–17 '83. facsim.

4774 **Kelley, Theresa M.** A minute particular in Blake's Songs of innocence,
copy O. (Minute particulars). Blake 17no1:18–19 '83. facsims.

4775 **Lange, Thomas V.** Two forged plates in America, copy B. [In Pierpont Morgan libr.]. Blake 16no4:212–17 '83. facsims.

4776 **Larrissy, Edward.** Blake's America; an early version. N&Q
228no3:217–19 Je '83.

4777 **Viscomi, Joseph.** Facsimile or forgery? An examination of America,
plates 4 and 9, copy B. [In Pierpont Morgan libr.]. Blake 16no4:218–
23 '83. facsims.
Plate measurements.–Plate numbers.–Binding.–The inscription.–Reproductive process used to make plates 4 and 9.–The original prints reproduced.–Conclusion.

4778 **Warner, Janet.** Trade cards of W.S. Blake. [Examples of possible Blake
cards]. (Note 449). Bk Coll 32no1:105–7 '83. facsims.

4779 **Bentley, Gerald E., jr.** The 1821 Edwards catalogue. [Described]. (Minute particulars). Blake 17n04:154–6 '84.

4780 —— Charles Parr Burney as a Blake collector. (Minute particulars). Blake 17n01:16 '84.

4781 **Essick, Robert N.** Some unrecorded states, prints, and impressions of Blake's graphic works. Blake 17n04:130–8 '84. facsims.

4782 **Greenberg, Mark L.** William Michael Rossetti's transcription and William Bell Scott's tracings from Blake's note book. Library ser6 6n03:254–70 S '84. table, facsims.

4783 **Essick, Robert N.** Blake's Job; some unrecorded proofs and their inscriptions. Blake 19n03:96–102 '84/5. facsims

4784 **Grant, John E.** A re-view of some problems in understanding Blake's Night thoughts. [Defense of and responses to revs. of Blake's designs to Young's Night thoughts, 1980]. (Discussion). Blake 18n03:155–81 '84/5; W.J.T. Mitchell, Reply to John Grant 18n03:181–3 '84/5; M.D. Paley, Further thoughts on Night thoughts 18n03:183–4 '84/5; D.W. Dörrbecker, Grant's 'Problems in understanding': some marginalia 18n03:185–90 '84/5. facsims.
   1. On the reproductions in the Clarendon edition.–2. Interpretation.–3. Some engraved copies, with particulars of three engraved designs.

4785 **Bentley, Gerald E., jr.** Keynes and Blake at Cambridge. [His colln. in C.U.L.]. (Minute particulars). Blake 19n02:69–71 '85.

4786 **Essick, Robert N.** The Four zoas; intention and production. Blake 18n04:216–20 '85.

4787 —— William Blake, William Hamilton, and the materials of graphic meaning. [And Thomson's The seasons]. Eng Lit Hist 52n04:833–72 '85. facsims.

4788 **Mann, Paul.** The final state of The four zoas. Blake 18n04:204–15 '85. facsims.

4789 **Viscomi, Joseph.** Recreating Blake's illuminated prints; the facsimiles of the Manchester etching workshop. Blake 19n01:4–23 '85.
   See also R.N. Essick's review, (p.39–51).

4790 **Bentley, Gerald E., jr.** From sketch to text in Blake; the case of The book of Thel. Blake 19n04:128–41 '86. facsims

4791 —— A new America. Blake 20n02:36–44 '86. facsims.

4792 **Essick, Robert N.** '8. How Blake's body means' *in* Hilton, Nelson and T.A. Vogler, *ed.* Unnam'd forms; Blake and textuality. Berkeley, University of California pr., [1986]. p.197–217.

4793 —— Variation, accident, and intention in William Blake's The book of Urizen. Stud Bib 39:230–5 '86. facsim.

4794 **Bindman, David**, *ed.* William Blake's illustrations of the Book of Job; the engravings and related material, with essays, catalogue of states and printings, commentary on the plates and documentary record by David Bindman, Barbara Bryant, Robert Essick, Geoffrey Keynes and Bo Lindberg. London, William Blake trust, 1987. 147p. facsims. 38cm. in slip case, accompanying separate v. of illus. (Ltd. to 387 copies).
Foreword: Charles Ryskamp..–Preface: David Bindman and John Commander.–The development of the Job designs: Geoffrey Keynes.–The Book of Job designs from Butts series to final engravings: David Bindman.–Blake's engravings to the Book of Job: An essay of their graphic form; Catalogue of states and printings: Robert Essick.– The Job designs; a documentary and bibliographical record: Barbara Bryant.
Rev: D.J. McKitterick Bk Coll 36:305–20 '87.

4795 **Ellis, Helen B.** Added and omitted plates in The book of Urizen. Colby Libr Q 23no02:99–107 Je '87.

4796 **McKitterick, David J.** Job and the Blake trust. [Rev. article]. Bk Coll 36no03:305–20 '87.

4797 **Otto, Peter**. Final states, finished forms, and The four zoas. (Discussion). Blake 20no04:144–6 '87.

4798 **Bentley, Gerald E., jr.** Blake's works as performances; intentions and inattentions. Text 4:319–41 '88. facsims., table.
'Appendix: Facsimiles of Blake's coloured works in illuminated printing' (p.338–9).

4799 **Butlin, Martin**. Notes on the Huntington Blakes. (Minute particulars). Blake 22no01:17–18 '88.

4800 **Essick, Robert N.** Dating Blake's 'Enoch' lithograph again. (Minute particular). Blake 22no02:71–3 '88. facsims.

4801 —— The resurrection of America, copy R. Blake 21no04:138–42 '88. facsims.

4802 **Heffernan, James A.W.** 'Text and design in Blake's Songs of innocence and of experience' *in* Möller, Joachim, *ed.* Imagination on a long rein; English literature illustrated. [Marburg], [1988]. p.94–109.

4803 **Read, Dennis M.** The rival Canterbury pilgrims of Blake and Cromek; Herculean figures in the carpet. Mod Philol 86no02:171–90 N '88.

4804 **Bentley, Gerald E., jr.** Blake's seven golden candlesticks and the engraver's craft. [Royal universal family Bible, 1785]. Bib Soc Aust & N.Z. Bull 13no3:86–100 '89. facsims.

4805 **Butlin, Martin**. The physicality of William Blake; the large color prints of '1795'. Huntington Libr Q 52no1:1–17 '89. facsims.

4806 **Hilton, Nelson**. Blake, books, and the press: material vehicles. Stud Voltaire & Eight Cent 264:619–20 '89.

4807 **Taylor, Dena B.** The deterioration of the 1951 Blake trust Jerusalem. [And Trianon pr.]. Blake 23no2:75–8 '89.

4808 **Viscomi, Joseph**. The myth of commissioned illuminated books; George Romney, Isaac D'Israeli, and 'one hundred and sixty designs...of Blake's'. Blake 23no2:48–74 '89. facsims.

BLISS, SIR ARTHUR EDWARD DRUMMOND, 1891–1930

4809 **Foreman, Laurie**. Arthur Bliss; catalogue of the complete works. With an introd. by George Darmatt. [Sevenoaks], Novello, [1980]. 159p. port. 28cm.

4810 [**Easterbrook, Giles** and **Trudy Bliss**]. Supplement to Arthur Bliss; catalogue of the complete works. Sevenoaks, Novello, [1982]. 12p. 26cm. Covertitle.

BLOMEFIELD, FRANCIS, 1705–52

4811 **Stoker, David**. The genesis of Collectanea Cantabrigiensia. Cambridge Bib Soc Trans 9pt4:372–80 '89.

BLOMEFIELD, MILES, 1525–1603

4812 **Baker, Donald C.** Myles Blomefylde's books. (Query 285). Bk Coll 29no1:115–16 '80.

4813 —— and **J.L. Murphy**. Myles Blomefylde, Elizabethan physician, alchemist, and book collector: a sketch of his life. Bodleian Libr Rec 11no1:35–46 N '82.

BLOW, JOHN, 1648–1708

4814 **Shaw, Watkins**. 'The harpsichord music of John Blow; a first catalogue' *in* Neighbour, Oliver W., *ed*. Music and bibliography; essays in honour of Alec Hyatt King. London, [1980]. p.[51]–68. music.

BLUNDEN, EDMUND CHARLES, 1896–1974

4815   **Mallon, Thomas**. 'Selected bibliography [of primary and secondary sources]' *in* Edmund Blunden. (Twayne's English authors, 344). Boston, Twayne, [1983]. p.127–31.

———

4816   **Prance, Claude A.** 'Edmund Blunden and cricket' *in* Essays of a book collector; reminiscences on some old books and their authors. West Cornwall, Conn., 1989. p.141–7.

BLUNT, WILFRED SCAWEN, 1840–1922

4817   **Going, William T.** Blunt's Esther; the making of a sonnet sequence. Vict Poet 20no1:63–72 '82.

BLYTON, ENID MARY, 1897–1968

4818   **Sesemann, Julia**. Enid Blyton; an introduction to collecting the many hundreds of books by the popular children's author. Bk & Mag Coll 4:4–14 Je '84. ports., facsims.
'Bibliography of some collectable Enid Blyton 1st editions' (p.13–14).

BOLINGBROKE, HENRY ST. JOHN, 1ST VISCOUNT, 1678–1751
see SAINT JOHN, HENRY, 1ST VISCOUNT BOLINGBROKE, 1678–1751.

BOLTON, EDMUND, 1575–1635?

4819   **Woolf, Daniel R.** Edmund Bolton, Francis Bacon, and the making of the Hypercritica, 1618–21. Bodleian Libr Rec 11no3:162–8 N '83.

BOND, EDWARD, 1934–

4820   **Hay, Malcolm** and **P. Roberts**. 'Bibliography' *in* Bond; a study of his plays. London, Methuen, [1980]. p.301–15.

4821   **Roberts, Philip**. '5. A select bibliography [of works and ana]' *in* Bond on file. (Writers on file). London, Methuen, [1985]. p.75–80.

BORROW, GEORGE HENRY, 1808–81

4822   **Collie, Michael**. George Borrow; a bibliographical study. [Winchester, Hants.], St. Paul's bibliographies, 1984. 231p. illus., facsims. 22cm. (St. Paul's Bibs, 9). (Ltd. to 750 copies).

Bibliogr. of principal prose works first publ. during Borrow's lifetime, trans. by, anonymously-publ. works associated with Borrow, letters, other pamphlets ptd. for T.J. Wise, other priv. ptd. pamphlets, other John Murray ed., collected ed., publs. in periodicals during Borrow's lifetime, articles containing previously unpubl. Borrow material, 19th cent. trans. of, select checklist of other posthumous publs. of Borrow's writings, checklist of publs. of bibliogr. interest, 1899–1982.
Rev: B. McTigue Am Bk Coll new ser 5:54–5 '84; T.A.J. Burnett TLS 4 Ja '85:23; B. Lake Bk Coll 34:244–6 '85; J.F. Fuggles Library ser6 8:186–7 '86.

4823 **Fraser, sir Angus M.** Some pitfalls in collecting George Borrow. Antiqu Bk Mnthly R 7no10:470–9 Oc '80. ports., illus., facsims.
Bibliographies of George Borrow.–Price levels.–Suspect attributions.–Edition qualities.–Binding and other variants.–Subsequent editions.
'Descriptive list of Borrow's main works' (p.477–9).

4824 **Ridler, Anne M.** Norwich libraries and George Borrow. Libr Hist 6no3:61–71 '83.

BOSWELL, JAMES, 1709–95

4825 (5:8719e) **Waingrow, Marshall**, *ed.* The correspondence and other papers of James Boswell relating to the making of the Life of Boswell. New York, McGraw-Hill; London, Heinemann, [1969]. lxxxv,659p. 23cm. (Yale editions of The private papers of James Boswell; research ed.).
Introduction.–1. The documents.–2. Boswell's research.–3. Boswell's editing.–4. Boswell's Johnson.–Chronology....–Editorial procedures.–....The correspondence.

4826 (7:3484) **Buchanan, David**. The treasure of Auchinleck, [1974].
Rev: D.J. Greene Stud Burke & Time 18:114–27 '77.

4827 **Pottle, Frederick A.** Pride and negligence; the history of the Boswell papers. New York, McGraw-Hill, [1982]. xiv,290p. 23cm. (Yale editions of The private papers of James Boswell).
Prologue.–1. Puzzles at the outset.–2. Johnson's portrait leaves Auchinleck.–3. 'To that request the editor has never received any answer.'–4. 'It is believed the whole were immediately destroyed'.–5. Tinker goes to Malahide.–6. Isham goes to Malahide.–7. Geoffrey Scott gets off to a brilliant start.–8. The croquet-box.–9. 'Times 9 March announces discovery Scotland many missing Boswell papers'.–10. 'Operation hush'.–11. The Fettercairn cause.–12. The stable-loft.–13. The advent of Donald Hyde.–14. Yale buys the Boswell papers.–Epilogue I: Yale's acquisition of papers since 1950. II. History of the publication of the Boswell papers.
Rev: J.A. Vance Sth Atlantic Bull 48:82–5 '83; F.V. Bogel Stud Scott Lit 20:294–8 '85.

4828 **Hillyard, Brian P.** Boswell's Account of Corsica. [Distinction of variants]. (Features). Factotum 18:16–18 Mr '84; Addenda and corrigenda 19:4 Oc '84.

4829 **Hook, David**. Mr. Boswell's books and the Inquisition. [British essays in favour of the brave Corsicans]. (Bibliographical notes). Library ser6 8no3:265–8 S '86.

BOWEN, ELIZABETH DOROTHEA COLE (MRS. A.C. CAMERON), 1899–1973

4830   **Texas. University at Austin. Harry Ransom humanities center.** Elizabeth Bowen; a bibliography. Comp. by J'nan M. Sellery and W.O. Harris. Austin, Tex., [1981]. 359p. port. 23cm.

Bibliogr. of books and pamphlets, contribs. to books, pamphlets and periodicals, trans. of, mss., radio and TV productions and appearances, anthologies, and writings about.

BOYER, ABEL, 1667–1729

4831   **Sill, Geoffrey M.** Abel Boyer's Essay towards the history; an echo not a choice. (Bibliographical notes). Pa Bib Soc Am 75no3:321–5 '81; H.L. Snyder; G.M. Sill (Correspondence) 76no3:351–2 '82.

BOYLE, ROBERT, 1627–91

4832   **Stewart, M.A.** The authenticity of Robert Boyle's anonymous writings on reason. [Discourse of things; Some advices, 1681]. Bodleian Libr Rec 10no5:280–9 Ag '81.

BRADDON, MARY ELIZABETH (MRS. JOHN MAWELL), 1837–1915

4833   **Edwards, Peter D.** M.E. Braddon manuscripts in Australia. N&Q 233no3:326–8 S '88.

BRAINE, JOHN, 1922–

4834   **Salwak, Dale.** John Braine and John Wain; a reference guide. Boston, Mass., G.K. Hall, [1980]. xiv,195p. 24cm. (Reference guide to literature).

Rev: R.F. Kiernan Lit Res Newsl 6:124–6 '81.

BRAMAH, Ernest, *pseud. of* ERNEST BRAMAH SMITH, 1868–1942

4835   **White, William.** Ernest Bramah, Max Carrados, and The news of the world. (Notes bibliographic). Bull Bib 43no3:189 S '86.

BRAND, CHRISTIANNA, 1907–88

4836   **Penzler, Otto.** Christianna Brand; in memoriam, 1907–1988. Armchair Detective 21no3:228–30 '88. port.

'The works of Christianna Brand' (p.229–30).

BRAZIL, ANGELA, 1868–1947

4837 **Wright, Mark**. Angela Brazil pulls it off. [Collecting]. Bk & Mag Coll
3:60–5 My '84. facsims.
'Angela Brazil bibliography' (p.65).

BRENT-DYER, ELINOR, 1894–1969 *see* DYER, ELINOR BRENT-,
1894–1969.

BRENTON, HOWARD, 1942–

4838 (7:3517m) **Mitchell, Tony**. Howard Brenton checklist. (Theatre checklist, 5). Theatrefacts 2no1:2–9 '75.

4839 —— 'Bibliography [of primary and secondary sources]' *in* File on
Brenton. (Writer-files). London, Methuen, [1987]. p.91–4.

BRERETON, FREDERICK SADLEIR, 1872–1957

4840 **Crewdson, William H.P.** F.S. Brereton. [Collecting]. Antiqu Bk Mnthly
R 14no9:332–7 Ag '87. port.
'A check-list of the first editions of Frederick Sadleir Brereton' (p.337).

BRETT, EDWIN JOHN, 1828–95

4841 **LeBlanc, Edward T.** Jack Harkaway. Dime Novel Roundup 58no1:2–
6 F '89.

BREWER, GEORGE, 1766–1816?

4842 **Pitcher, Edward W.** The miscellaneous publications of George Brewer,
1766–1816? (Bibliographical notes). Library ser6 4no3:320–3 S '82.

BRIDGES, ROBERT SEYMOUR, 1844–1930

4843 **Fike, Francis**. Robert Seymour Bridges; a bibliography of secondary
sources, 1874–1981. Bull Bib 41no4:207–15 D '84.

———————————

4844 **Stanford, Donald E.** Robert Bridges, poet-typographer. (On type).
Fine Print 9no1:7–9 Ja '83.

BRIDIE, JAMES, *pseud. of* OSBORNE HENRY MAVOUR, 1888–1951

4845   **Tobin, Terence A.** 'Selected bibliography [of primary and secondary sources]' *in* James Bridie (Osborne Henry Mavour). (Twayne's English authors, 293). Boston, Twayne, [1980]. p.170–8.

BRIGHT, RICHARD, 1789–1858

4846   **Bright, Pamela.** 'Richard Bright, MD, FRCP, FRS; a bibliography [of works and criticism of]' *in* Dr. Richard Bright, 1789–1858. London, Bodley head, 1983. p.299–302.

BRITTEN, BENJAMIN, 1913–76

4847   **Wilson, Paul S.**, *comp.* 'A select bibliography' *in* Evans, John [and others]. A Britten source book. Alderburgh, Publ. for the Britten-Pears library by the Britten estate, [1987]. (Rev. ed. 1987). p.[183]–282.

4848   ——, *comp.* 'A select bibliography' *in* Evans, John [and others]. A Britten source book. Rev. ed. Alderburgh, Publ. for the Britten-Pears library by the Britten estate, 1987. (First publ. 1987). p.[183]–308.

BRONTË, CHARLOTTE (MRS. A.B. NICHOLLS), 1816–55

4849   **Alexander, Christine.** A bibliography of the manuscripts of Charlotte Brontë. Haworth, Brontë society; [Westport, Conn.], Meckler, 1982. xx,205p. facsims. 25cm.
       Not indexed.
       Rev: Brontë Soc Trans 18:243–4 '83; Sue Hanson Bull Bib 41:47–8 '84; TLS 20 Ja '84:71.

4850   **Smith, Margaret.** The Poems of Charlotte Brönte. [Ed. T. Winnifrith]. (Letters). TLS 23 Ag '85:925.

4851   **Butler, Janet.** Charlotte Brontë manuscripts; two sketches and her holograph preface to The professor. [At the Pierpont Morgan libr.]. Stud Bib 40:201–7 '87.

4852   **Odom, Keith C.** Dating Charlotte Brontë's Villette; a reappraisal. (Bibliographical notes). Pa Bib Soc Am 82no3:341–7 S '88.

BRONTË, EMILY, 1818–48

4853   **Barclay, Janet M.** Emily Brontë criticism, 1900–1982; an annotated check list. Westport, Conn., Meckler, [1984]. 162p. 26cm.
       Rev: Sue Hanson Bull Bib 43:181–2 '86.

4854 **Chazal, Roger**. Wuthering heights: bibliographie sélective et critique. (Agregation d'anglais 1989). Cahiers Vict & Edouardiens 28:117–31 Oc '88.

4855 **Roper, Derek**. The revision of Emily Brontë's Poems of 1846. Library ser6 6no2:153–67 Je '84.

BRONTË FAMILY

4856 **Crump, Rebecca W.** Charlotte and Emily Brontë, 1846–1915; a reference guide. Boston, Mass., G.K. Hall, [1982]. xvii,194p. 24cm. (Reference guide to literature).
Rev: Brontë Soc Trans 18:158 '82; H. Rosengarten Analytical & Enum Bib 7:159–67 '83; C. Lemon Brontë Soc Trans 18:406–7 '85; T.J. Winnifrith Yrbk Eng Stud 16:326–7 '86.

4857 **Walker, Arthur D.** The correspondence of the Brontë family; a guide. Didsbury, Manchester, E.J. Morten, 1982. xvi,[273]p. facsim. 23cm. (Reprod. from typewriting).
Rev: Brontë Soc Trans 18:158–9 '82.

4858 **Gérin, Winifred**. The mystery of the Bronte mss. (To the editor). TLS 25 Ap '80:468; S.C. Massey 23 My '80:584.

4859 **Alexander, Christine**. Some new findings in Brontë bibliography. [Mss.]. N&Q 228no3:233–7 Je '83.

4860 **Adams, Amber M.** Patronage and poverty in county Down; the case of Patrick Brontë. Ulster Folklife 33:26–31 '84.

BROUGHAM, HENRY PETER, BARON BROUGHAM AND VAUX, 1778–1868

4861 **Browne, Ronald K.** [Brougham's On the foreign policiy of nations, 1803]. (Miscellanea). Factotum 20:7 My '85.

BROWN, GEORGE DOUGLAS, 1869–1902

4862 **Campbell, Ian**. The House with the green shutters; some second thoughts. Biblioth 10no4:99–106 '80.

4863 **McCleery, Alistair**. The composition of The house with the green shutters. Biblioth 12no2:36–45 '84.

BROWNE, SIR THOMAS, 1605–82

4864 **Donovan, Dennis G., Margaretha G.H. Herman** and **Ann E. Imbrie.** Sir Thomas Browne and Robert Burton; a reference guide. Boston, Mass., G.K. Hall, [1981]. xxiii,530p. 23cm. (Reference guide to literature).
Rev. P.J. Klemp Lit Res Newsl 8:123–5 '83; R. Robbins N&Q 228:79–80 '83; P. Baker Am N&Q 229:89–91 '84.

4865 **Finch, Jeremiah S.,** *ed.* A catalogue of the libraries of sir Thomas Browne and dr. Edward Browne, his son; a facsimile reproduction. Leiden, E.J. Brill, Leiden U.P., 1986. xiv,177p. facsims. 23cm. (Sir Thomas Browne Inst Publs new ser, 7).
Rev. G. Mandelbrote Bk Coll 37:279–81 '88.

4866 **Sununu, Andrea.** Recent studies in sir Thomas Browne, 1970–1986. (Recent studies in the English renaissance). Eng Lit Renaiss 19no1:118–29 '89.

4867 **Finch, Jeremiah S.** Sir Thomas Browne's library. Eng Lang Notes 19no4:360–70 Je '82.

4868 **Royal college of physicians of London.** Sir Thomas Browne (1605–1682) and the baroque, with a postscript on his son Edward as treasurer, 1694–1703/4 and president, 1704–8, of the College of physicians: catalogue of an exhibition, January, 1982. [London], 1982. v,35p. 30cm. (Duplicated typescript).

4869 **Post, Jonathan F.S.** Browne's revisions of Religio medici. Stud Eng Lit 25no1:145–63 '85.

BROWNING, ELIZABETH (BARRETT), 1806–61 *see also* BROWNING, ROBERT, 1812–89.

4870 **Hudson, Ronald.** 'The gleaner'. [Periodical publ. poem c.1829 sought]. (Readers' queries). N&Q 228no3:241 Je '83.

4871 **Sharp, Phillip.** A note on some recently discovered page proofs. [In Armstrong Browning libr.]. Stud Browning & Circ 13:20–3 '85. facsims.

4872 **Fredeman, William E.** Thomas J. Wise's last word on the Reading Sonnets. ['spurious']. (Note 422). Bk Coll 37no3:422–3 '88.

BROWNING, ROBERT, 1782–1866

4873 (7:3547*) **Maynard, John.** 'Appendix B: Checklist of sketchbooks, notebooks, and manuscripts of Robert Browning, sr.' *in* Browning's youth. Cambridge, Mass., Harvard U.P., 1977. p.376–8.

BROWNING, ROBERT, 1812–89

4874 (7:3562) **Kelley, Philip** and **R. Hudson**. The Brownings' correspondence, 1978.
Rev: Sue Hanson Bull Bib 41:239–40 '84.

4875 **Freeman, Ronald E.** A checklist of publications, …. Stud Browning & Circle 8no1:66–8 '80; 8no2:102–4 '80; 9no1:87–90 '81; 9no2:92–5 '81; 10no1:69–72 '82; 11no1:79–83 '83; 12:170–6 '84; P. Sharp, 1984–1985. 14:138–47 '86; Betty A. Coley, 15:73–6 '88; 16:131–4 '88.

4876 **Kelley, Philip** and **R. Hudson**. The Browning's correspondence; supplement no.3 to the Checklist. Browning Inst Stud 8:161–75 '80; no.4. 9:161–71 '81; no.5. 10:163–7 '82.

4877 **Munich, Adrienne**. Robert and Elizabeth Browning; an annotated bibliography for 1978[–88]. Browning Inst Stud 8:177–88 '80; 1979. 9:173–83 '81; 1980. 10:169–80 '82; 1981. 11:189–98 '83; 12:189–96 '84; with Virginia Garrison and Kevin Railey, 1983. 13:201–12 '85; with K. Railey, 1984. 14:157–70 '86; Virginia Garrison and K. Railey, 1985. 15:177–89 '87; 1986. 16:181–93 '88; Rose Antos, Donesse Champeau and K. Railey, 1987. 17:129–41 '89; Donesse Champeau, 1988. 18:151–71 '90.

4878 **Anderson, Vincent P.** Robert Browning as a religious poet; an annotated bibliography of criticism. Troy, N.Y., Whitston, 1983. [3]325p. 23cm.
Rev: Beverly Taylor Sth Atlantic R 49:166–8 '84.

4879 **Meredith, Michael**. Meeting the Brownings. Waco, Tex., Armstrong Browning library, Baylor university, Browning institute, Southwestern college, [1986]. 128p. illus., facsims. 23cm.
Rev: Margaret Smith R Eng Stud new ser 39:315 '88.

4880 **Collins, Thomas J.** Browning's text; a question of marks. (Bibliographical notes). Library ser6 4no1:70–5 Mr '80.

4881 **Kelley, Philip** and **R. Hudson**. Editing the Browning's correspondence; an editorial manual. Browning Inst Stud 9:141–61 '81. table.

4882 **Crowder, Ashby B.** Robert Browning and his new publisher. [Smith, Elder]. (Notes). Stud Browning & Circle 10no2:49–52 '82. facsims.

4883 **Baker, William** and **S. Glass**. Robert Browning's Iliad; an unnoticed copy. [Libr.]. Stud Browning & Circ 12:148–59 '84. facsims., table.

4884 **Kelley, Philip** and **Betty A. Coley**. The Browning collections; a reconstruction with other memorabilia –the library, first works, presentation

volumes, manuscripts...of Robert and Elizabeth Barrett Browning. [Waco, Tex.], Armstrong Browning library, Baylor university; The Browning institute; [London], Mansell; [Winfield, Kan.], Wedgestone pr., [1984]. lvi,708p. facsims. 23cm.
Rev. A.C. Dooley Bull Bib 41:99–102 '84; M. Hancher Am Bk Coll new ser 5:45–7 '84; J. Maynard Analytical & Enum Bib new ser 1:259–64 '87.

4885   **Meidl, Anneliese.** A Strafford manuscript in the Lord chamberlain's office records. [BL]. Browning Inst Stud 12:163–88 '84. table, facsim.

4886   **Gibson, Mary E.** The manuscripts of Robert Browning, sr.; a source for The ring and the book. Stud Browning & Circ 13:11–19 '85. facsims.

4887   **Meredith, Michael.** Learning's crabbed text; a reconsideration of 1868 edition of Browning's Poetical works. Stud Browning & Circ 13:97–107 '85.
(a). The nature of the 1888–89 text.–(b). Hidden variants within the 1868 edition.–(c). The significance of Browning's punctuation.

4888   **Bornstein, George.** 'The arrangement of Browning's Dramatic lyrics, 1842' *in* Fraistat, Neil, *ed.* Poems in their place; the intertextuality and order of poetic collections. Chapel Hill, University of North Carolina pr., [1986]. p.[273]–88.

4889   **Coley, Betty A.** Done into doggerel. [Browning items acquired by Armstrong Browning libr.]. Stud Browning & Circ 15:55–70 '88.

4890   **Meredith, Michael.** A botched job; publication of The ring and the book. Stud Browning & Circ 15:41–50 '88.

4891   **Crowder, Ashby B.** Browning, a decisive reviser. Browning Soc Notes 18:47–54 '88/9.

BRUCE, DORITA MORRIS FAIRLIE, 1885–1970

4892   **Godfrey, Monica.** Dorita Fairlie Bruce & her stories for girls. [Collecting]. Bk & Mag Coll 14:38–43 Ap '85. facsims.
'Complete bibliography of Dorita Fairlie Bruce' (p.42).

BUCHAN, JOHN, BARON TWEEDSMUIR, 1875–1940

4893   **Blanchard, Robert G.** The first editions of John Buchan; a collector's bibliography. [Hamden, Conn.], Archon books, 1981. xi,284p. 22cm.
List of 1st ed. of books and pamphlets, ed. works, contribs. to books, uncollected contribs. to periodicals and public documents, and contribs. to The spectator, *with bibliogr. notes.*

4894 (5:8922f) **Fyfe, Janet**. Scottish collections in Canadian libraries. [Buchan's libr., Queen's univ., Kingston, Ont.]. Libr R 20no3:175–7 '65.

4895 **MacGlone, James M.** The printed texts of John Buchan's The thirty-nine steps, 1915–1940. Biblioth 12no1:9–24 '84. diagrs.

4896 **Macleod, Helen**. John Buchan. [Collecting]. Bk & Mag Coll 10:18–26 D '84. port., facsims., illus.
'John Buchan bibliography' (p.25–6).

4897 **Brydon, Selwyn A.** Mr. Standfast. [Variant 1st ed.?]. (Letters). Antiqu Bk Mnthly R 12no5:192 My '85.

BUCHANAN, GEORGE, 1506–82

4898 **McFarlane, Ian D.** 'Appendix A: A preliminary check-list of works by Buchanan [with locations of copies]' *in* Buchanan. [London], Duckworth, [1981]. (Also in pb). p.[490]–518.
See also 'C. Books in Buchanan's library' (p.[527]–31).

4899 **Durkan, M. John, S. Rawles** and **N. Thorp.** George Buchanan, 1506–1582; renaissance scholar and friend of Glasgow university: a quatercentenary exhibition, Glasgow university library, 17 May–7 August 1982. [Glasgow, Glasgow university library], [1982]. 13p. 20cm. (Duplicated typescript).

4900 **Durkan, M. John.** George Buchanan; new light on the poems. [1568]. Biblioth 10no1:1–9 '80.

4901 **McFarlane, Ian D.** 'Pour une édition de Poemata de George Buchanan, 1506–1582' *in* Margolin, Jean-Claude, *ed.* Acta conventus neolatini Turonensis. Paris, J. Vrin, 1980. p.[77]–83.

4902 **Beattie, William** and **M.J. Durkan**. An early publication of Latin poems of George Buchanan in Scotland from the press of Lekpreuik. Biblioth 11no3:77–80 '82.

4903 **Green, Roger P.H.** The text of George Buchanan's Psalm paraphrases. Biblioth 13no1:3–29 '86.

BULMER, HENRY KENNETH, 19??–

4904 **[Robinson, Roger]**, *ed.* The writings of Henry Kenneth Bulmer. [Harold Wood, Essex, BECCON], [1983?]. (Rev. and updated ed., 1984). 51p. 21cm. (Beccon Publ, 3).

BULWER-LYTTON, EDWARD GEORGE EARLE LYTTON, 1ST BARON LYTTON, 1803–73 *see* LYTTON, EDWARD GEORGE EARLE LYTTON, 1ST BARON LYTTON, 1803–73.

BUNTING, BASIL, 1900–85

4905   **Guedella, Roger**. Books and pamphlets by or edited by Basil Bunting. Paideuma 91n01:173–200 '80.

4906   **Nord, Roland**, *comp.* 'A bibliography of works about Basil Bunting, with extended commentary' *in* Terrell, Carroll F., *ed.* Basil Bunting; man and poet. [Orono, Me.], National poetry foundation, [1981]. p.[375]–427.

4907   **Wilde, Dana**, *comp.* 'Year by year bibliography of Basil Bunting' *in* Terrell, Carroll F., *ed.* Basil Bunting; man and poet. [Orono, Me.], National poetry foundation, [1981]. p.[357]–73.

BUNYAN, JOHN, 1628–88

4908   **Cameron, William J.** Seventeenth and eighteenth century editions of the writings of John Bunyan in special collections, the University library, the University of Alberta, Edmonton, Alberta. [London, Ont., University of Western Ontario], 1984. 57p. 27cm. (WHSTC Libr Cat ser, 19). Duplicated typescript. (Not seen: ISBN 0–7714–0518–9).

4909   **Batson, E. Beatrice.** 'Annotated bibliography' *in* John Bunyan's Grace abounding and The pilgrim's progress; an overview of literary studies, 1960–1987. (Reference library of the humanities, 773). New York, Garland, 1988. p.175–239.

4910 (5:8959d)   **Offor, Richard**. The Offor Bunyan books at Elstow. Libr Assn Rec 62n04:117–21 Ap '60. illus.

1. George Offor.–2. The ill-fated library.–3. The gift by the British museum.–4. Elstow moot hall.–5. Details of seventeenth-century editions.–A statistical note.

4911 (5:8963e)   **Kaufman, Paul**. Revelation by subscribers; John Bunyan among the Welsh. [Doctrine of the law, 1767]. Libr R 21n05:227–9 '68; Eiluned Rees 21n08:408–9 '68.

4912 (7:3604t)   **Alblas, Jacques B.H.** The earliest editions (1682–4) of the first Dutch translation of Bunyan's The pilgrim's progress. Quærendo 5n04:321–35 Oc '75. facsims.

4913   **Mills, Trevor**. Eighteenth-century Lancashire editions of Bunyan's works. (Query 331). Bk Coll 29n01:117 '80.

4914 **Editions** of Bunyan's works collected by sir Leicester Harmsworth, in BL *see* Gould, Alison, Named special collections, 1981: no.818.

4915 **Alblas, Jacques B.H.** The Johannes van Paddenburgh edition (Utrecht 1684) of Bunyan's Eens Christens reyse rediscovered. (Varia bibliographica).Quærendo 12no3:246–2 '82.

4916 **McGee, J. Sears.** Editing John Bunyan; a neophyte editor's progress. [The holy city; The resurrection of the dead]. Soundings 18no24:60–6 '87.

4917 **Sharrock, Roger**. '"When at first I took my pen in hand": Bunyan and the book' *in* Keeble, N.H., *ed.* John Bunyan; Conventicle and Parnassus: tercentenary essays. Oxford, Clarendon pr., 1988. p.71–90.
Sermons and fictions.–The books and their publishers.–Printing and press revision.

BURGESS, ANTHONY, *pseud. of* JOHN ANTHONY BURGESS WILSON, 1917–93

4918 **Brewer, Jeutonne.** Anthony Burgess; a bibliography. With a foreword by Anthony Burgess. Metuchen, N.J., Scarecrow pr., 1980. xv,175p. 22cm. (Scarecrow author bibs, 47).

4919 **Coale, Samuel**. Criticism of Anthony Burgess; a selected checklist. Mod Fict Stud 27no3:533–6 '81.

4920 **Boytinck, Paul W.** Anthony Burgess; an annotated bibliography and reference guide. New York, Garland, 1985. xxxvi,349p. port. 26cm. (Reference library of the humanities, 406).
Rev: I.C. Todd Am Bk Coll new ser 6:42–5 '85.

4921 **Harrison, Phillipa** [and] **D.W. Nichol.** A Clockwork orange. (Letters to the editor). TLS 4 Ja '80:14; A. Burgess 11 Ja '80:38.

BURKE, EDMUND, 1729–97

4922 **Todd, William B.** A bibliography of Edmund Burke. [Reissued, with some new notes]. [Godalming, Sy.], St. Paul's bibliographies, 1982. (First publ. 1964). 316p. facsims. 22cm. ([St. Paul's Bibs, 5]).
Rev: F.P. Lock Yrbk Eng Stud 16:278–9 '86.

4923 **Fasel, George**. 'Selected bibliography [of primary and secondary works]' *in* Edmund Burke. (Twayne's English authors, 286). Boston, Twayne, 1983. p.142–9.

4924 **Gandy, Clara I.** and **P. Stanlis**. Edmund Burke; a bibliography of secondary studies to 1982. With a foreword by William B. Todd. New York, Garland, 1983. xxxi,357p. port. 21cm. (Reference library of the humanities, 358).

BURKE, Thomas, *pseud. of* **SYDNEY TERENCE BURKE, 1886–1943?**

4925 **Uden, B.G. Grant.** Thomas Burke of London. [Collecting]. Antiqu Bk Mnthly R 11no12:482–5 D '84. port., illus.

BURLEY, WALTER, d.1345?

4926 (5:8990) **Bühler, Curt F.** Literary research and bibliographical training, '57.
Repr. *in* Bibliographical society of America. Bibliographical society of America, 1904–79. Charlottesville, [1980]. p.363–71.

BURNET, BP. GILBERT, 1643–1715

4927 **Cameron, William J.** Seventeenth and eighteenth century editions of the writings of Gilbert Burnet, bishop of Salisbury, in the libraries of the University of Toronto, McMaster university, and the School of library and information science, the University of Western Ontario. [London, Ont., University of Western Ontario], 1982. 44p. 27cm. (WHSTC Libr Cat ser, 6). Duplicated typescript. (Not seen: ISBN 0–7714–0368–2).

BURNEY, CHARLES, 1726–1814

4928 **Duckles, Vincent.** 'A general plan for a history of music of dr. Charles Burney, with a catalogue of his music library' *in* Elvers, Rudolf, *ed.* Festschrift Albi Rosenthal. Tutzing, H. Schneider, 1984. p.131–8.

4929 **Lacroix, Jean-Michel.** Le fonds Burney a la British library de Londres. R Française d'Hist du Livre nouv sér 53no45: 713–26 '84. facsims.
1. La vie de Charles Burney.–2. L'historique du British museum.–3. Les journaux de la collection Burney.

BURNEY, FRANCES (MRS. D'ARBLAY), 1752–1840

4930 **Grau, Joseph A.** Fanny Burney; an annotated bibliography. New York, Garland, 1981. xvi,210p. 21cm. (Reference library of the humanities, 284).

4931 (5:9001b) **Hemlow, Joyce**. 'Letters and journals of Fanny Burney' *in* Conference on editorial problems, 3d, Toronto, 1967. Editing eighteenth-century texts; papers given…. Ed. by D.I.B. Smith. [Toronto], [1968]. p.[25]–43. facsim.

4932 **Ribeiro, Alvaro**. The publication date of Fanny Burney's Cecilia. [July, 1782]. N&Q 225n05:415–16 Oc '80.

BURNS, ROBERT, 1756–96

4933 **Bentman, Raymond**. 'Selected bibliography [of primary and secondary sources]' *in* Robert Burns. (Twayne's English authors, 452). Boston, Twayne, [1987]. p.148–51.

4934 **Hewitt, David S.** Burns and the argument for standardisation. Text 1:217–29 '84.

4935 **Roy, G. Ross.** Burns' second (Edinburgh) edition [1787]. (Notes and documents). Stud Scott Lit 21:293–4 '86.

4936 **Brown, Iain G.** The Coulter collection of Burns manuscripts. [Now in National libr., Edinburgh]. Stud Scott Lit 24:68–78 '89.

BURTON, Robert, 1577–1640

4937 **O'Connell, Michael**. 'Selected bibliography [of primary and secondary sources]' *in* Robert Burton. (Twayne's English authors, 426). Boston, Twayne, [1986]. p.117–25.

4938 **Sununu, Andrea**. Recent studies in Burton and Walton. (Recent studies in the English renaissance). Eng Lit Renaiss 17n02:243–55 '87.

4939 **Conn, Joey**. Robert Burton and the Anatomy of melancholy; an annotated bibliography of primary and secondary sources. New York, Greenwood pr., [1988]. xii,105p. 23cm. (Bibliographies and indexes in world literature, 15).

4940 **Kiessling, Nicolas K.** The library of Robert Burton. [Oxford], Oxford bibliographical society, 1988. xli,433p. facsims. 23cm. (Oxford Bib Soc Publs new ser, 22).
Rev: T.A. Birrell TLS 17 Je '88:686; D.J. McKitterick Bk Coll 38:307–8 '89; R. Robbins Bk Coll 38:550–1 '89; J. McConica London R Bks 11:14–15 '89; A. Morvain Étud Angl 43:472–3 '90; R.J. Roberts Library ser6 12:248–50 '90.

4941 **Faulkner, Thomas C.** Computer applications for an edition of Robert Burton's The anatomy of melancholy; a system for scholarly publishing. Comp & Humanit 15no03:163–82 N '81. facsims., diagr., tables.

4942 **Blair, Rhonda L.** Robert Burton's 'agony'; a pattern of revision made for the sixth edition of The anatomy of melancholy. [1651]. Pa Bib Soc Am 78no02:215–18 '84.

4943 **Kiessling, Nicolas K.** Two notes on Robert Burton's annotations; his date of conception, and a fragment of copy for the Anatomy of melancholy. (Notes). R Eng Stud new ser 36no143:375–9 Ag '85. facsim.

4944 **McQuillen, Connie.** Robert Burton's Philosophaster; holograph status of the manuscripts. Manuscripta 29no03:148–53 N '85. facsims.

4945 **Höltgen, Karl J.** Robert Burton's books. (Letters). TLS 29 Jl '88:831; T.A. Birrell 4 N '88:1227.

BURTON, SIR RICHARD FRANCIS, 1821–90

4946 **Prance, Claude A.** 'The explorer: Sir Richard Burton and his books' *in* Essays of a book collector; reminiscences on some old books and their authors. West Cornwall, Conn., 1989. p.131–9.
Orig. publ. as a rev. in Priv Libr ser3 2no04:155–9 '79.

BUSSY, DOROTHY STRACHEY, 1865–1960

4947 **Foulkes, Erica.** Esquisse bibliographique de l'œuvre de Dorothy Bussy. Bull des Amis d'André Gide 17no084:481–6 Oc '89.

BUTLER, SAMUEL, 1612–80

4948 **Wasserman, George R.** Samuel Butler and the earl of Rochester; a reference guide. Boston, Mass., G.K. Hall, [1986]. xx,176p. 24cm. (Reference guide to literature).
Rev: K. Combe N&Q 233:236 '88.

4949 **De Quehen, A.H.** An account of works attributed to Samuel Butler. R Eng Stud new ser 33no131:262–77 Ag '82.

BUTLER, SAMUEL, 1835–1902

4950 **Hammond, Wayne G.** Samuel Butler; a checklist of works and criticism. Samuel Butler Newsl 3no01:13–24 '80; 3no02:51–61 D '80; 4no02:6–20 Je '81.

4951 **Breuer, Hans-Peter**. Samuel Butler in the U.S.; a bibliographical survey. Samuel Butler Newsl 6no1:3–16 My '86. facsim.

BYRON, GEORGE GORDON, afterwards NÖEL, BARON BYRON OF ROCHDALE, 1788–1824

4952 **Hearn, Ronald B. [and others]**. Byron criticism since 1952; a bibliography. [Salzburg, Institut für Anglistik und Amerikanistik, Universität Salzburg], [1980]. viii,52p. 19cm. (Romantic assessment, 83:2).

4953 **Kohler, C.C., bksllr.**, DORKING. Lord Byron; a collection of 429 items. Introd. by Jerome J. McGann. Dorking, 1980. [200]p. illus., facsims. 30cm. (Reprod. from typewriting).

4954 **Marchand, Leslie A.**, *ed.* 'II. List of forgeries of Byron's letters' *in* Byron's letters and journals. V.10, 1822–1823. Cambridge, Mass., Belknap pr., Harvard U.P., 1980. p.225.

4955 **Jordan, Frank**, *ed.*, 1985: no.4375.

4956 **Warrington, Bernard**. Pickering's medal of lord Byron; an advertisement. [1824]. (Note 417). Bk Coll 34no2:251 '85.

4957 **Sullivan, Ernest W.** A fragment of a possible Byron poem in manuscript. [Univ. of Leicester ms.2]. Pa Bib Soc Am 80no1:55–73 '86.

4958 **Pevelka, Karen**. Conservation treatment of a bound manuscript in the Byron collection. [The siege of Corinth]. Libr Chron Univ Texas 44/5:23–39 '89.
Description of the manuscript.–Treatment objectives.–Treatment procedures.–Restoring the bound volume.–Conclusion.

BYRON, ROBERT, 1905–41

4959 **Gowen, Keith**. What no Byron? [Collecting]. (Letters). Antiqu Bk Mnthly R 14no9:330 S '87; D. Laker; J. Heath 14no10:370 Oc '87; W. Reese 15no1:6 Ja '88.

CAMPION, THOMAS, d.1619

4960 **Davis, Walter R.** 'Selected bibliography [of primary and secondary works]' *in* Thomas Campion. (Twayne's English authors, 450). Boston, Twayne, [1987]. p.182–5.

CANNING, ELIZABETH, 1734–73

4961 **Harvard. University. Libraries.** The virgin and the witch; an exhibition at the Harvard law school library of materials from the Hyde collection and Harvard libraries on the celebrated trial of Elizabeth Canning. [Introd. by Hugh Amory]. [Cambridge, Mass.], [1987]. 1 sheet, folded. ports. 21cm.

CAREY, JOHN PATRICK, 1623–57

4962 (7:3678*) **Willetts, Pamela J.** Patrick Carey and his Italian poems. Brit Libr J 2no2:109–19 '76; A sequel 4no2:148–60 '78. illus., ports., facsims.

CAREY, ROSA NOUCHETTE, 1840–1909

4963 **Crisp, Jane.** Rosa Nouchette Carey, 1840–1909. [St. Lucia], Dept. of English, University of Queensland, [1989]. iv, 49p. facsims. 19cm. (Vict Fict Res Guides, 16). (Reprod. from typewriting).
Classified checklist of 293 works and ana.

CARLETON, WILLIAM, 1794–1869

4964 **Sullivan, Eileen A.** 'Selected bibliography [of primary and secondary sources]' *in* William Carleton. (Twayne's English authors, 376). Boston, Twayne, [1983]. p.130–41.

4965 **Hayley, Barbara.** A bibliography of the writings of William Carleton. Gerrards Cross, C. Smythe, 1985. 241p. 22cm.
Bibliogr. of books, periodical contribs., subsequent ptgs. in periodicals and anthologies, trans., and criticisms of Carleton's works.
Rev: Anne Clune N&Q 232:561–2 '87.

4966 —— A detailed bibliography of editions of William Carleton's Traits and stories of the Irish peasantry published in Dublin and London during the author's lifetime. Long Room 32:28–55 '87; 33:20–40 '88. table.

4967 **Earls, Brian.** The Carleton canon; additions and substractions. Stud Hibernica 21:95–125 '81.

CARLYLE, JANE BAILLIE (WELSH), 1801–66

4968 **Tarr, Rodger L.** 'Jane Welsh Carlyle's publications' *in* Thomas Carlyle; a descriptive bibliography. [Pittsburgh], University of Pittsburgh pr., 1989. p.[469]–509.

CARLYLE, THOMAS, 1795–1881

4969 **California. University at Santa Cruz. Library.** Carlyle; books & margins, being a catalogue of the Carlyle holdings in the Norman and Charlotte Strouse Carlyle collection and the University library.... [Comp. by Charles S. Fineman and Jerry D. James]. Santa Cruz, University library, University of California, 1980. 128p. 28cm. (UCSC Bib ser, 3).
See also no.4972, 4974.

4970 **Tarr, Rodger L.** Carlyle bibliography, 1978–79. [Annotated]. Carlyle Newsl 2:32–9 Mr '80; 1979–1980. 3:33–9 '81; 1980–1981. 4:34–9 '83.

4971 **Scotland. National library,** EDINBURGH. Thomas Carlyle, 1795–1881 [exhibition catalogue]. [Comp. by A.S. Bell]. Edinburgh, 1981. 37p. ports., facsims. 24cm.

4972 **James, Jerry D.** and **C.S. Fineman**, *ed.* 'Second supplement (June 1982) to the catalogue of the Carlyle holdings in the Norman and Charlotte Strouse collection of Thomas Carlyle in the University library' *in* Lectures on Carlyle & his era.... Santa Cruz, University library, University of California, 1982. p.55–72.

4973 **Dillon, R.W.** A centenary bibliography of Carlylean studies: Supplement I, 1975–80. [Edinburgh, Carlyle newsletter], [1983]. iii,31p. 22cm. (Carlyle pamphlets, 4). (Reprod. from typewriting).

4974 **James, Jerry D.** and **Janet M. James.** 'Third supplement (February 1985) to the catalogue of the Carlyle holdings in the Norman and Charlotte Strouse collection of Thomas Carlyle in the University library' *in* Lectures on Carlyle & his era.... Santa Cruz, University library, University of California, 1985. p.77–96.

4975 **Tarr, Rodger L.** Thomas Carlyle; a descriptive bibliography. [Pittsburgh], University of Pittsburgh pr., 1989. xxi,543p. port., facsims. 23cm.
Classified bibliogr. of separate publications, first book and pamphlet appearances, first contribs. to journals and newspapers, collected works, miscellaneous collections, material attributed to, Jane Welsh Carlyle's publications, unpublished and presumably lost writings by Carlyle through 1834, and principal books about the Carlyles.
Rev: A.S. Bell TLS 13 Jl '90:762.

4976 **Skabarnicki, Anne M.** The Strouse collection at Santa Cruz. Carlyle Newsl 2:31–2 Mr '80.

4977 **Strouse, Norman H.** 'The Norman and Charlotte Strouse Carlyle collection; how it was formed and how it came to Santa Cruz' *in*

California. University at Santa Cruz. Library. Carlyle; books & margins, being a catalogue of the Carlyle holdings in the Norman and Charlotte Strouse Carlyle collection and the University library.... [Comp. by Charles S. Fineman and Jerry D. James]. (UCSC Bib ser 3). Santa Cruz, University library, University of California, 1980. [3]p. *at front.*

4978   **Baker, William**. The London library borrowings of Thomas Carlyle. Libr R 30:89–95 '81.

4979   **Bell, Alan S.** Thomas Carlyle and the London library. TLS 29 My '81:611–12. illus.

4980   **Tarr, Rodger L.** Emendation as challenge; Carlyle's 'Negro question' from journal to pamphlet. (Bibliographical notes). Pa Bib Soc Am 75no3:341–5 '81.

4981   **Sanders, Charles R.** A brief history of the Duke–Edinburgh edition of the Carlyle letters. Stud Scott Lit 17:1–12 '82.

4982   **Tarr, Rodger L.** Truth and fiction; Carlyle edited and re-edited. [Rev. art]. Review 7:239–58 '85.

4983   **Campbell, Ian**. Froude, Moncure Conway and the American edition of the Reminiscences. [Froude's My relations with Carlyle]. Carlyle Newsl 8:71–9 '87.

4984   **Fielding, Kenneth J.** Vernon Lushington, Carlyle's friend and editor. Carlyle Newsl 8:7–18 '87.

4985   **Ryals, Clyde de L.** Thomas Carlyle and the Squire forgeries. [Oliver Cromwell's Letters and speeches]. Vict Stud 30no4:495–518 '87.

CARPENTER, EDWARD, 1844–1929

4986   **Brown, Tony**. Figuring in history; the reputation of Edward Carpenter; 1883–1987; annotated secondary bibliography, 1. Eng Lit Transit 32no1:34–64 '89; 2. 32no2:170–210 '89.

CARROLL, LEWIS, *pseud. of* CHARLES LUTWIDGE DODGSON, 1832–98

4987 (7:3710b)   **Crutch, Denis H.** Alice in paperback. Penguin Collectors' Soc Newsl 1no3:36–40 Ja '75; Additions and corrections 2no2:22 D '75.

4988 (7:3719c)   **[Goodacre, Selwyn H.]**. The reviews of Alice's adventures in Wonderland. Jabberwocky 9no1:3–8 '79/80; 9no2:27–39 '80; 9no3:55–8 '80; 9no4:79–86 '80.

4989 (7:3719) **Williams, Sidney H.** and **F. Madan.** The Lewis Carroll handbook...rev. by Denis Crutch, 1979.
Rev. P. Heath Eng Lang N 20:126–30 '82.

4990 **Guiliano, Edward**. Lewis Carroll; an annotated international bibliography, 1960–1977. Charlottesville, Va., Publ. for the Bibliographical society of the University of Virginia and the Lewis Carroll society of North America by the U.P. of Virginia, [1980]. viii,253p. 23cm.
Rev. F. Huxley TLS 13 N '81:1334; T. Otten Analytical & Enum Bib 6:123–4 '82; P. Heath Eng Lang N 20:126–30 '82.

4991 **Goodacre, Selwyn H.**, *comp.* 'The listing of the Snark' *in* Tanis, James and J. Dooley, *ed.* The hunting of the snark. Los Altos, Calif., W. Kaufman with Bryn Mawr college library, [1981]. p.[119]–29.
Discursive checklist of English-language ed., tranlations, anthologies, and 'candle-ends'.

4992 **Stern, Jeffrey**, *ed.* Lewis Carroll's library; a facsimile edition of the catalogue of the auction sale following C.L. Dodgson's death in 1898, with facsimiles of three subsequent booksellers' catalogues offering books from Dodgson's library. [Silver Spring, Md.], Lewis Carroll society of North America and distrib. by the U.P. of Virginia, [1981]. xiv,95p. illus. 22cm. (Carroll Stud, 5).
Rev. P. Heath Eng Lang N 20:126–30 '82.

4993 **Cohen, Morton N.** Lewis Carroll and Alice, 1832–1982. [New York], Pierpont Morgan library, [1982]. 133p. illus., ports., facsims. 24cm.
Exhibition catalogue drawn from A.A. Houghton colln.
Rev. P. Heath Eng Lang N 20:126–30 '82.

4994 **Goodacre, Selwyn H.** The 1865 Alice; a new appraisal and a revised census. Eng Lang N 20no2:77–96 D '82.

4995 **Taylor, Robert H. [and others].** Lewis Carroll at Texas; the Warren Weaver collection and related Dodgson materials at the Harry Ransom Humanities research center. Austin, Tex., Humanities research center, University of Texas at Austin, [1985]. 233p. ports., facsims., table. 25cm. (Carroll Stud, 9).
Also publ. as Libr Chron Univ Texas new ser 32/3:1–233 '85.
'In pursuit of Lewis Carroll', by Warren Weaver (p.9–15), *repr. from* Libr Chron Univ Texas new ser 2:38–45 N '70.
Rev. Margaret Watson N&Q 233:113–14 '88.

4996 **[Corke, Shirley].** Lewis Carroll in Guildford muniment room. [Kingston upon Thames, Surrey record office], 1989. 119p. geneal.table. 30cm. (Surrey Rec Office Handlist, 1). (Duplicated typescript).

4997 (5:9334d) **Weaver, Warren** and **A.C. Berol**. The India Alice; the story of a recently discovered copy of the genuine first edition, 1865, of Alice's adventures in Wonderland, prepared...in connection with a dinner at the Grolier club...1963. [New York, Privately ptd. by the Marchbanks pr.], [1963]. 15p. 24cm. (Ltd. to 66 copies).

4998 (7:3721) **Weaver, Warren**. In pursuit of Lewis Carroll, '70.
 Repr. in Taylor, Robert N. [and others]. Lewis Carroll at Texas. Libr Chron Univ Texas new ser 32/3:1–233 '85, p.9–15.

4999 **Goodacre, Selwyn H.** The 'Alice' manuscript facsimiles; an expansion, and an addition. Jabberwocky 9no3:10–1 '80; D.H. Crutch, Another University microfilms version 9no3:72 '80; G.W. Martin A further 'Alice' manuscript facsimile extract 9no3:73 '80.

5000 **Schiller, Justin G.** Collecting the works of Lewis Carroll. Am Bkmn's Wkly 68no20:3383–90 N '81.
 Repr. in AB Bkmn's Yrbk 1982pt2:41–4 '82.

5001 **Sewell, Byron W.** American editions of Alice's adventures in Wonderland published by Lee & Shepard and Lee, Shepard & Dillingham. Jabberwocky 10no4:95–7 '81.

5002 —— Macmillan's American 1877 'new edition' of Alice's adventures in Wonderland. Jabberwocky 10no4:98–9 '81.

5003 **Goodacre, Selwyn H.**, *comp.* 'The 1865 Alice; a new appraisal and a revised census' *in* Guiliano, Edward and J.R. Kincaid, *ed.* Soaring with the dodo; essays on Lewis Carroll's life and art. (Eng Lang N 20no2 D '82). [Silver Spring, Md.], Lewis Carroll society of North America; distrib. by the U.P. of Virginia, [1982]. p.77–96.

5004 **Hancher, Michael**. The placement of Tenniel's Alice illustrations. Harvard Libr Bull 30no3:237–52 Jl '82. facsims.

5005 **Heath, Peter**. The Carrollian paperchase. Eng Lang N 20no2:126–30 D '82.
 Rev. article on The Lewis Carroll handbook, 1979, Edward Guiliano, Lewis Carroll; an international bibliography, 1980, Morton N. Cohen, Lewis Carroll and Alice, 1982, *and* Jeffrey Stern, Lewis Carroll's library, 1981.

5006 **Snelling, O. Fred.** Alice in Plunderland. [Bksllng.]. Antiqu Bk Mnthly R 8no2:49–53 F '82; J.G. Schiller; S.H. Goodacre (Letters) 8no4:152 Ap '82. facsims.

5007 **Hancher, Michael**. On the writing, illustration and publication of Lewis Carroll's Alice books. [London], Macmillan; New York, Knopf, [1984]. 11p. 18cm. (Covertitle).

5008 **Macleod, Helen**. Lewis Carroll's Alice books; a guide for collectors.... Bk & Mag Coll 9:4–14 N '84. ports., facsims.
 'Selected 1st editions of illustrated Alice books' (p.14).

5009 **Smith, Muriel**. Some omissions from Martin Gardner's The annotated Alice. N&Q 229no4:499 D '84.

5010 **McGuire, Patrick**. An ardent Lewis Carroll collector. [Alfred C. Berol]. Am Bk Coll new ser 6no1:19–26 Ja/F '85. facsims.
Colln. now in N.Y. university Fales libr.

5011 **Clark, Beverly L.** '7. What went wrong with Alice' *in* Morse, Donald E., *ed*. The fantastic in world literature and the arts; selected essays.... (Contribs Stud Sci Fict & Fantasy, 28). Westport, Conn., Greenwood pr., [1987]. p.87–101.
Repr. from Children's Lit Assn Q 11no1:29–33 '86.

5012 **Cohen, Morton N.** and **Anita Gandolfo**, *ed*. Lewis Carroll and the house of Macmillan. Cambridge, C.U.P., 1987. ix,384p. illus., ports. 32cm. (Cambridge Stud Publ & Ptg Hist).
The letters.–Appendix A: Excerpts from The bookseller.–B. List of letters omitted from the text.
Rev: H. Carpenter TLS 12 Je '87:645; Elizabeth James Bk Trade Hist Group Newsl 7:9–12 '88.

5013 **Goodacre, Selwyn H.** Alice / book jackets. (Letters). Antiqu Bk Mnthly R 16no4:126–7 Ap '89.

5014 **Stephenson, Jonathan**. The printing of the Alice engravings. [By the Rocket pr., in 1985–7]. Matrix 9:137–45 '89.

CARY, ARTHUR JOYCE LUNEL, 1888–1957

5015 **Roby, Kinley E.** 'Selected bibliography [of primary and secondary sources]' *in* Joyce Cary. (Twayne's English authors, 377). Boston, Twayne, [1984]. p.128–33.

5016 **Makinen, Merja A.** and **K. Harris**. Joyce Cary; a descriptive bibliography. London, Mansell, [1989]. x,254p. 20cm.
'Introduction: The publishing history of Joyce Cary' (p.1–16); *classified checklist of writings by, and annotated ana.*

CARY, LUCIUS, 2d VISCOUNT FALKLAND, 1610?–43

5017 **Woolf, Daniel R.** The true date and authorship of Henry, viscount Falkland's History of the life, reign and death of king Edward II. [1680; not by Falkland, nor early; by Elizabeth Falkland?]. Bodleian Libr Rec 12no6:440–52 Ap '88; Isobel Grundy (Notes and documents) 13no1:82–3 Oc '88.

CAUDWELL, CHRISTOPHER, *pseud. of* CHRISTOPHER ST.JOHN SPRIGG, 1907–

5018 **Munton, Alan** and **A. Young**, no.700.

CAVENDISH, GEORGE, 1500–61?

5019 **Burchfield, Robert W.** R.S. Sylvester: The editing of Cavendish's Life of Wolsey. Moreana 17no65/6:81–5 Juin '80.

CAVENDISH, MARGARET (LUCAS), DUCHESS OF NEWCASTLE, 1624?–1724

5020 (1:2747c) **Grant, Douglas**. 'Check-list of the works of Margaret Cavendish' *in* Margaret the first; a biography of Margaret Cavendish, duchess of Newcastle, 1623–1673. London, R. Hart-Davis, 1957. p.240–2.

CHALLONER, BP. RICHARD, 1691–1781

5021 **Browne, Ronald K.** Richard Challenor, 1691–1781. (Features). Factotum 12:17–22 Jl '81; 13:4 D '81.
'A short title list of works written, compiled, edited, revised, or translated by bishop Challenor' (p.20–2).

CHALMERS, ALEXANDER, 1759–1834

5022 **Willey, Edward P.** The works of Alexander Chalmers, journalist, editor, biographer. Bull Res Humanit 86no1:94–104 '83. port.
Chalmers as journalist.–Chalmers and the booksellers.

CHAMBERLAYNE, EDWARD, 1616–1703

5023 **Alsop, James D.** The 1710 edition of Chamberlayne's Present state of Great Britain. (Bibliographical notes). Library 2no4:466–8 D '80.

CHAPMAN, GEORGE, 1559?–1634

5024 (5:9379a) **Yamada, Akihiro**. Press-variants and emendations in Monsieur d'Olive, 1606. Faculty Liberal Arts & Sci Shinshu Univ J 1no13:49–70 '63. tables.
1. Press-variants.–2. Emendations of accidentals.–3. Emendations of substantives and semi-substantives.

5025 (5:9379b) —— The printing of sheet B in the W.A. Clark library copy of Monsieur d'Olive, 1606. [Incorrect imposition]. Faculty Liberal Arts & Sci Shinshu Univ J 1no13:43–7 '63. tables.

5026 —— The seventeenth-century manuscript leaves of Chapman's Mayday, 1611. Library ser6 2no1:61–9 Mr '80; P.S. Graham (Correspondence) 4no4:472 D '80. facsims.

5027 **Cummings, L.A.** Geo: Chapman, his crowne and conclusion; a study of his handwriting. Salzburg, Austria, Institut für Anglistik und Amerikanistik, Universität Salzburg, 1989. ix,230p. facsims. 21cm. (Salzburg Stud Eng Lit. Elizabethan & Renaiss Stud, 106).
1. Introducing the investigation.–2. Earlier notices of Chapman's hand.–3. Later notices of Chapman's hand.–4. Projecting a method.–5. Legitimatizing holograph from external evidence.–6. A basic chirography.–7. Reconstructing the Diary.–8. Reconsidering the Diary.–9. Tracing Chapman's hand in the Diary.–10. Authenticating the dedicatory inscriptions.–11. Summing up and projecting.–Appendix: Titles for some of Chapman's works. Quick list of Chapman items in Diary. Books by Chapman with MS corrections without inscriptions.

CHARLES I, KING OF GREAT BRITAIN AND IRELAND, 1600–49

5028 **Editions** of the Eikon basilike and related works collected by F.F. Madan, in BL *see* Gould, Alison, Named special collections, 1981: no.818.

CHARTERIS, LESLIE, 1907–

5029 **Lofts, William O.G.** and **D.J. Adley**. The Saint stories of Leslie Charteris. [Collecting]. Bk & Mag Coll 14:4–12 Ap '85. ports., facsims.
'Complete bibliography of Leslie Charteris UK 1st editions' (p.11–12).

CHATTERTON, THOMAS, 1752–70

5030 **Haywood, Ian**. Chatterton's plans for the publication of the forgery. R Eng Stud new ser 36no141:58–68 F '85.

CHAUCER, GEOFFREY, 1340?–1400

5031 **Fisher, John H.** An annotated Chaucer bibliography, 1977–1978[–1989]. Stud Age Chaucer 2:221–85 '80; 1979. 3:189–259 '81; 1980. 4:193–246 '82; Lorrayne Y. Baird, 1981. 5:217–74 '83; with Cynthia D. Myers, 1982. 6:233–82 '84; 1983. 7:283–338 '85; with B.K. Bowers, 1984. 8:279–341 '86; Lorayne Y. Baird-Lange and B.K. Bowers, 1985. 9:279–347 '87; 1986. 10:219–87 '88; 1987. 11:303–77 '89; 1988. 12:361–429 '90; with B.W. Hozcski, 1989. 13:293–362 '91.

5032 **Kirby, Thomas A.** Chaucer research, 1979; report no.40[–50]. Chaucer R 15no1:63–84 '80; ...1980, report no.41. 15no4:356–79 '81;
...1981, report no.42. 16no4:356–77 '82; ...1982, report no.43.
17no3:255–77 '83; ...1983, report no.44. 18no3:250–72 '84; B.K.
Bowers, ...1984, report no.45. 20no1:70–8 '85; ...1985, report no.46.
21no1:67–83 '86; ...1986, report no.47. 22no1:62–79 '87; ...1987,
report no.48. 23no2:162–79 '88; ...1988, report no.49. 24no1:77–
94 '89; ...1989, report no.50. 25no2:152–69 '90.

5033 **Giaccherini, Enrico**, *comp.* 'Chaucer and the Italian trecento; a bibliography' *in* Boitani, Piero, *ed.* Chaucer and the Italian trecento.
Cambridge, C.U.P., [1983]. p.297–304.

5034 **Peck, Russell A.** Chaucer's lyrics and Anelida and Arcite; an annotated bibliography, 1900 to 1980. Toronto, University of Toronto pr.,
[1983]. xx,226p. 23cm. ([Chaucer Bibs, 1]).
Rev: Lorrayne Y. Baird-Lange Stud Age Chaucer 6:216–19 '84.

5035 **Johnson, James D.** Identifying Chaucer allusions, 1953–1980; an
annotated bibliography. Chaucer R 19no1:62–86 '84.

5036 **Morris, Lynn C.K.** Chaucer source and analogue criticism; a cross-
referenced guide. New York, Garland, 1985. xvii,584p. 23cm. (Reference library of the humanities, 454).

5037 **Anderson, David**, *ed.* Catalogue of the exhibition Sixty bokes olde
and newe; manuscripts and early printed books from libraries in
and near Philadelphia illustrating Chaucer's sources, his works and
their influence. Knoxville, New Chaucer society, University of Ten-
nessee, [1986]. xviii,123p. facsims. 23cm.

5038 **Leyerle, John** and **Anne Quick.** Chaucer; a bibliographical introduction. Toronto, University of Toronto pr., [1986]. xx,321p. 21cm.
(Toronto Med Bib, 10).
Rev: Beryl Rowland Univ Toronto Q 57:101–4 '87; Helen Cooper R Eng Stud new ser
38:541 '87; M. Andrew Speculum 63:695–7 '88; J. Norton-Smith N&Q 234:79–81
'89.

5039 **Allen, Mark** and **J.H. Fisher**. The essential Chaucer; an annotated
bibliography of major modern studies. Boston, G.K. Hall; London,
Mansell, [1987]. xiii,243p. 23cm. (Reference Publ Lit).
Rev: C.C. Morse N&Q 234:489–90 '89; R.A. Peck Speculum 64:381 '89; Helen Cooper R Eng Stud new ser 41:113 '90.

5040 **Besserman, Lawrence L.** Chaucer and the Bible; a critical review of
research indexes, and bibliography. New York, Garland, 1988.
xix,432p. 19cm. (Reference library of the humanities, 839).

5041 **Lange, Lorrayne Y. Baird-** and **Hildegard Schnuttgen.** A bibliography of Chaucer, 1974–1985. [Hamden, Conn.], Archon books;

Woodbridge, Boydell & Brewer, 1988. lxxv,344p. 23cm.
Rev: M. Allen Stud Age Chaucer 12:248–50 '90; K. Bitterling Anglia 108:497–9 '90.

5042 **Peck, Russell A.** Chaucer's Romaunt of the rose & Boece, Treatise on the astrolabe, Equatorie of the planetis, lost works, and Chaucerian apocrypha; an annotated bibliography, 1900 to 1985. Toronto, University of Toronto pr., [1988]. xviii,402p. 23cm. ([Chaucer Bibs, 2]).
Rev: W. Ginsberg Stud Age Chaucer 11:273–6 '89; K. Bitterling Anglia 108:499–501 '90.

5043 **Rooney, Anne.** Geoffrey Chaucer; a guide through the critical maze. [Bristol], Bristol pr., [1989]. ix,132p. 21cm. (State of the art, [1]).
Bibliogr. essays, with selected bibliogr. at end (p.118–32); not indexed.

5044 (7:3786d) **Boyd, Beverly.** Chaucer and the medieval book. [San Marino, Calif.], Huntington library, 1973. xi,165p. illus., facsims., tables. 23cm.
1. Of 'bookes, clad in blak or reed'.–2. Pictures and decoration in books.–3. Writing in books.–4. Book trade and libraries.–5. Chaucer, published and printed.–Appendix [money and prices].

5045 (7:3788t) **Doyle, Anthony I.** and **M.B. Parkes.** 'The production of copies of the Canterbury tales and the Confessio amantis in the early fifteenth century' *in* Watson, Andrew G., *ed.* Medieval scribes, manuscripts and libraries: essays presented to N.R. Ker. London, Scolar pr., [1978]. p.163–203. facsims.

5046 (7:3791e) **Miskimin, Alice.** The illustrated eighteenth-century Chaucer. Mod Philol 77no1:26–55 '79. facsims.
Urry's edition.–Eighteenth-century gothic and Chaucer.–The booksellers' war and Bell's Chaucer.–Stothard's designs in Bell's Chaucer.–Stothard's and Blake's Pilgrims.

5047 (7:3791h) **Windeatt, Barry A.** The scribes as Chaucer's early critics. [Text]. Stud Age Chaucer 1:119–41 '79.

5048 **Brown, Emerson.** Thoughts on editing Chaucer; the electronic-information revolution and a proposal for the future. Chaucer Newsl 2no2:2–3 '80.

5049 **Benson, C. David** and **D. Rollman.** Wynkyn de Worde and the ending of Chaucer's Troilus and Criseyde. (Notes and documents). Mod Philol 78no3:275–9 F '81.

5050 **Bentley, Gerald E., jr.** Comment upon the illustrated eighteenth-century Chaucer. [Corrs. to A. Miskimin: no.5046]. (Notes and documents). Mod Philol 78no4:398 My '81.

5051 **Blake, Norman F.** 'On editing the Canterbury tales' *in* Heyworth, Peter L., *ed.* Medieval studies for J.A.W. Bennett aetatis suae LXX. Oxford, Clarendon pr.; London, O.U.P., 1981. p.101–19.

5052 —— The textual tradition of The book of the duchess. Eng Stud 62no3:237–48 Je '81. diagr.

5053 **Brewer, Derek S.** 'Observations on the text of Troilus' *in* Heyworth, Peter L., *ed.* Medieval studies for J.A.W. Bennett aetatis suae LXX. Oxford, Clarendon pr.; London, O.U.P., 1981. p.121–38.

5054 **Cowen, Janet M.** Eighteenth-century ownership of two Chaucer manuscripts. [Ralph Thoresby; Morell Thurston]. N&Q 226no5:392–8 Oc '81.

5055 **Neuss, Paula.** Images of writing and the book in Chaucer's poetry. R Eng Stud new ser 32no128:385–97 N '81.

5056 **Moorman, Charles.** Computing Housman's fleas; a statistical analysis of Manly's landmark manuscripts in the general prologue to the Canterbury tales. Assn Lit & Lingu Computing J 3no1:15–35 '82. diagrs., tables.

5057 **Owen, Charles A.** The alternative reading of The Canterbury tales; Chaucer's text and the early manuscripts. Publ Mod Lang Assn 97no2:237–50 Mr '82.

5058 **Ramsey, R. Vance.** The Hengwrt and Ellesmere manuscripts of the Canterbury tales. Stud Bib 35:133–54 '82.

5059 **Blake, Norman F.** The editorial assumptions in the Manly–Rickert edition of The Canterbury tales. Eng Stud 64no5:385–400 Oc '83. diagr.

5060 **Kane, George.** 'The text of The legend of good women in CUL ms. Gg.4.27' *in* Gray, Douglas and E.G. Stanley, *ed.* Medieval studies presented to Norman Davis in honour of his seventieth birthday. Oxford, Clarendon pr., 1983. p.[39]–58.
     Repr. in Chaucer and Langland; historical and textual approaches. London; Berkeley, Calif., 1989. p.[162]–77.

5061 **Samuels, M.L.** The scribe of the Hengwrt and Ellesmere manuscripts of The Canterbury tales. Stud Age Chaucer 5:49–65 '83. tables.

5062 **Ruggiers, Paul G.**, *ed.* Editing Chaucer; the great tradition. Norman, Okla., Pilgrim books, [1984]. 301p. facsims. 22cm.
     Editor's introduction.–1. William Caxton, Beverly Boyd.–2. William Thynne, James E. Blodgett.–3. John Stowe, Anne Hudson.–4. Thomas Speght, Derek Pearsall.–5. John Urry, William L. Alderson.–6. Thomas Tyrwhitt, B.A. Windeatt.–7. Thomas Wright, Thomas Ross.–8. Frederick James Furnivall, Donald C. Baker.–9. Walter W. Skeat, A.S.G. Edwards.–10. Robert K. Root, Ralph Hanna.–11. John M. Manly and Edith Rickert, George Kane. [Repr. in Chaucer and Langland; historical and textual approaches. London; Berkeley, Calif., 1989. p. [178]–205].–12. F.N. Robinson, George F. Reinecke.
     Rev: R.W. Clement Libr Q 55:469–72 '85; J.A. Dane Huntington Libr Q 48:179–86 '85; E.G. Stanley N&Q 230:393 '85; G.R. Keiser J Eng & Germ Philol 85:251–3 '86; A.I. Doyle Speculum 61:700–4 '86; J.H. Fisher Stud Age Chaucer 8:239–41 '86.

5063 **Blake, Norman F.** The textual tradition of The Canterbury tales. [London], E. Arnold, [1985]. xiii,222p. 21cm.

1. Editions of the Canterbury tales.–2. Scholarly opinion of the manuscript tradition.–3. Problems and proposals about the manuscript tradition.–4. The earliest manuscripts.–5. The formation of the text: Hengwrt.–6–7. The development of the text.–8. Other developments in the text.–9. A matter of copyists.–10. The evidence of other Chaucerian texts.

Rev. S.S. Hussey Times Higher Educ Suppl 6 D '85:17; S. Knight Australasian Univ Lang & Lit Assoc J 166:311–13 '86; A. Wawn TLS 28 N '86:1356; Heather Boyd Unisa Eng Stud 25: 35–6 '87; J.W. Nicholls Mod Lang R 83:663–4 '88; J. Sudo Stud Engl Lit Eng no. 128–33 '88; Helen Cooper R Eng Stud new ser 38:237–8 '87; N&Q 234:370 '89.

5064 **Hirsch, John C.** Chaucer's Man of Law's tale 847; a conjectural emendation. Chaucer R 20no1:68–9 '85.

5065 **Jones, Alexander I.** Ms. Harley 7334 and the contruction of The Canterbury tales. Eng Lang N 23no2:9–15 D '85.

5066 **Mosser, Daniel W.** Manly and Rickerts' collation of Huntington library Chaucer manuscript HM 144 (Hn). [Bibliogr descr.]. (Bibliographical notes). Pa Bib Soc Am 79no2:235–40 '85. diagr.

5067 **Tschann, Judith**. The layout of Sir Thopas in the Ellesmere, Hengwrt, Cambridge Dd.4.24 and Cambridge Gg.4.27 manuscripts. Chaucer R 20no1:1–13 '85. facsims.

5068 **Baker, Donald C.** William Thynne's printing of The squire's tale; manuscripts and printer's copy. Stud Bib 39:125–32 '86.

5069 **Blake, Norman F.** The Book of the duchess again. [Response to Phillips: no.5074]. Eng Stud 67no2:122–5 Ap '86. diagrs.

5070 **Brown, Emerson**. The Knight's tale, 2639; guilt by punctuation. [Text]. Chaucer R 21no2:133–41 '86.

5071 **Jennings, Margaret**. 'To "pryke" or to "prye"; scribal delights in the Troilus, book III [Text]' *in* Wasserman, Julian N. and R.J. Blanch, *ed.* Chaucer in the eighties. [Syracuse], Syracuse U.P., 1986. p.121–33.

5072 **Ludlum, Charles**. Chaucer's Criseyde: 'Hir name, allas! is published so wyde'. [Text]. Pacific Coast Philol 21no1/2:37–41 N '86.

5073 **Mosser, Daniel W.** The two scribes of the Cardigan manuscript and the 'evidence' of scribal supervision and shop production. Stud Bib 39:112–25 '86. facsims., diagr.

5074 **Phillips, Helen**. The Book of the duchess, lines 31–96; are they a forgery? [And Thynne]. Eng Stud 67no2:113–21 Ap '86.

5075 **Cowen, Janet M.** 'Metrical problems in editing The legend of good women' *in* Pearsall, Derek A., *ed.* Manuscripts and texts; editorial problems in later middle English literature. [Cambridge], [1987]. p.[26]–33.

5076 —— Samuel Pegge's ownership of a manuscript of Chaucer's Legend of good women. [In BL]. N&Q 232no2:152–3 Je '87.

5077 **Hanna, Ralph**. 'Problems of "best text" editing and the Hengwrt manuscript of the Canterbury tales' *in* Pearsall, Derek A., *ed.* Manuscripts and texts; editorial problems in later middle English literature. [Cambridge], [1987]. p.[87]–94.

5078 **Kamowski, William**. A suggestion for emending the epilogue of Troilus and Criseyde. Chaucer R 21no4:405–18 '87.

5079 **Matheson, Lister M.** The House of fame, 26; a Chaucer reading restored. N&Q 232no3:289–91 S '87.

5080 **Morse, Charlotte C.** 'The value of editing the Clerk's tale for the Variorum Chaucer' *in* Pearsall, Derek A., *ed.* Manuscripts and texts; editorial problems in later middle English literature. [Cambridge], [1987]. p.[122]–9.

5081 **Mosser, Daniel W.** The Cardigan Chaucer; a witness to the manuscript and textual history of the Canterbury tales. Libr Chron Univ Texas 41:82–111 '87. facsims.
   The manuscript and textual history.–The Cardigan manuscript.–Textual variants in the Alpha manuscripts.

5082 **Owen, Charles A.** Troilus and Criseyde; the question of Chaucer's revisions. Stud Age Chaucer 9:155–72 '87.

5083 **Wright, Constance S.** On the eighteenth-century ownership of a ms. of Chaucer's Legend of good women, British library additional 9832. [Samuel Pegge]. Stud Bib 40:70–1 '87.

5084 —— The prologue to Chaucer's Legend of good women in Cambridge university library ms. Gg.4.27 and John Urry's Works of Chaucer. N&Q 232no4:456 D '87.

5085 **Dane, Joseph A.** The reception of Chaucer's eighteenth-century editors. Text 4:217–36 '88. facsims.
   John Urry's 1721 edition; a consensus on the 'worst' edition.–Tyrwhitt and the modern edition.–Thomas Morrell and the open edition.

5086 **Edwards, Anthony S.G.** Chaucer's House of fame: lines 1709, 1907. Eng Lang N 26no1:1–3 S '88.

5087 —— The unity and authenticity of Anelida and Arcite; the evidence of the manuscripts. Stud Bib 41:177–88 '88.

5088 **Fisher, John H.** Animadversions on the text of Chaucer, 1988. Speculum 63n04:779–93 Oc '88.

5089 **Hanna, Ralph**. Authorial versions, rolling versions, scribal error? Or, the truth about Truth. Stud Age Chaucer 10:23–40 '88.

5090 **MacDonald, Alasdair A.** Chaucer's Man of law's tale 847; a reconsideration. Chaucer R 22n03:246–9 '88; J.C. Hirsh, A rejoinder 22n04:332–34 '88.

5091 **Owen, Charles A.** Pre-1450 manuscripts of the Canterbury tales: relationships and significance. Chaucer R 23n01:1–29 '88; 23n02:95–116 '88. diagrs.

5092 **Cureton, Kevin K.** Chaucer's revision of Troilus and Criseyde. Stud Bib 42:153–84 '89.

5093 **Edwards, Anthony S.G.** Pynson's and Thynne's editions of Chaucer's House of fame. [1526; 1532]. Stud Bib 42:185–6 '89.

5094 **Finlayson, John**. Textual variants in Chaucer's House of fame; Thynne as editor. Eng Stud 70n05:385–94 Oc '89.

5095 **Gourlay, Alexander S.** What was Blake's Chaucer? [1687 Speght]. Stud Bib 42:272–83 '89.
Urry and Tyrwhitt.–'Thynne in his glossary'.–Which Speght?–Later quotations.–Conclusion.

5096 **Hanna, Ralph**. The Hengwrt manuscript and the canon of The Canterbury tales. Eng Manuscr Stud 1:64–84 '89.

5097 **Kane, George**. Chaucer and Langland; historical and textual approaches. London, Athlone pr.; Berkeley, Calif., University of California pr., [1989]. x,302p. 20cm.
Includes 11. Conjectural emendation.–12. The text of The legend of good women in CUL ms. Gg.4.27 (1983).–13. John M. Manly (1865–1940) and Edith Rickert (1871–1938). (1984).–14. 'Good' and 'bad' manuscripts: texts and critics. (1986).

5098 **Machan, Timothy W.** Editorial method and medieval translations: the example of Chaucer's Boece. [1687 Speght]. Stud Bib 42:272–83 '89.

5099 —— Scribal role, authorial intention, and Chaucer's Boece. Chaucer R 24n02:150–62 '89.

5100 **Moorman, Charles**. One hundred years of editing the Canterbury tales. Chaucer R 24n02:99–114 '89.

5101   **Ramsey, R. Vance.** F.N. Robinson's editing of the Canterbury tales. Stud Bib 42:134–52 '89. tables.

A. The initial reception of Robinson's text.–B. Robinson's discussion of his editorial method.–C. Robinson's emendations.–D. Flaws in Robinson's editorial method and why they matter.

5102   **Wright, Constance S.** On the eighteenth-century ownership of a MS of the Canterbury tales, Phillipps 6570. Am N&Q 2no4:134 Oc '89.

CHESTERFIELD, PHILIP DORMER, 4TH EARL OF, 1694–1773
see STANHOPE, PHILIP DORMER, 4TH EARL OF CHESTERFIELD, 1694–1773.

CHESTERTON, GILBERT KEITH, 1874–1936

5103   **Sullivan, John.** Additions to Chesterton three. Chesterton R 7no3:225–8 Ag '81.

5104   **White, William.** G.K. Chesterton's Father Brown; a bibliography. Armchair Detective 16no3:251–6 '83. illus.

5105   **Sullivan, John.** Chesterton three; a bibliographical postscript. Bedford, Vintage publs., 1980. 46p. 18cm.

Repr. from Chesterton R. *Includes* The trials of bibliography; an address given to the Manchester society of book collectors.
Rev: Christine d'Haussy Seven 3:131 '82.

5106   —— Chesterton's political views. [Utopia of usurers, N.Y., 1917]. (Letters). Chesterton R 8no1:84–5 F '82.

5107   **Thomas, Lewis E.** G.K. Chesterton. [Collecting]. Bk & Mag Coll 12:4–14 F '85. ports., facsims.
'Complete bibliography of G.K. Chesterton' (p.12–14).

5108   **Boyd, Ian.** Chesterton on censorship. [Evidence to Joint select committee on censorship of drama]. Chesterton R 12no1:1–21 F '86. illus.

5109   **Mead, A.H.** G.K. Chesterton, writer and artist. [St. Paul's school, London, exhib. of]. Chesterton R 12no1:25–8 F '86.

5110   Cancelled.

5111   **Boyd, Ian.** Something to celebrate. [Discovery of H. Jackson's Platitudes in the making, 1911, annot. by Chesterton]. Chesterton R 14no4:553–6 N '88. facsim.

5112 **Kessler, Alfred R.** The finding of the book. [H. Jackson's Platitudes, annot. by Chesterton]. Chesterton R 14n04:552–3 N '88. port.

5113 **Miklas, Sebastian.** Copy of a treasure. [H. Jackson's Platitudes]. Chesterton R 14n04:561–5 '88.

CHEYNEY, REGINALD SOUTHOUSE   ('PETER'), 1896–

5114 **Gunn, Katharine.** Peter Cheyney, creator of Lemmy Caution. [Collecting]. Bk & Mag Coll 19:26–34 S '85. port., facsims.
'Complete Peter Cheyney bibliography' (p.33–4).

CHIBNALL, MARJORIE MCCALLUM, 1915–

5115 **Chibnall, Joan**, *comp.* 'A bibliography of the works of Marjorie Chibnall to the end of December 1983' *in* Greenaway, Diana, C. Holdsworth and Jane Sayers, *ed.* Tradition and change; essays in honour of Marjorie Chibnall presented by her friends on the occasion of her seventieth birthday. Cambridge, C.U.P., [1985]. p.263–9.
Chronol. checklist, 1938–83.

CHOLMONDELEY, MARY, 1859–1925

5116 **Crisp, Jane.** Mary Cholmondeley, 1859–1925; a bibliography. [St. Lucia], Dept. of English, University of Queensland, [1981]. 42p. port. 20cm. (Vict Fict Res Guides, 6). (Reprod. from typewriting).
Classified checklist of novels, short stories, other published work, letters and ana (125 items).

CHRISTIE, DAME AGATHA MARY CLARISSA (LADY MALLOWAN), 1890–1976

5117 **Barnard, Louise**, *comp.* 'Bibliography [checklist of books and short stories]' *in* Barnard, Robert. A talent to deceive; an appreciation of Agatha Christie. London, Collins, 1980. (Rev. ed. 1980). p.134–78.

5118 **White, William.** Agatha Christie; additions to secondary sources. Bull Bib 40n02:84–9 Je '83.

5119 **Williams, Richard A.H.** Agatha Christie in paperback. Antiqu Bk Mnthly R 10n01:16–21 Ja '83. facsims.
'Checklist' (p.20–1): *title list of original and paperback issues.*

5120 **Hall, Anthony.** Agatha Christie; the queen of crime. [Collecting]. Bk & Mag Coll 3:4–14 My '84. ports., illus., facsims.
'Agatha Christie's crime novels & collected stories' (p.12–14).

5121   **Barnard, Robert** and **Louise Barnard.** The Case of the two moving fingers. [Revisions in Am. ed. of The moving finger]. Armchair Detective 18no3:306–8 '85.

5122   **Thomas, Lewis E.** Agatha Christie & the Hercule Poirot books. [Collecting]. Bk & Mag Coll 25:4–14 Ap '86. illus., port., facsims.
'Complete bibliography of Agatha Christie's Hercule Poirot books' (p.14).

CHURCHILL, CARYL, 1938–

5123   **Fitzsimmons, Linda.** '5. A select bibliography [of primary and secondary sources]' *in* File on Churchill. (Writer-files). [London], Methuen, [1989]. p.92–5.

CHURCHILL, JOHN, 1ST DUKE OF MARLBOROUGH, 1650–1722

5124   **Hudson, J.P.** The Blenheim papers. [Marlborough family]. Brit Libr J 8no1:1–6 '82.

CHURCHILL, SIR WINSTON LEONARD SPENCER, 1874–1965

5125   **Thomas, David A.** The historical works of sir Winston Churchill. [Collecting]. Bk & Mag Coll 24:4–11 F '86. port., facsims.
'Complete bibliography of sir Winston Churchill's historical works' (p.11).

5126   **Cohen, Ronald J.** Letter to the editor. [Dust jackets and his Churchill bibliogr.]. Bk Coll 38no1:65 '89.

CIBBER, COLLEY, 1671–1757

5127   **Viator, Timothy J.** Colley Cibber; a bibliography, 1967–1987. Restor & 18th Cent Theat Res ser2 4no2:31–8 '89.

CLARE, JOHN, 1793–1864

5128   **Howard, William J.** 'Selected bibliography [of primary and secondary sources]' *in* John Clare. (Twayne's English authors, 312). Boston, Twayne, [1981]. p.198–201.

5129   **Crossan, Greg C.** John Clare; a bibliography of commentary on the poems, to 1982. Bull Bib 41no4:185–200 D '84.

5130   **Estermann, Barbara.** John Clare; an annotated primary and secondary bibliography. New York, Garland, 1985. xxviii,303p. 21cm. (Reference

library of the humanities, 581).
Rev. G. Crossan John Clare Soc J 6:50–1 '87; G. Crossan N&Q 232:268–9 '87.

5131 (5:9464e) **Powell, David**. The John Clare collection in Northampton public library. Libr World 65no767:362–3 My '64. illus., facsim.

5132 **Crossan, Greg C.** John Clare's poetry; an examination of the textual accuracy of some recent editions. (Review essay). Stud Romanticism 23no4:581–98 '84.

5133 ——— Some fugitive John Clare items, 1820–1977. N&Q 231no2:167–70 Je '86; D. Powell and E. Robinson 232no2:244–5 Je '87.
1. Uncollected poems and letters.–2. Biographical sources.

5134 **Powell, Margaret A.** Clare and his patrons in 1820; some unpublished papers. John Clare Soc J 6:4–9 Jl '87. facsim.

CLARKE, ARTHUR CHARLES, 1917–

5135 **Beatie, Bruce A.** Arthur C. Clarke and the alien encounter; the background of Childhood's end. Extrapolation 30no1:53–69 '89.
'Primary sources: Works by Arthur C. Clarke' (p.65–7).

CLARKE, AUSTIN, 1896–1974

5136 **Harmon, Maurice**. Austin Clarke, The sword of the west (1921, 1936, 1974). [Text]. Étud Irlandaises 10:93–104 D '85.

CLARKE, MARCUS ANDREW HISLOP, 1846–81

5137 **McLaren, Ian F.** Richard Bentley and the publication of His natural life. Bib Soc Aust & N.Z. Bull 6no1:3–21 '82. tables.

CLELAND, JOHN, 1709–89

5138 (1:2813gh) **Ashbee, Herbert S.** 'Appendix [on Memoirs of a woman of pleasure, extr. from Pisanus Fraxi's Catena librorum tacendorum, 1885]' *in* Memoirs of a woman of pleasure. With an introd. by Peter Quennell. New York, G.P. Putnams, [1963]. p.299–319.

5139 (1:2813gk) **Larsen, Poul S.** John Cleland's Memoirs of a woman of pleasure; a bibliography of the earliest editions. [Copenhagen], 1968. 8l. 30cm. (Typescript: BL 2785.cp.20).

5140   **McCorison, Marcus A.** Memoirs of a woman of pleasure or Fanny Hill in New England. Am Bk Coll new ser 1no3:29–30 My/Je '80.

5141   **Sabor, Peter**. The censor censured; expurgating Memoirs of a woman of pleasure. Eight Cent Life new ser 9no3:192–201 My '85.

5142   **Basker, James G.** 'The wages of sin'; the later career of John Cleland. [Publ.]. Étud Angl 40no2:178–94 Avril/Juin '87.

CLEVELAND, JOHN, 1613–58

5143   **Duffy, Helen** and **P.S. Wilson**. Two manuscripts of John Cleveland. [The rebel Scot; A dialogue]. N&Q 230no2:162–6 Je '85. diagrs.

CLOUGH, ARTHUR HUGH, 1819–61

5144   **Scott, Patrick G.** The editorial problem in Clough's Adam and Eve. Browning Inst Stud 9:79–104 '81. table.

COKE, DESMOND F.T., 1879–1931

5145   **Lamb, R.W.** Desmond Coke, novelist, collector, patron of the arts, philanthropist. Antiqu Bk Mnthly R 16no6:216–18 Je '89. port.
'Check-list of first editions of books by Desmond F.T. Coke' (p.217–18).

COLERIDGE, JOHN, 1719–81

5146   **Sherbo, Arthur**. John Coleridge and the Gentleman's magazine. [Attributions]. Bull Res Humanit 86no1:86–93 '83.

COLERIDGE, SAMUEL TAYLOR, 1772–1832.

5147   **Milton, Mary L.T.** The poetry of Samuel Taylor Coleridge; an annotated bibliography of criticism, 1935–1970. New York, Garland, 1981. xiv,251p. 21cm. (Reference library of the humanities, 247).

5148   **Crawford, Walter B. [and others].** Samuel Taylor Coleridge; an annotated bibliography of criticism and scholarship, II: 1900–1939, with additional entries for 1795–1899. Boston, G.K. Hall, [1983]. l,812p. 23cm. (Reference Guide to Lit).

5149   **Jordan, Frank**, *ed.*, 1985: no.4375.

5150 **Coffman, Ralph J.** Coleridge's library; a bibliography of books owned by Samuel Taylor Coleridge. Boston, G.K. Hall, 1987. xlvi,255p. 29cm.

5151 **Whalley, George**, *ed.* 'Annex B: The dispersal of Coleridge's books' *in* Marginalia, I: Abbot to Byfield. (The collected works of Samuel Taylor Coleridge, XII, 1). Princeton, N.J., Princeton U.P.; London, Routledge & K. Paul, [1980]. p.clvi–clxxiv.
'Chronological tables...Location and dispersal of Coleridge's books' (p.liii–lv).

5152 **Books** owned by S.T. Coleridge, 186v. many with ms. notes, in BL *see* Gould, Alison, Named special collections, 1981: no.818.

5153 **Bentley, Gerald E., jr.** Coleridge, Stothard, and the first illustrations of 'Christabel'. Stud Romanticism 20no1:111–16 '81. facsim.

5154 **Little, Geoffrey** and **Elizabeth Hall.** Coleridge's 'To the rev. W.L. Bowles'; another version? (Notes). R Eng Stud new ser 32no126:193–6 My '81.

5155 **Citron, Jo Ann**. Two unrecorded manuscripts of Christabel. Wordsworth & Circ 13no4:214–18 '82.

5156 **Huftel, Sheila**. Coleridge's books. [Libr.]. Contemp R 243no1413:206–8 Oc '83.

5157 **Whalley, George**. 'Coleridge and the self-unravelling clue' *in* Conference on editorial problems, 18th, Toronto, 1982. Editing polymaths, Erasmus to Russell; papers given.... Ed. by H.J. Jackson. Toronto, Committee for the conference on editorial problems, 1983. p.17–40.

5158 **Little, Geoffrey**. Coleridge's copy of Lyrical ballads, 1800 and his connection with the Irving family. [E. Irving's copy in State libr. of Victoria, Melbourne]. Bk Coll 33no4:457–69 '84.

5159 **Mays, James C.C.** Coleridge's borrowings from Jesus college library, 1791–94. [List]. Cambridge Bib Soc Trans 8pt5:557–81 '85.

5160 **Modiano, Raimonda**. Coleridge's marginalia. [Editing]. Text 2:257–68 '85.

5161 **Coffman, Ralph J.** The working library of Samuel Taylor Coleridge. J Libr Hist 21no2:277–99 '86. tables.
Coleridge's working libraries in London.–Coleridge's working libraries in Bristol.–...in Germany.–...in the north.–...in Malta....in Highgate.–Summary.

5162 **Wallen, Martin J.** Return and representation; the revisions of 'The ancient mariner'. Wordsworth & Circ 17no3:148–56 '86.

5163 **Nabholtz, John R.** The text of Coleridge's Essays on the principles of genial criticism. (Notes and documents). Mod Philol 85no2:187–92 N '87.

5164 **Woodring, Carl R.** Recording from Coleridge's voice. [Lectures and conversation]. Text 3:367–76 '87.

5165 **Walker, Eric C.** Biographia literaria and Wordsworth's revisions. Stud Eng Lit 28no4:569–88 '88.

5166 **Freeman, Arthur** and **T. Hoffman**. The ghost of Coleridge's first effort; 'A monody on the death of Chatterton.' [Offset text]. Library ser6 11no4:328–35 D '89. facsims.

5167 **Nye, Eric W.** Coleridge and the publishers; twelve new manuscripts. Mod Philol 87no1:51–72 Ag '89.

COLLIER, JOHN PAYNE, 1789–1883

5168 **Wellens, Oskar.** Thomas Barnes's and John Payne Collier's contributions to the British lady's magazine, 1815–1818. N&Q 229no1:62–3 Mr '84.

5169 —— The Colliers of London; early advocates of Wordsworth, Lamb, Coleridge, and other romantics. Bull Res Humanit 86no1:105–27 '85.
'Table A: John Payne Collier's contributions to the Critical review' (p.119–21); 'Table B: John Dyer Collier's contributions to the Critical review' (p.123–5); 'Appendix: John Payne Collier's contributions to the Critical's "Bibliotheca antiqua" (p.126–7).

5170 —— John Payne Collier and the British Lady's magazine, 1815–1818; new attributions. N&Q 230no3:338–41 S '85.

5171 **Ganzel, Dewey.** Fortune and men's eyes; the career of John Payne Collier. Oxford, O.U.P., 1982. x,454p. ports. 21cm.
Disgrace.–1. Fortune: 'Do you mean to breed him up to authorship?'–2. The History of English dramatic poetry: 'I have sometimes pcked up curiousities in the most beaten paths'.–3. The Works of William Shakespeare: 'Few know what it was, and fewer what I have made it.'–4. The Catalogue controversy: 'I entirely, and from the first, misunderstood.'–5. The Perkins folio: 'I at first repented my bargain...'.–6. The Ellesmere thefts and Literary cookery: 'I declare war to the knife...'.–7. The Museum acquisition: '...not a natural hand of any period'.–8. An Inquiry and A reply: 'In all probability mr. Rodd named you to me...'.–9. A Complete view: 'Let his slip down'.–10. Men's eyes: '...it is my tendency now to think worse of the world than it really deserves.'–Appendix [on posthumous attacks on Collier].
Rev: L. Marder Sh Newsl 32:27,35 '82; Claudia Nelson Plain Dealer 28 N '82:20–D; W.M. Baillie Renaiss & Reform 8:146–9 '84; K-H. Magister Sh Jahrb Weimar 120:189–91 '84; A.S. Bell Library ser6 6:413–14 '84; K. Muir Sewanee R 92: 270–3 '84; S. Bennett Vict Stud 27:260–1 '84.

5172 **Ganzel, Dewey**. John Payne Collier. (To the editor). TLS 20 My '83:516; A. Freeman 3 Je '85:573; D. Ganzel 24 Je '83:667; R.W. Connon; A. Freeman 8 Jl '83:729; G.V. Speaight 22 Jl '83:783.

5173 **Jenkins, David C.** The alleged Collier forgeries. [Report of MLA conference session]. Sh Newsl 33n04:39 '83.

5174 **Ganzel, Dewey**. The Collier forgeries and the Ireland controversy. [And G. Steevens]. Sh Newsl 34n01:6 '84.

5175 **Jones, G.P.** John Payne Collier's reputation; review article. [On D. Ganzel]. Med & Renaiss Drama Eng 3:255–63 '86.

5176 —— A Burbage ballad and John Payne Collier. ['The burning of the Globe']. (Notes). R Eng Stud new ser 40n0159:393–7 Ag '89.

COLLINGWOOD, ROBIN GEORGE, 1889–1942

5177 **Taylor, Donald S.** R.G. Collingwood, a bibliography; the complete manuscripts and publications, selected secondary writings, with selective annotation.. New York, Garland, 1988. xiv,279p. 21cm. ([Bibs of modern critics and critical schools]).

COLLINS, JOHN CHURTON, 1848–1908

5178 **Kearney, Anthony**. 'Select bibliography' *in* John Churton Collins; the louse on the locks of literature. Edinburgh, Scottish academic pr., 1986. p.[176]–81.
Classified checklist of books, works edited, uncollected articles and miscellaneous pieces, and ana.

COLLINS, WILLIAM WILKIE, 1824–89

5179 **Lonoff, Sue**. 'Selected bibliography [of primary and secondary works]' *in* Wilkie Collins and his Victorian readers; a study in the rhetoric of authorship. (AMS Stud Ninet Cent, 2). New York, AMS pr., [1982]. p.270–88.

5180 **Gasson, Andrew**. Wilkie Collins; a collector's and bibliographer's challenge. Priv Libr ser3 3n02:51–71 '80. illus., facsims.

5181 **Lohrli, Anne**. Wilkie Collins and Household words. [The dead secret]. Vict Pers R 15n04:118–19 '82.

5182 —— Wilkie Collins: two corrections. ['The double-bedded room'; 'The yellow tiger']. Eng Lang N 22n01:50–3 S '84.

5183 **Rude, Donald W.** and **N. Layne Neeper.** A unique copy of the first American edition of Wilkie Collins' The woman in white. [1860]. Analytical & Enum Bib new ser 2no3:107–9 '88.

5184 **Peters, Catherine.** Corrigendum to The Wellesley index. ['The midnight mass' by another]. N&Q 234no2:182 Je '89.

COMPTON, JAMES, 3D EARL OF NORTHAMPTON, 1622–81

5185 (7:3893*) **Kelliher, W. Hilton.** A hitherto unrecognised Cavalier dramatist; James Compton, third earl of Northampton. Brit Libr J 6no2:158–87 '80. facsims.
The Compton family and theatre.–Northampton and the players.–Northampton's writings in manuscript.–The political writings.–The plays in translation.–The original dramas.–List of the writings of James Compton 3rd earl of Northampton, now Add. MSS. 60276–82 among the Castle Ashby manuscripts.

5186 **Wolf, William D.** The authorship of The mandrake and Leontius, king of Cyprus. (Bibliographical notes). Library 2no4:456–60 D '80. facsims.

CONGREVE, WILLIAM, 1670–1729

5187 (7:3896) **Bartlett, Laurence.** William Congreve; a reference guide, [1979].
Rev: A. Wertheim Lit Res Newsl 6:112–13 '81.

5188 **Hughes, Leo** and **A.H. Scouten.** Congreve at Drury lane: two eighteenth-century promptbooks. [Revision]. Mod Philol 19no2:146–56 N '81.

5189 **McKenzie, Donald F.** 'Typography and meaning; the case of William Congreve' *in* Barber, Giles G. and B. Fabian, *ed.* Buch und Buchhandel in Europa im achtzehnten Jahrhundert; The book and the book trade in eighteenth-century Europe...proceedings of the fifth Wolfenbütteler symposium, November 1–3, 1977. (Wolfenbütteler Schriften zur Geschichte des Buchwesens, 4). Hamburg, [1981]. p.[81]–125. facsims.

5190 —— Six readings in a recent edition of Congreve's comedies. N&Q 229no3:373–6 S '83.

5191 —— 'The game of quadrille; an allegory: a Congreve attribution. [1729]. Bk Coll 34no2:209–13 '85.

CONRAD, JOSEPH, pseud. of TEODOR JÓZEF KONRAD KORZE-NIOWSKI, 1857–1924

5192 **Higdon, D. Leon** and **D.W. Rude**. Conrad bibliography, 1978–79, a continuing checklist. Conradiana 12no2:135–46 '80; D.L. Higdon..., 1979–80; a continuing checklist. 13no3:229–39 '81; ..., 1984–1986. 19no3:215–29 '87; with Amy L. Waugh, ..., 1986–1987. 20no3:229–38 '88.
For 1981–3, see no.5200.

5193 **Rude, Donald W.** Additions to a checklist of Joseph Conrad's works in author's corrected proofs. Analytical & Enum Bib 4no3/4:173–9 '80.
Notes on 21 items additional to BLB 1970–79: 3908; see also no.5202.

5194 —— Some additions to the bibliographies of Joseph Conrad...Ford Madox Ford and George Gissing. (Bibliographical notes). Pa Bib Soc Am 75no3:347–9 '81.

5195 **Gillon, Adam**. 'Selected bibliography [of primary and secondary sources]' *in* Joseph Conrad. (Twayne's English authors, 333). Boston, Twayne, [1982]. p.191–202.

5196 **Hamner, Robert D.** Joseph Conrad and the colonial world; a selected bibliography. Conradiana 14no3:217–29 '82.

5197 **Steele, Eugene**. Conrad studies in the Soviet union, 1966–1980. Conradiana 14no2:127–30 '82.

5198 **Rude, Donald W.** The Richard Gimbel collection of Conrad's manuscripts and typescripts at the Philadelphia free library. Conradiana 15no3:231–6 '83.

5199 —— Some additions to the bibliographies of Joseph Conrad,...George Gissing.... Amalytical & Enum Bib 8no4:248 '84.

5200 **Higdon, D. Leon**. Conrad in the eighties; a bibliography and some observations. [Checklist, 1981–3]. Conradiana 17no3:214–49 '85. tables.

5201 **Secor, Robert** and **Debra Moddelmorg**, *ed.* Joseph Conrad and American writers; a bibliographical study of affinities, influences and relations. Westport, Conn., Greenwood, [1985]. xxxv,258p. 23cm. (Bibs & Indexes to Am Lit, 5).

5202 **Rude, Donald W.** Additions to a checklist of Joseph Conrad's works in author's corrected proofs. Analytical & Enum Bib 4no3/4:173–9 '86.
Notes on 21 additional items to no.5193.

5203 **Knowles, Owen**. Conrad in some recent general studies and collections: brief notices. Conradian 11no2:194–5 N '87; 12no2:187–8 N '87.

5204 **Ray, Martin S.** Joseph Conrad and his contemporaries; an annotated bibliography of interviews and recollections. London, Joseph Conrad society, 1988. 123p. ports. 21cm. (Joseph Conrad Soc (UK). Monogr, 1). (Reprod. from typewriting).

5205 (5:9660e) **Ordoñez, Elmer A.** The early Joseph Conrad; revisions and style. Quezon City, University of the Philippines, 1968. viii,192p. 24cm. (Philippine Soc Sci & Humanit R 33no1/2:187–90 Mr/Je '68).
Includes 2. From manuscript to print.–3. From serial to book edition.

5206 **Higdon, D. Leon.** Joseph Conrad, Under western eyes; location of typescript. (Query 332). Bk Coll 29no1:117 '80.

5207 **Michael, Marion** and **W. Barry**. The typescript of The heart of darkness. Conradiana 12no2:147–55 '80.

5208 **Bateman, Paula A.** and **S.W. Reid**. The typescript leaf of Nostromo in the British library. Conradiana 13no2:149–50 '81.

5209 **Hobson, Robert W.** Conrad's first story and the Savoy; typescript revisions of 'The idiots'. Stud Short Fict 18no3:267–72 '81.

5210 **Rude, Donald W.** Two unreported Conrad manuscripts in the George B. Arents research library at Syracuse university. Analytical & Enum Bib 5no2:98–9 '81.

5211 **Sizemore, Christine W.** Ridway's militant weekly and the serial version of Conrad's Secret agent. Analytical & Enum Bib 5no3:143–52 '81.

5212 **Epps, Edwin C.** Lost Conrad typescript rediscovered. [Suspense, pt.3, ch.3]. Conradiana 14no1:51–2 '82.

5213 **Rude, Donald W.** Additions [to] Lindstrand's survey of Conrad Manuscripts. (Note 445). Bk Coll 31no4:505–6 '82; Further additions 33no2:236–8 '84.

5214 —— Conrad literary manuscripts. [Sought]. (Queries). Pa Bib Soc Am 76no1:83 '82; Conrad's manuscripts. (Query 355). Bk Coll 31no3:377 '82; Joseph Conrad manuscripts and typescripts. (Reader's queries). N&Q 227no4:352 Ag '82.

5215 —— From the library of Frank J. Hogan; two lost Conrad items. Analytical & Enum Bib 6no3:181–2 '82.

5216 **Reid, Sidney W.** The first editions of The secret agent. Library ser6 5no3:237–53 S '83. table.

5217 **Rude, Donald W.** Conrad's The Torrens; a personal tribute. [Ms.]. (Bibliographical notes). Library ser6 5no2:169–70 Je '83.

5218 **Stape, John H.** Conrad 'private printed'; the Shorter and Wise limited edition pamphlets. Pa Bib Soc Am 77no3:317–32 '83.
'Appendix: The Shorter and Wise pamphlets' (p.329–32): *chronol. checklist, with locations of proofs.*

5219 —— Conrad's Notes on life & letters; some revised dates of composition. Conradiana 15no2:153–5 '83.

5220 **Rude, Donald W.** The first American edition of Conrad's 'author's note' to Nostromo. Conradiana 16no1:79–80 '84.

5221 —— Three lost pieces of Conradiana. Analytical & Enum Bib 8no3:171–2 '84.

5222 **Siegle, Robert.** The two texts of Chance. Conradiana 16no2:83–99 '84.

5223 **Stape, John H.** The writing and publication of Conrad's 'Poland revisited'. Conradiana 16no2:155–9 '84.

5224 **Brown, Geoffrey.** Joseph Conrad. [Collecting]. Bk & Mag Coll 22:4–10 D '85. port., facsims.
'Complete bibliography of Joseph Conrad's first editions' (p.10).

5225 **Carabine, Keith.** Conrad, Pinker, and Under western eyes, a novel. Conradian 10no2:144–53 N '85.

5226 **Higdon, D. Leon.** Edward Garnett's copy of Under western eyes. Conradian 10no2:139–43 N '85.

5227 **Knowles, Owen.** Conrad in some recent general studies and collections; brief notices. Conradian 10no2:179–80 N '85.

5228 **Rude, Donald W.** Some ghosts laid to rest; a note on Gordon J. Lindstrand's survey of Conrad's manuscripts and typescripts. Conradiana 17no2:147–8 '85.

5229 **Stevens, H. Ray.** Joseph Conrad's Last essays. [Mss. sought]. (Readers' queries). N&Q 230no2:251 Je '85.

5230 **Sullivan, Ernest W.** The genesis and evolution of Joseph Conrad's 'Youth'; a revised and copy-edited typescript page. R Eng Stud new ser 36no144:522–34 N '85. facsim.

5231 **Higdon, D. Leon.** 'Word for word'; the collected editions of Conrad's Under western eyes. Conradiana 18no2:129–36 '86.

5232 **Lowens, Peter J.** The Conrad-Pinker relationship; an unpublished letter. Conradiana 18no1:45–7 '86.

5233 **Rude, Donald W.** Joseph Conrad letters, typescripts, and proofs in the Texas tech Conrad collection. Conradian 11no2:136–54 N '86.

5234 ——Joseph Conrad typescripts at Fales library. (Bibliographical notes). Library ser6 8no4:360–2 D '86.

5235 —— Three bibliographical notes on Conrad. Conradiana 18no2:144–6 '86.
> 1. The fragmentary typescript of 'Typhoon.'–2. 'Legends', a Conrad manuscript recovered.–3. 'Geography and some explorers', a note and an query.

5236 **Stape, John H.** The date and writing of Conrad's 'Stephen Crane: a note without dates'. [1919]. N&Q 231no2:184–5 Je '86.

5237 **Szczypien, Jean M.** Untyrannical copy-texts for the prefatory essays to Joseph Conrad's A personal record. Conradian 11no1:16–23 My '86.

5238 **Canterbury. Museums.** Joseph Conrad; the Canterbury collection. [Descr. brochure to accompany an exhibition]. [Canterbury], Canterbury heritage, [1987]. 8p. illus., ports. 30cm. Covertitle.

5239 **Carabine, Keith.** 'The secret sharer'; a note on the dates of its composition. Conradiana 19no3:209–13 '87.

5240 **Hawthorn, Jeremy.** Conrad and lintels; a note on the text of The shadow-line. Conradian 12no2:178–9 N '87.

5241 **Higdon, D. Leon.** The unrecognized second edition of Conrad's Under western eyes. [Cheap ed., 1917]. Stud Bib 40:220–5 '87. table.

5242 **Higdon, D. Leon** and **R.F. Sheard.** Conrad's 'unkindest cut': the canceled scenes in Under western eyes. Conradiana 19no3:167–81 '87.

5243 **Purdy, Dwight H.** Conrad at work; the two serial texts of Typhoon. Conradiana 19no2:99–119 '87.

5244 **Rude, Donald W.** 'The Texas tech Conrad collection; its history and significance' *in* Sullivan, Ernest W. and D.J. Murrah, *ed.* The Donne Dalhousie discovery. Lubbock, Texas tech pr., 1987. p.11–20.

5245 **Stape, John H.** The textual history of Notes on life & letters; the book text. [1921]. Conradiana 19no2:121–38 '87. diagr., tables.
> The making of Notes on life & letters.–The first English edition.–The first American edition.–The limited collected editions. The collected editions.

5246 **Szczypien, Jean M.** New light on the composition of Joseph Conrad's A personal record. [Ms.]. N&Q 232no1:50–1 N '87.

5247 **Teets, Bruce E.** Joseph Conrad; an annotated bibliography, 1971. [On its compilation]. Conradiana 19no1:41–7 '87.

5248 **Carabine, Keith**. 'The black mate', June-July, 1886, January, 1908. Conradian 13no2:128–48 D '88.

5249 **Fraser, Gail**. Conrad's revisions to Amy Foster. Conradiana 20no3:181–93 '88.

5250 **Higdon, D. Leon.** Conrad, Under western eyes, and the mysteries of revision. R Eng Stud new ser 39no054:231–44 My '88. tables.

5251 **Rude, Donald W.** Some unrecorded Joseph Conrad typescripts and proofs. (Bibliographical notes). Library ser6 10no1:44–51 Mr '88.

5252 **Stape, John H.** The Joseph Conrad collection at Syracuse university. Courier (Syracuse) 23no1:27–32 '88. illus., facsim.
First editions.–Privately printed and limited editions.–Letters.–Manuscript and type-script materials.

5253 —— Conrad to T.F. Unwin and Neil Munro: two unpublished letters. N&Q 234no2:192 Je '89.

COOPER, ANTHONY ASHLEY, 3D EARL SHAFTESBURY, 1671–1713

5254 **Chapin, Chester**. British references to Shaftesbury, 1700–1800; additions, with commentary, to A.O. Aldridge's list. Philos Res Archives 13:315–29 '87/8.

5255 (7:3940) **Wright, William C.** Piere Desmaizeaux. N&Q '74; H. Meyer 219no12:471 D '74.

5256 **Meyer, Horst E.** Ein Philosoph gestaltet seine Bucher: Shaftesbury und die Drucklegung der Characteristicks, 1711/14. Imprimatur neue Folge 11:255–68 '84. facsims.

5257 **Wolf, Richard B.** The first two editions of Shaftesbury's Characteristics; corrigenda and addenda to Meyer's Limae labor. (Bibliographical notes). Pa Bib Soc Am 78no3:349–54 '84.

COPPARD, ALFRED EDGAR, 1878–1957

5258 **Cave, Roderick G.J.M.** Adam & Eve & Golden cockerel. Matrix 7:42–56 '87.

CORNIER, VINCENT WILLIAM, 1898–1976

5259 **Leadbetter, Stephan**. Vincent Cornier rediscovered. [With checklist]. Armchair Detective 21no4:426–30 '88.

CORRY, JOHN, 1760?–1825?

5260 **Pitcher, Edward W.** The miscellaneous works of John Corry, 1760?–1825? (Bibliographical notes). Pa Bib Soc Am 80no1:83–90 '86.
'Checklist' (p. 89–90): *c.1780–1825*.

COTTON, CHARLES, 1630–87

5261 **Parks, Stephen**. 'Charles Cotton and the Derby manuscript' *in* Parks, Stephen and P.J. Croft. Literary autographs. Los Angeles, 1983. p.[1]–35. facsims.
Rev: Katherine Duncan-Jones TLS 2 Mr '84:231.

5262 **Dust, Alvin I.** The Derby ms. book of Cotton's poems and Contentation reconsidered. Stud Bib 37:170–80 '84. table.

COUTTS, ANGELA GEORGINA BURDETT-, BARONESS BUR DETT-COUTTS, 1814–1906

5263 **Orton, Diana**. 'Select bibliography' *in* Made of gold; a biography of Angela Burdett Coutts. London, H. Hamilton, [1980]. p.[267]–70.

COWARD, SIR NÖEL PIERCE, 1899–1973

5264 **Russell, Jacqui**. '5. A select bibliography [of primary and secondary sources]' *in* File on Coward. (Writer-files). London, Methuen, [1987]. p.92–6.

COWLEY, ABRAHAM, 1618–67

5265 **Pritchard, Allen**. 'Editing from manuscript; Cowley and Cowper papers [The civil war]' *in* Conference on editorial problems, 16th,

Toronto, 1980. Editing poetry from Spenser to Dryden; papers given.... Ed. by A.H. de Quehen. New York, 1981. p.[46]–76.

COWPER, WILLIAM, 1731–1800

5266 **Sherbo, Arthur**. William Cowper and the European magazine. [Unnoticed contributions, 1789]. Stud Bib 34:238–41 '81.

5267 **Rogers, Deborah D.** Cowper's 'Ode on reading Richardson's History of Charles Grandison' again. [Ms. in Berg colln., N.Y.P.L.]. Pa Lang & Lit 18no4:416–20 '82.

CRAIG, EDWARD GORDON, 1872–1966

5268 **Franklin, Colin**. Fond of printing; Gordon Craig as typographer & illustrator. With a foreword by Edward Craig and an essay by Gordon Craig on illustrations in general. London, Hurtwood publs., 1980. 89p. illus., facsims. 19cm. (And anr. issue ltd. to 125 copies).
Also issued San Francisco, Book club of California, 1980. (Bk Club California Publ, 164); New York, The typophiles, 1980. (Typophiles chap book, 54).

5269 **Craig, Edward G.** Gordon Craig prints The mask in Italy. [Publ.]. Matrix 1:6–11 '81. facsims.

5270 **Newman, L.M.** Artist and printer; a problem of the Cranach press Hamlet resolved. Matrix 4:1–12 '84. facsims.

5271 **Thompson, Edward**, *ed.* Edward Gordon Craig: letters concerning On the art of the theatre. [Publ.]. Matrix 7:57–68 '87.

CRAIK, DINAH MARIA (MULOCK), 1826–87

5272 **Mitchell, Sally**. 'Selected bibliography [of primary and secondary works]' *in* Dinah Mulock Craik. (Twayne's English authors, 364). Boston, Twayne, [1983]. p.131–41.

CRAKANTHORPE, RICHARD, 1567–1624

5273 **Linnell, Naomi**. A unique copy of Richard Crakanthorp's Logic. [With authorial annotations]. (Bibliographical notes). Library ser6 4no3:323–6 S '82. facsim.

CRANE, RALPH, fl.1575–1632

5274 **Haas, Virginia J.** Ralph Crane, a status report. Analytical & Enum Bib new ser 3no1:3–10 '89.

CRANMER, ARCHBP. THOMAS, 1489–1556

5275 **Cambridge. University. Library.** Cranmer, primate of all England; catalogue of a quincentenary exhibition at the British library, 27 October –21 January, 1990. Comp. by Paul Ayris. Ed. with an introd. and chronology by Peter Newman Brooks. [London], British library, 1989. 47p. illus., facsims., ports. 24cm.

CRASHAW, RICHARD, 1612?–49

5276 **Roberts, John R.** Richard Crashaw; an annotated bibliography of criticism, 1632–1980. Columbia, University of Missouri pr., 1985. 477p. 23cm.
Rev: R. Boston Choice 24:53–4 '86; D.R. Dickson Lit Res Newsl 10:40–1 '85; P.A. Parrish Sevent Cent New 44:12–13 '86; G. Soldano Lingue del Mondo 1/2:108 '86; R.V. Young J Eng & Germ Philol 86:245–7 '87; A.C. Labriola Mod Philol 84:431–4 '87; T.F. Healy N&Q 232:538–9 '87; G.A. Stringer Sth Carolina R 14:107–8 '87; E.R. Cunnar John Donne J 6:147–9 '87; R. Ellrodt Études Angl 42:214 '89; M.G. Brennan Analytical & Enum Bib new ser 1:82–3 '87.

5277 **White, William.** Dissertations on Richard Crashaw: addenda to Robert's bibliography. (Notes bibliographic). Bull Bib 42no4:221–2 D '85.

5278 **Knowles, Sebastian.** 'Only connect...'; Crashaw and four elegies in Bodleian ms. Tanner 465. Pa Bib Soc Am 81no4:433–50 '87.

CRAWFORD, FRANCIS MARION, 1854–1909

5279 **Moran, John C.** A note on F. Marion Crawford and Henry Brokman, with an unrecorded preface by Crawford. (Bibliographical notes). Pa Bib Soc Am 74no2:155–6 '80.

5280 ——An F. Marion Crawford miscellany: notes on the P.F. Collier edition, Arethusa, and some unrecorded contributions to periodicals. (Bibliographical notes). Pa Bib Soc Am 75no1:86–92 '81.

CREMER, ROBERT WYNDHAM KETTON-, 1906–69

5281 **Gretton, John R.** 'R.W. Ketton-Cremer' *in* Essays in book-colllecting. [Dereham, Norf.], 1985. p.41–7.
'A checklist of the books of R.W. Ketton-Cremer' (p.46–7) *with ana.*

CROFT, SIR HERBERT, 1751–1816

5282 **Todd, William B.** The Abbey of Kilkhampton; a register of epitaphs, 1780–1980. (Bibliographical notes). Pa Bib Soc Am 74no4:386–401 '80. facsim.
Summary list of references.–Register of epitaphs.–Index.

5283 **Garratt, John G.** The Abbey of Kilkhampton. Antiqu Bk Mnthly R 9no10:380–3 Oc '82. facsims.

CROMEK, ROBERT HARTLEY, 1770–1812

5284 **Reid, Dennis M.** Practicing the necessity of purification; Cromek, Roscoe, and The reliques of Burns. Stud Bib 35:306–19 '82.

CROMPTON, RICHMAL, *pseud. of* RICHMAL CROMPTON LAM-BURN, 1890–1969

5285 **Howman, Gary**. Richmal Crompton and the William books. [Collecting]. Bk & Mag Coll 2:23–31 Ap '84. facsims.
'Complete bibliography of the original William series' (p.30–1).

CRONIN, ARCHIBALD JOSEPH, 1896–1981

5286 **Salwak, Dale**. A.J. Cronin; a reference guide. Boston, Mass., G.K. Hall, [1982]. xv,185p. 23cm. (Reference guide to literature).
Rev: Isobel Murray Scott Lit J Suppl 20:23–4 '84.

5287 **Macleod, Helen**. A.J. Cronin. [Collecting]. Bk & Mag Coll 25:16–22 Ap '86. port., facsims.
'Complete UK bibliography of A.J. Cronin' (p.22).

DABORNE, ROBERT, d.1628

5288 **Holloway, Peter**. Scribal dittography; Daborne's The poor man's comfort. (Bibliographical notes). Library ser6 3no3: 233–9 S '81.

DANIEL, SAMUEL, 1562–1619

5289 **Harner, James L.** Samuel Daniel and Michael Drayton; a reference guide. Boston, Mass., G.K. Hall, [1980]. xviii,338p. 23cm.
Rev: P.J. Klemp Lit Res Newsl 7:116–17 '82; J. Buxton Yrbk Eng Stud 14:311–12 '84.

5290   **Pitcher, John**. Samuel Daniel: the Brotherton manuscript; a study in authorship. [Leeds], University of Leeds, School of English, 1981. xii,214p. illus., facsims. 33cm. (Leeds texts and monographs, new ser, 7).
1. The manuscript.–2. Evidence for ascription.–3. Samuel Daniel and the Brotherton manuscript.
Rev: W.P. Williams Analytical & Enum Bib 6:256–8 '82; B. Juel-Jensen Library ser6 5:428–30 '83; S.W. May Mod Philol 80:411–13 '83; D.B.J. Randall Renaiss Q 36:145–8 '83.

5291   **Shapiro, Isaac A.** The dedication of Daniel's Collection, 1618. Library ser6 3no1:62–4 Mr '81.

5292   **Jensen, Bent Juel-**. Daniel's First part of the historie of England, 1612, and Collection, ?1618. (Correspondence). Library 4no4:425 D '82.

5293   **Pitcher, John**. 'Editing Daniel' *in* Renaissance English text society. The 1985 forum.... [Chicago, Newberry library], 1986. l.1–12. facsims., diagrs.

DARTON, FREDERICK JOSEPH HARVEY, 1878–1936

5294   **Alderson, Brian W.**, *comp.* 'A listing of books by F.J. Harvey Darton' *in* Darton, F.J. Harvey. Children's books in England. 3d ed., rev. Cambridge, [1982]. p.336–8.
Chronol. checklist of books only, 1901–36.

DARWIN, CHARLES ROBERT, 1809–82

5295   **Toronto. University. Thomas Fisher rare book library.** Charles Darwin; a centenary exhibition in commemoration of the life and work of Charles Robert Darwin. [Comp. by Richard Landon and Philip Oldfield]. [Toronto], 1982. 35p. 27cm. (Reprod. from typewriting).

5296 (5:9826f)   **Mann, Sherrill** and **D.E. Fitch**. Darwin and evolution. [Colln. comp. by Peter Eaton mainly from J. Huxley libr.]. Soundings (UCLA Santa Barbara) 1no2:20–34 '69.

5297   **Landon, Richard G.** Charles Darwin; some bibliographical problems and textual implications. Bib Soc Canada Pa 20:21–40 '81. facsims.

5298   **Baker, William**. Microdarwiniana. [Borrowings from London library]. (Letters). TLS 23 N '84:1342; P. Reading 23 N '84:1342.

5299   **Burkhardt, Frederick**. Editing the correspondence of Charles Darwin. Stud Bib 41:149–59 '88.

DAVENANT, SIR WILLIAM, 1606–68

5300 **Blaydes, Sophia B.** and **P. Bordinat.** Sir William Davenant; an annotated bibliography, 1629–1985. New York, Garland, 1986. xx,370p. port., facsims. 21cm. (Reference library of the humanities, 525).
Rev: J. Egan Sevent Cent Newsl 45:69–70 '87; R. Dutton Sh Surv 40:221–2 '88.

———————

5301 **Gellert, James.** Davenant's The law against lovers; a 'lost' Herringman quarto. [1676 TP counterfeited in 1908]. (Bibliographical notes). Library ser6 5no1:57–60 Mr '83. facsims.

5302 **Gellert, James.** The sources of Davenant's The law against lovers. [And Measure for measure]. (Bibliographical notes). Library ser6 8no4:351–7 D '86. tables.

DAVENPORT, ROBERT, fl.1623

5303 **Tricomi, Albert H.** Watermark dating of Robert Davenport's literary manuscripts. (Bibliographical notes). Pa Bib Soc Am 83no3:359–64 S '89.

DAVIDSON, JOHN, 1857–1909

5304 **Uden, B.G. Grant.** The greatest of a doomed generation. Antiqu Bk Mnthly R 12no2:472–5 D '85. port., facsims.
'Check list' (p.475).

DAVIES, EDWARD TEGLA, 1880–

5305 **Davies, Pennar.** 'Select bibliography' *in* E. Tegla Davies. (Writers of Wales). [Cardiff], University of Wales pr. on behalf of the Welsh arts council, 1983. p.97–100.

DAVIES, IDRIS, 1905–53

5306 **Harris, Sylvia.** A bibliography of Idris Davies. Poet Wales 16no4:76–84 '81.

DAVIES, JOHN, 1565?–1618

5307 **Sawday, Jonathan.** Unattributed manuscript corrections to a poem by John Davies of Hereford. [Mirum in modum, in BL]. N&Q 226no1:40–1 '81.

DAVIES, WILLIAM HENRY, 1871–1940

5308   **Hollingdrake, Sybil**. Bibliography of works by W.H. Davies. Poet Wales 18no2:89–91 '83.

5309   **Nickson, Richard**. A poet not for all seasons; Shaw as trumpeter and censor. [Publ. of W.H. Davies' Autobiography; Young Emma]. Independent Shavian 19no2:35 '81.

DEFOE, DANIEL, 1661?–1731

5310   **Downie, J. Alan.** and **J.P.W. Rogers**. Defoe in the pamphlets; some additions and corrections. [To W.L. Payne, BLB 1970–79: 4018]. Philol Q 59no1:38–43 '80.

5311   **Rogers, J. Patrick W.** Addenda and corrigenda: Moore's Checklist of Defoe. (Bibliographical notes). Pa Bib Soc Am 75no1:60–4 '81.

5312   **Hammerschmidt, Hildegard**. Daniel Defoe; articles in periodicals, 1950–1980. Bull Bib 40no2:90–102 Je '83.

5313   **Stoler, John A.** Daniel Defoe; an annotated bibliography of modern criticism, 1900–1980. New York, Garland, 1984. xv,424p. 21cm. (Reference library of the humanities, 430).

5314   **Halimi, Suzy.** Daniel Defoe, The true-born Englishman, 1701: bibliographie sélective et critique. Soc d'Étud Anglo-Am Bull 21:21–43 N '85.

5315   **Peterson, Spiro.** Daniel Defoe; a reference guide, 1731–1924. Boston, G.K. Hall, 1987. xxxiii,455p. 23cm. (Reference guide to literature).

5316   **Richetti, John J.** 'Selected bibliography [of primary and secondary sources]' *in* Daniel Defoe. (Twayne's English authors, 453). Boston, Twayne, [1987]. p.146–51.

5317   **Rothman, Irving N.** Defoe's The family instructor; a response to the Schism act. Pa Bib Soc Am 74no3:202–20 '80.

5318   **Wilkie, Everett C.** Eidous' translation of Defoe's A general history of discoveries and improvements. [Histoire des principales découvertes, 1767]. (Bibliographical notes). Pa Bib Soc Am 74no1:67–70 '80.

5319   **Alsop, James D.** New light on Nathaniel Mist and Daniel Defoe. (Bibliographical notes). Pa Bib Soc Am 75no1:57–60 '81.

5320 **Backscheider, Paula R.** Defoe and the Edinburgh town council. [Patronage]. Scriblerian 14no1:44–6 '81.

5321 **Ellis, Frank H.** Notes for an edition of Defoe's verse. [Hologr. of 'The vision']. R Eng Stud 32no128:398–407 N '81. facsims.

5322 **MacAree, David.** Variant titles of a tract ascribed to Daniel Defoe. [The apparent danger of an invasion, 1701]. (Note 445). Bk Coll 31no3:371–5 '82.

5323 **Pickering, Samuel F.** The early editors of Robinson Crusoe. AB Bkmn's Wkly 72no2:3509–28 N '83.

5324 **Owens, W.R.** and **P.N. Furbank**. A Vindication of the press, 1718; not by Defoe? (Bibliographical notes). Pa Bib Soc Am 78no3:355–60 '84.

5325 **Rogers, J. Patrick W.** Defoe's Tour, 1742, and the chapbook trade. [Thomas Harris, publ.]. (Bibliographical notes). Library 6no3:275–9 S '84; R.C. Alston, Thomas Harris, publisher. (Correspondence) 7no1:63 Mr '85.

5326 **Rothman, Irving N.** Donald Govan; Defoe's Glasgow printer of The family instructor. [1717]. Biblioth 12no3:70–83 '84. facsim., illus.

5327 **Wood, J. Laurence.** Defoe serialized. [Novels in periodicals]. (Features). Factotum 19:21–3 Oc '84.

5328 **MacAree, David.** Title and text variants of a pamphlet ascribed to Daniel Defoe. [The Apparent danger of an invasion, 1701]. (Notes and documents). Huntington Libr Q 48no2:172–7 '85. facsims.

5329 **Rogers, J. Patrick W.** 'Moll in the chapbooks' *in* Literature and culture in eighteenth century England. [Brighton], Sussex, Harvester pr.; [Totowa], N.J., Barnes & Noble, [1985]. p.183–97.

5330 **Blewett, David.** 'Robinson Crusoe, Friday, and the noble savage; the illustration of the rescue of Friday scene in the eighteenth century' *in* Annandale, E.T. and R.A. Lebrun, *ed.* L'homme et la nature/Man and nature. (Proc Canadian Soc Eighteenth-century Stud, 5). Edmonton, Alberta, Publ. for the Society by Academic printing and publishing, 1986. p.[29]–49. facsims.

5331 **Furbank, P.N.** and **W.R. Owens**. What if Defoe did not write the History of the wars of Charles XII? Pa Bib Soc Am 80no3:333–47 '86.

5332 —— William Lee of Sheffield; sanitary reformer and Defoe bibliographer. Bk Coll 37no2:185–206 '87.

5333 **McLean, Ruari.** Collecting Robinson Crusoe. Antiqu Bk Mnthly R 14no5:178–81 My '87. facsims., illus.

5334 **Novak, Maximilian E.** A Vindication of the press and the Defoe canon. Stud Eng Lit 27no3:399–411 '87.

5335 **Blewett, David.** 'The illustration of Robinson Crusoe, 1719–1840' *in* Möller, Joachim, *ed.* Imagination on a long rein; English literature illustrated. [Marburg], [1988]. p.66–81. facsims.

5336 **Curtis, Laura A.** The attribution of A vindication of the press to Daniel Defoe. [1718]. Stud Eight Cent Culture 18:433–44 '88.

5337 **Furbank, P.N.** and **W.R. Owens**. The canonisation of Daniel Defoe. New Haven, Conn., Yale U.P., 1988. ix,210p. 23cm.
1. Doubts about the Defoe 'canon'.–2. Case-study; William Lee and The history of the wars of Charles XII.–3. Principles of author-attribution.–4. George Chalmers.–5. Walter Wilson.–6. William Lee.–7. James Crossley.–8. W.P. Trent.–9. John Robert Moore.–10. Defoe and prose style.–11. Defoe as poet.–12. Defoe as a man.–13. 'Knowing your author'.–14. Towards a new Defoe bibliography.–Appendices: A. Stylometry and Defoe. B. James Crossley's manuscript list of attributions.
Rev: D. Trotter TLS 20 My '88:551; H. Amory Bk Coll 38:410–14 '89; J.P.W. Rogers London R Bks 11:16–17 '89; A. Varney N&Q 234:514–15 '89; F.H. Ellis R Eng Stud new ser 40:419–22 '89; M.G.H. Pittock Brit J Eight Cent Stud 13:119–21 '90; P-G. Boucé Étud Angl 43:475–7 '90.

5338 —— The Defoe canon again. [A Vindication of the press, 1718]. (Bibliographical notes). Pa Bib Soc Am 82no1:95–8 Mr '88.

DEIGHTON, LEN, 1929–

5339 **Oliver, Edward Milward-.** Len Deighton; an annotated bibliography, 1954–1985. [London], Sammler pr.; Maidstone, Oliver, 1985. 64p. 20cm. (375 no. copies signed).

5340 —— 'Bibliography' *in* The Len Deighton companion. London, Grafton, [1987]. p.[309]–26.
'Twenty-five year chronology of British and American first editions' (p.[27]–9).

DEKKER, THOMAS, 1570?–1641?

5341 **Adler, Doris R.** Thomas Dekker; a reference guide. Boston, Mass., G.K. Hall, [1983]. xxiii,309p. 23cm. (Reference guide to literature).
Rev: M.R. Woodhead N&Q 230:521–2 '85; N.A. Brittin Sh Q 39:260–2 '88.

5342 **Adler, Doris R.** Thomas Dekker and bibliography. Res Opportunities Renaiss Drama 26:3–12 '83.

5343 **Mulholland, Paul.** The Roaring girl; new readings and further notes. Stud Bib 37:159–70 '84. facsim

5344 **Evans, Robert C.** Jonson, Satiromastix, and the poetomachia; a patronage perspective. Iowa State J Res 60no3:369–83 F '86.

5345 **Gasper, Julia**. A surplus coronation in Dekker's If this be not a good
play. ['crownde' for 'drownde' in 4.2.63]. N&Q 233no4:490–1 D '88.

DELIUS, FREDERICK, 1862–1934

5346 (7:4049d) **Threlfall, Robert**. A catalogue of the compositions of Frederick Delius; sources and references. London, Delius trust, 1977. 206p.
facsims., port., music. 25cm.

5347 **Lowe, Rachel**. A descriptive catalogue with checklists of the letters
and related documents in the Delius collection of the Grainger
museum, University of Melbourne. London, Delius trust, 1981.
v,233p. facsims., ports. 26cm. (Reprod. from typewriting). Ltd. to
500 no. copies.
Not indexed.

5348 —— Frederick Delius, 1862–1934; a repr. of the catalogue of the
musical archives of the Delius trust (1974) with minor corrs. London, Delius trust, 1986. (First publ. 1974). 183p. music. 23cm.
Adds index.

5349 **Threlfall, Robert**. Frederick Delius, a supplementary catalogue. London, Delius trust, 1986. 252p. music., port. 26cm. (Ltd. to 1000
copies).

DENHAM, SIR JOHN, 1615–69

5350 **Kelliher, W. Hilton**. John Denham; new letters and documents. Brit
Libr J 12no1:1–20 '86. ports., facsims.

DE QUINCEY, THOMAS, 1785–1859

5351 **Woof, Robert S.** Thomas De Quincey, an English opium eater, 1785–
1859; [exhibition] at the Grasmere and Wordsworth museum, at the
National library of Scotland...1986. [Grasmere], Trustees of Dove
cottage, [1985]. 115p. + errata. ports., facsims., geneal.table. 19cm.

5352 **Byrns, Richard H.** Some unrepublished articles of De Quincey in
Blackwood's magazine. Bull Res Humanit 85no3:344–51 '82. table.

5353 **Lindop, Grevel**. Newfound mid-brown manuscripts. [Holograph Confessions, 1st part, at Dove cottage]. TLS 14 Jl '89:772.

DEVEREAUX, ROBERT, 2D EARL OF ESSEX, 1566–1601

5354 **Davids, Roy**. The handwriting of Robert Devereux, second earl of Essex. Bk Coll 37no3:351–65 '88. facsims.

DIBDIN, THOMAS FROGNALL, 1776–1847

5355 **Priddy, John C.** Dibdin's Typographical antiquities; large paper copies. [Sought]. (Query 339). Bk Coll 29no4:594 '80.

5356 —— I. [i.e. T.] F. Dibdin's edition of Typographical antiquities. [Large paper copies sought]. (Query 354). Bk Coll 31no3:376–7 '82.

5357 **Windle, John R.** Bibliography of Dibdin. [Bibliogr. queries]. (Queries). Pa Bib Soc Am 76no1:84–7 '82.

5358 **Lister, Anthony**. A bibliomaniac abroad. Antiqu Bk Mnthly R 11no8:300–5 Ag '84; 11no9:346–9 S '84. port., facsims.

5359 **Rabaiotto, Renato**. A Dibdin collection. Priv Libr ser3 10no2:65–80 '87. illus.
      'A Dibdin collection in 1987' (p.76–80): *44 items*.

5360 **Hendricks, Donald D.** An unpublished Dibdin fragment. [Ms. in copy of Bibliomania]. (Note 424). Bk Coll 37no4:572–4 '88.

5361 **Rabaiotto, Renato**, *ed.* Thomas Frognall Dibdin: Horae bibliographicae Cantabrigienses; a facsim. of Dibdin's Cambridge notebook, 1823, with readings from The library companion, 1824. Containing a current finding-list of the books, mss. and prints examined by Dibdin in Cambridge libraries, comp. by David McKitterick. New Castle, Del., Oak Knoll books, 1989. 79p. port., facsims. 23cm. (Ltd. to 250 copies).
      'Finding-list' (p.[75]–[80]).

DICKENS, CHARLES JOHN HUFFAM, 1817–70

5362 **Cohn, Alan M.** and **K.K. Collins**. The Dickens checklist. Dickens Stud Newsl 11no1:29–32 Mr '80; 11no2:61–4 Je '80; 11no3:93–6 S '80; 11no4:125–6 D '80; 12no1:29–32 Mr '81; 12no2:62–4 Je '81; 12no3:94–6 S '81; 12no4:123–5 D '81; 13no1:27–30 Mr '82; 13no2:60–4 Je '82; 13no3:90–3 S '82; 13no4:123–5 D '82; 14no1:28–32 Mr '83; 14no2:75–9 Je '83; 14no3:125–7 S '83; 14no4:162–4 D '83.
      See no.5371.

5363 **Yale university. Library.** Dickens and Dickensiana; a catalogue of the Richard Gimbel collection in the Yale university library. Comp. by John B. Podeschi. New Haven, Yale university library, 1980. xxiii,570p. ports. 23cm.
Bibliogr. catalogue of major ed., minor ed., trans. and adaptations of, collected ed. and selections, periodicals, mss., autograph letters and documents, and Dickensiana.
Rev: K.J. Fielding Dickens Stud Newsl 13:54–7 '82.

5364 **Dunn, Richard J.** David Copperfield; an annotated bibliography. New York, Garland, 1981. xxv,256p. 21cm. (Dickens Bibs, 8).
Rev: D. Paroissien Dickensian 79:165–7 '83.

5365 **Gresh, Richard H.** Charles Dickens, The posthumous papers of the Pickwick club, 1836–7. [Census and collation of 'prime' copies]. (Query 343). Bk Coll 30no1:101 '81.

5366 **Nelson, Harland S.** 'Selected bibliography' *in* Charles Dickens. (Twayne's English authors, 314). Boston, Twayne, [1981]. p.249–56.

5367 **Cohn, Alan M.** and **K.K. Collins.** The cumulated Dickens checklist, 1970–1979. Troy, N.Y., Whitston, 1982. vi, 391p. facsim. 23cm.
Accumulated from Dickens Stud Newsl.
Rev: S. Monod Yrbk Eng Stud 16:321–2 '86; P. Preston N&Q 231:254–5 '86.

5368 **Smith, Walter E.** Charles Dickens in the original cloth; a bibliographical catalogue. Los Angeles, Heritage books, 1982–3. 2pts.(xvi,120; xvi,95p.) illus., facsims. 28cm.
1. The novels with Sketches by Boz. (1982).–2. The Christmas books and selected secondary works. (1983).
Rev: J. Stephens Dickensian 79:118–19 '83.

5369 **Bomans, Godfried.** Catalogus Dickens-collectie van Godfried Bomans; catalogue of the Dickens-collection.... [Ed. by] J.F.M. Olsthoon and J.M.L. Schoolmiesters. Tilburg, [Netherlands], Bibliotheek Katholieke hogeschool, 1983. 73p. 22cm. (Reprod. from typewriting).
English summary (p.13).

5370 **Brattin, Joel J.** and **B.G. Hornback.** Our mutual friend; an annotated bibliography. New York, Garland, 1984. xxi, 197p. 21cm. (Dickens Bibs, 1).

5371 **Cohn, Alan M.** The Dickens checklist. Dickens Q 1no1:37–40 Mr '84; 1no2:75–9 Je '84; 1no3:116–20 S '84; 1no4:153–6 D '84; 2no1:30–3 Mr '85; 2no2:71–4 Je '85; 2no3:109–11 S '85; 2no4:148–50 D '85; 3no1:67–71 Mr '86; 3no2:105–8 Je '86; 3no3:149–52 S '86; 3no4:197–9 D '86; 4no1:34–8 Mr '87; 4no2:123–6 Je '87; 4no3:180–3 S '87; 4no4:219–21 D '87; 5no1:40–4 Mr '88; 5no2:99–103 Je '88; 5no3:166–9 S '88; 5no4:204–7 D '88; 6no1:31–5 Mr '89; 6no2:72–9 Je '89.

5372   **Manning, Sylvia B.** Hard times; an annotated bibliography. New York, Garland, 1984. xxiii,296p. 22cm. (Reference library of the humanities, 515; Dickens Bib, 3).
Rev: J.G. Watson N&Q 232:558–9 '87.

5373   **Glancy, Ruth F.** Dickens's Christmas books, Christmas stories and other short fiction; an annotated bibliography. New York, Garland, 1985. xxxiii,610p. 23cm. (Dickens Bibs, 4).

5374   **Paroissien, David.** Oliver Twist; an annotated bibliography. New York, Garland, 1986. xxxvi,313p. 21cm. (Reference library of the humanities, 385; Dickens Bibs, 2).

5375   **Worth, George J.** Great expectations; an annotated bibliography. New York, Garland, 1986. xxii,346p. 21cm. (Reference library of the humanities, 555: Dickens Bibs, 5).

5376   **Rice, Thomas J.** Barnaby Rudge; an annotated bibliography. New York, Garland, 1987. xxxvii,351p. 21cm. (Reference library of the humanities, 630; Dickens Bibs, 6).
Rev: TLS 13 Ja '84:47; I. Crawford Dickensian 84:182–3 '88.

5377   **Schlicke, Priscilla** and **P. Schlicke**. The Old curiosity shop; an annotated bibliography. New York, Garland, 1988. xxi,495p. 21cm. (Reference library of the humanities, 708; Dickens Bibs, 9).

5378   **Bick, W., B. Czennia** and **S.R. Gaur**. Bibliographie der deutschen Übersetzungen der Romane von Charles Dickens, folge I. Anglia 107hft1/2:65–88 '89; II. 107hft3/4:430–51 1989.

5379   **Chittick, Kathryn**. The critical reception of Charles Dickens, 1833–1841. New York, Garland, 1989. xvi,277p. 22cm. (Reference library of the humanities, 900).

5380   **Jarndyce antiquarian booksellers,** LONDON. The Dickens catalogue. [London], [1989]. [140]p. facsims. 25cm. (Catalogue LXI). Covertitle.
Classified catalogue of works and ana; 1008 items.

5381 (5:10186g) **Bentley, Nicolas**. 'Dickens and his illustrators' *in* Tomlin, Eric W.F., *ed*. Charles Dickens, 1812–1870; a centenary volume. London, Weidenfeld & Nicolson; New York, Simon and Schuster, [1969]. p.196–227. facsims.

5382 (7:4107) **Patten, Robert L.** Charles Dickens and his publishers, [1978].
Rev: Deborah A. Thomas Stud Novel 14:126–8 '82.

5383 (7:4107d) **Steig, Michael**. Dickens and Phiz. Bloomington, Indiana U.P., 1978. x,340p. facsims. 23cm.

1. Dickens and Browne: illustration, collaboration, and iconography.–2. The beginnings of Phiz. Pickwick, Nickleby, and the emergence from caricature.–3. From caricature to progress: Master Humphrey's clock and Martin Chuzzlewit.–4. Dombey and son: iconography of social and sexual satire.–5. David Copperfield: progress of a confused soul.–6. Bleak house and Little Dorrit: iconography of darkness.–7. Phiz the illustrator: an overview and summing up.–Appendix: A checklist of the work of Hablot Knight Browne, 1836–1859 (p.317–22).

Rev: G. Reynolds Apollo 110:82 '79; J. Gold Univ Toronto Q 49:279–82 '80; J.H. Gardner Dickens Stud Newsl 11:58–61 '80; R.D. McMaster Eng Stud Canada 6:506–11 '80; P. Preston N&Q 225:557–8 '80; J.D. Hunt Dickensian 76:51–2 '80; Rachel Bennett R Eng Stud new ser 31:484–5 '80; S. Monod Mod Lang R 76:171–3 '81; Deborah A. Thomas Stud Novel 14:126–8 '82.

5384 **Cohen, Jane R.** Charles Dickens and his original illustrators. Columbus, Ohio state U.P., [1980]. xxv,295p. illus., facsims. 29cm.

1. Dickens and his early illustrators. 1. George Cruikshank. 2. Robert Seymour. 3. Robert Buss.–2. Dickens and his principal illustrator. 4. Hablot Browne.–3. Dickens and his other illustrators. The other illustrators of Master Humphrey's clock. 5. George Cattermole. 6. Samuel Williams. The illustrators of the Christmas books. 7. John Leech. 8. Richard Doyle. 9. John Tenniel. 10. Daniel Maclise. 11. Edwin Landseer. 12. Clarkson Stanfield. 13. Frank Stone. The illustrators of Pictures from Italy and A child's history of England. 14. Samuel Palmer. 15. Francis Topham. The illustrators of Our mutual friend and The mystery of Edwin Drood. 16. Marcus Stone. 17. Charles Collins. 18. Luke Fildes.–Conclusion: Dickens and the decline of the English illustrated novel after 1870.–Appendix: Dickens and his would-be illustrator, William Thackeray.

Rev: D. Alexander TLS 12 Je '81:680; A. Powell Apollo 113:125–7 '81; N.K. Hill Eng Lang N 19:73–5 '81; A. Sanders Dickensian 77:41–2 '81; Celina Fox Burlington Mag 124:778–9 '82; M. Baumgarten Western Humanities R 36:279–81 '82; Alice Schreyer Am Bk Coll new ser 4:42–51 '83.

5385 **Lutman, Stephen**. 'Reading illustrations; pictures in David Copperfield' *in* Gregor, Ian, *ed.* Reading the Victorian novel; detail into form. London, Vision; Totowa, N.J., Barnes & Noble, 1980. p.196–225. illus.

5386 **Solberg, Sarah A.** Dickens and illustration; a matter of perspective. J Narrative Technique 10:128–37 '80.

5387 —— 'Text dropped into the woodcuts'; Dickens' Christmas books. Dickens Stud Ann 8:103–18 '80. facsims.

5388 **Turpin, John**. Maclise as a Dickens illustrator. Dickensian 76no2:66–77 '80. facsims.

5389 **Translations** of Dickens's works, collected by lady Marie T.L. Dickens, c.100v., letters to her, and ms. catalogue of her libr., in BL *see* Gould, Alison, Named special collections, 1981: no.818.

5390 **Works** of and relating to Charles Dickens, collected by J.F. Dexter, in BL *see* Gould, Alison, Named special collections, 1981: no.818.
See also publ. catalogue, BLB 1970–79: 4073.

5391 **Casey, Ellen**. 'That specially trying mode of publication'; Dickens as editor of the weekly serial. Vict Pers R 14no3:93–101 '81.

5392 **Manning, Sylvia B.** Dickens' illustrators. [Review article]. Centrum new ser 1no2:133–41 '81.

5393 **Maxwell, Richard.** Dickens, the two Chronicles, and the publication of Sketches by Boz. [Morning chronicle; Evening Chronicle]. Dickens Stud Ann 9:21–32 '81. table.
'Publication in the Evening and republication in the Morning chronicle' (p.27).

5394 **Moss, Sidney P.** Charles Dickens and Frederick Chapman's agreement with Ticknor & Fields. Pa Bib Soc Am 75no1:33–8 '81.

5395 **Rosenberg, Edgar.** Last words on Great expectations; a textual brief on the six endings. [Revision]. Dickens Stud Ann 9:87–115 '81.

5396 **Collins, K.K.** and **A.M. Cohn.** Charles Dickens, Harriet Martineau, and Angela Burdett Coutts's Common things. [Dickens as editor]. Mod Philol 19no4:407–13 My '82.

5397 **Hill, C.W.** [Stamps featuring Dickens] (Ephemera). Antiqu Bk Mnthly R 9no1:22 Ja '82. facsim.

5398 **Makinen, Merja A.** Parodies of Dickens. [Leslie Staples bequest, Dickens house museum]. (Letters). Antiqu Bk Mnthly R 10no2:628 F '82.

5399 **Hoefnagel, Dick.** The bookplate of Charles Dickens. (Note 453). Bk Coll 32no3:349–51 '83. facsims.

5400 **Wheeler, Burton M.** The text and plan of Oliver Twist. Dickens Stud Ann 12:41–61 '83.

5401 **Adams, William.** Charles Dickens. [Collecting]. Bk & Mag Coll 2:32–40 Ap '84. ports., facsims.
'Bibliography of Charles Dickens' 1st editions in book form' (p.40).

5402 **Davis, Paul B.** Dickens, Hogarth, and the illustrated Great expectations. Dickensian 80no3:130–43 '84. facsims.

5403 **Harris, Kevin.** Bibliographic classification and cataloguing in Dickens studies. Dickensian 80no3:163–4 '84.

5404 **Mann, James Pace-.** A Christmas carol. [Points]. (Letters). Antiqu Bk Mnthly R 11no4:153 Ap '84; B. Lake 11no5:195 My '84.

5405 **Moss, Sidney P.** South Carolina contemplates banning Dickens's American notes. Dickensian 80no3:156–62 '84.

5406 **Mott, Graham.** The first publication of 'Our next door neighbours'. [Sketches by Boz]. Dickensian 80no2:114–16 '84.

5407 **Brattin, Joel J.** A map of the labyrinth; editing Dickens's manuscripts. Dickens Q 2n01:3–11 Mr '85. facsims.

5408 **Sutherland, John A.** Dickens, Reade and Hard cash. [Dickens as editor]. Dickensian 81n01:5–12 '85.

5409 **Bump, Jerome.** Parody and the Dickens–Collins collaboration in No thoroughfare. Libr Chron Univ Texas new ser 37:38–53 '86. facsim., port.

5410 **Glancy, Ruth F.** Dickens at work on The haunted man. [Revision]. Dickens Stud Ann 15:66–85 '86.

5411 **Keitt, Diane.** Charles Dickens and Robert Seymour; the battle of wills. [Illus.]. Dickensian 82n01:2–11 '86. facsims.

5412 **Collins, Philip A.W.** Dickensian errata. [Textual status of popular ed.]. TLS 20 N '87:1278; The Oxford illustrated Dickens, P. Rowland (Letters) 11 D '87:1377; P.A.W. Collins 18 D '87:1403;   D. Attwooll 1 Ja '88:88.

5413 **Glancy, Ruth F.** The shaping of The battle of life: Dickens' manuscript revisions. Dickens Stud Ann 17:67–89 '88.

5414 **Hollington, Michael.** 'Dickens, "Phiz" and physiognomy' in Möller, Joachim, ed. Imagination on a long rein; English literature illustrated. [Marburg], [1988]. p.125–35. facsims.

5415 **Kelly, Dawn P.** 'Image and effigy; the illustrations to The old curiosity shop' in Möller, Joachim, ed. Imagination on a long rein; English literature illustrated. [Marburg], [1988]. p.136–47. facsims.

5416 **Lettis, Richard.** 'The illustrated Dickens; "Exactly what I meant"' in Möller, Joachim, ed. Imagination on a long rein; English literature illustrated. [Marburg], [1988]. p.120–4.

5417 **Meckier, Jerome.** Dickens and the newspaper conspiracy of 1852, part I. Dickens Q 5n01:3–17 Mr '88; II. 5n02:51–64 Je '88.

5418 **Easson, Angus.** Towards the celestial city; the Pilgrim edition of Dickens's letters. Dickensian 85n01:18–28 '89.

5419 **Hoefnagel, Richard.** Charles Dickens's annotated copy of Pepys' Memoirs. [At Dartmouth college]. Dickensian 85n03:162–6 '89. facsim.

DIDSBURY, PETER, 1946–

5420 **Cooley, P.A.** Peter Didsbury; a bibliography. Bête Noire 6:53–60 '88.

DIGBY, SIR KENELM, 1603–65

5421 (5:10198) **Rhodes, Dennis E.** Sir Kenelm Digby and Siena, '58.
Repr. in Rhodes, Dennis E. Studies in early European printing and book collecting.
London, 1983. p.[161]–2.

DILKE, CHARLES WENTWORTH, 1789–1864

5422 **Garrett, William**. A checklist of the writings of Charles Wentworth Dilke, 1789–1864. Vict Pers R 14no3:111–18 '81.

5423 —— 'Selected bibliography [of primary and secondary sources]' in Charles Wentworth Dilke. (Twayne's English authors, 300). Boston, Twayne, [1982]. p.233–54.

DILL, SÃIRSÃL AGUS, fl.1945–81

5424 **Sãirsãl** agus Dill, 1945–1981. Comhar 41no5:256 '82.

DOBRÉE, BONAMY, 1891–1969

5425 **Morrish, P.S.** Bonamy Dobrée, theatre critic of The nation & athenaeum. [List of publ. notices]. N&Q 227no4:344–5 Ag '82.

DOBSON, HENRY AUSTIN, 1840–1921

5426 **Prance, Claude A.** On Austin Dobson and some of his books. Priv Libr ser3 4no2:116–32 '81. port., facsims.
Repr. in Essays of a book collector; reminiscences on some old books and their authors. West Cornwall, Conn., 1989. p.21–35.

DODD, WILLIAM, 1729–77

5427 **Barker, A.D.** The early career of William Dodd. [Publs.]. Cambridge Bib Soc Trans 8pt2:217–35 '82.

DONLEAVY, JAMES PATRICK, 1926–

5428 **Madden, David W.** A bibliography of J.P. Donleavy. Bull Bib 39no3:170–8 S '82. port.

DONNE, JOHN, 1573–1631

5429 (7:4125) **Roberts, John R.** John Donne; an annotated bibliography of modern criticism, 1912–1967, 1973.
Rev: D.G. Donovan SHR 8:236–7 '74; Barbara K. Lewalski Stud Engl Lit 14:158 '74; C. Mann Am Ref Bks Ann 521 '74; W. White Am Bk Coll new ser25:7 '74; Milton Q 8:23–4 '74; Françoise Gaudet Bull Bibliotheques de France 19:item 1325 '74; P. Legouis Études Angl 28:83–4 '75; A.J. Smith Yrbk Eng Stud 278–9 '75.

5430 ——— John Donne; an annotated bibliography of modern criticism, 1968–1978. Columbia, University of Missouri pr., [1982]. 434p. 22cm.
Rev: G. Soldano Lingue del Mondo 48:270–1 '83; E.W. Sullivan Lit Res Newsl 8:83–4 '83; J.T. Shawcross Analytic & Enum Bib 7:156–8 '83; Choice 20:11113 '83; A.W. Fields Round Table Sth Central Engl Assn 24:5 '83; A.C. Labriola John Donne J 3:113–15 '84; G.H. Carruthers Renaiss & Reformation 8:149–51 '84; P.R. Rider Am Ref Bks Ann 15:588 '84; E. Miner Mod Philol 82:323–5 '85; R. Ellrodt Études Angl 39:94 '86; W. White Bull Bib 43:59 '86; A. Rudrum Yrbk Eng Stud 17:272–3 '87.

5431 **Llasera, Margaret** and **Marie-Madeleine Martinet.** John Donne, Poems: bibliographie sélective et critique. Soc d'Étud Anglo-Am Bull 23:7–16 N '86.

5432 **Sullivan, Ernest W.** Updating the John Donne listings in Peter Beal's Index of English literary manuscripts. John Donne J 6no2:219–314 '87.

5433 **Warnke, Frank J.** 'Selected bibliography [of primary and secondary sources]' *in* John Donne. (Twayne's English authors, 444). Boston, Twayne, [1987]. p.133–9.

5434 **Hobbs, Mary.** More books from the library of John Donne. [Now in Chichester cathedral library]. (Note 419). Bk Coll 29no4:590–2 '80.

5435 **Sullivan, Ernest W.** John Donne's Probleme, 'Why was Sr Walter Raleigh thought ye fittest Man, to write ye Historie of these Times?'. (Bibliographical notes). Pa Bib Soc Am 74no1:63–7 '80.

5436 **Hobbs, Mary.** 'To a most dear friend'; Donne's Bellarmine. [i.e. sir Thomas Roe; libr.]. R Eng Stud 32no128:435–8 N '81.

5437 **Marotti, Arthur F.** 'John Donne and the rewards of patronage' *in* Lytle, Guy F. and S. Orgel, *ed.* Patronage in the renaissance. Princeton, Princeton U.P., [1981]. p.207–34.

5438 **Roberts, Mark.** 'Problems in editing Donne's Songs and sonets' *in* Conference on editorial problems, 16th, Toronto, 1980. Editing poetry from Spenser to Dryden; papers given…. Ed. by A.H. de Quehen. New York, 1981. p.[15]–45.

Appendix 1: 'A Valediction forbidding mourning'; principal variants.–2. 'The flea': two versions.

5439   **Shapiro, Isaac A.** Donne and Walton forgeries. [Inscription in copy of Gregory's De cura pastorali]. (Bibliographical notes). Library ser6 3no3:232 S '81; Jonquil Bevan [and] I. A. Shapiro (Correspondence) 4no3:329–39 S '82.

5440   **Sullivan, Ernest W.** The problem of text in familiar letters. Pa Bib Soc Am 75no2:115–26 '81.

5441   —— Bibliographical evidence in presentation copies; an example from Donne. [Biathanatos]. Analytical & Enum Bib 6no1:17–22 '82.

5442   —— A Donne saying. [Inscription in copy of Biathanatos by Thomas Martin]. (Bibliographical notes). Library 4no3:314–16 S '82; W.R. Le Fanu (Correspondence) 5no2:176 Je '83. facsim.

5443   **Shawcross, John T.** A text of John Donne's poems; unsatisfactory compromise. John Donne J 2no1:1–19 '83.

5444   **Sullivan, Ernest W.** Donne manuscripts: Dalhousie II. John Donne J 2no2:79–89 '83.

5445   —— Replicar editing of John Donne's texts. John Donne J 2no1:21–9 '83.

5446   **Woudhuysen, Henry R.** Two more books from the library of John Donne. (Note 452). Bk Coll 32no3:349 '83.

5447   **Baumlin, James S.** A note on the 1649/1650 editions o[f] Donne's Poems. [Ptg.]. John Donne J 3no1:97–8 '84.

5448   **Pebworth, Ted-Larry.** Manuscript poems and print assumptions; Donne and his modern editors. John Donne J 3no1:1–22 '84.

5449   **Shawcross, John T.** The making of the Variorum text of the Anniversaries. John Donne J 3no1:63–72 '84.

5450   **Sullivan, Ernest W.** Donne manuscripts: Dalhousie I. [At Texas tech university]. John Donne J 3no2:203–19 '84.

5451   **Clark, William B.** An interview with Gary A. Stringer on the Variorum Donne. (Special feature). Sth Central R 2no2:80–93 '85.

5452   **Patrides, C.A.** John Donne methodized, or, how to improve Donne's impossible text with the assistance of his several editors. Mod Philol 82no4:365–73 My '85.

5453 **Shapiro, Isaac A.** 'Huyghen's copy of Donne's Letters, 1651' *in* Motten, J.P. Vander, *ed*. Elizabethan and modern studies; presented to professor Willem Schrickx on the occasion of his retirement. Ghent, Seminarie voor Engelse en Amerikaanse literatur, R.U.G., 1985. p.229–34. facsim.

5454 **Daalder, Joost**. The prosodic significance of Donne's accidentals. [Letter to the lady Carey and mrs. Essex Rich]. Pargeron new ser 4:87–101 '86.

5455 **Pearson, David**. An unrecorded book from the library of John Donne. (Note 419). Bk Coll 35no2:246 '86.

5456 **Shawcross, John T.** 'The arrangement and order of John Donne's poems' *in* Fraistat, Neil, *ed*. Poems in their place; the intertextuality and order of poetic collections. Chapel Hill, University of North Carolina pr., [1986]. p.119–63.

5457 **Beal, Peter**. More Donne manuscripts. John Donne J 6no2:213–18 '87.

5458 **Hill, W. Speed.** John Donne's Biathanatos; authenticity, authority, and context in three editions. [Rev. art.]. John Donne J 6no1:109–33 '87. diagrs.

5459 **Pebworth, Ted-Larry**. The editor, the critic; and the multiple texts of Donne's 'A hymne to God the father'. Sth Central R 4no2:16–34 '87. diagr.
     Appendix: The textual apparatus of the three texts of Donne's Hymne.

5460 **Stringer, Gary A.** and **W.R. Vilberg**. The Donne Varioum textual collation program. Comp & Humanit 21no2:83–9 Ap/Je '87.

5461 **Sullivan, Ernest W.** and **D.J. Murrah**, *ed*. The Donne Dalhousie discovery; proceedings of a symposium on the acquisition and study of the John Donne and Joseph Conrad collections at Texas technological university. [Lubbock, Tex.], Friends of the University library, Southwest collection, [1987]. vii,71p. 23cm.
     Includes 'And having that, thou hast done': Locating, acquiring, and studying the Dalhousie Donne manuscripts, Ernest W. Sullivan.–'What do you read?' 'Words' – Ah, but are they Donne's?, John T. Shawcross.–Editing literary texts on the microcomputer; the example of Donne's poetry, Ted-Larry Pebworth.–When its done, it will be Donne; the Variorum edition of the poetry of John Donne, Gary A. Stringer.
     Rev: P. Parrish Sevent Cent Newsl 47:9 '89.

5462 **Bennett, Stuart**. An intermediate state of Donne's Paradoxes, 1652. [Corr. to Keynes's bibliogr.]. (Query 375). Bk Coll 37no2:273 '88.

5463 **Shawcross, John T.** But is it Donne's? The problem of titles on his poems. John Donne J 7no2:141–9 '88.

5464   **Marotti, Arthur F.** John Donne, author. [Publ.]. J Med & Renaiss Stud 19no1:69–82 '89.

5465   **Pebworth, Ted-Larry**. John Donne, coterie poetry, and the text as performance. Stud Eng Lit 29no1:61–75 '89.

5466   **Walby, Celestin J.** The Westmoreland text of Donne's first epithalamion. John Donne J 8no1/2:17–35 '89. diagr.

5467   **Wright, Nancy E.** The figura of the martyr in John Donne's sermons. [Censorship]. Eng Lit Hist 56no2:293–309 '89.

DOUGHTY, CHARLES MONTAGU, 1843–1926

5468   **O'Brien, Philip M.**, *comp.* 'Charles M. Doughty's Travels in Arabia deserta and its abridgments; a descriptive bibliography' *in* Tabachnik, Stephen E., *ed.* Explorations in Doughty's Arabia deserta. Athens, University of Georgia pr., [1987]. p.[223]–53.
See also 'A selected bibliography of works about Travels in Arabia deserta' (p.[255]–8).

DOUGLAS, LORD ALFRED BRUCE, 1870–1945

5469   **Paterson, Gary H.** Lord Alfred Douglas, an annotated bibliography of writings about him. Eng Lit Transit 23no3:168–200 '80.

DOUGLAS, BP. GAVIN, 1474?–1522

5470   **Scheps, Walter** and **J. Anna Looney**, [1986]: no.905.

DOUGLAS, George, *pseud.*, *see* BROWN, GEORGE DOUGLAS, 1869–1902.

DOUGLAS, KEITH, 1920–44

5471   **Graham, Desmond**. Keith Douglas's books. Bk Coll 30no2:103–76 '81.
'Check-list: Books belonging to Keith Douglas' (p. 170–6): *presentation, signed, and other copies.*

DOUGLAS, NORMAN, *pseud. of* DOUGLASS, GEORGE NORMAN, 1886–1952

5472   **Toronto. University. Thomas Fisher rare book library.** Grand man: Norman Douglas, 1868–1952. [By Luba Hussell]. [Toronto], 1982. [v],13p. 27cm. (Reprod. from typewriting).

DOYLE, SIR ARTHUR CONAN, 1859–1930

5473 **De Waal, Ronald B.** The international Sherlock Holmes; a companion volume to The world bibliography of Sherlock Holmes and dr. Watson. Hamden, Conn., Archon books; London, Mansell, 1980. 621p. 24cm.

Post-1971 Sherlockiana, with addenda to The world bibliography: BBLB 1970–79: 4160.

5474 **Stix, Thomas L.** Baker street inventory; conducted by…. [Annotated checklist of Holmesiana]. Baker St J 31no2:126–7 Je '81; 31no3:190–1 S '81; 32no1:61–3 Mr '82; 32no2:117–21 Je '82; 32no4:245–7 D '82; 33no1:54–8 Mr '83; 33no2:112–18 Je '83; 33no3:184–7 S '83; 34no1:46–56 Mr '84; 34no2:117–22 Je '84; 34no3:186–8 S '84; 34no4:251 D '84; 35no1:54–60 Mr '85; P.E. Blau 35no2:119–23 Je '85; 35no3:180–5 S '85; 35no4:244–7 D '85; 36no1:53–60 Mr '86; 36no2:124–5 Je '86; 36no3:182–8 S '86; 36no4:244–7 D '86; 37no1:57–61 Mr '87; 37no2:121–4 Je '87; 37no3:183–9 S '87; 37no4:251 D '87; 38no1:58–61 Mr '88; 38no2:123–5 Je '88; 38no3:184–8 S '88; 38no4:251 D '88; 39no1:57–60 Mr '89; 39no2:124–5 Je '89; 39no3:183–7 S '89.

5475 **Green, Roger L.** and **J.M. Gibson**. A bibliography of A. Conan Doyle. With a foreword by Graham Greene. Oxford, Clarendon pr., 1983. xvi,712p. port., facsims. 21cm. ([Soho Bibs, 23]).

Descr. bibliogr. of works of fiction, and miscellaneous works, with minor contribs., periodical and newspaper contribs., and biogr. sources; appendices include notes on British colonial, continental and North American publishers.

Rev. Paulette Greene Am Bk Coll new ser 4:56–8 '83; E.S. Lauterbach Mod Fict Stud 30:379–80 '84; T. d'A. Smith TLS 10 F '84:131; J.G. Watson N&Q 231:258–6 '86.

5476 **Lellenberg, Jon L.** and **W.O.G. Lofts.** The Adventures of Herlock Sholmes; a history and bibliography. [Parodies by C.H.St.J. Hamilton]. Baker St J new ser 34no2:73–86 Je '84.

5477 **Nielsen, Bjarne**. Sherlock Holmes in Denmark; a check-list of Danish editions of the canon and the writings about the writings in Denmark. [Copenhagen], Pinkerton, 1987. 66p. 20cm.

Rev. from Sherlock Holmes i Danmark, 1981.

5478 **Wertheim, Stanley**. The Arthur Conan Doyle mystery; towards a resolution. [Bookplate]. Am Bk Coll new ser 1no5:38–42 S/Oc '80. facsim.

5479 **Gregor, D.B.** Conan Doyle. [Misprint in 'The adventure of the blue carbuncle']. (To the editor). TLS 14 Ag '81:934; R.L. Green 28 Ag '81:983.

5480   **Redmond, Donald A.** Textual variations in 'The missing three-quarter'. Baker St. J 35no1:9–11 Mr '85.

5481   Cancelled.

DRABBLE, MARGARET, 1939–

5482   **Rose, Ellen C.** 'List of works cited [by and about]' *in* The novels of Margaret Drabble; equivocal figures. [London], Macmillan; Totowa, N.J., Barnes & Noble, [1980]. p.130–4.

5483   **Schmidt, Dorey**, *comp.* 'A bibliography update, 1977–1981' *in* Schmidt, Dorey and Jan Seale, *ed.* Margaret Drabble: Golden realms. Edinburg, Tex., School of humanities, Pan American university, [1982]. p.186–93.

5484   **Korenman, Joan S.**, *comp.* 'A Margaret Drabble bibliography' *in* Rose, Ellen C., *ed.* Critical essays on Margaret Drabble. Boston, Mass., G.K. Hall, [1985]. p.181–202.
        Classified checklist of works, interviews, and ana.

5485   **Martin, Gyde C.** Margaret Drabble; a bibliography. Bull Bib 45no1:21–32 Mr '88.

5486   **Packer, Joan G.** Margaret Drabble; an annotated bibliography. New York, Garland, 1988. xvi,189p. 21cm.
        Annotated checklist of works and works about.

DRAYTON, MICHAEL, 1563–1631

5487   **Brennan, Michael G.** The 1602 edition of Drayton's Idea. [Ptg.]. (Bibliographical notes). Library ser6 4no1:42–7 Mr '82. table.

DRINKWATER, JOHN, 1882–1937

5488   **Prance, Claude A.** John Drinkwater and some of his books. Priv Libr ser3 9no2:71–8 '86. facsims.
        'Some association books' (p.87–8). *Repr. in* Essays of a book collector; reminiscences on some old books and their authors. West Cornwall, Conn., 1989. p.171–90.

DRUMMOND, WILLIAM, 1585–1649

5489   **Edinburgh. University. Library.** William Drummond of Hawthornden (1585–1649), book collector and benefactor; an exhibition of books and manuscripts from the Drummond collection…. [Comp. by J.T.D. Hall]. Edinburgh, 1985. [24]p. facsims. 20cm.

5490 (7:4179k) **Simpson, Murray C.T.** Don Murmidumilla, book-collector; three newly-acquired volumes from the library of William Drummond of Hawthornden in Edinburgh university library. Univ Libr J 29n01:42–8 Je '79. facsims.

5491 **Fowler, Alastair** and **M. Leslie**. Drummond's copy of The faerie queene. [Edinburgh U.L.]. TLS 17 Jl '81:821–2.

DRYDEN, JOHN, 1631–1700

5492 **California. University at Los Angeles. William Andrews Clark memorial library.** Annus notabilis; an exhibition of books and manuscripts at... commemorating the 350th anniversary of the birth of John Dryden. Los Angeles, [William Andrews Clark memorial library], 1981. 47p. illus., port., facsims. 26cm.

5493 **Hall, James M.** John Dryden; a reference guide. Boston, Mass., G.K. Hall, [1984]. xix,424p. 23cm. (Reference guide to literature).
Rev: S. Archer Sevent Cent Newsl 43:43–4 '85.

5494 **Rigaud, Nadia J.** Dryden, All for love: bibliographie sélective et critique. Soc d'Étud Anglo-Am Bull 21:9–19 N '85.

———

5495 (5:10393a) **Crinò, Anna M.** Uno sconosciuto autografo Drydeniano al British museum. [Heroic stanzas, Lansdowne ms.1045]. Eng Misc 17:311–20 '66.

5496 **Cameron, William J.,** *comp.* 'The future of Dryden bibliography' *in* Coleman, Antony and A. Hammond, *ed.* Poetry and drama, 1570–1700; essays in honour of Harold F. Brooks. London, Methuen, [1981]. p.[200]–32.
The 'business of bibliography'.–An exploratory approach to a bibliography of Dryden and Drydeniana.–Minimum standards for bibliographical description.–The ingressive principle as appplied to bibliographical notes.–Arrangement of the bibliographically augmented entries.–A bibliography of Drydeniana.–A posthumous author bibliography.

5497 **Eversole, Richard**. The Traquair manuscript of Dryden's The hind and the panther. (Bibliographical notes). Pa Bib Soc Am 75n02:179–91 '81. tables.

5498 **Frost, William**. 'On editing Dryden's Virgil' *in* Conference on editorial problems, 16th, Toronto, 1980. Editing poetry from Spenser to Dryden; papers given.... Ed. by A.H. De Quehen. New York, 1981. p.99–126.

5499   **Hammond, Paul**. The autograph manuscript of Dryden's Heroique stanza's and its implications for editors. (Bibliographical notes). Pa Bib Soc Am 76no4:457–70 '82.

5500   —— Dryden's library. N&Q 229no3:344–5 S '84.

5501   —— Dryden's revision of To the lady Castlemain. (Bibliographical notes). Pa Bib Soc Am 78no1:81–90 '84. diagrs.

5502   **Sherbo, Arthur**. Dryden as a Cambridge editor. [Writers associated with him in collns.]. Stud Bib 38:251–61 '85.

5503   —— Dryden's translation of Virgil's Eclogues and the tradition. Stud Bib 38:292–76 '85. tables.

5504   —— Dryden and the fourth earl of Lauderdale. [Trans. of Aeneid]. Stud Bib 39:199–210 '86.

5505   **Hammond, Paul**. The prologue and epilogue to Dryden's Marriage a-la-mode and the problem of Covent garden drollery. Pa Bib Soc Am 81no2:155–72 '87. diagrs.

DUCK, STEPHEN, 1705–56

5506   **McGonigle, Peter J.** Stephen Duck and the text of The thresher's labour. Library ser6 4no3:288–96 S '82.

5507   **Musty, John**. The labouring poets: Stephen Duck, Robert Bloomfield and John Clare. (Collecting country writers, 6). Antiqu Bk Mnthly R 13no1:4–15 Ja '86; A. Bridge (Letters) 13no2:64–5 F '86; S.H. Goodacre 13no3:105 Mr '86. facsims., ports.
'Check lists of first editions' (p.14–15).

DU MAURIER, DAME DAPHNE, 1907–89

5508   **Macleod, Helen**. Daphne du Maurier. [Collecting]. Bk & Mag Coll 11:19–25 Ja '85. port., facsims., illus.
'Complete UK bibliography of Daphne Du Maurier 1st editions' (p.25).

DU MAURIER, GEORGE LOUIS PALMELLA BUSSON, 1834–96

5509   **Kelly, Richard**. 'Selected bibliography [of primary and secondary sources]' *in* George Du Maurier. (Twayne's English authors, 355). Boston, [Mass.], Twayne, [1983]. p.168–73.

DUNBAR, WILLIAM, 1465?–1530?

5510 **Scheps, Walter** and **J. Anna Looney**, [1986]: no.905.

5511 **Bawcutt, Priscilla**. The text and interpretation of Dunbar. (Review article). Medium Ævum 50no1:88–100 '81.

DURRELL, LAWRENCE GEORGE, 1912–

5512 **Koger, Grove**. Some contributions to the Lawrence Durrell bibliography. Deus Loci 3no3:11–20 Mr '80.

5513 **Feistel, Hartmut-Ortwin**. Lawrence Durrell in the German speaking countries; a preliminary bibliography. Deus Loci 6no263:1–27 D/ Mr '82/3.

5514 **Thomas, Alan G.** and **J.A. Brigham**. Laurence Durrell; an illustrated checklist. Carbondale, Southern Illinois pr., [1983]. x,198p. facsims. 21cm.
'An illustrated expansion and updating of the Durrell bibliography by Alan G. Thomas originally published in Lawrence Durrell; a study, by G.S. Fraser.'
Rev: Bull Bib 41:245–6 '84; G. Bixby Am Bk Coll new ser 5:53–6 '84; A. Rota Bk Coll 33:379–82 '84.

5515 **Koger, Grove**. 1981–1982 Durrell bibliography. Deus Loci 7no3:25–32 Je '84.

5516 **Brigham, James A.** At work in the Durrell factory; editing the Collected poems. Deus Loci 5no1:260–8 '81.

5517 **Thomas, Alan G.** Preserving the archive. [Mss. now at Southern Illinois univ.]. Twent Cent Lit 33no3:345–7 '87.

DYER, ELINOR BRENT-, 1894–1969

5518 **Godfrey, Monica**. Elinor Brent-Dyer & the Chalet school stories. [Collecting]. Bk & Mag Coll 10:40–7 D '84. port., facsims.
'Complete bibliography of Elinor Brent-Dyer 1st editions' (p.45–7).

DYER, JOHN, 1700?–58

5519 **Humfrey, Belinda**. 'A selected bibliography' *in* John Dyer. (Writers of Wales). [Cardiff], University of Wales pr. on behalf of the Welsh arts council, 1980. p.113–15.

ELIOT, GEORGE, *pseud. of* **MARY ANN (EVANS) CROSS, 1819–80**

5520 **Higdon, D. Leon.** A bibliography of George Eliot criticism, 1971–1977. Bull Bib 39no2:90–103 Ap/Je '80.

5521 **Preston, John** and **Audrey Cooper.** George Eliot: the making of a novelist, a centenary exhibition. Coventry, University of Warwick library, [1980]. 14p. illus., facsim. 21cm. (Reprod. from typewriting).

5522 **Baker, William.** The libraries of George Eliot and George Henry Lewes. [Victoria, B.C.], English literary studies, University of Victoria, 1981. 146p. 23cm. (ELS Monogr, 24).
Rev: W. Myers Yrbk Eng Stud 15:320–1 '85.

5523 **Ermarth, Elizabeth D.** 'Selected bibliography [of primary and secondary sources]' *in* George Eliot. (Twayne's English authors, 414). Boston, [Mass.], Twayne, [1985]. p.146–60.

5524 **Griffith, George V.** George Eliot's American reception, 1858–1981; a bibliography. Bull Bib 44no3:193–6 S '87.

5525 **Levine, George** and **Patricia O'Hara.** An annotated critical bibliography of George Eliot. New York, St. Martin's pr., [1988]. xi,128p. 21cm.

———

5526 **Baker, William.** 'A new George Eliot manuscript [in the Hugh Walpole colln., King's school, Canterbury]' *in* Smith, Anne, *ed.* George Eliot; centenary essays…. [Totowa, N.J.], Barnes & Noble, [1980]. p.9–20.

5527 **Meikle, Susan.** 'Fruit and seed; the finale to Middlemarch [Revision]' *in* Smith, Anne, *ed.* George Eliot; centenary essays…. [Totowa, N.J.], Barnes & Noble, [1980]. p.181–95.

5528 **Millet, Stanton.** The union of Miss Brooke and Middlemarch; a study of the manuscript. J Eng Germ Philol 79no1:32–57 Ja '80.

5529 **Waley, Daniel.** The Department of manuscripts' George Eliot holdings. Brit Libr J 6no2:123–9 '80.

5530 **Baker, William.** A George Eliot manuscript. [Partly in J.W. Cross's hand]. (To the editor). TLS 4 D '81:1419.

5531 **Dodd, Valerie A.** A George Eliot notebook. [Nuneaton libr., Warws., G. Eliot colln.]. Stud Bib 34:258–62 '81.

5532 **Anderson, Roland F.** 'Things wisely ordered'; John Blackwood, George Eliot, and the publication of Romola. Publ Hist 11:5–39 '82.

5533 **Baker, William**. George Eliot; notebooks—and blotter. [Review article]. Library ser6 4no1:80–4 Mr '82.

5534 **Collins, K.K.** Sources of remaining unidentified serial offprints in the George Eliot–George Henry Lewes library. (Bibliographical notes). Pa Bib Soc Am 77no4:486–9 '83.

5535 **Feltes, Norman N.** One round of a long ladder; gender, profession, and the production of Middlemarch. [Publishing]. Eng Stud Canada 12no2:210–28 Je '86.
Also in Modes of production of Victorian novels, 1986; *see* no.3785.

5536 **Baker, William**. Some Eliot inscribed copies. (Note 420). Bk Coll 36no1:124–7 '87; An addendum 38no2:253–7 '89. facsims.

5537 **Handley, Graham**. The manuscript of Daniel Deronda; a change in sequence? [Revision]. George Eliot Fellowship 18:61–5 '87.

ELIOT, THOMAS STEARNS, 1888–1968

5538 **Ricks, Beatrice**. T.S. Eliot; a bibliography of secondary works. Metuchen, N.J., Scarecrow, 1980. xxiii,366p. 23cm. (Scarecrow author bibs., 45).

5539 **Edwards, Anthony S.G.** Addenda to Gallup: T.S. Eliot. (Bibliographical notes). Pa Bib Soc Am 75no1:93 '81.

5540 **Davies, Alastair**, [1982]: no.704.

5541 **Frank, Armin P.** T.S. Eliot in Germany, 1965 to the present; an estimate and a bibliography. Yeats Eliot R 7no1/2:123–37 Je '82.
'Bibliography [comp. by Brigitt Feldmann and Hanna Niehus]' (p.127–37).

5542 ——T.S. Eliot criticism and scholarship in German; a descriptive survey, 1923–1980. With reference to the holdings of the Niedersächsische Staats- und Universitätsbibliotheket at Göttingen. Ed. by Erika Hulpke. Göttingen, Vanderhoeck & Ruprecht, 1986. ix,[215]p. 22cm. (Arbeiten aus der Nierdersächsische Staats- und Universitätsbibliotheket at Göttingen, 20).

5543 **Herrick, Casey**. Four quartets; an annotated bibliographical supplement, 1980–1986. Bull Bib 46no2:122–8 Je '89.

5544 **Magoon, Joseph**. Bibliography of writings about T.S. Eliot for the years 1970 to 1987; subject bibliography and indexes. [Bournemouth, J. Magoon], 1989. xi,95p. in various pagings. 30cm. (Duplicated typescript).

5545 **Aithal, S. Krishnamoorthy.** The typewriters in the making of The waste land. Stud Bib 33:191–3 '80.

5546 **Baker, William**. T.S. Eliot and Emily Hale; some fresh evidence. [Inscribed copies]. Eng Stud 66no5:432–6 Oc '85.

5547 **Du Sautoy, Peter**. T.S. Eliot and publishing. Agenda 23no1/2:171–6 '85.

5548 **Ali, Agha Shahid**. T.S. Eliot as editor. Ann Arbor, Mich., U.M.I. research pr., [1986]. x,173p. 22cm. (Stud Mod Lit, 60).
Introduction.–The European Criterion.–The new and monthly Criterion.–3. The quarterly Criterion.–4. The Marxist Criterion.–5. The failed Criterion.–Conclusion.
Rev: G.W. Clift Midwest Q 28:283–7 '87.

5549 **Brown, Geoffrey**. T.S. Eliot. [Collecting]. Bk & Mag Coll 24:44–51 F '86. port., facsims.
'Complete UK bibliography of T.S. Eliot' (p.50–1).

5550 **George, Alexander**. 'It's' misspelled; history of an error in The waste land. Bib Soc Aust & N.Z. Bull 11no4:169–70 '87.

5551 **Brenchley, Frank**. Collecting mr. Eliot. Priv Libr ser4 1no3:103–13 '88. illus.

5552 **Gallup, Donald C.** The Eliots and the T.S. Eliot collection at Harvard. Harvard Libr Bull 36no3:233–47 '88.

5553 **Smith, A.R. Jabez-.** T.S. Eliot. [Copyright]. (Listener letters). Listener 120no3086:25 Oc '88.

ELLIOTT, MARY (BELSON), 1794–1870

5554 **Moon, Marjorie**. The children's books of Mary (Belson) Elliott, blending sound Christian principles with cheerful cultivation; a bibliography. [Winchester], St. Paul's bibliographies, 1987. xxix,142p. illus., facsims. 23cm.
Classified checklists by titles, with bibliogr. notes and location of copies, for books, French and German translations. 'Indexes of publishers and booksellers,' (p.139–40); 'Index of printers...and of engravers, artists, &c.' (p.141–2).
Rev: M.H. Junior Bkshlf 51:157 '87; C. Hurst Bk Coll 37:281–2 '88; J. Barr Library ser6 11:75–7 '89.

ELYOT, SIR THOMAS, 1490?–1546

5555 **Dees, Jerome S.** Sir Thomas Elyot and Roger Ascham; a reference guide. Boston, G.K. Hall, [1981]. xvii,186p. 25cm. (Reference guide to literature).
'Elyot' (p.[1]–66); 'Ascham' (p.[67]–156).
Rev: P. Hyland Seventh Cent News 41:54 '83; J. McConica Mod Lang R 80:900–1 '85.

EMPSON, SIR WILLIAM, 1906–84

5556 **Day, Frank**. Sir William Empson; an annotated bibliography. New York, Garland, 1984. xli,229p. 21cm. (Bibs Mod Critics & Critical Schools, 8. Reference library of the humanities, 376).
Classified checklists of primary and secondary works.
Rev. R.M. Adams N.Y. R Bks 32:32–5 '85.

ESSEX, ROBERT DEVEREAUX, 2D EARL OF, 1566–1601 *see* DE-VEREAUX, ROBERT, 2D EARL OF ESSEX, 1566–1601.

ETHEREGE, SIR GEORGE, 1636–91/2

5557 **Mann, David D**. Sir George Etherege; a reference guide. Boston, Mass., G.K. Hall, [1981]. xxxii,135p. 23cm. (Reference guide to literature).

5558 **Rigaud, Nadia J**. Etherege; The man of mode; bibliographie sélective et critique. Soc d'Étud Anglo-Am Bull 25:7–17 N '87.

5559 **Beal, Peter**. 'The most constant and best entertainment'; Sir George Etherege's reading in Ratisbon. Library ser6 10no2:122–44 Je '88. facsims.
'A catalogue of Sr. George's Bookes' (p.131–44).

EVELYN, JOHN, 1655–99

5560 **Blackwell, B.H., bksllrs.**, OXFORD. John Evelyn, 1620–1706. [Oxford], [1981]. 35p. 22cm. (Blackwell's rare books. Catalogue, A20).
103 items, mainly from the Evelyn library, including works by, books from his library, and Evelyniana, with Wing and Keynes nos.

5561 **Sherbo, Arthur**. Thomas Holt White and the 1772 reprint of John Evelyn's Fumifugium. [And Samuel Pegge]. N&Q 225no1:57–9 F '80.

5562 **Nucleus** of Evelyn's library consisting mainly of annotated copies, purchased at Christie's sales, 1977–8, 262v. in BL *see* Gould, Alison, Named special collections, 1981: no.818.

5563 **Rostenberg, Leona**. Restoration bibliophily; the libraries of John Evelyn, Samuel Pepys, and Robert Hooke: [1. John Evelyn]. Am Bk Coll new ser 7no7:21–8 Jl '86. illus., port., facsims.

FAIRLIE, ALISON, fl.1947–81

5564 **Austin, L.J.**, *comp.* 'Select bibliography of the works of Alison Fairlie [1947–81]' *in* Bowie, Malcolm, *ed.* Imagination and language; collected essays of Alison Fairlie. Cambridge, C.U.P., 1981. p.[461]–70.

FALLON, PADRAIC, 1906–

5565 **Grennam, Eamon**. Affectional truth; critical intelligence in the poetry of Padraic Fallon. Irish Univ R 12no2:173–88 '82.
'Appendix 1. [Dates of composition and publication of poems in Poems, 1974].–2. [Dates of first broadcasts of radio plays]. (p.185–8).

FAQUES, WILLIAM, fl.1504–8

5566 (7:4258) **Rhodes, Dennis E.** William Menyman and William Faques, '76.
Repr. in Rhodes, Dennis E. Studies in early European printing and book collecting. London, 1983. p.[46]–8.

FARQUHAR, GEORGE, 1678–1707

5567 **James, Eugene N.** George Farqhuar; a reference guide. Boston, Mass., G.K. Hall, [1986]. xxiii,112p. 23cm. (Reference guide to literature).

FELLTHAM, OWEN, 1602?–68

5568 **Pebworth, Ted-Larry**. An Anglican family worship service of the interregnum; a canceled early text and a new edition of Owen Felltham's 'A form of prayer'. Eng Lit Renaiss 16no1:206–33 '86.

5569 **Stewart, Stanley**. Authorial representation and Owen Felltham's Resolves. [Revision]. Cithara 28no2:7–35 My '89. facsims.

FENN, GEORGE MANVILLE, 1831–1909

5570 **Crewdson, William H.P.** George Manville Fenn. Antiqu Bk Mnthly R 14no1:8–15 Ja '87; R. Dalby (Letters) 14no2:46 F '87; W.H.P. Crewdson 14no3:87 Mr '87. port., facsims.
'A short-title list of the first editions of George Manville Fenn' (p.15).

FERGUSON, JAMES, 1710–76

5571 **Millburn, John R.** A bibliography of James Ferguson, F.R.S., 1710–1776; astronomical & philosophical lecturer. Aylesbury, Bucks., John R. Millburn, 1983. 28p. + 2 microfiches at back. 22cm.

FERRIER, SUSAN EDMONSTONE, 1782–1854

5572 **Scotland. National library,** EDINBURGH. Susan Ferrier, 1782–1854. [With exhib. catalogue]. Edinburgh, 1982. 51p. illus., facsims. 25cm. ([Exhibition catalogues, 22]).

5573 **Cullinan, Mary**. 'Selected bibliography [of primary and secondary sources]' *in* Susan Ferrier. (Twayne's English authors, 392). Boston, Twayne, [1984]. p.129–32.

FIELDING, HENRY, 1707–54

5574 (7:4273) **Hahn, H. George**. Henry Fielding; an annotated bibliography, 1979.
Rev: J.P.W. Rogers N&Q 226:80–1 '81; D.L. Vander Meulen Eight Cent Stud 16:439–42 '83.

5575 **Ducrocq, Jean**. Fielding: Tom Jones; bibliographie sélective et critique. Soc d'Étud Anglo-Am Bull 17/18no11:55–74 N '80.

5576 **Morrissey, L.J.** Henry Fielding; a reference guide. Boston, Mass., G.K. Hall, [1980]. 560p. 23cm. (Reference guide to literature).
Rev: H. Amory N&Q 227:82–3 '82; P.-G. Boucé Études Angl 36:79–80 '83; D.L. Vander Meulen Eight Cent Stud 16:439–42 '83; C.J. Rawson Mod Lang R 79:421–3 '84.

5577 **Stoler, John A.** and **R.D. Fulton**. Henry Fielding; an annotated bibliography of twentieth-century criticism, 1900–1977. New York, Garland, 1980. xvi,386p. 23cm. (Reference library of the humanities, 147).
Rev: J.C. Beasley Lit Res Newsl 7:39–43 '82; D.L. Vander Meulen Eight Cent Stud 16:439–42 '83; P.-G. Boucé Études Angl 36:79–80 '83; C.J. Rawson Mod Lang R 79:421–3 '84.

5578 **Harvard. University. Houghton library.** New books by Fielding; an exhibition of the Hyde collection...January 12–March 6 1987. [Comp. by Hugh Amory]. Cambridge, [Mass.], Houghton library, [1987]. 56p. illus., port., facsims. 19x22cm.

5579 (7:4274) **Bowers, Fredson T.** 'Textual introduction' *in* Miller, Henry K., *ed.* Miscellanies, by Henry Fielding. (Wesleyan ed. of the works of Henry Fielding). Oxford, Clarendon pr.; Middletown, Conn., Wesleyan U.P., [1972]. p.l–lv.

5580 (7:4274c) —— 'Textual introduction' *in* Battestin, Martin C., *ed.* Henry Fielding: The history of Tom Jones, a foundling (Wesleyan ed. of the works of Henry Fielding, 4). Oxford, Clarendon pr.; Middletown, Conn., Wesleyan U.P., [1974]. V.1, p.lxii–lxxxiv.
1. The copy-text and its treatment.–2. The apparatus.–3. Collation.–4. Appendix.

5581   **Battestin, Martin C.** and **Ruth R. Battestin.** A Fielding discovery, with some remarks on the canon. [Letter in Common Sense, 13 My 1738]. Stud Bib 33:131–43 '80. facsims

5582   **Amory, Hugh.** Fatum libelli; Tom Jones in Italy. Harvard Libr Bull 29no1:44–70 Ja '81.

5583   —— In the stacks; on a copy of Fielding's Works. [With bibliogr. descr.]. (Notes). Harvard Libr Bull 29no4:445–50 Oc '81. illus., facsims.

5584   —— Fielding's copy of the Covent garden journal. [Notes and documents]. Bodleian Libr Rec 11no2:126–8 '83.

5585   —— What Murphy knew; his interpolations in Fielding's Works, 1762, and Fielding's revision of Amelia. Pa Bib Soc Am 77no2:133–66 '83.
Demonstrable authorial revisions, demonstrable editorial interpolations, and uncanonical variants in the 1762 Works.–The main tendencies of the revision of Amelia.–What Murphy knew.–Appendix [of variants].

5586   **Battestin, Martin C.** Four new Fielding attributions; his earliest satires of Walpole. [In The craftsman, Mist's weekly journal, and Fog's weekly journal]. Stud Bib 36:69–109 '83.
I. The Norfolk lanthorn, July 1728.–II. On the benefit of laughing, August 1728.–III. The physiognomist, July 1730.–IV. On hunters and politicians, October 1730.

5587   **Amory, Hugh.** 'De facto copyright'? Fielding's Works in partnership, 1769–1821. Eight Cent Stud 17no4:449–76 '84. table.
Fielding in law and fact.–Appendix A: Synopsis of editions, 1762–1821 (p.469–73). B: Partners in Fielding's Works, 1769–74.

5588   **Bowers, Fredson T.** 'Textual introduction' *in* Battestin, Martin C., *ed.* Joseph Andrews, by Henry Fielding. (Wesleyan ed. of the works of Henry Fielding). Oxford, Clarendon pr.; Middletown, Conn., Wesleyan U.P., [1984]. (First publ. 1967). p.3–13.

5589   —— 'Textual introduction' *in* Battestin, Martin C., *ed.* Amelia, by Henry Fielding. (Wesleyan ed. of the works of Henry Fielding). Oxford, Clarendon pr., [1983]; Middletown, Conn., Wesleyan U.P., [1984]. p.lxii–lxxx.
1. The copytext and its treatment.–2. The apparatus.–3. Collation.–4. Revised text not in the first edition.

5590   **Rizzo, Betty W.** Notes on the war between Henry Fielding and John Hill, 1752–53. Library ser6 7no4:338–53 D '85.

5591   **Amory, Hugh.** The evidence of things not seen; concealed proofs of Fielding's Juvenal. Pa Bib Soc Am 80no1:15–33 '86.
1. The sources of Fielding's text and annotation.–2. The bibliographical evidence of revision.–3. The significance of the revision.–Appendix: Text of the Sixth satire.

5592 **Battestin, Martin C.** Fielding's contributions to the Universal spectator, 1736–7. Stud Philol 83no1:88–116 '86.
1. An essay on eating, 1736.–2. The physiognomist's academy, 1737.

5593 **Harvard. University. Houghton library.** Henry Fielding: An institute of the pleas of the crown; an exhibition of the Hyde collection at the Houghton library. [Introd. by Charles Donahue]. [Cambridge, Mass., Houghton library], [1987]. [v],30p. facsims. 35cm.
'Textual note' *by* Hugh Amory (p.[v]).

5594 **Lockwood, Thomas.** Henry Fielding and the History of our own times, 1741. [As editor]. J Newsp & Per Hist 3no3:2–11 '87.

5595 **Battestin, Martin C.** Dating Fielding's letters to lady Mary Wortley Montagu. Stud Bib 42:246–8 '89.

FINCH, ANN, COUNTESS OF WINCHILSEA, 1661–1720

5596 **Messenger, Ann.** Publishing without perishing; Lady Winchilsea's Miscellany poems of 1713. Restor 5no1:27–37 '81.

FIRBANK, ARTHUR ANNESLEY RONALD, 1886–1926

5597 **Benkovitz, Miriam J.** Supplement to A bibliography of Ronald Firbank. London, Enitharmon pr., 1980. 55p. 23cm. (Ltd. to 400 copies)

5598 —— A bibliography of Ronald Firbank. 2d ed. Oxford, Clarendon pr., 1982. (First publ. 1963; Suppl. 1980). xv,106p. 21cm. (Soho Bibs, 16).
Bibliogr. of books and pamphlets, contribs. to books, contribs. to periodicals, mss. and typescripts, and supposititious works; with extensive bibliogr. notes and discussion.
Rev: J.G. Watson N&Q 228:556–7 '83.

FISHER, ROY, 1930–

5599 **Slade, Derek.** Roy Fisher; a bibliography. [London], D. Slade, 1987. 32l. 30cm. (Duplicated typescript).
Checklist with some bibliogr. notes, of books and pamphlets, collaborations of artists, book contribs. by, contribs. to periodicals, recorded readings and broadcasts, interviews, revs. of, articles and essays on, and critical studies of, with miscellanea and addenda.

FITZGERALD, EDWARD, 1809–83

5600 **Bridge, Alexander.** Edward FitzGerald; ghost editions. (Query 44). Bk Coll 29no2:279 '80.

FITZMAURICE, GEORGE, 1878–1963

5601 (5:10556k) **Miller, Liam**. George Fitzmaurice; a bibliographical note. Irish Writing 15:47–8 Je '51.

FLEMING, IAN LANCASTER, 1908–64

5602 **Upton, John**. Ian Fleming and the James Bond books. [Collecting]. Bk & Mag Coll 1:4–13 Mr '84. port., illus., facsims.
'Complete bibliography of James Bond 1st editions' (p.13).

FLETCHER, JOHN, 1579–1625 *see also* BEAUMONT, FRANCIS, 1584–1616, AND JOHN FLETCHER, 1579–1625.

5603 **Squier, Charles L**. 'Selected bibliography [of primary and secondary sources]' *in* John Fletcher. (Twayne's English authors, 433). Boston, Twayne, [1986]. p.162–4.

5604 **Eade, J.C**. Astrological analysis as an editorial tool; the case of Fletcher's The bloody brother. Stud Bib 34:198–204 '81.

5605 **Turner, Robert K**. Revisions and repetition brackets in Fletcher's A wife for a month. Stud Bib 36:178–90 '83.

5606 **Hill, Trevor H. Howard-**. Buc and the censorship of Sir John van Olden Barnavelt in 1619. R Eng Stud new ser 39no153:39–63 F '88.

FLETCHER, JOHN, 1729–85

5607 **John** Fletcher, 1729–1785; a library exhibition. (Notes and news). John Rylands Univ Libr Manchester Bull 67no2:569–71 '85.

FOOTE, SAMUEL, 1720–77

5608 **Chatten, Elizabeth N**. 'Selected bibliography [of primary and secondary sources]' *in* Samuel Foote. (Twayne's English authors, 285). Boston, Twayne, [1980]. p.153–7.

FORD, FORD MADOX (formerly HUEFFER), 1873–1939

5609 **Stang, Sondra J**. 'Chronological list of Ford's books' *in* The presence of Ford Madox Ford; a memorial volume of essays, poems, and memoirs. Philadelphia, University of Pennsylvania pr., 1981. p.240–2.
'Books in print' (p.243).

5610 **Tamkin, Linda**. A secondary source bibliography on Ford Madox Ford, 1962–1979. Bull Bib 38no1:20–5 Ja/Mr '81.

5611 **Longrie, Michael**. A secondary source bibliography on Ford Madox Ford, 1985–1988. Contemp Lit 30no2:328–33 '89.

5612 **Krickel, Edward**. 'Lord Plushbottom in the service of the kingdom; Ford as editor' *in* Stang, Sondra J. The presence of Ford Madox Ford; a memorial volume of essays, poems, and memoirs. Philadelphia, University of Pennsylvania pr., 1981. p.98–108.

5613 **Naumburg, Edward**. 'A collector looks at Ford again' *in* Stang, Sondra J., *ed*. The presence of Ford Madox Ford; a memorial volume of essays, poems, and memoirs. Philadelphia, University of Pennsylvania pr., 1981. p.161–85. facsims.

5614 **Higdon, D. Leon**. The Macmillan reader's report on Romance. (Notes and discussion). Mod Fict Stud 30no2:274–7 '84.

FORD, JOHN, fl.1602–39

5615 **Monsarrat, G.D.** Printed texts and presentation manuscripts; the case of John Ford's Fame's memorial and A line of life. (Bibliographical notes). Library ser6 2no1:80–5 Mr '80.

5616 **Fehrenbach, Robert J.** 'Typographical variation in Ford's texts; accidentals or substantives [Italics]' *in* Anderson, Donald K., *ed*. 'Concord in discord'; the plays of John Ford, 1586–1986. New York, AMS pr., [1986]. p.265–94.

FORSTER, EDWARD MORGAN, 1879–1970

5617 **McDowell, Frederick P.W.** 'Selected bibliography [of primary and secondary works]' *in* E.M. Forster. Rev. ed. (Twayne's English authors, 89). Boston, [Mass.], Twayne, [1982]. (First publ. 1969). p.160–7.

5618 **Lago, Mary**. Calendar of the letters of E.M. Forster. London, Mansell, [1984]. xxiii,199p. 28cm.
Rev: J. Batchelor R Eng Stud new ser 38:103–5 '87.

5619 **Kirkpatrick, Brownlee J.** A bibliography of E.M. Forster. 2d ed. Oxford, Clarendon pr., 1985. (First publ. 1968). xiv,327p. port. 21cm. (Soho Bibs, 19).
Adds F. Audio-visual material and G. Manuscripts to BBLB2 3351; *section E (Miscellaneous printed material) is expanded.*
Rev: T. Brown R Eng Stud new ser 38:408–9 '87.

5620 —— E.M. Forster's broadcast talks. [Extr. from bibliogr.]. Twent Cent Lit 31no2/3:329–41 '85.

5621 (7:4331) **Stallybrass, Oliver G.W.** The manuscripts of A passage to India, [1978].
Rev: M. Bowen Mod Philol 89:61–76 '82; P.A. Burger Unisa Eng Stud 21:49–51 '83.

5622 **Halls, Michael.** The Forster collections at King's; a survey. [Cambridge]. Twent Cent Lit 31no2/3:147–60 '85.
1. Introduction.–2. The novels.–3. Other books.–4. Short stories.–5. Plays and poems.–6. Diaries and journals.–7. Memoirs.–8. Essays and talks; notebooks, etc.–9. Correspondence.–10. Other materials.

5623 **Lohrli, Anne.** Chapman and Hall. [Names in Forster's Maurice: Christopher Hall]. N&Q 230no3:377–8 S '85.

5624 **Hegazi, Safaa.** The date and first publication of two essays by E.M. Forster. ['Shakespeare and Egypt', 1916; 'Eliza in Egypt', 1917]. N&Q 231no2:191–2 Je '86; A. Aly 232no4:506 D '87.

FOTHERGILL, JESSIE, 1851–91

5625 **Crisp, Jane.** Jessie Fothergill, 1851–1891; a bibliography. [St. Lucia], Dept. of English, University of Queensland, [1980]. 27p. port., illus. 19cm. (Vict Fict Res Guides, 2).
Classified checklist of 110 works and ana.
Rev: Joanne Shattock Mod Lang R 79:682–3 '84.

FOWLES, JOHN, 1926–

5626 **Huffaker, Robert.** 'Selected bibliography [of primary and secondary sources]' *in* John Fowles. (Twayne's English authors, 292). Boston, Twayne, [1980]. p.147–61.

5627 **Olshen, Barry N.** and **Toni A. Olshen.** John Fowles; a reference guide. Boston, Mass., G.K. Hall, [1980]. xix,86p. 23cm. (Reference guides to literature).
Rev: R.F. Kiernan Lit Res Newsl 6:124–6 '81; J.G. Wason N&Q 227:474 '82; J.L. Halio Yrbk Eng Stud 13:357–9 '83.

5628 **Roberts, Ray A.** John Fowles; a bibliographical checklist. Am Bk Coll new ser 1no5:26–37 S/Oc '80.

5629 **Dixon, Ronald C.** Criticism of John Fowles; a selected checklist. Mod Fict Stud 31no1:205–10 '85.

5630 **Sullivan, Paula**. The manuscripts for John Fowles' The French lieutenant's woman. (Bibliographical notes). Pa Bib Soc Am 74n03:272-7 '80.

5631 **Smith, Frederick N.** The endings of The French lieutenant's woman; another speculation on the manuscript. [Revision]. J Mod Lit 14n04:579-84 '88; Elizabeth Mansfield 14n04:584 '88.

FOX, CHARLES JAMES, 1749-1806

5632 **Pomeroy, John**. Charles James Fox; a bibliography. [Australia, J. Pomeroy], [1988]. 32p. port. 19cm.

FOX, RALPH WINSTON, 1900-37

5633 **Munton, Alan** and **A. Young**, no.700.

FOXE, JOHN, 1516-87

5634 **Wooden, Warren W.** Recent studies in Foxe. (Recent studies in the English renaissance). Eng Lit Renaiss 11n02:224-32 '81.

5635 —— 'Selected bibliography [of primary and secondary sources]' *in* John Foxe. (Twayne's English authors, 345). Boston, Twayne, [1983]. p.134-9.

FRANCIS, RICHARD ('DICK'), 1920-

5636 **Macleod, Helen**. Dick Francis. [Collecting]. Bk & Mag Coll 11:35-40 Ja '85. port., facsims.
'Complete Dick Francis UK bibliography (p.40).

FRANCIS, STEPHEN DANIEL, 1917-

5637 **Lofts, William O.G.** and **D.J. Audley**. The pulp fiction of Hank Janson, popular paperback writer of the forties and fifties. [Collecting]. Bk & Mag Coll 18:52-7 Ag '85. facsims.
'Collectable Hank Janson pulp fiction books' (p.57).

GALSWORTHY, JOHN, 1867-1933

5638 **Stevens, Earl E.** and **H.R. Stevens**. John Galsworthy; an annotated bibliography of writings about him. De Kalb, Ill., Northern Illinois U.P., [1980]. xii,483p. 23cm. (Annotated Secondary Bib Ser Eng Lit Transit 1880-1920).
Rev: D.L. Higdon Lit Res Newsl 6:73-7 '81.

5639 (5:10623m) **Evans, D. Wyn.** The Galsworthy collection in Birmingham university library. Open Access new ser 17no1:12–13 '68.

5640 **Small, Ian.** Special collections report; the Galsworthy collection and its fate. [University of Birmingham]. Eng Lit Transit 27no3:236–8 '84.

GALT, JOHN, 1779–1839

5641 **Gordon, Ian A.** Galt and Constable; two new Galt attributions. [Articles in Edinburgh gazeteer]. Scott Lit J 8no1:5–9 My '81.

5642 **Wilson, Patricia J.** John Galt at work; comments on the ms. of Ringan Gilhaize. [Revision]. Stud Scott Lit 20:160–76 '85. facsims.

GARDNER, DAME HELEN LOUISE, 1908–86

5643 **Peters, Helen**, *comp.* 'A select list of the published writings of dame Helen Gardner...[1933–79]' *in* [Carey, John], *ed.* English renaissance studies presented to dame Helen Gardner in honour of her seventieth birthday. Oxford, Clarendon pr., 1980. p.[291]–8.

GARNETT, DAVID, 1892–1981

5644 **Hosking, Michael, bksllr.** David Garnett, C.B.E.; a writer's library. [Catalogue, with introd. by Nicolas Barker]. Deal, Kent, 1983. 179p. 23cm. (Catalogue, 22).
'Part three: A check-list of books by members of the Garnett family' (p.174–9).

GARNETT, RICHARD, 1835–1906

5645 **McCrimmon, Barbara.** Richard Garnett as censor. [At BM.]. Brit Libr J 12no1:64–75 '86. port.

GARRICK, DAVID, 1717–79

5646 **Berkowitz, Gerald M.** David Garrick; a reference guide. Boston, Mass., G.K. Hall, [1980]. xvi,309p. 23cm. (Reference Publ in Lit).
Rev: C.J.L. Price N&Q 227:556–7 '82.

5647 **Dircks, Phyllis T.** 'Selected bibliography [of primary and secondary sources]' *in* David Garrick. (Twayne's English authors, 403). Boston, Twayne, [1985]. p.143–7.

GARTH, SIR SAMUEL, 1661–1719

5648 **Cook, Richard I.** 'Selected bibliography [of primary and secondary sources]' *in* Sir Samuel Garth. (Twayne's English authors, 276). Boston, Twayne, [1980]. p.162–5.

GASCOYNE, DAVID EMERY, 1916–

5649 **Benford, Colin T.** David Gascoyne; a bibliography of his works, 1929–1985. Ryde, I.O.W., Heritage, [1986]. xvi,148p. illus. 23cm. (Ltd. to 350 no. copies).
Quasifacsim. TP transcrs., contents, and bibliogr. notes and discussion of ptd. books and pamphlets, contribs. to books and papmphlets, anthologies and collections, trans. by, periodical contribs., miscellaneous, broadcasts, recordings and a play, works trans. into foreign languages, anthologies and periodicals, and biographical and critical sources.

GASKELL, ELIZABETH CLEGHORN (STEVENSON), 1810–65

5650 **Lansbury, Coral**. 'Selected bibliography [of primary and secondary sources]' *in* Elizabeth Gaskell. (Twayne's English authors, 371). Boston, [Mass.], Twayne, [1984]. p.123–8.

5651 **Crick, Brian**. The implications of the title changes and textual revisions in mrs. Gaskell's Mary Barton, a tale of Manchester life. N&Q 225no6:514–19 D '80.

5652 **Unsworth, Anna** and **A.Q. Morton**. Mrs. Gaskell anonymous; some unidentified items in Fraser's magazine. Vict Pers R 14no1:24–31 '81. tables.

5653 **Collin, Dorothy M.** The composition and publication of Elizabeth Gaskell's Cranford. John Rylands Libr Bull 69no1:59–95 '86.
'Appendix 1: A census of Cranford holdings with descriptions' (p.87–94).

5654 **Ruddick, Bill**. George de Maurier; illustrator and interpreter of mrs. Gaskell. Gaskell Soc J 1:48–69 '87.

5655 **Lingard, Christine**. The Gaskell collection in Manchester central library. Gaskell Soc J 2:59–75 '88.

5656 **Shelston, Alan**. The Moorland cottage; Elizabeth Gaskell and Myles Birket Foster. [Illus.]. Gaskell Soc J 2:41–58 '88. facsims.

5657 **Hodgson, John**. A Gaskell collection at Canterbury. Gaskell Soc J 3:42–5 '89.

GAY, JOHN, 1685–1732

5658 **Lanoix, Louis.** John Gay, The Beggar's opera; bibliographie sélective et critique. Soc d'Étud Anglo-Am Bull 29:25–43 N '89. facsim.

5659 **Hammond, Brean S.** "A poet, and a patron, and ten pound'; John Gay and patronage' *in* Lewis, Peter and N. Wood, *ed.* John Gay and the Scriblerians. London, Vision; New York, St. Martin's pr., [1988]. p.23–43.

GEDDES, WILLIAM, 1600?–94

5660 **Nash, N. Frederick.** A case of declining patronage; William Geddes's The saints recreation of 1683. [Issues and dedications]. Biblioth 11no3:59–72 '82. facsims.

GIBBON, EDWARD, 1737–94

5661 **Keynes, sir Geoffrey L.,** *ed.* The library of Edward Gibbon; a catalogue. 2d ed. [Winchester], St. Paul's bibliographies, [1980]. (First publ. 1940). 293p. illus., port., facsims. 21cm. (St. Paul's Bibs, 2).
'Appendix to the second edition' (p.289–93).
Rev: G. Naylor TLS 23 Ja '81:95; Yvonne Noble Am Bk Coll new ser 2:44–8 '81; R. Norris Libr R 30:119–20 '81; T. Hofmann Bk Coll 31:247–51 '82; W.B. Carnochan Mod Lang R 78:685–7 '83.

5662 **Craddock, Patricia B.** and **Margaret C. Huff.** Edward Gibbon; a reference guide. Boston, Mass., G.K. Hall, 1987. xlix, 476p. 23cm. (Reference guide to literature).
Ref: M. Baridon Étud Angl 42:103–4 '89; J.M. Black Durham Univ J 82:270–1 '90.

5663 **Bennett, Jack A.W.** 'Bookman and bibliophile' *in* Essays on Gibbon. Cambridge, Privately ptd., 1980. p.11–27.

GIBBON, LEWIS GRASSIC, *pseud. of* JAMES LESLIE MITCHELL, 1901–35

5664 **Malcolm, William K.** James Leslie Mitchell/Lewis Grassic Gibbon checklist: Additions III. Biblioth 11no6:149–56 '83.

5665 **Campbell, Ian.** Lewis Grassic Gibbon correspondence; the background and a checklist. Biblioth 12no2:46–57 '84.
'Checklist' (p.52–7).

5666 —— Gibbon and MacDiarmid at play; the evolution of Scottish scene. Biblioth 13no2:46–55 '86.

GIBBON, WILLIAM MONK, 1896–

5667 **MacKenzie, Norman H.** The Monk Gibbon papers. [Queen's university]. Canadian J Irish Stud 9no2:5–24 D '83.

GILBERT, SIR WILLIAM SCHWENCK, 1836–1911

5668 **Works** of W.S. Gilbert collected by C.P. Johnson, in BL *see* Gould, Alison, Named special collections, 1981: no.818.

GILL, ARTHUR ERIC ROWTON, 1882–1940 *see* BOOK PRODUCTION AND DISTRIBUTION—Printers, etc.

GISSING, GEORGE ROBERT, 1857–1903

5669 **Selig, Robert L.** 'Selected bibliography [of primary and secondary sources]' *in* George Gissing. (Twayne's English authors, 346). Boston, Twayne, [1983]. p.161–70.

5670 **Collie, Michael.** George Gissing; a bibliographical study. [New ed., rev. and extended]. Winchester, St. Paul's bibliographies, 1985. (First publ. 1976). [ix],167p. facsims. 22cm. (St. Paul's Bibs, 12).
Bibliogr. of principal works publ. during Gissing's lifetime, principal works publ. posthumously, posthumous publications containing original work publ. for the first time, letters, short stories, and appendices: 1. Select checklist of books and articles about Gissing. 2. Colonial issues. 3. Some early translations.
Rev. P. Coustillas Library ser6 9:75–7 '87; Susan A. Porterfield Analytical & Enum Bib new ser 1:265–7 '87.

5671 **Coustillas, Pierre** and **R. Hoefnagel**. The presentation copies of Gissing's works in the Darmouth college library. [Checklist of 7 copies]. Gissing Newsl 21no4:18–24 Oc '85.

5672 **Coustillas, Pierre**. Gissing's novels in paperback. Gissing Newsl 23no1:28–30 Ja '87.

5673 —— The new Japanese translations of Gissing's works. [Listed]. Gissing Newsl 24no2:21–3 Ap '88. [Sg.: P.C.].

5674 **Wyatt, C.M.** and **P. Coustillas**. Gissing down under. [Austr. and N.Z. reviews, etc.]. Gissing Newsl 24no4:8–38 Oc '88; 25no1:13–42 Ja '89; 25no2:14–37 Ap '89; 25no3:11–29 Jl '89.

5675   **Coustillas, Pierre** and **R.L. Selig**. Gissing in America; two tales res-
cued from oblivion. [In The alliance, 1877]. Gissing Newsl 16no1:1–
5 Ja '80.

5676   —— Gissing's American short stories. (Note 430). Bk Coll 29no3:428 '80.

5677   **Partridge, Colin**. Will Warburton; deletions from the manuscript.
[Revision]. Gissing Newsl 16no2:14–25 Ap '80.

5678   **Coustillas, Pierre**. 'Bibliographical note' *in* Collis, John S., *ed*. The
private papers of Henry Rycroft. [Brighton], Harvester pr., 1982.
p.[xxv]–xxvi.

5679   **Selig, Robert L.** An unknown Gissing story from the Chicago Daily
news. ['Too wretched to live']. Stud Bib 36:205–12 '83.

5680   **Brattin, Joel J.** A lost Gissing manuscript discovered. [Introd. to
Martin Chuzzlewit, at Stanford]. Gissing Newsl 20no4:15–17 Oc '84.

5681   **Coustillas, Pierre**. The 'explosion' continues; forthcoming editions
of Gissing's works. [Publ.]. Gissing Newsl 22no2:35–7 Ap '86 '86.

5682   —— Sidelights on Gissing's publishing career. Gissing Newsl 22no3:1–
32 Jl '86.

5683   **Selig, Robert L.** A further Gissing attribution from the Chicago Post.
['One farthing damages']. (Bibliographical notes). Pa Bib Soc Am
80no1:100–4 '86.

5684   **Coustillas, Pierre**. 'The publication of The private life of Henry Mait-
land; a literary event' *in* Brack, O M, *ed*. Twilight of dawn; studies in
English literature in transition. Tucson, Publ. for the Arizona state university centennial by the University of Arizona pr., [1987]. p.137–52.

5685   **Selig, Robert L.** Unconvincing Gissing attributions: 'The death-clock',
'The serpent-charm', 'Dead and alive'. (Bibliographical notes).
Library ser6 9no2:169–72 '87; P. Coustillas; R.L. Selig (Correspon-
dence) 9no3:274–7 S '87.

5686   **Coustillas, Pierre**. The romance of Japanese editions; the Selected
works of George Gissing in their bibliographical context. Gissing
Newsl 24no3:35–43 Jl '88.

GLADSTONE, WILLIAM EWART, 1809–98

5687   **Dobson, Caroline J.** Gladstoniana; a bibliography of material relating to W.E. Gladstone at St. Deiniol's library. Haward, St. Deiniol's
library, [1983?]. ii,38p. 30cm. Covertitle. (Duplicated typescript).

5688 **Foot, M.R.D.** 'Mr. Gladstone and his publishers' *in* Myers, Robin and M.R.A. Harris, *ed.* Author/publisher relations during the eighteenth and nineteenth centuries. [Oxford], 1983. p.[156]–75.

GODWIN, MARY (WOLLSTONECRAFT), 1759–97

5689 **Duket, Paule-Marie**. Mary Wollstonecraft, A vindication of the rights of woman, 1792: bibliographie sélective et critique. Soc d'Étud Anglo-Am Bull 23:25–36 N '86.

5690 **Windle, John R.** Mary Wollstonecraft [Godwin]; a bibliography of her writings, 1787–1982. Los Angeles, 1988. 29[3]p. facsims. 22cm. (Ltd. to 200 no. copies).

5691 **Maison, Margaret**. Mary Wollstonecraft and mr. Cresswick. [The Female reader, 1789, not by her]. N&Q 232no4:467–8 D '87; Isobel Grundy 234no2:166 Je '89.

5692 **Taylor, Julia**. The early publishing history of Mary Wollstonecraft's Vindication. Factotum 27:13–16 N '88.

GODWIN, MARY WOLLSTONECRAFT (MRS. P.B. SHELLEY), 1797–
1851 *see* SHELLEY, MARY WOLLSTONECRAFT (GODWIN), 1797–1851.

GODWIN, WILLIAM, 1756–1836

5693 **Tysdahl, B.J.** 'Bibliography [of Godwin's works and secondary sources]' *in* William Godwin as novelist. London, Athlone, [1981]. p.192–9.

5694 **St.Clair, William**. 'William Godwin as children's bookseller' *in* Avery, Gillian and Julia Biggs, *ed.* Children and their books; a celebration of the work of Iona and Peter Opie. Oxford, 1989. p.165–79. facsim.
'William Godwin's books for children' (p.179).

GOLDING, WILLIAM GERALD, 1911–

5695 **Dick, Bernard F.** 'Selected bibliography [of primary and secondary sources]' *in* William Golding. Rev. ed. (Twayne's English authors, 57). Boston, Twayne, [1987]. p.162–5.

5696 **Gunn, Katharine**. William Golding. [Collecting]. Bk & Mag Coll 24:21–7 F '86. port., facsims.
'Complete UK bibliography of William Golding' (p.27).

5697 **Monteith, Charles**. 'Strangers from within' into Lord of the flies; on William Golding's 75th birthday, Charles Monteith recalls how he came to publish Lord of the flies. TLS 19 S '86:1030.

5698 **Bode, Christoph**. Goldings verächtlicher sisyphos; Text und Autorenintention in Pincher Martin. Germanisch-Romanische Monatschrift 38no1/2:151–67 '88.

GOLDSMITH, OLIVER, 1728–74

5699 **Woods, Samuel H.** Oliver Goldsmith; a reference guide. Boston, Mass., G.K. Hall, 1982. xxiii,208p. 25cm. (Reference guide to literature).
Rev: P. Dixon Yrbk Eng Stud 16:277–8 '86.

5700 **Soupel, Serge**. Oliver Goldsmith 1730?–1774, The vicar of Wakefield 1766: bibliographie sélective et critique. Soc d'Étud Anglo-Am Bull 23:17–24 N '86.

———

5701 **Pitcher, Edward W.** Lyttelton, Goldsmith, and 'The story of Zelis'. (Bibliographical notes). Pa Bib Soc Am 74no3:259–62 '80.

5702 **Jannetta, Mervyn J.** An annotated copy of Goldsmith's Life of Nash, 1762. Brit Libr J 10no1:63–7 '84. facsim.

5703 **Pointon, Marcia**. 'On reading Rowlandson's The vicar of Wakefield; challenging and subverting the narrative' *in* Möller, Joachim, *ed.* Imagination on a long rein; English literature illustrated. [Marburg], [1988]. p.110–19. facsims., diagr.

GOODACRE, NORMAN WILLIAM, 1907–

5704 **Goodacre, Selwyn H.** Norman W. Goodacre; an annotated hand-list of the printed writings. [Burton-on-Trent, Staffs.], Privately ptd., 1982. 43p. 21cm. (Reprod. from typewriting). Ltd. to 400 no. copies.

GOSSE, PHILIP HENRY, 1810–88

5705 **Freeman, Richard B.** and **D.L. Wertheimer**. P.H. Gosse; a bibliography. [Folkestone], Dawson, [1980]. x,148p. illus., facsims. 21cm.
Classified checklist of books and pamphlets, tracts, contribs. to serials, and biographies of, with discursive bibliogr. etc. notes and note of copy seen.
Rev: Library ser6 2:478–9 '80.

GOULD, JOHN, 1804-81

5706 **Kansas. University. Kenneth Spencer research library.** John Gould; his birds & beasts: an exhibit in the Department of special collections. [Lawrence, Friends of the library, University of Kansas], 1981. 6p. 27cm. Covertitle.

5707 **Sauer, Gordon C.** John Gould, the bird man; a chronology and bibliography. London, H. Sotheran; [Lawrence, Kan.], U.P. of Kansas, [1982]. xxiv,416p. illus., facsims., ports. 27cm.

5708 **Sauer, Gordon C.** John Gould's prospectuses and lists of subscribers to his works on natural history.... [Kansas city, Mo.], Privately ptd., 1980. v,12,26p. facsims. 25cm. (Ltd. to 350 no. copies).

5709 **McEvey, Allan.** A note on early and late states of plates and text pages for John Gould's The birds of Australia. Bib Soc Aust & N.Z. Bull 11no2:69-75 '87. facsims.

5710 **Sauer, Gordon C.** and **D. Evans.** John Gould's The birds of Australia in the original 36 parts, with notes on the cancelled plates and text. Bib Soc Aust & N.Z. Bull 11no2:67-9 '87.

5711 **Sauer, Gordon C.** Prospectus for John Gould's A century of birds hitherto unfigured from the Himalaya mountains, 1830-1833. Archiv Nat Hist 15no1:89-91 F '88. facsim.

GOULDING, RICHARD WILLIAM, 1868-1929

5712 **Jefferson, J.K.** Richard William Goulding collection; a handlist. [Lincoln], Lincolnshire library service, [1980]. 150p. port. 29cm.

GOWER, JOHN, 1325?-1408

5713 **Yeager, Robert F.** John Gower materials; a bibliography through 1979. New York, Garland, 1981. xi,155p. 23cm. (Reference library of the humanities, 266).
Rev: Pamela Gradon N&Q 227:357-8 '82.

5714 **Nicholson, Peter.** An annotated index to the commentary on Gower's Confession amantis. Binghamton, N.Y., Medieval and renaissance texts and studies, 1989. ix,593p. 24cm. (Med & Renaiss Texts & Stud, 62).
Notes and annotations to the text, arranged in text order, with references to a checklist of c.357 books, articles, editions and selections since 1900.

5715 **Doyle, Anthony I.** 'Early 15th-century copies of Gower's Confessio amantis and Chaucer's Canterbury tales' *in* Hellinga, Lotte and H. Härtel, *ed.* Buch und text im 15. Jahrhundert / Book and text in the fifteenth century. Hamburg, 1981. p.47–50.

   Summary of Doyle, Anthony I.H. and M.B. Parkes, 'The production of copies of the Canterbury tales and the Confessio amantis in the early fifteenth century' *in* Watson, Andrew G. Medieval scribes, manuscripts and libraries; essays presented to N.R. Ker. London, Scolar pr., 1978. p.163–203.

5716 **Gardiner, Eileen**. The recension of the Confessio amantis in the Plimpton Gower. [Columbia univ.]. Manuscripts 25no2:107–12 Jl '81.

5717 **Harris, Kate**. 'John Gower's Confessio amantis; the virtues of bad texts' *in* Pearsall, Derek A., *ed.* Manuscripts and readers in fifteenth-century England. [Cambridge], [1983]. p.[27]–40.

5718 **Nicholson, Peter**. Gower's revisions in the Confessio amantis. Chaucer R 19no2:123–43 '84.

5719 —— 'Poet and scribe in the manuscripts of Gower's Confession amantis' *in* Pearsall, Derek A., *ed.* Manuscripts and texts; editorial problems in later middle English literature. [Cambridge], [1987]. p.[130]–42.

GRAHAM, ROBERT BONTINE CUNNINGHAME, 1852–1936

5720 **Walker, John**. Cunninghame Graham and Scotland; an annotated bibliography. Dollar, D.S. Mack, 1980. 33p. 28cm. (Duplicated typescript).

   Rev: J. Kidd Biblioth 10:82–3 '80.

5721 **Jefferson, George**. Cunninghame Graham; a British conquistador. (Unappreciated authors, 9). Antiqu Bk Mnthly R 14no7:252–7 Jl '87. ports., facsims.

   'Select bibliography' (p.257).

GRAHAM, WILLIAM SYDNEY, 1918–

5722 **Lopez, Tony**. 'Bibliography' *in* The poetry of W.S. Graham. [Edinburgh], Edinburgh U.P., [1988]. p.138–68.

   Classified checklist with some bibliogr. notes of books and pamphlets, works ed. or with contribs. by, contribs. to periodicals, ms. collns., and ana.

GRAHAME, KENNETH, 1859–1932

5723 **Kuznets, Lois R.** 'Selected bibliography [of primary and secondary sources]' *in* Kenneth Grahame. (Twayne's English authors, 449). Boston, Twayne, [1986]. p.146–50.

5724 **Macleod, Helen**. Kenneth Grahame. [Collecting]. Bk & Mag Coll 18:15–24 Ag '85. port., facsims.

5725 **Bridge, Alexander**. Kenneth Grahame on my shelves. [Libr.]. Antiqu Bk Mnthly R 13no8:301–5 Ag '86. illus., facsim.

5726 ——A Wind in the willows point? (Letters). Antiqu Bk Mnthly R 15no4:126 Ap '88.

GRAND, SARAH, *pseud. of* FRANCES ELIZABETH (CLARKE) McFALL, 1854–1943

5727 (7:4443) **Huddleston, Joan**. Sarah Grand...; a bibliography, 1979.
Rev: Shirley Foster Yrbk Eng Stud 13:338–42 '83.

GRANGER, FRANCIS S., 1864–

5728 **Nottingham. University. Library. Manuscripts department.** Manuscripts of professor Frank S. Granger, c.1710–1980. [Nottingham], [1980?]. 13p. 30cm. (Duplicated typescript).

GRAVES, ROBERT VON RANKE, 1895–1985

5729 (7:4446c) **Pownall, David E.** An annotated bibliography of articles on Robert Graves. Focus on Graves [1no]2:17–23 D '73.

5730 (7:4450) **Presley, John W.** The Robert Graves manuscripts and letters at Southern Illinois university; an inventory, 1976.
Rev: W.A. Dolid Focus 6:91–4 '82.

5731 **Edwards, Anthony S.G.** Robert Graves bibliography; addenda and corrigenda. Analytical & Enum Bib 4no1:37–8 '80.

5732 ——Further addenda to Higginson; The bibliography of Robert Graves. (Bibliographical notes). Pa Bib Soc Am 75no2:210–11 '81.

5733 **Presley, John W.** A preliminary list of the SIU Robert Graves collection. [Mss. and letters]. Focus Robert Graves 6:95–102 S '82.

5734 **Ahearn, Allen** and **Patricia Hearne.** Author price guides: Robert Graves. Bethesda, Md., [Quill & Brush], [1984]. 15p. 28cm.
Rev: G. Bixby Am Bk Coll 7:47–50 '86.

5735 **Bryant, Hallman B.** Robert Graves; an annotated bibliography. New York, Garland, 1986. xvi,206p. port. 22cm. (Reference library of the humanities, 671).
Rev: A.S.G. Edwards Analytical & Enum Bib new ser 2:36–43 '88; K. Quinlan Sth Carolina R 22:144–5 '89.

5736 **Higginson, Fred H.** and **W.P. Williams**. Robert Graves; a biblio- gra-
phy. Rev. and enl. [Winchester, Hants.], St. Paul's bibliographies,
1987. (First publ. 1966). vi,354p. illus., facsims. 22cm.
Rev: M. Seymour-Smith TLS 15 Ap '88:434; S. Hills Bk Coll 38:119–22 '89.

5737 (7:4452u) **Collections**. [Graves collns. at librs., incl. SUNY Buffalo, Southern Illinois, and the University of Victoria]. Focus on Graves [1no]1:12–
14 Ja '72.

5738 (7:4452v) **Private** collections. [Holdings listed]. Focus on Graves
[1no]2:28–32 D '72.

5739 (7:4453c) **Gerwing, Howard B.** The Robert Graves collection at the
University of Victoria. Focus on Graves [1no]3:45–6 D '73.

5740 (7:4453d) **Cohn, Alan M.** Glanville-Hicks' Nausicaa and Graves (Higginson D76). Focus on Graves [1no]4:71–3 Je '74.

5741 **Petter, Christopher G.** Graves manuscripts at the University of Victoria: addendum. Focus on Graves [1no]6:102–4 S '82.

5742 **Rooksby, Rikky**. A Graves revision. ['In dedication']. Eng Lang N
21no3:53–7 Mr '84.

5743 **Brown, Geoffrey**. Robert Graves. [Collecting]. Bk & Mag Coll 19:42–
51 S '85. port., facsims., illus.
'Complete bibliography of Robert Graves first editions' (p.49–51).

5744 **Bertz, Dietrich**. Graves manuscripts. (Letters). TLS 15 Jl '88:781.

5745 **Mason, Ellsworth**. Expanding the Robert Graves canon. Focus Robert Graves & Contemps 1no7:1–9 Je '88.

5746 **Baker, William**. An addition to Robert Graves bibliography. [In Libr
R]. Analytical & Enum Bib new ser 3no2:66–7 '89.

5747 **Cox, Shelley**. The Robert Graves collections at Southern Illinois
university, Carbondale. Focus Robert Graves & Contemps 1no9:4–
10 My '89.

5748 **Gerwing, Howard B.** Graves manuscripts at the University of Victoria:
fourth report. Focus Robert Graves & Contemps 1no10:1 '89/90.

5749 **Hayes, Deborah**. Glanville-Hicks' Nausicaa, Graves and Reid. Focus
Robert Graves & Contemps 1no9:11–14 My '89.

GRAY, John, 1866–1934

5750 **Cevasco, George A.** 'Selected bibliography [of primary and secondary sources]' *in* John Gray. (Twayne's English authors, 353). Boston, Twayne, [1982]. p.156–60.

GRAY, THOMAS, 1716–71

5751 **McKenzie, Alan T.** Thomas Gray; a reference guide. Boston, Mass., G.K. Hall, [1982]. xxii,334p. 25cm. (Reference guide to literature). *Rev*: R. Lonsdale Mod Lang R 80:126–7 '85.

5752 **Rogers, Deborah D.** The problem of copy-texts for Gray's epitaph on mrs. Clerke. [Epitaph copied from a tombstone]. Eng Lang N 26no2:30–4 D '88.

GREEN, Henry, *pseud. of* **HENRY YORKE, d.1973**

5753 **Heinzkill, Richard**. Henry Green; a checklist. [Of primary and secondary sources]. Twent Cent Lit 29no4:465–70 '83.

GREENAWAY, CATHERINE ('KATE'), 1846–1901

5754 **Hunt institute for botanical documentation,** PITTSBURGH. Kate Greenaway; catalogue of an exhibition of original artworks and related materials selected from the Frances Hooper collection at the Hunt institute. With essays by miss Hooper, Rodney Engen and John Brindle and a summary register of the full collection. Ed. by Robert Kiger. Comp. by Bernadette Callery [and others]. Pittsburgh, Hunt institute for botanical documentation, Carnegie-Mellon university, 1980. 106p. facsims. 26cm. *Rev*: Ellin Greene Libr Q 52:204–5 '82.

5755 **Engen, Rodney K.** 'Appendix: Illustrated books' *in* Kate Greenaway; a biography. London, Macdonald, [1981]. p.228–34.

5756 **Schuster, Thomas E.** and **R.K. Engen**. Printed Kate Greenaway; a catalogue raisonné. London, T.E. Schuster, 1986. 304p. illus., facsims. 26cm. *Classified checklists of books, black and white plates, posthumous, greeting cards, colour plates, calendars, trade cards, book plates, periodicals, ephemera, spinoffs, card spinoffs, ana, collectors guides, and exhibition catalogues, with bibliogr. notes and refs., and location of copy.* *Rev*: B.W. Alderson Bk Coll 37:581–2 '88.

5757 (7:4463) **Henderson, Geoffrey**. Was W.G., K.G....? Antiqu Bk Mnthly R '79; S.J. Robinson; R. Cooper (Letters) 7no3:154 Mr '80.

5758   **Engen, Rodney K.** Charting the course of the Greenaway legend. Antiqu Bk Mnthly R 7no3:114–23 Mr '80. facsims.

5759   —— Kate Greenaway; a biography. London, Macdonald, [1981]. 240p. illus., facsims., ports. 25cm.

5760   **Macleod, Helen**. The illustrated books of Kate Greenaway; a guide.... [Collecting]. Bk & Mag Coll 14:14–21 Ap '85. port., facsims.
'Bibliography of books written and illustrated by Kate Greenaway' (p.21).

5761   **Engen, Rodney K.** The myth of Kate Greenaway. Am Bk Coll new ser 7no7:3–11 Jl '86. port., facsims.

GREENE, HENRY GRAHAM, 1904–91

5762   **Cassis, A.F.** Graham Greene; an annotated bibliography of criticism. Metuchen, N.J., Scarecrow pr., 1981. xx,401p. 21cm. (Scarecrow author bibs, 55).
Rev: E.L. Chapman Christianity & Lit 31:101–2 '82; P. Stratford Eng Stud Canada 9:378–80 '83; R.H. Miller Lit Res Newsl 8:32–4 '83.

5763   **Costa, Richard H.** Graham Greene; a checklist. (Bibliography). College Lit 12no1:85–94 '85.

5764   **DeVitis, A.A.** 'Selected bibliography [of primary and secondary sources]' *in* Graham Greene. Rev. ed. (Twayne's English authors, 3). Boston, [Mass.], Twayne, [1986]. (First publ. 1964). p.204–14.

5765   **Higdon, D. Leon.** A textual history of Graham Greene's The power and the glory. Stud Bib 33:222–39 '80.

5766   **Redway, Alan R.** Graham Greene mss. [Sold at auction]. (Letters). Antiqu Bk Mnthly R 7no11:533 N '80.

5767   **Higdon, D. Leon.** The McFarlin library Graham Greene collection. [Univ. of Tulsa colln.]. N&Q 228no04:334–45 Ag '83.

5768   **Macleod, Helen**. Graham Greene. [Collecting]. Bk & Mag Coll 13:4–11 Mr '85. port., facsims.
'Complete bibliography of UK Graham Greene 1st editions' (p.10–11).

5769   **Antin, Charles**. A publishing mystery unraveled. [Eyre & Spottiswoode's Atlantis ser. publ. by Greene]. Am Bk Coll new ser 8no3:10–12 Mr '87. facsims.

5770 **Higdon, D. Leon.** "I try to be accurate'; the text of Greene's Brighton rock' *in* Wolfe, Peter, *ed.* Essays in Graham Greene; an annual review. Greenwood, Fla., Penkevill pr., [1987]. p.[169]–86.

5771 **Greene, H. Graham.** and **D. Low**. Dear David, dear Graham; a bibliophilic correspondence. Oxford, Alembic pr. with the Amate pr., 1989. 91p. ports. 24cm. (Ltd. to 250 no. copies).

GREENE, ROBERT, 1560?–92

5772 **Dean, James S.** Robert Greene; a reference guide. Boston, G.K. Hall, [1984]. xxv,258p. 25cm. (Reference publication in literature).
Rev: M.G. Brennan Analytical & Enum Bib new ser 1:79–80 '87.

5773 **Crupi, Charles W.** 'Selected bibliography [of primary and secondary sources]' *in* Robert Greene. (Twayne's English authors, 416). Boston, Twayne, [1985]. p.169–79.

5774 (7:4479) **Bratchell, D.F.** Robert Greene's Planetomachia, [1979].
Rev: J.P. Feather N&Q 227:69–70 '82.

5775 **Coggins, Gordon**. Greene's Pandosto; a ghost of 1584. (Bibliographical notes). Library ser6 2no4:448–56 D '80.

5776 ——Greene's repetitions as solutions to textual problems; a catalogue of repetitions. Analytical & Enum Bib 5no1:3–15 '81. tables.

GREGORY, ISABELLA AUGUSTA (PERSE), LADY, 1852–1932

5777 **Mikhail, Edward H.** Lady Gregory; an annotated bibliography of criticism. Troy, N.Y., Whitston, 1982. viii,258p. 23cm.
Rev: H. Adams Analytical & Enum Bib 6:269–71 '82.

5778 **Smythe, Colin S.**, *comp.* 'Lady Gregory's contributions to periodicals; a checklist' *in* Saddlemyer, Ann and C.S. Smythe, *ed.* Lady Gregory; fifty years after. (Irish Lit Stud 13). Gerrard Cross, C. Smythe; Totowa, N.J., Barnes & Noble, 1987. p.322–45.

GRENVILLE, WILLIAM WYNDHAM, BARON GRENVILLE, 1759–1834

5779 **Harvey, A.D.** Lord Grenville, 1759–1834; a bibliography. Westport, Conn., Meckler, [1989]. 94p. port. 23cm. (Bibs of Brit statesmen, 2).

GREVILLE, SIR FULKE, 1ST BARON BROOKE, 1554–1628

5780 **Klemp, Paul J.** Fulke Greville and sir John Davies; a reference guide. Boston, Mass., G.K. Hall, [1985]. xix,128p. 23cm. (Reference guide to literature).

Rev. Sara J. Steen Sevent Cent N 44:43 '86; Joan Rees Mod Lang R 83:666 '88; C.S. Hunter Sidney Newsl 10:36–42 '89.

GRIFFITH, ELIZABETH, 1720?–93

5781 **Massefski, Heidi M.** From London to Philadelphia; the misattribution of Elizabeth Griffith's Essays, addressed to young married women, 1782. N&Q 234no4:480–2 D '89.

GRIFFITH, LLEWELYN WYN, 1890–1977

5782 **Hill, Greg.** 'Bibliography [of works]' *in* Llewelyn Wyn Griffith. (Writers of Wales). Cardiff, University of Wales pr. on behalf of the Welsh arts council, 1984. p.65–8.

GRYMESTON, ELIZABETH, d.1603

5783 **Fletcher, Bradford Y.** and **Christine W. Sizemore.** Elizabeth Grymeston's Miscelanea, meditations, memoratives; introduction and selected text. Libr Chron Univ Pennsylvania 45no1/2:53–83 '81.

'Note on the text' (p.57–8).

GUNN, NEIL MILLER, 1891–1973

5784 **Stokoe, C.J.L.** A bibliography of the works of Neil M. Gunn. [Aberdeen], Aberdeen U.P.; Aberdeen U.P. in association with Aberdeen city library, [1987]. x,245p. 23cm. (Reprod. from typewriting).

Quasifacsim. TP transcrs., collations, contents and some bibliogr. notes and discussion, of books and short stories, plays, dramatisations and film scripts, verse, articles in newspapers and periodicals, broadcast material, and miscellaneous.

5785 **McCleery, Alistair.** The early novels of Neil M. Gunn. Biblioth 10no5:126–38 '81.

'Appendix: Table showing serial publication of The lost glen and The poaching at Grianan in The Scots magazine' (p.137–8).

GUNN, THOMSON WILLIAM, 1929–

5786 **Hagstrom, Jack W.C.** Thom Gunn. [Collecting]. Am Bk Coll new ser 1no5:12 S/Oc '80.

5787 **Traister, Daniel**. Addendum to the Thom Gunn bibliography. [Hagstrom and Bixby, BLB 1970–79: 4491]. (Bibliographical notes). Pa Bib Soc Am 75no3:354 '81.

HAGGARD, SIR HENRY RIDER, 1856–1925

5788 **Higgins, D.S.** 'Haggard's published works' *in* Rider Haggard, the great storyteller. London, Cassell, [1981]. p.[xi–xiii].

5789 **Etherington, Norman**. 'Selected bibliography [of primary and selected texts]' *in* Rider Haggard. (Twayne's English authors, 383). Boston, [Mass.], Twayne, [1984]. p.127–30.

5790 **Whatmore, Denys E.** H. Rider Haggard; a bibliography. [London], Mansell; [Westport, Conn.], Meckler, [1987]. xix,187p. 23cm.
Classified bibliogr. with extensive bibliogr. descriptions of principal fiction and non-fiction works, poems and reports, The African review, miscellaneous writings, letters to newspapers and periodicals, selected reports of speeches, films, plays and radio broadcasts based on his works, material about, parodies and lampoons of, theses, some popular ed. of note, and mss. in Norfolk record office.
Rev: Susan J. Navarette Lit Res 14:42–4 '89.

5791 **Allen, Roger**. Rider Haggard, the author of King Solomon's mines. [Collecting]. Bk & Mag Coll 4:16–23 Je '84. port., facsims.
'Rider Haggard: complete bibliography of novels and non-fiction works' (p.22–3).

5792 **Dalby, Richard**. King Solomon's mines; a centenary remembered. Antiqu Bk Mnthly R 12no10:390–3 Oc '85. port., facsims.

5793 **Whatmore, Denys E.** Some remarks on the adventures of Allan Quatermain. [With checklist]. Antiqu Bk Mnthly R 15no3:98–103 Mr '88. illus., port., facsim.

HAKLUYT, RICHARD, 1552?–1616

5794 **Garratt, John G.** Richard Hakluyt. Antiqu Bk Mnthly R 11no5:180–5 My '80. facsims.
'A list of Hakluyt's principal works' (p.183, 185).

HALES, STEPHEN, 1677–1761

5795 **Jensen, Bent Juel-.** A Friendly admonition to the drinkers of brandy. [With list of ed.]. (Query 381). Bk Coll 38no4:546–7 '89.

HALIFAX, GEORGE, MARQUIS OF, 1633–95 *see* SAVILE, GEORGE, MARQUIS OF HALIFAX, 1633–95.

HALL, ANNA MARIA (FIELDING), 1800–81

5796 **Newcomer, James.** Mr. and mrs. S.C. Hall; their papers at Iowa. Bks at Iowa 43:15–23 N '85. facsims.

HALL, BP. JOSEPH, 1574–1656

5797 **Wands, John M.** The early printing history of Joseph Hall's Mundus alter idem. Pa Bib Soc Am 74no1:1–12 '80. facsims.

5798 (5:10914n) **Wallis, Peter J.** Some provisional notes on the works of Joseph Hall, STC2 12635–40.7. Newcastle upon Tyne, Dept. of education, 1967. 5p. 30cm. Headtitle. (Duplicated typescript).

HALLAM, ARTHUR HENRY, 1811–33

5799 **Elliott, Philip L.** Materials for a life of A.T. [Publ.]. N&Q 226no5:415–18 Oc '81.

HAMILTON, PATRICK, 1904–62

5800 **Snelling, O. Fred.** Patrick Hamilton. (Unappreciated authors, 1). Antiqu Bk Mnthly R 11no1:8–13 Ja '84. port., facsims., illus.

HANDEL, GEORGE FREDERICK, 1685–1759

5801 **Hall, Mary A. Parker-.** G.F. Handel; a guide to research. New York, Garland, 1988. xvii,294p. illus., port. 23cm. (Composer resource manual, 19).
    Includes '4. List of Handel's works' (p.103–25); '5. Studies of Handel's music' (p.126–210).

5802 (5:10937b) **Tobin, John**. Handel's Messiah; a critical account of the manuscript sources and printed editions. London, Cassell, 1969; New York, St. Martin's pr., [1969]. xii,279p. facsims., music, port. 26cm.

Includes The source manuscripts.–2. The printed editions....–Appendixes [A. Alternative settings. I. Table of manuscript sources and their contents. II. Table of contents of the principal editions from 1749 to 1854.–C. Seriatim list of textual variants].

5803 **Illing, Robert**. Performing Messiah as Handel wished. Bib Soc Aust & N.Z. Bull 4no4:241–53 N '80. music.

1. Studies and editions.–2. Instruments and voices.–3. Establishing the text.–4. Comparative study of the editions.

5804 **Hill, Cecil**. Early engravers of Handel's music. Bib Soc Aust & N.Z. Bull 11no4:125–40 '87. facsims.

HANLEY, JAMES, 1901–85

5805 **Stape, John H.** James Hanley, William Golding, Muriel Spark: additional primary works. Analytical & Enum Bib new ser 2no3:110–12 '88.

––––––––––––

5806 **Harrington, Frank G.** Considering and collecting James Hanley. Am Bk Coll new ser 8no5:3–10 My '87. illus., ports, facsims.

HARDING, DENYS WYATT, 1906–

5807 **Grosman, Meta**. Denys Wyatt Harding and his work. Acta Neophilologica (Ljubljana) 15:63–95 '82.

'Bibliography of D.W. Harding's works' (p.84–95): chronol. checklist, 1929–81.

HARDY, THOMAS, 1840–1928

5808 **Davis, W. Eugene** and **H.E. Gerber**. Thomas Hardy; an annotated bibliography of writings about him: vol.2, 1970–1978 and Supplement for 1871–1969. DeKalb, Ill., Northern Illinois U.P., [1983]. x,735p. 25cm. (Annotated secondary bibliography series on English literature in transition).

Rev: D.J. Winslow Analytical & Enum Bib 8:45–8 '84; C.P.C. Pettit Thomas Hardy J 1:16–19 '87.

5809 **Foote, I.P.** Thomas Hardy in Russian translation and criticism to 1978. Thomas Hardy Yrbk 11:6–27 '84.

'Translations of Hardy's works' (p.14–23).

5810   **Furukawa, Takao**, *ed.* Thomas Hardy; a bibliography about his poetry in Japan, 1912–1984. Tokyo, Kirihara shoten, 1984. 256p. (Not seen: OCLC 2380592).

5811   **Pettit, Charles P.C.** A catalogue of the works of Thomas Hardy, 1840–1928, in Dorchester reference library. [Dorchester], Dorchester county library, 1984. iv,86p. facsims. 30cm. (Reprod. from typewriting).

5812   **Magoon, Joseph**. A bibliography of writings about Thomas Hardy for 1970 to 1985. [Bournemouth, J. Magoon], [1988 i.e. 1989]. vii,72; iv,63; 11p. 29cm. (Reprod. from typewriting).
'Supplement: Thomas Hardy society publications, 1970–1985' (p.1–11 *at end*), 1989.

5813   **Draper, Ronald P.** and **M.S. Ray**. An annotated critical bibliography of Thomas Hardy. London, Harvester wheatsheaf, 1989. vi,227p. 22cm. (Annotated critical bibliographies).

––––––––––

5814 (5:10982c)   **Hodgson and company, bksllrs.**, LONDON. The library of Thomas Hardy. Ed. by J. Stevens Cox. New ed. St. Peter Port, Toucan pr., 1969. (First publ. 1938). 193–216p. 19cm. (Monogrs. on...Hardy, 52).

5815   **Jackson, Arlene M.** Illustration and the novels of Thomas Hardy. Totowa, N.J., Rowman and Littlefield, [1980]. xiii,151p. facsims. 23cm.
1. Introduction: Thomas Hardy and the pictorial imagination.–2. English magazine illustration: the historic context.–3. Hardy and his illustrators.–4. Illustration and the novel.–5. Conclusion.
Rev. M. Milgate Ninet Cent Fict 37:119–22 '82; Alice Schreyer Am Bk Coll new ser 4:42–51 '83; L. Elsbree Vict Stud 26:454–6 '83; M. Steig Thomas Hardy Ann 2:236–41 '84.

5816   **Laird, J.T.** New light on the evolution of Tess of the d'Urbervilles. R Eng Stud new ser 31no124:414–35 N '80.

5817   **Ahmad, Suleiman M.** The genesis of the Wessex edition of Hardy's works. [Proposed Anglo-Am. ed.]. (Bibliographical notes). Pa Bib Soc Am 75no3:350–1 '81.

5818   **Schweik, Robert C.** and **M. Piret**. Editing Hardy. Browning Inst Stud 9:15–41 '81.
Materials not intended for publication.–Hardy's published writings.–Scholarly editions published and in preparation.–Editing Far from the madding crowd.

5819   **Manford, Alan L.** The texts of Thomas Hardy's map of Wessex. Library ser6 4no3:297–306 S '82. facsims.

5820   –––– Thomas Hardy's later revisions in A pair of blue eyes. (Bibliographical notes). Pa Bib Soc Am 76no2:209–20 '82.

5821 **Grindle, Jane** and **S.J. Gatrell**, *ed.* 'General introduction' [and] 'Editorial introduction' *in* Tess of the D'Urbervilles. Oxford, Clarendon pr., 1983. p.1–103.

General introduction. 1. The writing and publication of the novel.–2. Revision in the novel.–Editorial introduction. 1. Description of the principal texts.–2. Substantive readings in the edited text.–3. The choice of copy-text.–4. Some features of the manuscript punctuation.–5. Editorial conventions in the presentation of variant readings.

5822 **Bies, Werner**. 'MS before revision' oder die ungenutzte Chance; Textkritische Anmerkungen zur Variorum edition of the Complete poems of Thomas Hardy. [1979]. Archiv 221no2:311–19 '84.

5823 **Brown, Geoffrey**. Thomas Hardy. [Collecting]. Bk & Mag Coll 14:22–9 Ap '85. port., facsims.

'Complete bibliography of Thomas Hardy first editions' (p.28).

5824 **Gatrell, Simon J.** Editing Thomas Hardy; a review essay. Eng Lit Transit 31no2:174–85 '88.

5825 —— Hardy the creator; a textual biography. Oxford, Clarendon pr., 1988. [xv],260p. facsims. 22cm.

Introduction: The author and publishing in late Victorian England.–1. Beginnings, 1868–1875: Under the greenwood tree....–2. Intermission, 1876: Dealings with America.–3. The manuscript of The return of the native, 1877–1878.–4. Research the story, 1878–1882: The trumpet-major.... Two on a tower....–5. Hardy and the Graphic, 1883–1891.–6. From Tess to Jude, 1892–1894.–7. A first collected edition, 1895–1897.–8. The last novels, 1895–1897.–9. Paperback editions and the move to Macmillan, 1898–1928.–10. Two on a tower, 1881–1912.–11. Editing Hardy.–12. Conclusion.–Appendix I: A chronology of the writing of Hardy's fictional prose. II. The proofs for the first edition of Jude the obscure.

Rev. R.C. Schweik Thomas Hardy J 5:79–82 '89; P.J. Casagrande Stud Novel 22:452–5 '90; M. Williams N&Q 37:235–7 '90.

5826 **Greenland, R.E.** Hardy in the Osgood, McIlvaine and Harper (London) editions. Thomas Hardy J 4no3:57–60 Oc '88.

'A checklist of the Osgood, McIlvaine editions' (p. 59–60).

5827 —— A preliminary note on the Tauchnitz editions of Thomas Hardy's works. Thomas Hardy J 4no1:69–71 Ja '88.

5828 **Mason, Michael**. The burning of Jude the obscure. N&Q 233no3:332–4 S '88.

5829 **Nemesvari, Richard**. Editing Hardy and classroom texts. Thomas Hardy J 4no1:50–3 Ja '88.

5830 **Dalziel, Pamela**. Hardy as collaborator; the composition of 'The spectre of the real'. Pa Bib Soc Am 83no4:473–501 D '89.

5831 **Nemesvari, Richard**. Choice of copy-text and treatment of accidentals in Thomas Hardy's The trumpet-major. (Bibliographical notes). Library ser6 11no4:357–62 D '89.

HARE, HENRY, 2D BARON COLERAINE, 1636–1708

5832 **McCabe, Richard A.** Meditation, pilgrimage, and paradise; the literary career of Henry Hare, second lord Coleraine. (Bibliographical notes). Library ser6 8no1:59–67 Mr '86.

HARINGTON, SIR JOHN, 1561–1612

5833 **Craig, David H.** 'Selected bibliography [of primary and secondary sources]' *in* Sir John Harington. (Twayne's English authors, 386). Boston, [Mass.], Twayne, [1985]. p.156–62

5834 **Alsop, James D.** A manuscript copy of John Harington's Of the death of master Deuerox. Manuscripta 24no3:145–54 N '80.

5835 **Cauchi, Simon**. Orlando furioso. (Correspondence). Library ser6 3no3:244–5 S '81.

5836 **Miller, Robert H.** Harington's Supplie or addicion to the catalogue of bishops. [Ms.]. Stud Bib 35:171–2 '82.

5837 **Cauchi, Simon**. The 'setting foorth' of Harington's Ariosto. Stud Bib 36:137–68 '83.

5838 **Miller, Robert H.** Sir John Harington's manuscripts in italic. [Not in his hand]. Stud Bib 40:101–6 '87. facsims.

5839 **Cauchi, Simon**. Sir John Harington and Virgil's Aeneid IV. [Ms. in BL not by him]. (Shorter articles and notes). Eng Manuscr Stud 1:242–9 '89. facsim.
      Provenance.–Handwriting.–Style.–Harington and Virgil.

HARLEY, ROBERT, 1ST EARL OF OXFORD, 1661–1724

5840 **Jones, Clyve**. The Harley family and the Harley papers. Brit Libr J 15no2:123–33 '89. geneal. table.
      The Harley family.–Robert Harley, 1st earl of Oxford and earl Mortimer.–The Harley papers.–The Portland collection.–Brampton Bryan Harley papers.–Other Harley papers.

HARRIS, JOHN WYNDHAM PARKES LUCAS BENYON, 1903–69
see Wyndham, John, *pseud.*

HARRISON, FREDERIC, 1831–1923

5841 **Sullivan, Harry R.** 'Selected bibliography [of primary and secondary sources]' *in* Frederic Harrison. (Twayne's English authors, 341). Boston, Twayne, [1983]. p.198–203.

HARRISON, TONY, 1937–

5842 **Kaiser, John R.** Tony Harrison; a bibliography, 1957–1987. London, Mansell, [1989]. xii,105p. 21cm.
Bibliogr. of books, pamphlets and broadsheets by; books and pamphlets ed. or combining original contribs. or first book appearances of poems or prose by; contribs. to periodicals and newspapers by; miscellany, and criticism.

HARTLEY, LESLIE POLES, 1895–1972

5843 **The L.P.** Hartley collection. (News and notes). John Rylands Univ Libr Manchester Bull 69no1:7–8 '86.

HARVEY, GABRIEL, 1535?–1630?

5844 **Baker, William** and **J.C. Ross**. Gabriel Harvey's Il cortegiano. [In University coll. libr., London]. (Note 443). Bk Coll 31no2:244–5 '82.

5845 **Kratzmann, Gregory**. An addition to the catalogue of Gabriel Harvey's library; The dialogues of creatures moralysed. [At Univ. of Queensland]. N&Q 227no5:413–15 Oc '82.

HARVEY, WILLIAM, 1578–1657

5846 **Keynes, sir Geoffrey L.** A bibliography of the writings of dr. William Harvey, 1578–1657. 3d ed. rev. by Gweneth Whitteridge and Christine English. [Winchester, Hants.], St. Paul's bibliographies, 1989. (First publ. 1931). xvi,136p. port., facsims. 23cm.

5847 **Gaskell, Roger**. The errata leaf of Harvey's De motu cordis, Frankfurt, 1628. Bk Coll 38no1:60–5 '89.

HAWES, STEPHEN, d.1523?

5848 **Edwards, Anthony S.G.** 'Selected bibliography [of primary and secondary sources]' *in* Stephen Hawes. (Twayne's English authors, 354). Boston, Twayne, [1983]. p.119–25.

HAWKESWORTH, JOHN, 1720–73

5849   **Abbott, John L.** and **G.J. Finch**. A checklist of the correspondence of John and Mary Hawkesworth. John Rylands Univ Libr Manchester Bull 66no2:10–39 '84.

HAYDN, FRANZ JOSEF, 1732–1809

5850   **Poole, H. Edmund**. 'Music engraving practice in eighteenth-century London; a study of some Forster editions of Haydn and their manuscript sources' *in* Neighbour, Oliver W., *ed.* Music and bibliography; essays in honour of Alec Hyatt King. London, 1980. p.[98]–131. facsims., tables.

HAYES, JAMES MILTON, 1884–1940

5851   **Haymon, Sylvia**. In search of Milton Hayes. [Collecting]. Antiqu Bk Mnthly R 8no8:296–9 Ag '81; A. Wanford *ib*. (Letters) 8no10:392 Oc '81. ports.

HAYLEY, WILLIAM, 1745–1820

5852   **Bishop, Morchard**. William Hayley & his last printer. [William Mason, Chichester]. Bk Coll 31no2:187–200 '82. illus., facsims.

HAYWOOD, ELIZA (FOWLER), 1693?–1756

5853   **Schofield, Mary A.** 'Selected bibliography [of primary and secondary sources]' *in* Eliza Haywood. (Twayne's English authors, 411). Boston, [Mass.], Twayne, [1985]. p.129–36.

HAZLITT, WILLIAM, 1778–1830

5854   **Keynes, sir Geoffrey L.** A bibliography of William Hazlitt. 2d ed., rev. [Godalming, Surrey], St. Paul's bibliographies, 1981. (First publ. 1931; 3d ed. 1989). xx,152p. facsims. 21cm. (St. Paul's Bibs, 4). Ltd. to 750 copies.
    Rev: T. Hofman Bk Coll 31:247–51 '82; S. Jones Analytical & Enum Bib 6:272–6 '82; J.H. Alexander Mod Lang R 79:911–12 '84.

5855   **Jones, Stanley**. The dating of a Hazlitt essay; bibliography and biography. [On reading new books]. Étud Angl 33no2:188–98 Av/Juin '80.

5856 —— 'Bad English in the Scotch novels.' [Articles in Examiner on Waverley novels attrib. to Hazlitt]. Library ser6 3no3:202–16 S '81.

5857 —— Some notes on the letters of William Hazlitt. (Bibliographical notes). Library ser6 5no3:269–75 S '83.

5858 —— A Hazlitt anomaly. [Text of My first acquaintance with poets]. (Bibliographical notes). Library ser6 7no1:60–2 Mr '85.

5859 **Gates, Payson G.** Hazlitt's Select British poets; an American publication. Keats-Sh J 35:168–82 '86.

5860 **Jones, Stanley.** The 'suppression' of Hazlitt's New and improved grammar of the English tongue; a reconstruction of events. Library ser6 9no1:32–43 Mr '87.

5861 **Robinson, Charles E.** William Hazlitt to his publishers, friends and creditors; twenty-seven new holograph letters. [Printed here]. Keats-Sh R 2:1–47 '87.

HAZLITT, WILLIAM CAREW, 1834–1913

5862 **Books** with marginalia by W.C. Hazlitt, in BL *see* Gould, Alison, Named special collections, 1981: no.818.

HEAD, RICHARD, 1637?–86?

5863 **Salzman, Paul.** Alterations to The English rogue. (Bibliographical notes). Library ser6 4no1:49–56 Mr '82.

HEANEY, SEAMUS, 1939–

5864 **Curtis, Tony,** *ed.* 'Bibliography [of primary and secondary sources]' *in* The art of Seamus Heaney. [Bridgend], Poetry Wales; [Chester Springs, Pa.], Dufour editions, 1982. (2d ed. 1985). p.[139]–45.

5865 **Pearson, Henry.** Seamus Heaney; a bibliographical checklist. [Primary and secondary works]. Am Bk Coll new ser 3no2:31–42 Mr/Ap '82.

5866 **Curtis, Tony,** *ed.* 'Bibliography [of primary and secondary sources]' *in* The art of Seamus Heaney. [2d ed.] [Bridgend], Poetry Wales; [Chester Springs, Pa.], Dufour editions, 1985. (First publ. 1982). p.[165]–71.

5867 **Durkan, M. John.** Seamus Heaney; a checklist for a bibliography. Irish Univ R 16no1:48–76 '86.

5868 **Foster, Thomas C.** 'Selected bibliography [of primary and secondary sources]' *in* Seamus Heaney. (Twayne's English authors, 468). Boston, [Mass.], Twayne; Dublin, O'Brien, [1989]. p.148–51.

5869 (7:4560*) **McGuinness, Arthur E.** The craft of diction; revision in Seamus Heaney's poems. [With texts]. Irish Univ R 9no1:62–91 '79.

HEATH-STUBBS, JOHN FRANCIS ALEXANDER, 1918–*see* STUBBS, JOHN FRANCIS ALEXANDER HEATH-, 1918– .

HENRYSON, ROBERT, 1430?–1506?

5870 **Scheps, Walter** and **J. Anna Looney**, [1986]: no.905.

5871 **Mapstone, Sally**. The Testament of Cresseid, lines 561–7; a new manuscript witness. N&Q 230no3:307–10 S '85.

HENTY, GEORGE ALFRED, 1832–1902

5872 **Bethnal Green museum of childhood,** LONDON. The Renier collection of historic and contemporary children's books: G.A. Henty. [Comp. by Tessa Rose Chester]. [London], 1988. 28p. facsims. 20cm. (Occas list, 4). Covertitle. (Duplicated typescript).

5873 **Crewdson, William H.P.** George Alfred Henty. Antiqu Bk Mnthly R 15no3:88–97 Mr '88. port., illus.
'A short-title list of the first editions of George Alfred Henty' (p.97).

HERBERT, SIR ALAN PATRICK, 1890–1971

5874 **Dalby, Richard**. A.P. Herbert. [Collecting]. Bk & Mag Coll 21:44–50 N '85. port., facsims.
'Complete A.P. Herbert bibliography' (p.49–50).

HERBERT, EDWARD, 1ST BARON HERBERT OF CHERBURY, 1583–1648

5875 (5:11040c) **Maggs bros., bksllrs.,** LONDON. Books from the library of Edward, first lord Herbert of Cherbury, 1583–1648, together with works by him and his friends.... London, [1956]. 18p. facsim. 22cm. (Catalogue 837). Not seen.

5876 **Hill, Eugene D.** 'Selected bibliography [of primary and secondary sources]' *in* Edward, lord Herbert of Cherbury. (Twayne's English authors, 439). Boston, Twayne, [1987]. p.134–6.

HERBERT, GEORGE, 1593–1633

5877 **Miller, Edmund**. 1987 bibliography of new and forthcoming works on Herbert. Cross Bias 9:9–12 '86; 11:9–12 suppl '87.

5878 **Stewart, Stanley**. 'Selected bibliography [of primary and secondary sources]' *in* George Herbert. (Twayne's English authors, 428). Boston, Twayne, [1987]. p.169–76.

5879 **Ray, Robert H.** Recent studies in Herbert, 1974–1986. (Recent studies in the English renaissance). Eng Lit Renaiss 18no3:460–75 '88.

5880 **Roberts, John R.** George Herbert; an annotated bibliography of modern criticism. Rev. ed., 1905–1984 Columbia, University of Missouri pr., 1988. (First publ. 1978). xix,433p. 23cm.
Rev: J. Johnson Christianity & Lit 38:85–6 '89; E.J. Devereux Renaiss & Reformation 14:334–6 '90; R. Ellrodt Étud Angl 44:214–15 '91.

5881 **Miller, Edmund**. Thom. Buck, the anagram, and the editing of The temple. (Bibliographical notes). Library ser6 2no4:446–8 D '80.

5882 **Shawcross, John T.** 'Herbert's double poems; a problem in the text of The temple' *in* Summers, Claude J. and T.-L. Pebworth, *ed*. 'Too rich to clothe the sunne'; essays on George Herbert. [Pittsburgh], University of Pittsburgh U.P., [1980]. p.211–28.

5883 **Charles, Amy M.** 'The original of mr. George Herbert's Temple'. George Herbert J 6no2:1–14 '83.
The Bodleian manuscript.–Provenance.–Date.–Herbert and the Ferrars.–Herbert and the original of the Bodleian manuscript.

5884 **Di Cesare, Mario A.** The Bodleian manuscript and the text of Herbert's poems. George Herbert J 6no2:15–35 '83.

5885 **Dinshaw, Fram**. A lost ms. of George Herbert's occasional verse and the authorship of 'To the l. chancellor'. N&Q 228no5:423–5 Oc '83.

5886 **Idol, John L.** The 1894 sale of a first edition of The temple in New York. [C.B. Foote sale]. George Herbert J 6no2:47–8 '83.

5887   **Lull, Janis**. Expanding 'The poem itself'; reading George Herbert's revisions. [And authors' intentions]. Stud Eng Lit 27no1:71–87 '87.

5888   **Piret, Michael**. Canon Hutchinson and the Outlandish proverbs. [In Wits' recreations, 1640]. N&Q 232no3:312–13 S '87.

HERBERT, MARY (SIDNEY), COUNTESS OF PEMBROKE, 1561–1621

5889   **Roberts, Josephine A.** Recent studies in women writers of Tudor England. Part II: Mary Sidney, countess of Pembroke. (Recent studies in the English renaissance). Eng Lit Renaiss 14no3:426–39 '84.

5890   **Kinnamon, Noel J.** A variant of the Countess of Pembroke's Psalm 85. Sidney Newsl 2no2:9–12 '81.

5891   **Lamb, Mary E.** The Countess of Pembroke's patronage. Eng Lit Renaiss 12no2:162–79 '82.

HERRICK, ROBERT, 1591–1674

5892   **Hageman, Elizabeth H.** Robert Herrick; a reference guide Boston, Mass., G.K. Hall, 1983. xix,245p. 23cm. (Reference guide to literature).
Rev: R.B. Rollin Sevent Cent Newsl 42:35–6 '84; Z. Stribny Seven Cent Newsl 43:8 '85.

5893   **Martinet, Marie-Madeleine**. Robert Herrick: bibliographie sélective et critique. Soc d'Étud Anglo-Am Bull 19:9–15 N '84.

5894   **Soldana, Giuseppe**. Robert Herrick; bibliografia scelta e commentata, 1648–1980. Cerignola, Istituto tecnico commerciale e per Geometri Dante Aligheri, 1984. viii,133p. 24cm.

5895   **Gertzman, Jay A.** Fantasy, fashion and affection; editions of Robert Herrick's poetry for the common reader, 1810–1968. Bowling Green, Ohio, Bowling Green state university Popular pr., [1986]. 240p. illus., facsims. 23cm.
'Appendix: Reprints of Herrick's poetry, 1810–1980; an annotated checkllist' (p.193–239).
Rev: E.D. Mackerness N&Q 233:402–4 '88.

5896   **Gertzman, Jay A.** 'Life's sweet without its sting'; a Victorian illustrator's recreation of Robert Herrick's time and place. [E.A. Abbey's illus. of Dobson's Selections, 1882]. Stud Humanit (Indiana, Pa.) 10no2:68–86 '83. illus.

HEYER, GEORGETTE, 1902–74

5897 **Macleod, Helen**. Georgette Heyer. [Collecting]. Bk & Mag Coll 10:27–
34 D '84. port., facsims.
'Complete bibliography of Georgette Heyer U.K. 1st editions' (p.303–4).

HEYWOOD, JOHN, 1497?–1580?

5898 **Kolin, Philip C.** Recent studies in John Heywood. (Recent studies in
the English renaissance). Eng Lit Renaiss 13n01:113–23 '83.

HEYWOOD, THOMAS, 1575–1641

5899 **Baines, Barbara J.** 'Selected bibliography [of primary and secondary
sources]' *in* Thomas Heywood. (Twayne's English authors, 388).
Boston, Twayne, [1984]. p.168–74.

5900 **Wentworth, Michael**. Thomas Heywood; a reference guide. Boston,
Mass., G.K. Hall, [1986]. xxxii,315p. 23cm. (Reference guide to literature).

5901 **Janzen, Henry D.** 'Preparing a diplomatic edition: Heywood's The
escapes of Jupiter' *in* Shand, G.B. and R.C. Shady, *ed.* Play-texts in
old spelling; papers from the Glendon conference. (AMS pr. Studies in the renaissance, 6). New York, [1984]. p.73–9.

5902 **Bergeron, David M.** Patronage of dramatists; the case of Thomas
Heywood. Eng Lit Renaiss 18n02:294–304 '88.

HILL, AARON, 1685–1750

5903 **Belcher, William F.** Aaron Hill's earliest poems. [In British Apollo,
listed]. N&Q 227n06:531–2 D '82.

HILL, GEOFFREY, 1932–

5904 **Gallet, René**, *comp.* 'Geoffrey Hill; esquisse de bibliographie' *in* Genet,
J. and R. Gallet, *ed.* Poètes anglais contemporains; études. [Caen,
Centre de recherches de littérature et linguistique des pays de langue
anglaise de l'université de Caen], [1982]. p.51–3.

5905 **Horne, Philip**, *comp.* 'Bibliography of works by and about Geoffrey Hill' *in* Robinson, Peter, *ed.* Geoffrey Hill; essays on his work. Milton Keynes, Open U.P., [1985]. p.[237]–51.
Chronol. checklist, 1951–84, with trans. and musical settings of, and ana.

HOBBES, THOMAS, 1575?–1641

5906 **Hinnant, Charles H.** Thomas Hobbes; a reference guide. Boston, Mass., G.K. Hall, [1980]. xviii,275p. 23cm. (Reference guide to literature).
Rev: C. Cantalupo Sevent Cent Newsl 41:76 '83.

5907 **Warrender, Howard**. The early Latin versions of Thomas Hobbes's De cive. [1642]. Library ser6 2no1:40–52 Mr '80.
1. The early versions.–2. MS.: The Chatsworth manuscript.–3. L1: the first edition.–4. L2: the second edition.–5. L2a: variants of the second edition.–6. The third edition.–7. Some problems concerning the Amsterdam editions of 1647.–8. A note on Molesworth's edition.

5908 **Schoneveld, Cornelis W.** 'Some features of the seventeenth-century editions of Hobbe's De cive printed in Holland and elsewhere' *in* Bend, J.G. van der, *ed.* Thomas Hobbes, his view of man; proceedings of the Hobbes symposium.... (Elementa, 21). Amsterdam, Rodopi, 1982. p.125–42. facsims.

5909 **Berman, David**. A disputed deistic classic. [Essay 1693 possibly by Hobbes]. (Bibliographical notes). Library ser6 7no1:58–9 Mr '85.

HOCCLEVE, THOMAS, 1368?–1426?

5910 **Harris, Kate**. The patron of British library ms. Arundel 38. [Regiment of princes; J. Mowbray, duke of Norfolk]. N&Q 229no4:462–3 D '84.

5911 **Greetham, David C.** 'Challenges of theory and practice in the editing of Hoccleve's Regement of princes' *in* Pearsall, Derek A., *ed.* Manuscripts and texts; editorial problems in later middle English literature. [Cambridge], 1987. p.[60]–86. diagrs.

5912 **Marzec, Marcia S.** Scribal emendations in some later manuscripts of Hoccleve's Regement of princes. Analytical & Enum Bib new ser 1no2:41–51 '87.

5913 **Bowers, John**. Hoccleve's two copies of 'Lerne to dye': implications for textual critics. [And revision]. Pa Bib Soc Am 83no4:437–72 D '89.
1. Monogenous descent.–2. The author's manuscript.–3. Final intentions.–4. Authorial versions.–5. Formal and social contexts.

HODGSON, RALPH, 1871–1962

5914 **Sweetser, Wesley D.** Ralph Hodgson; a bibliography. Rev. and enl.
ed. New York, Garland, 1980. (First publ. privately, 1974). xxxvi,148p.
port., facsims. 20cm.
*Classified checklist of books, chapbooks, and broadsides; anthologies; contribs. to periodicals,
miscellanea, and works about, with various bibliogr. etc. notes.*

HOEY, FRANCES SARAH (CASHEL), 1830–1908

5915 **Edwards, Peter D.** Frances Cashel Hoey, 1830–1908; a bibliography.
[St. Lucia], Dept. of English, University of Queensland, [1982].
iii,62p. 19cm. (Vict Fict Res Guides, 8). Reprod. from typewriting.
'Bibliography' (p.36–62): *classified checklist with some bibliogr. notes.*

HOFLAND, BARBARA, 1770–1844

5916 **Butts, Dennis**. Barbara Hofland, the Sheffield skylark. Antiqu Bk
Mnthly R 10no7:252–7 Jl '83. port., facsims.
'A checklist of mrs. Hofland's books' (p.255–7): *chronol. checklist, 1805–46.*

HOGG, JAMES, 1770–1835

5917 **Smith, Nelson C.** 'Selected bibliography [of primary and secondary
sources]' *in* James Hogg. (Twayne's English authors, 311). Boston,
[Mass.], Twayne, [1981]. p.181–3.

5918 **Mack, Douglas S.** James Hogg's reminiscences of sir Walter Scott.
[The domestic manners and private life, 1834]. Biblioth 11no4:81–
92 '82.
The early texts: the first version.–…the second version.–The two manuscripts.–Editing the texts: the first version.–…the second version.

5919 **Hughes, Gillian H.** The Spy and literary Edinburgh. Scott Lit J
10no1:42–53 My '83.

5920 **Mack, Douglas S.** Notes on editing James Hogg's 'Storms'. Biblioth
12no6:140–9 '85.

5921 ——James Hogg's second thoughts on The three perils of man.
[Revision]. Stud Scott Lit 21:167–75 '86.

5922 **Groves, David**. James Hogg and the Scots magazine. [Lament for the
old Scots magazine, 1829]. (Bibliographical notes). Library ser6
9no2:164–9 Je '87.

5923 ——James Hogg, London, and the Royal lady's magazine. [And 'O Kitty dinna frown on me']. Library ser6 10no4:339–46 D '88.

5924 **Garside, Peter D.** Notes on editing James Hogg's Ringan and May. Biblioth 16no1/3:40–53 '89. tables.

HOLTBY, WINIFRED, 1898–1935

5925 **[Crowther, Jill].** Winifred Holtby, 1898–1935; a catalogue of the book and manuscript collection in the Hull local studies library, produced to commemorate the 50th anniversary of her death. [Hull], Humberside leisure services, 1985. 21p. facsim. 21cm.

HOOD, THOMAS, 1799–1845

5926 **Gatton, John S.** Of publishing, polkas and prudery; a restored letter by Thomas Hood. [On ed. of Hood's magazine]. Kentucky R 12no2:89–97 '81.

5927 **Thorogood, Peter.** 'Thomas Hood; a nineteenth-century author and his relations with the book trade to 1835' *in* Myers, Robin and M.R.A. Harris, *ed.* Development of the English book trade, 1700–1899. [Oxford], 1981. p.[106]–72. facsim.
1. The rise and fall of Vernor, Hood and Sharpe.–2. Thomas Hood, the poet, and his relations with the book trade to 1835.

HOOKE, ROBERT, 1635–1703

5928 **Rostenberg, Leona.** Robert Hooke's scientific library; books from Duck lane and Moorfields. Bks at Iowa 33:3–21 N '80.

5929 ——Book collecting in 17th-century England. [Hooke's libr.]. AB Bkmn's Wkly 72no14:2027–44 Oc '83.
Library literature.–Book shelving.

5930 ——Robert Hooke, restoration bibliophile. Am Bk Coll new ser 8no4:9–15 Ap '84. facsims.

5931 ——The library of Robert Hooke; the scientific book trade of restoration England. Santa Monica, Calif., Modoc pr., 1989. xix,257p. facsims. 23cm.
Preface by Nicolas Barker.–Introduction.–Pt.I. The scientific book trade of restoration England: the background. 1. Robert Hooke, F.R.S.–2. John Martyn, 'printer to the Royal society'.–3. Moses Pitt, publisher and purveyor of mathematical texts.–4. William Cooper, alchemical specialist.–5. Book stalls of Duke lane and Moorfields.–6. Book auctions and auctioneers.–7. Domestic circulation, exportation and importation of foreign books.–8. The Philosophical transactions.–Pt.II. The library of Robert Hooke.–9. The collector.–Pt.III. The Bibliotheca Hookiana. (p.[141]–221).

HOOKER, RICHARD, 1554?–1600

5932 **Archer, Stanley**. 'Selected bibliography [of primary and secondary sources]' *in* Richard Hooker. (Twayne's English authors, 350). Boston, Twayne, [1983]. p.131–7.

5933 **Hill, W. Speed.** Casting off copy and the composition of Hooker's Book V. [Of the laws of ecclesiastical polity, 1597, ptd. by J. Windet]. Stud Bib 33:144–61 '80. facsims., tables.

HOOKER, THOMAS, 1586–1647

5934 (7:4633) **Bush, Sargent, comp**. 'A bibliography of the published writings of Thomas Hooker' *in* Williams, George H. [and others], *ed*. Thomas Hooker: writings in England and Holland, 1626–1633. (Harvard Theol Stud). [Cambridge, Mass., Harvard U.P.], [1975]. p.390–425.
Chronol. by date of 1st ed.; quasi-facsim. TP transcrs., formats, collations, locations of copies, bibiogr. refs. and discussion.

5935 —— 'Thomas Hooker's works' *in* The writings of Thomas Hooker; spiritual adventure in two worlds. [Madison, Wisc.], University of Wisconsin pr., [1980]. p.373–5.

HOPKINS, GERARD MANLEY, 1844–89

5936 **Foltz, William**. Further correspondence of Manley Hopkins. Hopkins Q 9no2:51–77 '82.

5937 **Seelhammer, Ruth**. A Hopkins bibliography for 1980. Hopkins Q 9no2:43–50 '82.

5938 **Bender, Todd K.** The emergence of Gerard Manley Hopkins from obscurity to recognition, 1889–1918. Libr Chron Univ Texas new ser 46/7:40–9 '89. facsims.
'Books published before 1918 with poems by Hopkins' (p.49).

5939 **Feeney, Joseph J.** The Gerard Manley Hopkins archive of the Harry Ransom humanities research center. [Listed]. Libr Chron Libr Texas new ser 46/7:10–39 '89. facsims.

5940 **Giles, Richard F.** Significant books on Gerard Manley Hopkins, 1844–1988. Libr Chron Univ Texas new ser 46/7:74–121 '89. facsims.

5941 **Sutton, Carl**. The presence of Hopkins in the world today. Libr Chron Univ Texas new ser 46/7:132–82 '89. facsims.

5942 ——Significant association items. Libr Chron Univ Texas new ser 46/7:122–31 '89. facsims.

5943 **Feeney, Joseph J.** The Blandyke papers; an addition to the bibliography of essays on Hopkins. Hopkins Q 9n04:127–32 '83.

5944 **Litzinger, Boyd**. Two notes on on The wreck of the Deutschland. Vict Poetry 21n02:191–5 '83.
'2. Shire, shore, and shower in ...' (p.193–5).

5945 **Quinn, William A.** The crux of The windhover. Hopkins Q 10n01:7–22 '83.

5946 **White, Norman**. A newly discovered version of a verse translation by Gerard Manley Hopkins. ['Adore te devote']. N&Q 230n03:363–4 S '85.

5947 **Cohen, Edward H.** Hopkins, Bridges, and the editing of Ashboughs. (Bibliographical notes). Pa Bib Soc Am 83n03:353–8 S '89.

5948 **MacKenzie, Norman H.** From manuscript to printed text; the hazardous transmission of the Hopkins canon. Libr Chron Univ Texas new ser 46/7:50–73 '89. facsims.
'The Hopkins canon' (p.72–3).

HOUGHTON, WILLIAM STANLEY, 1881–1913

5949 **Mortimer, Paul**. W. Stanley Houghton; an introduction and bibliography. Mod Drama 28n03:474–89 S '85.
Appendix 1. The works of Stanley Houghton.–2. The Stanley Houghton collection, University of Salford library.–3. Special articles...in The Manchester guardian.

HOUSMAN, ALFRED EDWARD, 1859–1936

5950 **Carter, John W.** and **J.H.A. Sparrow**. A.E. Housman; a bibliography. 2d ed. rev. by William White. [Godalming], St. Paul's bibliographies, 1982. xvii,94p. illus., facsims. 21cm. ([St.Paul's Bibs, 6]).
Rev: Bull Bib 41:175 '84; R.J. Roberts TLS 4 My '84:503; P.G. Naiditch Classical J 79:269–72 '84; T.J. Winnifrith Yrbk Eng Stud 17:337–8 '87.

5951 **Bryn Mawr college**. The name and nature of A.E. Housman; from the collection of Seymour Adelman. [Bryn Mawr, Pa.], Bryn Mawr college library; [New York], Pierpont Morgan library, 1986. ix,54p. illus., facsims., ports. 26cm.
Rev: N. Jenkins TLS 24 Oc '86:1193.

5952 **Heap, G.V.** Housman's alterations in the text of A Shropshire lad. Housman Soc J 7:70–80 '81.

5953 **Maas, Henry**. On editing A.E. Housman's letters. Housman Soc J 7:19–21 '81.

5954 **Naiditch, Peter G.** Owen's review of Housman's Juvenal. Am N&Q 20no5/6:76–7 Ja/F '82.

5955 **White, William**. Misprints in Harrap's A Shropshire lad. [1980]. Housman Soc J 8:52–3 '82.

5956 **Eaton, P.D.** The mystery of the missing article; a last note on the diaries of A.E. Housman. [Unpubl. proof of article by J.W. Carter, 1968]. Housman Soc J 9:49–51 '83.

5957 **Fisher, Benjamin F.** The Housmans; texts and criticism since the mid-seventies. Housman Soc J 9:41–9 '83.

5958 **Naiditch, Peter G.** The earliest specimen of A.E. Housman's handwriting. Am N&Q 21no7/8:106–7 Mr/Ap '83.

5959 **Symons, Robert E.** Some thoughts on being A.E. Housman's literary executor. Housman Soc J 9:15–22 '83.

5960 **Burnett, Archibald**. Errors in Housman bibliography. [Corrs. to Carter and Sparrow: no.5950]. Housman Soc J 10:49–52 '84.

5961 **Naiditch, Peter G.** A chronological analysis of A.E. Housman's notebook. Housman Soc J 10:7–24 '84.

5962 —— A.E. Housman's 'prize books.' Housman Soc J 11: 98–100 '85. facsim.

5963 —— Three notes on the library of A.E. Housman. Housman Soc J 12:33–53 '85; Correction 12:143 '86. facsim.

5964 **Tunnicliffe, J.D.** and **M. Buncombe**. A.E. Housman and the failure of Grant Richards limited in 1926. Housman Soc J 11:101–6 '85.

5965 **Burnett, Archibald**. Seymour Adelman and the Adelman collection of A.E. Housman. Housman Soc J 12:71–6 '86.

5966 **Burch, Francis F.** A.E. Housman's signature of approval. [Signed copies]. N&Q 232no1:55 Mr '87; G.R. Woodward 233no3:341–2 S '88.

5967 **White, William**. Misprints in Horwood's A.E. Housman; poetry and prose. [1971]. Housman Soc J 13:53 '87.

5968 —— Misprinting A Shropshire lad. [J. Wain's Oxford library of English poetry, 1986]. Housman Soc J 14:73 '88.

HOUSMAN, CLEMENCE, 1865–1955

5969 **Fisher, Benjamin F.** An excursus on Clemence Housman. [Checklist of major works, reviews and criticism of]. Housman Soc J 10:38–48 '84.

HOUSMAN, LAURENCE, 1865–1959

5970 **Engen, Rodney K.** 'Appendices: A. Books designed and illustrated by Laurence Housman. B. Magazines and journal illustrations by.... C. Laurence Housman, the critic. D. Book-plate designs by... E. Wood engravings by...' *in* Laurence Housman. Stroud, Glos., Catalpa books; New Castle, Del., Oak Knoll books, 1983. p.152–7.

5971 **Bies, Werner.** Laurence Housman; an annotated bibliography of writings about him. Housman Soc J 7:47–53 '81; 11:81–90 '85.

HOWARD, HENRY, EARL OF SURREY, 1517?–47

5972 **Sessions, William A.** 'Selected bibliography [of primary and secondary sources]' *in* Henry Howard, earl of Surrey. (Twayne's English authors, 429). Boston, [Mass.], Twayne, [1986]. p.165–8.

5973 **Caldwell, Ellen C.** Recent studies in Henry Howard, earl of Surrey, 1970–1989. (Recent studies in the English renaissance). Eng Lit Renaiss 19no3:389–401 '89.

5974 **Evans, J.M.** The text of Surrey's 'The meanes to attain happy life'. N&Q 228no5:409–11 Oc '83; W.D. McGaw, A reply 230no4:456–8 D '85. table.

5975 **McGaw, William D.** Surrey's 'Love that doth raine'; the history of a mistranscription. AUMLA 67:82–8 My '87.

HUDSON, WILLIAM HENRY, 1841–1922

5976 **Shrubsall, Dennis.** Updating W.H. Hudson's bibliography. Eng Lit Transit 31no2:186–6 '88; 31no4:437–44.

HUGHES, RICHARD ARTHUR WARREN, 1900–76

5977 **Poole, Richard**, *ed.* 'Bibliography [of books, books ed. by, prefaces, articles, and reviews]' *in* Fiction as truth; selected literary writings by Richard Hughes. Bridgend, Poetry Wales pr., 1983. p.[171]–4.

5978 **Morgan, Paul B.** Richard Hughes; an author's library. Nat Libr Wales J 25no3:341–6 '88.

HUGHES, TED, 1930–

5979 **Sagar, Keith M.** and **S. Tabor**. Ted Hughes; a bibliography, 1946–1980. [London], Mansell, [1983]. xiv,260p. port. 21cm.
Classified bibliogr. of books, pamphlets and broadsides; works ed. or with contribs. by; contribs. to periodicals; translations of; interviews, recordings, broadcasts, miscellaneous, settings, and works about.
Rev: B.C. Bloomfield Library ser6 6:200–1 '84; G. Bixby Am Bk Coll new ser 5:45–8 '84; J.G. Watson N&Q 230:411–12 '85; E. Larrissy Yrbk Eng Stud 17:362–5 '87; J.W.C. Hagstrom Analytical & Enum Bib new ser 1:99 '87.

HUGHES, THOMAS, 1822–96

5980 **Crewdson, William H.P.** Thomas Hughes. Antiqu Bk Mnthly R 15no12:462–9 D '88. port., illus.
'A check-list of the first editions of Thomas Hughes' (p.469).

HULME, THOMAS ERNEST, 1883–1917

5981 **Csengeri, Karen E.** T.E. Hulme; a bibliographical note. [Checklist]. N&Q 230no3:379–80 S '85.

5982 —— T.E. Hulme; an annotated bibliography of writings about him. Eng Lit Transit 29no4:388–428 '86.

5983 **Csengeri, Karen E.** The chronology of T.E. Hulme's Speculations. (Bibliographical notes). Pa Bib Soc Am 80no1:105–9 '86.

HUME, DAVID, 1711–76

5984 (1:3758) **Jessop, Thomas E.** A bibliography of David Hume and of Scottish philosophy, 1938. (Repr. New York, Garland, 1983).

5985 **Cameron, William J.** Eighteenth century editions of the writings of David Hume in special collections, McGill university libraries, Montreal, Quebec. [London, Ont., University of Western Ontario], 1982. 26p. 27cm. (WHSTC Libr Cat ser, 7). Duplicated typescript. (Not seen: ISBN 0–7714–0378–X).

5986 **Chuo university,** Tokyo. David Hume and eighteenth century British thought; an annotated catalogue. [Comp. by Sadao Ikeda]. Tokyo, Chuo university library, [1986]. xix,560p. tables. 21cm.
The J.V. Price colln.

5987 —— David Hume and eighteenth century British thought; an annotated catalogue: Supplement. [Comp. by Sadao Ikeda, Michihiro Otonashi and Tamihiro Shigemori]. Tokyo, Chuo university library, [1988]. v,214p. 21cm.

———

5988 **[Morton, David F.].** The works of David Hume. [Materials sought]. (Help wanted). Factotum 2:14 D '85; (Query 370) Bk Coll 35no4:523 '86; (Correspondence) Pa Bib Soc Am 80no2:241–2 '86.

5989 **Norton, David F.** Lost books. [Treatise of human nature, 1739, with hologr. corrs.]. (Letters). TLS 19 Je '87:661.

5990 **Cunningham, Ian C.** The arrangement of the Royal society of Edinburgh's David Hume collection. Biblioth 15no1:8–22 '88. table.

HUMPHREYS, EMYR, 1919–

5991 **Williams, Ioan M.** 'Select bibliography [of primary and secondary works]' *in* Emyr Humphreys. (Writers of Wales). [Cardiff], University of Wales pr. on behalf of the Welsh arts council, 1980. p.89–93.

HUNT, JAMES HENRY LEIGH, 1784–1859

5992 **Lulofs, Timothy J.** and **H. Ostrom**. Leigh Hunt; a reference guide. Boston, Mass., G.K. Hall, [1985]. xxix,264p. 23cm. (Reference guide to literature).

5993 **Waltman, John L.** and **G.G. McDaniel**. Leigh Hunt; a comprehensive bibliography. New York, Garland, 1985. xxv,273p. 21cm. (Reference library of the humanities, 551).
Rev: W. St.Clair TLS 18 Ap '86:428.

———

5994 **Thomas, Donald**. Leigh Hunt and The prince on St. Patrick's day. [Libellous editorial]. (Bibliographical notes). Library ser6 3n02:145–6 Je '81.

5995 **Cheney, David R.** 'Advantages and problems of editing letters on the computer' *in* Burton, Sarah K. and D.D. Short, *ed.* Sixth international conference on computers and the humanities. [Rockville, Md.], Computer science pr., [1983]. p.89–93.

5996 **Cheyney, David R.** The Leigh Hunt letters. [Editing]. Keats-Sh Mem Bull 35:40–53 '84.

5997 **Stam, David H.** 'The doors and windows of the library; Leigh Hunt and special collections [i.e. the librs. of his time]' *in* McCown, Robert A., *ed.* The life & times of Leigh Hunt; papers delivered at a symposium.... Iowa City, Friends of the University of Iowa libraries, 1985. p.101–8.

5998 **Quinn, Mary A.** Leigh Hunt's presentation copy of Shelley's Alastor volume. (News). Keats-Sh J 35:16–20 '86. facsims.

5999 **Stam, David H.** The doors and windows of the library; Leigh Hunt and special collections. [His experience of librs.]. Bk Coll 35n01:67–75 '86.

6000 **Bentley, Gerald E., jr.** Robert and Leigh Hunt and Benjamin West's Gallery of pictures. (Note 423). Bk Coll 37n04:571–2 '88.

HUTCHESON, ARCHIBALD, 1659?–1740

6001 **Alsop, James D.** Archibald Hutcheson's Letters...to the late earl of Sunderland, 1722. [Text]. (Bibliographical notes). Library ser6 4n01:61–5 Mr '80.

HUTCHESON, FRANCIS, 1694–1746

6002 **Stephens, John.** Hutcheson's Inquiry, 1738. [Collation]. (Note 450). Bk Coll 32n02:228 '83.

6003 —— Francis Hutcheson and the early history of the Foulis press; some overlooked evidence. (Notes). Bib Soc Aust & N.Z. Bull 8n04:213–15 '84.

HUXLEY, ALDOUS LEONARD, 1894–1963

6004 **Bass, Eben E.** Aldous Huxley; an annotated bibliography of criticism. New York, Garland, 1981. xvi,221p. 21cm. (Reference library of the humanities, 198).
Rev: J. Meckier Lit Res N 7:34–9 '82; P. Miles Library ser6 5:77–9 '83.

HUXLEY, SIR JULIAN SORELL, 1887–1975

6005   **Green, Jens-Peter**. 'Abkürzungs- und Literaturverzeichnis' *in* Krise und Hoffnung; der Evolutionshumanismus Julian Huxleys. (Anglistische Forschungen, 151). Heidelberg, C. Winter, 1981. p.[341]–407.

HYDE, EDWARD, EARL OF CLARENDON, 1609–74

6006   **Roebuck, Graham**. Clarendon and cultural continuity; a bibliographical study. New York, Garland, 1981. xxi,309p. port. 20cm. (Reference library of the humanities, 168).

––––––––––

6007   **Green, Ian**. The publication of Clarendon's autobiography and the acquisition of his papers by the Bodleian library. Bodleian Libr Rec 10no6:349–67 '82.

INCHBALD, ELIZABETH (SIMPSON), 1753–1821

6008   **Moreux, Françoise**. Bibliographie sélective d'Elizabeth Inchbald, auteur dramatique et romancière, 1753–1821. Soc d'Étud Anglo-Am Bull 13:81–105 '81.

––––––––––

6009   **Sigl, Patricia**. The Elizabeth Inchbald papers. N&Q 227no3:220–4 Je '82.

ISHERWOOD, CHRISTOPHER WILLIAM BRADSHAW-, 1904–86

6010   **White, James** and **W.H. White**, *ed.* Christopher Isherwood; a bibliography of his personal papers. [Montrose, Ala.], Texas center for writers pr., [1987]. 77p. 21cm.

ISLES, FRANCIS, *pseud. of* ANTHONY BERKELEY COX, 1893–1971

6011   **Moy, Paul R.** A bibliography of the works of Anthony Berkeley Cox (Francis Isles). Armchair Detective 14no3:236–8 '81.

JACK THE RIPPER, fl.1888

6012   **Kelly, Alexander G.** Jack the ripper; a bibliography and review of the literature. Fully rev. and expanded ed. including the original introd. to the murders and the theories by Colin Wilson. London, Association of assistant librarians, S.E.D., 1984. (First publ. 1973). 83p. facsims. 21cm.

JACKSON, HOLBROOK, 1874–1948

6013 (5:11313d) **Jackson, Holbrook**. The Holbrook Jackson library; a memorial catalogue, with an appreciation by sir Francis Meynell. Bishop's Stortford, E. Mathews, 1951. 101p. port. 22cm. (Catalogue, 119). Covertitle.

'The Burton collection' (p.4–5).

JACKSON, JOHN EDWARD, 1805–91

6014 **Stratford, A. Jenny L.**, *ed.* 'Checklist of canon Jackson's works' *in* Catalogue of the Jackson collection of manuscript fragments in the Royal library, Windsor castle, with a memoir of canon J.E. Jackson.... [London], Academic pr., 1981. p.43–61.

Classified chronol. checklist of books and pamphlets on antiquarian subjects, ptd. sermons, contribs. to periodicals and newspapers, and offprints from the Wiltshire Archæol & Nat Hist Mag.

JACOBS, WILLIAM WYMARK, 1863–1943

6015 **Lamerton, Christopher**. W.W. Jacobs; a bibliography. [Margate], Greystone pr., [1988]. 172p. 28cm. (Reprod. from typewriting).

Bibliogr. of novels, novelettes and short story collections; anthologies; plays; contribs. by; and uncollected works, with appendices on collected short stories, British reprints series, illustrated books by, and selected works about.

6016 **James, A.R.** The W.W. Jacobs book hunter's field guide. Southwick, E. Sussex, A.R. James, 1989. (Rev. ed. 1990). (Not seen).

Rev: R. Dalby Antiqu Bk Mnthly R 16:313 '89.

6017 **James, A.R.** W.W. Jacobs. [Collecting]. Bk & Mag Coll 17:32–7 Jl '85. port., facsims.

'Complete W.W. Jacobs UK bibliography' (p.37).

6018 **James, A.R.** and **C. Lamerton**. W.W. Jacobs & his illustrators. Antiqu Bk Mnthly R 13no11:408–14 N '86. ports., facsims.

JAMES, HENRY, 1843–1916

6019 **Babüha, Thaddeo K.** 'Appendix: Chronological list of James's writings on and references to Hawthorne' *in* The James-Hawthorne relation; bibliographical essays. Boston, Mass., G.K. Hall, [1980]. p.[281]–3.

6020 **Cadbury, Vivian [and others].** A bibliography of the writings on Henry James by Leon Edel, with some annotations. Henry James R 3no3:176–99 '82.

6021 **Edel, Leon** and **D.H. Laurence.** A bibliography of Henry James. 3d ed. Rev. with the assistance of James Rambeau. Oxford, Clarendon pr., 1982. (First publ. 1957; 2d ed. 1961). 428p. port. 21cm. (Soho Bibs, 8).

The standard bibliogr. of original works, contribs. to books, published letters, contribs. to periodicals, translations of, and miscellanea.

Rev. R.J. Roberts TLS 4 My '84:503; D. Seed Analytical & Enum Bib 8:49–56 '84; A.W. Bellringer Yrbk Eng Stud 16:336–8 '86.

6022 **Taylor, Linda J.** Henry James, 1866–1916; a reference guide. Boston, Mass., G.K. Hall, [1982]. xxvi,533p. 23cm.

Rev. R.L. Gale Am Lit R 16:151–4 '83.

6023 **Budd, John.** Henry James; a bibliography of criticism, 1975–1981. Westport, Conn., Greenwood pr., [1983]. xx,190p. 24cm.

Rev. Bull Bib 41:174 '84; A.W. Bellringer Mod Lang R 82:938–9 '87.

6024 **Richmond, Marion.** Henry James's The portrait of a lady; a bibliography of primary material and annotated criticism. Henry James R 7no2/3:164–95 '86.

6025 **Bradbury, Nicola.** An annotated critical bibliography of Henry James. [Brighton], Harvester wheatsheaf; New York, St. Martin's pr., 1987. vii,142p. 21cm. (Annotated critical bibs.).

Rev. R.A. Hocks Am Lit Realism 21:83–5 '88.

6026 **Edel, Leon** and **Adeline R. Tintner.** The library of Henry James. Comp. and ed. with essays by…. Ann Arbor, UMI research pr., [1987]. x,106p. illus., facsims. 22cm. (Stud Mod Lit, 90).

The two libraries of Henry James, Leon Edel.–Henry James's library: titles from the original inventory and various collections, augmented from other sources.–The books in the books: what Henry Jamess's characters read and why, Adeline R. Tintner.

Rev. P.N. Furbank TLS 25 Mr '88:335–6; E. Wagenknecht Am Lit Realism 23:90–3 '90.

6027 **Hocks, Richard, Karen R. Hamer** and **W.D. Brown.** James studies, 1983–1984; an analytic bibliographical monograph. Henry James R 8no3:155–88 '87; 9no1:35–76 '88.

6028 **Hewitt, Rosalie.** Henry James's 'Autumn impression'; the history, the manuscript, the Howells relation. Yale Univ Libr Gaz 57no1/2:39–51 Oc '82.

6029 **Von Frank, Albert J.** James studies 1980; an analytical bibliographical essay. Henry James R 3no3:210–28 '82.

6030 **Edel, Leon** and **Adeline R. Tintner.** The library of Henry James, from inventory, catalogues, and library lists. Henry James R 4n03:158–90 '83.

6031 **Hewitt, Rosalie.** Henry James, the Harpers, and The American scene. [1907]. Am Lit 55n01:41–7 Mr '83.

6032 **Tintner, Adeline R.** A textual error in The spoils of Poynton. [N.Y. ed.]. Henry James R 5n01:65 '83.

6033 **Whiteman, Bruce.** The Henry James collection at McMaster university. Henry James R 5n01:66–7 '83.

6034 **Bogardus, Ralph F.** 'The illustrated James' *in* Pictures and texts; Henry James, A.L. Coburn, and new ways of seeing in literary culture. (Stud Photography 2). Ann Arbor, UMT research pr., [1984]. p.[67]–83. illus.
See also 'James and the art of illustration' (p.[51]–66).

6035 **Nordloh, David J.** First appearances of Henry James's 'The real thing'; the McClure papers as a bibliographical resource. (Bibliographical notes). Pa Bib Soc Am 78n01:69–71 '84.

6036 **Parker, Hershel.** Henry James In the wood; sequence and significances of his literary labors, 195–1907. [Revision]. Ninet Cent Fict 38n04:492–513 Mr '84.

6037 **Anesko, Michael W.** 'Friction with the market'; Henry James and the profession of authorship. New York, O.U.P., 1986. xii,258p., [2]p. of plates. illus., facsims. 25cm.
1. Introduction.–2. Stuff as dreams are made on: Henry James and his audience.–3. Henry James and the profession of authorship.–4. James's Hawthorne: the last primitive man of letters.–5. Melodrama in the marketplace: the making of The Bostonians.–6. Between the worlds of beauty and necessity: Hyacinth Robinson's problem of vocation.–7. Accommodating art and the world: the primary motive of the tragic muse.–8. The eclectic architecture of Henry James's New York edition.–Appendix A. Henry James and the movement for international copyright. B. Henry James's literary income.
Rev. R.E. Long New England Q 60:317–20 '87; P. Horne Lit Res Newsl 9:14–16 '87; J.A. Sutherland TLS 19 Je '87:672; H. Parker Review 10:211–17 '88; P.B. Armstrong Am Lit Realism 20:93–4 '88; Nina Baym J Eng & Germ Philol 87:140–1 '88; Jean Gooder Cambridge Q 17:177–86 '88; C.B. Cox Sewanee R 96:505–6 '88; Susan M. Griffin Mod Philol 86:321–3 '89; Nicola Bradbury R Eng Stud new ser 39:582–3 '89; Marcia Jacobson Henry James R 11:72–3 '90.

6038 **Milligan, Ian.** Some misprints in The awkward age. [1898–9]. N&Q 231n02:177–8 Je '86.

6039 **Powers, Lyall H.** Visions and revisions; the past rewritten. [Revision of Portrait]. Henry James R 7n02/3:158–63 '86.

6040 **Griffin, Susan M.** James's revisions of 'The novel in The ring and the book'. (Notes and documents). Mod Philol 85n01:57–64 Ag '87.

6041 **Martin, W.R.** and **W.U. Ober**. '5 pages'; Henry James's addition to 'A day of days'. [Revision]. Stud Short Fict 25no2:153–5 '88.

JAMES I, KING OF ENGLAND, 1566–1625

6042 **Akrigg, G.P.V.**, *ed*. 'Finding list' *in* Letters of king James VI and I. Berkeley, University of California pr., [1984]. p.[457]–528.
Chronol. checklist, with note of contents.

6043 **Dunne, Adair M.** An unnoticed portrait of James I by an anonymous artist, printed in 1605. [In R. Vennard's The true testimony of a faithful subject]. (Bibliographical notes). Library ser6 5no2:256–9 Je '83. port.

6044 **Stewart, Alisdair M.** Basilicon doron in Germany, 1604. Scott Lit J 11no2:83 D '84.

JAMES I, KING OF SCOTLAND, 1394–1437

6045 **Scheps, Walter** and **J. Anna Looney**, [1986]: no.905.

JAMES, MONTAGUE RHODES, 1862–1936

6046 **Pfaff, Richard W.** 'Bibliography of the scholarly writings of M.R. James' *in* Montague Rhodes James. London, Scolar pr., [1980]. p.[427]–38.
Chronol. checklist, 1887–1936.

6047 **Dalby, Richard**. The ghost stories of M.R. James. [Collecting]. Bk & Mag Coll 16:46–53 Je '85. port., facsims.
'M.R. James bibliography' (p.53).

JAMES, P.D. *pseud. of* PHYLLIS DOROTHY JAMES WHITE, 1920–

6048 **Siebenheller, Norma**. 'Bibliography [of primary and secondary sources]' *in* P.D. James. (Recognitions). New York, F. Ungar, [1981]. p.145–9.

JAMES VI, KING OF SCOTLAND, 1566–1625 *see* JAMES I, KING OF ENGLAND, 1566–1625.

JEFFERIES, JOHN RICHARD, 1848–87

6049 **Taylor, Brian**. 'Selected bibliography [of primary and secondary works]' *in* Richard Jefferies. (Twayne's English authors, 329). Boston, Twayne, [1982]. p.168–72.

6050 **Musty, John**. Richard Jefferies and Alfred Williams. (Collecting country writers, 1). Antiqu Bk Mnthly R 11no6:222–9 Je '84; Nicole Gill (Letters) 11no7:279–80 Jl '84. port., facsims.
The genre.–Origins.–Jefferies the writer.–Alfred Williams.–Pioneer Jefferies collectors.–Collecting Jefferies and Williams today.
'Checklist of first editions' (p.228–9).

JENKINS, JOHN EDWARD, 1838–1910

6051 **Maidment, Brian E.** Victorian publishing and social criticism: the case of Edward Jenkins. Publ Hist 11:41–71 '82. illus., facsims.
'Appendix I: A list of Jenkins's main publications' (p.[64]).

JENNER, EDWARD, 1749–1823

6052 **LeFanu, William R.** A bibliography of Edward Jenner. 2d ed. [Winchester, Hants.], St. Paul's bibliographies, 1985. (First publ. 1951). xv,160p. port., facsims. 21cm. ([St. Paul's Bibs, 10]). (Ltd. to 500 copies).

JENYNS, SOAME, 1704–87

6053 **Rompkey, Ronald**. A draft of Soame Jenyn's Free inquiry into the nature and origin of evil, 1757. [Bottisham hall, Cambr.]. N&Q 231no4:518–21 D '86.

JEROME, JEROME KLAPKA, 1859–1927

6054 **Markgraf, Carl**. Jerome K. Jerome; an annotated bibliography of writings about him. Eng Lit Transit 26no2:83–132 '83.

6055 ——Jerome K. Jerome; update of a bibliography of writings about him. Eng Lit Transit 30no2:180–211 '87; 2, by C. Markgraf and R. Wiebe 31no1:64–76 '88.

6056 **Henderson, Geoffrey** [and] **M. Collins.** Three men in a boat; first state or first issue? (Letters). Antiqu Bk Mnthly R 8n07:272–3 Jl '81.

6057 **Macleod, Helen**. Jerome K. Jerome. [Collecting]. Bk & Mag Coll 16:4–12 Je '85. port., facsims.
'Complete Jerome K. Jerome UK bibliography (p.12).

JERROLD, DOUGLAS WILLIAM, 1803–57

6058 **White, Bruce A.** Douglas Jerrold's 'Q' papers in Punch. Vict Pers R 15n04:130–7 '82. port., facsim.
'Chronological list of 'Q' papers' (p.136–7).

JOHN, GWEN, fl.1912–28

6059 **Morgan, Ceridwen L.** Gwen John papers at the National library of Wales. Aberystwyth, National library of Wales, 1988. 52p. facsims. 24cm.
'Appendix: Summary of holdings' (p.44–5).

JOHNS, WILLIAM EARL, 1893–1968

6060 **Winstanley, F.H.** Capt. W.E. Johns' Biggles stories. [Collecting]. Bk & Mag Coll 4:4–11 Jl '84. port., facsims.

JOHNSON, BRIAN STANLEY, 1933–73

6061 **D'Eath, Paul M.** B.S. Johnson; a select bibliography. R Contemp Fict 5n02:109–11 '85.

JOHNSON, PAMELA HANSFORD, 1912–81

6062 **Lindblad, Ishrat**. 'Selected bibliography [of primary and secondary sources]' *in* Pamela Hansford Johnson. (Twayne's English authors, 291). Boston, Twayne, [1982]. p.187–99.

6063 **Franks, Mildred M.** Pamela Hansford Johnson; secondary sources, 1934–1981. Bull Bib 40n02:73–82 Je '83.

JOHNSON, SAMUEL, 1709–84

6064 (7:4773e) **Eddy, Donald D.** 'Appendix B: Chronological list of book and pamphlets [reviewed]' *in* Samuel Johnson, book reviewer in the Literary magazine or Universal review, 1756–1758. New York, Garland, 1979. p.[127]–42.

6065　**Maggs bros., bksllrs.,** LONDON. Samuel Johnson, LL.D., 1709–1784. London, 1983. 174p. facsims. 25cm. (Catalogue, 1038).

6066　**Arts council of Great Britain,** LONDON. Samuel Johnson, 1709–84; a bicentenary exhibition. [Comp. by Kai Kin Yung]. [London], [1984]. 144p. illus., ports., facsims. 21cm.
Rev. I. Ehrenpreis London R Bks 6:5–6 '84/5.

6067　**Birmingham. Public library.** Dr. Samuel Johnson, 1709–1784; a bicentenary exhibition. Birmingham, Public libraries, 1984. 15p. 19cm. (Reprod. from typewriting).

6068　**Cameron, William J.** Eighteenth century editions of dr. Samuel Johnson's Dictionary in special collections, the library of the School of library and information science, the University of Western Ontario. [London, Ont., University of Western Ontario], 1984. 22p. 27cm. (WHSTC Libr Cat ser, 26). Duplicated typescript. (Not seen: ISBN 0–7714–0684–3).

6069　**Courtney, William P.** and **D.N. Smith.** A bibliography of Samuel Johnson; with Johnsonian bibliography, a supplement to Courtney, by R.W. Chapman with the collaboration of Allen Hazen. Repr. with a new introd. [New Castle, Del.], Oak Knoll books and G.M. Goldberg, 1984. (First publ. 1915, 1968). viii,186; 120–66p. facsims. 23cm.
See BBLB2 3838.

6070　**Fleeman, J. David.** A preliminary handlist of copies of books associated with dr. Samuel Johnson. Oxford, Oxford bibliographical society, Bodleian library, 1984. vii,101p. 24cm. (Reprod. from typewriting).
Rev. J.P.W. Rogers TLS 14 S '84:1039; Isobel Grundy New Rambler 25:48–9 '84; I. Ehrenpreis London R Bks 6:5–6 '84/5; D. Wheeler Brit J Eight Cent Stud 9:254–6 '86; O M Brack Library ser6 9:72–5 '87.

6071　**Harvard. University. Houghton library.** He has long outlived his century; [the 200th anniversary of Johnson's death: an exhibition of books & mss. collected by Mary & Donald Hyde, Arthur A. Houghton, jr., Robert Metzdorf, Amy Lowell, Harold Murdock, Houghton Mifflin co. & others]. [Introd. by Hugh Amory]. [Cambridge, Mass., Houghton library], [1984]. iv,15p. 25cm. Covertitle.

6072　**Manchester. University. John Rylands university library.** Samuel Johnson, 1709–1784; a bicentenary exhibition. [Manchester, Manchester U.P.], [1984]. 22p. 30cm. (Duplicated typescript).

6073　**Samuel Johnson society of Southern California.** Samuel Johnson, 1709–1764; an appreciation. An exhibition of manuscripts, books, & graphic images held at the Huntington library, San Marino, and the William Andrews Clark memorial library, Los Angeles, Fall & winter 1984–1985. [Comp. by Robert Allen]. Los Angeles, 1984. 46p. illus., ports., facsims. 25cm.

6074 **[Soupel, Serge].** Samuel Johnson, Rasselas: bibliographie sélective. Soc d'Étud Anglo-Am Bull 19:17–42 N '84.

6075 **Fleeman, J.David.** 'Johnsonian prospectuses and proposals' *in* Patey, Douglas L. and T. Keegan, *ed.* Augustan studies; essays in honor of Irvin Ehrenpreis. Newark, N.J., University of Delaware pr.; London, Associated U.P., [1985]. p.215–38.

6076 **Greene, Donald J.** and **J.A. Vance**. A bibliography of Johnsonian studies, 1970–1985. [Victoria, B.C.], English literary studies, University of Victoria, 1987. vi,116p. 22cm. (ELS Monogr ser, 39).

6077 **Fleeman, J. David.** Memorabilia. [Adds. and corrs. to Clifford, 1970 and D.J. Greene, 1987]. N&Q 234no1:1–5 Mr '89.

———

6078 (5:11523d) **Greene, Donald J.** 'No dull duty; the Yale edition of the works of Samuel Johnson' *in* Conference on editorial problems, 3d, Toronto, 1967. Editing eighteenth-century texts; papers.... Ed. by D.I.B. Smith. [Toronto], [1968]. p.[92]–123.

6079 **Fleeman, J. David.** A Johnsonian crux. [Journey to the western islands, 1775]. N&Q 225no1:48–9 F '80.

6080 **Lonsdale, Roger**. Johnson as subscriber; some additions. N&Q 225no5:410–12 Oc '80; H. Forster, Another Johnson subscription 228no1:54–5 F '83.

6081 **Wendorf, Richard**. The making of Johnson's 'Life of Collins'. [In Lives of the English poets]. Pa Bib Soc Am 74no2:95–115 '80. table.

6082 **Barker, A.D.** The printing and publishing of Johnson's Marmor Norfolciense, 1739, and London, 1738 and 1739. Library ser6 3no4:287–304 D '81. facsims.

6083 **Cole, Richard C.** Samuel Johnson and the eighteenth-century Irish book trade. Pa Bib Soc Am 75no3:235–55 '81.

6084 **McCarthy, William**. The composition of Johnson's Lives; a calendar. Philol Q 60no1:53–67 '81.

6085 **Samuel** Johnson; a bicentenary exhibition. (Notes and news). John Rylands Univ Libr Manchester Bull 67no1:286–9 '84.

6086 **Alkon, Paul**. 'Illustrations of Rasselas and reader-response criticism' *in* Alkon, Paul and R. Folkenflik. Samuel Johnson: pictures and the word; papers presented at a Clark library seminar, 23 October 1982. Los Angeles, William Andrews Clark memorial library, University of California, 1984. p.3–62. facsims.

6087 **Congleton, J.E.** and **Elizabeth C. Congleton**, *ed.* Johnson's Dictionary; bibliographical survey, 1746–1984, with excerpts for all entries. [Terre Haute, Ind.], Dictionary society of North America, 1984. xiii,197p. facsim. 22cm.
'Known surviving books marked by Johnson while compiling the Dictionary' (p.92).

6088 **Nicholls, Graham** and **J. Sanders**. Samuel Johnson and the Midlands; a bi-centenary exhibition, 9 July to 29 September, 1984, Lichfield art gallery. [Lichfield], Johnson bi-centenary committee, [1984]. 59p. port., facsims. 20cm.

6089 **Sherbo, Arthur**. Another book owned by Samuel Johnson. N&Q 229no3:402–3 S '84.

6090 **Reddick, Allen H.** Hopes raised for Johnson; and example of misleading descriptive and analytical bibliography. [Beinecke libr. copy of Dictionary]. Text 2:245–9 '85.

6091 **Ruml, Treadwell**. The younger Johnson's texts of Pope. [Libr.]. R Eng Stud new ser 36no142:180–98 My '85.
1. The problem.–2. General data.–3. Early poems and translations.–4. Motte's Miscellanies.–5. Moral essays.–6. Imitations of Horace.–7. Martinus Scriblerus and The dunciad.–8. Conclusion.

6092 **Rizzo, Betty W.** 'Innocent frauds' by Samuel Johnson. [Literary forgeries in the Gentleman's magazine]. Library ser6 8no3:249–64 S '86.

6093 **Sharma, T.R.**, *ed.* 'Dr. Johnson and defeudalization of literature [Patronage]' *in* Essays on dr. Samuel Johnson. Meerut, Shalabh book house, [1986]. p.109–18.

6094 **Stewart, Charlotte A.** The life of a Johnsonian collection. [A.G. Rippey colln. now at McMaster univ.]. Am Bk Coll new ser 7no6:9–17 Je '86. facsims.

6095 **Johnson** and Boswell; the Rippey collection at McMaster. (Notes and news). John Rylands Univ Libr Manchester Bull 69no2:320–3 '87.

6096 **Brownell, Morris R.** 'Dr. Johnson's ghost': genesis of a satirical engraving. Huntington Libr Q 50no4:338–57 '87. facsims.
1. The ghost and rival biographers.–2. ' Dr. Johnson's ghost' and Boswell's Tour, 1785.–3. A portrait ghost of dr. Johnson.

6097 **Kernan, Alvin B.** Printing technology, letters, & Samuel Johnson.
Princeton, N.J., Princeton U.P., 1987. xvi,357p. illus., facsims. 21cm.
Introduction: Print and letters in eighteenth-century England.–1. The King of England
meets the great cham of literature.–2. Printing, bookselling, readers and writers in eighteenth-century London.–3. Making the writer's role in a print culture.–4. The writer as
culture hero: Boswell's Johnson.–5. Creating an aura for literary texts in print culture.–
6. Reading and readers: the literacy crisis of the eighteenth-century.–7. The place and
purpose of letters in print society.–8. The social construction of romantic literature.
Rev. C.J. Rawson London R Bks 9:18–19,21 '87; D. Womersley R Eng Stud new ser 39:
559–60 '88; P. Alkon Eng Lang N 26:73–5 '88; G.J. Kolb J Eng & Germ Philol 88:241–
6 '89; C.J. Sommerville Am Hist R 94:133–4 '89; Isobel Grundy Age Johnson 3:455–61
'90.

6098 **Clingham, G.J.** and **N. Hopkinson.** Johnson's copy of the Iliad at
Felbrigg hall, Norfolk. [Annotated by R. Creighton and son]. Bk
Coll 37n04:503–21 '88. facsims.

6099 **Powell, Paul Jeffreys-**. A grammatical error in Johnson's Ode on the
isle of Skye ('Ponti profundis clausa recessibus'). [Misprint]. N&Q
233n02:190–1 Je '88.

JOHNSTON, DENIS, 1901–

6100 **Ronsley, Joseph,** *ed.* 'Check-list: Denis Johnston's writings' *in* Denis
Johnston, a retrospective. (Irish Lit Stud 8). Gerrards Cross, C.
Smythe; Totowa, N.J., Barnes & Noble, 1981. p.245–62.
*Checklist of books of plays, books other than plays, plays and stories in collections, articles,
reviews by, drama reviews by, unpublished plays, ballet, and broadcasts.*
'Appendix and errata to The dramatic works [A bride for the unicorn]' (p.263–6).

JOHNSTONE, CHARLES, 1719?–1800?

6101 **Bartz, F.K.** A new edition and new identifications; Johnstone's Chrysal.
[1761]. N&Q 225n01:46–7 F '80.

JONES, DAVID MICHAEL, 1895–1974

6102 **Delaney, J.G. Paul.** David Jones. (Great illustrators). Antiqu Bk Mnthly
R 7n010:480–7 Ag '80; T.D.J. Cleverdon; D.M. Blamires (Letters)
7n012:571–2 D '80. facsims.
'Books illustrated by David Jones' (p.485): *checklist of 20 items, 1922–69.*

6103 **Dilworth, Thomas.** A book to remember by; David Jones's glosses on
a history of the great war. [In parenthesis]. Pa Bib Soc Am 74n03:221–
34 '80.

6104 —— David Jones's glosses in The anathemata. Stud Bib 33:239–53 '80.

JONES, GWYN, 1907–

6105 **Morgan, Paul B.** The writings of Gwyn Jones; a checklist. [Principal works and 1st ed.]. New Welsh R 1no3:39–41 '88.

JONES, JOHN MORRIS-, 1864–1929

6106 **Walters, Huw.** John Morris-Jones, 1864–1929; llfrddiaeth anodiadol. Aberystwyth, Llyfrgell genedlaethol Cymru, 1986. 166p. 21cm. (Reprod. from typewriting).
977 items.

JONES, ROBERT AMBROSE, 1851–1906

6107 **Clwyd county council. Library service.** Emrys ap Iwan llyfryddiaeth. [Mold], Gwasaneth llyfrgell Clwyd, [1980]. i,20p. 29cm.
'Llfrau' (p.1–2); 'Llythyrau ac erthyglau' (p.2–10), *and works about.*

JONES, THOMAS GWYNN, 1871–1949

6108 **Roberts, D. Hywel E.** Llyfryddiaeth Thomas Gwynn Jones; The bibliography of Thomas Gwynn Jones. Caerdydd, Gawsg Prifysgol Cymru, 1981. xvi,350p. 23cm.
'A brief introduction' (p.xv–xvi): *in English.*

JONES, SIR WILLIAM, 1746–94

6109 **British library. Reference division.** Sir William Jones and the Asiatic society of Bengal; an exhibition.... London, British library, 1984. [4]p. illus., port. 21cm. (Not seen).

JONSON, BENJAMIN, 1573?–1637

6110 **Carrive, Lucien.** Ben Jonson The alchemist; bibliographie sélective et critique. Soc d'Étud Anglo-Am Bull 11:7–30 N '80.

6111 **Lehrman, Walter D., Dolores J. Sarafinski** and **Elizabeth Savage.** The plays of Ben Jonson; a reference guide. Boston, Mass., G.K. Hall, [1980]. xix,311p. 24cm. (Reference guide to literature).
Rev: Sara Pearl N&Q 228:165–6 '83; I. Donaldson Yrbk Eng Stud 16:244–5 '86.

6112 **Judkins, David C.** The nondramatic works of Ben Jonson; a reference guide. Boston, Mass., G.K. Hall, [1982]. xix, 260p. 23cm. (Reference guide to literature).

6113   **Kelly, Joseph**. A book from the libraries of Ben Jonson and John Aubrey. Sevent Cent Newsl 39no2/3:44 '81.

6114   **Dunlap, Rhodes**. Honest Ben and royal James; the poetics of patronage. Iowa State J Res 57no2:143–51 N '82.

6115   **Newton, Richard C.** 'Jonson and the (re-)invention of the book' *in* Summers, Claude J. and T.-L. Pebworth, *ed.* Classic and cavalier; essays on Jonson and the sons of Ben. [Pittsburgh], University of Pittsburgh U.P., [1982]. p.31–55.

6116   **Miller, Anthony**. The text of Ben Jonson's translation of Martial, Epigrams X.xlvii. Eng Lang N 21no2:8–10 D '83.

6117   **Murray, Timothy**. From foul sheets to legitimate model; anti-theater, text, Ben Jonson. New Lit Hist 14no3:641–64 '83.

6118   **Reichert, John**. An early text of Jonson's 'A hymne to God the father'. [In Thomas Myriell's Tristitiae remedium, 1616]. N&Q 228no2:147–8 Ap '83.

6119   **Gerritsen, Johan**. 'A Jonson proof-sheet: Neptune's triumph' *in* Janssens, G.A.M. and F.G.A.M. Aarts, *ed.* Studies in seventeenth-century English literature, history and bibliography; festschrift for professor T.A. Birrell on the occasion of his sixtieth birthday. (Costerus new ser 46). Amsterdam, Rodopi, 1984. p.[107]–17. facsims.

6120   **Evans, Robert C.** 'Men that are safe, and sure'; Jonson's 'Tribe of Ben' epistle in its patronage context. Renaiss & Reformation new ser 9no4:235–54 N '85.

6121   **Murray, Timothy**. 'Ben Jonson's folio as textual performance' *in* International comparative literature association. Congress, 10th, New York, 1982. Proceedings.... Ed. by Anna Balakian [and others]. New York, Garland, 1985. V.1, p.325–30.

6122   **Riddell, James A.** Variant title-pages of the 1616 Jonson folio. (Bibliographical notes). Library ser6 8no2:152–6 Je '86; J. Gerritsen; J. A. Riddell (Correspondence) 8no2:363 D '86.

6123   **Bracken, James K.** Ben Jonson's 'y' spellings in the Masque of queens holograph. Analytical & Enum Bib new ser 1no1:17–19 '87.

6124   —— The preference for 'y' spellings in Ben Jonson's autographs. Analytical & Enum Bib new ser 1no4:237–46 '87.
'Appendix: "y" spellings and variants in Johnson's autographs' (p.242–5).

6125   **Donovan, Kevin J.** The final quires of the Jonson 1616 Workes; headline evidence. Stud Bib 40:106–20 '87. illus.

6126 **Evans, Robert C.** Ben Jonson's library and marginalia; new evidence from the Folger collection. (Brief articles and notes). Philol Q 66no4:521–8 '87.

6127 —— Literature as equipment for living; Ben Jonson and the poetics of patronage. CLA J 30no3:379–94 Mr '87.

6128 —— 'Making just approaches'; Ben Jonson's poems to the earl of Newcastle. [Patronage]. Renaiss Pa 1988:63–75 '88.

6129 **Jowett, John**. 'Fall before this Booke'; the 1605 quarto of Sejanus. Text 4:279–95 '88. facsims.

6130 **Loewenstein, Joseph**. 'The script in the marketplace [Patronage, and the 1616 Folio]' *in* Greenblatt, Stephen, *ed*. Representing the English renaissance. Berkeley, Calif., University of California pr., [1988]. p.265–78.

6131 **Ostovich, Helen**. 'Manfrede'? reconstruction of a misprint in Jonson's Every man out his humour? [4.8.110]. N&Q 234no3:320–1 S '89.

JOYCE, JAMES AUGUSTINE, 1882–1941

6132 **Cohn, Alan M.** Current JJ checklist.... James Joyce Q 17no2:207–11 '80; 17no3:293–9 '80; 17no4:419–26 '80; 18no1:69–77 '80; 18no2:189–98 '81; 18no3:339–48 '81; 18no4:433–8 '81; 19no1:63–8 '81; 19no2:141–9 '82; 19no3:331–7 '82; 19no4:439–52 '82; 20no2:209–21 '83; 20no3:337–47 '83; 20no4:443–54 '83; 21no1:69–79 '83; 21no2:155–63 '84; 21no3:267–74 '84; 21no4:357–67 '84; 22no1:67–74 '84; 22no2:213–21 '85; 22no3:307–12 '85; 22no4:405–12 '85; 23no1:67–75 '85; 23no2:201–8 '86; 23no3:337–8 '86; 23no4:479–85 '86; 24no1:73–8 '86; 24no2:201–9 '87; 24no3:351–8 '87; 24no4:457–64 '87; 25no1:105–13 '87; 26no2:271–7 '89; 26no3:425–34 '89; 26no4:573–81 '89.

6133 **Groden, Michael**. James Joyce's manuscripts; an index. New York, Garland, 1980. xv,173p. 21cm. (Reference library of the humanities, 186). *Rev*: A.W. Litz TLS 12 D '80:1403.

6134 **Woolmer, J. Howard.** Ulysses at auction, with a preliminary census. James Joyce Q 17no2:141–8 '80.

6135 **Gilvarry, James**. The James Joyce exhibition at the Grolier club. Grolier Club Gaz new ser 33/4:19–49 '81/2.

6136 **Bushrui, Suheil B.**, *comp*. 'Joyce in the Arab world [including bibliogr. of works by and about in Arabic]' *in* Bushrui, Suheil B. and B. Benstock, *ed*.

James Joyce; an international perspective: essays in honor of the late sir Desmond Cochrane. (Irish Lit Stud 10). Gerrards Cross, Bucks., C. Smythe; Totowa, N.J., Barnes and Noble, 1982. p.232–49.

6137 **Cambridge. University. Library.** James Joyce, 1882–1941; a handlist of an exhibition at Cambridge university library, January to March 1982. Cambridge, 1982. [29]p. 30cm. Headtitle. (Duplicated typescript). [Sg.: S.J.H. i.e. Hills].

6138 **Caspel, Paul van.** 'Joyce studies in the Netherlands' *in* Bushrui, Suheil B. and B. Benstock, *ed.* James Joyce; an international perspective. Gerrards Cross, C. Smythe; Totowa, N.J., Barnes & Noble, 1982. p.215–21.
'Bibliography or list of works referred to in the text' (p.220–1).

6139 **Peterson, Richard F., A.M. Cohn** and **S. Cox.** James Joyce, 1882–1941; a centenary exhibit. Carbondale, Friends of Morris library, Southern Illinois university, 1982. 54p. ports., facsims. 25cm.

6140 **Soar, Geoffrey** and **R. Brown.** Joyce and the Joyceans; an exhibition...Flaxman gallery, University college, London library.... [London, University college], [1982]. ii,20p.+ errata slip. 30cm. (Reprod. from typewriting).

6141 **Toronto. University. Thomas Fisher rare book library.** Re Joyce; an exhibition celebrating the hundredth anniversary of the birth of James Joyce. [By Rachel Grover]. [Toronto], 1982. [iv],15p. plan. 28cm. (Reprod. from typewriting).

6142 **Kemnitz, Charles.** James Joyce at 101; an exhibition...February–April 1983. [Tulsa], University of Tulsa, McFarlin library, [1983]. 44p. illus., ports., facsims. 18x22cm.

6143 **Nadel, Ira B.** Lucia Joyce; archival material at the James Joyce centre, University college, London. [Listed]. James Joyce Q 22n04:397–404 '85.

6144 **Gillespie, Michael P.** and **E.B. Stocker.** James Joyce's Trieste library; a catalogue of materials at the Harry Ransom humanities research center, the University of Texas at Austin. [Austin, Tex., HRHRC, University of Texas], [1986]. 276p. facsims. 25cm.
'An appraisal of James Joyce's personal library, 1904–1920' (p.9–23).
Rev. Mary T. Reynolds James Joyce Q 24:483–8 '87; J.C.C. Mays R Eng Stud new ser 39:589 '88; M.H. Begnal Éire-Ireland 23:149–50 '88.

6145 **Staley, Thomas F.** An annotated critical bibliography of James Joyce. London, Harvester wheatsheaf; New York, St. Martin's pr., [1989]. viii,182p. 21cm.
Rev. M. Groden James Joyce Q 27:411–14 '90.

6146 **Groden, Michael**. Editing Joyce's Ulysses, an international effort. Schol Publ 12no1:37–54 Oc '80. facsims., diagr.

6147 **Gabler, Hans W.** 'Prospekt und Perspektiven der kritischen Ulysses-edition' *in* Grabes, Herbert, *ed.* Anglistentag 1980 Giessen; Tagungs-beiträge und Berichte im Auftrage des Vorstandes. Grossen-Linden, Hoffmann, [1981]. p.[227]–39.

6148 **Gillespie, Michael P.** A critique of Ellmann's list of Joyce's Trieste library. James Joyce Q 19no1:27–36 '81.

6149 **Groden, Michael**. 'Editing Joyce's Ulysses; an international effort' *in* Langlois, Ethel G., *ed.* Scholarly publishing in an era of change; proceedings of the second annual meeting, Society for scholarly publishing.... Washington, D.C., Society for scholarly publishing, [1981]. p.27–34. diagr., facsims.
Literary editing.–Joyce's writing of Ulysses.–The continuous manuscript.–The TU–Step process.–Editing Ulysses.–The edited text.–Conclusion.

6150 **Zahorí, H.** Shakespeare & company; tras las huellas de Ulises. [Publ.]. Quimera 5:4–7 Mr '81. illus., ports.

6151 **Cahoon, Herbert**. The Joyce bibliography. Grolier Club Gaz new ser 33/4:3–5 '81/2.

6152 **Koch, David V.** The Harley K. Croessmann collection of James Joyce at Southern Illinois university, Carbondale. Grolier Club Gaz new ser 33/4:91–6 '81/2.

6153 **Mason, Alexandra**. The James Joyce collection at the University of Kansas. [Kenneth Spencer research libr.]. Grolier Club Gaz new ser 33/4:87–90 '81/2.

6154 **Slocum, John J.** Collecting James Joyce. Grolier Club Gaz new ser 33/4:6–18 '81/2.

6155 **Tatum, G. Marvin.** The James Joyce collection at Cornell university. Grolier Club Gaz new ser 33/4:78–83 '81/2.

6156 **Turner, Decherd**. The James Joyce collection at the Humanities research center. Grolier Club Gaz new ser 33/4:84–6 '81/2.

6157 **Wynne, Marjorie G.** and **Mary T. Reynolds.** James Joyce, 1882–1941; a centenary exhibition at the Beinecke rare book and manuscript library, Yale university. Grolier Club Gaz new ser 33/4:50–77 '81/2.

6158 **Banta, Melissa W.** The James Joyce–Sylvia Beach correspondence at Buffalo. (Notes). James Joyce Q 19no4:453–5 '82.

6159   **Ford, Jane**. James Joyce's Trieste library; some notes on its use. Libr Chron Univ Texas 20/1:140–57 '82. port., facsims.

6160   **Kidd, John**. Joyce's copy of François Rabelais's Les cinq livres. [In HRC]. Libr Chron Univ Texas 20/1:158–70 '82. port., facsim.

6161   **Fitch, Noel R.** '4. The battle of Ulysses' and '6. Selling and smuggling Ulysses' *in* Sylvia Beach and the lost generation; a history of literary Paris in the twenties and thirties. New York, W.W. Norton, 1983. (Also publ. London, Souvenir pr., 1984; [Harmondsworth], Penguin, [1985]). p.[65]–92, [115]–40.

6162   **Gillespie, Michael P.** Inverted volumes improperly arranged; James Joyce and his Trieste library. Ann Arbor, Mich., UMI research pr., [1983]. 122p. 22cm. (Stud Mod Lit, 10).

   Appendix A: Books Joyce owned in Zurich.–B. Books Joyce consulted while writing Ulysses.–C. Books referred to in Ulysses.

   Rev: C. Hart Library ser6 7:287–8 '85; C.W. Barrow Éire–Ireland 20:152–3 '85.

6163   **Oliphant, Dave** and **T. Zigal**, *ed.* Joyce at Texas; essays on the James Joyce materials at the Humanities research center. Austin, Humanities research center, University of Texas, [1983]. 172p. illus., facsims., ports. 25cm.

   Roy Gottfried, 'Le point doit être plus visible': The Texas page proofs of Ulysses.–John L. Brown, Ulysses into French.–Richard Ellmann, Joyce's aunt Josephine.–David Hayman, Shadow of his mind: The papers of Lucia Joyce.–Nancy Cunard and James Joyce.–Nancy Cunard, On James Joyce – for professor Ellmann.–Kenneth R. Stevens, Ulysses on trial.–Joseph Evans Slate, The Reisman–Zukofsky screenplay of Ulysses; its background and significance.–Jane Ford, James Joyce's Trieste library; some notes on its use.–John Kidd, Joyce's copy of François Rabelais's Les cinq livres.

   Rev: A.M. Cohn James Joyce Q 22:332–4 '85.

6164   **Bauerle, Ruth.** Editing Ulysses. (Letters). TLS 10 Ag '84:893; H. Kenner 17 Ag '84:917.

6165   **Brown, Richard.** To administer correction. [Gabler's Ulysses and editing]. James Joyce Broadsheet 15:1 Oc '84.

6166   **Gabler, Hans W.** The synchrony and diachrony of texts; practice and theory of the critical edition of James Joyce's Ulysses. Text 1:305–26 '84.

6167   **Heltche, Walter** and **C. Melchior**. A famous fighter and Mairy's drawers; Joyce's corrections for the 1936 John Lane edition of Ulysses. (Notes). James Joyce Q 21no2:165–9 '84.

6168   **Moscato, Michael** and **Leslie Le Blanc**, *ed.* The United States of America v. one book entitled Ulysses by James Joyce: documents and commentary; a 50 year retrospective. Introd. by Richard Ellmann. [Frederick, Md.], University publications of America, [1984]. xxvii,482p. map. 23cm.

   Rev: Alison Rieke Am N&Q 22:155–6 '84.

6169 **Sarkany, Stéphane**. 'Qu'en est-il d'une institution littéraire internationale? A propos de l'histoire éditoriale de Dubliners e Joyce et les
structure de l'institution anglo-saxonne' *in* Heyndels, Ralph and E.
Cros, *ed.* Opérativité des méthodes sociocritiques. (Études socioc-
rites. Actes 3). Montpellier, Centre d'études et recherches socioc-
rits, 1984. p.189–204.

Préalables.–Données.–L'institution anglo-saxonne: interprétation des donnés et théorie.–...l'institution internationale.–Théorie; l'épreuve a contrario.

First publ. in Zagadnienia Rodzajów Literackich 25no1:72–83 '82.

6170 **Benstock, Bernard**. Bedeviling the typographer's ass; Ulysses and
Finnegan's wake. [Ptg.]. J Mod Lit 12no1:3–33 Mr '85. illus.

6171 **Fitch, Noel R.** '4. The battle of Ulysses [and] 6. Selling and smuggling
Ulysses' *in* Sylvia Beach and the lost generation; a history of literary
Paris in the twenties and thirties. [Harmondsworth], Penguin, [1985].
(First publ. New York, W.W. Norton, 1983). p.65–92, 115–40.

6172 **Groden, Michael**. Foostering over those changes; the new Ulysses.
[Gabler's ed.]. James Joyce Q 22no2:137–59 '85. diagr., facsims.

6173 **McGann, Jerome J.** Ulysses as postmodern text; the Gabler edition.
Criticism 27no3:283–305 '85.

Trans. by Judit Friedrich *as* Az Ulysses mint postmodern szöveg: a Gabler-féle kiadás.
Helikon 35no3/4:429–52 '89.

6174 **HRHRC** acquires additional materials relating to James Joyce. (Collections at Texas). Libr Chron Univ Texas new ser 37:9–10 '86.

6175 **Buning, Marius**. Ulysses's textual homecoming. [On the Gabler
Ulysses]. Dutch Q R 16no2:145–52 '86.

6176 **Groden, Michael**. 'James Joyce conference, Philadelphia, Pennsylva-
nia: 12–16 June, 1985 [and Gabler's Ulysses]' *in* Ross, Jean W., *ed.*
Dictionary of literary bibliography yearbook, 1985. Detroit, Mich.,
Gale research, [1986]. p.162–8. facsims.

6177 **Hayman, David**. 'Shadow of his mind; the papers of Lucia Joyce' *in*
Beja, Morris [and others], *ed.* James Joyce; the centennial symposium. Urbana, University of Illinois pr., [1986]. p.[193]–206.

Repr. from Joyce at Texas, ed. D. Oliphant and T. Zigal, 1983: no.6163.

6178 **McCullough, Ann**. 'Joyce's early publishing history in America' *in*
Beja, Morris [and others], *ed.* James Joyce; the centennial symposium. Urbana, University of Illinois pr., [1986]. p.[184]–92.

BWH: person and publisher.–Publishing the early Joyce.–Publishing negotiations:
Ulysses.–Postscript: Finnegan's wake.

6179 **O'Halpin, Eunan**. British patronage and an Irish writer; the award of
a government grant to James Joyce in 1916. (Notes). James Joyce Q
24no1:79–83 '86.

6180 **Pugliatti, Paola**. Il nuovo Ulysses e la critica del testo. Strumenti Critici nuova ser 1fasc2:187–224 Maggio '86. facsims.

1. La vulgata.–2. La pubblicazione della prima editione.–3. La costituzione dell'avantexto.–4. Documenti di composizione e documenti di trasmissione.–5. Il dibattito sul nuovo Ulysses.

6181 **Sandulescu, C. George** and **C. Hart**, *ed*. Assessing the 1984 Ulysses. Gerrards Cross, Bucks., C. Smythe; Totowa, N.J., Barnes & Noble, 1986. xxiv,247p. facsims., diagrs. 20cm. (Princess Grace Irish Libr ser, 1).

A Finnegan's wake approach to Ulysses: foreword, Anthony Burgess.–How this particular funforall came about, C. George Sandulescu.–Ulysses: how many texts are there in it?, Bernard Benstock.–Joyce the scribe and the right hand reader, Rosa Maria Bollettieri Bosinelli.–Typography underrated; a note on Aelus in Gabler's edition, Giovanni Cianci.–On Mondadori's Telemachia, Carla de Petris.–A crux in the new edition, Richard Ellmann.–Unanswered questions about a questionable answer; the restored 'love'-passage of the new Ulysses in the light of speech-act theory, Wilhelm Füger.–Why does one re-read Ulysses?, Michael Patrick Gillespie.–Art thou real, my ideal?, Clive Hart.–Balancing the book, or pro and contra the Gabler Ulysses, David Hayman.–Reconstructing Ulysses in a deconstructive mode, Suzette Henke.–Dublin, 1904, Richard M. Kain.–Italics in Ulysses, Carla Marengo Vaglio.–Textual criticism, literary theory, and the new Ulysses, Ira B. Nadel.–From Telemachus to Penelope; episodes anonymous?, Patrick Parrinder.–Some critical comments on the Telemachia in the 1984 Ulysses, Charles Peake.–Curios of sings I am here to rede!, C. George Sandulescu.–Ulysses between corruption and correction, Fritz Senn.–Ulysses in Spanish, Francisco Garcia Tortosa.–The 1922 and 1984 editions; some philosophical considerations, Donald Philip Verene.

Rev: C. Murray Stud 76:361–2 '87; Carol Shloss James Joyce Q 25:395–401 '88.

6182 **Shloss, Carol**. 'Finnegan's wake as a history of the book' *in* Beja, Morris [and others], *ed*. James Joyce; the centennial symposium. Urbana, University of Illinois pr., [1986]. p.[102]–99. facsims.

6183 **Storhaug, Glenn**. 'Seems to see with his fingers'; the printing of Joyce's Ulysses. Matrix 6:50–6 '86. illus., facsim.

6184 **Banta, Melissa W.** and **O.A. Silverman**, *ed*. James Joyce's letters to Sylvia Beach, 1921–1940. Bloomington, Indiana U.P., [1987]. xvi,221p. illus., ports., facsims. 24cm.

Rev: Bonnie K. Scott James Joyce Q 26:141–5 '88.

6185 **Ford, Jane**. A note on the new edition of Ulysses as a research tool. (Notes). James Joyce Q 24no02:216–17 '87.

6186 **Jacquet, Claude**. Les textes de Ulysses. [And Gabler's ed.]. Étud Angl 40no03:294–300 Jl/S '87.

6187 **Kain, Richard M.** 'Fifty years of Joyce; 1934–1984' *in* Newman, Robert D. and W. Thornton, *ed*. Joyce's Ulysses; the larger perspective. [Publ.]. Newark, University of Delaware pr.; London, Associate U.P., [1987]. p.74–88.

6188 **Nadel, Ira B.** Textual criticism, literary theory, and the new Ulysses. Contemp Lit 28no01:111–20 '87. diagr.

6189 **Pugliatti, Paola**. The new Ulysses between philology, semiotics and textual genetics. Dispositio 12no30/2:113–40 '87.

1. Philology semiotics and genetics.–2. Ulysses, the textual problem.–3. The critical edition of Ulysses.

6190 **Rose, Danis**. Mr. Dignam's change of address. [Revision in Ulysses]. (Notes). James Joyce Q 25no1:126–8 '87.

6191 —— The source of mr. Blooms's wealth. [Revision in Ulysses]. (Notes). James Joyce Q 25no1:128–32 '87.

6192 **Ryder, John**. Editing Ulysses typographically. [Design of Gabler ed., 1984]. Schol Publ 18no2:108–24 Ja '87. facsims., table.

6193 **Fitch, Noel R.** 'The first Ulysses [and Sylvia Beach]' *in* International James Joyce symposium, 9th, Frankfurt-am-Main, 1984. James Joyce; the augmented ninth; proceedings…. Ed. by Bernard Benstock. Syracuse, N.Y., Syracuse U.P., 1988. p.349–61.

6194 **Ford, Jane [and others]**. 'The new edition of Ulysses; an assessment of its usefulness one year later' *in* Scott, Bonnie K., *ed.* New alliances in Joyce studies: 'When it's aped to foul a Delfian'. Newark, N.J., University of Delaware pr.; London, Associate U.P., [1988]. p.219–29.

6195 **Gabler, Hans W.** Editing Ulysses. (Letters). TLS 1 Jl '88:733; P. Du Sautoy 8 Jl '88:755; J. Kidd 22 Jl '88:805,818; H.W. Gabler 12 Ag '88:883; J. Kidd 19 Ag '88:907; C. Rosman 2 S '88:963; P. du Sautoy; S.J. Joyce 9 S '88:989; M. Groden 7 Oc '88:1109,1132; J. Kidd 21 Oc '88:1175; I. Gunn 4 N '88 1227; P. du Sautoy and C. Hart 2 D '88:1344; H.W. Gabler 16 D '88:1395.

6196 **Kenner, Hugh**. Reflections on the Gabler era. James Joyce Q 26no1:11–20 '88.

6197 **Kidd, John**. An inquiry into Ulysses; the corrected text. [H.W. Gabler's ed.]. Pa Bib Soc Am 82no4:411–584 D '88. tables.

Introduction.–What is a critical edition?–The rationale of copytext.–An imaginary continuous manuscript text.–Re-assembling the copytext.–Transcribing the Rosenbach manuscript.–Single Rosenbach leaves as typist's copy: Nausicaa leaf 55.–Nausicaa 55: Paleography and paper.–The peril of working from facsimiles.–Wandering rocks; Joyce's or Budgen's hand?–Spurious erasures.–Undetected erasures.–More transcription problems; the Telemachiad.–Paper folds.–A late addition to Sirens?–Joyce to typist Claude Sykes.–A sampling of transcription errors.–The imaginary level R.–Shifting levels.–Whose style? Joyce or his typist?–Too many levels, too little clarity.–Lost & found typescripts; Wandering rocks.–A missing link in Cyclops.–Penelope's kidney transplant.–Apparent ghost variants in the 1984 historical collation.–Eyeing the printing history.–Thirteen unacknowledged classes of emendation.–One last example: The hangman's letter.–Appendix 1. Preliminary comments on the 1984 list of editions. 2. Errors in recording hyphenation. 3. Variation in ellipses not reported in 1984. Glossary of symbols and abbreviations. Select table of editions and impressions of Ulysses. [Tables].

6198 **Levitt, Morton P.** Editor's introduction. [On Gabler Ulysses]. J Mod
      Lit 15no1:3–6 '88.

6199 **Osteen, Mark.** Gabriel's sarcasm; a lost line in The dead. [Text].
      (Notes). James Joyce Q 25no2:259–62 '88.

6200 **Ryder, John.** Unpublished illustrations by Charles Mozley for Janes
      Joyce's Ulysses. Matrix 8:164–5 + 8p. illus. '88. facsims.

6201 **Suzuki, Takashi.** James Joyce's unpublished letters in the National
      library of Ireland. N&Q 233no3:337–8 S '88.

6202 **Woodnutt, Roma.** James Joyce family copyright. (Letters). TLS 25 N
      '88:1313.

6203 **Du Sautoy, Peter.** Editing Ulysses; a personal account. [Gabler's ed.].
      James Joyce Q 27no1:69–76 '89.

6204 **Gaskell, J. Philip W.** and **C. Hart**. Ulysses; a review of three texts:
      proposals for alterations to the texts of 1922, 1961, and 1984. Ger-
      rards Cross, C. Smythe; Totowa, N.J., Barnes & Noble, [1989].
      xvii,232p. 21cm. (Princess Grace Irish Libr ser, 4).

6205 **Hayman, David.** Ulysses and Motherwell; illustrating an affinity. [Il-
      lus. ed.]. James Joyce Q 26no4:582–605 '89. facsims.

6206 **Kain, Richard M.** The case of the lost cyclist, or, what happened to
      Harry Thrift, U. 10:1259. [Misreading]. (Notes). James Joyce Q
      26no4:607 '89.

6207 **Kopff, E. Christian.** Publishers and sinners. [Ulysses and other cor-
      rupted texts]. Chronicles Mag Am Culture 13no1:16–18 Ja '89.

6208 **Pesch, Josef W.** Dot dropping(s)...a 'Pre-text'. [Ulysses]. James Joyce
      Q 27no1:136–7 '89.

6209 **Pugliatti, Paola.** Who's afraid of the 1984 Ulysses? James Joyce Q
      27no1:41–54 '89; W. Steppe, Reply to... 27no1:55–68 '89. facsims.

6210 **Rossman, Charles.** The critical reception of the Gabler Ulysses, or,
      Gabler's Ulysses Kidd-napped. Stud Novel 21no2:154–81 '89.

JUNIUS, *pseud.*

6211 **Cordasco, Francesco G.M.** Junius; a bibliography of the letters of
      Junius, with a checklist of Junian scholarship and related studies.
      Fairview, N.J., Junius–Vaughan pr., 1986. xx,454p. 24cm. (Not seen).
      Rev: J. Black N&Q 233:241 '88.

6212 —— and **G. Simonson**. Junius and his works; a history of the letters of Junius and the authorship controversy. Fairview, N.J., Junius–Vaughan pr., 1986. xx,454p. facsims. 24cm.
  Includes 1. The Junian text.–2. Junius in the letters.–3. Junius and Henry Sampson Woodfall.
  Rev: J. Black N&Q 233:241 '88.

6213 **Cordasco, Francesco G.M.** Political poems compiled by Junius, 1772; a further note. N&Q 231no4:523 D '86.

6214 —— An unrecorded Bensley edition of Junius. [1799]. N&Q 231no1:84 Mr '86.

6215 —— The vellum Junius. [1772]. N&Q 232no3:348–52 S '87.

KAVANAGH, PATRICK JOSEPH GREGORY, 1931–

6216 (7:4872k) **Nemo, John.** 'Selected bibliography [of primary and secondary sources]' *in* Patrick Kavanagh. (Twayne's English authors, 267). Boston, Mass., Twayne, [1979]. p.155–61.

6217 **Kavanagh, Peter**, *ed.* 'An annotated bibliography of Patrick Kavanagh' *in* Patrick Kavanagh, man and poet. Orono, Me., National poetry foundation, University of Maine, 1986. p.[389]–450.

KAYE-SMITH, SHEILA KAYE- (MRS. T.P. FRY), 1887–1956 *see* SMITH, SHEILA KAYE- (MRS. T.P. FRY), 1887–1956.

KEATS, JOHN, 1795–1821

6218 **Hearn, Ronald B. [and others].** Keats criticism since 1954; a bibliography. [Salzburg, Institut für Anglistik und Amerikanistik, Universität Salzburg], [1981]. ix,52p. 20cm. (Salzburg Stud Eng Lit. Romantic reassessment, 83:3).

6219 **Rhodes, Jack W.** Keats's major odes; an annotated bibliography of the criticism. Westport, Conn., Greenwood pr., [1984]. 224p. 23cm.
  Rev: W.H. Hildebrand Bull Bib 41:238–9 '84.

6220 **Jordan, Frank**, *ed.*, 1985: no.4375.

6221 **Stillinger, Jack.** The manuscripts of Keats's letters, an update. (Notes). Keats-Sh J 36:16–19 '87.

6222 **Owings, Frank N.** Keats, Lamb, and a black-letter Chaucer. [1598, in Lilly library]. Pa Bib Soc Am 75no2:147–55 '81.

6223 **Jackson, David H.** Line indentation in Stillinger's The poems of Keats. Stud Bib 36:200–5 '83.

6224 **Powell, Margaret K.** Keats and his editor; the manuscript of Endymion. [Influence of John Taylor]. Library ser6 6no2:139–52 Je '84.

6225 **Stillinger, Jack**. Stop-press corrections in Keat's Poems, 1817. (Bibliographical notes). Pa Bib Soc Am 79no2:235–5 '85.

6226 **Morpurgo, Jack E.** 'The poet and Barabbas; Keats, his publishers and editors' *in* Welch, Robert and S.B. Bushrui, *ed*. Literature and the art of creation; essays and poems in honour of A. Norman Jeffares. Gerrard's Cross, Bucks., C. Smythe; Totowa, N.J., Barnes & Noble, 1988. p.112–23.

6227 **Sato, Toshihiko**. A revaluation of Keats's 'Ode on indolence' with special attention to its stanzaic order. Philol Q 68no2:195–217 '89.

KELLY, HUGH, 1739–77

6228 **Bataille, Robert R.** Hugh Kelly, 1739–1777; a bibliography. Bull Bib 43no4:228–34 D '86.

KETTON-CREMER, ROBERT WYNDHAM, 1906–69 *see* CREMER, ROBERT WYNDHAM KETTON-, 1906–69.

KEYNES, JOHN MAYNARD, 1ST BARON KEYNES, 1883–1946

6229 **Toronto. University. Thomas Fisher rare book library.** John Maynard Keynes, 1883–1946; an exhibition of books, pamphlets, manuscripts and ephemera primarily from the collection of professor John G. Slater, on the occasion of the Keynes centenary symposium...1983. [By D.E. Moggridge]. [Toronto], [1983]. 23p. 28cm. (Reprod. from typewriting).

6230 **Moggridge, Donald E.** Bibliography and index. [London], Macmillan; [New York], C.U.P. for the Royal economic society, [1989]. xvi,557p. 22cm. (Collected writings of John Maynard Keynes, 30). 'Bibliography' (p.29–160): *classified checklist of writings, with* 'Chronological list of published material' (p.154–60).

6231 **Scrase, David** and **P. Scott**. Maynard Keynes, collector of pictures, books and manuscripts; catalogue of an exhibition held at the Fitzwilliam museum, Cambridge, 5 July – 29 August 1983. [Cambridge, King's college], [1983]. 112p. port., facsims. 25cm.
'Maynard Keynes; a personal note' *by* George Rylands (p.708).
Rev: Frances Spalding TLS 5 Ag '83:832.

6232 **Moggridge, Donald E.** 'On editing Keynes' *in* Conference on editorial problems, 22d, Toronto, 1986. Editing modern economists; papers given.... Ed. by D.E. Moggridge. New York, [1988]. p.[67]–90.
'Appendix 1: The Collected writings of John Maynard Keynes' (p.88–9).

6233 **Rymes, T.K.** 'Keynes's lectures, 1932–35; notes of a representative student: problems in construction of a synthesis' *in* Conference on editorial problems, 22d, Toronto, 1986. Editing modern economists; papers given.... Ed. by D.E. Moggridge. New York, [1988]. p.[91]–127.
The setting.–The objective of the synthesis of the lecture notes.–Major problems....–History of the lecture notes.–An exemplary treatment, 1933.–Conclusion.

KIDD, BENJAMIN, 1858–1916

6234 **Crook, D.P.** and **D. O'Donnell**. A checklist of the publications of Benjamin Kidd, 1858–1916. Vict Pers R 16no1:27–31 '83. port.

KILLIGREW, THOMAS, 1612–83

6235 **Cutbirth, Nancy**. Thomas Killingrew's commonplace book? Libr Chron Univ Texas new ser 13:31–8 '80. facsims.

KILLIGREW, SIR WILLIAM, 1606–95

6236 **Vander Motten, J.P.** Some problems of attribution in the canon of sir William Killigrew's works. [With list of reattribs. to W. Killigrew the younger]. Stud Bib 33:161–8 '80.

6237 —— and **J.S. Johnston**. Sir William Killigrew's unpublished revisions of The seege of Urbin. (Bibliographical notes). Library ser6 5 2no2:159 Je '83.

6238 **Horden, John R.B.** Sir William Killigrew's Four new playes, 1666, with his Imperial tragedy, 1669; a second annotated copy. (Bibliographical notes). Library ser6 6no3:271–5 S '84.

6239 **Vander Motten, J.P.** Another annotated copy of sir William Killigrew's Four new playes, 1666. (Bibliographical notes). Library ser6 8no1:53–8 Mr '86.

6240 **Horden, John R.B.** and **J.P. Vander Motten**. Five new plays; sir William Killigrew's two annotated copies. [Revision]. Library ser6 11no3:253–71 S '89.

'Appendix: Killigrew's annotations in the Brotherton copy of Four new playes (press mark: MS Lit.q 16)' (p.266–71).

KINGLAKE, ALEXANDER WILLIAM, 1809–91

6241 **Jewett, Iran Banu Hassani**. 'Selected bibliography [of primary and secondary sources]' *in* Alexander W. Kinglake. (Twayne's English authors, 324). Boston, Twayne, 1981. p.162–6.

KINGSLEY, CHARLES, 1819–75

6242 **Harris, Styron**. Charles Kingsley; a reference guide. Boston, Mass., G.K. Hall, [1981]. xxiii,163p. 23cm. (Reference guide to literature).

Rev: M. Reboul Étud Angl 36:90 '83; Joanne Shattuck Mod Lang R 79:683 '84.

6243 **Macleod, Helen**. Charles Kingsley & The water babies. [Collecting]. Bk & Mag Coll 23:36–43 Ja '86. port., facsims.

'Collectable editions of Charles Kingsley's The water babies' (p.42).

6244 **Uffelman, Larry K.** Kingsley's Hereward the wake; from serial to book. Vict Inst J 14:147–56 '86. port.

6245 —— and **P.G. Scott**. Kingsley's serial novels, 2: The water-babies. Vict Pers R 19no4:122–31 '86. table.

'Table 1: Serial and book texts of Kingsley's The water-babies' (p.131).

KIPLING, JOSEPH RUDYARD, 1865–1936

6246 **Harrison, James**. 'Selected bibliography [of primary and selected texts]' *in* Rudyard Kipling. (Twayne's English authors, 339). Boston, [Mass.], Twayne, [1982]. p.163–6.

6247 **Feeley, Margaret P.** The Kim that nobody reads. [Ms.]. Stud Novel 13no3:266–81 '81.

6248 **Lyman, Philip**. Notes on American notes. Kipling J 49no222:26–32 Je '82.

Chronology of the texts.–The famous Yokohama curse [against book piracy].–Other omissions in the 1899 editions.–Errors and corrections in the Oklahoma edition.

6249 **[Webb, G.H.]**. The context of the curse. [Copyright]. Kipling J 56no224:29–30 D '82.

6250 **Burt, John**. The Kipling papers in Sussex university. Kipling J 57no225:12–33 Mr '83. facsims.
1. Introduction.–2. Lockwood Kipling's papers.–3. Rudyard Kipling's papers other than personal letters.–4. The personal correspondence.

6251 **Newsom, Margaret**. The Kipling society library. Kipling J 58no230:45–7 Je '84.

6252 **Ardley, C.M.** A bibliographical query. [Land and sea tales in Uniform ed. format]. (Letters to the editor). Kipling J 59no234:27 Je '85; J.E. Phillips; G.L. Wallace 59no235:51–2 S '85.

6253 **Lewis, L.A.F.** A Syracuse university collection. Kipling J 59no235:58–61 S '85.

6254 **Dalby, Richard**. Rudyard Kipling's novels and stories. [Collecting]. Bk & Mag Coll 23:4–12 Ja '86. port., facsims.
'Complete bibliography of Rudyard Kipling's novels and stories' (p.12).

6255 **Pinney, Thomas**. Kipling in the libraries. Eng Lit Transit 29no1:83–90 '86.
1. England.–2. North America and elsewhere.–3. The manuscripts of Kipling's major works.

6256 **Wilson, Keith M.** The manuscript of 'The English flag'. Kipling J 60no237:23–31 Mr '86. facsims.

6257 **Simpson, Donald H.** A librarian's view of Kipling. [And Royal commonwealth society libr.]. Kipling J 61no242:11–29 Je '87.

KLICKMANN, FLORA, 1857–1958

6258 **Lazell, David**. Flora Klickmann and the Girl's own paper. [Collecting]. Bk & Mag Coll 6:52–9 Ag '84. port., facsims.
'Bibliography of collectable Flora Klickmann titles' (p.59).

KNOX, JOHN, 1505–72

6259 **Hazlett, Ian**. 'A working bibliography of writings by John Knox' *in* Schnucker, Robert V., *ed*. Calviniana; ideas and influence of Jean Calvin. (Sixteenth century essays & studies, 10). [Kirksville, Mo., Sixteenth century journal publications], [1988]. p.185–93.

KOESTLER, ARTHUR, 1905–83

6260 **Day, Frank**. Arthur Koestler; a guide to research. New York, Garland, 1987. xxi,248p. 21cm. (Reference library of the humanities, 376).
Rev. P.G. Reeve Sth Carolina R 22:140–1 '89.

6261 **[Smyth, Susan J.]**. The Koestler archive in Edinburgh university library; a checklist. Edinburgh, Edinburgh university library, 1987. 95p. + errata tipped in. illus., port. 20cm.
Not indexed.

L'ESTRANGE, SIR ROGER, 1616–1704

6262 **Hetet, John**. Roger L'Estrange and No blinde guides. Turnbull Libr 16no1:20–37 My '83. port.

LAMB, CHARLES, 1775–1828

6263 (5:11858e) **Prance, Claude A.** 'A Charles Lamb library' *in* Peppercorn papers; a miscellany.... Cambridge, Golden head pr., 1964. p.50–63.

6264 **Marrs, Edwin W.** The Peal collection of Lamb letters. [Univ. of Kentucky]. Charles Lamb Bull new ser 43:49–54 Jl '83.

6265 **Finch, Jeremiah S.** The Taylor Lamb collection. [At Princeton]. Charles Lamb Bull new ser 55:229 Jl '86.

6266 **Prance, Claude A.** 'Charles Lamb and John Linnell' *in* Essays of a book collector; reminiscences on some old books and their authors. West Cornwall, Conn., 1989. p.55–63.

6267 —— 'Charles Lamb and The retrospective review' *in* Essays of a book collector; reminiscences on some old books and their authors. West Cornwall, Conn., 1989. p.97–103.

6268 —— 'Charles Lamb's Free thoughts' *in* Essays of a book collector; reminiscences on some old books and their authors. West Cornwall, Conn., 1989. p.93–5.

6269 —— 'Charles Lamb's "golden year"' *in* Essays of a book collector; reminiscences on some old books and their authors. West Cornwall, Conn., 1989. p.65–92.

6270 **Russell, Gillian.** Lamb's Specimens of English dramatic poets; the publishing context and the principles of selection. Charles Lamb Bull new ser 65:1–8 Ja '89.

LANDOR, A. HENRY SAVAGE, 1865–1924

6271 **Dalby, Richard**. A. Henry Savage Landor. [Collecting]. Bk & Mag
Coll 13:30–7 Mr '85. ports., facsims.
'Complete bibliography of the works of Savage Landor' (p.37).

LANDOR, WALTER SAVAGE, 1775–1864

6272 **Books** belonging to W.S. Landor; c.45v. with ms. notes, in BL *see*
Gould, Alison, Named special collections, 1981: no.818.

LANG, ANDREW, 1844–1912

6273 **Pearce, Michael**. The bibliography of Andrew Lang. Priv Libr ser3
9no3:132–9 '86. illus., facsim.

LANGLAND, WILLIAM, 1330–1400?

6274 (7:4941*) **Bourquin, Guy**. 'References bibliographiques' *in* Piers Plowman; études sur la genèse littéraire des trois versions. Lille, Atelier
réproductions des thèses de Lille III; Paris, H. Champion, 1978. V.2,
p.825–902.

6275 **DiMarco, Vincent**. Piers Plowman; a reference guide. Boston, Mass.,
G.K. Hall, [1982]. xxviii,384p. 24cm. (Reference guide to literature).
Rev. D.C. Fowler Analytical & Enum Bib 7:137–55 '83; S.S. Hussey Yrbk Eng Stud
17:246–7 '87.

6276 **Adams, Robert**. Annual bibliography: 1985. Yrbk Langland Stud
1:161–73 '87; 1986, by V. DiMarco 1:174–89 '87; 1987, by V. DiMarco 2:179–203 '88; 1988, by V. DiMarco 3:181–213 '89; 1989, by V.
DiMarco 4:189–209 '90.

6277 (5:11903*) **Donaldson, E. Talbot**. Mss. R and F in the B-tradition of Piers
Plowman. Connecticut Acad Arts & Sci Trans 39:177–22 S '55. diagr.

6278 (5:11903*b) **Russell, George H.** The evolution of a poem; some reflections on the textual tradition of Piers Plowman. Arts 2:33–46 '62.
(Not seen).

6279 (7:4941*t) **Fowler, David C.** A new edition of the B text of Piers Plowman. [Kane and Donaldson's ed., 1975]. Yrbk Eng Stud 7:23–42 '77.
Manuscripts R and F.–Appendix: Classification of emendations in the Kane–Donaldson edition of the B version of Piers Plowman.

6280 **Schmidt, A.V.C.** The C-version of Piers plowman; a new edition. [By Derek A. Pearsall, 1978]. N&Q 225no2:102–10 Ap '80.

6281 **Kane, George**. The Z version of Piers Plowman. [Rev. art. on A.C. Rigg and Charlotte Brewer's ed., 1983]. Speculum 60no4:910–30 Oc '85.

6282 **Patterson, Lee**. 'The logic of textual criticism and the way of genius; the Kane-Donaldson Piers Plowman' *in* McGann, Jerome J., *ed.* Textual criticism and literary interpretation. Chicago, University of Chicago pr., 1985. p.55–91.

6283 **Doyle, Anthony I.** 'Remarks on surviving manuscripts of Piers Plowman' *in* Kratzmann, Gregory and J. Simpson, *ed.* Medieval English religious and ethical literature; essays in honour of G.H. Russell. [Cambridge], D.S. Brewer, [1986]. p.35–48.

6284 **Thorne, J.R.** and **Marie-Claire Uhart.** Robert Crowley's Piers Plowman. [Text]. (Notes). Medium Ævum 55no2:248–54 '86.

6285 **Scase, Wendy**. Two Piers Plowman C-text interpolations; evidence for a second textual tradition. N&Q 232no4:456–63 D '87.

6286 **Kane, George**. '7. The text' *in* Alford, John A., *ed.* A companion to Piers Plowman. Berkeley, Calif., University of California pr., [1988]. p.175–200.
      Early study.–Skeat's achievement.–Sequence of versions.–Authorial and scribal differentiation of texts.–Manuscript traditions.–Date and origin of the versions.–Dissemination of the versions.–Scribal 'correction'.–The A tradition.–The B tradition.–The C tradition.–Scribes and the text.–The textual problem.–The character of textual criticism.

6287 **Regan, Catharine A.** The shaping and reshaping of Piers Plowman; interaction of editors and audiences. L Per* 8no2:1–13 N '88.

6288 **Russell, George H.** 'The imperative of revision in the C version of Piers Plowman' *in* Kennedy, Edward D. [and others]. Medieval English studies presented to George Kane. [Woodbridge], D.S. Brewer, [1988]. p.233–42.

6289 **Brewer, Charlotte**. The textual principles of Kane's A text. Yrbk Langland Stud 3:67–90 '89.

LARKIN, PHILIP ARTHUR, 1922–85

6290 (7:4943) **Bloomfield, Barry C.** Philip Larkin; a bibliography, [1979].
      Rev: Jean Peters Am Bk Coll new ser 3:50–2 '82.

6291 **Tierce, Michael**. Philip Larkin; secondary sources, 1950–1984. Bull Bib 67–75 Je '86.

6292 **Monteith, Charles**. 'Publishing Larkin [at Faber]' *in* Thwaite, Anthony, *ed.* Larkin at sixty. [London], Faber and Faber, [1982]. p.38–47.

6293 **Whitehead, John**. Philip Larkin's Collected poems. [Publ.]. TLS 4 N '88:1227; A. Thwaite 11 N '88:1251; 18 N '88:1279.

6294 **Hartley, Jean**. Philip Larkin, the Marvel press, and me. [London], Carcanet pr., [1989]. 208p. illus., ports. 21cm.
    Rev. B. Morrison TLS 7 Jl '89:740; P. Taylor-Martin Listener 121:28 '89; J. Wiltshire Cambridge Q 19:255–65 '90.

LAWRENCE, DAVID HERBERT, 1885–1930

6295 **Cooke, Sheila M.** D.H. Lawrence, a finding list; a catalogue of printed material in the County and University libraries of Nottingham. 2d ed. Nottingham, Nottinghamshire county council, 1980. (First publ. 1969). vi,121p. 30cm.

6296 **Davies, Alastair**, [1982]: no.704.

6297 **Roberts, Warren.** A bibliography of D.H. Lawrence. 2d ed. Cambridge, C.U.P., [1982]. (First publ. 1963). xvii,626p. port., facsims. 21cm.
    Descriptive bibliogr. of books and pamphlets; contribs. to books; contribs. to periodicals; translations of; mss. and ana; appendices: parodies of Lady Chatterley's lover, *other spurious works and* The phoenix; *with extensive bibliogr. notes.*
    Rev. B.C. Bloomfield Bk Coll 33:240–5 '84; R.J. Roberts TLS 4 My '84:503; R.A. Gekoski Mod Lang R 79:170–4 '84; A. Sullivan D.H. Roberts R 18:79–81 '85/6.

6298 **Cowan, James C.** D.H. Lawrence; an annotated bibliography of writings about him. DeKalb, Ill., Northern Illinois U.P., [1982–5]. 2v.(xxvi,612; xxxvi,768p.) 24cm. (Annotated secondary bibliography series on English literature in transition).
    Rev. J.B. Humma Stud Novel 16:115 '84.

6299 **Nottingham. University. Library. Manuscripts department.** D.H. Lawrence collection catalogue, vol.2. [Nottingham], 1983. vi,51p. ports., facsims. 30cm.
    With combined index to v.1 (1979): BLB 1970–79: 6973.

6300 **Rice, Thomas J.** D.H. Lawrence; a guide to research. New York, Garland, 1983. xxiii,484p. 21cm. (Reference library of the humanities, 412).
    Rev. TLS 13 Ja '84:47; G. Bixby Am Bk Coll new ser 5:53–6 '84; J.E. Tanner D.H. Lawrence R 18:82–3 '85/6; J.G. Watson N&Q 231:129 '86; B.L. Smith Bull Bib 43:185 '86.

6301 **Cambridge. University. Library.** D.H. Lawrence, 1885–1930; catalogue of an exhibition at Cambridge university library, September–November, 1985. [By S.J. Hills]. Cambridge, Cambridge university library, 1985. [i],43p. 22cm. (Reprod. from typewriting).

6302 **Preston, Peter.** 'Lawrence and mr. Noon [Publ.]' *in* Cooper, Andrew, *ed*. D.H. Lawrence, 1885–1930; a celebration. [Nottingham], D.H. Lawrence society, [1985]. p.77–88.

6303 **Rosenthal, Rae, D. Jackson** and **B. Howard**. Bibliography: checklist of D.H. Lawrence criticism and scholarship, 1979–1983. D.H. Lawrence R 18no1:37–74 '85/6; Rae Rosenthal and D. Jackson, 1984–1985. 19no2:195–218 '87; Rae Rosenthal, 1986–1987. 20no3:315–30 '88; 1988. 21no3:323–36 '89.

6304 **Filippis, Simonetta de.** A checklist of D.H. Lawrence criticism and scholarship in Italy, 1976–1985. D.H. Lawrence R 19no3:309–16 '87.

6305 **Ôhashi, Yosuichirô.** Checklist of graduate theses on D.H. Lawrence in Japan, 1976–1985. D.H. Lawrence R 19no2:227–8 '87.

6306 **Gouirand, Jacqueline.** A checklist of D.H. Lawrence translations, criticism, and scholarship published in France, 1976–1985. D.H. Lawrence R 20no3:331–5 '88.

6307 **Jackson, Dennis** and **Lydia Blanchard.** Mr. Noon's critical reception, 1984–1988. D.H. Lawrence R 20no2:133–52 '88.
'Bibliography of writings on Mr. Noon, 1984–88' (p.150–2).

6308 **Meyers, Jeffrey.** Imaginative portraits of D.H. Lawrence. [Works based on his life]. Bull Bib 45no4:271–3 D '88.

6309 **Ôhashi, Yosuichirô** and **H. Yoshimura.** A checklist of D.H. Lawrence articles in Japan, 1976–1985. D.H. Lawrence R 20no1:79–99 '88.

6310 **Worthen, John.** Catalogue of some letters and postcards relating to the Lawrence family, 1897–1910. (New materials in the biography of D.H. Lawrence, 1). D.H. Lawrence R 20no3:269–74 '88.

6311 **Concha, Angeles de la.** D.H. Lawrence in Spanish; a checklist of works by and about him. D.H. Lawrence R 21no1:55–65 '89.

6312 **Gertzman, Jay A.** A descriptive bibliography of Lady Chatterley's lover; with essays towards a publishing history of the novel. Westport, Conn., Greenwood pr., [1989]. xiii,296p. facsims. 23cm. (Bibs & Indexes in World Lit, 23).
Introd. essays and bibliogr. descriptions, with note of copies examined, for 1st ed. and autho-rized impressions, piracies, etc., 1928–50; authorized abridged ed., 1932–68; continental ed. in England, 1933–60; post-censorship U.S. ed., 1959–88; post-censorship British ed., 1960–88; The First Lady Chatterley, 1944–88; John Thomas and lady Jane, 1972–88.

6313 **Worthen, John.** Catalogue of the papers of Louie Burrows relating to D.H. Lawrence. (New materials in the biography of D.H. Lawrence, 2). D.H. Lawrence R 21no1:47–53 '89. port., facsim.

6314 (7:4994f) **Cox and Wyman, ltd.** The production of Lady Chatterley's lover. [Ptg.]. Penguin Collectors' Soc Newsl 2n04:54–8 D '76.

6315 (7:4998) **Ross, Charles L.** The composition of The rainbow and Women in love, [1979].
Rev: J.C.F. Littlewood Essays in Crit 32:191–4 '82; J. Worthen N&Q 227:263–5 '82.

6316 **Crumpton, Philip**. D.H. Lawrence's 'mauled history'; the Irish edition of Movements in European history. [1926]. D.H. Lawrence R 13n02:105–18 '80.

6317 **Partlow, Robert B.** and **H.T. Moore**, *ed.* D.H. Lawrence, the man who lived; papers delivered at the D.H. Lawrence conference at Southern Illinois university, Carbondale, April, 1979. Carbondale, Southern Illinois U.P., [1980]. xviii,302p. illus. 23cm.
Includes The Lawrence estate, Gerald Pollinger.–The works of D.H. Lawrence: the Cambridge edition, Michael H. Black.–Problems in editing D.H. Lawrence, Warren Roberts.–Editing Lady Chatterley's lover, Michael Squire.–The Cambridge university edition of Lawrence's letters, part 4, James T. Boulton.–The case for an edition of The letters of D.H. Lawrence, Gerald M. Lacy.–Editing Lawrence's letters: the strategy of volume division, George J. Zytaruk.–The Cambridge university press edition of The letters of D.H. Lawrence: sources for the edition, David Farmer.

6318 **Ruderman, Judith G.** Tracking Lawrence's Fox; an account of its composition, evolution, and publication. Stud Bib 33:206–21 '80.

6319 —— The 'trilogy' that never was; The rainbow, Women in love and Aaron's rod. [Publ.]. (Bibliographical notes). Pa Bib Soc Am 74n01:76–80 '80.

6320 **Steele, Bruce**. The manuscript of D.H. Lawrence's Saga of Siegmund. [= The trespasser, 1912]. Stud Bib 33:193–205 '80. table.

6321 **Vitoux, Pierre**. Women in love; from typescripts into print. Texas Stud Lit & Lang 23n04:577–93 '81.

6322 **Finney, Brian H.** Aspects of copyright. [And Lawrence]. (To the editor.). TLS 17 S '82:1000; M. Le Fanu 17 S '82:1000; C. Middleton Murry; E. Mendelson; E. Delavenay 24 S '82:1036.

6323 **Holroyd, Michael** and **Sandra Jobson.** Copyrights and wrongs: D.H. Lawrence. TLS 3 S '82:943–4.

6324 **Sagar, Keith M.** The Cambridge Lawrence. [To the editor]. TLS 8 Oc '82:1102.

6325 **Saunders, David**. The trial of Lady Chatterley's lover; limiting cases and literary canons. [Censorship]. Sthn R (Adelaide) 15n02:161–77 Jl '82.

6326   **Holroyd, John**. D.H. Lawrence and Australia. [Publ.]. Bib Soc Aust &
N.Z. Bull 7no4:178–9 '83.

6327   **Steele, Bruce**. The Bancroft library typescript of D.H. Lawrence's
Study of Thomas Hardy. Bib Soc Aust & N.Z. Bull 7no4:143–50 '83.

6328   **Templeton, Wayne**. The Sons and lovers manuscript. Stud Bib 37:234–
43 '84. table.

6329   **Wade, Graham**. D.H. Lawrence. [Collecting]. Bk & Mag Coll 10:4–
12 D '84. ports., illus., facsims.
   'Complete bibliography of D.H. Lawrence U.K. 1st editions' (p.11–12).

6330   **Baron, Helen V.** Sons and lovers; the surviving manuscripts from three
drafts dated by paper analysis. Stud Bib 38:289–328 '85. tables.
   The paper research.–The composition stages.–Jessie Chambers and stage II.–Stage
   IIIa: the start.–Stage IIIa: the completion.–The remains of stage IIIa.–The remains
   of stage IIIb.–Edward Garnett's notes on stage IIIb.–The survival of the manuscripts.–
   Table 1: the paper.–Table 2: the mss.

6331   **Caffrey, Raymond T.** Lady Chatterley's lover; the Grove press publication of the unexpurgated text. Courier (Syracuse) 20no1:49–79
'85. illus.

6332   **Mehl, Dieter**. Editing a 'constantly revising author'; The tales of Henry
James (Oxford) and The works of D.H. Lawrence (Cambridge).
Archiv 222no1:128–36 '85.

6333   **Munro, Craig**. 'Lady Chatterley in London; the secret third edition
[1929]' *in* Squire, Michael and D. Jackson, *ed.* D.H. Lawrence's Lady;
a new look at Lady Chatterley's lover. Athens, University of Georgia
pr., [1985]. p.222–35. port.

6334   **Nottingham. University. Library.** D.H. Lawrence; a life in literature:
catalogue of the centenary exhibition held in the University of Nottingham, 7 September–13 October, 1985. Ed. by Alan Cameron.
[Nottingham], Nottingham university library, [1985]. ix,61p. illus.,
port., facsims. 24cm.

6335   **Pollinger, Gerald J.** 'Lady Chatterley's lover; a view from Lawrence's
literary executor [L.E. Pollinger]' *in* Squire, Michael and D. Jackson, *ed.* D.H. Lawrence's Lady; a new look at Lady Chatterley's lover.
Athens, University of Georgia pr., [1985]. p.236–41.

6336   **Rota, Anthony**. D.H. Lawrence; the George Lazarus collection of
books and manuscripts. Renaiss & Mod Stud 29:101–19 '85.
   2. Manuscripts.–3. Letters.–4. Printed books.–5. Books and other material about
   Lawrence.–6. Foreign language editions.–7. Miscellanea.

6337 **Cushman, Keith**. D.H. Lawrence in Chapala; an unpublished letter to Thomas Seltzer and its context. [Publ.]. (Notes). D.H. Lawrence R 18no1:25–31 '85/6.

6338 **Black, Michael H.** 'Editing a constantly-revising author; the Cambridge edition of Lawrence in historical context' *in* Kalnins, Mara, *ed.* D.H. Lawrence; centenary essays. [Bristol], Bristol classical pr., [1986]. p.191–210.

6339 **Roberts, Warren E.** D.H. Lawrence at Texas; a memoir. [Colln.]. Libr Chron Univ Texas new ser 34:22–37 '86. ports.

6340 **Worthen, John**. Reading Women in Love. D.H. Lawrence Soc J 4no1:5–12 '86.

6341 **Gertzman, Jay A.** The piracies of Lady Chatterley's lover, 1928–1950. D.H. Lawrence R 19no3:267–99 '87. facsims.
Importation.–Domestic distribution.–Bibliographical descriptions of piracies.

6342 **Kay, Wallace G.** Two printer's errors in Sons and lovers. (Notes). D.H. Lawrence R 19no2:185–7 '87.

6343 **Saxena, H.S.** 'A study of the facsimile of the manuscript of Sons and lovers [and censorship]' *in* Sharma, T.R., *ed.* Essays on D.H. Lawrence. Meerut, India, Shalabh book house, [1987]. p.[79]–88.

6344 **Eggert, Paul**. The literary work of a readership: The Boy in the bush in Australia, 1924–1926. Bib Soc Aust & N.Z. Bull 12no2:146–66 '88 [i.e. Je '90].

6345 —— The reviewing of the Cambridge edition of Women in Love. [Text]. (Notes). D.H. Lawrence R 20no3:297–303 '88.

6346 **Gouirand, Jacqueline**. Les chemins de l'écriture; les chapitres 'Man to man' et 'Gladitorial', des avant-textes à la version finale de Women in love. [Revision]. Étud Lawrenciennes 3:79–97 My '88.

6347 **Jackson, Dennis** and **Lydia Blanchard.** Mr. Noon's critical reception, 1984–1988. D.H. Lawrence R 20no2:133–52 '88.
'Bibliography of writings on Mr. Noon, 1984–88' (p.150–2).

6348 **Vasey, Lindeth** and **J. Worthen.** *Mr Noon*/Mr Noon. [Additions, etc. to Cambridge ed.]. D.H. Lawrence R 20no2:179–89 '88. facsims.

6349 **Scott, James B.** The Norton distortion; a dangerous typo in 'The rockinghorse winner'. (Notes). D.H. Lawrence R 21no2:175–7 '89.

6350 **Whitehouse, Carol S.** D.H. Lawrence's The first lady Chatterley; conservation treatment of a twentieth-century bound manuscript. Libr Chron Univ Texas new ser 44/5:40–55 '89. facsim., illus.

LAWRENCE, THOMAS EDWARD, afterwards SHAW, 1888–1935

6351 **[Simmons, John S.G.].** T.E. Lawrence; a modest exhibition in the Codrington library, All souls college, Oxford, 21–23 October 1981. Oxford, Codrington library, All souls college, 1981. [12]p. 21cm. (Reprod. from typescript). Ltd. to 66 copies.

6352 **Tabachnik, Stephen E.**, *ed.* 'The T.E. Lawrence revival, 1969–1983; a selected bibliography' *in* The T.E. Lawrence puzzle. Athens, University of Georgia pr., 1984. p.[313]–21. facsims., illus.

6353 **Meyers, Jeffrey.** Imaginative portraits of T.E. Lawrence. [Works based on his life]. Bull Bib 45no1:15–16 Mr '88.

6354 **O'Brien, Philip M.** T.E. Lawrence; a bibliography. Winchester, St. Paul's bibliographies; Boston, Mass., G.K. Hall, [1988]. xii,724p. facsims. 23cm.
   Bibliogr. of books, prefaces; introds., translations, etc. by; newspaper articles by; incidental works containing writings of, with North American locations only; and works about.
   Rev: A.J. Flavell Library ser6 12:67–72 '90.

6355 **Oxford. University. Bodleian library.** T.E. Lawrence, the legend and the man; an exhibition...12 September to 26 November 1988 to mark the centenay of the birth of Thomas Edward Lawrence, Lawrence of Arabia. [Comp. by A.J. Flavell]. Oxford, 1988. 112p. ports., facsims. 19cm.

6356 **Grosvenor, Charles.** 'The subscribers' Seven pillars of wisdom; the visual aspect [1926]' *in* Tabachnik, Stephen E., *ed.* The T.E. Lawrence puzzle. Athens, University of Georgia pr., 1984. p.[159]–84. facsims., illus.

6357 **Richards, Vyvyan W.** T.E. Lawrence, book designer; his friendship with Vyvyan Richards. [Wakefield], Fleece pr., [1985]. 20p. illus., port. 20cm. (Ltd. to 250 copies).
   Repr. from T.E. Lawrence, by his friends. Ed. by A.W. Lawrence. (London, 1937), p. [381]–92.

6358 **Wilson, Jean M.** T.E. Lawrence and the printing of Seven pillars of wisdom. Matrix 5:55–69 '85. illus.

6359 **Thompson, V.M.** 'Not a suitable hobby for an airman'; T.E. Lawrence as publisher. [Oxford], Orchard books, [1986]. xii, 173p. illus., port. 21cm.

LEAR, EDWARD, 1812–88

6360 (7:5009*) **Sibley, Brian**. Leaves from the Leary paperbackins. [With checklist]. Penguin Collectors' Soc Newsl 11:2–4 N '78.

6361 **Noakes, Vivien**, *ed.* 'Bibliographies' *in* Edward Lear, 1812–1888; catalogue. London, Royal academy of arts in association with W. Weidenfeld and Nicolson, 1985. p.207–11.

> Ornithology and natural history, comp. by R.D. Wise. I. Books illustrated by Lear. II. Books to which Lear contributed. III. Books with illustrations copied from Lear's plates. IV. Birds named after Lear.–Travel books.–Nonsense. Comp. by Justin G. Schiller [and others].–Exhibitions.

6362 **Schiller, Justin G.**, *ed.* 'A book of nonsense; census of the 1846 first edition' *in* Nonsensus; cross-referencing Edward Lear's original 116 limericks with eight holograph manuscripts.... New Castle, Del., Oak Knoll books; Stroud, Catalpa pr., 1988. p.118–19.

6363 **Hearn, Michael P.** How pleasant it is to know mr. Lear? Am Bk Coll new ser 7no1:21–7 Ja '86. facsims.

6364 **Gallup, Donald C.** Collecting Edward Lear. Yale Univ Libr Gaz 61no3/4:125–42 Ap '87. facsims.

LEAVIS, FRANK RAYMOND, 1895–1978

6365 **Baker, William**. F.R. Leavis, 1965–1979, & Q.D. Leavis, 1922–1979; a bibliography of writings by and about them. Bull Bib 37no4:185–208 Oc/D '80.

6366 **Diaz Fernández, José R.** F.R. Leavis; bibliografía de sus estudios críticos. R Alicantina Estudios Ingleses 2:175–202 N '89.
> *Abstract in English* (p.175).

6367 **Kinch, M.B.,W. Baker** and **J. Kimber**. F.R. Leavis and Q.D. Leavis; an annotated bibliography. New York, Garland, 1989. xxiii,531p. 20cm. (Bibs Mod Critics & Critical Schools, 12).

LE CARRÉ, JOHN, *pseud. of* DAVID JOHN MOORE CORNEALL, 1931–

6368 **Lewis, Peter**. 'Bibliography [of novels, short stories, miscellaneous non-fiction, letters to the press, major interviews, and criticism about]' *in* John le Carré. New York, F. Ungar, [1985]. p.219–21.

LEE, VERNON, *pseud. of* VIOLET PAGET, 1856–1935

6369   **Manocchi, Phillis F.** Vernon Lee; a reintroduction and primary bibliography. Eng Lit Transit 26no4:231–67 '83.
Classif. checklist of books, eds. of, pamphlets, papers by, contribs., articles by, letters to the editor, and mss.

6370   **Markgraf, Carl**. Vernon Lee; a commentary and an annotated bibliography of writings about her. Eng Lit Transit 26no4:268–312 '83.

LEECH, JOHN, 1817–64

6371   **Houfe, Simon**. 'Bibliography of John Leech' *in* John Leech and the Victorian scene. Woodbridge, 1984. p.245–60.
Chronol. annotated checklist, 1835–69, based on S.K. Wilson's catalogue, 1914.

LEFANU, JOSEPH SHERIDAN, 1814–73

6372   **Melada, Ivan**. 'Selected bibliography [of primary and secondary sources]' *in* Sheridan Le Fanu. (Twayne's English authors, 438). Boston, [Mass.], Twayne, [1987]. p.136–9.

6373   **Gates, David**. An addition to the Le Fanu bibliography. ['Modern novel and romance', 1863]. N&Q 229no4:491 D '84.

6374   **Hall, Wayne**. Le Fanu's house by the marketplace. [As ed. of Dublin university magazine]. Éire 21no1:55–72 '86.

LEICESTER, ROBERT, EARL OF, 1532?–88 *see* DUDLEY, ROBERT, EARL OF LEICESTER, 1532?–88.

LELAND, JOHN, 1506?–52.

6375   **Carley, James P.** The manuscript remains of John Leland, 'The king's antiquary'. Text 2:111–20 '85.
'Principal manuscripts (autograph & early copies)' (p.115).

LEONARD, TOM, 1944–

6376   **Bibliography** of works by Tom Leonard. Edinburgh R 77:72–3 '87.

LEVERSON, ADA ESTHER (BEDDINGTON), 1862–1933

6377 **Speedie, Julie**. The sphinx of modern life; Ada Leverson, 1862–1933.
Antiqu Bk Mnthly R 15no1:8–15 Ja '88. ports., facsim.
'[Bibliography]: Books by Ada Leverson; contributions to books; books about...'
(p.15).

LEWIS, CECIL DAY-, 1904–72

6378 **Gunn, Katharine**. The detective novels of Nicholas Blake. [Collect-
ing]. Bk & Mag Coll 20:12–18 Oc '85. port., facsims.
'Nicholas Blake: complete UK bibliography' (p.18).

LEWIS, CLIVE STAPLES, 1898–1963

6379 **Christopher, Joe R.** Letters from C.S. Lewis in the Humanities research center, the University of Texas at Austin; a checklist. CSL
New York C.S. Lewis Soc Bull 12no1:1–7 N '80.

6380 **New York C.S. Lewis society**. Bibliography of the works of C.S. Lewis.
[New Haven, Conn.], [1980]. 10p. 28cm. Headtitle. (Duplicated
typescript).

6381 **Thorson, Stephen** and **J. Daniel**. Bibliographic notes. [Supplement-
ing Hooper, 1979: BLB 1970–79: 5027]. CSL New York C.S. Lewis
Soc Bull 17no9:5–6 Jl '86; 17no10:6–8 Ag '86; 18no1:15–18 N '86;
18no2:6–7 D '86; 18no5:6–7 Mr '87.

6382 **Christopher, Joe R.** 'Selected bibliography [of primary and secondary sources]' *in* C.S. Lewis. (Twayne's English authors, 442). Boston,
Twayne, 1987. p.136–44.

6383 **Schildroth, Lisa**. An annotated bibliography of criticism of C.S. Lewis's
Chronicles of Narnia. CSL New York C.S. Lewis Soc Bull 18no9:1–6
Jl '87; 18no10:1–5 Ag '87.

6384 **Como, James T.** The Screwtape letters; a description of the manu-
script in the Berg collection of the New York public library. CSL
New York C.S. Lewis Soc Bull 11no12:2–8 '80.
General characteristics.–Particular characteristics.–Emendations [List of variants].

6385 **Murdoch, Brian**. C.S. Lewis. [Collecting]. Bk & Mag Coll 13:22–9 Mr
'85. ports., facsims.
'C.S. Lewis bibliography' (p.29).

LEWIS, MATTHEW GREGORY, 1775–1818

6386 **Levy, Maurice**. Matthew G. Lewis, The monk: bibliographie sélective et critique. Soc d'Étud Anglo-Am Bull 21:69–83 N '85.

6387 **Carnochan, W.B.** and **D.W. Donaldson**. The presentation copy of Monk Lewis's Oberon's henchman, 1803. [Ms.]. Bk Coll 30no3:346–59 '81. facsims.

6388 **Edwards, Rosa**. James Edwards, Giambattista Bodoni, and The castle of Otranto: some unpublished letters. Publ Hist 18:5–48 '85.

LEWIS, PERCY WYNDHAM, 1882–1957

6389 (7:5034) **Pound, Omar S.** and **P. Grover**. Wyndham Lewis; a descriptive bibliography, [1978].
Rev: T. Materer Paideuma 8:353–6 '79.

6390 (7:5033) **Morrow, Bradford** and **B. Lafourcade**. A bibliography of the writings of Wyndham Lewis, 1979.
Rev: T. Materer Paideuma 8:353–6 '79.

6391 **Meyers, Jeffrey**. Wyndham Lewis, a bibliography of criticism, 1912–1980. Bull Bib 37no1:33–52 Ja/Mr '80.

6392 **Davies, Alastair**, [1982]: no.704.

6393 **Fox, C.J.** 'The enemy' in his books; a Wyndham Lewis collection. [From libr. of mrs. Lewis]. Libr Chron Univ Texas new ser 14:14–21 '80. port.

LINDSAY, DAVID, 1876–1945

6394 **Sellin, Bernard**. 'Bibliography [of works, letters, and criticism of]' *in* The life and works of David Lindsay. Cambridge, C.U.P., [1981]. p.249–50.

LINGARD, JOHN, 1771–1851

6395 **Chinnici, Joseph P.** 'Bibliography [of primary and secondary sources]' *in* English Catholic enlightenment; John Lingard and the Cisalpine movement, 1780–1850. Shepherdstown, Patmos pr., 1980. p.[225]–50.

LISTER, MARTIN, 1638?–1712

6396 **Keynes, sir Geoffrey L.** Dr. Martin Lister; a bibliography. [Godalming, Sy.], St. Paul's bibliographies, 1981. xii,52p. facsims. 21cm. ([St. Paul's Bibs, 3]). (Ltd. to 350 copies).
Partly repr. from BLB 1970–79: 5046.
Rev: T. Hofmann Bk Coll 31:247–51 '82.

6397 **Jefcoate, Graham P.** Addendum to Keynes's bibliography of Lister. (Note 446). Bk Coll 31n04:506 '82; [same] (Note 459) 33n04:527 '84.

LIVINGSTONE, DAVID, 1813–73

6398 **Clendennen, Gary W.** Livingstone's second book. [Analysis of the language of the Bechuanas, 1858]. Biblioth 10n01:10–19 '80.
'Appendix: the twenty-five copies of the Analysis' (p.16–18).

6399 —— Who wrote Livingstone's Narrative? Biblioth 16n01/3:30–9 '89.

LOCKE, JOHN, 1632–1704

6400 **Hall, Roland** and **R. Woolhouse**. 80 years of Locke scholarship; a bibliographical guide. Edinburgh, U.P., [1983]. x,215p. 20cm.
Rev: J.W. Oliver Stud Scot Lit 17:296–7 '82; G. Kemerling Analytical & Enum Bib ?:42–4 '84.

6401 **Bots, Hans.** 'Jean Leclerc as journalist of the Bibliothèques; his contribution to the spread of English learning on the European continent' *in* Janssens, G.A.M. and F.G.A.M. Aarts, *ed.* Studies in seventeenth-century literature, history and bibliography; festschrift for professor T.A. Birrell on the occasion of his sixtieth birthday. (Costerus new ser 46). Amsterdam, Rodopi, 1984. p.[53]–66.
'a list of all the works that relate to John Locke and that were reviewed in the three Bibliothèques' (p.63–4): *12 items in* Bibliothèque universelle, Bibliothèque choisie, *and* Bibliothèque ancienne.

6402 **Attig, John C.** The works of John Locke; a comprehensive bibliography from the seventeenth century to the present. Westport, Conn., Greenwood pr., [1985]. xx,185p. 24cm. (Bibs & Indexes Philos 1).
Rev: Jean S. Yolton Library ser6 8:381–2 '86.

6403 (5:12030e) **Fitch, Donald E.** Milton from Locke's library. [Complete collection, 1698]. (Briefer notes). Soundings (UCLA, Santa Barbara) 1n01:32–4 My '69.

6404 **Yolton, Jean S.** The first editions of John Locke's Some thoughts concerning education. (Bibliographical notes). Pa Bib Soc Am 75no3:315–21 '81. table.

6405 **Printed** books; English books before 1700. [i.e., books from Locke's libr.]. (Notable accessions). Bodleian Libr Rec 10no6:376–82 My '82.

LOCKHART, JOHN GIBSON, 1794–1854

6406 **Mack, Douglas S.** Hogg, Lockhart, and Familiar anecdotes of sir Walter Scott. Scott Lit J 10no1:5–13 '83.

LODGE, THOMAS, 1558?–1625

6407 (5:12043f) **Hayashi, Tetsumaro.** A textual study of A looking glasse for London by Thomas Lodge and Robert Greene. Muncie, Ind., Ball state university, 1969. ix,38p. facsim. 23cm. (Ball state Monogr 17 Publs Eng, 11).
1. Authorship.–2. Date of composition.–3. Collaboration between Thoms Lodge and Robert Greene.–4. Type of work and literary background.–5. Sources.–6. Bibliographical descriptions of early editions.–7. Bibliographical analysis of early editions.

6408 **Addison, James C.** A textual error in Thomas Lodge's A margarite of America, 1596. (Bibliographical notes). Library ser6 3no2:142–3 Je '81.

LOWRY, CLARENCE MALCOLM, 1909–57

6409 **Maurey, Pierre.** Lowry's library; an annotated catalogue of Lowry's books at the University of British Columbia. Malcolm Lowry Newsl 7:3–10 '80.

6410 **Yandle, Anne.** Bibliography. Malcolm Lowry Newsl 7:22–5 '80; 9:35–8 '81; 11/13:21–3,31–8 '82/3; 17/18:145–50 '85/6.

––––––––––

6411 **Doyle, Margaret E.** Malcolm Lowry's library. Malcolm Lowry Newsl 9:23–31 '81.

6412 **Tiessen, Paul.** The composition of Under the volcano; graphic evidence. Malcolm Lowry Newsl 13:10–11 '83.

6413 **Yandle, Anne** and **Grace Sherrill.** Guide to the William Templeton collection at UBC library. Malcolm Lowry Newsl 13:8–10 '83.

6414 **Thomas, Mark**. Redgrave as Lowry's editor. Malcolm Lowry Newsl 17/18:54 '85/86.

LUBBOCK, JOSEPH GUY, fl.1967–83

6415 **Mason, Roger B.** The illuminated book today; the books of J.G. Lubbock. Albion 8no2:[12–13] '84.
'A checklist of books by J.G. Lubbock': *7 titles, 1967–83.*

LUCAS, EDWARD VERRALL, 1868–1938

6416 **Prance, Claude A.** E.V. Lucas and his books. West Cornwall, Conn., Locust Hill pr., 1988. xxvi,243p. 21cm.
Chronol. list of books and pamphlets, some contribs. to periodicals, selected works about, some books reprinting his work, and alphabetical lists of books and pamphlets, books ed., selected, or introd. by; essays, sketches, and short stories; verses by; and selected subjects and genres covered by his books and essays. Appendices include '3. Illustrators of E.V. Lucas's books' (p.241–3). *Not indexed.*
Rev: Mary Wedd Charles Lamb Bull 67:103–5 '89.

LYDGATE, JOHN, 1370?–1451?

6417 **Ebin, Lois A.** 'Selected bibliography [of primary and secondary sources]' *in* John Lydgate. (Twayne's English authors, 407). Boston, Twayne, [1985]. p.155–9.

6418 **Edwards, Anthony S.G.** Additions and corrections to the bibliography of John Lydgate. N&Q 230no4:450–2 D '85.

———

6419 **Edwards, Anthony S.G.** 'Lydgate manuscripts: some directions for further research' *in* Pearsall, Derek A., *ed.* Manuscripts and readers in fifteenth-century England. [Cambridge], 1983. p.[15]–26.

6420 **Lawton, Lesley**. 'The illustration of late medieval secular texts, with special reference to Lydgate's Troy book' *in* Pearsall, Derek A., *ed.* Manuscripts and readers in fifteenth-century England. [Cambridge], 1983. p.[41]–69. facsims., table.

6421 **Vowles, Margaret S.** The Fall of princes; an 18th copy. (Note 451). Bk Coll 32no2:228 '83.

6422 **Blake, Norman F.** John Lydgate and William Caxton. [And patronage]. Leeds Stud Eng new ser 16:272–89 '85.

6423 **Horrall, Sarah M.** Lydgate's 'Verses on the kings of England'; a new
manuscript. [At Hatfield house]. N&Q 233no4:441 D '88.

LYLY, JOHN, 1554?–1606

6424 **[Harner, James L.].** Two bibliographies: John Lyly. Eng Renaiss Prose
3no1:40–50 Oc '89.

————————————

6425 **Bevington, David M.** The first edition of John Lyly's Sappho and
Phao, 1584. Stud Bib 42:187–99 '89.

LYONS, ALBERT MICHAEL NEIL, 1880–1940

6426 **Richardson, Alan.** A note on A. Neil Lyons, 1880–1940. Eng Lit Transit
23no4:208–14 '80. port.
'Neil Lyons; a checklist' (p. 212–14).

LYTTON, EDWARD GEORGE EARLE LYTTON BULWER-, 1ST
BARON LYTTON, 1803–73

6427 **Campbell, James L.** 'Selected bibliography [of primary and secondary sources]' *in* Sir Edward Bulwer-Lytton. (Twayne's English authors, 420). Boston, Twayne, [1987]. p.144–51.

MACAULAY, THOMAS BABINGTON, 1ST BARON MACAULAY,
1800–59

6428 **Pinney, Thomas**, *ed.* 'List of Macaulay's published writings' *in* The
letters of Thomas Babington Macaulay. Volume 6. Cambridge, C.U.P.,
1981. p.289–302.
Classified checklist of juvenilia, essays, history, speeches, minutes and other official papers,
verses, miscellaneous, and attributed writings.

————————————

6429 **Gray, Donald J.** 'Macaulay's Lays of ancient Rome and the publication of nineteenth-century poetry' *in* Kincaid, James R. and A.J. Kuhn,
ed. Victorian literature and society; essays presented to Richard D.
Altick. [Columbus], Ohio state U.P., [1984]. p.73–93.

MACDIARMID, HUGH, *pseud. of* CHRISTOPHER MURRAY
GRIEVE, 1892–1978

6430 **Hall, John T.D.** Hugh MacDiarmid, author and publisher. Stud Scott
Lit 21:53–88 '86.

MACDONAGH, TERENCE, fl.1936–57

6431 **Checklist** of published works and contribs. to. Donegal Hist Soc J 4no1:[ii–iii] '58.

MACDONAGH, THOMAS, 1878–1916

6432 **Norstedt, Johann A.** 'B. Previously published portions of Literature in Ireland' and 'C. Thomas MacDonagh's contributions to the Irish review' *in* Thomas MacDonagh; a critical biography. Charlottesville, U.P. of Virginia, [1980]. p.154–5.

MACDONALD, GEORGE, 1824–1905

6433 **Stewart, Seumas**. My Macdonald collection. Antiqu Bk Mnthly R 9no5:220–1 Je '82. port., illus.

MACHEN, ARTHUR LLEWELYN JONES, 1863–1947

6434 **Dobson, Roger**. Arthur Machen, the wizard from Gwent. Antiqu Bk Mnthly R 12no7:268–73 Jl '85.
'Checklist of Machen's major works' (p.273).

MACKENZIE, HENRY, 1745–1831

6435 **Pitcher, Edward W.** Henry Mackenzie and the essays signed 'Z' in the Westminster magazine, 1773–1785. [With list]. (Bibliographical notes). Library ser6 4no4:415–17 D '82.

MACKENZIE, SIR EDWARD MONTAGUE COMPTON, 1883–1972

6436 **Thomas, David A.** and **Joyce Thomas.** Compton Mackenzie; a bibliography. London, Mansell, [1986]. x,309p. 22cm.
Bibliogr. of works entirely by, forewords and contribs. to other books, contribs. to press and periodicals, radio broadcasts, television broadcasts, books and articles about, and reprints and anthologies. Rev: A.S. Bell TLS 16 Ja '87:71.

6437 **Thomas, David A.** Sir Compton Mackenzie. [Collecting]. Bk & Mag Coll 22:28–35 D '85. port., facsims.
'Complete UK bibliography of sir Compton Mackenzie (p.34–5).

MACLAURIN, COLIN 1648–1746

6438   **Mills, Stella**, *ed.* 'Bibliography' and 'Manuscript source list' *in* The collected letters of Colin MacLaurin. Nantwich, Shiva, 1982. p.469–78.

MACLEAN, ALISTAIR, 1921–

6439   **The adventure** stories of Alistair Maclean. [Collecting]. Bk & Mag Coll 21:4–11 N '85. illus., port., facsims.
'Complete bibliography of Alistair Maclean's 1st editions' (p.11).

6440   **DeGategno, Paul J.** 'Selected bibliography [of primary and secondary sources]' *in* James Macpherson. (Twayne's English authors, 467). Boston, [Mass.], Twayne, [1989]. p.158–65.

MAINWARING, ARTHUR, 1668–1712

6441   **Harris, Frances**. For Arthur read Author. [Queries, 1710]. (Features). Factotum 10:14–16 D '80.

6442   —— Robert Walpole, Arthur Maynwaring, and the Letter to a friend concerning the publick debts. [1711]. (Features). Factotum 11:22–3 Ap '81.

MALORY, SIR THOMAS, d.1471

6443   **Life, Page W.** Sir Thomas Malory and the Morte darthur; a survey of scholarship and annotated bibliography. Charlottesville, Publ. for the Bibliographical society of the University of Virginia by the U.P. of Virginia, [1980]. xiii,297p. 21cm.
Rev: B. Gaines Sth Atlantic R 46:109–12 '81; P. Brown Library ser6 3:248–9 '81.

6444   **Takamiya, Toshiyuki**, *comp.* 'A bibliography to Aspects of Malory' *in* Takamiya, Toshiyuki and D.S. Brewer, *ed.* Aspects of Malory. (Arthurian Stud 1). [Cambridge], D.S. Brewer; [Totowa, N.J.], Rowman & Littlefield, [1981]. p.179–86.

———————

6445   **Hellinga, Lotte**. Two Malory facsimiles. [Review]. Library ser6 2no1:92–8 Mr '80.

6446   **Takamiya, Toshiyuki** and **D.S. Brewer**, *ed.* Aspects of Malory. [Cambridge], D.S.Brewer; [Totowa, N.J.], Rowman & Littlefield, [1981]. x,232p. illus., facsims. 21cm. (Arthurian Stud, 1).

Includes 9. The Malory manuscript and Caxton, Lotte Helinga.–10. The early history of the Malory manuscript, W. Hilton Kelliher.–11. The authorship question reconsidered, Richard R. Griffin.–A bibliography to Aspects of Malory, Toshiyuki Takamiya.

6447 **La Farge, Catherine**. Two suggested emendations in Malory. N&Q 227no1:14 F '82.

6448 **Evans, Murray J.** The two scribes in the Winchester ms.; the ninth explicit and Malory's 'hoole book'. Manuscripta 27no1:38–44 Mr '83. table.

6449 **Goodman, Jennifer R.** 'Malory and Caxton's chivalric series, 1481–85' *in* Spisak, James W., *ed.* Studies in Malory. Kalamazoo, Mich., Medieval institute publs., Western Michigan university, 1985. p.257–74.

6450 **Meale, Carol M.** Manuscripts, readers, and patrons in fifteenth-century England: Sir Thomas Malory and Arthurian romance. Arthurian Lit 4:93–126 '85.

6451 **Whitaker, Muriel A.I.** 'Illustrating Caxton's Malory' *in* Spisak, James W., *ed.* Studies in Malory. Kalamazoo, Mich., Medieval institute publs., Western Michigan university, 1985. p.297–319 + 6l. illus.

6452 **Fries, Maureen**. 500 years of Caxton's Malory; a celebration of the Morte darthur. Avalon to Camelot 2no2:11–14 '86. illus.

6453 **Lumiansky, R.M.** A different view of the Winchester manuscript of sir Thomas Malory's Le morte darthur. [Ptg.]. N&Q 232no2:153–4 Je '87.

6454 —— Sir Thomas Malory's Le morte darthur, 1947–1987: author, title, text. Speculum 62no4:878–97 Oc '87.
The author.–The title.–The text.

6455 **Moorman, Charles**. Caxton's Morte darthur; Malory's second edition. [Revision]. Fift Cent Stud 12:99–113 '87.

6456 **Lumiansky, R.M.** 'Concerning three names in Le morte darthur: 'Roome', 'The Welsh kyng', and 'Chastelayne', and Malory's possible revision of his book' *in* Kennedy, Edward D. [and others], *ed.* Medieval English studies presented to George Kane. [Woodbridge], D.S. Brewer, [1988]. p.301–8.

6457 **Parins, Marilyn J.** 'Malory's expurgators' *in* Braswell, Mary F. and J. Bugge, *ed.* The Arthurian tradition; essays in convergence. Tuscaloosa, University of Alabama pr., [1988]. p.144–62.

MALTHUS, THOMAS ROBERT, 1766–1834

6458 **Gray, Edward**, *ed.* The Malthus library catalogue; the personal collection of Thomas Robert Malthus of Jesus college, Cambridge; with

invited contributions by John Harrison, Ryotaro Minami, Patricia
James, William Petersen, John Pullen.... [Elmsford, N.Y.], Pergamon pr., [1983]. lxii,232p. 23cm.

'Supplementary list of books published before 1835 registered in the Dalton Hill
catalogue but not forming part of Jesus college collection' (p.189–205).

MANDEVILLE, BERNARD, 1670?–1733

6459 **Wood, Michael B.** Bernard Mandeville; sources, 1924–1979. Bull Bib
40no2:103–7 Je '83.

MANLEY, DE LA RIVIÈRE, 1663–1724

6460 **[Harris, Frances]**. Sunderland v. Manley. [The new Atlantis, 1709].
(Features). Factotum 21:22–3 D '85.

MANLEY, SIR ROGER, 1626?–88

6461 **Köster, Patricia**. The correspondence of sir Roger Manley. Bull Bib
42no4:179–86 D '85. facsim.

MANNING, OLIVIA, 1908?–80

6462 **Martin, Gyde C.** Olivia Manning, a bibliography. Bull Bib 46no3:160–
72 S '89.

MANSFIELD, KATHERINE, *pseud. of* KATHLEEN (BEAUCHAMP) MURRY, 1888–1923

6463 **Gabel, Gernot U.** Canadian theses on Katherine Mansfield, 1941–
1979. (Notes bibliographic). Bull Bib 43no2:124–5 Je '86.

6464 **Alexander Turnbull library,** WELLINGTON, N.Z. Katherine Mansfield;
manuscripts in the Alexander Turnbull library. Wellington, Alexander Turnbull library, National library of New Zealand, 1988.
xii,136p.illus., ports., facsims. 27cm.

6465 **Kirkpatrick, Brownlee J.** A bibliography of Katherine Mansfield. Oxford, Clarendon pr., 1989. xxviii,396p. port., facsims. 21cm. (Soho Bibs).

*Bibliogr. of books and pamphlets, contribs. to books and books trans. by, contribs. to periodicals
and newspapers, selections, translations of, foreign ed. in English, educational and shorthand
ed., large print etc. ed., extracts, reported speech, music, stage and film scripts, recorded sound,
radio and TV productions, ballet etc. productions, films, and mss.*
Rev: S. Hills TLS 10 Ag '90:858; J.G. Watson N&Q 38:552–3 '91.

6466 **Alpers, Antony**. ...and Mansfield. [Editing]. (Letters). TLS 12 Ag '88:883; Cherry Hankin 9 S '88:989.

6467 **Brown, Sally**. 'Hundreds of selves'; the British library's Katherine Mansfield letters. Brit Libr J 14no2:154–64 '88. port., facsim.

MARLOWE, CHRISTOPHER, 1564–93

6468 **Levao, Ronald**. Recent studies in Marlowe, 1977–1986. (Recent studies in the English renaissance). Eng Lit Renaiss 18no2:329–42 '88.

———

6469 **Allen, Michael J.** Doctor Faustus; the old man and the text. Eng Lit Renaiss 11no2:111–47 '81.

6470 **Covella, Francis D.** The choral nexus in Doctor Faustus. [Text]. Stud Eng Lit 26no2:201–15 '86.
'Appendix: Outline of a hypothetical version of Marlowe's original Doctor Faustus based on the 1604 A-text ... (p.213–15).

6471 **Daalder, Joost** and **G. Harris**. Doctor Faustus and the colossus of Rhodes. [Text]. Bib Soc Aust & N.Z. Bull 10no4:113–19 '86.

6472 **Ronan, Clifford**. Pharsalia 1.373–378; Roman parricale and Marlowe's editors. [Text]. Classical & Mod Lit 6no4:305–9 '86.

6473 **Empson, sir William**. Faustus and the censor; the English Faust-book and Marlowe's Doctor Faustus. Recovered and ed. with an introd. and postscript by J.H. Jones. [Oxford], B. Blackwell, [1987]. viii,226p. tables. 21cm.
Introduction.–The English Faust-book and Marlowe's Doctor Faustus. 1. The problem.–2. The translator.–3. The censor.–4. The spirits.–5. The play.–6. The sadistic additions.–Appendix 1: Additional material. 2. 'Kill-devil all the parish over'. 3. Concordance of acts and scenes.–Postscript.
Rev: C. Nicholl London R Bks 9:6–8 '87; D. Fuller Durham Univ J 80:343–4 '88; J. Jowett N&Q 234:94–5 '89; Roma Gill R Eng Stud new ser 40:551–3 '89.

6474 **Gill, Roma**. Doctor Faustus; the textual problem. Univ Hartford Stud Lit 20no1:52–60 '88.

6475 **Shawcross, John T.** 'Signs of the times; Christopher Marlowe's decline in the seventeenth century' *in* Friedenreich, Kenneth [and others], *ed*. 'A poet and a filthy play-maker'; new essays on Christopher Marlowe. New York, AMS pr., 1988. p.63–71.

MARRYAT, FREDERICK, 1792–1848

6476 **California. University at Los Angeles. Library.** Captain Marryat; a bio-bibliographical essay to accompany an exhibition.... By Allan Buster. With a prefatory note by Wilbur Smith & a list of additions to the Marryat collection by Brooke Whiting. Los Angeles, University of California library, 1980. 48p. + errata slip. facsims. 19cm.

6477 **Crewdson, William H.P.** Frederick Marryat. Antiqu Bk Mnthly R 14n04:128–35 Ap '87. ports., facsims.
'A check-list of the first editions of Captain Frederick Marryat' (p.135).

MARSH, Richard, *pseud. of* RICHARD BERNARD HELDMANN, 1857–1915

6478 **Dalby, Richard**. Richard Marsh and The beetle. (Unappreciated authors, 8). Antiqu Bk Mnthly R 13n04:136–41 Ap '86. illus., facsims.
'Bernard Heldmann/Richard Marsh: complete checklist' (p.141).

MARSHALL, EMMA (MARTIN), 1830–99

6479 **Wanford, Arthur**. Bristol's Emma; a forgotten story-teller. Antiqu Bk Mnthly R 14n04:140–3 Ap '87. ports., illus.
'Emma Marshall: list of known titles' (p.142–3).

MARSTON, JOHN, 1575?–1634

6480 **Dineen, Marcia B.** An annotated bibliography of criticism of John Marston's Antonio plays. Bull Bib 38n02:71–81,91 Ap/Je '81.

6481 **Tucker, Kenneth**. John Marston; a reference guide. Boston, G.K. Hall, 1985. xxii,204p. 25cm. (Reference guide to literature).

6482 **Tricomi, Albert H.** John Marston's manuscripts. [Collier, and The mountebank's masque]. Huntington Libr Q 43n02:87–102 '80. facsims.

6483 **West, Michael** and **Marilyn Thorssen**. Observations on the text of Marston's Sophonisba. Anglia 98hft3/4:348–56 '80.

6484 **Yamada, Akihiro**. 'Q1–3 of The malcontent, 1604, and the compositors' *in* Nakanori, Koshi and Y. Tamaizumi, *ed.* Poetry and drama in the English renaissance, in honour of professor Jiro Ozu. Tokyo, Kinokuniya Shoten, 1980. p.107–32.

1. The printing order of Q1–3.–2. The nature of the printer's copy behind Q1–3.–3. A compositorial analysis of Q1–3.–4. Spelling characteristics of the compositors.–5. Identification of the compositors.–6. Compositor A's fidelity to his copy.–7. Why reconsider edited texts.

MARTINEAU, HARRIET, 1802–76

6485 **Thomas, Gillian**. 'Selected bibliography [of primary and secondary sources]' *in* Harriet Martineau. (Twayne's English authors, 404). Boston, Twayne, [1985]. p.138–42.

MARVELL, ANDREW, 1621–78

6486 **Collins, Dan S.** Andrew Marvell; a reference guide. Boston, Mass., G.K. Hall, 1981. xiv,449p. 23cm. (Reference guide to literature). *Rev:* W.H. Kelliher N&Q 228:471–2 '83.

6487 **Barnard, John**. The 1665 York and London editions of Marvell's The character of Holland. (Bibliographical notes). Pa Bib Soc Am 81no4:459–64 '87.

6488 **Miller, Clarence H.** The misprint 'not compare' for 'nought compare' in line 303 of Marvell's Upon Appleton house. Eng Lang N 25no3:26–8 Mr '88.

MASEFIELD, JOHN EDWARD, 1878–1967

6489 **Wight, Crocker**. John Masefield; a bibliographical description of his first, limited, signed and special editions. Boston, Library of the Boston athenæum, 1986. xxxii,214p. illus., facsims. 22cm. (Ltd. to 500 copies). *Errata tipped in after TP; 'Alphabetical listing of Masefield's works' (p.xix–xxxii). Chronol. arrangement with quasifacsim. TP transcrs., contents, collation & some bibliogr. notes; not indexed.*

MASSINGER, PHILIP, 1583–1640

6490 **Gibson, Colin A.** The new Massinger elegy. [Text of Elegy on sir Warham St.Leger]. N&Q 227no6:289–90 D '82.

6491 —— A New way to pay old debts, V.i.321–3; a proposed emendation. N&Q 227no6:490–1 D '82.

6492 **Turner, Robert K.** 'Accidental evils' *in* Shand, G.B. and R.C. Shady, *ed.* Play-texts in old spelling; papers from the Glendon conference. [Treatment of accidentals in Edwards and Gibson Massinger]. (AMS pr. Studies in the renaissance, 6). New York, [1984]. p.27–33.

MASSINGHAM, HAROLD JOHN, 1888–1952

6493 (1:4169p) [**Sherwood, John**]. 'Bibliography of the works of H.J. Massingham, 1888–1952' *in* Wessex letters from Springhead, no.4, midwinter, 1952. Springhead, Fontmell Magna, Dorset, R. Gardiner, [1952]. p.87–90.
Chronol. checklist, 1913–52.

6494 **Musty, John**. H.J. Massingham and W. Beach Thomas. (Collecting country writers, 3). Antiqu Bk Mnthly R 12no3:94–101 Mr '85. facsims.
'Checklists of first editions: Massingham' (p.100–1); '...Beach Thomas' (p.101).

MASTERS, JOHN WHITE, 1791–1873

6495 **Goulden, Richard J.** Dick & Sal at Canterbury fair. Antiqu Bk Mnthly R 10no6:218–21 Je '83. illus., facsims.

MATHEWS, CHARLES, 1776–1835

6496 **Degen, John A.** Charles Mathews' At homes; the textual morass. Theat Surv 28no2:75–88 N '87.

MATURIN, CHARLES ROBERT, 1780–1824

6497 **Harris, John B.** 'A selected annotated bibliography [of primary and secondary sources]' *in* Charles Robert Maturin; the forgotten imitator. (Gothic Stud & Dissertations). New York, Arno pr., 1980. p.[336]–56.

6498 **Henderson, Peter M.** 'Bibliography [of primary and secondary sources]' *in* A nut between two blades; the novels of Charles Robert Maturin. (Gothic Stud & Dissertations). New York, Arno pr., 1980. p.252–62.

MAUDSLEY, HENRY, 1835–1918

6499 **Collie, Michael**. Henry Maudsley, Victorian psychiatrist; a bibliographical study. [Winchester], St. Paul's bibliographies, [1988]. xviii,205p. illus., port., facsims. 22cm.
Quasifacsim. TP transcrs., collations, contents, bibliogr. notes and extensive discussions of principal works; pamphlets, etc., with annotated checklist of articles, early revs. by, and letters on professional subjects.

MAUGHAM, WILLIAM SOMERSET, 1874–1963

6500 (5:12219b) **Canterbury. King's school.** Books given by W. Somerset Maugham. [Canterbury], [1966]. 32l. 32cm. Covertitle. (Duplicated typescript).

6501 **Komolova, Maryna.** Bridging the abyss; William Somerset Maugham in the USSR. Cahiers Vict & Edouardiens 22:87–102 Oc '85.
'Bibliography [of USSR ed. of] W.S. Maugham's writings' (p.96–102).

6502 **William** Somerset Maugham, Of human bondage; bibliographie sélective: Agregation 1987/1988. Cahiers Vict & Edouardiens 26:136–43 Oc '87.

6503 **Stott, Raymond T.** Maugham's Of human bondage, Canadian edition. [1915]. (Note 435). Bk Coll 30no1:100–1 '81.

6504 —— The collections of Somerset Maugham. Antiqu Bk Mnthly R 9no8:300–5 Ag '82; H. Abromson (Letters) 9no10:391 Oc '82. ports.
Repr. from Soundings (UCLA Santa Barbara) 3no1:6–17 My '71.
'Bibliographical note' (p.304–5).

6505 **Thomas, Lewis E.** W. Somerset Maugham. [Collecting]. Bk & Mag Coll 9:32–41 N '84. port., illus., facsims.
'Complete UK bibliography of W. Somerset Maugham 1st editions' (p.40–1).

MCCOSH, JAMES, 1811–94

6506 **Hoeveler, J. David.** 'McCosh bibliography' *in* James McCosh and the Scottish intellectual tradition; from Glasgow to Princeton. Princeton, N.J., Princeton U.P., [1981]. p.[351]–9.
Classified checklist of books, pamphlets, essays and articles, anthologies, and unpublished material by.

MERCER, CECIL WILLIAM, 1885–1960 *see* YATES, DORNFORD, *pseud.*

MEREDITH, GEORGE, 1828–1909

6507 (7:5199) **Olmsted, John C.** George Meredith, 1978.
Rev. R.F. Giles Lit Res Newsl 8:24–6 '83.

6508 **Muendel, Renate.** 'Selected bibliography [of primary and secondary sources]' *in* George Meredith. (Twayne's English authors, 434). Boston, Twayne, [1986]. p.140–6.

6509   **Spånberg, Sven-Johan**. George Meredith to Smith, Elder & co: eighteen unpublished letters. Stud Neophilol (Stockholm) 52n01:103–14 '80.

6510   **Baker, William**. Some additions to Phyllis B. Bartlett's edition of the poems of George Meredith. Browning Inst Stud 9:105–13 '81.

6511   **Roth, Lorie**. A compositorial error in The egoist. [Ch.2]. N&Q 228n04:310 Ag '83.

6512   **Stone, James S.** Errata in Michael Collie's bibliography of George Meredith. Bull Bib 43n01:44–53 Mr '86.
       See BLB 1970–79: 5198.

MEREDITH, LOUISA ANNE (TWAMLEY), 1812–95

6513   **Miller, David C.** Mrs. Louisa Anne Meredith & her colour printed books. Antiqu Bk Mnthly R 14n03:88–95 F '87. port., facsims.
       'Check list of works by mrs. Meredith' (p.95).

MERRICK, LEONARD, *pseud. of* LEONARD MILLER, 1864–1939

6514   **Baker, William**. Leonard Merrick, a forgotten master. Antiqu Bk Mnthly R 15n04:140–4 Ap '88. port., facsims.
       'A check list of the major writings of Leonard Merrick' (p.144).

MIDDLETON, CONYERS, 1683–1750

6515   **Clarke, M.L.** Conyers Middleton's alleged plagiarism. [Of W. Bellenden's De tribus luminibus Romanorum, in the life of Cicero]. N&Q 228n01:44–6 F '83.

6516   **Levine, Joseph M.** '"Et tu Brute?" History and forgery in 18th-century England' *in* Myers, Robin and M.R.A. Harris, *ed.* Fakes and frauds; varieties of deception in print & manuscript. Winchester; Detroit, 1989. p.71–97. facsim.

MIDDLETON, THOMAS, 1570?–1627

6517   **Fuzier, Jean** and **A. Bry**. The Changeling de Thomas Middleton et William Rowley; bibliographie sélective et critique. Soc d'Étud Anglo-Am Bull 15:7–33 N '82.

6518   **Brooks, John B.** Recent studies in Middleton, 1971–1981. (Recent studies in the English renaissance). Eng Lit Renaiss 14n01:114–28 '84.

6519 **Wolff, Dorothy**. Thomas Middleton; an annotated bibliography. New York, Garland, 1985. xv,138p. 21cm. (Reference library of the humanities, 554).
Rev: R.A. Aken Choice 23:1662 '86.

6520 **Craik, Thomas W.** Further proposed emendations in The changeling. N&Q 225no4:324–7 '80.

6521 **Jackson, MacDonald P.** Compositorial practices in The revenger's tragedy, 1607–08. (Bibliographical notes). Pa Bib Soc Am 75no2:157–70 '81.

6522 **Zimmerman, Susan**. The Folger manuscripts of Thomas Middleton's A Game at Chesse; a study in the genealogy of texts. Pa Bib Soc Am 76no2:159–95 '82. tables.
Archdall-Folger V.a.231.–Rosenbach-Folger V.a.342–Conclusion.–Methodology of collation: introduction to the table.

6523 **Hill, Trevor H. Howard-.** The Bridgewater-Huntington ms. of Middleton's Game at chess. Manuscripta 28no3:145–56 N '84.

6524 **Mulholland, Paul**. Notes on several derivatives of Crane's manuscript of Middleton's The witch. (Bibliographical notes). Pa Bib Soc Am 78no1:75–81 '84. facsim.

6525 **Hill, Trevor H. Howard-.** Auction catalogue of Edw. Lewis, c. 1735 listing Middleton mss. (Query 367). Bk Coll 35no4:522 '86.

6526 **Kaplan, Joel H.** Thomas Middleton's epitaph on the death of Richard Burbage, and John Payne Collier. [Probable forgery]. (Bibliographical notes). Pa Bib Soc Am 80no2:225–32 '86.

6527 **Mulholland, Paul**. Thomas Middleton's The two gates of salvation, 1609; an instance of running-title rotation. Library ser6 8no1:18–31 Mr '86. facsims.

6528 **Hill, Trevor H. Howard-.** The author as scribe or reviser? Middleton's intentions in A Game at Chess. Text 3:305–18 '87.

6529 **Kaplan, Joel H.** Printer's copy for Thomas Middleton's The ant and the nightingale. (Bibliographical notes). Pa Bib Soc Am 81no2:173–5 '87.

6530 **Daalder, Joost**. Emending The changeling. Bib Soc Aust & N.Z. Bull 13no4:136–45 '89.

6531 —— Punctuating The changeling. Bib Soc Aust & N.Z. Bull 13no1:11–26 '89.
The status of the Q punctuation.–Editorial vs. Q punctuation.

6532 **Rasmussen, Eric**. Shakespeare's hand in The second maiden's tragedy. Sh Q 40no1:1–26 '89. facsims.

The addition slips: texts and contexts.–The revisions in the manuscript.–Evidence against Middleton as author of the additions.–Evidence for Shakespeare as author of the additions.–Evidence against Shakespeare's authorship of the additions.–The revisions in The second maiden's tragedy and Sir Thomas More.–Conclusions.–Old-spelling version of the additions....

MILL, JOHN STUART, 1806–73

6533 **Laine, Michael**. Bibliography of works on John Stuart Mill. Toronto, University of Toronto pr., [1982]. viii,173p. 23cm.

Rev: C. Spandoni Bib Soc Canada Pa 21:96–8 '83; W. Thomas TLS 15 Ap '83:387.

6534 **Robson, John M.** A Mill for editing. Browning Inst Stud 9:1–13 '81.

6535 **Boylan, Thomas A.** and **T.P. Foley**. Notes on Ireland for John Stuart Mill; the Cairnes-Longfield manuscript. Hermathena 138:28–39 '85.

6536 **Robson, John M.** Practice, not theory; editing J.S. Mill's newspaper writings. Stud Bib 41:160–76 '88.

Description of materials.–Treatment.–Conclusion.

MILNE, ALAN ALEXANDER, 1882–1956

6537 **Smith, Tori Haring-**. A.A. Milne; a critical bibliography. New York, Garland, 1982. xxxvii,344p. 21cm. (Reference library of the humanities, 305).

Classified annotated checklists of writings by, about, 'Pooh without Milne', *and* 'The writings of Milne's family', *Christopher Robin, Kenneth J. and Dorothy DeSelincourt Milne.*

MILTON, JOHN, 1608–74

6538 **Alexander Turnbull library,** WELLINGTON, N.Z. A descriptive catalogue of the Milton collection in the Alexander Turnbull library describing works printed before 1801 held in the library at December 1975. Comp. by K.A. Coleridge. [Oxford], Publ. for the Alexander Turnbull library, National library of New Zealand by O.U.P., 1980. xxv,562p. + 27l. of plates. facsims. 21cm.

Bibliogr. catalogue with full descrs., bibliogr. notes and refs.

6539 **Camé, Jean-François**. Milton: Paradise lost, books IV & IX; bibliographie sélective et critique. Soc d'Étud Anglo-Am Bull 13:9–42 N '81.

6540 **MacLaren, I.S.** Milton's Nativity ode; the function of poetry and structures of response in 1629, with a bibliography of twentieth-century criticism. Milton Stud 15:181–200 '81.

'A chronological bibliography of twentieth-century criticism' (p.195–8).

6541 **Cameron, William J.** Seventeenth and eighteenth century editions of the writings of John Milton in special collections, Douglas library, Queen's university, Kingston, Ont. [London, Ont., University of Western Ontario], 1982. 17p. 27cm. (WHSTC Libr Cat ser, 2). Duplicated typescript. (Not seen: ISBN 0–7714–0334–8).

6542 **Amory, Hugh.** Things unattempted yet; a bibliography of the first edition of Paradise lost. Bk Coll 32no1:41–66 '83. illus., facsims.
'Postscript [Vertue–Holland, Quaritch–Furthman copies]' (p.57–61); 'Bibliography' (p.62–6).

6543 **Dillon, John B.** Milton's Latin and Greek verse; an annotated bibliography. Milton Stud 19:227–307 '84.

6544 **Shawcross, John T.** Milton; a bibliography for the years 1624–1700. Binghamton, N.Y., Medieval & renaissance texts & studies, 1984. xiv,452p. 23cm. (Medieval & Renaiss Texts & Stud, 30).
Classified arrangements of primary works, with quasi-facsim. TP transcrs., collations, bibliogr. notes and refs., and secondary bibliogr., with full indexes.
Rev: Am N&Q 23:93–4 '85.

6545 **Jones, Edward.** A checklist of recent work on Milton. Milton Q 19no4:118–20 D '85.

6546 **Shawcross, John T.** The collection of the works of John Milton and Miltoniana in the Margaret I. King library, University of Kentucky. [Lexington, University of Kentucky libraries], [1985]. 113p. facsims. 27cm. (Univ Kentucky Occas Pa, 8).

6547 —— Milton, a bibliography for the years 1624–1700: Corrigenda and addenda. Milton Q 19no1:21–2 Mr '85.
See no.6544.

6548 **Ravenstree company, bksllrs.,** YUMA. John Milton, 1608–1674, and Miltoniana; books by, about, and concerning John Milton in first and early editions. [Yuma, Ariz.], 1986. ii,43p. 21cm. (Catalogue, 135). 229 items.

6549 **Patrides, C.A.** An annotated critical bibliography of John Milton. New York, St. Martin's pr.; Brighton, Harvester pr., [1987]. xii,200p. 21cm.
Rev: M. Fixler R Eng Stud new ser 39:604 '88; T. Healy Mod Lang R 84:717–18 '89.

6550 **Himy, Armand.** Poems mineurs de John Milton, Comus, Lycidas, L'allegro, Il penseroso: bibliographie sélective et critique. Soc d'Étud Anglo-Am Bull 29:7–24 N '89.

6551 (5:12420d) **Adams, Robert M.** '3. The text of Paradise lost' in Ikon; John Milton and the modern critics. Ithaca, Cornell U.P., [1955]; London,

G. Cumberlege, O.U.P., [1956]. (2d paperback ed., Ithaca, Cornell U.P., 1966). p.60–111.

6552 (5:12425a) **Fletcher, Harris F.** '215. Inter bibliopolas [Milton and the booksellers]' *in* The intellectual development of John Milton. Urbana, University of Illinois pr., 1956. V.1, p.398–404.

6553 (5:12439h) —— '21. Milton's acess to books' *in* The intellectual development of John Milton. Urbana, University of Illinois pr., 1961. V.2, p.367–81.

6554 (5:12453c) **Hyman, Lawrence W.** The publication of Paradise lost, 1667–1674. J Hist Stud 1no1:50–64 '67. facsims.

6555 (5:12455a) **Shawcross, John T.** 'Orthography and the text of Paradise lost' *in* Emma, Ronald D. and J.T. Shawcross, *ed.* Language and style in Milton; a symposium in honor of the tercentenary of Paradise lost. New York, F. Ungar, [1967]. p.120–53.

6556 (7:5234*) **Hanford, James H.** and **J.G. Taaffe.** 'Appendix D: Milton's private library' *in* A Milton handbook. 5th ed. New York, Appleton-Century-Crofts, [1970]. (First publ. 1926). p.317–19.

6557 (7:5234*b) —— 'Appendix E: Milton and his printers' *in* A Milton handbook. 5th ed. New York, Appleton-Century-Crofts, [1970]. (First publ. 1926). p.321–7.

6558 **Moyles, R. Gordon.** The text of Paradise lost; a stemma for the early editions. Stud Bib 33:168–82 '80. diagr.

6559 **Cameron, William J.** Milton redivivus; a review of Coleridge's descriptive catalogue. [And descr. bibliogr.]. Bib Soc Aust & N.Z. Bull 5no4:125–48 '81. tables.
'A thorough full-scale bibliography'.–Application of the 'degressive principle' in an author bibliography.–Arrangement of entries in a comprehensive full-scale bibliography.–Miltoniana.–Adequacy of the Alexander Turnbull library collection.

6560 **Dust, Philip.** Another copy of Milton's Pro populo anglicano defensio. (Bibliographical notes). Library ser6 3no2:143–4 Je '81; Kathleen A. Coleridge (Correspondence) 4no3:327–8 S '82.

6561 **Elliott, Victor G.** Catalogues, bibliographies and early printed books. [Largely on K. Coleridge's Descriptive catalogue of the Milton collection, no.6538]. N.Z. Libs 43no7:114–17 S '81.

6562 **Hale, John K.** Thomas Bentley to dr. Pearce; new light on Richard Bentley's edition of Paradise lost. Turnbull Libr Rec 14no1:23–34 My '81. facsims.

'Thomas Bentley to dr. Pearce; some comments on the bibliographical evidence', *by* Kathleen Coleridge (p.31–4).

6563 **McKenzie, Donald F.** John Milton, Alexander Turnbull, and Kathleen Coleridge. Turnbull Libr Rec 14no2:106–11 '81.

6564 **Moyles, R. Gordon.** 'Iconoclast and catalyst: Richard Bentley as editor of Paradise lost' *in* Conference on editorial problems, 16th, Toronto, 1980. Editing poetry from Spenser to Dryden; papers given…. Ed. by A.H. De Quehen. New York, 1981. p.[99]–126. facsims.

6565 **Shawcross, John T.** Some inferences about literary history from the John Milton collection in the Margaret I. King library. (Library notes). Kentucky R 2no3:85–99 '81.

6566 **Yeandle, Laetitia**. Milton's library. [The plot discovered, 1640]. (To the editor). TLS 21 Ag '81:958.

6567 **Burnett, Archibald**. A textual crux in 'L'allegro'. N&Q 227no1:495–8 D '82; J. Creaser, A reply 229no3:327–30 S '84.

6568 **Creaser, John**. Textual cruces in Milton's shorter poems. N&Q 227no1:26–8 F '82.

6569 **Gatti, Hilary**. Some amendments to E. Sirluck's textual notes on Areopagitica. N&Q 227no6:499–500 D '82.

6570 **Ravenhall, Mary D.** Sources and meaning in dr. Aldrich's 1688 illustrations of Paradise lost. Eng Lang N 19no3:208–18 Mr '82. facsims.

6571 **Creaser, John**. Editorial problems in Milton. R Eng Stud new ser 34no135:279–303 Ag '83; 35no137:45–60 F '84.

6572 **Corns, Thomas N.** The Complete prose works of John Milton in retrospect. [Review art]. Prose Stud 7no2:179–86 S '84.

6573 **Hale, John K.** Notes on Richard Bentley's edition of Paradise lost, 1732. Milton Q 18no2:46–50 My '84.

6574 **Miller, Leo**. Some inferences from Milton's Hebrew. [Ptg. errors]. Milton Q 18no2:41–6 My '84.

6575 **Hunter, William B.** A bibliographical excursus into Milton's Trinity manuscript. Milton Q 19no3:61–71 Oc '85.

6576 **Miller, Leo**. Establishing the text of Milton's state papers. Text 2:181–6 '85.

6577 **Moyles, R. Gordon.** The text of Paradise lost; a study in editorial procedure. Toronto, University of Toronto pr., [1985]. x,188p. facsims., tables, diagr. 22cm.

1. The original texts; a question of authority.–2. The transmission of Paradise lost; the early editors, 1678–1720.–3. Towards the definitive text: Richard Bentley to Thomas Newton, and after.–4. Orthography: the modern editorial preoccupation.–5. Punctuation: a question of grammar and rhetoric.–6. Editing Paradise lost.–Appendix [on ptg. of 1st ed.].–Bibliography [including Editions of Paradise lost from 1667 to 1749].

Rev: A.S.G. Edwards TLS 13 D '85:1436; T.N. Corns Times Higher Educ Suppl 18 Oc '85:20; R. Flannagan Milton Q 19:22–3 '85; C.A. Thompson Eng Stud Canada 12:346–50 '86.

6578 **Shawcross, John T.** Early Milton bibliography, its nature and implications. Text 2:173–80 '85.

6579 **Brown, Cedric C.** Milton's Arcades in the Trinity manuscript. (Notes). R Eng Stud new ser 37no148:542–9 N '86.

6580 **Kelley, Maurice.** A review of four entries on the Milton mss. in A Milton encyclopedia. [Corrections]. Milton Q 20no1:32 Mr '86.

6581 **Miller, Leo.** Milton's Defensio ordered wholesale for the states of Holland. N&Q 231no1:33 Mr '86.

6582 **Blum, Abbe.** 'The author's authority; Areopagitica and the labour of licensing' *in* Nyquist, Mary and Margaret W. Ferguson. Re-membering Milton; essays on the texts and traditions. New York, Methuen, [1987]. p.74–96. facsim. as frontispiece.

Milton and the printing controversy.–Transgressive signature in Areopagitica.–Tokens of manly prowess: erasure, naming, and the monumentalizing of the author.–The author as licenser.

6583 **Helgerson, Richard.** Milton reads the king's book; print, performance, and the making of a bourgeois idol. Criticism 29no1:1–25 '87. facsims.

6584 **Miller, Leo.** The burning of Milton's books in 1660; two mysteries. [Pro populo Anglicano defensio; Eikonoklastes]. Engl Lit Renaiss 18no3:424–37 '88.

6585 **Schoenberg, Estella.** 'Picturing Satan for the 1688 Paradise lost' *in* Labriola, Albert C. and E. Sichi, *ed.* Milton's legacy in the arts. University Park, Pennsylvania state U.P., [1988]. p.[1]–20. facsims.

6586 **Fletcher, Harris F.** John Milton's copy of Lycophron's Alexandra in the library of the University of Illinois. Milton Q 23no4:129–58 D '89.

Ed. by John T. Shawcross.

John Milton's copy of Lycophron.–The provenance of the Foster–White–Vand Sinderin Lycophron.–Description of Milton's Lycophron.–Milton's Greek studies and Lycophron.–Milton's holograph marginalia.

6587 **Hale, John K.** The punctuating of Milton's Latin verse; some prolegomena. Milton Q 23no1:7–19 Mr '89.

6588 **Miller, Leo.** Milton and Vlacq: addenda 1644–1668. [To BLB 1970–79: 5256]. (Bibliographical notes). Pa Bib Soc Am 83no4:533–8 D '89.
Vlacq in France, 1644–1645.–Vlacq and the Salmasius circle.–An author deals with Vlacq [Robert Creighton, 1593–1672].–The posthumous catalogues.

6589 **Noble, Margaret.** Twentieth-century illustrated editions of Samson Agonistes. Am N&Q new ser 2no3:97–100 Jl '89.

6590 **Watt, R.J.C.** The lacuna in Milton's 'On the death of a fair infant'. N&Q 234no1:30–1 Mr '89.

MIRK, JOHN, fl.1403?

6591 (7:5257b) **Blake, Norman F.**, *ed.* 'Introduction' *in* Quattuor sermones; printed by William Caxton. (Middle Eng Texts). Heidelberg, C. Winter, 1975. p.7–17.
Editions of Caxton's Qs.–Description of the first edition.–The title.–Relation with the Festial and date of Qs.–Qs and other texts of instruction.

6592 **Kaimowitz, Jeffrey H.** A newly identified copy of Mirk's Liber festivalis and Quattuor sermones (STC 17970.5). [In Watkinson libr., Trinity coll., Hartford]. (Bibliographical notes). Pa Bib Soc Am 76no2:221–2 '82. table.

MITFORD, NANCY FREEMAN, 1904–73

6593 **Parise, Marina P.** Nancy Mitford; a bibliography. Bull Bib 46no1:3–9 Mr '89.

6594 **Gunn, Katharine.** Nancy Mitford. [Collecting]. Bk & Mag Coll 13:45–9 Mr '85. port., facsims.
'Complete bibliography of Nancy Mitford' (p.49).

MOIR, JOHN, fl.1776–1802

6595 **Pitcher, Edward W.** Some contributions to eighteenth-century magazines by John Moir. N&Q 231no1:75–6 Mr '86.

6596 —— A note on the periodical and miscellaneous publications of John Moir, fl.1776–1802. N&Q 225no1:62–3 F '80.

MONTAGU, LADY MARY WORTLEY (PIERREPONT), 1689–1762

6597 **Grundy, Isobel**. New verse by lady Mary Wortley Montagu. Bodleian Libr Rec 10no4:210–11 F '81.

6598 —— The politics of female authorship; lady Mary Wortley Montagu's reaction to the printing of her poems. Bk Coll 31no1:19–37 '81. illus., facsims.

MONTAGU, RALPH, 1ST DUKE OF MONTAGU, 1638–1709

6599 **Metzger, Edward C.** Ralph Montagu, first duke of Montagu, 1638–1709; a bibliography. Bull Bib 43no4:248–59 D '86.

MONTAGUE, JOHN, 1929–

6600 **Redshaw, Thomas D.** Books by John Montague; a descriptive checklist, 1958–1988. Irish Univ R 19no1:139–58 '89.
Quasifacsim. TP transcrs. with bibliogr. notes on 58 titles.

MOORCOCK, MICHAEL, 1939–

6601 **Hinton, Brian**. Michael Moorcock; a bibliography, based on the Moorcock deposit, Bodleian library, Oxford. [Brighton, J.L. Noyce], [1983]. 55p. 30cm. Covertitle. (Reprod. from typewriting).

MOORE, BRIAN, 1921–

6602 **Dahlie, Hallvard**. 'Selected bibliography [of primary and secondary works]' *in* Brian Moore. (Twayne's world authors, 632). Boston, Twayne, [1981]. p.158–65.

6603 **McIlroy, Brian**. A Brian Moore bibliography, 1974–1987. [Primary and secondary]. Irish Univ R 18no1:106–33 '88.

MOORE, GEORGE AUGUSTUS, 1852–1933

6604 **Langenfeld, Robert**. George Moore; an annotated secondary bibliography of writings about him. New York, AMS pr., [1987]. xii,531p. 25cm. (AMS Stud Mod Lit, 13).

6605 **Gilcher, Edwin, R.S. Becker** and **C.K. Strauss**. Supplement to A bibliography of George Moore. Westport, Conn., Meckler books; Gerrards Cross, C. Smythe, [1988]. xii,95p. illus. 23cm.

6606 **Thomas, Sue**. A study of George Moore's revisions of The lake. Eng Lit Transit 24no4:174–84 '81.
The first English edition compared with the 1906 Tauchnitz edition.–The first compared with the second English edition.–The second English edition compared with the 1921 edition.

6607 **Gilcher, Edwin**. 'Collecting Moore' *in* Dunleavy, Janet E., *ed.* George Moore in perspective. (Irish Lit Stud 16). Naas, co. Kildare, Malton pr.; Gerrard's Cross, Bucks., C. Smythe; Totowa, N.J., Barnes & Noble, [1983]. p.[132]–52.

6608 —— 'Some bibliographical notes' *in* Dunleavy, Janet E., *ed.* George Moore in perspective. (Irish Lit Stud). Naas, co. Kildare, Malton pr.; Gerrard's Cross, Bucks., C. Smythe; Totowa, N.J., Barnes & Noble, [1983]. p.[155]–61.

6609 —— A note on Arizona state university's George Moore collection. Eng Lit Transit 29no4:386–7 '86.

6610 **Gerber, Helmut E.**, *ed.* George Moore on Parnassus; letters (1900–1933) to secretaries, publishers, printers, agents, literati, friends, and acquaintances. Newark, N.J., University of Delaware pr., [1988]. 896p. 25cm.
Appendixes. A. Census of recipients. B. Census of writers.
Rev: J. Kelly TLS 28 Ap '89:451.

MOORE, JOHN, fl.1930–66

6611 **Musty, John**. John Moore and Fred Archer. (Collecting country writers, 4). Antiqu Bk Mnthly R 12no5:172–7 My '85. illus., port., fascims.
'Check lists of first editions: John Moore' (p.177); '...Fred Archer' (p.177).

MORE, SIR THOMAS, 1478–1535

6612 **Delendick, Patricia** and **Marie-Claude Rousseau.** Utopiana in Moreana; articles only; suelement les articles. Moreana 18no69:163–5 Mr '81.

6613 **Smith, Constance**. An updating of R.W. Gibson's St. Thomas More, a preliminary bibliography. St. Louis, Center for reformation research, 1981. iii,46p. 21cm. (Sixt Cent Bib, 20). (Reprod. from typewriting).

6614 (5:12511c) **Marc'hadour, Germain**. 'Three Tudor editors of Thomas More' *in* Conference on editorial problems, 1st, Toronto, 1965. Editing sixteenth century texts; papers.... Ed. by R.J. Schoeck. [Toronto], [1966]. p.59–71.

6615 (7:5299c) **Schuster, Louis A.** and **J.P. Lusardi**. 'Appendix D: 1. Press-variants in the 1532 Confutation, 2. Press-variants in Glosses, 1532, 3. A selective list of press-variants in the second part of the Confutation, 1533' *in* Schuster, Louis A. [and others], *ed.* The complete works of St. Thomas More. (Yale ed. of The complete works, 8pt2). New Haven, Yale U.P., 1973. p.1123–34. facsims.

6616 **Williams, Franklin B.** Surreptitious London editions of Fisher and More. Moreana 17n065/6:113–15 Juin '80.

6617 **McCutcheon, Elizabeth**. A mid-Tudor owner of More's Utopia, sir William More. Moreana 18n070:32–5 Junio '81.

6618 **Hanna, Ralph**. Two new texts of More's Dialogue of comfort. Moreana 19n074:5–11 Je '82. diagr.

6619 **Keen, Ralph**. A correction by hand in More's Supplication, 1529. [By ptr., Rastell]. Moreana 20n077:100 F '83.

6620 **Billingsley, Dale B.** The editorial design of the 1557 English Works. [Ed. by W. Rastell]. Moreana 23n089:39–48 F '86.
French summary (p.109–10).

6621 **Kinney, Daniel**. Rewriting Thomas More; a devotional anthology. [Cambridge U.L.]. Manuscripta 33n01:29–35 Mr '89.

MORGAN, EDWIN, 1920–

6622 **Whyte, Hamish**. Edwin Morgan; a selected bibliography, 1950–1980. Glasgow, H. Whyte, 1980. 25l. 30cm. Covertitle. (Duplicated typescript).

MORRIS, MAY, 1862–

6623 **Masterman, Elizabeth**. May Morris; some notes for collectors. Bk Coll 33n02:163–78 '84. illus.
'Checklist' (p.174–8): *list of 15 items, 1888–1973, with some bibliogr. notes.*

MORRIS, WILLIAM, 1834–96 *see also* BOOK PRODUCTION AND DISTRIBUTION—Printers, etc.–Kelmscott press, Hammersmith, 1891–8.

6624 (7:5318d) **Kirchhoff, Frederick**. 'Selected bibliography [of primary and secondary sources]' *in* William Morris. (Twayne's English authors, 262). Boson, Mass., Twayne, [1979]. p.176–9.

6625 **George Washington university**, WASHINGTON, D.C. **Library**. A collector's choice; the John J. Walsdorf collection of William Morris in private press and limited editions; an exhibition held…26 November 1979 to

15 February 1980. Washington, 1980. 62p. 21cm. (George Washington university Friends of the libraries Collectors ser Keepsake 1979–80). Covertitle.

6626 **Robinson, Duncan** and **S. Wildman**, *ed*. Morris & company in Cambridge; catalogue by...; exhibition organised by the Fitzwilliam museum, Cambridge.... Cambridge, C.U.P., [1980]. xiv,113p. illus., facsims. 28cm.

6627 **Goodwin, Kenneth L.** A preliminary handlist of manuscripts and documents of William Morris. [London], William Morris society, [1983]. v,107p. 20cm. (Reprod. from typewriting).

6628 **Latham, David** and **Sheila Latham.** William Morris; an annotated bibliography, 1978–80. Wm Morris Soc J 5no3:23–4 '83; 1981–3. 6no4:1–24 after p.14 '85/6; 1984–5. 7no3:i–xxiv after p.18 '87; 1986–87. 8no3:i–xvi after p.20 '89; 1988–89. 9no2:i–xviii after p.20 '91.

6629 **Walsdorf, John J.** William Morris in private press and limited editions; a descriptive bibliography of books by and about William Morris, 1891–1981. London, Library association; Phoenix, Ariz., Oryx pr., 1983. xxvi,602p. illlus., facsims. 24cm.
Rev: D.J. McKitterick TLS 6 Ap '84:387; Susan O. Thompson Fine Print 11:127–8 '85.

6630 **Banham, Joanna** and **Jennifer Harris.** William Morris and the middle ages; a collection of essays together with a catalogue of works exhibited at the Whitworth art gallery, 28 September – 8 December 1984. [Manchester], Manchester U.P., [1984]. xii,225p. illus., facsims. 23cm.
'Catalogue' (p.[65]–225).
Rev: J.R. Dunlap Am Bk Coll 7:40–5 '86.

6631 **Aho, Gary L.** William Morris; a reference guide. Boston, Mass., G.K. Hall, [1985]. xliii,428p. 23cm. (Reference guide to literature).

6632 **Doheny, Estelle**. The Estelle Doheny collection.... Part VI: Printed books and manuscripts concerning William Morris and his circle...Friday, 19 May, 1989. New York, Christie, Manson & Woods international, [1989]. 1v.(unpaged) illus., port., facsims. 28cm.

6633 (1:4301) **Vallance, Aylmer**. William Morris; his art, his writings and his public life, 1897. (Repr. London, Studio editions, 1986).

6634 **Fifty** items by or about William Morris, collected by sir Sydney Cockerell, in BL *see* Gould, Alison, Named special collections, 1981: no.818.

6635 **Kelvin, Norman**. 'Editing the letters of William Morris' *in* Brody, Saul N. and H. Schechter, *ed*. CUNY English forum, 1. New York, AMS pr., 1985. p.275–85. facsims.

6636 **Felsenstein, Frank**. William Morris and the Brotherton collection. Univ Leeds R 28:97–113 '85/6. illus., facsims.

6637 **Liberman, Michael**. Major textual changes in William Morris's News from nowhere. (Notes). Ninet Cent Fict 41no3:349–56 D '86.

6638 **Latham, David**. Paradise lost; Morris's re-writing of The earthly paradise. J Pre-Raphaelite & Aesthet Stud 1no1:67–75 '87.

6639 **Schulte, Edvige**. Morris in Italian today. William Morris Soc J 7no2:29 '87.

MORRIS-JONES, John, 1864–1929 *see* JONES, JOHN MORRIS-, 1864–1929.

MORRISON, ARTHUR, 1863–1945

6640 **Calder, Robert**. Arthur Morrison; a commentary with an annotated bibliography of writings about him. Eng Lit Transit 28no3:276–97 '85.

MORTIMER, RAYMOND, 1895–1980

6641 **Preston, Jean F.** The Raymond Mortimer papers. [New & notable]. Princeton Univ Libr Chron 47no3:364–6 '86.

MORTON, THOMAS, d.1647

6642 **Sternberg, Paul R.** The publication of Thomas Morton's New English Canaan reconsidered. (Bibliographical notes). Pa Bib Soc Am 80no3:369–74 '86.

MUIR, EDWIN, 1887–1959

6643 **Robertson, Ritchie**. Some revisions and variants in the poetry of Edwin Muir. Biblioth 10no1:20–6 '80.

MUNDAY, ANTHONY, 1553–1633

6644 **Metz, G. Harold.** The Master of the revels and The Booke of sir Thomas Moore. (Notes). Sh Q 33no4:493–5 '82.

6645 **Jackson, MacDonald P.** Anthony Munday and the play of Thomas More. Moreana 22no85:83–4 Ap '85.

6646 **Melchiori, Giorgio**. The Booke of sir Thomas Moore; a chronology of revision. Sh Q 37no3:291–308 '86.

1. Paper, watermarks, and chain-lines.–2. The hands in the additions.–3. The sequence of revising: the later part.–4. The sequence of revisions: the early part.–5. The process of revising: a recapitulation.–6. The problem of dating.

MURDOCH, JEAN IRIS (MRS. J.O. BAYLEY), 1919–

6647 **Begnal, Kate**. Iris Murdoch; a reference guide. Boston, Mass., G.K. Hall, [1987]. xvii,198p. 23cm. (Reference guide to literature).

6648 **Brown, Geoffrey**. Iris Murdoch. [Collecting]. Bk & Mag Coll 25:42–7 F '86. port., facsims.

'Complete UK bibliography of Iris Murdoch' (p.46).

NAIPAUL, VIDIADHAR SURAT PRASAD, 1932–

6649 **Mann, Harveen S.** Primary works of and critical writings on V.S. Naipaul; a selected checklist. Mod Fict Stud 30no3:581–91 '84.

6650 **Jarvis, Kelvin**. V.S. Naipaul; a selective bibliography with annotations, 1957–1987. Metuchen, N.J., Scarecrow pr., 1989. xvii,205p. 21cm. (Scarecrow author bibs., 83).

'Works by...' (p.11–32).

NASHE, THOMAS, 1567–1601

6651 **Fehrenbach, Robert J.** Recent studies in Nashe, 1968–1979. (Recent studies in the English renaissance). Eng Lit Renaiss 11no3:344–50 '81.

NEEDHAM, MARCHAMONT, 1620–78

6652 **Frank, Joseph**. '3. Marchamont Nedham' *in* Cromwell's press agent; a critical biography of Marchamont Nedham, 1620–1678. [Lanham, Md.], U.P. of America, 1980. p.196–9.

NESBIT, EDITH (MRS. HUBERT BLAND), 1858–1924

6653 **Goodacre, Selwyn H.**, *comp.* 'Bibliography' *in* Briggs, Julia. A woman of passion; the life of E. Nesbitt, 1858–1924. London, Hutchinson; New York, New Amsterdam books, 1987. p.453–65.

Chronol. checklist, 1885–1925, with ana.

6654 **Macleod, Helen**. The children's books of E. Nesbit. [Collecting]. Bk & Mag Coll 17:46–53 Jl '85. ports., facsims.
'Major collectable children's books of E. Nesbit' (p.53).

NEUBURG, VICTOR BENJAMIN, 1883–1940

6655 **Neuburg, Victor E.R.P.** 'Books...a list of books by (or mainly by) Vickybird...' *in* Vickybird; a memoir of Victor B. Newburg by his son. [London], Polytechnic of North London, 1983. p.13–[15].
Checklist, 1908–22, with bibliogr. annotations.

NEWMAN, CARD. JOHN HENRY, 1801–90

6656 **Earnest, James D.** and **G. Tracey**. John Henry Newman; an annotated bibliography of his tract and pamphlet collection [in Birmingham oratory]. New York, Garland, 1984. xx,234p. 21cm. (Reference Libr Soc Sci, 239).

6657 **Litvak, Leon**. A brief alliance; Pugin, Newman and the English Saints. Antiqu Bk Mnthly R 12no10:376–81 Oc '85. ports., facsims.

NEWTON, SIR ISAAC, 1642–1727

6658 **Cohen, I. Bernard.** Newton's copy of Leibniz's Théodicée; with some remarks on the turned-down pages of books in Newton's library. (Notes & correspondence). Isis 73:410–14 S '82.

6659 —— 'The thrice-revealed Newton' *in* Conference on editorial problems, 17th, Toronto, 1981. Editing texts in the history of science and medicine. Ed. by Trevor H. Levere. New York, 1982. p.[117]–84.
'Bibliography' (p.169–84).

NICHOLS, PETER, 1927–

6660 **Clayton, Thomas S.** The texts and publishing vicissitudes of Peter Nichols's Passion play. Library ser6 9no4:365–83 D '87. facsims., diagr.

NORTHAMPTON, JAMES COMPTON, 3D EARL OF, 1622–81
see COMPTON, JAMES, 3D EARL OF NORTHAMPTON, 1622–81.

NORTON, CAROLINE JULIA, 1808–77

6661 **Casper, Dale E.** Caroline Norton: the writings. Bull Bib 40no2:113–16 Je '83.

O'BRIAN, PATRICK, 1899–1983.

6662 **Cunningham, A.E.** Patrick O'Brian; a bibliography of first printings and first British printings. [Newton-on-Ouse, Thrommett books], [1986]. 28p. 21cm. (Thrommett Bibs, 1). (Duplicated typescript).

O'CASEY, SEAN, 1880–1964

6663 (7:5406) **Ayling, Ronald F.** and **M.J. Durkan**. Sean O'Casey; a bibliography, 1978.
Rev: C.A. Carpenter Mod Drama 24:119–21 '81.

6664 **Lowery, Robert G.** 'Sean O'Casey at the Abbey theatre [checklist of productions]' *in* Krause, David and R.G. Lowery, *ed*. Sean O'Casey; centenary essays. Gerrards Cross, C. Smythe; Totowa, N.J., Barnes & Noble, [1980]. p.228–49.

6665 **Mikhail, Edward H.** Sean O'Casey; an annual bibliography. O'Casey Ann 1:180–91 '82; 2:166–71 '83; 3:186–9 '84; 4:111–15 '85.

6666 **Ayling, Ronald F.** and **M.J. Durkan**. Sean O'Casey; a bibliographical update. [To BLB 1970–79: 5406]. O'Casey Ann 2:149–65 '83.

6667 **Mikhail, Edward H.** Sean O'Casey and his critics; an annotated bibliography, 1916–1982. Metuchen, N.J., Scarecrow pr., 1985. x,348p. 21cm. (Scarecrow author bibliogrs., 67).
Rev: R.E. Ward Éire–Ireland 20:154–6 '85.

6668 **Jones, Nesta**. '5. A select bibliography of primary and secondary sources' *in* File on O'Casey. (Writer-files). London, Methuen, [1986]. p.90–6.

6669 **Ayling, Ronald F.** '1. The origin and evolution of a Dublin epic [his autobiogr.]' *in* Lowery, Robert G., *ed*. Essays on Sean O'Casey's autobiographies. Totowa, N.J., Barnes & Noble, [1981]. p.[1]–34.

6670 **Schrank, Bernice**. O'Casey's The silver tassie; from manuscripts to published texts. [Revision]. Bull Res Humanit 87no2/3:237–50 '86/7. facsim.

O'CONNOR, FRANK, *pseud. of* MICHAEL O'DONOVAN, 1903–66

6671 **Alexander, James**. An annotated bibliography of works about Frank O'Connor. J Irish Lit 16no3:40–8 S '87.

6672 **Steinham, Michael**. Frank O'Connor at work; 'The genius'. [Revision]. Éire 20no4:24–32 '85.

O'DONNELL, ELLIOTT, 1872–1965

6673 **Dalby, Richard**. Elliott O'Donnell. [Collecting]. Bk & Mag Coll 22:38–43 D '85. facsims.
'Complete Elliott O'Donnell bibliography' (p.43).

O'FLAHERTY, LIAM, 1896–1984

6674 **Jefferson, George**. Liam O'Flaherty; the man from Aran. Antiqu Bk Mnthly R 12no9:348–53 S '85. port., facsims.
'Liam O'Flaherty bibliography' (p.353).

O'NEILL, JOSEPH, 1883–1953

6675 **Giffuni, Cathy**. Joseph O'Neill; a bibliography. J Irish Lit 16no2:14–19 My '87.
Checklist of writings, poems, articles and stories by, and ana.

O'SULLIVAN, TIMOTHY, 1715–95

6676 **Ó Gadhra, Nollaig**. Stair fhoilsitheoireachta an Pious miscellany san 19ú aois. [19th cent. publ. hist., with checklist]. An tUltach 65no7:3–6 Jl '88; 65no8:2–6 Ag '88; 65no9:19–22 S '88.

Ó TUAIRISC, EOGHAN, 1919–82

6677 **Nugent, Martin**. Eoghan Ó Tuairisc; a bibliography. Poet Ireland R 13no117–30 '85.

OLDHAM, JOHN, 1653–3

6678 **Zigerell, James**. 'Selected bibliography [of primary and secondary sources]' *in* James Oldham. (Twayne's English authors, 372). Boston, Twayne, [1983]. p.139–43.

6679 **Brooks, Harold F.** and **R. Selden**. Correspondence. [On Oldham's text]. R Eng Stud new ser 40no160:538–9 N '89.

OLDMIXON, JOHN, 1673–1742

6680 **Black, Jeremy** and **J.P.W. Rogers**. Oldmixon incurs 'the displeasure of the most honourable house of peers'. [Letter, 1716]. (Features). Factotum 24:5–9 Ag '87.

OLIPHANT, MARGARET OLIPHANT (WILSON), 1828–97

6681 **Clarke, John S.** Margaret Oliphant, 1828–1897; a bibliography. [St. Lucia], Dept. of English, University of Queensland, [1986]. 102p. + 4p. Addenda, May 1990. port. (Reprod. from typewriting).
Classified checklist of 728 works and ana; 'Appendix C: Littell's living age' (p.2–4); 'D. Novels by William Wilson' (p.95–6).

6682 **Haythornthwaite, Jo Ann**. The wages of success: Miss Marjoribanks, Margaret Oliphant and the house of Blackwood. Publ Hist 15:91–107 '84. tables.

6683 —— A Victorian novelist and her publisher: Margaret Oliphant and the house of Blackwood. Biblioth 15no2:37–50 '88.

OLIVIER, EDITH MAUD, 1872–1948

6684 **Gilson, David J.** Edith Olivier. (Some uncollected authors, 55). Bk Coll 35no3:305–25 '86. facsims.
'Bibliographical checklist of Edith Olivier's writings' (p.309–25): *quasifacsim. TP transcrs., format, collations and bibliogr. notes on books, contribs. to books and to periodicals.*

OPPENHEIM, EDWARD PHILLIPS, 1866–1946

6685 **Wellman, Ellen** and **W.D. Brown**. Collecting E. Phillips Oppenheim, 1866–1946. Priv Libr ser3 6no2:82–9 '83. illus.

ORCZY, BARONESS EMMUSKA MAGDALENA ROSALIA MARIE JOSEPHA BARBARA (MRS. MONTAGUE BARSTOW), 1865–1947.

6686 **Allen, Roger**. Baroness Orczy. [Collecting]. Bk & Mag Coll 8:42–50 Oc '84. port., facsims., illus.
'Complete bibliography of baroness Orczy' (p.49–50).

ORMOND, JOHN, 1923–

6687 **O'Neill, Christopher**. Notes towards a bibliography of John Ormond's works. Poet Wales 16no2:34–8 '80.

ORWELL, GEORGE, *pseud. of* ERIC BLAIR, 1903–50

6688 **Karel, Thomas A.** George Orwell; a pre-1984 bibliography of criticism, 1975–1983. Bull Bib 41no3:133–47 S '84.

6689 **Bloxom, Marguerite D.** 'Bibliography; a select list of references' *in* George Orwell & Nineteen eighty-four; the man and the book. Washington, D.C., Library of Congress, 1985. p.123–50.

6690 **Schlueter, Paul**, *comp.* 'Bibliography: Trends in Orwell criticism, 1968–1984' *in* Oldsey, Bernard and J. Browne, *ed.* Critical essays on Orwell. Boston, Mass., G.K. Hall, [1986]. p.229–49.
Enl. from Coll Lit 11no1:94–112 '84.

6691 **Berga i Bagué, Miguel**. The publishing of George Orwell's books, a political tell-tale. [Barcelona]. Anuario del Departamento de Ingles 1979:71–84 '80.

6692 **Klitzke, Robert**. Why is the Collected Orwell not the complete Orwell? Int Fict R 10no2:125–9 '83.

6693 **Willison, Ian R.** 'Bibliographie et biographie littéraire: le cas de George Orwell' *in* Laufer, Roger, *ed.* La bibliographie matérielle. Paris, 1983. p.53–61.

6694 **Davison, Peter H.** Editing Orwell; eight problems. Library ser6 6no3:217–28 S '84.

6695 **Duhar, Alenkar**. Orwell in Yugoslavia. [Editions]. (Letters). TLS 12 Oc '84:1159.

6696 **Greene, Jo-Ann**. George Orwell. [Collecting]. Bk & Mag Coll 6:33–42 Ag '84. ports., facsims.
'Complete George Orwell bibliography' (p.42).

6697 **Puhar, Alenkar**. Orwell in Yugoslavia. [Editions]. TLS 12 Oc '84:119.

6698 **Shelden, Michael**. Orwell and his publishers; new letters. [In Lilly libr]. (Letters). TLS 6 Ja '84:15–16; M. Muggeridge 13 Ja '84:37.

6699 **Davison, Peter H.** 'What Orwell really wrote' *in* George Orwell & Nineteen eighty-four; the man and the book. Washington, D.C., Library of Congress, 1985. p.5–21.

6700 —— (Re-)publishing Orwell. [Research]. Dict Lit Biogr Yrbk 1986:127–32 '87. facsims.

OSBORNE, DOROTHY(LADY TEMPLE), 1627–95

6701 **Prance, Claude A.** 'Concerning Dorothy Osborne' *in* Essays of a book collector; reminiscences on some old books and their authors. West Cornwall, Conn., 1989. p.37–53.

OSBORNE, JOHN JAMES, 1929–

6702 **Page, Malcolm.** '5. A select bibliography [of primary and secondary sources]' *in* File on Osborne. (Writer-files). London, Methuen, [1988]. p.86–91.

OTWAY, THOMAS, 1652–85

6703 **Warner, Kerstin P.** 'Selected bibliography [of primary and secondary sources]' *in* Thomas Otway. (Twayne's English authors, 335). Boston, Twayne, [1982]. p.156–9.

OWEN, WILFRED EDWARD SALTER, 1893–1918

6704 **Hibberd, Dominic.** Wilfred Owen's letters; some additions, amendments and notes. Library ser6 4no3:273–87 S '82.

6705 **Norgate, Paul.** 'Dulce et decorum est' and some amendments to the dating of Wilfred Owen's letters. [With list]. N&Q 231no2:186–90 Je '86.

6706 **Stafford, Fiona.** Wilfred Owen. [Collecting]. Bk & Mag Coll 23:45–51 Ja '86. port., facsims.
'Wilfred Owen bibliography' (p.51).

6707 **Stallworthy, Jon.** Aspects of copyright. [Editing Owens's Poems]. TLS 15 Ag '86:889; J. Silkin; J.A.C. Greppin 29 Ag '86:939.

6708 **Stephens, John** and **Ruth Waterhouse.** Authorial revision and constraints on the role of the reader; some examples from Wilfred Owen. Poetics Today 8no1:65–83 '87.
'Appendix: 'Anthem for doomed youth' (p.81–2).

6709 **Hibberd, Dominic**. A donation to the Wilfred Owen collection at Oxford. [English faculty libr]. N&Q 234no2:197–8 Je '89.

OXENHAM, ELSIE JEANETTE, *pseud. of* **ELSIE JEANETTE DUNKERLEY, 1880–1960**

6710 **Godfrey, Monica**. Elsie J. Oxenham & her schoolgirl stories. [Collecting]. Bk & Mag Coll 8:51–7 Oc '84. facsims., illus.
'Complete bibliography of Elsie J. Oxenham' (p.56–7).

OXLEY, WILLIAM, 1939–

6711 '**Bibliography** of William Oxley' *in* A vitalist seminar; studies in the poetry of Peter Russell, Anthony L. Johnson and William Oxley. Salzburg, Institut für Anglistik und Amerikanistik, Universität Salzburg, 1984. p.296–313.
Classified checklist of books, pamphlets and broadsides, trans. by, prose, magazines, etc. ed. by, anthologies contrib. to, poems in periodicals, and selected reviews, articles and letters by.

PALMER, SAMUEL, 1805–81

6712 **Lister, Raymond**. 'The book illustrations' *in* A catalogue raisonné of the works of Samuel Palmer. Cambridge, C.U.P., 1988. p.253–63. facsims.
'Checklist of the published writings of Samuel Palmer' (p.270).

PARHAM, DAME MARGERY FREDA, 1895–1982

6713 **Oxford. University. Bodleian library**. A catalogue of the papers of dame Margery Parham, 1895–1982, in Rhodes house library, Oxford. Comp. by Patricia Pugh. Oxford, 1989. 498p. 22cm. (Reprod. from typewriting).
'Bibliography' (p.21–3).

PARKER, ARCHBP. MATTHEW, 1504–75

6714 **Page, R. Ivan**. The Parker register and Matthew Parker's Anglo-Saxon manuscripts. [Corpus Christi, Cambr]. Cambridge Bib Soc Trans 8pt1:1–17 '81.

6715 —— Matthew Parker's copy of Prosper his meditation with his wife. Cambridge Bib Soc Trans 8pt3:342–9 '83. facsim.

6716 **Hagedorn, Suzanne C**. Matthew Parker and Asser's Ælfredi regis res gestæ. [Publ]. Princeton Univ Libr Chron 51no1:74–90 '89. facsims.

PARNELL, THOMAS, 1679–1718

6717 **Matteson, Robert S.** Books from the library of Thomas Parnell. [In Cashel diocesan libr., with list]. (Bibliographical notes). Library ser6 6no4:372–6 D '84.

6718 **Woodman, Thomas M.** 'Select bibliography [of primary and secondary sources]' *in* Thomas Parnell. (Twayne's English authors, 397). Boston, Twayne, [1985]. p.130–2.

6719 **Finlay, Nancy.** Parnell's 'Hermit'; illustrations by Stothard. Scriblerian 18no1:1–5 '85. facsims.

PARTRIDGE, ERIC HONEYWOOD, 1894–1977

6720 **Crystal, David,** *ed.* 'A Partridge bibliography' *in* Eric Partridge in his own words; with appreciations.... [London], A. Deutsch, 1980; New York, Macmillan, [1981]. p.239–44.
Chronol. checklist, 1914–77.

PATER, WALTER HORATIO, 1839–94

6721 **Court, Franklin E.** Walter Pater; an annotated bibliography of writings about him. DeKalb, Ill., Northern Illinois U.P., [1980]. vii,411p. 23cm. (Annotated Secondary Bib ser on Eng Lit in Transition, 1880–1920).

6722 **Inman, Billie A.** Walter Pater's reading; a bibliography of his library borrowings and literary references, 1858–1873. New York, Garland, 1981. xliii,380p. 22cm. (Reference library of the humanities, 152).
Rev: E.R. Hall Arnoldian 10:36–44 '83.

6723 **Seiler, R.M.** Editing Walter Pater. Prose Stud 4no1:78–80 My '81.

6724 **Ward, Hayden.** The 'paper in ms.'; a problem in establishing the chronology of Pater's composition. Prose Stud 4no1:81–3 My '81.

6725 **Falsey, Elizabeth A.** Special collections report; the Pater manuscripts at Houghton, Harvard university. Eng Lit Transit 24no2:152–5 '84.

6726 **Richards, Bernard.** Special collections report: the Pater collections in Oxford. Eng Lit Transit 24no4:149–51 '84.

PEAKE, MERVYN LAURENCE, 1911–68

6727 **Berkeley, Dee** and **G.P. Winnington.** Peake in print; an annotated checklist of Mervyn Peake's works, of books he illustrated, and of his contributions of books and periodicals, with some of the reviews and articles they occasioned. Mervyn Peake R 13:8–36 '81; 14:15–35 '82; 15:18–29 '82; 16:20–36 '83; 17:14–28 '83.

6728 **Winnington, G. Peter.** The Mervyn Peake manuscripts at University college, London. Mervyn Peake R 12:29–30 '81. [Sg: G.P.W].

6729 **Winnington, G. Peter.** Editing Peake. Mervyn Peake R 13:2–7 '81.

6730 **Turner, Pauline.** Peake in the saleroom. Mervyn Peake R 14:43–4 '82.

6731 **Winnington, G. Peter.** Penguin Peakes. [Text]. Penguin Collectors' Soc Newsl 18:255–7 My '82. facsims.

6732 **Sotheby** Peakes. Mervyn Peake R 16:38–40 '83.

6733 **Sarzano, Frances.** The book illustrations of Mervyn Peake. Mervyn Peake R 17:4–8 '83.

6734 **Kennedy, Veronica M.S.** The graphic art of Mervyn Peake. Peake Stud 1no3:17–24 '89. facsim.

6735 **Scott, Tanya Gardiner-.** Through the maze; textual problems in Mervyn Peake's Titus alone. Extrapolation 30no1:70–83 '89.

PEELE, GEORGE, 1558?–1597?

6736 **Nellis, M.K.** Peele's night; dumb or divine architect? [Battle of Alcazar, act 2]. N&Q 228no2:132–3 Ap '83.

PEMBERTON, JESSE, MANCHESTER, 1864–1922

6737 **Goodman, Jonathan.** The publications of Jesse Pemberton. Antiqu Bk Mnthly R 12no1:16–19 Ja '85. illus.

PENN, WILLIAM, 1644–1718

6738 **Bronner, Edwin B.** and **D. Fraser.** William Penn's published writings, 1660–1726; an interpretive bibliography. [Philadelphia], University of Pennsylvania pr., 1986. xxvi,545p. facsims. 24cm. (Papers of William Penn, 5).
TP facsims. in place of transcrs., collations, some bibliogr. notes and discussion, in chronol. order.

PENNANT, THOMAS, 1726–98

6739 **Noblett, William**. Pennant and his publisher; Benjamin White, Thomas Pennant and Of London. Archiv Nat Hist 11no1:61–8 Oc '82.

6740 **Roberts, Thomas Lloyd-**. American annals and Miscellanies by Thomas Pennant; an attempt to determine a possible chronology. (Features). Factotum 24:24–7 Ag '87.

PEPYS, SAMUEL, 1633–1703

6741 (5:12730c) **Ladborough, Richard W.** The sanctum of Samuel Pepys. [Libr]. Author 77no3:13–16 '66.

6742 **Wilson, Edward M.** and **D.W. Cruickshank**. Samuel Pepys's Spanish plays. London, Bibliographical society, 1980. [viii],196p. 22cm.
Rev: J.E. Varey Mod Lang R 77:977 '82; Szilvia E. Szmuk Am Bk Coll new ser 3:56–8 '82.

6743 **Rivington, Charles A.** Samuel Pepys and the Oxford university press. [With documents]. N&Q 229no3:356–72 S '84.

6744 **Waals, Jan Van der**. The print collection of Samuel Pepys. [Libr]. Print Q 1no4:236–57 D '84. illus., facsims.

6745 **Rostenberg, Leona**. A look at Pepys. [Libr]. Am Bk Coll new ser 7no10:17–24 Oc '86. illus., port., facsims.

PERCY, BP. THOMAS, 1729–1811

6746 **Davis, Bertram H.** 'Selected bibliography [of primary and secondary sources]' in Thomas Percy. (Twayne's English authors, 313). Boston, Twayne, [1981]. p.158–66.

6747 (5:12752c) **Robinson, M.G.**, ed. 'The history of Percy's edition of Buckingham' in The correspondence of Thomas Percy & Thomas Warton. [Baton Rouge], Louisiana state U.P., 1951. p.148–67.

6748 **Manning, John**. Notes and marginalia in bishop Percy's copy of Spenser's Works, 1611. [At Queen's university, Belfast]. N&Q 229no2:225–7 Je '84.

6749 **Knapman, Zinnia**. A reappraisal of Percy's editing. Folk Mus J new ser 5no2:202–14 '86.

6750   **Smith, Margaret M.** Thomas Percy, William Shenstone, Five pieces of
runic poetry, and the Reliques. Bodleian Libr Rec 12no6:471–7 Ap
'88.

PHILIPS, KATHERINE (FOWLER), 1631–64

6751   **MacLean, Gerald M.** What is a restoration poem? Editing a discourse,
not an author. [Upon his majesty's most happy restoration]. Text
3:319–46 '87. facsims.

PINDAR, PETER, *pseud. of* JOHN WOLCOT, 1738–1819

6752   **Ikin, Bridget**. Peter Pindar and the pirates. (Features). Factotum
9:27–31 Ag '80.

PINERO, SIR ARTHUR WING, 1855–1934

6753   **Weaver, Jack W.** and **E.J. Wilcox**. Arthur Wing Pinero, an annotated
bibliography of writings about him. Eng Lit Transit 23no4:231–59 '80.

PINTER, HAROLD, 1930–

6754   **Hinchcliffe, Arnold P.** 'Selected bibliography [of primary and secondary sources]' *in* Harold Pinter. Rev. ed. (Twayne's English authors, 51). Boston, Twayne, [1981]. (First publ. 1967). p.169–75.

6755   **Merritt, Susan H.** Harold Pinter bibiography, 1986–1987. Pinter R
1no1:77–82 '87.

PIOZZI, HESTER LYNCH (SALUSBURY), FORMERLY MRS. THRALE, 1741–1821

6756   **McCarthy, William**. The writings of Hester Lynch Piozzi; a bibliography. Bull Bib 45no2:129–41 Je '88.

6757   **Hester** Lynch Piozzi; some new letters. [Acquired]. (News and notes).
John Rylands Univ Libr Manchester Bull 67no2:566–7 '85.

6758   **Brownley, Martino W.** Samuel Johnson and the printing career of
Hester Lynch Piozzi. [Publ.]. John Rylands Univ Libr Manchester
Bull 67no2:623–40 '85.

PITCAIRNE, ARCHIBALD, 1652–1713

6759 **Appleby, John H.** Archibald Pitcairne re-encountered; a note on his manuscript poems and printed library catalogue. Biblioth 12no6:137–9 '85.

PITT, WILLIAM, 1759–1806

6760 **Harvey, A.D.** William Pitt the younger, 1759–1806; a bibliography. Westport, Conn., Meckler, [1989]. vi,80p. port. 22cm. (Bibs Brit statesmen, 1).

POPE, ALEXANDER, 1688–1744

6761 **Kowalk, Wolfgang.** Alexander Pope; an annotated bibliography of twentieth-century criticism, 1900–1979. Frankfurt am Main, P.D. Lang, [1981]. ix,371p. 21cm.
Rev: J. McLaverty N&Q 228:81–2 '83; C.J. Rawson Yrbk Eng Stud 15:302–3 '85.

6762 **Laprevotte, Guy.** A. Pope, Essay on man: bibliographie sélective et critique. Soc d'Étud Anglo-Am Bull 21:45–62 N '85.

6763 **Cassetta, Richard.** The Rape of the lock in the 1980s; an annotated bibliography. New Orleans R 15no4:78–9 '88.

6764 **Mack, Maynard.** The world of Alexander Pope; exhibitions in the Beinecke rare book and manuscript library 8 April–5 August and the Yale center for British art, 8 April–29 May 1988. Yale Univ Libr Gaz 62no3/4:[after p.84] Ap '88. ports., facsims.

6765 **Richmond upon Thames. Libraries dept.** Alexander Pope, 1688–1744; catalogue of the Pope collection. Comp. by Brian Reid. Richmond-upon-Thames, 1989. 53l. 29cm. (Reprod. from typewriting).

6766 (5:13745) **Mack, Maynard.** The first printing of the Letters of Pope and Swift, '39.
Repr. in Collected in himself; essays.... Newark; London, [1982]. p.93–105.

6767 (5:12843) —— Pope's Horatian poems; problems of bibliography and text, '43.
Repr. in Collected in himself; essays.... Newark; London, [1982]. p.106–21.

6768 (5:12848) —— A manuscript of Pope's imitation of the First ode of the fourth book of Horace, '45.
Repr. in Collected in himself; essays.... Newark; London, [1982]. p.122–4.

6769 (5:12867) —— Some annotations in the second earl of Oxford's copies of Pope's Epistle to dr. Arbuthnot and Sober advice from Horace, '57.
Repr. in Collected in himself; essays.... Newark; London, [1982]. p.134–8.

6770 (5:12868) —— Two variant copies of Pope's Works...volume II; further light on some problems of authorship, bibliography, and text, '57.
Repr. in Collected in himself; essays.... Newark; London, [1982]. p.139–44.

6771 **Halsband, Robert**. The Rape of the lock and its illustrations, 1714–1896. Oxford, Clarendon pr., 1980. vii,160p. facsims. 23cm.
1. Publication of The rape of the lock.–2. The illustrations of 1714.–3. Later eighteenth century illustrations.–4. Fuseli and The rape of the lock.–5. Fuseli's disciples.–6. Romantic and Victorian illustrations.–7. Embroidered by Aubrey Beardsley.–Appendix I. Illustrations in German, French and Italian translations....
Rev: P. Conrad TLS 7 N '80:1255–6; P. Quennell Apollo 112:214 '80; D. Traister Bk Coll new ser 2:60–73 '81; M.R. Brownell Eight Cent Stud 16:90–3 '82; R. Paulson J Eng & Germ Philol 80:417–19 '81.

6772 **McLaverty, James**. The first printing and publication of Pope's letters. Library ser6 2no3:264–80 S '80. facsims.

6773 —— Pope's Horatian poems; a new variant state. [Ed. 507x, 1739]. Mod Philol 77no3:304–6 F '80.

6774 **Vander Meulen, David L.** Pope's revisions during printing; a variant section in The dunciad. (Notes and documents). Mod Philol 78no4:393–8 My '81.

6775 **Winn, James A.** On Pope, printers and publishers. Eight Cent Life new ser 6no2/3:93–101 Ja/My '81.

6776 **Mack, Maynard**. Collected in himself; essays critical, biographical, and bibliographical on Pope and some of his contemporaries. Newark, N.J., University of Delaware pr.; London, Associated U.P., [1982]. 569p. 23cm.
Includes The first printing of the Letters of Pope and Swift (1939).–Pope's Horatian poems; some problems of bibliography and text (1943).–A manuscript of Pope's imitation of the First ode of the fourth book of Horace (1945).–Some annotations in the second earl of Oxford's copies of Pope's Epistle to dr. Arbuthnot and Sober advice from Horace (1957).–Two variant copies of Pope's Works...volume II; further light on some problems of authorship, bibliography, and text (1957).–Pope's copy of Chaucer (1979).–Books and the man; Pope's library.–The last and greatest art; Pope's poetical manuscripts.–Appendix A: A finding list of books surviving from Pope's library with a few that may not have survived.
Rev: J.P.W. Rogers Mod Lang R 79:419–21 '84.

6777 **Vander Meulen, David L.** The printing of Pope's Dunciad, 1728. Stud Bib 35:271–85 '82. table.

6778 **Nichol, Donald W.** A misplaced plate in Warburton's Pope IV. [1751]. N&Q 228no1:34–5 F '83.

6779 **Vander Meulen, David L.** The identification of paper without watermarks; the example of Pope's Dunciad. Stud Bib 37:58–81 '84.

6780 **Cartwright, Graham.** Pope's books; a postscript to Mack. [Pope's libr.]. N&Q 231no1:56–8 Mr '86.

6781 **Knapp, Elise F.** Community property; the case for Warburton's 1751 edition of Pope. Stud Eng Lit 26no3:455–68 '86.

6782 **Nichol, Donald W.** Piracy of Pope's Homer. [By T. Johnson, The Hague]. N&Q 231no1:54–6 Mr '86.

6783 **Hunter, David.** Pope v. Bickham; an infringement of An essay on man alleged. [Copyright]. (Bibliographical notes). Library ser6 9no3:268–73 S '87.

6784 **Nichol, Donald W.** '"So proper for that constant pocket use"; posthumous editions of Pope's Works, 1751–1754' *in* Graham, Kenneth W. and N. Johnson, *ed.* L'homme et la nature/Man and nature. (Proc Canadian Soc Eighteenth-Cent Stud, 6). Edmonton, Academic ptg. & publ., 1987. p.81–92. table.

6785 **McLaverty, James.** Pope's text; life after Twickenham? Scriblerian 21no1:1–3 '88.

6786 **Philips, Michael.** '11. The composition of Pope's Imitation of Horace, satire II, 1' *in* Nicholson, Colin, *ed.* Alexander Pope; essays for the tercentenary. [Aberdeen], Aberdeen U.P., [1988]. p.171–94. facsims.

6787 **Sorrell, Paul.** Pope's Odyssey; a new manuscript fragment in Dunedin, New Zealand. [Dunedin public libr.]. Scriblerian 20no2:137–44 '88.

6788 **Vander Meulen, David L.** Where angels fear to tread: descriptive bibliography and Alexander Pope; an Engelhard lecture of the book, presented on February 25, 1987, at the Library of Congress. Washington, D.C., Library of Congress, 1988. 29p. 21cm. ([Center for the book Viewpoint ser, 19]).

6789 **Nichol, Donald W.** Pope, Warburton, Knapton, and Cole; a longstanding connection. N&Q 234no1:54–6 Mr '89.

6790 **Vander Meulen, David L.** The Dunciad in four books and the bibliography of Pope. Pa Bib Soc Am 83no3:293–310 S '89. diagrs.

POTOCKI, GEOFFREY WLADISLAS VAILE, COUNT POTOCKI DE MONTALK, 1903–

6791 **Macalister, John.** Count Potocki of Montalk; a private library in Provence. Priv Libr ser3 7no1:30–42 '84. port., facsims.

POTTER, HELEN BEATRIX, 1866–1943

6792 (1:4450*) **Linder, Leslie C.** The Beatrix Potter papers at Hill Top; a catalogue of the manuscripts, miscellaneous drawings and papers at Hill Top, Sawrey, belonging to the National trust. [n.p.], Privately comp., 1954. (2d ed. 1987). 54p. 30cm. (Ltd. to 17 copies).

6793 (1:4450) **Quinby, Jane.** Beatrix Potter; a bibliographical check list, 1954. (Repr. Stroud, I. Hodgkins, 1983).

6794 **Victoria and Albert museum,** SOUTH KENSINGTON, LONDON. Beatrix Potter; the V & A collection; the Leslie Linder bequest of Beatrix Potter material.... Comp. by Anne S. Hobbs and Joyce I. Whalley.... Ed. by Joyce I. Whalley. London, Victoria and Albert museum and F. Warne, 1985. 240p. illus., facsims. 26cm.
Rev: M. C[ouch] Junior Bkshelf 50:137 '86.

6795 **MacDonald, Ruth K.** 'Selected bibliography [of primary and secondary sources]' *in* Beatrix Potter. (Twayne's English authors, 442). Boston, Twayne, [1986]. p.140–4.

6796 **Linder, Leslie.** The Beatrix Potter papers at Hill Top; a catalogue of the manuscripts, miscellaneous drawings and papers at Hill Top, Sawrey, belonging to the National trust. Stroud, I. Hodgkins, 1987. (First publ. privately, 1954). xi,28p. 23cm. (Ltd. to 450 copies).
With foreword by Margaret Lane *on Linder.*

6797 (7:5543m) **Lane, Margaret.** The magic years of Beatrix Potter. London, F. Warne, 1978. (Pbk ed. London, Fontana, 1980). 216p. illus., ports., facsims. 26cm.
1. The third-floor nursery.–2. The young naturalist.–3. The secret apprenticeship.– 4. Children as audience.–5. Sawrey discovered.–6. The doll's house.–7. Sawrey and its animal characters.–8. The path to Castle cottage.–Epilogue: The ghost of Beatrix Potter.–The Beatrix Potter books [listed] (p.[211]–12).
Rev: Violet Powell Apollo 110:156 '79.

6798 **Greene, Jo-Ann.** The books of Beatrix Potter. [Collecting]. Bk & Mag Coll 7:11–18 S '84. facsims., ports.
'Bibliography of Beatrix Potter 1st editions' (p.18).

POWYS, JOHN COWPER, 1872–1963

6799 **Peltier, Jacqueline.** Powys R 6no4:31–8 '89. facsim.
'French trans. of the works of John Cowper Powys and T.F. Powys since 1967: a list [and French ana]' (p.34–8).

6800 **Moran, Margaret**. The vision and revision of John Cowper Powys's Weymouth sands. [= Jobber Skald]. Powys R 11:18–31 '82/3. illus., table.
'Appendix: Jobber Skald: table of alterations' (p.26–31).

6801 **Hart, Thomas C.** A printer and a Powys. [The Welsh review]. Powys R 13:49–58 '83/4.

PRATT, SAMUEL JACKSON, 1749–1814

6802 **Pitcher, Edward W.** Samuel Jackson Pratt's prose contributions to The Westminster magazine, 1772–85. (Bibliographical notes). Pa Bib Soc Am 74no2:137–43 '80.

PRICE, RICHARD, 1723–91

6803 **Stephens, John**. Richard Price's Two tracts, 1778. Bib Soc Aust & N.Z. Bull 9no1:23–30 '85. tables.

PRIESTLEY, JOHN BOYNTON, 1894–1984

6804 **Day, Alan E.** J.B. Priestley; an annotated bibliography. Introd. by J.B. Priestley. Stroud, Hodgkins; New York, Garland, 1980. xi,360p. 23cm. (Reference library of the humanities, 145).
Classified checklist of books and pamphlets; contribs. to books and pamphlets; contribs. to newspapers, journals and magazines; theatre programs, advertisements, non-print publications; Priestley the painter; studies of; Priestleyana, and index of books rev. by.

PRIESTLEY, JOSEPH, 1733–1804

6805 **Oxford. University. Manchester college.** Joseph Priestley, 1733–1804, scientist, teacher and theologian; a 250th anniversary exhibition organised by Manchester college, Oxford, at the Bodleian library. Oxford, Manchester college, 1983. 35p. illus., facsims., port. 21cm. Covertitle. (Reprod. from typewriting).

6806 **Lancaster, John.** 'The transatlantic printing history of Joseph Priestley's Discourses relating to the evidences of revealed religion, 1794–99' *in* [Amory, Hugh and R.G. Dennis], *ed.* Essays in honor of James Edward Welsh on his sixty-fifth birthday. Cambridge, [Mass.], Goethe institute of Boston and the Houghton library, 1983. p.221–30.

PRIOR, MATTHEW, 1664–1721

6807 **Wright, H. Bunker** and **P.J. Croft**. Matthew Prior's last manuscript: Predestination. Brit Libr J 11no2:99–112 '85. facsims.

PUGIN, AUGUSTUS WELBY NORTHMORE, 1812–52

6808 **Belcher, Margaret**. A.W.N. Pugin; an annotated bibliography. London, Mansell, [1987]. xxiii,495p. facsims. 22cm.

PYM, BARBARA MARY CRAMPTON, 1913–80

6809 **Peterson, Lorna**. Barbara Pym; a checklist, 1950–1984. Bull Bib 41no4:201–6 D '84.

6810 **Nardin, Barbara**. 'Selected bibliography [of primary and secondary sources]' *in* Barbara Pym. (Twayne's English authors, 406). Boston, Twayne, [1985]. p.151–2.

6811 **Berndt, Judy**. Barbara Pym; a supplementary list of secondary sources. Bull Bib 43no2:76–80 Je '86.

6812 **Rossen, Janice**. '15. The Pym papers [in Bodleian libr.]' *in* Salwak, Dale, *ed*. The life and work of Barbara Pym. [London], Macmillan; Iowa city, University of Iowa pr., [1987]. p.156–67.

6813 **Macleod, Helen**. Barbara Pym. [Collecting]. Bk & Mag Coll 23:30–5 Ja '86. port., facsims.
'Complete Barbara Pym bibliography (p.35).

QUARLES, FRANCIS, 1592–1644

6814 **Höltgen, Karl J.** 'Francis Quarles's second emblem book: Hieroglyphikes of the life of man' *in* Höltgen, Karl J., W. Lottes and P.M. Daly, *ed*. Word and visual imagination; studies in the interaction of English literature and the visual arts. Erlangen, Universitätsbibliothek Erlangen-Nürnberg, 1988. p.183–207. facsims.

QUIN, ANN, 1936–73

6815 **Willmott, R.D.** A bibliography of works by and about Ann Quin. [London], School of library & information studies, Ealing college of higher education, [1982]. 13p. 30cm. (Ealing miscellany, 13). (Duplicated typescript).

RALEIGH, SIR WALTER, 1552?–1618

6816 **Mills, Jerry L.** Recent studies in Ralegh. (Recent studies in the English renaissance). Eng Lit Renaiss 15no2:225–44 '85.

6817 —— Sir Walter Raleigh; a reference guide. Boston, Mass., G.K. Hall, 1986. xxi,116p. facsim. 23cm. (Reference guide to literature).

6818 **Armitage, Christopher M.** Sir Walter Ralegh; an annotated bibliography. Chapel Hill, University of North Carolina pr., 1987. xiii,236p. 23cm.
Rev: W.J. Scheick Sevent Cent Newsl 46:50–1 '88; Judith H. Anderson Stud Eng Lit 29:192 '89; C.S. Hunter Sidney Newsl 10:36–42 '89.

6819 **Tennenhouse, Leonard**. 'Sir Walter Ralegh and the literature of clientage' *in* Lytle, Guy F. and S. Orgel, *ed.* Patronage in the renaissance. Princeton, Princeton U.P., [1981]. p.235–58.

6820 **Clanton, Stacy M.** The 'number' of sir Walter Raleigh's Booke of the ocean to Scinthia. Stud Philol 82no2:200–11 '85. facsims.

6821 **Rudick, Michael**. The text of Ralegh's lyric 'What is our life'. Stud Philol 83no1:76–87 '86. diagrs.

RAMSAY, ALLEN, 1713–84

6822 **MacLaine, Allan H.** 'Selected bibliography [of primary and secondary sources]' *in* Allan Ramsay. (Twayne's English authors, 400). Boston, Twayne, [1985]. p.152–5.

6823 **Brown, Iain G.** The pamphlets of Allen Ramsey the younger. Bk Coll 37no1:54–85 '88. ports., facsim.
'Part II: Annotated hand–list of works' (p.66–80): *20 works, 1753–84, with locations of copies seen*; 'Note A: The provenance of Ramsey's own set of his pamphlets' (p.80–1); 'Note B: A lost volume of Ramsey pamphlets' (p.81–2); 'Appendix I: Pamphlets attributed at various times to Ramsay' (p. 82–4); 'II: Unpublished essays of Ramsay' (p.84–5).

6824 **Law, Alexander**. Allan Ramsay; Edinburgh university's recent acquisitions. (Notes and documents). Stud Scott Lit 20:248–56 '85.

RANSOME, ARTHUR MITCHELL, 1884–1967

6825 **Macleod, Helen**. Arthur Ransom. [Collecting]. Bk & Mag Coll 12:26–33 F '85. ports., facsims.
'Complete Arthur Ransom bibliography' (p.33).

RAWNSLEY, HARDWICKE DRUMMOND, 1850–1920

6826 **Wilson, Andrew F.** A checklist of the principal publications of Hardwicke Drummond Rawnsley. London, 1985. 47p. 21cm. (Duplicated typescript).
Chronol. checklist of 380 items, 1877–1968.

REDLICH, MONICA MARY (MRS. SIGURD CHRISTENSEN), 1909–65?

6827 (7:5578*) **Christensen, Sigurd**, *ed.* 'Bibliography' *in* Redlich, Monica. The unfolding years. London, G. Duckworth, 1970. p.54–6.

6828 **Wickham, D.E.** Monica Redlich; an uncollected treasure. Priv Libr ser3 10no4:170–5 '87. port.
'Handlist of books by Monica Redlich' (p.175): *chronol. checklist, 1932–70.*

REDMON, ANNE, *pseud. of* ANNE (REDMON) NIGHTINGALE, 1943–

6829 **Drinkwater, Catherine**. A bibliography of writings by Anne Redmon. Texas Stud Lang & Lit 25no2:364–5 '83.

REED, ISAAC, 1742–1807

6830 **Sherbo, Arthur**. Isaac Reed and the European magazine. Stud Bib 37:210–27 '84. table.
With lists of Reed's contribs. as C.D. *(51 items), and articles adapted for* Biographia dramatica.

REED, TALBOT BAINES, 1852–93

6831 **Crewdson, William H.P.** Talbot Baines Reed. Antiqu Bk Mnthly R 16no12:452–9 D '89. port., illus.
'A check-list of the first editions of Talbot Baines Reed' (p.459).

REID, THOMAS, 1710–96

6832 **Toronto. University. Thomas Fisher rare book library.** Thomas Reid and the Scottish enlightenment; an exhibition to celebrate the 200th anniversary of the publication of Thomas Reid's Essays on the intellectual powers of man, 1785. Prepared by P.B. Wood. Toronto, 1985. 33p. 28cm. (Reprod. from typewritng).

REYNOLDS, GEORGE WILLIAM MACARTHUR, 1814–79

6833 **Baker, William**. Reynolds vs Dickens; Chambers's London journal in
      1843. Antiqu Bk Mnthly R 11no1:14–19 Ja '84. facsims.
      'A checklist of G.W.M. Reynolds' Chambers's London journal contributions' (p.18–19).

6834 **Winn, Sharon A.** G.W.M. Reynolds papers. [Sought]. (Notes and
      queries). Bk Trade Hist Group Newsl 3:40 Oc '86.

RHYS, ERNEST PERCIVAL, 1859–1946

6835 **Roberts, J. Kimberley.** 'A selected bibliography' *in* Ernest Rhys.
      (Writers of Wales). Cardiff, University of Wales pr. on behalf of the
      Welsh arts council, 1983. p.67–71.

RHYS, JEAN, *pseud. of* ELLA GWENDOLEN REES WILLIAMS, 1894–1979

6836 **Roberts, Ray A.** Jean Rhys; bibliographical checklist. Am Bk Coll new
      ser 3no6:35–8 N/D '82.

6837 **Mellown, Elgin W.** Jean Rhys; a descriptive and annotated bibliogra-
      phy of works and criticism. New York, Garland, 1984. xxvii,218p.
      21cm. (Reference library of the humanities, 435).
      Rev: G. Bixby Am Bk Coll 7:47–50 '86.

6838 **Gaines, Nora.** Bibliography. Jean Rhys R 1no1:29–35 '86; 2no1:15–
      20 '87; 3no1:14–20 '88.

6839 **Bateman, Jean.** Jean Rhys. [Collecting]. Bk & Mag Coll 18:46–51 Ag
      '85. port., facsims.
      'Complete Jean Rhys bibliography' (p.51).

6840 **Chartier, Delphine.** Jean Rhys; l'auto-censure créatrice; analyse des
      versions successives de la nouvelle Rapunzel Rapunzel. [Revision].
      Jean Rhys R 1no1:15–29 '86.

6841 **Webb, Ruth.** Swimming the wide Sargasso sea; the manuscripts of
      Jean Rhys's novel. Brit Libr J 14no2:165–77 '88. facsims.

RICHARDSON, SAMUEL, 1689–1761

6842 **Hannaford, R.G.** Samuel Richardson; an annotated bibliography of
critical studies. New York, Garland, 1980. xxii,292p. 21cm. (Reference library of the humanities, 150).
Rev: A. Varney N&Q 227:447–8 '82; Sarah W.R. Smith Scriblerian 15:47–8 '82.

6843 **Brophy, Elizabeth B.** 'Select bibliography [of primary and secondary
sources]' *in* Samuel Richardson. (Twayne's English authors, 454).
Boston, Twayne, [1987]. p.131–4.

6844 **Warde, William B.** Revisions in the published texts of volume one of
Samuel Richardson's Clarissa. Libr Chron Univ Pennsylvania 45no1/
2:92–103 '81.

6845 **Doherty, Francis**. An autograph of Samuel Richardson. N&Q
230no2:220–1 Je '85.

6846 **Stuber, Florian.** On original and final intentions, or can there be an
authoritative Clarissa? Text 2:229–44 '85.

6847 **Doody, Margaret A.** and **F. Stuber**. Clarissa censored. [G. Sherburn's
1962 ed.]. Mod Lang Stud 18no1:74–88 '88.

6848 **Maslen, Keith I.D.** Samuel Richardson's books. Bib Soc Aust & N.Z.
Bull 12no2:85–9 '88.

6849 **Marks, Patricia H.** Lady Bradshaigh's copy of Clarissa. [Acquired].
(New and notable). Princeton Univ Libr Chron 50no3:285–7 '89.

RICKETTS, CHARLES DE SOUSY, 1866–1931

6850 **Delaney, J.G. Paul.**, *ed.* Letters from Charles Ricketts to 'Michael
Field', 1903–1913. Edinburgh, Tragara pr., 1981. 30p. 22cm. (Ltd.
to 145 no. copies).

RICKWOOD, JOHN EDGELL, 1898–

6851 **Munton, Alan** and **A. Young**, no.700.

RIDDELL, MARIA, 1776–1818

6852 **Truckell, A.E.** The Maria Riddell collection. [Libr.]. Dumfriesshire
& Galloway Nat Hist & Antiqu Soc Trans ser3 57:92–6 '82.

RITCHIE, ANNE ISABELLA THACKERAY, LADY, 1837–1919

6853 **Callow, Steven D.** [Annotated bibliography of lady Ritchie]. Virginia
      Woolf Q 2no3/4:288–93 '80.

6854 **Gérin, Winifred.** 'Bibliography' *in* Ann Thackeray Ritchie; a biogra-
      phy. Oxford, O.U.P., 1981. p.[297]–9.
      Checklist of unpubl. material, major publ. works, and some works about.

6855 **MacKay, Carol H.** 'Only connect'; the multiple roles of Anne Thack-
      eray Ritchie. [Colln. at HRC]. Libr Chron Univ Texas new ser 30:82–
      112 '85. port., facsims.

ROBERTS, MICHAEL, 1902–48

6856 **Frubb, Frederick**, *ed.* 'Bibliography [checklist of books and antholo-
      gies, essays and reviews, and ana]' *in* Selected poems and prose [of]
      Michael Roberts. [Manchester], Carcenet pr., [1980]. p.196–202.

ROBERTS, MORLEY, 1857–1942

6857 **Boll, Theophilus E.M.** The childhood of Morley Roberts. Libr Chron
      Univ Pennsylvania 45no1/2:115–28 '81.
      'Appendix: Stories of revenge; Psychological stories; Didactic stories' (p.126–8).

ROBERTSON, JOHN MCKINNON, 1856–1933

6858 **Wells, G.A.**, *ed.* 'Bibliography of works by J.M. Robertson' *in* J.M.
      Robertson, 1856–1933; liberal, rationalist and scholar: an assessment
      by several hands. London, Pemberton, 1987. p.3–9.
      Classified checklist of 116 items.

ROBERTSON, THOMAS WILLIAM, 1829–71

6859 **Tydeman, William**, *ed.* 'The principal plays of' and 'Select bibliography'
      in Plays by Tom Robertson.... Cambridge, C.U.P., [1982]. p.234–7.

6860 **Barrett, Daniel.** T.W. Robertson's plays; addenda to Nicoll's Han-
      dlist. Ninet Cent Theat Res 11no2:93–103 '83.

ROBINSON, HENRY CRABB, 1775–1867

6861 **Wellens, Oskar**. Henry Crabb Robinson, reviewer of Wordsworth, Coleridge, and Byron in the Critical review; some new attributions. Bull Res Humanit 84no1:98–120 '81. port.

'Henry Crabb Robinson's contributions to the Critical review' (p.101–2).

ROHMER, SAX, *pseud. of* ARTHUR SARSFIELD WADE, 1883–1959

6862 **Warren, Alan**. On compiling a Sax Rohmer collection. Armchair Detective 13no2:148–9 '80. facsims.

ROLFE, FREDERICK WILLIAM SERAFINO AUSTIN LEWIS MARY ('BARON CORVO'), 1860–1913

6863 **Gilsdorf, Jeanette W.** and **N.A. Salerno**. Frederick W. Rolfe, baron Corvo; an annotated bibliography of writings about him. Eng Lit Transit 23no1:3–83 '80.

6864 (7:5626) **Weeks, Donald**. Frederick Rolfe/baron Corvo. Antiqu Bk Mnthly R '79; D. Weeks 7no2:92 F '80.

6865 **James, G.P.** The date of composition of Frederick Rolfe's Nicholas Crable. [c.1901–4]. Eng Lit Transit 23no2:125–30 '80.

6866 **Weeks, Donald**. Frederick Rolfe's commonplace book. [Ms.]. Bk Coll 30no3:360–8 '81.

6867 —— Baron Corvo's onion top. [Pirated stories in Dutch]. Antiqu Bk Mnthly R 10no10:368–73 Oc '83. facsims.

6868 **Benkovitz, Miriam J.** Baron Corvo in Holland. [Stories publ. by P.L. Tak, 1898]. Bull Res Humanit 86:335–7 '83/5.

6869 **Jones, G.P.** The text of The desire and pursuit of the whole. [Revised by A.J.A. Symons, 1934]. N&Q 232no4:504–5 D '87.

ROLT, LIONEL THOMAS CASWALL, 1910–74

6870 **Rogerson, Ian** and **G. Maxim**. L.T.C. Rolt; a bibliography. Ed. and with an introd. by Mark Baldwin. Cleobury Mortimer, Shrop., M. & M. Baldwin, 1986. 48p. illus., facsims., ports. 21cm.

Classified checklist (523 items) of books and booklets, non-fiction periodical contribs., fiction, and biogr. material.

Rev: G. Weiner Antiqu Bk Mnthly R 14:69 '87.

ROLT, RICHARD, 1724–70

6871 **Black, Jeremy**. Richard Rolt, 'patriot' historian. [And his Memoirs of the life of...Crawford and Lindesay, 1735]. (Features). Factotum 16:19–23 F '85.

6872 **Rizzo, Betty W.** Richard Rolt and David Garrick; Rolt's 1750 Rosciad, other attributions, and his Drury lane career. Pa Bib Soc Am 79no4:489–98 '85.

ROSSETTI, CHRISTINA GEORGINA, 1830–94

6873 **Lasner, Mark S.** Christina Rossetti's 'common looking booklet'; a new letter about her Verses of 1847. N&Q 226no5:420–1 Oc '81.

ROSSETTI, DANTE GABRIEL, 1828–82

6874 **Fennell, Francis L.** Dante Gabriel Rossetti; an annotated bibliography. New York, Garland, 1983. xvi,282p. 21cm. (Reference library of the humanities, 286).

———————

6875 (5:13097c) **Fredeman, William E.** Rossetti's In memoriam; an elegaic reading of The house of life. John Rylands Libr Bull 47no2:298–341 Mr '65. table.
'Bibliographical chart...to facilitate the comparison of the three published versions of The house of life' (p.335–41).

6876 **Goldberg, Gail L.** Dante Gabriel Rossetti's revising hand; his illustrations for Christina Rossetti's poems. Vict Poet 20no3/4:145–59 '82. facsims.

6877 **Lewis, Roger C.** The making of Rossetti's Ballads and sonnets and Poems, 1881. [Publ.]. Vict Poet 20no3/4:199–212,216 '82. diagr.
'Editor's note' (p.212–15) *by* W.E. Fredeman.

6878 **Life, Allan R.** The art of not going halfway; Rossetti's illustration for The maids of Elfen-mere. Vict Poet 20no3/4:65–87 '82. facsims.

6879 **Riede, David**. A juvenile affair; D.G. Rossetti's 'Sacred to the memory of Algernon R.G. Stanhope.' [And W.M. Rossetti as editor]. Vict Poet 20no3/4:187–98 '82.

6880 **Gates, Barbara**. Revising The house of life; a look at seven unpublished sonnets. [Text]. Vict Poet 21no1:65–78 '83. facsims.

6881 **Ullmann, S.O.A.** Rossetti, Stillman and the Union college 'Willowood' manuscripts. [With transcripts]. Schenectady, [N.Y.], Friends of the Union college library, 1985. 24p. facsims. 24cm.

6882 **Keane, Robert N.** D.G. Rossetti in Texas. [Colln.]. Libr Chron Univ Texas 41:62–81 '87. ports., facsims.

6883 **Slayton, William T.** 'Roderick and Rosalba'; D.G. Rossetti's first juvenile work. [Descr. and ed.]. Vict Inst J 17:181–91 '89.

ROSSETTI, WILLIAM MICHAEL, 1829–1919

6884 **Lasner, Mark S.** William Rossetti's Swinburne's poems and ballads, a criticism. [1866]. (Note 444). Bk Coll 31no3:370–1 '82.

6885 **Peattie, Roger W.** W.M. Rossetti's contributions to the Edinburgh weekly review. Vict Pers R 19no3:108–10 '86. port.

6886 **Fredeman, William E.** William Michael Rossetti and the Wise-Forman conspiracy; a footnote to A sequel. Bk Coll 36no1:55–71 '87.

ROWE, NICHOLAS, 1674–1718

6887 **Shawcross, John T.** An apparently unrecorded item in the Margaret I. King library. [The fair penitent, ptd. by T. Sabine]. (Library notes). Kentucky R 9no2:97–8 '89.

ROWLEY, WILLIAM, 1585?–1625

6888 **Cheatham, George.** The date of William Rowley's A new wonder, a woman never vext. [1611–14]. (Bibliographical notes). Pa Bib Soc Am 75no4:437–42 '81.

6889 —— Confused lineation; an indication of Rowley's hand in collaboration. Library ser6 7no1:16–37 Mr '85. tables.

6890 **Darby, Trudi** [and] **G. Cheatham.** Rowley's hand in collaboration. ["I'l" as indication of scribe]. (Bibliographical notes). Library ser6 8no1:68–9 Mr '86.

RUSKIN, JOHN, 1819–1900

6891 **Recent** books and articles. Ruskin Newsl 22:8–9 '80; 23:10 '80; 24:18 '81; 25:12–13 '81; 26/7:13–15 '82; 28/9:26–8 '83; 30/1:22–4 '86; 32/3:23–5 '87.

6892 **Rochester. University. Rush Rhees library.** The Sydney Ross collection of John Ruskin; a catalogue of an exhibition held in the Department of rare books…. [Prepared by Ernest Bevan and David Riede].
[Rochester], 1981. 31p. port., facsims. 21cm. (Ltd. to 1000 copies).

6893 **Harmon, Robert B.** The impact of John Ruskin on literature; a selected bibliography. [Monticello, Ill.], Vance bibliographies, 1982.
12p. 28cm. (Architecture ser bib, A–751). (Duplicated typescript).

6894 **Kirchhoff, Frederick.** 'Selected bibliography [of primary and secondary sources]' *in* John Ruskin. (Twayne's English authors, 369).
Boston, Twayne, [1984]. p.149–56.

6895 **Cate, George A.** John Ruskin, a reference guide; a selective guide to
significant and representative works about him. Boston, Mass., G.K.
Hall, [1988]. xix,146p. 22cm. (Reference guide to literature).

6896 (7:5660c) **Benjamin, R. Dyke.** Ruskin observed. [Colln., with a descr.
checklist of the exhibition, 24 January–1 April 1978]. Grolier Club Gaz
new ser 28/9:3–56 Je/D '78. illus., ports., facsims.

6897 (7:5660f) —— 'John Ruskin: The development of a private collection'
in Fletcher, H. George, *ed.* A miscellany for bibliophiles. New York,
[1979]. p.[96]–125. illus.

6898 **Ruskin** in the sale rooms. Ruskin Newsl 22:7 '80; 23:8–10 '80; 24:18
'81; 25:11–12 '81; 26/7:11–12 '82; 28/9:24–6 '83; 30/1:19–22 '86;
32/3:21–3 '87.

6899 **Burd, Van A.** The Sydney Ross collection of Ruskiniana. [At University of Rochester]. Ruskin Newsl 24:7–8 '81.

6900 **Dearden, James S.** Ruskin's The ethics of the dust; an unrecorded
impression. [1866]. (Note 436). Bk Coll 30no2:254–5 '81.

6901 **Maidment, Brian E.** John Ruskin, George Allen and American printed books. Publ Hist 9:5–20 '81.

6902 —— '2. Readers fair and foul; John Ruskin and the periodical press'
in Shattock, Joanne and M. Wolff, *ed.* The Victorian periodical press;
samplings and soundings. [Leicester], Leicester U.P.; [Toronto],
Toronto U.P., 1982. p.[29]–58.

6903 —— 'Interpreting Ruskin, 1870–1914 [Publ.]' *in* Hunt, John D. and
Faith M. Holland, *ed.* The Ruskin polygon; essays on the imagination of
John Ruskin. [Manchester], Manchester U.P., [1982]. p.[158]–71.

6904   **...and** a new Ruskin library. [Ruskin library, Tokyo, based on Ryuzo Mikimoto colln.]. Ruskin Newsl 28/9:2–5 '83; Ruskin library, Tokyo. 30/1:17–18 '86.

6905   **Arts council of Great Britain,** LONDON. John Ruskin; an Arts council exhibition 1983. [Comp. by Jeanne Clegg]. [London, Arts council], [1983]. 88p. illus., facsims., ports. 26cm.

6906   **Dearden, James S.** John Ruskin and Bernard Quaritch; some additional letters. (Notes and documents). Bodleian Libr Rec 11no4:264–9 My '84.

6907   ——John Ruskin's Salsette and Elephanta. [1839]. Bk Coll 34no2:173–86 '85. facsims.
'...list of editions...' (p.182); 'Appendix: Present Location of copies...' (p.185–6).

6908   **Hilton, Timothy.** In the Ruskin archive. [Ruskin galleries, Bembridge school]. TLS 24 My '85:578,591.

6909   **Dearden, James S.** John Ruskin's Poems, 1850. [With note of addit. copies]. (Note 425). Bk Coll 38no1:114–16 '89.

6910   **Hayman, John.** John Ruskin's Hortus inclusus; the manuscript sources and publication history. [1887]. Huntington Libr Q 52no3:363–87 '89.
The relationship of John Ruskin and Susanna Beever.–The relationship of John Ruskin and Albert Fleming.–Hortus inclusus: publication; reception and revision.–Additions to Hortus inclusus; proposed and suppressed.–Conclusion.

RUSSELL, BERTRAND ARTHUR WILLIAM, 3D EARL RUSSELL, 1872–1970

6911   **Blackwell, Kenneth.** Recent bibliographical discoveries. Russell 37/40:47–9 '80/1. [Sg.: K.B.].

6912   **Spadoni, Carl.** Recent acquisitions; manuscripts, typescripts and proofs. Russell 37/40:51–8 '80/1. facsim. [Sg.: C.S.].

6913   **Martin, Werner.** Bertrand Russell; a bibliography of his writings/ Eine Bibliographie seiner Schrifte, 1895–1976. München, K.G. Saur; Hamden, Conn., Linnet books, 1981. xlv,332p. 21cm.

6914   **Blackwell, Kenneth.** A secondary bibliography of Russell's 'The essence of religion'. (Bibliographies/archival inventories). Russell new ser 1no2:143–6 '81/2.

6915   **Harley, David** and **C. Spadoni.** A secondary educational bibliography of Bertrand Russell. (Bibliographies/ archival inventories). Russell new ser 2no1:59–68 '82.

6916 **Toronto. University. Thomas Fisher rare book library.** Bertrand Russell, polymath; an exhibition of books, pamphlets and ephemera from the collection of John G. Slater, November 1982–January 22, 1983, on the occasion of the seventeenth annual Conference on editorial problems,…1982. [Toronto], [1982]. 30p. 28cm. (Reprod. from typewriting).
Rev: K. Blackwell Russell new ser 3:78–80 '83.

6917 **Spadoni, Carl**. Rupert Crawshay-Williams's bequest. (Bibliographies/ archival inventories). Russell new ser 3n01:29–40 '83. facsims.
1. A brief biography.–2. Checklist of publications by R. Crawshay-Williams (p.31–2).–3. The papers.

6918 —— A checklist of theses and dissertations on Bertrand Russell. (Bibliographies/archival inventories). Russell new ser 4n02:289–301 '84/5.

6919 **Kuntz, Paul G.** 'Selected bibliography [of primary and secondary sources]' *in* Bertrand Russell (Twayne's English authors, 421). Boston, Twayne, [1986]. p.171–7.

6920 **Blackwell, Kenneth**. Recent additions to the bibliography. (Bibliographies/archival inventories). Russell new ser 6n02:165–8 '86/7.

6921 **Turcon, Sheila**. Recent acquisitions: manuscripts, typescripts and proofs. (Bibliographies/archival inventories). Russell new ser 6n02:154–64 '86/7; 7n01:79–85 '87. facsims.

6922 **Anderson, Stefan**. A secondary religious bibliography of Bertrand Russell. (Bibliography/archival inventories). Russell new ser 7n02:147–61 '87/8.

6923 **Blackwell, Kenneth**. Addenda to the checklist of theses and dissertations on Bertrand Russell. (Bibliographies/ archival inventories). Russell new ser 7n02:162–6 '87/8.

6924 —— Recent acquisitions: manuscripts, typescripts and proofs in the Dora Russell papers. (Bibliographies/archival inventories). Russell new ser 9n02:165–7 '89/90.

6925 **Turcon, Sheila**. Recent acquisitions: Russell's correspondence in the Dora Russell papers. (Bibliographies/ archival inventories). Russell new ser 9n02:156–64 '89/90.

———

6926 (5:13129p) **The Bertrand** Russell archive. McMaster Univ Libr Res News 1n01:[1–4] '68/9. ports., facsim.

6927 **Blackwell, Kenneth**. '"Perhaps you will think me fussy..."; three myths in editing Russell's Collected papers' *in* Conference on editorial problems, 18th, Toronto, 1982. Editing polymaths; Erasmus to Russell: papers given.... Ed. by H.J. Jackson. Toronto, Committee for the Conference on editorial problems, 1983. p.99–138.

6928 —— Russell's mathematical proofreading. Russell new ser 3n02:157–8 '83/4. facsim.

6929 —— Part 1 of The principles of mathematics. (Textual studies). Russell new ser 4n02:271–88 '84/5.
'Variants between The principles of mathematics and its ms.' (p.284–8).

6930 —— The finding-aids of the Russell archives. [McMaster univ.]. (Bibliographies/archival inventories). Russell new ser 5n01:66–71 '85.
1. The physical arrangement of the Russell archives.–2. The catalogues of archives 1 and 2.–3. The bibliography.–4. Other finding-aids.

6931 **Spadoni, Carl** and **D. Harley**. Bertrand Russell's library. [At McMaster university]. J Libr Hist 20n01:25–45 '85.
Russell family.–Cobden-Sanderson material.–History and politics.–Literature.–Philosophy.–General science.–Religion.–Wittgenstein's books.

6932 **Spadoni, Carl**. Who wrote Bertrand Russell's Wisdom of the west? [Paul Foulkes]. Pa Bib Soc Am 80n03:349–67 '86.

6933 **Blackwell, Kenneth**. Part II of The principles of mathematics. (Textual studies). Russell new ser 7n01:60–70 '87.
'Variants between The principles of mathematics, part KK, "Number", and its ms.' (p.68–70).

6934 **Spadoni, Carl**. Kate Amberley's album. (Bibliographies/archival inventories). Russell new ser 7n01:71–8 '87.

RUSSELL, ERIC FRANK, 1905–78

6935 **Payne, Philip Stephensen-**. Eric Frank Russell; a working bibliography. [2d ed.] [Leeds], 1988. (First publ. 1986). 31p. 20cm. (Galactic Central Bibs). (Duplicated typescript).

RUSSELL, WILLIAM CLARK, 1844–1911

6936 **Crewdson, William H.P.** William Clark Russell. Antiqu Bk Mnthly R 15n08:302–7 Ag '88. port., illus.
'A check-list of the first editions of William Clark Russell' (p.307).

SAINT JOHN, HENRY, 1ST VISCOUNT BOLINGBROKE, 1678–1751

6937 **Clingham, G.J.** Bolingbroke's copy of Pope's Works, 1717–1735, in Tonbridge school library. N&Q 231no4:500–2 D '86. facsim.

SAINTSBURY, GEORGE EDWARD BATEMAN, 1845–1933

6938 (1:4576d) **Parker, W.M.** 'A Saintsbury bibliography' *in* Oliver, John W. [and others], *ed.* The last vintage; essays and papers by George Saintsbury. London, Methuen, [1950]. p.244–55.
Classified checklist of literary histories, biogr. and critical works, miscellaneous works, introds., prefaces and edited matter, and articles by.

SALISBURY, ENOCH ROBERT GIBBON, 1819–90

6939 **James, Brian Ll.** The Salisbury collection. [University college, Cardiff]. New Welsh R 1no2:71–3 '88. facsims.

SANDYS, SIR EDWIN, 1561–1629

6940 **Ellison, James.** The order of editions of sir Edwin Sandy's Relation of the state of religion, 1605. (Bibliographical notes). Library ser6 2no2:208–11 Je '80.

SANDYS, GEORGE, 1578–1644

6941 **Hoppe, Jody.** Illustrations in George Sandys' translation of Ovid's Metamorphosis. Soundings 20no26:29–36 '89. facsims.

SAVILE, GEORGE, MARQUIS OF HALIFAX, 1633–95

6942 **Emmerson, John McL.** The rare ninth edition. [G. Savile's Advice to a daughter, 1716 and rarity]. (Notes). Bib Soc Aust & N.Z. Bull 8no4:215–18 '84.

SAYERS, DOROTHY LEIGH (MRS. I. FLEMING), 1893–1947

6943 (7:5694) **Gilbert, Colleen B.** A bibliography of the works of Dorothy L. Sayers, 1978.
Rev: G.A. Lee Seven 1:126–8 '80.

6944 **Christopher, Joe R.** A Sayers checklist. [Annotated]. Sayers R 4no1:13–25 '80; 4no2:18–32 Ja '81.

6945 **Durkin, Mary B.** 'Selected bibliography [of primary and secondary sources]' *in* Dorothy L. Sayers. (Twayne's English authors, 281). Boston, Twayne, [1980]. p.189–200.

6946 **Youngberg, Ruth T.** Dorothy L. Sayers; a reference guide. Boston, Mass., G.K. Hall, 1982. xxi,178p. 23cm. (Reference guide to literature).
Rev: J. Breen Wilson Libr Bull 56:615 '82; G.A. Lee Seven 4:119–21 '83; Nancy M. Tischler Christianity & Lit 32:72 '83; Nancy-Lou Patterson Mythlore 10:38 '84.

6947 **Hoy, Peter C.** Addenda to C. Gilbert, A bibliography of the works of Dorothy L. Sayers. Bib Soc Aust & N.Z. Bull 10no2/3:89–91 '86.

6948 **Hall, Trevor H.** '3. The singular affair of the verso signature [Dr. Watson, widower]' *in* Dorothy L. Sayers; nine literary studies. [London], Duckworth, [1980]. p.29–34.

6949 **Macleod, Helen.** Dorothy L. Sayers. [Collecting]. Bk & Mag Coll 12:42–9 F '85. ports., facsims.
'Complete bibliography of Dorothy L. Sayers 1st editions' (p.49).

SCOTT, MARY, fl.1774–88

6950 **Fullard, Joyce.** Notes on Mary Whateley and Mary Scott's The female advocate. (Bibliographical notes). Pa Bib Soc Am 81no1:74–6 '87.

SCOTT, PAUL, 1928–78

6951 **Rao, K. Bhaskara.** 'Selected bibliography [of primary and secondary sources]' *in* Paul Scott. (Twayne's English authors, 285). Boston, Twayne, [1980]. p.157–64.

SCOTT, SIR WALTER, 1771–1832

6952 **Edinburgh. University. Library.** Catalogue of an exhibition of some unique or unusual items from the Corson sir Walter Scott collection. Edinburgh, 1980. vii,14p. 21cm. Covertitle. (Duplicated typescript).
Foreword by James C. Corson.

6953 **Mitchell, Jerome,** *comp.* 'A list of Walter Scott operas' *in* Alexander, J.H. and D.S. Hewitt, *ed.* Scott and his influence; papers of the Aberdeen Scott conference, 1982. (Occas Pa 6). [Aberdeen], Association for Scottish literary studies, [1983]. p.[511]–17.

6954 (5:13242d) **Beckwith, Frank.** The Leeds library and sir Walter Scott. [Its colln.]. Univ Leeds R 11no2:152–61 D '68.

6955 (7:5718c) **Gamerschlag, Kurt**. Die Korrektur der Waverley Novels; Tex-tkritische untersuchungen zur einer Autor-Korrektor-Beziehung. Bonn, Bouvier, 1979. x,378p. 22cm. (Studien zur englischen Literatur, 16).

1. Einleitung.–2. Ballantyne und Scott.–3. Der Korrekturengang.–4. Die Korrektur der Setzfehler.–5. Die Korrektur der Sprache.–6. Die Stilkorrektur.–7. Die Korrektur der Erzählstruktur.–8. Stoff und Inhalt.

6956 **Bruckner, Ursula**. Walter Scott, Dichter und Bibliophile. Marginalien 79hft3:54–83 '80.

6957 **Finley, Gerald**. Landscapes of memory; Turner as illustrator to Scott. London, Scolar pr., [1980]. 272p. facsims. 25cm.

1. Introduction: Turner, Scotland and Scott.–2. The background to Turner as illus-trator.–3. The Provincial antiquities.–4. The Poetical works.–5. Turner's visit to Ab-botsford in 1831.–6. Berwick-on-Tweed, Edinburgh, and the northern tour.–7. The conclusion of the 'poetry' business; Turner's 'Smailholm gift'.–8. Turner's tour of Scotland in 1831; its artistic significance.–9. Turner's tour of Scotland in 1834; the 'Waverley' commission; the Prose works.–10. Turner's illustrations to Lockhart's Memoirs of the life of sir Walter Scott.–Appendices: 1. The Turner–Tilt affair. 2. The Scott monument. 3. The selection of the subjects illustrated in Lockhart's edition of Scott's Poetical works.–4. Periods of use of some sketch books in the Turner bequest (British museum).

Rev: Evelyn Joll Burlington Mag 123:244 '81; J. Bayley Listener 105:115–16 '81; K. Kroeber Scott Lit J 16:13–16 '82; Alice Schreyer Am Bk Coll new ser 4:42–51 '83.

6958 **Garside, Peter D.** 'Rob's last raid; Scott and the publication of the Waverley novels' *in* Myers, Robin and M.R.A. Harris, *ed*. Author/ publisher relations during the eighteenth and nineteenth centuries. [Oxford], [1983]. p.[88]–118.

6959 **Kelly, Gary**. 'A proposal to carry out a critical edition of sir Walter Scott's Waverley novels at the University of Alberta' *in* Alexander, J.H. and D.S. Hewitt, *ed*. Scott and his influence; papers of the Aberdeen Scott conference, 1982. (Occas Pa 6). [Aberdeen], Association for Scottish literary studies, [1983]. p.13–19.

6960 **Pinkerton, J.M.** Demonology in the library of Abbotsford. [Biblio-thèques écossaises]. Bull Bibliophile 3:312–19 '84. facsim.

'Resumé' (p.319).

6961 **Millgate, Jane**. Scott as innovator; the example of Rob Roy. Biblioth 12no4:93–102 '85.

6962 **Bell, Alan S.** Scott for Scotland. [Interleaved set of Waverley novels with revisions, and mss. from Pforzheimer library to NLS]. Bk Coll 35no3:281–92 '86. [Sg.: A.S.B.]

6963 **Garside, Peter D.** Dating Waverley's early chapters. Biblioth 13no3:61–81 '86.

6964   **Scotland. National library,** EDINBURGH. Sir Walter Scott's magnum opus and the Pforzheimer manuscript. Ed. by M.F. Strachan. Edinburgh, 1986. 27p. illus., facsims. 25cm.
> The interleaved Waverley novels, Jane Millgate.–The exile and return of the magnum, Iain Gordon Brown.–The Pforzheimer Scott manuscripts, Patrick Cadell.

6965   **Brown, Iain G.** Scott's interleaved Waverley novels, the 'magnum opus': National library of Scotland mss. 23001–41; an introd. and commentary. [Aberdeen], Pergamon/Aberdeen U.P. in association with the National library of Scotland, [1987]. xi,131p. illus., facsims. 29cm.
> The interleaved Waverley novels, Jane Millgate.–Descriptive guide to the interleaved set, J.H. Alexander.–The exile and return of the 'magnum opus': episodes in the life of a literary wanderer, Iain Gordon Brown.–Related material in American collections, Claire Lamont.–'My own right hand shall do it': an anthology of extracts from Scott's Journal and Letters, 1825–1831, comp. by Iain Gordon Brown.–An illustrated commentary on the interleaved set....–Concordance....
> *Rev*: Fiona Robertson R Eng Stud new ser 40:133–4 '89.

6966   **Key, Neil.** Sir Walter Scotts Bibliothek in Abbotsford. Imprimatur neue Folge 12:249–59 '87. ports., facsims.

6967   **Mayer, Robert.** The internal machinery displayed; The heart of Midlothian and Scott's apparatus for the Waverley novels. Clio 17no1:1–20 '87.

6968   **Millgate, Jane.** Adding more buckram; Scott and the amplification of Peveril of the park. [Revision]. Eng Stud Canada 13no2:174–81 Je '87.

6969   —— Scott's last edition; a study in publishing history. Edinburgh, Edinburgh U.P., [1987]. x,154p. 19cm.
> 1. The conception and planning of the edition.–2. Working on the magnum.–3. James Ballantyne and the printing of the magnum.–4. Robert Cadell and the ownership of the magnum.–5. Scott at work: interleaved set, transcription, and proofs.–6. The author's correcting hand: revision and annotation in the magnum.–7. Publishing context and later influence.–8. Conclusion.
> *Rev*: Fiona Robertson R Eng Stud new ser 40:134–5 '89; K. Gamerschlag Scott Lit J Suppl 32:2–4 '90.

6970   **Hewitt, David S.** Scott and textual multiplepoinding. Text 4:361–73 '88.

6971   **Kelly, William A.** Scott in the National library of Scotland. [Significant acquisitions]. Biblioth 15no2:51 '88.

6972   **Tait, Margaret.** Illustrated editions of The surgeon's letter. Scott Newsl 13:8–11 '88.

6973   **McMullin, Brian J.** The publication of Scott's, The pirate 1822. [With bibliogr. descrs.]. Biblioth 16no1/3:1–29 '89. facsims.

6974   **Millgate, Jane.** Scott the cunning tailor; refurbishing the Poetical works. [Publ. R. Cadell, 1829–39]. Library ser6 11no4:336–51 D '89.

SCROPE, GEORGE JULIUS POULETT, 1797–1876

6975 **Sturges, Paul**. A bibliography of George Poulett Scrope, geologist, economist and local historian. Boston, Baker library, Harvard business school, 1984. 83p. port., facsims. (Kress Libr Publ, 24).
Chronol. checklist, with locations of copies.

SEELEY, SIR JOHN ROBERT, 1834–95

6976 **Wormell, Deborah**. 'Bibliography [of works, press reports of, reviews of, and ana]' *in* Sir John Seeley and the uses of history. Cambridge, C.U.P., [1980]. p.211–24.

SEWARD, ANNA, 1747–1809

6977 **Douglas, Aileen**. Anna Seward's annotated copy of Caleb Williams. Princeton Univ Libr Chron 49no1:74–7 '87.

SHAFFER, PETER, 1926–

6978 (7:5725*) **Klein, Dennis A.** 'Selected bibliography [of primary and secondary sources]' *in* Peter Shaffer. (Twayne's English authors, 261). Boston, Twayne, [1979]. (Rev. ed. 1993). p.155–61.

6979 **Cooke, Virginia** and **M. Page**. '5. Select bibliography [of primary and secondary sources]' *in* File on Shaffer. (Writer-files). London, Methuen, [1987]. p.86–8.

6980 **Gianakaris, C.J.** Shaffer's revisions in Amadeus. Theat J 35no1:88–101 Mr '83.

SHAKESPEARE, WILLIAM, 1564–1616

The following entries represent additions to Shakespearian bibliography and textual criticism; a bibliography (1971). *Items published before 1969 have the prefix '2' of that volume of the* Index *and numbers to indicate their place in the volume. Corrections and additions to items in* British literary bibliography, 1970–79 (1992), *and additional items, have the prefix '7'.*

SHAKESPEARE—GENERAL BIBLIOGRAPHIES OF AND GUIDES TO SHAKESPEARIAN LITERATURE

—SERIAL BIBLIOGRAPHIES

6981 **Boltz, Ingeborg**. Shakespeare-bibliographie für 1978[–81/2] wit Nachtragen aus früheren Jahren. (Bibliographie). Sh Jahrb (Heidelberg) 1980:275–333 '80; 1981:230–63 '81; 1982:253–89 '82; Shakespeare auf der Bühne Spielzeit 1981/1982... 1983:269–95 '83; Verzeichnis der

Shakespeare-Inszenierungen und Bibliographie der Kritiken, Spielzeit 1982/1983, von Ingeborg Boltz und Christian Jauslin 1984:207–24 '84; ...1983/1984... 1985:194–212 '85; ...1984/1985... 1986:177–97 '86; ...1985/1986... 1987:151–70 '87; ...1986/1987... 1988:217–34 '88; ...1987/1988... 1989:311–31 '89; ...1988/1989... 1990:203–27 '90; ...1989/1990... 1991:211–31 '91.

6982 **Magister, Karl-Heinz.** Shakespeare-Bibliographie für 1978[–89] mit Nachträgen aus früheren Jahren. Sh-Jahrb (Weimar) 116:193–274 '80; 117:227–307 '81; 118:209–91 '82; 119:205–86 '83; 120:209–78 '84; 121:235–302 '85; 122:243–30 '86; 123:225–99 '87; 124:303–71 '88; 125:225–302 '89; 126:239–320 '90; 127:227–303 '91.

6983 **Williams, George W.** and **MacD.P. Jackson.** 3. Textual studies. (The year's contributions to Shakespearian study). Sh Surv 33:205–11 '80; 34:187–97 '81; 35:179–91 '82; 36:181–95 '83; MacD.P. Jackson 37:202–19 '84; 38:238–54 '85; 39:236–52 '86; 40:224–36 '87; 41:228–45 '88; 42:200–13 '89.

6984 (2:21) '**Shakespeare**, an annotated bibliography for 1949–80, 1981–<9>' *in* Shakespeare Quarterly. 1no1 Ja '50–22no4 '71, 23no1–32no4 '81 1972–81; 33no5– . Bethlehem, Pa. [etc.], Shakespeare association of America, 1950–71; Washington, D.C., Folger Shakespeare library, 1982–<90>.

6985 **A Shakespeare** bibliography of periodical publications in South Africa in 1985 and 1986. Sh in Southern Africa 1:85–7 '87; ...in 1987. 2:131–4 '88; ...in 1988. 3:113–15 '89.

SHAKESPEARE—GENERAL BIBLIOGRAPHIES AND GUIDES

—BIBLIOGRAPHIES

6986 (7:5753) **Elton, William R.** and **Giselle Schlesinger.** Shakespeare's world. Renaissance intellectual contexts; a selective annotated guide, 1966–1971, 1979.
Rev: W. Habicht Mod Lang R 78:426 '83; Charlotte Spivack Lit Res Newsl 7:161–2 '82; K.S. Cahn, M. Pons Ann Scholarship 3:110–22 '84.

6987 **Lenz, Carolyn, Ruth Swift, Gayle Greene [and others]**, *ed.* 'Women and men in Shakespeare; a selective bibliography' *in* The women's part; feminist criticism of Shakespeare. Urbana, University of Illinois pr., [1980]. p.314–35.

6988 **McLean, Andrew M.** Shakespeare; annotated bibliographies and media guide for teachers. Urbana, Ill., National council of teachers of English, 1980. ix,277p. 22cm.
Rev: Choice 18:374 '80; H.E. Jacobs Sh Stud 14:339–41 '81; P.R. Rider Am Ref Bks Ann 12:602 '81; Dorothy E. Litt Renaiss & Reformation 7:295–7 '83.

6989 **Willbern, David**, *comp.* 'A bibliography of psychoanalytic and psychological criticism, 1964–1978' *in* Schwartz, Murray M. and Coppélia Kahn, *ed.* Representing Shakespeare; new psychoanalytic essays. Baltimore, Johns Hopkins pr., [1980]. p.264–88.
Rev. and enl. from Int R Psycho-analysis 51:361–72 '78.

6990 **Kolin, Philip C.** Shakespeare and the computer; a checklist of scholarship. Sh Newsl 31no3:22 My '81; 31no4/5:28 N '81; 31no6:36 D '81.

6991 **Ziegler, Georgianna**. A supplement to the Lenz-Greene-Neely bibliography on Women and men in Shakespeare, based on the collections of the Furness Shakespeare library. Women's Stud 9no2:203–13 '82.

6992 **Chen Xiongshang.** Books and articles on Shakespeare published in People's republic of China. Sh Trans 9:33–41 '83.

6993 **Studing, Richard** and **Carolyn Merlo.** Shakespeare and pictorial art. Bull Bib 40no2:108–12 Je '83.

6994 **Lautermilch, Steven [and others].** A check list of explication, 1983: Shakespeare. Explicator 44no1:2–48 '85.

6995 **McRoberts, J. Paul.** Shakespeare and the medieval tradition; an annotated bibliography. New York, Garland, 1985. xix,256p. 20cm. (Reference library of the humanities, 603).
Rev. Marjorie E. Bloss Am Ref Bks Ann 17:463–4 '86; Carolyn VanDyke Sh Bull 4:21 '86; Barbara Cohen-Stratyner Theat J 38:496–8 '86; L.R.N. Ashley Biblioth d'Humanisme & Renaiss 49:443–4 '87.

6996 **Champion, Larry S.** The essential Shakespeare; an annotated bibliography of major modern studies. Boston, G.K. Hall, 1986. (2d ed. 1993). xiv,463p. 23cm. (Reference Publ Lit).
Rev. Francine Fialkoff, Janet Fletcher, Barbara Hoffert Libr J 112:34 '87; T. Hawkes TLS 10 Ap '87:390,392–3 '87; D.C. Reading Choice 24:860 '87; G.U. de Sousa Am Ref Bks Ann 18:467 '87; L.R.N. Ashley Biblioth d'Humanisme & Renaiss 50:156 '88; A. Leggatt Lit Res Nesl 11:274–7 '86 [i.e. '88].

6997 **Liu Houling.** Shakespeare in China, 1982–1983. Sh Worldwide 11:99–109 '86.

6998 **Coates, Richard**. A provincial bibliography on names in the works of Shakespeare. Names 35no3/4:203–23 S/D '87.

6999 **Rajec, Elizabeth M.** A selected bibliography of Shakespeare and literary onomastics. Names 35no3/4:224–31 S/D '87.

7000 **Terris, Olwen.** Shakespeare; a list of audio-visual materials available in the U.K. 2d ed. London, British universities film and video council, 1987. (First publ. 1986). vi,41p. 30cm.
Rev. Sh on Film Newsl 13:5 '89.

7001 **Woodbridge, Linda**. Shakespeare; a selective bibliography of modern criticism. West Cornwall, Conn., Locust Hill pr., 1988. xiv,266p. 16cm.
Rev: P. Kujoory Choice 25:1541 '88; F. Occhigrosso Sh Bull 6:27 '88; J.E. Stephenson Am Ref Bks Ann 20:450–1 '89.

7002 **Wells, Stanley W.** Shakespeare; a bibliography. [London, British council], [1989]. 54p. 21cm.

7003 **Meserole, Harrison T.** and **J.B. Smith**. 'Yet there is method in it'; the cumulative Shakespeare bibliography, a product of project planning in the humanities. Perspectives Computing 1no2:4–11 Ap '81. facsims.
Coordination and administration.–System design.–Work flow.–Conclusion.

—GUIDES

7004 **Bergeron, David M.** and **G.U. de Sousa**. Shakespeare; a study and research guide. 2d ed., rev. Lawrence, U.P. of Kansas, 1987. (First publ. 1975). viii,202p. 20cm. 20cm.
Rev: L.R.N. Ashley Bull d'Humanisme 50:731–2 '88; J.J. Yoch Sh Q 40:113–15 '89.

SHAKESPEARE—WORKS

7005 **[Marder, Louis]**. Pergamon's Shakespeare microfiche library. [Bibliotheca Shakespeariana]. Sh Newsl 35no2:21 '85; 35no3:28 '85.

—BIBLIOGRAPHIES

7006 **Heun, Hans G.** Probleme der deutschen Shakespeare-Übersetzung, VIII: eine Bibliographie. Sh Jahrb (Heidelberg) 1980:260–74 '80.

7007 **Meisei university,** Токуо. **Kodama memorial library.** Shakespeare and Shakespeariana, no.I. Hino, Tokyo, 1980. xv,451p. illus., facsims. 24cm.
Catalogue based on acquisitions from Folger Sh. libr. and Allardyce Nicoll's libr.; not indexed.

7008 **Priessnitz, Horst,** *ed*. 'Anglo-amerikanische Shakespeare-Bearbeitungen des 20. Jahrhunderts; ein bibliographischer Versuch' *in* Anglo-amerikanische Shakespeare-Bearbeitungen des 20. Jahrhunderts. [Modern adaptations of Sh.'s works]. (Ars interpretandi, 9). Darmstadt, Wissenschaftliche Buchgesellschaft, 1980. p.413–32.

7009 **Lehnert, Martin**. Shakespeares Werke in modernenglischer Schreibweise. Zeitschrift Angl & Amerikanistik 29hft1:5–11 '81.

7010 **Meisei university,** TOKYO. **Kodama memorial library.** Selected Shakespeariana. Preface by Mitsuo Kodama. Tokyo, Japan, 1986. 32p. largely plates. illus., facsims. 25cm.

7011 —— Shakespeare and Shakespeariana, no.II. Hino, Tokyo, 1986. xxvi,760p. illus., facsims. 24cm.

7012 **Newlin, Jeanne T.** Shakespeare promptbooks in the Harvard theatre collection; a catalogue. With the assistance of Martha R. Mahard and Robin L. Baker. [Cambridge, Mass., Harvard university library], [1988]. 133p. facsims. 25cm. (Harvard Libr Bull 35no1 Special issue, 1987). *Annotated classified checklist of 403 items.*

7013 **Drama** on the world stage: prompt books and performance records. Series one: The Folger Shakespeare library, Washington, D.C.; an inventory to the Research publications microform collection. [Reading], Research publications, [1989]. xxvi,91p. 20cm. (Reprod. from typewriting).

7014 **Thatcher, David S.** The 1988 Shakespeare music catalogue; aims, methods, and progress to date. Sh Jahrb (Bochum) 1985:166–77 '85.

—COLLECTIONS AND LIBRARIES

7015 (2:348) **Swaim, Elizabeth A.** The Curtis Bacon-Shakespeare collection. Wesleyan Libr N 3:13–16 '69. [Sg.: E.A.S.]

7016 **Cerasano, Susan P.** Joseph Crosby's green boxes, his Shakespeare collectanea. (A nineteenth-century bardolator). Michigan Academician 14:81–92 '81/2.

7017 **Fox, Levi.** In honour of Shakespeare; the history and collections of the Shakespeare birthplace trust. [Enl. ed.]. Norwich, Jarrold in association with the Shakespeare birthplace trust, 1972 [i.e. 1983]. (First publ. 1972). 160p. illus., facsims. 24cm.

7018 **Twentieth** anniversary; the Shakespeare library in Munich. Sh Newsl 34no3:34 '84.

7019 **Rathbone, Niky.** The Birmingham Shakespeare library. Theatrephile 1no2:21–4 Mr '84. facsims.

7020 **Schoenbaum, Samuel.** '12. The Folger at fifty' *in* Shakespeare and others. Washington, Folger books; London, Scolar pr., [1985]. p.161–8. *Repr. from* Smithsonian 13:118–24 '82.

7021 **Marder, Louis**. Pforzheimer Shakespeareana sold to University of Texas–Austin. Sh Newsl 36no1:12 '86. [Sg.: L.M.].

7022 **Birmingham. Public libraries. Shakespeare library.** The Shakespeare library. Birmingham, Birmingham public libraries, 1987. [8]p. facsims. 21cm. (Covertitle).

7023 **Burdette, Livia**. The Hillier Shakespeare collection; origin, scope and prospects. Sh in Southern Africa 1:62–4 '87.

7024 **Pafford, John H.P.** Shakespeare and the Burghley or Cope library. [Thomas Burghley's libr.]. N&Q 232no2:219 Je '87.

7025 **Kamps, Ivo** and **Lisa Schnell**. 'The bitter-sweet of this Shakespearean fruit'. [Princeton's Sh. colln., and preservation]. Princeton Univ Libr Chron 49no3:273–88 '88. table., facsims.
The Shakespeare project.–The book and society.–The collection and scholarship.

7026 **Lidholm, Elaine**. Shakespeare in Washington; the fabulous Folger Shakespeare Library. Brit Heritage 9no4:34–9 Je/Jl '88. illus.

7027 **Wolpers, Theodor**. Die Shakespeare-Sammlung der Göttinger Universitäts-bibliothek im 18. Jahrhundert. Sh Jahrb (Bochum) 1988:58–84 '88.
'Anhang: Englische Shakespeare-Kritik des 18. Jhs. und der Göttinger Bestand' (p.81–4).

7028 **An exhibition** of Shakespeare materials in the HRHRC collections. (Collections at Texas). Libr Chron Univ Texas new ser 48:6–7 '89. illus.

—GENERAL

7029 (2:938c) **McManaway, James G.** The authorship of Shakespeare. [Washington, D.C.], Folger Shakespeare library, [1962]. (4th ptg. 1974; 5th ptg. 1979). 54p. illus., facsims. 20cm.

7030 **Playbills**, illustrations, etc. related to the 1769 Shakespeare jubilee, particularly D. Garrick's participation, 1746–1860?; collected by G. Daniel; in BL *see* Gould, Alison, Named special collections, 1981: no.818.

7031 **Alsop, James D.** The Shakespearian forgeries of 1796; an insertion in a Tudor manuscript. [In BL]. N&Q 226no4:315 Ag '81.

7032 **Thomas, David**. Shakespeare in the public records. Section on the will and signatures by Jane Cox. London, H.M.S.O., [1985]. 39p. facsims. 26cm.
Rev. Inga-Stina Ewbank TLS 25 Ap '86:451–2.

7033 **Wickenden, Dorothy**. Bowdlerizing the bard; how to protect your kids from Shakespeare. [Censorship]. New Republic 3:16–19 Je '85.

7034 **Williams, George W.** The craft of printing and the publication of Shakespeare's works. Washington, D.C., Folger Shakespeare library; London, Associated U.P., 1985. 103p. illus., facsims., tables. 24cm.
1. The invention of printing.–2. The craft of printing.–3. Printing in England.–4. The printing and publishing of Shakespeare's works.
Rev: Inga-Stina Ewbank TLS 25 Ap '86:451–2; MacD.P. Jackson Sh Surv 40:235 '88.

7035 —— 'The publishing and editing of Shakespeare's plays' *in* Andrews, John F., *ed.* William Shakespeare; his world, his work, his influence. New York, C. Scribner's, [1985]. V.3, p.589–601.

7036 **Sherbo, Arthur**. The earliest(?) critic of the Ireland Shakespeare forgeries. [K.S., fl.1795, possibly Malone]. N&Q 233no4:498–500 D '88.

—QUARTOS

7037 **Cloud, Random**, *pseud. of* Randall McLeod. The marriage of good and bad quartos. Sh Q 33no4:421–31 '82. facsims.

7038 **Johnson, Alfred F.** Shakespeare and the pirates. Knebworth, Herts., Lytton pr., 1982. 11p. facsim. 19cm.

7039 **Berger, Thomas L.** Press variants in substantive Shakespearian dramatic quartos. Library ser6 10no3:231–41 S '88.
1. 'Good' and 'doubtful' quartos not reprinted before the Folio.–2. 'Bad' quartos reprinted before the Folio.–3. 'Bad' quartos followed by 'good' quartos before the Folio.–4. 'Good' quartos reprinted before the Folio.–5. 'Doubtful' quartos reprinted before the Folio.–6. The Pavier quartos.

7040 **Forse, James H.** The 'mole' in Shakespeare's company. [i.e. Will Kemp, source of pirated ed.]. Sh & Renaiss Assn West Virginia Selected Pa 13:39–47 '88.

7041 **Urkowitz, Steven**. 'Good news about bad quartos' *in* Charney, Maurice, *ed.* 'Bad' Shakespeare; revaluations of the Shakespeare canon. Madison, Fairleigh Dickinson U.P.; London, Associated U.P., [1988]. p.189–206.

—FOLIOS

—FIRST

7042 (2:594) **Prouty, Charles T.** 'Introduction' *in* Mr. William Shakespeares Comedies, histories, & tragedies; a facsimile ed. prepared by Helge Kökeritz. New Haven, Yale U.P.; London, G. Cumberlege, O.U.P., [1954]. p.vii–xxix.

7043 (2:621g) **Hinman, Charlton J.K.**, *ed.* 'Introduction' *in* The First folio of Shakespeare. (The Norton facsimile). New York, W.W. Norton; London, P. Hamlyn, [1968]. p.vii–xxix.

1. The First folio and its contents: the value and authority of the text.–2. The printing and proofing.–3. The facsimile.–4. Appendix A. [Some variant states of the Folio text].

7044 **Hill, Trevor H. Howard-.** New light on compositor E of the Shakespeare First folio. Library ser6 2n02:156–78 Je '80; (Correspondence) 4n03:328 S '82.

1. Compositorial analysis. A. Typographical evidence.–B. Other typographical or orthographical evidence.–C. Orthographical features influenced by copy.–2. Reattributions and the printing of the tragedies.

7045 **Werstine, E. Paul.** An unrecorded state in the Shakespeare First folio. (Bibliographical notes). Pa Bib Soc Am 74n02:133–4 '80.
Huntington Church copy shows qq1v:6 (Lr.) *was corrected not three but four times.*

7046 **Myers, Robin.** A new way of looking at Shakespeare First folios; the Hinman collator. Charlton Hinman, The printing... 2 vols. Oxford, Clarendon pr., 1963. (Key works in bibliography, [10]). Antiqu Bk Mnthly R 8n06:219–23 Je '81; H. Gent [Blink comparator]. (Letters) 8n010:392 Oc '81.
'Selected checklist of articles by Charlton Hinman' (p.223).

7047 **Taylor, Gary.** The shrinking compositor A of the Shakespeare First folio. Stud Bib 34:96–117 '81. tables.

7048 **Connell, Charles.** They gave us Shakespeare; John Heminge & Henry Condell. London, Oriel pr., 1982. xiii,110p. illus., ports., facsims. 21cm.
Rev: Choice 20:1286 '83; M. Grivelet Études Angl 37:93 '84; T.H. Howard–Hill Sh Q 35:345–6 '84; Susan P. Cerasano Biogr 7:259–64 '84; G.E. Bentley Mod Philol 82:421–2 '85; J. Blom Eng Stud 66:73 '85; Ann J. Cook Mod Lang R 81:714–15 '86.

7049 **Werstine, E. Paul.** Cases and compositors in the Shakespeare First folio comedies. [Quires H, G, I, K–Q, A–F]. Stud Bib 35:206–34 '82. tables.

7050 —— More unrecorded states in the Folger Shakespeare library's collection of First folios. (Bibliographical notes). Library ser6 11n01:47–51 Mr '89. facsims.
In 3a3v and 4r (Cym.) *and cc3v* (Cor.)

—SECOND

7051 **Ganzel, Dewey.** 'The Perkins folio: "I at first repented my bargain..."' *in* Fortune and men's eyes; the career of John Payne Collier. Oxford, O.U.P., 1982. p.[133]–75.

7052 **[Marder, Louis].** Historic folio facsimilied. [Charles I's copy]. Sh Newsl 37n04:46 '87.

—OTHER EDITIONS

7053 **Cameron, William J.** Editions of individual plays and parts of books that went to make up John Bell's acting edition of Shakespeare's plays, 1773–1779, in the Scott library, York university, the library of the School of library and information science, the University of Western Ontario, and the D.B. Weldon library, the University of Western Ontario. [London, Ont., University of Western Ontario], 1983. 35p. 27cm. (WHSTC Libr Cat ser, 15). Duplicated typescript. (Not seen: ISBN 0–7714–0457–3).

7054 ——James Barker's continuation (1794–1800) of John Bell's acting edition of Shakespeare's plays (1773–1779); a bibliography in short-title catalog form. Reissued. [London, Ont., University of Western Ontario], 1987. (First publ. 1983). 15p. 27cm. (WHSTC Bib, 13). Duplicated typescript. (Not seen: ISBN 0–7714–0456–5).

7055 (7:5835g) **Goldstein, Melvin**. On the state of American Shakespeare scholarship, 1950–1970: The Pelican books Complete Shakespeare. [Rev. article]. J Aesthetic Educ 5no3:109–37 Jl '71.

7056 (7:5852h) **Hardy, J.P.** 'Edition of Shakespeare' *in* Samuel Johnson; a critical study. London, Routledge & K. Paul, [1979]. p.149–77.

7057 **Turner, Robert K.** Shakespeare. [Appeal for NV ed.]. (Letters to the editor). TLS 29 F '80:236.

7058 **Fanego, Teresa**. Las notas de Pope a su edición de Shakespeare. Scenara R Filoxía 4:191–203 '82. tables.

7059 **Ganzel, Dewey**. 'The Works of William Shakespeare: "Few know what it was, and fewer what I have made it"' *in* Fortune and men's eyes; the career of John Payne Collier. Oxford, O.U.P., 1982. p.[69]–107.

7060 **Zall, Paul M.** The cool world of Samuel Taylor Coleridge; George Steevens, antic antiquarian. Wordsworth & Circ 13no4:211–13 '82.

7061 **Davies, H. Neville.** 'Fakesimile' title-pages. [In the Bankside-restoration Shakespeare, 1908]. (Correspondence). Library ser6 5no3:279 S '83.

7062 **Edwards, Paul C.** Shopping Shakespeare; a consumer's encounter with the paperbacks. (Book reviews). Lit in Performance 4no1:85–9 N '83.

7063 **Honigmann, Ernst A.J.** The Arden Shakespeare, mark II and III. [On completion of series]. (Review article). Durham Univ J 75no2:95–9 Je '83.

7064 **Paul, Angus**. Proliferation of Shakespeare editions; sure to be or not to be as you like it. Chron Higher Educ 25no20:27–8 Ja '83.

7065 **Sen, Sailendra K.** When Malone nods. (Notes). Sh Q 34no2:212–14 '83.

7066 **Williams, William P.** Oxford Shakespeare. [Need for old-spelling text]. (To the editor). TLS 19 Ag '83:822; S.W. Wells 26 Ag '83:907.

7067 **Eberstadt, Fernanda**. Shakespeare in the original. [Survey of 20th cent. ed.]. Commentary 78no6:40–7 D '84.

7068 **Johnston, Shirley W.** 'From preface to practice; Samuel Johnson's editorship of Shakespeare' in Korshin, Paul J. and R.R. Allen, *ed.* Greene centennial studies; essays presented to Donald Greene.... Charlottesville, Va., University of Virginia pr., [1984]. p.250–70.
Title pages.–Prefatory materials.–The annotation in Lear and The tempest.–Johnson's successors.

7069 **Marder, Louis**. Editions of Shakespeare. [Modern]. Sh Newsl 34no4:40 '84. [Sg.: L.M.].

7070 —— The Variorum Shakespeare; plans and problems. Sh Newsl 34no2:14 '84. [Sg.: L.M.].

7071 **Jones, Herbert**. Arthur Henry Bullen and the Stratford town Shakespeare. [1907]. Antiqu Bk Mnthly R 12no4:128–33 Ap '85. illus., facsims.

7072 **Sen, Sailendra K.** Malone and his Boswell. [1821]. N&Q 230no2:246–50 Je '85.

7073 **Corballis, Richard**. Copy-text for Theobald's Shakespeare. (Bibliographical notes). Library ser6 8no2:156–9 Je '86.
Pope's Shakespeare, 2d ed., 1728, in 8 vols.

7074 **Seary, Peter**. '11. The early editors of Shakespeare and the judgments of Johnson' in Korshin, Paul J., *ed.* Johnson after two hundred years. Philadelphia, University of Pennsylvania pr., 1986. p.175–86.

7075 **Turner, Robert K.** 'The New Variorum Shakespeare' in Ross, Jean W., *ed.* Dictionary of literary biography yearbook, 1985. Detroit, Gale, [1986]. p.153–8. facsims.

7076 **Woodson, William C.** Isaac Reed's 1785 variorum Shakespeare. Stud Bib 39:220–9 '86.

7077 **Bevington, David M.** Determining the indeterminate; the Oxford Shakespeare. Sh Q 38no4:501–19 '87.

7078 **Black, Stephen A.** 'Henry Norman Hudson' *in* Rathbun, John W. and Monica M. Grecu, *ed.* American literary critics and scholars, 1800–1850. (Dictionary of literary biography, 64). Detroit, Mich., Gale research, [1987]. p.130–6. port., facsims.

7079 **Howard, Anne B.** 'Oliver William Bourn Peabody' *in* Rathbun, John W. and Monica M. Grecu, *ed.* American literary critics and scholars, 1800–1850. [1st Amer. ed.]. (Dictionary of literary biography, 59). Detroit, Mich., Gale research, [1987]. p.250–3. facsim.

7080 **Knowles, Richard A.J.** Dates for some serially published Shakespeares. Stud Bib 40:181–201 '87.
1. Charles Knight, ed. The pictorial edition of the works of Shakspere. 8 vols. [1839–43]. Serially issued in 55 parts, 1838–43.–2. Gulian C. Verplanck, ed. The illustrated Shakespeare. 3 vols. New York: Harper & brothers, 1847. Serially issued in 138(?) parts, 1844–47.–3. Howard Staunton, ed. Plays of Shakespeare. 3 vols. 1858–60. Serially issued in 50 parts, 1856–60.–4. Charles and Mary Cowden Clarke, eds. The plays of Shakespeare. Cassell's illustrated Shakespeare. 3 vols. n.d. Serially issued in 270 weekly parts, 1864–69.–5. John Payne Collier, ed. Plays and poems. 8 vols. Serially issued in 1864–69 in 43 parts, 1875–78.

7081 **Marder, Louis.** Stanley Wells on the Complete Oxford Shakespeare. [Report of lecture]. Sh Newsl 37no2:21 '87. [Sg.: L.M.].

7082 **Pérez Gállego, Cándido.** The Oxford Shakespeare; la edición esperada. Insula 42no483:19 '87.

7083 **Sams, Eric.** Where there's a Will–The Oxford or the Stratford Shakespeare? Encounter 69no1:54–7 Je '87.

7084 **Winston, Robert P.** 'Gulian C. Verplanck' *in* Rathbun, John W. and Monica M. Grecu, *ed.* American literary critics and scholars, 1800–1850. (Dictionary of literary biography, 59). Detroit, Mich., Gale research, [1987]. p.317–23. port.

7085 **Bevington, David M.** Editing Renaissance drama in paperback. [Bantam Shakespeare]. Renaiss Drama new ser 19:127–47 '88.

7086 **Hammond, Paul.** Review article: The Oxford Shakespeare. Sevent Cent (Durham) 3:85–107 '88.

7087 **Laird, David.** 'Horace Howard Furness' *in* Rathbun, John W. and Monica M. Grecu, *ed.* American literary critics and scholars, 1850–1880. (Dictionary of literary biography, 64). Detroit, Mich., Gale research, 1988. p.66–70.

7088 **Lim, C.S.** Emendation of Shakespeare in the eighteenth century: the case of Johnson. Cahiers Elisabéthains 33:23–30 Ap '88.
Abstrs. in Fr. and Eng. (p.x).

7089 **Mehl, Dieter**. Eine neue Shakespeare-Edition. [Oxford Complete works]. Archiv 225:128–37 '88.

7090 **Gabler, Hans W.** Assumptions fruitfully disturbed; the one-volume Oxford Shakespeares. Sh Jahrb (Bochum) 1989:344–50 '89.

7091 **Hiltscher, Michael**. Nicolaus Delius, 1813–1888. (Aus der Geschichte des deutschen Shakespeare-Forschung). Sh Jahrb (Bochum) 1989:386–97 '89.
'Bibliographie der Schriften Delius' zur englischen Philologie' (p.396–7).

7092 **Ioppolo, Grace J.** 'Old' and 'new' revisionists; Shakespeare's eighteenth-century editors. Huntington Libr Q 52no3:347–61 '89.

7093 **Williams, George W.** Review article [on Oxford Shakespeares]. Cahiers Elisabéthains 35:103–17 Ap '89.

SHAKESPEARE—TEXTUAL STUDIES

7094 (7:5888) **Wells, Stanley W.** Modernising Shakespeare's spelling, 1979.
Rev: E.P. Werstine Sh Stud 16:382–91 '83; G.W. Williams Yrbk Eng Stud 13:307–8 '83.

7095 **Bowers, Fredson T.** Establishing Shakespeare's text; notes on short lines and the problem of verse division. Stud Bib 33:74–130 '80.

7096 **Werstine, E. Paul.** Modern editions and historical collation in old-spelling editions of Shakespeare. Analytical & Enum Bib 4no2:95–106 '80.

7097 **Bertram, Paul**. White spaces in Shakespeare; the development of the modern text. Cleveland, Ohio, Bellflower pr., Case western reserve university, [1981]. x,86p. facsims. 21cm.
Rev: G. Taylor N&Q 228:463–5 '83; S. Orgel Renaiss Q 36:302–7 '83; A. Schlösser Sh Jahrb (Weimar) 119:169–70 '83; E.A.J. Honigmann Yrbk Eng Stud 15:280–2 '85.

7098 **Craik, Thomas W.** A fly in Shakespeare's amber; an inaugural lecture...11th November, 1980. [On textual emendation]. Durham, Ptd. for the University of Durham by T. Wilson, Kendal, [1981]. 16p. 22cm.

7099 **Beaurline, Lester A.** In search of Shakespeare's anonymous editors. [Rev. art. on Prosser, 7198]. Virginia Q R 58no4:715–19 '82.

7100 **Binns, James W.** Shakespeare's Latin citations; the editorial problem. Sh Surv 35:119–28 '82.
1. Shakespeare's original Latin.–2. Classical Latin quotations.–3. Citations from renaissance Latin authors.–4. Miscellaneous words and phrases.

7101 **Marder, Louis**. Thoughts on a definitive edition of Shakespeare; is it possible? Sh Newsl 32no5/6:27,29 '82.

7102 **McLeod, Randall**. UN Editing Shak-speare. Sub-Stance 33/4:26–55 '82. facsims.
Keatspeare.–Text in the age of photographic reproduction.–Shakestext.–Textgate.– Godspeare.

7103 **Sams, Eric**. Viewpoint: Shakespeare's text and common sense. TLS 2 S '83:933–4.

7104 **Martinez Luciano, Juan V.** Shakespeare en la critica bibliotextual. [Guide]. [Valencia], Instituto Shakespeare, Biblioteca de la Universitat de Barcelona, 1984. 96p. 19cm. (Serie critica, 2).
Ediciones de Shakespeare hasta el siglo XX.–La critica bibliotextual en el siglo XX. (a). The new bibliography.–(b). The newer bibliography.–(c). Nuevas aportaciones.

7105 **Spevack, Marvin**. Shakespeare; editions and textual scholarship, II. (Bücherschau). Sh Jahrb (Bochum) 1984:225–35 '84.
Review article on Bertram, White spaces (7099), Bowers, 'Establishing...', 1980 (7095), Wells's Modernising (7094), Prosser's Sh's anonymous editors (7198), Urkowitz's Lear (7228), and Blayney (7231).

7106 **Wells, Stanley W.** Re-editing Shakespeare for the modern reader; based on lectures given at the Folger Shakespeare library, Washington, D.C. Oxford, Clarendon pr., 1984. vi,131p. 21cm. (Oxford Sh Stud, [2]).
Introduction.–1. Old and modern spelling.–2. Emending Shakespeare.–3. The editor and the theatre; editorial treatment of stage directions.–4. The editor and the theatre; act one of Titus Andronicus.–Appendix: Shakespeare's first draft of act one of Titus Andronicus; a conjectural reconstruction.
Rev. Ann Thompson Times Higher Ed Suppl 23 N '84:20; T.W. Craik Brit Bk News D '84; P. Edwards Analytical & Enum Bib 8:260–3 '84; D. Traister Sh Bull 2:41–3 '84/5; L. Beaurline Renaiss Q 38:573–6 '85; D. Birch Theat Res Int 10:166–72 '85; L.R.N. Ashley Biblioth d'Humanisme & Renaiss 48:185–6 '86; D. Mehl Archiv 223:470–1 '86; P. Bertram Eng Lit N 23:68–71 '86; H. Henning Sh Jahrb (Weimar) 122:201–2 '86; P.C. McGuire Centennial R 30:423–5 '86; D. Bevington Mod Lang R 82:704–5 '87; H.W. Gabler Sh Jahrb (Bochum) 1987:215–19 '87; MacD.P. Jackson Sh Surv 39:236–8 '87; R. Todd Dutch Q R 17:262–82 '87; M.J. Warren J Eng & Germ Philol 87:111–13 '88.

7107 **Werstine, E. Paul.** Line division in Shakespeare's dramatic verse; an editorial problem. Analytical & Enum Bib 8no2:73–125 '84. tables.
(a). Divided verse lines: the reprints. Compositors A and B in eleven plays.–(b). Prose set as verse: the reprints. Compositors A and B in eleven plays.–(c). Verse set as prose: the reprints.....–(d). Line division in prose.....–(e). Two lines of verse set as one line.....–(f). Irregular verse patterns.–Conclusion.

7108 **Honigmann, Ernst A.J.** 'Shakespeare as a reviser' *in* McGann, Jerome J., *ed.* Textual criticism and literary interpretation. Chicago, University of Chicago pr., 1985. p.1–22.

7109 **Warren, Michael J.** 'Textual problems, editorial assertions in editions of Shakespeare' *in* McGann, Jerome J., *ed.* Textual criticism and literary interpretation. Chicago, University of Chicago pr., 1985. p.23–37.

7110   **Wells, Stanley W.** Editing Shakespeare. (Letters). TLS 18 Ja '85:63; A.L. Rowse; T. Hawkes; E. Sams 1 F '85:119; S.W. Wells 8 F '85:145; E. Sams 22 F '85:201.

7111   **Werstine, E. Paul.** Edward Capell and metrically linked speeches in Shakespeare. (Bibliographical notes). Library ser6 7n03:259–61 S '85; R. Knowles (Correspondence) 7n04:354–5 D '85.

7112   **Bibliographers'** nightmares; problematic speech-headings in Shakespeare. [Report of Shakespeare association seminar, 1986]. Sh Newsl 36n03:44 '86.

7113   **Bowers, Fredson T.** 'Authority, copy, and transmission in Shakespeare's texts' *in* Ziegler, Georgianna, *ed.* Shakespeare study today; the Horace Howard Furness memorial lectures. (AMS Stud Renaiss 13). New York, AMS pr., [1986]. p.7–36.

7114   —— 'A search for authority; the investigation of Shakespeare's printed texts' *in* Tyson, Gerald P. and Sylvia S. Wagonheim, *ed.* Print and culture in the renaissance; essays on the advent of printing in Europe. Newark, N.J., University of Delaware pr.; London, Associated U.P., [1986]. p.17–44.
On 'identification of compositors, which...rests on three bases: (1) spelling characteristics; (2) typographical characteristics; and (3) certain mechanical details in the printing process' (p.19).

7115   **Goldberg, Jonathan.** Textual properties. (Issues). Sh Q 37n02:213–17 '86.

7116   **Taylor, Gary.** Inventing Shakespeare. Sh Jahrb (Bochum) 1986:26–4 '86.

7117   **Bowers, Fredson T.** Readability and regularization in old-spelling texts of Shakespeare. Huntington Libr Q 50n03:199–227 '87.

7118   **Kerrigan, John.** 'Shakespeare as reviser' *in* Ricks, Christopher, *ed.* English drama to 1710. (The new history of literature, 3). New York, P. Bedrick, [1987]. p.[255]–75.

7119   **Munkelt, Margarete.** Disambiguation and conjecture; modes of editorial decision in Shakespeare's early plays. Analytical & Enum Bib new ser 1n02:52–74 '87.
1. Expanded abbreviations.–2. Names.–3. Possible spelling variants.–4. Nonce-forms and cruxes.–Conclusion.

7120   **Spevack, Marvin.** The editor as philologist. Text 3:91–106 '87.

7121   **Taylor, Gary.** Revising Shakespeare. Text 3:285–304 '87. facsims.
Examines instances of substantial textual variation that demonstrate that Sh. 'habitually' revised his texts.

7122 **Wells, Stanley W.** Revisionist Shakespeare. Oxford Mag 24:10–13 '87; E. Sams (To the editor) 25:7 '87; S.W. Wells 26:15 '87; E. Sams 27:15 '87; S.W. Wells 28:13 '87.

Revision during composition.–Between first composition and performance.–How to treat theatrical revision.–Two text plays.–Implications.–The two texts of King Lear.

7123 **Wells, Stanley W., G. Taylor, [and others].** William Shakespeare: A textual companion. With John Jowett and William Montgomery. Oxford, Clarendon pr., 1987. x,671p. illus., facsims., diagrs., tables. 26cm.

General introduction, [Gary Taylor].–The canon and chronology of Shakespeare's plays, [Gary Taylor].–Summary of control-texts, [Gary Taylor, W.L. Montgomery].–Attributions to compositors of the First folio.–Editorial procedures.–Works cited.–[Textual introductions to individual works].

Rev: D. Bevington Sh Q 38:501–17 '87; J. Wilders TLS 30 Oc '87:1197–9; M. Baron Eng (London) 37:82–8 '88; P.H. Davison Library ser6 10:255–67 '88; B. Engler Eng Stud 6:277–80 '88; P. Hammond Seibt Cent 3:85–107 '88; F. Kermode London R Bks 21 Ap '88:8–9; 19 My '88:4; D. Mehl Archiv 225:128–37 '88; Lois Potter TLS 23 S '88:1056; R.J. Weis Times Higher Ed Suppl 25 Mr '88; G.B. Evans J Eng & Germ Philol 88:401–7 '89; H.W. Gabler Sh Jahrb (Bochum) 1989:344–50 '89; E.A.J. Honigmann N&Q 234:95–8 '89; MacD.P. Jackson Sh Surv 41:228–41 '89; J.L. Simmons Stud Engl Lit 29:359–61 '89; B. Vickers R Eng Stud new ser 40:402–11; G.W. Williams Cahiers Elisabéthains 35:103–17 '89.

7124 **Grazia, Margreta de.** The essential Shakespeare and the material book. ['New' bibliography]. Text Practice 2no1:69–86 '88.

7125 **Orgel, Stephen.** The authentic Shakespeare. Representations 21:1–26 '88. facsims., illus.

Discusses the question 'what does a play represent' (p.13), *with observations on text and performance.*

7126 **Sams, Eric.** William Shakespeare; a textual companion. [Disputes use of memorial reconstruction]. (Letters). TLS 11 N '88:1251.

7127 **Smidt, Kristian.** Repetition, revision, and editorial greed in Shakespeare's play texts. Cahiers Elisabéthains 34:25–37 Oc '88.

Abstrs. in Fr. and Eng. (p.xi).

Suggests F's incorrect retention of passages marked for omission at 1H6 4.5–7 (scenes), TGV 2.1.14–81, R3 4.4.197–431, 2H4 4.4.12–80, Ham. 2.2.239–310, Oth. 1.3.189–220, Tim. 4.3.289–400, Tit. 1.1.292–5 *and* 341–5, MV 5.5.36–49, *and* Tro. 5.10.21–31 *(New Arden line nos.).*

7128 **Taylor, Gary.** 'Praestat difficilior lectio': All's well that ends well and Richard III. Renaiss Stud 2no1:27–46 Mr '88. facsim.

7129 **Thomson, Leslie.** Broken brackets and 'mended texts; stage directions in the Oxford Shakespeare. Renaiss Drama new ser 19:175–93 '88.

Particularly for Lr., R2, 1H4, Tmp., Oth. Tro. *and* R3.

7130 **Wells, Stanley W.** 'Revision in Shakespeare's plays' *in* Conference on editorial problems, 21st, Toronto, 1985. Editing and editors, a retrospect; papers given.... Ed. by Richard Landon. New York, [1988]. p.[67]–97.

7131 —— 'The unstable image of Shakespeare's text' *in* Habicht, Werner, D.J. Palmer and R. Pringle, *ed.* Images of Shakespeare; proceedings of the third congress of the International Shakespeare association, 1986. Newark, N.J., University of Delaware pr.; London, Associated U.P., [1988]. p.305–13.

7132 **Altman, Joel H.** The practice of Shakespeare's text. Style 23no3:466–500 '89.
1. Practice, ethics, criticism.–2. Action, production, art.–3. Ingenuity, imitation, performance.

7133 **Sams, Eric**. Shakespeare, or Bottom? The myth of memorial reconstruction. (Books & writers). Encounter 72no1:41–5 Ja '89.

7134 **Spevack, Marvin.** The other Shakespeare; some observations on the vocabulary and text. Analytical & Enum Bib new ser 3no2:41–65 '89.
Considers treatment in modern ed. of words bracketed in Riverside Sh., hapax legomena, and emended after F1.

7135 **Urkowitz, Steven**. Memorial reconstruction; decline of a theory. Sh Newsl 39no1/2:10 '89.

—COLLECTED EMENDATIONS

7136 **Cunningham, J.V.** 'Shakespeare: three textual notes' *in* Smith, John H., *ed.* Brandeis essays in literature. Waltham, Mass., Brandeis university, Dept. of English and American literature, 1983. p.23.
Proposes 'Rod. O wretched villain! (Two or three groans) / Lod. 'Tis a heavy night:' at Oth. 5.1.41–2 (TLN 3131–2); at TN 4.2.12 (TLN 1995) 'The Competitors enter.' is a SD; at Oth. 5.2.101–2 (TLN 3364–6) proposes '…alterations. / Emil. [within] Good my lord, / I do…with you.'

7137 **Fisher, Sidney T.** Some proposed Shakespeare emendations and notes. [Montreal, Halcyon pr.], [1984]. (2d ed. 1985). 40p. 20cm.

7138 —— Some proposed Shakespeare emendations and notes. 2d ed. [Montreal, Halcyon pr.], [1985]. (First publ. 1984). 23p. 20cm.

7139 —— Some new notes on Shakespeare's text. [Montreal], [1986]. 7p. 29cm. (Duplicated typescript).

7140 —— Some proposed Shakespeare emendations. [Montreal], [1986]. 22p. 29cm. (Duplicated typescript).

7141 **Proudfoot, G. Richard.** 'Two notes on Shakespeare's text' *in* KM80; a birthday album…. [Liverpool, Liverpool U.P. for private circulation], [1987]. p.[119]–20.
Suggests 'every' for 'and the', Tro., 1.3.63 (TLN 522), and supports 'autumn' for 'Anthony' in Ant., 5.2.87 (TLN 3305).

—HANDWRITING AND PALÆOGRAPHY

7142 **Marder, Louis**. Shakespeare signatures (?) seven, eight, and nine! Sh Newsl 34no2:13–14 '84. [Sg.: L.M.].

7143 **Hamilton, Charles**. A letter in Shakespeare's hand. [Signed by Southampton]. Sh Newsl 36no3:37 '86; L. Marder, The expert and the skeptic 36no3:37 '86.

7144 **Dawson, Giles**. Shakespeare's handwriting. Sh Surv 42:119–28 '89. facsims.

SHAKESPEARE—INDIVIDUAL TEXTS

—ALL'S WELL THAT ENDS WELL

7145 **Fuzier, Jean** and **F. Laroque**, *comp.* 'Bibliographie' *in* Fuzier, Jean, *ed.* All's well that ends well; nouvelles perspectives critiques. (Université Paul Valéry. Collection Astrea, 1). Montpellier, Centre d'études et de recherches Elisabèthaines, [1985]. p.137–44.

7146 **Bowers, Fredson T.** 'Shakespeare at work; the foul papers of All's well that ends well' *in* [Carey, John], *ed.* English renaissance studies presented to dame Helen Gardner in honour of her seventieth birthday. Oxford, Clarendon pr., 1980. p.[56]–73.

7147 **Walker, Alice**. Six notes on All's well that ends well. Sh Q 33no3:339–42 '82.
1.3.207f. (TLN 532f.); 2.1.12–17 (TLN 609–14); 2.1.172–7 (TLN 779–85); 4.2.38–9 (TLN 2063–4); 4.4.28–34 (TLN 2471–8); 5.1.6 SD (TLN 2601).

7148 **Fraser, Russell**, *ed.* 'Textual analysis' *in* All's well that ends well. (New Cambridge Sh). Cambridge, C.U.P., [1985]. p.149–52.
F1 was set from Sh's foul papers.

7149 **Taylor, Gary**. 'Textual double knots: "make rope's in such a scarre"' *in* Dotterer, Ronald, *ed.* Shakespeare: Text, subtext, and context. Selinsgrove, Susequehanna U.P.; London, Associated U.P., [1989]. p.163–85.
Proposes 'toys e'en such a surance' at 4.2.38 (TLN 2063).

—ANTONY AND CLEOPATRA

7150 **Swander, Homer**. Menas and the editors; a Folio script unscripted. [On editorial treatment of character]. Sh Q 36no2:165–87 '85.

—AS YOU LIKE IT

7151 **Halio, Jay L.** and **Barbara C. Millard.** As you like it; an annotated bibliography, 1940–1980. New York, Garland, 1985. viii,744p. 21cm. (Sh Bibs, 8).
Rev: L.R.N. Ashley Biblioth d'Humanisme & Renaiss 47:659–96 '85; L.S. Champion Sth Atlantic R 50:107–9 '85; Helen Gregory Am Ref Bks Ann 17:463 '86.

—COMEDY OF ERRORS

7152 **Dorsch, Theodore S.**, ed. 'Text; its nature and origin' in The comedy of errors. (New Cambridge Sh). Cambridge, C.U.P., [1988]. p.34–8.
F1 was ptd. from an authorial ms.

7153 **Taylor, Gary.** Textual and sexual criticism; a crux in The comedy of errors. Renaiss Drama new ser 19:195–225 '88.
After a review of womens' involvement in editing Sh., resolves the compound crux at 2.1.95–9 (TLN 371–5) as in the Oxford ed., 2.1.109–13.

7154 **Werstine, E. Paul.** 'Foul papers' and 'prompt-books'; printer's copy for Shakespeare's Comedy of errors. Stud Bib 41:232–46 '88. table, facsim.

—CORIOLANUS

7155 **Leggatt, Alexander** and **Lois Norem.** Coriolanus; an annotated bibliography. New York, Garland, 1989. xxviii,738p. 21cm. ([Garland Sh Bibs, 17]).

7156 **Riehle, Wolfgang.** Coriolanus, I.i.217 'unroof'd'. N&Q 225no2:174 Ap '80.
Theobald's emendation is unnecessary as F reads 'vnroof't' at TLN 232 (1.1.222).

—CYMBELINE

7157 **Jacobs, Henry E.** Cymbeline. New York, Garland, 1982. xlviii,591p. 20cm. (Sh Bibs, 3).
Rev: Janet R. Ivey Am Ref Bks Ann 14:580–1 '83; L.S. Champion Sth Atlantic R 50:107–9 '85.

—HAMLET

7158 **Hunter, Glen D.** Shakespeare's Hamlet; a comprehensive bibliography of editions and paraphrases in English, 1876–1981. Bull Bib 38no4:157–72 Oc/D '81.

7159 **Robinson, Randal F.** Hamlet in the 1950s; an annotated bibliography. New York, Garland, 1984. xxvi,383p. 22cm. (Sh Bibs, 7).
Rev: L.R.N. Ashley Biblioth d'Humanisme & Renaiss 47:659–96 '85; Janet R. Ivey Am Ref Bks Ann 16:406–7 '85.

7160 **Levine, Robert T.** Honesty and beauty; an emendation for Hamlet, III.i.109–10. N&Q 225no2:166–9 Ap '80.
Proposes that Q2 compositor memorially transposed words in TLN 1764–5.

7161 **Spencer, Terence J.B.**, *ed.* 'An account of the text' *in* Hamlet. (New Penguin Sh.). Harmondsworth, Penguin, [1980]. p.362–[84].
The reported Q1 represents an early version of the play; Q2 comes from Sh's ms.; and F1 was ptd. from the promptbook (or a transcript of it) with consultation of Q2.

7162 **Melchiori, Giorgio.** 'Solid/sullied', Hamlet I.ii. La Cultura 19:203–6 '81.
In Italian.

7163 **Jenkins, Harold.** '3. The texts; 4. The editorial problem and the present text' *in* Hamlet. (Arden Sh.). London, Methuen, [1982]. p.18–82.
Q1 was memorially reconstructed by the actor who played Marcellus, probably for a provincial tour; it is valuable for recollections of performances of the original. Q2 was ptd. from Sh's foul papers, partially annotated by the book-keeper before being transcribed for a promptbook. The Q2 compositors set from a copy of Q1 which had been annotated from the ms., in act 1, but thereafter consulted Q1 intermittently. F1 'is a very mixed text. It differs from Q2 partly by preserving what Q2 omits or misrepresents...'. It may have been ptd. from 'a fair copy which was preparation for but did not become the promptbook, and a subsequent transcript of this' (p.64). F 'depends, though not necessarily directly, upon a copy of Q2 which had been collated with the manuscript and emended to conform with it' (p.68).

7164 **Lee, Kyng-shik.** Hamlet's solid / sullied flesh. Lang R 18no1:121–37 Je '82.
English summary (p.136–7).

7165 **Bowers, Fredson T.** William Shakespeare, Hamlet, edited by Harold Jenkins. New Arden edition.... (Reviews). Library ser6 5no3:282–96 S '83.

7166 **Schrickx, Willem.** The date of Dekker's The meeting of gallants and the printing of Hamlet. Hamlet Stud 5no1/2:82–6 '83.
Q2 Ham. was ptd. in 1605, before 25 March.

7167 **Edwards, Philip.** 'Shakespeare's alterations in Hamlet' *in* Scattergood, V. John, *ed.* Literature and learning in medieval and renaissance England; essays presented to Fitzroy Pyle. [Blackrock, co. Dublin], Irish academic pr., [1984]. p.175–84.

7168 **Rasmussen, Eric.** 'Pollux' for 'pollax'; an emendation of Hamlet 1.1.66. (Note). Hamlet Stud 6no1/2:72–4 '84.

7169   **Edwards, Philip**, *ed.* 'The play's shape' *in* Hamlet, prince of Denmark. (New Cambridge Sh). Cambridge, C.U.P., [1985]. p.8–32. diagr.

Q2 (1604/5) was ptd. from Sh's foul papers with passages marked for deletion but overlooked by the Q compositors; they consulted a copy of Q1 (1603), especially in act 1. The scribal fair copy of Sh's ms., with two cuts and an additional passage, was again transcribed by a careless scribe, who attempted to reduce the number of minor parts. F1 was ptd. from the second transcript, with recourse to a copy of Q2. Q1 is a corrupt, abbreviated and adapted version of the play represented by F1.

7170   **Zitner, Sheldon P.** Four feet in the grave; some stage directions in Hamlet V.i. Text 2:139–48 '85.

7171   **Hibbard, George R.** Common errors and unusual spellings in Hamlet Q2 and F. (Notes). R Eng Stud new ser 37no145:55–61 F '86.

No strong evidence for consultation of Q during F ptg.

7172   **Rasmussen, Eric**. The relevance of cast-off copy in determining the nature of omissions: Q2 Hamlet. Stud Bib 39:133–5 '86.

7173   **Urkowitz, Steven**. '"Well-sayd olde Mole"; burying three Hamlets in modern editions' *in* Ziegler, Georgianna, *ed.* Shakespeare study today; the Horace Howard Furness memorial lectures. (AMS Stud Renaiss 13). New York, AMS pr., [1986]. p.37–70.

7174   **Hibbard, George R.**, *ed.* 'Textual introduction' *in* Hamlet. (Oxford Sh). Oxford, Clarendon pr., 1987. p.67–130.

The text of Q1 'is a completely illegitimate and unreliable one, having no direct contact with any Shakespearian manuscript, or with any transcript of such a manuscript' (p.69): it is, as Duthie showed, an abbreviated text memorially-reconstructed by the player who acted Marcellus, Lucianus and Voltemar, for a provincial tour, and 'stems from the text behind F' (p.88). On the other hand, Q2 was ptd. from Sh's foul papers, with the aid of a copy of Q1 in act 1. The F text represents Sh's revision of his early draft; F was ptd. from his fair copy (which was not used as a promptbook).

7175   **Everett, Barbara**. New readings in Hamlet, and some principles of emendation. R Eng Stud new ser 39no154:177–98 My '88.

7176   **Loewenstein, Joseph**. Plays agonistic and competitive; the textual approach to Elsinore. Renaiss Drama new ser 19:63–96 '88.

Through consideration of 'the late innovation' Fl Oo3v, locates Ham. 'within the cultural economy of the English Renaissance' (p.64).

7177   **Mowat, Barbara**. The form of Hamlet's fortunes. Renaiss Drama new ser 19:97–126 '88.

Surveys editorial history.

7178   **Roatcap, Adela S.** Designing literature: The book as theatre; the Cranach press Hamlet. Fine Print 14no1:26–33 Ja '88. illus., facsims.

7179   **Sams, Eric**. Taboo or not taboo? The text, dating and authorship of Hamlet, 1589–1623. Hamlet Stud 10no1/2:12–46 '88.

7180 **Werstine, E. Paul.** The textual mystery of Hamlet. Sh Q 39no1:1–26 '88; (To the editor) 39no4:522 '88.

7181 **Bowers, Fredson T.** 'Hamlet's 'sullied' or 'solid' flesh; a bibliographical case study' *in* Hamlet as minister and scourge and other studies in Shakespeare and Milton. Charlottesville, U.P. of Virginia, 1989. p.[155]–62.
Repr. from SBTC: 1237.

7182 **Jackson, MacDonald P.** Editing Hamlet in the 1980s; textual theories and textual practices. (Notes). Hamlet Stud 11no1/2:60–72 '89.

—HENRY IV

7183 **Reid, Sidney W.** B and 'J'; two compositors in two plays of the Shakespeare First folio. [Henry IV]. Library ser6 7no2:126–36 Je '85. table.
'Appendix: Summary of evidence for compositor J in Folio 1 Henry IV and 2 Henry IV' (p.134–6).

7184 **Taylor, Gary.** The fortunes of Oldcastle. [Censorship]. Sh Surv 38:85–100 '85.

7185 **Melchiori, Giorgio.** 'Reconstructing the ur-Henry IV' *in* Bilton, Peter [and others], *ed*. Essays in honour of Kristian Smidt. [Oslo], University of Oslo, Institute of English studies, 1986. p.59–77.

7186 **Yeandle, Laetitia.** The dating of sir Edward Dering's copy of The history of King Henry the fourth. [1623]. (Notes). Sh Q 37no2:224–6 '86. facsim.

——1 HENRY IV

7187 **Bowers, Fredson T.** Establishing Shakespeare's text; Poins and Peto in 1 Henry IV. Stud Bib 34:189–98 '81.
'...the actor of Poins had to be withdrawn before the end of II.iv in order to double the part of another character,' (p.191–2) *and variation of SPs is not a consequence of compositional or scribal error.* 'A note on 2 Henry IV' (p.196–8): '2 Henry IV...has no direct application' (p.197) *to the Poins/Peto problem in* 1H4.

7188 **Antoni, Robert** [and] **G.W. Williams.** Gadshill's question in 1 Henry IV. [2.4.192]. Cahiers Elisabéthaines 23:99–103 Ap '83.

7189 **Zimmerman, Susan.** The uses of headlines; Peter Short's Shakespearian quartos 1 Henry IV and Richard III. Library ser6 7no3:218–55 S '85. tables.
1. Compositor analysis: 1H4.–Summary of evidence: 1H4.–2. Compositor analysis: Richard III.–Conclusions.
The 'headlines bear no discernible relationship either to the number of compositors or to the order of composition' (p.238); 1H4 *was set by a single compositor and* R3 *possibly was also.*

7190 **Jackson, MacDonald P.** The manuscript copy for the quarto (1598) of Shakespeare's 1 Henry IV. N&Q 231no3:353–4 S '86.

Spellings indicate that Q was set from a scribal transcript.

7191 **Bevington, David M.**, *ed.* 'The text' *in* Henry IV, part 1. (Oxford Sh). Oxford, Clarendon pr., 1987. p.85–110.

'We appear to have in Q0 and Q1 a text based either on Shakespeare's corrected papers and hence close to his original, or on a scribal copy that imposed relatively few changes in its orginal' (p.90). *F was set up from a copy of Q5 (1613), edited.*

7192 **Jowett, John.** The thieves in 1 Henry IV. [Revision for censorship]. R Eng Stud 38no151:325–33 Ag '87.

7193 —— The transformation of Hal. N&Q 232no2:208–10 Je '87.

Revives Malone's suggestion that a line was lost after 4.1.98 (TLN 2329).

7194 **Taylor, Gary.** William Shakespeare, Richard James and the house of Cobham. [Censorship]. R Eng Stud new ser 38no151:334–54 Ag '87.

7195 **Goldberg, Jonathan.** Rebel letters; postal effects from Richard II to Henry IV. Renaiss Drama new ser19:3–28 '88.

'III. The purloined paper' (p.20–4) *discusses crux at* 1H4 2.4.585–90 (TLN 1503–7): *Peto as reader of* 'Item a capon...'.

7196 **Kelliher, W. Hilton.** Contemporary manuscript extracts from Shakespeare's Henry IV, part 1. [In BL]. Eng Manuscr Stud 1:144–81 '89. facsims.

The 'Harriot' notes.–The extracts from Henry IV, part 1.–The nature of the extracts.–Possible source of the extracts.–Copying in the playhouse.–Henry's speech on statecraft.–Summary.

—2 HENRY IV

7197 **Berger, Thomas L.** and **G.W. Williams**. Variants in the quarto of Shakespeare's 2 Henry IV. Library ser6 3no2:109–18 Je '81.

I. Press variants in the first quarto.–II. The relationship of Q(a) and Q(b).

7198 **Prosser, Eleanor.** Shakespeare's anonymous editors; scribe and compositor in the Folio text of 2 Henry IV. Stanford, Calif., Stanford U.P., 1981. ix,219p. tables, facsims. 21cm.

1. The textual problem.–2. Reflections of stage practice in the Folio.–3. Textual changes by the Folio compositors.–4. Textual changes by the scribe.–5. Conclusion.–Appendixes: A. The nature of the copy underlying Folio additions. B. The placement of stage directions in Elizabethan manuscripts. C. Recommended adoptions.

Rev: A.E. Craven Analytical & Enum Bib 5:241–5 '81; L.R. Ashley Bibliothèque d'Humanisme & Renaiss 44:472–4 '82; L.A. Beaurline Virginia Q R 58:715–19 '82; P. Bertram Renaiss Q 35:332–6 '82; T.L. Berger Sh Stud 15:369–80 '82; E.A.J. Honigmann N&Q 227:539–40 '82; W.C. McAvoy Manuscripta 28:58–60 '84; M. Spevack Sh Jahrb West 119:225–35 '84; E.P. Werstine Mod Philol 81:419–22 '84.

7199 **Melchiori, Giorgio**. Sir John Umfrevile in Henry IV, part 2, I.i.161–
79. [Text]. REAL 2:199–209 '84.

7200 **Jowett, John** and **G. Taylor**. The three texts of 2 Henry IV. Stud Bib
40:31–50 '87.
*Rather than a censorial excision in 1600, the scene (F 3.1) added in Q1(b) was Sh.'s addition
in foul papers; this suggests that F preserves other authorial revisions.*

7201 **Jowett, John**. Cuts and casting; author and book-keeper in the folio
text of 2 Henry IV. AUMLA 72:275–95 N '89. table.
Discusses influence of promptbook on F text.

7202 **Melchiori, Giorgio**, *ed.* 'Textual analysis' *in* The second part of King Henry
IV. (New Cambridge Sh). Cambridge, C.U.P., [1989]. p.189–202.
*Q was ptd. from foul papers revised for the preparation of the prompt-book; F was set from a
transcript prepared by a literary scribe (following Prosser) who consulted a* 'supplementary
manuscript, probably Shakespeare's foul papers' *(p.191), and has* 'no real authority'
(p.192) except for eight passages that had been deleted from Q copy.

—HENRY V

7203 **Candido, Joseph** and **C.R. Forker**. Henry V; an annotated bibliogra-
phy. New York, Garland, 1983. xxiv,815p. 21cm. (Sh Bibs, 4).
Rev. L.R.N. Ashley Biblioth d'Humanisme & Renaiss 46:433–71 '84; Janet Ivey Am
Ref Bks Ann 16:405–6 '85.

7204 **Craik, Thomas W.** Henry V. (To the editor). TLS 29 F '80:236; Priscilla
Bawcutt; I.E. Jones 21 Mr '80:324; H. Jenkins 11 Ap '80:415; T.W.
Craik 13 Je '80:672; I.E. Jones 11 Jl '80:782.
Jamy's 'ay or goe to death' (3.1.124, TLN 1233) *is a misreading of* 'I owe God a death'.

7205 **Fuzier, Jean**. Ie quand sur le possession de Fraunce; a French crux in
Henry V solved? Sh Q 32no1:97–100 '81.
F compositor misread 'Ie quand suis le possesseur de Fraunce, & quand vous aues le
possession de moy' *at* 5.2.187–8 (TLN3169–71).

7206 **Taylor, Gary**, *ed.* 'Text and interpretation' *in* Henry V. (Oxford Sh).
Oxford, Clarendon pr., 1982. p.12–26.
F derives from an authorial draft; Q 'represents a transcript...by two men whose living
depended on their memories, and who had acted in Henry V within a year or so of its
first performance. This makes Q an historical document of far more authority than
the hypotheses of any twentieth-century scholar' (p.23).

7207 **Patterson, Annabel**. Back by popular demand; the two versions of
Henry V. Renaiss Drama new ser 19:29–62 '88.
*Examines G. Taylor's argument in Oxford ed. (1982) in the light of historical evidence; suggests
that the Q1 abridgement* 'was a tactical retreat from one kind of play to another' (p.41)

—HENRY VI

7208   **Hinchcliffe, Judith**. King Henry VI, parts 1, 2, and 3; an annotated bibliography. New York, Garland, 1984. xix,368p. 21cm. ([Garland Sh Bibs, 5]).
Rev: R.A. Aken Choice 22:1474 '85; L.R.N. Ashley Biblioth d'Humanisme & Renaiss 47:659–96 '85; Janet R. Ivey Am Ref Bks Ann 16:406–7 '85.

7209   **Urkowitz, Steven**. 'If I mistake in those foundations which I build upon'; Peter Alexander's textual analysis of Henry VI parts 2 and 3. Eng Lit Renaiss 18no2:230–56 '88.
Examination of Alexander's Shakespeare's Henry VI and Richard III, 1929 (SBTC 1341) casts doubt on theories of memorial reconstruction.

—1 HENRY VI

7210   **Sanders, Norman**, *ed.* 'An account of the text' *in* The first part of king Henry the sixth. (New Penguin Sh). [Harmondsworth, Middlesex], Penguin, [1981]. p.239–[50].
F1 was set up either from Sh's own ms. or an edited transcript of it, with some theatrical annotation.

—2 HENRY VI

7211   **Sanders, Norman**, *ed.* 'An account of the text' *in* The second part of king Henry the sixth. (New Penguin Sh.). [Harmondsworth, Middlesex], Penguin, [1981]. p.279–[302].
Q1 'looks as though it is a deliberately shortened version of the original play' (p.284); F1 was ptd. from a ms. of theatrical origin but 'no theory…has won general acceptance' (p.286).

—3 HENRY VI

7212   **Sanders, Norman**, *ed.* 'An account of the text' *in* The third part of king Henry the sixth. (New Penguin Sh). [Harmondsworth], Penguin, [1981]. p.283–97.
Q1 was ptd. from a shortened version of the play, F1 from authorial copy, but 'at the moment there is no theory concerning the genesis and early history of the play which has won general acceptance' (p.286).

—HENRY VIII

7213   **Micheli, Linda McJ**. Henry VIII; an annotated bibliography. New York, Garland, 1988. xxxii,444p. 20cm. (Sh Bibs, 15).
Rev: L.R.N. Ashley Biblioth d'Humanisme & Renaiss 51:426 '89; J.D. Cox Sh Q 40:509–11 '89; P. Kujoory Choice 26:923 '89; G.U. de Sousa Am Ref Bks Ann 20:449 '89.

7214 **Bowers, Fredson T.**, *ed.* 'Textual introduction' *in* Henry VIII. (The dramatic works in the Beaumont and Fletcher canon, 7). Cambridge, C.U.P., 1989. p.3–20.
The F text was set from a scribal transcr. of a Fletcher–Shakespeare collaboration.

—JULIUS CAESAR

7215 **Rogers, J.K.** The folio compositors of Julius Caesar; a quantitative analysis. Analytical & Enum Bib 6no3:143–72 '82. tables.

7216 **Clayton, Thomas S.** 'Should Brutus never taste of Portia's death but once?' Text and performance in Julius Caesar. Stud Eng Lit 23no2:237–55 '83.

7217 **Pulbrook, Martin.** A textual rearrangement in Julius Caesar, act IV scene 3. [Dublin], Dublin U.P., 1983. [2]p. 24cm. Covertitle.
Suggests l.35–50 (TLN 1951–66) *mislocated (from between l.62–3* [TLN 2039–40]) *on account of eye-skip.*

7218 **Humphreys, Arthur R.**, *ed.* 'The First folio text' *in* Julius Caesar. (Oxford Sh). Oxford, Clarendon pr.; New York, O.U.P., 1984. p.72–83.
'The somewhat tentative assumption is that a clean scribal transcript of Shakespeare's working papers was either, as Fredson Bowers indicates, "partly marked up by the book-keeper with a view to the later inscription from it of the official prompt-book, and then preserved in the theatre as a substitute file copy for the working papers", or else partially annotated from the prompt-book in preparation for the printer' (p.77).

7219 **Jowett, John.** Ligature shortage and speech-prefix variation in Julius Caesar. Library ser6 6no3:244–53 S '84. tables.
Analysis of composition does not support the theory that 'either of the episodes concerning Portia's death is a revision' (p.253).

7220 **Velz, John W.** Disambiguation in recent editions of Shakespeare's Julius Caesar; the silent tradition. Analytical & Enum Bib new ser 2no1:1–11 '88.

—KING JOHN

7221 **Sams, Eric.** The troublesome wrangle over King John. N&Q 233no1:41–4 Mr '88.
F King John is Sh.'s revision of his own Troublesome reign.

7222 **Braunmuller, Albert R.** 'Editing the staging / staging the editing [and King John]' *in* Thompson, Marvin and Ruth Thompson, *ed.* Shakespeare and the sense of performance; essays in the tradition of performance criticism in honor of Bernard Beckerman. Newark, University of Delaware pr.; London, Associated U.P., [1989]. p.139–47.

7223   ——, *ed.* 'The text' *in* The life and death of king John. (Oxford Sh).
Oxford, Clarendon pr., 1989. p.19–36.

> *F copy was written by two scribes (roughly TLN 1–1893, 1941–end); F compositors* 'B and C
> were setting from copy that was prepared or revised after 1606, with at least a faint
> sense that the play might be spoken from the stage; it is probable, however, that the
> compositors' copy (and perhaps the text(s) underlying their copy) had not been
> used in the theatre' (p.25).

—KING LEAR

7224   **Champion, Larry S.** King Lear; an annotated bibliography. New York,
Garland, 1980. 2v. (vi,484; 425p.) 23cm. (Garland Sh Bibs, 1).

> *Rev:* TLS 1 My '81:477; Choice 18:1232 '81; Ruth L. Widmann Libr J 106:543 '81;
> L.R.N. Ashley Biblioth d'Humanisme & Renaiss 44:474–6 '82; Dorothy E. Litt Am
> Ref Bks Ann 13:680 '82; Elizabeth H. Hageman Sh Stud 16:329–34 '83; A. Wertheim
> Lit Res Newsl 8:87–9 '83.

7225   **Warren, Michael J.**, *ed.* 'Annotated bibliography, 1885–1896' *in*
William Shakespeare: The complete King Lear, 1608–1623. Berkeley, University of California pr., 1989. p.xxiii–xxxiii.

> *Selective bibliogr. illustrating* 'the chronological development of thinking about the
> texts of *King Lear*' (p.xxiii).

7226   **Stone, Peter W.K.** The textual history of King Lear. London, Scolar
pr, [1980]. viii,280p. tables. 23cm.

> 1. The textual problem.–2. The first quarto.–3. The derivation of the Folio text.–4. The
> Folio additions.–5. The manuscript source of corrections in F.–6. The manuscript 'copy'
> for F.–7. The textual history of F.–8. The relationship between F and Q2.–9. The distri-
> bution of F 'copy'.–10. Editorial principles.–Appendices: A1. Misreadings in Q1. A2.
> Misreadings in Q1 implying misdivision or misplacement of words in the copy. A3. Pho-
> netic errors in Q1. A4. Complex errors in Q1. A5. Miscellaneous errors in Q1. A6.
> Cruxes. A7. Q1 readings unnecessarily altered. A8. Q1/F 'true' variants. B1. Ascription
> of speeches in Q1 and F. B2. Omissions and additions in F. C1. Qa/Qb/F variants. C2.
> Unmetrical lines in F the result of interpolation or omission. D1. Q2/Q1 punctuation
> variants. D2. Q1/F and Q2/F anomalies in punctuation. D3. The evidence of dashes and
> brackets in Q1, Q2 and F. D4. The division of F copy.

> *Argues that* 'the text of Q1 derives from a theatrical report: from *verbatim* notes, that is,
> taken down at an actual performance or performances in the theatre' (p.13). *This manu-*
> *script was used, with the printed Q1, in the preparation of a promptbook to replace the earlier one*
> *which was lost* (p.112); *afterwards, these materials were given to another dramatist for revision*
> (p.114). *F1 was set in type from a copy of Q2 amended from the promptbook, by compositor E, but*
> *compositor B used a ms. derived from Q1, i.e., the promptbook itself* (p.138–40).

> *Rev:* D.J. Palmer Times Higher Educ Suppl 24 Ap '81:12; N. Alexander TLS 27 Mr
> '81:359; P. Edwards Mod Lang R 77:694–8 '82; J. Reibetantz Renaiss & Reform 6:294–
> 300 '82; S.W. Reid Sh Stud 15:327–39 '82; MacD.P. Jackson Sh Q 34:121–6 '83; G.
> Taylor R Eng Stud new ser 34:68–71 '83.

7227   **Taylor, Gary.** The war in King Lear. Sh Surv 33:27–34 '80.

> *Significance of Q/F variations.*

7228 **Urkowitz, Steven.** Shakespeare's revision of King Lear. [Princeton, N.J.], Princeton U.P., 1980. 168p. 19cm. (Princeton essays in literature).

1. Current opinions on the texts of King Lear.–2. Textual variants in dramatic contexts.–3. Textual variants and players' entrances and exits.–4. Interrupted exits and the textual variants in act three, scene one.–5. The role of Albany in the quarto and Folio.–6. Contemporary bibliographical theories and editorial practices and the case for authorial revision.

Rev: S.W. Wells TLS 13 F '81:176; R. Knowles Mod Philol 79:197–200 '81; R. Berry Queen's Q 88:536–9 '81; H.-J. Colmsee Sh Jahrb (Weimar) 118:171–2 '82; P. Edwards Mod Lang R 77:694–8 '82; G.P. Jones Univ Toronto Q 52:106–14 '82; J. Reibetanz Renaiss & Reformation 6:294–300 '82; S.W. Reid Sh Stud 15:327–39 '82; J.W. Velz Comp Drama 16:79–82 '82; L.A. Beaurline Renaiss Q 36:290–5 '83; G. Taylor R Eng Stud new ser 34:68–71 '83; M. Spevack Sh Jahrb (Bochum) 119:225–35 '84; E.P. Werstine Sh Q 36:368–70 '85; L.R.N. Ashley Bull d'Humanisme & Renaiss 50:402–3 '88; J. Wasson Comp Drama 23:102–3 '89.

7229 **Bhattacharya, Jyoti.** Kenneth Muir's edition of King Lear; a few questions. (Calcutta). J Dept Eng 16no2:97–105 '80/1.

7230 **Clayton, Thomas S.** Old light on the text of King Lear. Mod Philol 78no4:347–67 My '81. table., diagr.

Particular attention to 4.2.28: 'my foot usurps my body' (TLN 2297)

7231 **Blayney, Peter W.M.** The texts of King Lear and their origins. Vol. 1: Nicholas Okes and the first quarto. Cambridge, C.U.P., [1982]. xxi,740p. + errata p. tipped in. facsims., diagr., tables. 23cm. (New Cambr Sh Stud & Suppl Texts 1).

Introduction.–1. The printing house and its owners.–2. Printing-house methods.–3. Okes at work, 1607–8.–4. The printing of King Lear.–5. The compositors.–6. Proofreading, revising, and press-correcting.–7. Proofsheets and miscorrections.–8. Printers' copy.–9. Epilogue: Okes's later career.–Appendixes.–Addenda.

Rev: G.R. Proudfoot TLS 9 D '83:1381; C.L. Taylor Brit Bk News My '83:324; P. Bertram Renaiss Q 37:658–62 '84; G.B. Evans Mod Lang R 79:901–4 '84; A. Hammond Library ser6 6:89–93 '84; Bk Coll 33:7–24 '84; W.C. Ferguson Analytical & Enum Bib 8:138–41 '84; S.W. Reid Pa Bib Soc Am 78:489–93 '84; M. Spevack Sh Jahrb (Weimar) 119:225–35 '84; J. McLaverty N&Q 230:112–13 '85.

7232 **Hill, Trevor H. Howard-.** The problem of manuscript copy for Folio King Lear. Library ser6 4no1:1–24 Mr '82. tables.

Analysis of spellings, particularly the compositors' treatment of uncommon words, indicates that Q2 rather that Q1 lies behind F; but F was printed from a ms. prepared by concurrent collation and transcription of Q2 and the promptbook.

7233 **Honigmann, Ernst A.J.** Shakespeare's revised plays, King Lear and Othello. Library ser6 4no2:142–73 Je '82.

Review of recent scholarship suggests likelihood of revision.

7234 **Knowles, Richard A.J.** The printing of the second quarto of King Lear, 1619. Stud Bib 35:191–6 '82. diagr.

Proposes that Q2 Lr. 'was set from two type cases by two compositors working concurrently throughout sheets A to H, and thereafter from one of these type cases by a third compositor who by himself set the last three sheets, I to L' (p.191).

7235 **Reid, Sidney W.** The texts of King Lear; a review essay. [On Stone, no.7226 and Urkowitz, no.7228]. Sh Stud 15:327–39 '82.

7236 **Taylor, Gary**. Four new readings in King Lear. N&Q 227no2:121–3 Ap '82.

    In Q1, 'benefacted' *for* 'beniflicted' *at* 4.4.45; 'scrine' (shrine) *for* 'fruit' *in* 2.4.13; 'now' *for* 'not' *at* 2.2.167; *and* 'retinue' *for* 'returne' *at* 1.4.40.

7237 **Muir, Kenneth**. The texts of King Lear; an interim assessment of the controversy. Aligarh J Eng Stud 8:99–13 '83.

7238 **Taylor, Gary** and **M.J. Warren**, *ed.* The division of the kingdoms; Shakespeare's two versions of King Lear. Oxford, Clarendon pr., 1983. xii,489p. facsims., diagrs., tables. 21cm. (Oxford Sh Stud).

    Introduction: The once and future King Lear, Stanley Wells.–The base shall to th' legitimate: The growth of an editorial tradition, Steven Urkowitz.–The Folio omission of the mock trial: Motives and consequences, Roger Warren.–The diminution of Kent, Michael Warren.–Monopolies, show trials, disaster, and invasion: King Lear and censorship, Gary Taylor.–'Is this the promis'd end?': Revision in the role of the king, Thomas Clayton.–*Cor*.'s rescue of Kent, Beth Goldring.–*Gon*. No more, the text is foolish, Randall McLeod.–Revision, adaptation, and the fool in King Lear, John Kerrigan.–Folio editors, Folio compositors, and the Folio text of King Lear, Paul Werstine.–Fluctuating variation: Author, annotator, or actor?, MacD. P. Jackson.– King Lear: The date and authorship of the Folio version, Gary Taylor.–Select bibliography.–Index of passages discussed.–Addenda.

    Rev: J.R. Mulryne Times Higher Educ Suppl 4 My '84:24; P. Edwards Times Educ Suppl 9 Mr '84:257; E.A.J. Honigmann N.Y. R Bks 2 F '84:16–18; J. Seabrook Christian Sci Monitor 11 Jl '84:21–2; A.E. Craven Analytical & Enum Bib new ser 8:202– 3 '84; T.W. Craik Durham Univ J 77:271–2 '85; B.S. Hammond TRI 10:231–4 '85; T.H. Howard–Hill Library ser6 7:161–79 '85; K. Tetzeli von Rosador Sh Jahrb (Heidelburg) 1985:229–37 '85; G.W. Williams Mod & Renaiss Drama England 2:343–50 '85; K. Bartenschlager Anglia 104:229–35 '86; M. Charney N.Y. Sh Soc Bull 4:23 '86; M. Hattaway R Eng Stud new ser 37:256–8 '86; J.L. Halio Sh Stud 18:295–303 '86; J.L. Murphy Pa Bib Soc Am 81:53–63 '87.

7239 **[Barker, Nicolas J.]**. The Lear revolution. [On Blayney, no.7231 and The division, no.7238]. Bk Coll 33no1:7–24 '84.

7240 **Blayney, Peter W.M.** The texts of King Lear. (Letters). TLS 27 Ja '84:85.

7241 **Clayton, Thomas S.** Disemending King Lear in favour of Shakespeare; 'Edmund the base shall to th' legitimate'. N&Q 229no2:207– 8 Je '84.

    Retains 'to' *at* 1.2.21 (TLN 315).

7242 **Pittock, Malcolm**. 'Top the legitimate'? N&Q 229no2:208–10 Je '84.

    Retains 'to' *at* 1.2.21 (TLN 315).

7243 **Thomas, Sidney**. Shakespeare's supposed revision of King Lear. (Perspective). Sh Q 35no4:506–11 '84.

7244 **Warren, Michael J.** King Lear, IV.vi.83; the case for 'crying'. (Notes). Sh Q 35no3:319–21 '84.
Supports F reading at TLN 2530.

7245 **Foakes, Reginald A.** Textual revision and the fool in King Lear. Trivium: Stage screen and society; essays in honour of Peter Davison 20:33–47 My '85.

7246 **Hill, Trevor H. Howard-.** The challenge of King Lear. (Reviews). Library ser6 7no2:161–79 Je '85.
On the bibliographical arguments of G. Taylor and M. Warren, ed. The division of the kingdoms; Shakespeare's two versions of King Lear. Oxford, O.U.P., 1983: no.7238.

7247 **Taylor, Gary.** Folio compositors and folio copy; King Lear and its context. Pa Bib Soc Am 79no1:17–74 '85. tables, facsims., diagrs.
Detailed analysis of compositorial practices shows that 'both compositor B and his partner [E] appear to have worked from the same kind of copy. That copy was either (most probably) Q2, or some sort of transcript which had been influenced by Q2 to an extraordinary extent' (p.71).

7248 **Hill, Trevor H. Howard-.** Q1 and the copy for Folio Lear. Pa Bib Soc Am 80no4:419–35 '86. table., diagr.
Analysis of proofvariants and their transmission by Q2 strongly suggests that the printing of F1 was not directly influenced by Q1.

7249 **Trousdale, Marion.** A trip through the divided kingdoms. (Issues). Sh Q 37no2:218–23 '86.

7250 **Warren, Michael J.** 'Teaching with a proper text' *in* Ray, Robert H., *ed.* Approaches to teaching Shakespeare's King Lear. New York, Modern language association of America, 1986. p.105–10.

7251 **West, Gillian.** 'My father, poorly led?' A suggested emendation to King Lear IV.i.10. Eng Lang N 23no3:22–3 Mr '86.
Suggests 'purblid-eied' for 'purblind-eyed' at Q TLN 2189.

7252 **Murphy, John L.** Sheep-like goats and goat-like sheep; did Shakespeare divide Lear's kingdom. [On Taylor and Warren, The division of the kingdoms, no.7238]. (Review essay). Pa Bib Soc Am 81no1:53–63 '87.

7253 **Bartenschlager, Klaus** and **H.W. Gabler**. Die zwei Fassungen von Shakespear's King Lear; Zum neuen Verhältnis von Textkritik und Literaturkritik. (Aus der forschung). Sh Jahrb (Heidelberg) 1988:163–86 '88.

7254 **Carroll, William C.** New plays vs. old readings; The division of the kingdoms and folio deletions in King Lear. Stud Philol 85no2:225–44 '88.
Argues that some F revised passages are not improvements.

7255 **Gabler, Hans W.** The two versions of King Lear; a review article. Archiv 225nr1:137–44 '88.

—LOVE'S LABOURS LOST

7256 **Harvey, Nancy L.** and **Anna K. Carey.** Love's labor's lost; an annotated bibliography. New York, Garland, 1984. xiv, 220p. 21cm. (Sh Bibs, 6).
Rev: L.R.N. Ashley Biblioth d'Humanisme & Renaiss 47:659–96 '85; L.S. Champion Sth Atlantic R 50:107–9 '85; Janet R. Ivey Am Ref Bks Ann 16:406–7 '85; D.C. Redding Choice 22:1304 '85.

7257 **Draudt, Manfred.** Printer's copy for the quartos of Love's labour lost, 1598. Library ser6 3no2:119–31 Je '81.
Concludes that 'setting began from the lost Bad quarto, concluded from foul papers, and occasionally involved consultation of the source not in use for setting' (p.131).

7258 —— The Rosaline-Katherine tangle of Love's labour's lost. Library ser6 4no4:381–96 D '82.
'...the so-called "Rosaline-Katherine tangle" is, in spite of minor inconsistencies and imperfections, not "inexcusably muddled" but an actable scene that makes perfectly good sense within the context of the play, as a whole' (p.395).

7259 **Kerrigan, John,** ed. 'An account of the text' in Love's labour's lost. (New Penguin Sh). Harmondsworth, Penguin books, 1982. p.241–[60].
Q 1598 replaces a lost quarto and was set from foul papers; F was set from an annotated copy of Q.

7260 —— Love's labor's lost and Shakespearean revision. Sh Q 33no3:337–9 '82.
Attributes 'immediately post-foul-paper' revision to an annotator 'who worked from his memory of the play in performance' but denies J.W. Lever's suggestion of revision in 1597–8.

7261 —— Shakespeare at work; the Katharine-Rosaline tangle in Love's labour's lost. R Eng Stud new ser 33no130:129–36 My '82.

7262 **Wells, Stanley W.** The copy for the Folio text of Love's labour's lost. R Eng Stud new ser 33no130:137–47 My '82.
Concludes that 'the Quarto from which the Folio was printed had been compared with a manuscript and that this manuscript was one which presented the play in a form closer to that in which it was performed than the foul papers from which the Quarto was printed' (p.146).

7263 **Wells, Stanley W., J. Kerrigan** and **M. Draudt.** The 'Rosaline-Katherine tangle'; a correspondence. (Correspondence). Library ser6 5no4:399–404 D '83.

7264 **Werstine, E. Paul.** 'The editorial usefulness of printing house and and compositor studies' in Shand, G.B. and R.C. Shady, ed. Play-texts in old spelling; papers from the Glendon conference. [Illus. by W. White's LLL Q1]. (AMS pr. Studies in the renaissance, 6). New York, [1984]. p.27–33.

7265 —— The Hickmott–Dartmouth copy of Love's labour's lost, Q1. [1598]. N&Q 230:473 '85.

7266 **Draudt, Manfred**. The rationale of current bibliographical methods; printing house studies, computer-aided compositor studies, and the rise of statistical methods. Sh Surv 40:145–53 '87.

7267 **Scragg, Leah**. 'Rosaline's "pertaunt like"; a possible emendation' *in* KM80; a birthday album for Kenneth Muir. Liverpool, Liverpool U.P. for private circulation, [1987]. p.[129]–30.
Suggests 'Pertelot-like' *at* 5.2.67 (TLN 1957).

—MACBETH

7268 (2:1524) **Spangenberg, Heidemarie**. Illustrationen zu Shakespeare's Macbeth. Marburg, Lahn, 1967. 251 + 17p. illus. 19cm.
Einleitung.–A. Deskriptive Sichtung und Zuordnung des Materials.–B. Auswertung. 1. Die Motivwahl des Illustrators und ihre Voraussetzungen.–2. Die kostümkunkundliche Bedeutung der Illustrationen zum Text.

—MEASURE FOR MEASURE

7269 **Eccles, Mark**, *ed.* 'The text' *in* Measure for measure. (New variorum ed.). [New York], Modern language association of America, [1980]. p.291–8.

7270 **Marder, Louis**. Variorum Measure for measure published; new editors appointed. Sh Newsl 30no5:37,44 N '80. [Sg.: L.M.].

7271 **Walker, Alice**. The text of Measure for measure. R Eng Stud new ser 34no133:1–20 F '83.
1. Suspected textual corruptions.–2. Cruces and controversial readings.–3. Notes on ancilliary questions.–Appendix: The date of Measure for measure [1603].

7272 **Watt, R.J.C.** Three cruxes in Measure for measure. (Notes). R Eng Stud new ser 38no150:227–33 My '87.
1.2.112 (TLN 211), 2.4.88 (TLN 1096), 3.2.266 (TLN 1758).

7273 **Bawcutt, Nigel W.** A ghost press-variant in Folio Measure for measure. Sh Q 39no3:360 '88.
Uncorr. variant 'stings' *for* 'strings' (TLN 1760) *in Yale copy is product of crease in leaf.*

—MERCHANT OF VENICE

7274 **Wheeler, Thomas**. The Merchant of Venice; an annotated bibliography. New York, Garland, 1985. xxiii,386p. 23cm. ([Garland Sh Bibs, 9]).
Rev. D.C. Redding Choice 23:1662 '86; Janet R. Ivey Am Ref Bks Ann 18:468 '87; L. Engle Sh Q 40:244–5 '89.

7275 **Mahood, M.M.**, *ed.* 'Textual analysis' *in* The Merchant of Venice. (New Cambridge Sh). Cambridge, C.U.P., [1987]. p.168–83. facsim.
The Heyes-Roberts quarto (Q1).–The copy for Q1.–The Pavier quarto of 1619 (Q2).–The Folio of 1623 (F).–The quarto of 1637 (Q3).–Salarino, Solanio, Salerio.
Q1 was ptd. from Sh's ms., F1 from an edited copy of Q1.

—MERRY WIVES OF WINDSOR

7276 **Evans, Gwynne B.** 'The Merry wives of Windsor; the Folger manuscript [c.1660]' *in* Fabian, Bernhard and K. Tetzeli von Rosador, *ed.* Shakespeare: Text, language, criticism; essays in honour of Marvin Spevack. New York, Olms-Weidmann; Zurich, Hildesheim, 1987. p.[57]–79.

7277 **Craik, Thomas W.**, *ed.* 'The quarto and Folio texts' *in* The Merry wives of Windsor. (Oxford Sh). Oxford, Clarendon pr., 1989. p.48–63. facsims.
Q1 is a 'corrupt text reconstructed from memory' (p.48); *F was set from Crane's transcript of Sh's ms.*

—MIDSUMMER NIGHT'S DREAM

7278 **Carroll, D. Allen.** and **G.J. Williams**. A Midsummer night's dream; an annotated bibliography. New York, Garland, 1986. xxxvii,641p. 20cm. (Sh Bibs, 12).
Rev: Janet R. Ivey Am Ref Bks Ann 18:466–7 '87; L.R.N. Ashley Biblioth d'Humanisme & Renaiss 50:726–7 '88.

7279 **Foakes, Reginald A.**, *ed.* 'Textual analysis' *in* A Midsummer night's dream. (New Cambridge Sh). Cambridge, C.U.P., 1984. p.135–43.
Q1 was probably set from foul papers, F from a copy of Q2 'haphazardly corrected and expanded by an editor who was able to compare it with a manuscript marked up for use in the theatre' (p.139).

7280 **Taylor, Gary**. A crux in A midsummer night's dream. N&Q 230no1:47–9 Mr '85.
Proposes 'No, no, Sir, yield' *at* 3.2.257 (TLN 1289).

—MUCH ADO ABOUT NOTHING

7281 **Wells, Stanley W.** Editorial treatment of foul-paper texts: Much ado about nothing as test case. R Eng Stud new ser 31no121:1–16 F '80.

7282 **Humphreys, Arthur R.**, *ed.* '10. The text' *in* Much ado about nothing. (Arden Sh). London, Methuen, [1981]. p.75–84.
1. The quarto.–2. The Folio.
Q1 was ptd. from Sh's ms., F1 from a copy of Q somewhat marked up from the prompt-book.

7283 **Werstine, E. Paul.** The Bodmer copy of Shakespeare's Much ado about nothing, Q1. N&Q 228no2:123–4 Ap '83.

7284 **Mares, F.H.**, *ed.* 'Textual analysis' *in* Much ado about nothing. (New Cambridge Sh). Cambridge, C.U.P., [1988]. p.148–53.
The nature of the copy for Q and the problems of the text for editor and producer. *Q was ptd. from foul papers.*

7285 **Werstine, E. Paul.** McKerrow's 'suggestion' and twentieth-century Shakespeare textual criticism. Renaiss Drama new ser 19:149–73 '88.
Analysis of McKerrow's hypothesis and Ado. *suggests that* "'Bad quartos', 'foul papers', and 'prompt-copy' tend to coalesce. The quest for a stable entity called a 'performing text' thus becomes as quixotic as the abandoned quest for authorial intention" (p.169).

—OTHELLO

7286 **Levin, Richard**. The Indian/Iudean crux in Othello. Sh Q 33no1:60–7 '82; An addendum. (Notes) 34no1:72 '83; cf. G.W. Williams, Yet another early use of Iudean 34no1:72 '83.
Supports Q 'Indian' *at* 3.2.346 (TLN 3658).

7287 **Sanders, Norman**, *ed.* 'Textual analysis' *in* Othello. (New Cambridge Sh). Cambridge, C.U.P., [1984]. p.193–207. facsims.
The 1622 quarto.–The 1623 Folio.–Substantive variants.–Editorial procedure.–Later seventeenth-century editions.
Q1 was set by three compositors from a transcript of Sh's ms. made by two scribes; F1 was set from ms. copy: 'what we are dealing with is Shakespeare's first version of the play (behind Q1) and his own transcription of it (behind F), during the process of making which he not only created additions for dramatic clarification or imaginative amplification but was also enticed into changes in words and phrases which appeared to him at the time as improvements on his first thoughts' (p.206).

7288 **Amneus, Daniel**. The three Othellos. [Alhambra, Calif.], Primrose pr., [1986]. vi,194p. + corrigenda slip pasted in. 21cm.
1. Shakespeare's revision of Othello.–2. The Othello ballad.–3. The double attack on Iago.–4. The brawl.–5. Othello without Roderigo.–6. The handkerchief.–7. The landing.–8. The double time scheme.–9. The scene in the Senate chamber.–10. The Folio scribe.–11. The quarto and Folio texts.–12. The three Othellos.–Appendix 1. 'Othello, or fine fleecy hosiery'. 2. Dittographic errors (echoes) in F.

7289 **Everett, Barbara**. Two damned cruces: Othello and Twelfth night. R Eng Stud 37no146:184–97 My '86.
Reads 'limned' *for* 'dambd' *at* 1.1.23 (TLN 23), *and* 'limond' (lemon) *for* 'dam'd' *at* TN 1.3.145 (TLN 243).

7290 **Jackson, MacDonald P.** Printer's copy for the First folio text of Othello; the evidence of misreadings. (Bibliographical notes). Library ser6 9no3:262–7 S '87.
Analysis suggests that F was set from ms. rather than ptd. copy.

7291 **Berger, Thomas L.** The second quarto of Othello and the question of textual authority. [1630]. Analytical & Enum Bib new ser 2n04:141–59 '88.

Believes the Q 'to be a document that in its history reflects a definitive theatrical existence and in its adherence to Q readings attendance to an authorial presence' (p.156), *but would not base an ed. on it.*

7292 **Fleissner, Robert F.** 'Base Iúdean' in Othello again; misprint or, more likely, misreading. [5.1.356 (TLN 3658)]. N&Q 233n04:475–9 D '88.

7293 **Jackson, MacDonald P.** India and Indian or Judea and Judean? Shakespeare's Othello V.ii.356 and Peele's Edward I i.107. N&Q 233n04:479–80 D '88.

'Judea's' *misprinted* 'Indiaes' *in Edw.*

—PERICLES

7294 **Michael, Nancy C.** Pericles; an annotated bibliography. New York, Garland, 1987. xxii,289p. 21cm. (Garland Sh Bibs, 13).

Rev: L.R.N. Ashley Biblioth d'Humanisme & Renaiss 50:718–19 '88; J.K. Bracken Choice 25:1223 '88; R. Hillman Sh Q 40:117–21 '89; Janet R. Ivey Am Ref Bks Ann 20:449 '89.

7295 **Thomas, Sidney.** The problem of Pericles. Sh Q 34n04:448–50 '83.

Disputes bibliogr. arguments in F.D. Hoeniger's 'Gower and Shakespeare in Pericles' Sh Q 33n04:461–79 '82.

7296 **Taylor, Gary.** The transmission of Pericles. Pa Bib Soc Am 80n02:193–217 '86.

Per. 'was reported by a boy actor who doubled Lychorida and Marina' (p.217), *memorially reconstructed with the aid of the part of Gower.*

7297 **Jackson, MacDonald P.** Compositors' stints and the spacing of punctuation in the first quarto, 1609, of Shakespeare's Pericles. Pa Bib Soc Am 80n01:17–23 '87. table.

—RICHARD II

7298 **Roberts, Josephine A.** Richard II; an annotated bibliography. New York, Garland, 1988. 2v.(xxxviii,593; 656p.) 21cm. (Sh Bibs, 14).

Rev: E.J. Carpenter Choice 26:468 '88; L. Marder Sh Newsl 39:32 '89; G.U. de Sousa Am Ref Bks Ann 20:450 '89.

7299 **Craven, Alan E.** Compositor analysis to edited text; some suggested readings in Richard II and Much ado about nothing. [Simmes's compositor A]. Pa Bib Soc Am 26no1:43–62 '82.

7300 **Gurr, Andrew**, *ed.* 'Textual analysis' *in* King Richard II. (New Cambridge Sh). Cambridge, C.U.P., [1984]. p.175–83 facsims.
Q1 was ptd. from authoritative copy; F1 was ptd. from a copy of Q3 corrected by 'another text with some authority' (p.176). *The deposition scene was set up from an authoritative ms.*

7301 **Heinemann, Margot.** Shakespeare und die Zensur; Sir Thomas More und Richard II. Sh-Jahrb (Weimar) 121:77–88 '85.

7302 **Jowett, John** and **G. Taylor**. Sprinklings of authority; the Folio text of Richard II. Stud Bib 38:151–200 '85. tables.
1. Q5 and the abdication episode.–2. Q5 and act V.–3. The pattern of annotation: Compounded error; share error; manuscript misreadings; lineation; profanity; cuts; corrections of Q1 error; preliminary summary; stage directions; speech prefixes; act and scene divisions; hypothesis.–4. Authoritative F readings.–5. Censorship and the abdication episode.–6. Textual history of Richard II.
'On the most economical assumptions…Q1 was set from foul papers, or a transcript of them, censored for printing; F was set from an exemplar of Q3 which had been collated against an autograph prompt-book, containing a version of the abdication episode and one short passage transcribed from Q5' (p.200).

—RICHARD III

7303 **Moore, James A.** Richard III; an annotated bibliography. New York, Garland, 1986. li,867p. 21cm. ([Garland Sh Bibs, 11]).
Rev: G.U. de Sousa Am Ref Bks Ann 18:467–8 '87; L.R.N. Ashley Biblioth d'Humanisme & Renaiss 50:718–19 '88.

7304 **Hammond, Antony**, *ed.* '2. The text' *in* King Richard III. (Arden Sh). London, Methuen, [1981]. p.1–50.
The two texts.–Q1 and Patrick's theory of memorial reconstruction.–Was Q based on a prompt-book?–The printing of Q.–The compositors of Q.–The derivative quartos.–Was Q6 the copy for F?–Was Q3 the copy?–F copy: was it a transcript?–The F manuscript.–The printing of F.–The 'stability' of the text.–Summary.
Q1 represents a text reconstructed from memory by the Chamberlain's men; F1 was set from copies of Q3 and Q6 (or a transcript made from them) corrected from a ms. that was probably the 'author's "foul papers"' (p.43).

7305 **Jackson, MacDonald P.** Two Shakespeare quartos: Richard III and Henry IV. Stud Bib 35:173–90 '82. tables.
'…two compositors (N and D) set Richard III, Q1 (1957), sheets H–M, and…1 Henry IV, Q1 (1598), another product of Peter Short's printing house, was also set by two men (X and Y).… The surviving fragment of 1 Henry IV, Q0, was probably set by two compositors, who may plausibly be identified with X and Y. It is possible, even likely, that compositors X and N are one and the same man' (p.189).

7306 **Taylor, Gary**. Humphrey Hower. Sh Q 33no1:95–7 '82.
Suggests 'Hewer' for 'Hower' at 4.4.175 (TLN 2952).

7307 **Hammersmith, James P.** 'This Son of Yorke'; textual and literary criticism again. Sh Q 37no3:359–65 '86.

7308 **Urkowitz, Steven**. Reconsidering the relationship of quarto and folio texts of Richard III. Eng Lit Renaiss 16no3:442–66 '86.
Opposing D. L. Patrick (SBTC 1674), offers 'instead a model of Richard III as a work in progress, an early state in the Quarto, a later state in the Folio' (p.466), with analysis of recent ed.

—ROMEO AND JULIET

7309 **Gibbons, Brian C.**, *ed.* 'The text' *in* Romeo and Juliet. (Arden Sh). London, Methuen, 1980. (Repr. Routledge, 1988). p.1–26.
Q2 was ptd. from Sh.'s own ms., with consultation of Q1.

7310 **Reid, Sidney W.** The editing of Folio Romeo and Juliet. Stud Bib 35:43–46 '82.
Concludes 'an editor...worked through Q3's text with (for his day) considerable care, annotating the printer's copy where it struck him as deficient and relying mainly on the context to do so, though perhaps occasionally...consulting a playhouse manuscript' (p. 66).

7311 —— McKerrow, Greg, and quarto copy for Folio Romeo and Juliet. Library ser6 5no2:118–25 Je '83.
Rejects 'the notion that F1 depends on Q4' (p.124) since the variants which appear to indicate use of Q4 were not beyond the capacity of a compositor or editor to effect.

7312 **Evans, Gwynne B.**, *ed.* 'Textual analysis' *in* Romeo and Juliet. (New Cambridge Sh). Cambridge, C.U.P., 1984. p.206–12.
Q1 is a memorially reported text; Q2 was set from foul papers apart from a section in act 1 that was set from a copy of Q1, but with intermittent consultation of Q1 where Sh.'s ms. was illegible. F1 was ptd. from Q3 (1609).

7313 **Logan, Maureen F.** Star-crossed platonic Lovers, or Bowdler redux. [Censorship in anthology]. Eng J 74no1:53–5 Ja '85.

7314 **Ferguson, W. Craig.** Compositor identification in Romeo Q1 and Troilus. Stud Bib 42:211–18 '89. tables.
Modifies Hoppe's compositor attributions in Rom. and detects a third compositor in Tro. Q1 (1609).

—TAMING OF THE SHREW

7315 **Morris, Brian**, *ed.* '1. The text' *in* The Taming of the shrew. (Arden Sh). London, Methuen, [1981]. p.1–12.
F1 was ptd. from a scribal transcript of foul papers, annotated by the book-keeper.

7316 **Oliver, Harold J.**, *ed.* 'Introduction to the text' *in* The Taming of the shrew. (Oxford Sh). Oxford, Clarendon pr.; New York, O.U.P., 1982. p.1–29.

The play in the First folio.–The quarto: The taming of a shrew.–The relation of quarto and Folio.

F1 was ptd. from a revised author's ms.; A Shrew is a report of an earlier Sh. form of the play.

7317 **Martin, R.W.F.** A proposed emendation for The taming of the shrew, IV.iii.91. N&Q 229n02:184–6 Je '84.

Proposes 'scissor' for' censor' at TLN 2076.

7318 **Thompson, Ann**, *ed.* 'Textual analysis' *in* The taming of the shrew. (New Cambridge Sh.). Cambridge, C.U.P., 1984. p.155–74.

The nature of the copy and its transmission.–Is the Folio text an incomplete or revised version?–The relationship of The shrew and A shrew.–Conclusions.

F was ptd. from a transcript of a cut (but not substantially revised) longer play; A Shrew derives from the F play, with some rewriting.

7319 **Witworth, Charles W.** The editing of The shrew; a comparative review of the Arden, Oxford, and Cambridge editions. Cahiers Elisabéthains 27:101–5 Avril '85.

7320 **Wells, Stanley W.** and **G. Taylor**. 'No shrew, a shrew, and the shrew; internal revision in The taming of the shrew' *in* Fabian, Bernhard and K. Tetzeli von Rosador, *ed.* Shakespeare: Text, language, criticism; essays in honour of Marvin Spevack. New York, Olms–Weidmann; Zurich, Hildesheim, 1987. p.[351]–70.

—TEMPEST, THE

7321 **Roberts, Jeanne A.** Ralph Crane and the text of The Tempest. Sh Stud 13:213–33 '80. facsims.

7322 **Jowett, John**. New created creatures; Ralph Crane and the stage directions in The tempest. Sh Surv 36:107–20 '83.

7323 **Orgel, Stephen**. 'Text and date' *in* The tempest. (Oxford Sh). Oxford, Clarendon pr., 1987. p.56–62.

F1 was ptd. from Crane's transcript of a non-playhouse ms.

—TIMON OF ATHENS

7324 **Ruszkiewicz, John**. Timon of Athens; an annotated bibliography. New York, Garland, 1986. xxvii,274p. 21cm. ([Garland Sh Bibs, 10]).

Rev: W.R. Elton Sh Q 38:381–2 '87; Janet R. Ivey Am Ref Bks Ann 18:486 '87; L.R.N. Ashley Bull d'Humanisme & Renaiss 50:718–19 '88.

7325   **Hinman, Charlton J.K.**, *ed.* 'Note on the text' *in* The life of Timon of Athens. [Rev. ed.] (Pelican Sh). [Harmondsworth], Penguin books, [1982]. (First publ. 1964; repr. 1983). p.25–7.
Concludes that 'various parts of Shakespeare's incompletely revised autograph version were found so untidy and illegible' *that scribal transcription was necessary; the 'second hand' is* 'sometimes found in the most peculiarly Shakespearean passages in the play' (p.26).

—*TITUS ANDRONICUS*

7326   **Metz, G. Harold.** How many copies of Titus Andronicus Q3 are extant? [17]. (Bibliographical notes). Library ser6 3no4:336–40 D '81.

7327   **Hill, Trevor H. Howard-.** Compositor E and page dd3v of F Troilus. [i.e. Tit.]. Library ser6 4no3:328 '82.

7328   **Waith, Eugene M.**, *ed.* 'Text' *in* Titus Andronicus (Oxford Sh). Oxford, Clarendon pr.; New York, O.U.P., 1984. p.39–43.
Q1 was ptd. from foul papers, F1 from Q3 revised from a playhouse ms.

7329   **Metz, G. Harold.** Titus Andronicus; a watermark in the Longleat manuscript. (Notes). Sh Q 36no4:450–3 '85. facsims.

7330   **Holdsworth, Roger V.** A crux in Titus Andronicus. N&Q 233no1:44–5 Mr '88.
Questions S. Well's emendation of 'figure' *for* 'vigour' *in Q1 4.2.108 (TLN 1791).*

—*TROILUS AND CRESSIDA*

7331 (2:1829)   **Greg, sir Walter W.** The printing of Shakespeare's Troilus and Cressida, 1951.
Repr. in Bibliographical society of America. The Bibliographical society of America, 1904–79. Charlottesville, [1980]. p.266–75.

7332   **Muir, Kenneth**, *ed.* 'Text' *in* Troilus and Cressida. (Oxford Sh). Oxford, Clarendon pr.; New York, O.U.P., 1982. p.1–5. facsims.
'we do not know for certain the nature of the manuscript which formed the copy for the Quarto (1609) or of the manuscript by which a copy of that edition was corrected for the First folio' (p.1).

7333   **Palmer, Kenneth**, *ed.* 'The text' *in* Troilus and Cressida. (Arden Sh). London, Methuen, [1982]. p.1–17.
Q1 copy was possibly a transcript of Sh's draft; F1 was ptd. from copy of Q1 through the first 3 pages, then some other text, with some reference to Q1 (following Greg).

7334   **Taylor, Gary.** Troilus and Cressida; bibliography, performance and interpretation. Sh Stud 15:99–136 '82. table, diagr.

7335 **Honigmann, Ernst A.J.** 'The date and revision of Troilus and Cressida' *in* McGann, Jerome J., *ed.* Textual criticism and literary interpretation. Chicago, University of Chicago pr., 1985. p.38–54.
Tro. 'was written in the early months of 1601 and privately performed' (p.53); Sh. later wrote out a fair copy for a patron, the copy for Q; F was ptd. from a scribal copy of foul papers.

7336 **Riemer, A.P.** Some Shakespearean boxes; Troilus and Cressida, V.i.15–6. Sydney Stud Eng 12:119 '86/7.

7337 **Foakes, Reginald A.**, *ed.* 'An account of the text' *in* Troilus and Cressida. (New Penguin Sh). [London], Penguin, [1987]. (Repr. 1988). p.229–[53].
Q1 was ptd. from foul papers; the first 3p. of F was ptd. from Q1, the rest from a copy of Q annotated from a scribal ms. marked up for stage use.

—TWELFTH NIGHT

7338 **McAvoy, William C.** Twelfth night, or, What you will; a bibliography to supplement the New Variorum edition of 1901. New York, Modern language association of America, 1984. vi,57p. 22cm.
Rev: Jeanne M. Roberts Analytical & Enum Bib 8:264–7 '84; Am N&Q 24:60 '84; Janet R. Ivey Am Ref Bks Ann 16:407 '85; L.R.N.Ashley Biblioth d'Humanisme & Renaiss 50:423–4 '88.

—TWO GENTLEMEN OF VERONA

7339 **Pearson, D'Orsay W.** Two gentlemen of Verona; an annotated bibliography. New York, Garland, 1988. xv,251p. 21cm. ([Garland Sh. Bibs, 16]).
Rev: T.H. Howard-Hill Analytical & Enum Bib new ser 3:20–3 '89; J.E. Stephenson Am Ref Bks Ann 20:450 '89.

—APOCRYPHA

7340 **Metz, G. Harold.** Four plays ascribed to Shakespeare: The reign of king Edward III, Sir Thomas More, The history of Cardenio, and The two noble kinsmen; an annotated bibliography. New York, Garland, 1982. xxiv,193p. 20cm. (Sh Bibs, 2).
Rev: D. Rosenbaum Am Ref Bks Ann 14:581 '83.

7341 **Hamlin, Will.** 'A select bibliographical guide to The two noble kinsmen' *in* Frey, Charles H., *ed.* Shakespeare, Fletcher, and The two noble kinsmen. Columbia, University of Missouri pr., 1989. p.186–216.

7342 **Melchiori, Giorgio**. Hand D in Sir Thomas More; an essay in misinterpretation. Sh Surv 38:101–14 '85. fascims.

The first layer: alterations in Hand D.–Line 144: How say you now.–Lines 160–1: No, no, no, no, no, Shrewsbury, Shrewsbury!–Line 236: In, in to your obedience!–Line 245: Alas! alas!–The second layer of alterations: Hand C.–Munday's lost original.–The editor's problem.

7343 **Proudfoot, G. Richard**. The reign of king Edward the third, 1590, and Shakespeare. (Ann Sh lecture). Brit Acad Proc 71:159–85 '85.

7344 **Melchiori, Giorgio**. 'The Master of the revels and the date of the additions to The book of Sir Thomas More' *in* Fabian, Bernhard and K. Tetzeli von Rosador, *ed.* Shakespeare: Text, language, criticism; essays in honour of Marvin Spevack. New York, Olms-Weidmann; Zurich, Hildesheim, 1987. p.[164]–79.

The Master of the revels.–The date of the additions.–Conclusion.

7345 **Bowers, Fredson T.**, *ed.* 'Textual introduction' *in* The Two noble kinsmen. (The dramatic works in the Beaumont and Fletcher canon, 7). Cambridge, C.U.P., 1989. p.147–68.

F copy was most likely the '1623 prompt-book annotated by Knight' (p.150).

7346 **Hill, Trevor H. Howard-**, *ed.* Shakespeare and 'Sir Thomas More'; essays on the play and its Shakespearian interest. Cambridge, C.U.P., [1989]. ix,210p. tables. 23cm. (New Cambridge Sh Stud & Suppl Texts).

Introduction, T.H. Howard–Hill.–'Voice and credyt': the scholars and Sir Thomas More, G. Harold Metz.–2. The occasion of The book of Sir Thomas More, William B. Long.–3. The Book of Sir Thomas More: dates and acting companies, Scott McMillan.–4. The Book of Sir Thomas More: dramatic unity, Giorgio Melchiori.–5. The date and auspices of the additions to Sir Thomas More, Gary Taylor.–6. Henry Chettle and the original text of Sir Thomas More, John Jowett.–7. Webster or Shakespeare? Style, idiom, vocabulary and spelling in the additions to Sir Thomas More, Charles R. Forker.–8. Sir Thomas More and the Shakespeare canon: two approaches, John W. Velz.–Appendix: A table of sources and close analogues for the text of The book of Sir Thomas More, Giorgio Melchiori and Vittorio Gabrieli.

Rev: D.W. Foster Renaissance Q 44:369–72 '91; E.A.J. Honigmann Yrbk Eng Stud 21: 359–60 '91.

7347 **Waith, Eugene M.**, *ed.* 'Text' *in* The Two noble kinsmen, by William Shakespeare and John Fletcher. (Oxford Sh). Oxford, Clarendon pr., 1989. p.23–6.

Q 1634 was ptd. from a scribal ms. annotated by the book-keeper Edward Knight for revival in 1625–6.

7348 **Werstine, E. Paul**. '1. On the compositors of The two noble kinsmen' *in* Frey, Charles H., *ed.* Shakespeare, Fletcher, and The two noble kinsmen. Columbia, University of Missouri pr., 1989. p.6–30. facsims., tables.

—SONNETS

7349 **Jones, Katherine Duncan-**. Was the 1609 Shake-speares sonnets really unauthorized? R Eng Stud new ser 34no134:151–71 My '83.

1. The text of the Sonnets.–2. The career of Thomas Thorpe.–3. The structure of Shake-speares sonnets, 1609.

7350 **Taylor, Gary**. Shakespeare's sonnets; a rediscovery. [With text of Son. 2]. TLS 19 Ap '85:450; P. Beal 10 My '85:521 '85; G. Taylor 17 My '85:549.

7351 —— Some manuscripts of Shakespeare's Sonnets. John Rylands Univ Libr Manchester Bull 68no1:210–46 '85. table., facsim., diagrs.

SHAW, GEORGE BERNARD, 1856–1950

7352 **Pfeiffer, John R.** A continuing [annotated] checklist of Shaviana. Shaw 23no1:40–4 Ja '80; 23no2:95–9 My '80; 23no3:151–6 S '80; new ser 1:255–8 '81; 2:207–17 '82; 3:251–9 '83; 4: 211–24 '84; 5:325–40 '85; 6:169–79 '86; 7:355–66 '87; 8:163–75 '88; 9:223–35 '89;....

7353 **Carpenter, Charles A.** Shaw and religion/philosophy; a working bibliography. Shaw new ser 1:225–46 '81.

7354 **Rosenburg, Edgar**. The Shaw/Dickens file, 1914 to 1950; an annotated checklist, concluded; addenda, 1885 to 1919. Shaw 2:101–45 '82.

7355 **Laurence, Dan H.** Bernard Shaw; a bibliography. Oxford, Clarendon pr., 1983. 2v.(xxiii,1058p.) port., facsims. 21cm. (Soho Bibs, 22).
1.A. Books and ephemeral publications.–AA. Rough proofs/rehearsal copies.–B. Contributions to books....–BB. Works edited by Shaw.–2. C. Contribs. to periodicals and newspapers.–D. Stereotyped postcards.–E. Blurbs.–F. Broadcasts.–G. Recordings.–H. Wraiths and strays.–J. Manuscripts.–K. Works on Shaw.–L. Misattribution.
Quasifasim. TP transcrs., collations, bibliogr. notes and discussion.
Rev. S. Weintraub TLS 18 My '84:563; T. Kidd Time Higher Educ Suppl 4 My '84:26; M. Holroyd London R Bks 6:16–17 '84; B.F. Dukore Theat J 36:547–8 '84; J. Barzun Am Sch 53:546–9 '85; D. Leary Independent Shavian 23:13–16 '85; J. Stokes Yrbk Eng Stud 17:335–7 '87; F.P.W. McDowell Philol Q 66:509–13 '87.

7356 **Amalric, Jean-Claude**. B. Shaw, Man and superman: bibliographie sélective. Cahiers Vict & Edouardiens 24:153–60 Oc '86.

7357 **Carpenter, Charles A.** Studies of Shaw's neglected plays and mini-plays. Shaw 7:331–47 '87.

7358 **Morgan, Margery**. '5. A select bibliography [of primary and secondary sources]' *in* File on Shaw. (Writer-files). [London], Methuen, [1989]. p.116–24.

7359 **Wood, Roma**. The Society of authors. ['Fair use' in quoting unpubl. Shaw material]. (To the editor). TLS 15 Ag '80:916.

7360 **Bradford, Sarah**. Sale of autograph letters and mss. [Shaw and mrs. Campbell]. TLS 11 Mr '83:252.

7361 **Gibbs, A.M.** Pygmalion. [Text]. (Letters). TLS 13 Jl '84:783.

7362 **Joyce, Steven**. The ice age cometh; a major emendation of Buoyant billions in critical perspective. [Revision]. Shaw 7:279–99 '87. facsims.

7363 **McDowell, Frederick P.W.** A Bernard Shaw bibliography. [Rev. article on Laurence, no.7355]. Philol Q 66no4:509–20 '87.

7364 **Albrecht, Michael von**. Fate or hate? A textual problem in Shaw's Major Barbara. [3.3.117–18]. N&Q 234no2:196–7 Je '89.

7365 **Colby, Robert A.** Socialist to carbonato; George Bernard Shaw's dealings with Paul Reynolds. [About serialization in U.S.]. Columbia Libr Cols 38no3:2–14 My '89. ports., facsims.

7366 **Summers, Ellen**. Shaw and Henderson; autobiographer versus biographer. Stud Bib 42:284–93 '89.

SHEDDEN, WILLIAM RALSTON, 1828–89 *see* RALSTON, WILLIAM RALSTON SHEDDEN, *pseud*.

SHELLEY, MARY WOLLSTONECRAFT   (GODWIN), 1797–1851

7367 **Frank, Frederick S.** Mary Shelley's Frankenstein; a register of research. Bull Bib 40no3:163–88 S '83.

7368 **Glut, Donald F.** The Frankenstein catalog; being a comprehensive list of novels, translations, adaptations, stories, critical works…featuring Frankenstein's monster and/or descended from Mary Shelley's novel. Jefferson, N.C., McFarland, [1984]. xiii,525p. illus., facsims. 23cm.

7369 **Sunstein, Emily W.** Sketchbook used by Mary Shelley. [Sought]. (Query 342). Bk Coll 29no4:595 '80.

7370 **Murray, E.B.** Changes in the 1823 edition of Frankenstein. Library ser6 3no4:320–7 D '81. tables.

SHELLEY, PERCY BYSSHE, 1792–1822

7371 (1:4657) **Carl H. Pforzheimer library**, NEW YORK. Shelley and his circle, 1773–1822. Ed. by Donald H. Reiman and Doucet D. Fischer. Cambridge, Mass., Harvard U.P., 1961–86. 8v. illus., ports., facsims. 30cm.

For v.1–4, see BBLB2 4657.–V. Manuscripts and essays, 1816–1818. (1973).–VI. Manuscripts and essays, 1818–1819.–Appendix: Byron manuscripts, 1807–1815. (1973).–VII. Retrospective: miscellaneous manuscripts and essays, 1815–1819.–Retrospective: Byron and Guiccioli papers, 1816–1819. (1986).–VIII. Manuscripts and essays, 1820. (1986).

7372 **Jordan, Frank**, *ed.*, 1985: no.4375.

7373 **Engelberg, Karsten K.** Making the Shelley myth; an annotated bibliography of criticism of Percy Bysshe Shelley, 1822–1860. [London], Mansell; [Westport, Conn.], Meckler, 1988. xxiv,468p. 23cm.
Rev: Elizabeth James Bk Coll 38:124 '89.

7374 (7:6029) **Reiman, Donald H.** Editing Shelley, '72.
Repr. in Romantic texts and contexts. Columbia, University of Missouri pr., 1987. p.17–32.

7375 **Tetreault, Ronald**. Shelley's folio Plato. (News and notes). Keats-Sh J 30:17–21 '81.

7376 **Adamson, Carlene A.** The watermarks of Ms. Shelley adds.e.6 and Ms. Shelley Adds.e.8 and the dating of their texts. [Shelley notebooks]. Keats-Sh Mem Bull 33:70–1 '82. facsim.

7377 **Curtis, F.B.** Shelley and the Holkham circulating library in old Bond street. Keats-Shelley Mem Bull 33:25–35 '82.

7378 **Benfield, Bruce C.Barker-**. A Shelley fake. [Letter, 23 F 1822]. Bodleian Libr Rec 11no2:99–104 My '83.

7379 **Handrea, Mihai H.** Out of bounds. [Vols. annotated by Shelley sold in 1829]. (Letters). Antiqu Bk Mnthly R 8no6:232 Je '83; Searching for Shelley (Letters) 9no2:60 F '82; 9no4:155 Ap '82.

7380 **Murray, E.B.** Shelley's Notes on sculptures; the provenance and authority of the text. [And H.B. Forman; 1879]. Keats-Sh J 32:150–71 '83.

7381 **Vance, Thomas H.** Shelley's copy of Dante's works. [Sought]. (Readers' queries). N&Q 228no3:239–40 Je '83.

7382 **Murray, E.B.** The dating and composition of Shelley's The assassins. (Notes). Keats-Sh J 34:14–17 '85.

7383 **Burling, William J.** New light on Shelley's 'Lines to —'. [Revision]. (Notes). Keats-Sh J 35:20–3 '86.

7384 **Benfield, Bruce C. Barker-**. Shelley's Bodleian visits. Bodleian Libr Rec 12no5:381–99 Oc '87.

7385 **Glickman, Susan**. Roberts as editor; Shelley's Adonais and Alastor. Canadian Poet 25:56–65 '89.

7386 **Murray, E.B.** A suspect title-page of Shelley's History of a six weeks' tour. [1817]. (Bibliographical notes). Pa Bib Soc Am 83no2:201–6 Je '89. facsims.

SHERIDAN, RICHARD BRINSLEY, 1751–1816

7387 **Durant, Jack D.** Richard Brinsley Sheridan; a reference guide. Boston, Mass., G.K. Hall, [1981]. xxxi,312p. 24cm. (Reference guide to literature).

7388 **Redford, Bruce**. 'A peep behind the curtain at Drury lane'; the Richard Brinsley Sheridan archive at Princeton. Princeton Univ Libr Chron 46no3:248–68 '85. facsims.

7389 **Dixon, Peter** and **Vicky Dancroft**. Sheridan's second prologue to The rivals; a case for emendation. N&Q 234no4:479–80 D '89.

7390 **Murray, Geraldine**. A Sheridan emendation. [The school for scandal]. N&Q 234no4:482–3 D '89.

SHIEL, MATTHEW PHIPPS, 1865–1947

7391 **Morse, A. Reynolds**. The works of M.P. Shiel updated; a study in bibliography. 2d and updated ed. [Cleveland, Reynolds Morse foundation], 1980. 2v.(858p.) illus., ports., facsims. 28cm. (The works of M.P. Shiel update, 2–3). (Ltd. to 900 no. and signed copies).
Discursive bibliogr. of works and criticism.

7392 **Tyson, Jon Wynne-**. M.P. Shiel, right royal fantasist. Antiqu Bk Mnthly R 8no11:412–17 N '81. ports., illus.

7393 —— Two kings of Redonda: M.P. Shiel and John Gawsworth. Bks at Iowa 36:15–22 Ap '82. illus.

SHIRLEY, JAMES, 1596–1666

7394 **Zimmer, Ruth K.** James Shirley; a reference guide. Boston, G.K. Hall, [1980]. 132p. 23cm. (Reference guide to literature).
Rev: R. Morton Analytical & Enum Bull 6:32–6 '82; B.J. McMullin N&Q 227:78–9 '82; A. Wertheim Lit Res Newsl 7:43–5 '82.

7395 **Lucow, Ben**. 'Selected bibliography [of primary and secondary works]' *in* James Shirley. (Twayne's English authors, 321). Boston, Twayne, [1981]. p.165–72.

7396 **Walker, Kim**. Press variants and proof correction in Shirley's The dukes mistris, 1638. Long Room 31:19–33 '86. table.

7397 **Burner, Sandra**. James Shirley; a study of literary coteries and patronage in seventeenth-century England. Lanham, [Md.], U.P. of America, [1988]. xiv,234p. 21cm.

7398 **Walker, Kim**. The printing and publishing of James Shirley's The dukes mistris, 1638. Library ser6 10no4:317–38 D '88. facsims., tables.
Publication.–The publishers.–Manuscript copy.–The printer.–The printed text.–Variant states.–Bibliographical description and collation.–The preliminaries.–Compositorial and printing analysis.–Spelling variation and the number of compositors.

SHORE, JANE, d.1527?

7399 **Harner, James L.** Jane Shore in literature; a checklist. N&Q 226no6:496–507 D '81.

SIDNEY, SIR PHILIP, 1554–86

7400 **Lamb, Mary E. [and others]**. Recent studies of Sidney and his circle; an annotated bibliography. Sidney Newsl 1no1:15–24 '80; 1no2:61–9 '80; 2no2:20–6 '81; 3no1:27–37 '82; 4no1:20–9 '83; 4no2:27–33 '83; 5no1:28–37 '84; 6no1:25–41 '85; 9no2:67–73 ['88]; 10no1:57–69 '89.

7401 **Oxford. University. Bodleian library.** Sir Philip Sidney, life, death and legend; an exhibition to celebrate the 400th anniversary of the death of...23 September 1986 to 31 January 1987. [Introd. by Katherine Duncan-Jones]. Oxford, 1986. 64p. illus., map, music, facsims. 21cm.

7402 **Jensen, Bent Juel-**, *comp.* 'Sir Philip Sidney, 1554–1586; a check-list of early editions of his works' *in* Kay, Dennis, *ed.* Sir Philip Sidney; an anthology of modern criticism. Oxford, Clarendon pr., 1987. p.[289]–322.
Repr. with adds. and corrs. from Bk Coll 11no4:468–79 '62; 12no2:196–201 '63 (BBLB2: 4687–8).

7403 **Alwes, Derek B.** and **W.L. Godshalk**, *comp.* 'Recent studies in Sidney, 1978–86' *in* Kinney, Arthur F. [and others], *ed.* Sidney in retrospect; selections from English literary renaissance. Amherst, Mass., University of Massachusetts pr., 1988. p.[242]–63.

7404 **Robertson, Jean**. A note on Poems by sir Philip Sidney; the Ottley manuscript. [See BBTC 6054]. (Bibliographical notes). Library ser6 2no2:202–5 Je '80; P. Beal (Correspondence) 3no2:157 Je '81.

7405 **Warkentin, Germaine**. Sidney's Certain sonnets; speculations on the evolution of the text. Library ser6 2no4:430–44 D '80.
'Appendix: I. The Ottley manuscript.–II. Other manuscripts containing several poems.

7406 **DeNeef, A. Leigh.** Opening and closing the Sidneian text. [Editing the Defence]. Sidney Newsl 2no1:3–6 '81; J. A. van Dorsten, How not to open the Sidnean text 2no2:4–7 '81.

7407 **Lamb, Mary E.** The Houghton sale; items of interest to Sidney scholars. [Principally the Helmington hall ms. of Arcadia]. Sidney Newsl 2no2:7–9 '81.

7408 **Croft, Peter J.** 'Sir John Harington's manuscript of sir Philip Sidney's Arcadia' *in* Parks, Stephen and P.J. Croft. Literary autographs. Los Angeles, 1983. p.[37]–75. facsims.

7409 **Alton, Reginald E.** Sidney's Old Arcadia. [Phillips ms. transcribed by Harington and others]. (Letters). TLS 16 Mr '84:275; Katherine Duncan-Jones; H.R. Woudhuysen 30 Mr '84:345; R.E. Alton 13 Ap '84:404.

7410 **Brennan, Michael G.** Licensing the Sidney Psalms for the press in the 1640s. N&Q 229no3:304–5 S '84.

7411 **Chaudhuri, Sukanta**. The eclogues in Sidney's New Arcadia. [Editing]. R Eng Stud new ser 35no138:183–202 My '84.

7412 **Woudhuysen, Henry R.** A crux in the text of Sidney's A letter to queen Elizabeth. [At 53.6]. N&Q 229no2:172–3 '84.

7413 **Warkentin, Germaine**. Ins and outs of the Sidney family library. [Penshurst]. TLS 6 D '85:1394,1411.

7414 ——— Patrons and profiteers; Thomas Newman and the 'violent enlargement' of Astrophil and Stella. [And Francis Flower]. Bk Coll 34no4:461–87 '85.

7415 **Skretkowicz, Victor**. 'Building Sidney's reputation; texts and editors of the Arcadia' *in* Dorsten, Jan A. van, *ed*. Sir Philip Sidney: 1586 and the creation of a legend. (Sir Thomas Browne Inst Publs 9). Leiden, Publ. for the Sir Thomas Browne institute by E.J. Brill, 1986. p.[111]–24. facsims.

SIDNEY, ROBERT, VISCOUNT LISLE, 1ST EARL OF LEICESTER, 1563–1626

7416 (7:6056*) **Kelliher, W. Hilton** and **Katherine Duncan-Jones.** A manuscript of poems by Robert Sidney; some early impressions. [Add. ms. 58435]. Brit Libr J 1no2:107–44 '75. facsims.

The provenance.–The manuscript.–The poetry.–A selection from the poems.–Commentary.

7417 **Wright, Deborah K.** Modern-spelling text of Robert Sidney's poems proves disappointing. [Ed. Katherine Duncan-Jones, 1981]. Sidney Newsl 3no1:12–16 '82.

7418 **Brennan, Michael G.** Sir Robert Sidney and sir John Harington of Kelston. [Patronage]. N&Q 232no2:233–7 Je '87.

SILKIN, JON, 1930–

7419 **Jon Silkin**, a bibliography. Poetry R 69no4:30,75–6 Je '80.

SILLITOE, ALAN, 1928–

7420 **Gerard, David.** Alan Sillitoe, a bibliography. [London], Mansell; [Westport, Conn.], Meckler, [1988]. xx,175p. 20cm.

Classified bibliogr. of books (with quasi-facsim. TP transcrs., collations and bibliogr. notes and discussion), contribs., materials of critical and biogr. interest, reviews of, films and plays, radio etc. recordings. Rev: L. Bonnerot Étud Angl 44:234–5 '91.

SITWELL, DAME EDITH LOUISA, 1887–1964

7421 **Elborn, Geoffrey.** 'Bibliography [checklist of original works, books ed. by or with contribs. by, periodical contribs by, books announced but not publ., trans. of, and musical settings]' *in* Edith Sitwell, a biography. London, Sheldon pr.; New York, Doubleday, 1981. p.[295]–310.

7422 **Cevasco, G.A.** 'Selected bibliography [of primary and secondary sources]' *in* The Sitwells: Edith, Osbert, and Sacheverell. (Twayne's English authors, 457). Boston, [Mass.], Twayne, [1987]. p.153–8.

SITWELL, SIR FRANCIS OSBERT SACHEVERELL, 1892–1969

7423 **Abraham, Mildred K.** Sir Osbert Sitwell and his artists. Libr Chron Univ Texas new ser 30:38–55 '85. port., facsims.

7424 **Ritchie, Neil.** Collecting Sitwelliana. Priv Libr ser4 2no4:178–85 '89.

SITWELL, SIR SACHEVERELL, 1897–1988

7425 **Ritchie, Neil**. Sacheverell Sitwell; an annotated and descriptive bibliography, 1916–1986. [Florence], Giardo pr., 1987. 391p. + errata and addenda slip. illus., facsims., ports. 24cm. (Ltd. to 425 no., 400 signed, copies).

Quasi-facsim. TP transcrs., collations, contents, and bibliogr. notes and discussion for books, contribs. to books, contribs. to periodicals, and radio and television appearances.
Rev: A.R.A. Hobson TLS 21 Ap '89:437.

7426 **Abraham, Mildred K.** Sacheverell Sitwell and his artists. Am Bk Coll new ser 3no1:23–31 Ja/F '82. facsims.

SKELTON, JOHN, 1460?–1529

7427 **Carlson, David R.** Joseph Haslewood's manuscript collection of unpublished poems by John Skelton. (Bibliographical notes). Pa Bib Soc Am 81no1:65–74 '87.

SLADEN, DOUGLAS, 1856–1947

7428 **Eliot, Simon**. The sunny side of new Grub street; the writing of Douglas Sladen's autobiography. [1915]. Publ Hist 23:95–100 '88.

SMART, CHRISTOPHER, 1722–71

7429 **Mahony, Robert** and **Betty W. Rizzo**. Christopher Smart; an annotated bibliography, 1743–1983. New York, Garland, 1984. xxi,671[12]p. port., facsims. 21cm. (Reference library of the humanities, 214).

Classified annotated checklist of bibliogr. articles and canonical evidence, separate publications, general publications, refs. to and criticism of, census of mss., and alphabetical title checklist of published appearances of individual works.

7430 **Pitcher, Edward W.** Additions for Christopher Smart; an annotated bibliography, 1743–1983 (1984); the 'General publications' lists. Am N&Q new ser 24no5/6:71–2 Ja/F '86.

7431 **Williamson, Karina**. Christopher Smart's Hymns for children. [C.H. Wilkinson's copy sought]. (Readers' queries). N&Q 225no2:182 Ap '80.

7432 **Mahony, Robert**. Revision and correction in the poems of Christopher Smart. (Bibliographical notes). Pa Bib Soc Am 77no2:196–206 '83.

7433 **Rizzo, Betty W.** Christopher Smart, the C.S. poems, and Molly Leapor's epitaph. Library ser6 5no1:22–31 Mr '83.

7434 **Stewart, Mary M.** Smart, Kenrick, Carnan and Newbery; new evidence on the paper war, 1750–51. [And The midwife]. Library ser6 5no1:32–43 Mr '83.

7435 —— Christopher Smart's Proposals for A collection of original poems. (Bibliographical notes). Library ser6 10no3:253–4 S '88.

SMITH, ADAM, 1723–90

7436 (7:6076e) **Rechtenwald, Horst C.** An Adam Smith renaissance anno 1976? The bicentenary output—a reappraisal of his scholarship. J Econ Lit 16no1:56–83 Mr '78.
'References' (p.76–83).

7437 (7:6076f) **West, Edwin G.** Scotland's resurgent economist; a survey of the new literature on Adam Smith. Sthn Econ J 45no2:343–69 Oc '78.
'References' (p.367–9).

7438 **Lightwood, Martha B.** A selected bibliography of significant works about Adam Smith. Basingstoke, Macmillan, 1984; Philadelphia, University of Pennsylvania pr., [1985]. xvi,82p. 22cm.

7439 **McMullin, Brian J.** Another volume from Adam Smith's library. Bib Soc Aust & N.Z. Bull 4no3:212 My '80.

SMITH, ALEXANDER, 1829–67

7440 **Mackay, Kay.** In appreciation of Dreamthorp. Antiqu Bk Mnthly R 7no9:430–6 S '80. port., illus., facsims.
'A contribution towards a checklist of the works of Alexander Smith' (p.435–6).

SMITH, CHARLES ROACH, 1807–90

7441 **Gretton, John R.** 'Charles Roach Smith; a nineteenth-century archaeologist and his books' in Essays in book-collecting. [Dereham, Norf.], 1985. p.71–5. port. after p.40.
'Appendix: A checklist of Charles Roach Smith's books' (p.74): *18 items, 1848–86, and 3 books ed., and biography.*

SMITH, CHARLOTTE (TURNER), 1749–1806

7442 **Hardy, J.C.** Charlotte Smith's Letters of a solitary wanderer; dates of publication. [1800–2]. (Note 437). Bk Coll 30no2:256–7 '81.

7443 **Stanton, Judith P.** Charlotte Smith's 'literary business'; income, patronage, and indigence. Age Johnson 1:375–401 '87.

SMITH, FLORENCE MARGARET ('STEVIE'), 1902–71

7444 **Barbera, Jack W.McB.** and **Helen Bajan**. Stevie Smith; a bibliography. [London], Mansell; [Westport, Conn.], Meckler, [1987]. xvii,183p. 21cm.
Classified checklists of published works, publ. interviews, publ. works about, discography, and written archives.
Rev: S. Hills Bk Coll 37:136–7 '88.

SMITH, SHEILA KAYE- (MRS. T.P. FRY), 1887–1956

7445 **Walker, Dorothea.** 'Selected bibliography [of primary and secondary sources]' *in* Sheila Kaye-Smith. (Twayne's English authors, 278). Boston, Twayne, 1980. p.163–6.

SMOLLETT, TOBIAS GEORGE, 1721–71

7446 **Spector, Robert D.** Tobias Smollett; a reference guide. Boston, Mass., G.K. Hall, [1980]. xiv,341p. 24cm. (Reference publication in literature).
Rev: J.C. Beasley Lit Res Newsl 6:113–17 '81; J.V. Price N&Q 227:450–1 '82; P.-G. Boucé Mod Lang R 79:423–4 '84.

7447 **Boucé, Paul-Gabriel.** Smollett: Roderick Random, 1748; a selective critical bibliography. Soc d'Étud Anglo-Am Bull 13:43–51 N '81.

7448 **Wagoner, Mary.** Tobias Smollett; a checklist of editions of his works and an annotated secondary bibliography. New York, Garland, 1984. xvi,753p. 21cm. (Reference library of the humanities, 431).

7449 **Spector, Robert D.** 'Selected bibliography [of primary and secondary works]' *in* Tobias George Smollett. Updated ed. (Twayne's English authors, 75). Boston, Twayne, [1989]. (First publ. 1968). p.140–51.

7450 **Fitzpatrick, Barbara L.** The revision of a chapter heading in Smollett's Sir Launcelot Greaves; evidence from an Irish edition. N&Q 233no2:184–7 Je '88.

SNOW, CHARLES PERCY, BARON SNOW, 1905–80

7451 **Boytinck, Paul W.** C.P. Snow; a reference guide. Boston, Mass., G.K. Hall, [1980]. xxvii,381p. 24cm. (Reference guide to literature).
Rev: J.G. Watson N&Q 228:266–7 '83.

SORLEY, GEORGE HAMILTON, 1895–1915

7452 [Wilson, Jean M. and C. Woolf]. Charles Hamilton Sorley; catalogue of an exhibition held by Cecil Woolf publishers in association with the Central library, Cambridge…. London, C. Woolf, 1985. 31p. 15x22cm.

SOUTHERNE, THOMAS, 1660–1746

7453 Jordan, R.J. Oroonoko, the first fifty years. Bib Soc Aust & N.Z. Bull 6no2:53–63 '82.
Checklist of 20 ed., with collations, locations of copies and some bibliogr notes and discussion.

7454 Cameron, William J. Thomas Southerne's Oroonoko; a bibliography in short-title catalog form. [London, Ont., University of Western Ontario], 1983. 22p. 27cm. (WHSTC Bib, 14). Duplicated typescript. (Not seen: ISBN 0–7714–0465–4)

7455 Armistead, J.M. Thomas Southerne; three centuries of criticism. [Annotated]. Bull Bib 41no4:216–37 D '84.

———————

7456 Spector, Stephen. New light on Southerne's The disappointment, 1684. [Ptg.]. (Bibliographical notes). Library ser6 4no2:465–6 D '80; F.T. Bowers (Correspondence) 3no4:347 D '81.

7457 Blayney, Peter W.M. The Disappointment; a disappointment. [Ptg.]. Library ser6 6no1:50–60 Mr '84.

SOUTHEY, ROBERT, 1774–1843

7458 Priestley, Mary E. The Southey collection in the Fitz park museum, Keswick, Cumbria. [Catalogue]. Wordsworth & Circle 11no1:43–64 '80. illus., facsims.

———————

7459 Baine, Rodney M. The Southey-Sargent copy of Lewis and Clark's Travels. [In Libr.]. (Notes). Harvard Libr Bull 29no4:450–2 Oc '81.

7460 Curry, Kenneth. The text of Robert Southey's published correspondence; misdated letters and missing names. Pa Bib Soc Am 75no2:127–46 '81.

7461 Prance, Claude A. 'Southey's The doctor' *in* Essays of a book collector; reminiscences on some old books and their authors. West Cornwall, Conn., 1989. p.105–11.

SOUTHWELL, ROBERT, 1561?–95

7462 **King, John N.** Recent studies in Southwell. (Recent studies in the English renaissance). Eng Lit Renaiss 13no2:221–7 '83.

SPARK, MURIEL SARAH, 1918–

7463 **Spence, Martin**. Muriel Spark. [Collecting]. Bk & Mag Coll 24:61–8 F '86. port., facsims.
'Complete Muriel Spark UK bibliography' (p.68).

SPENCER, HERBERT, 1820–1903

7464 **Books** from Spencer's library, mainly editions of his works, in BL *see* Gould, Alison, Named special collections, 1981: no.818.

SPENSER, EDMUND, 1552?–99

7465 **Moore, John W.** Spenser bibliography update. Spenser Newsl 11no1:19–128 '80; 12no3:66–84 '81; 13no3:66–76 '82; 14no3:77–86 '83; 15no3:76–86 '84; 16no3:76–84 '85; 17no3:72–81 '86; 18no3:73–81 '87; 19no3:67–81 '88; 20no3:64–71 '88; 21no3:12–19 '90; 22no3:14–21 '91.

7466 **Sipple, William L.** Edmund Spenser, 1900–1936; a reference guide. With the assistance of Bernard J. Vondersmith. Boston, Mass., G.K. Hall, [1984]. xxxviii,244p. 25cm. (Reference guide to literature).
Rev: W.F. McNeir Spenser Newsl 15:67–9 '84; M.G. Brennan N&Q 230:396 '85; G. Morgan Mod Lang R 82:443 '87.

7467 **Shaheen, Naseeb**. The 1590 and 1596 texts of The faerie queene. (Bibliographical notes). Pa Bib Soc Am 74no1:57–63 '80.

7468 **Williams, Franklin B.** The iconography of Una's Lamb. [George-and-dragon woodcut in Sarum missals, 1500–20]. Pa Bib Soc Am 74no4:301–5 '80. facsim.

7469 **Luborsky, Ruth S.** The illustrations to The Shepheardes calender. Spenser Stud 2:3–53 '81. fascims.

7470 **Suzuki, Toshiyuki**. The influence of rhymes on the compositors of The faerie queene, 1590. Treatises & Stud by the Faculty of Kinjo Gahuin Univ 95:79–94 '81. (Not seen)

7471 **Yamashita, Hiroshi**. The printing of the first part (books I–III) of The faerie queene, I. Stud Lang & Cultures (Inst Mod Lang & Cultures, Univ Tsukuba) 11:143–76 '81. (Not seen).

7472 **Quitslund, Jon A.** '"Ornaments of all true love and beautie"; the patronesses of the Fowre hymnes [Anne Dudley, countess of Warwick and Margaret Clifford, countess of Cumberland]' *in* International congress on medieval studies. Spenser at Kalmazoo; proceedings of special sessions. Ed. by Russell J. Meyer. [Clarion, Dept. of English, Clarion state college], 1982. p.54–70.

7473 **Yamashita, Hiroshi**. The printing of The first part (books I–III) of The faerie queene in 1590, II. Stud Lang & Cultures (Inst Mod Lang & Cultures, Univ Tsukuba) 13:231–84 '82. diagrs.

7474 **Stillman, Carol A.** Politics, precedence, and the order of the dedicatory sonnets in The faerie queene. Spenser Stud 5:143–8 '85.

7475 **Rogers, David M.** Edmund Spenser and Gabriel Harvey; a new find. [Donation in Harvey's libr.]. (Notes and documents). Bodleian Libr Rec 12no4:334–7 Ap '87. facsims.

7476 **Bath, Michael**. 'Verse for and pictorial space in Van der Noot's Theatre for worldlings' *in* Höltgen, Karl J., W. Lottes and P.M. Daly, *ed*. Word and visual imagination; studies in the interaction of English literature and the visual arts. Erlangen, Universitätsbibliothek Erlangen-Nürnberg, 1988. p.73–105. facsims.

7477 **Gilman, Ernest B.** 'A Theatre for voluptuous worldlings (1569) and the origins of Spenser's iconoclastic imagination' *in* Möller, Joachim, *ed*. Imagination on a long rein; English literature illustrated. [Marburg], 1988. p.45–55. facsims.

7478 **Heninger, S.K.** 'The typographical layout of Spenser's Shepherdes calender' *in* Höltgen, Karl J., L. Wolfgang and P.M. Daly, *ed*. Word and visual imagination; studies in the interaction of English literature and the visual arts. Erlangen, Universitätsbibliothek Erlangen-Nürnberg, 1988. p.33–71. facsims.

STABLES, WILLIAM GORDON, 1840–1910

7479 **Crewdson, William H.P.** Stables the steadfast. Antiqu Bk Mnthly R 12no4:134–7 Ap '85. illus.

'A short-title list of the first edition of the adventure fiction of William Gordon Stables' (p.137).

STANHOPE, PHILIP DORMER, 4TH EARL OF CHESTERFIELD, 1694–1773

7480 (7:6122) **Gulick, Sidney L.** A Chesterfield bibliography to 1800, [1979].

Rev. Yvonne Noble Am Bk Coll new ser 2:44–8 '81; C.J.L.Price Mod Lang R 77:926–7 '82.

STAPLEDON, WILLIAM OLAF, 1886–1950

7481 **McCarthy, Patrick A.** 'Selected bibliography [of primary and secondary sources]' *in* Olaf Stapledon. (Twayne's English authors, 340). Boston, Twayne, 1981. p.158–62.

7482 **Satty, Harvey J.** and **C.C. Smith**. Olaf Stapledon; a bibliography. Westport, Conn., Greenwood pr., [1984]. xxxviii,167p. port. 24cm.
Bibliogr. of books and pamphlets, omnibus collns. and complete novel reprs., contribs. to books, pamphlets, periodicals and newspapers, mss., translations, bibliogrs. and works about.
Rev. R. Dalby Antiqu Bk Mnthly R 13:390 '86.

7483 **Smith, Curtis C.** The manuscript of Last and first men; towards a variorum. Sci Fict Stud 9no3:265–73 N '82.

STARK, DAME FREYA MADELINE (MRS. S.H. PEROWNE), 1893–1993

7484 **Macleod, Helen**. The travel books of Freya Stark. [Collecting]. Bk & Mag Coll 21:12–18 N '85. port., facsims.
'Complete Freya Stark bibliography' (p.18).

STEAD, WILLIAM THOMAS, 1849–1912

7485 **Wood, Sally**. W.T. Stead and his 'Books for the bairns'. Edinburgh, Salvia books, 1987. iv,60p. illus., facsims., port. 21cm.
Biography of W.T. Stead.–Bibliography: Books for the bairns.–New series.–Ernest Benn's edition.–Collection Stead; edition française: *checklists.*
Partly repr. from Antiqu Bk Mnthly R 14no8:292–9 Ap '87.

7486 (7:2352g) **Baylen, Joseph O.** Stead's penny Masterpiece library. [Review of reviews publishing co.]. J Pop Culture 9no3:710–25 '75.

7487 **Jones, Victor P.** Saint or sensationalist? the story of W.T. Stead, 1849–1912. [Chichester], Gooday, [1988]. [10]116p. illus., ports., facsims. 22cm.

STEELE, SIR RICHARD, 1672–1729

7488 **Dammers, Richard H.** 'Selected bibliography [of primary and secondary sources]' *in* Richard Steele. (Twayne's English authors, 351). Boston, [Mass.], Twayne, [1982]. p.144–56.

7489 **Alsop, James D.** Richard Steele and the reform of the London gazette. [Bibliographical notes]. Pa Bib Soc Am 8no4:455–61 '86.

7490 **May, James E.** Cancellanda in the first edition of Steele's Poetical miscellanies. Pa Bib Soc Am 82no1:71–82 Mr '88.

STEPHEN, SIR LESLIE, 1832–1904

7491 **Huber, Werner.** Towards a James Stephens bibliography; a checklist of criticism, 1958–1978. Irish Bklore 4no2:123–35 '80.

STERNE, LAURENCE, 1713–68

7492 (7:6154b) **Monkman, Kenneth**, *comp.* 'Appendix five: Bibliographical descriptions' *in* New, Melvyn and Joan New, *ed.* The life and opinions of Tristram Shandy, gentleman. [Gainesville, University pr. of Florida], [1978]. V.2, p.907–38. facsims.

7493 **Bony, Alain.** Laurence Sterne; The life and opinions of Tristram Shandy, gentleman; bibliographie sélective et critique. Soc d'Étud Anglo-Am Bull 17:35–64 N '83.

7494 (7:6154c) **New, Melvyn** and **Joan New**, *ed.* 'Introduction to the text' *in* The life and opinions of Tristram Shandy, gentleman. [Gainesville, University pr. of Florida], [1978]. V.2, p.814–42.
Composition and publication.–The copy-text.–The apparatus.–Collation.
See also 'Appendix nine: The 1780 edition' (p.958–66).

7495 **New, Melvyn.** Whim-whams and flim-flams; the Oxford university press edition of Tristram Shandy. [Ed. by Ian C. Ross, 1983]. Review 7:1–18 '85; I.C. Ross, New puzzles over the editing of Tristram Shandy; a response. 9:329–51 '87.

7496 **Brack, O M.** A book for a parlour window. [Rev. art. on Univ. of Florida Tristram Shandy, 1978–84]. Review 8:273–301 '86.

7497 **Meyer, Horst E.** Das Geheimnis der marmorierten Seite oder Tristram Shandys typographische Extravaganzen. (Buchillustration). Aus dem Antiquariat 3:A130–4 '86.

7498 **Vande Berg, Michael.** 'Pictures of pronunciation'; typographical travels through Tristram Shandy and Jacques le fataliste. Eight Cent Stud 21no1:21–47 '87.

7499 **Voogd, Peter J. de.** Tristram Shandy as aesthetic object. [Text]. Word & Image 4no1:38–92 Ja/Mr '88. facsims.

STERRY, PETER, d.1672

7500 **Croft, Peter J.** and **N. Matar**. The Peter Sterry mss. at Emmanuel college, Cambridge. Cambridge Bib Soc Trans 7pt1:42–46 '81. facsims.
'Appendix: Letters of Peter Sterry, in the National Library of Wales' (p.55–6).

STEVENSON, ROBERT LOUIS, 1850–94

7501 **Swearingen, Roger G.** The prose writings of Robert Louis Stevenson; a guide. [Hamden, Conn.], Archon books; [London], Macmillan, 1980. xxiii,217p. 23cm.
Rev: P. Keating TLS 26 Je '81:715; L.K. Uffelman Analytical & Enum Bib 6:39–45 '82; E.M. Eigner Ninet Cent Fict 36:492–6 '82.

7502 **Naugrette, Jean-Pierre**. Robert Louis Stevenson, The master of Ballantrae: bibliographie. (Agregation 1990). Cahiers Vict & Edouardiens 30:177–87 Oc '89.

7503 **Monteiro, George**. R.L. Stevenson to a book-owner; a new letter. [And Ballads of books, ed. J.B. Matthews, 1887]. N&Q 225no3:217 Je '80.

7504 **Swearingen, Roger G.** 'An old song', 1877; Robert Louis Stevenson's first published story, a new discovery in the Yale libraries. Yale Univ Libr Gaz 54no3:101–13 Ja '80.

7505 **Royle, Trevor**. 'The literary background to Stevenson's Edinburgh [and authors and publishers]' *in* Calder, Jenni, *ed*. Stevenson and Victorian Scotland. Edinburgh, U.P., [1981]. p.[48]–61.

7506 **Carpenter, Kevin**. R.L. Stevenson and the Treasure island illustrations. [1885]. N&Q 227no4:322–5 '82.

7507 **Wanford, Arthur**. A Stevenson serial. [David Balfour/Catriona]. (Letters). Antiqu Bk Mnthly R 10no6:226 Je '83; E. Mehew 10no7:269 Jl '83.

7508 **Menikoff, Barry**. Robert Louis Stevenson and The beach of Falesá; a study in Victorian publishing…. Stanford, Calif., Stanford U.P.; Edinburgh, Edinburgh U.P., 1984. viii,199p. illus., ports., facsims. 20cm.
Includes Part one: A study in Victorian publishing. 1. Introduction.–2. The context.–3. The accidentals.–4. The language.–5. Conclusion.
Rev: K. Gelder Stud Scott Lit 20:311–15 '85; B. Morton Times Higher Educ Suppl 1 Mr '85:19; J.A. Sutherland TLS 21 Je '85:705; N. Rankin London? R 27–8 Mr '85; D.H. Jackson Review 8:79–92 '86; D.S. Mack N&Q 232:271–2 '87.

7509 **Allen, Roger**. Robert Louis Stevenson. [Collecting]. Bk & Mag Coll 11:4–10 Ja '85. port., facsims., illus.
'Robert Louis Stevenson bibliography' (p.10).

7510 **Gelder, Kenneth**. Robert Louis Stevenson's revisions to 'The merry men.' [With collation]. Stud Scott Lit 21:262–87 '86.

7511 **Hardesty, Patricia W., W.H. Hardesty** and **D.D. Mann**. Doctoring the doctor; how Stevenson altered the second narrator of Treasure island. Stud Scott Lit 21:1–22 '86.
1. Revisions of the doctor in Jim's narrative chapters 1–15.–2. Revisions in the doctor's narrative.–3. Revisions of the doctor in Jim's narrative, chapters 19–34.–4. The effect of the revisions on doctor Livesey.–Textual collation.

7512 **Jackson, David H.** The Stanford Falésa [sic] and textual scholarship. Review 8:79–92 '86.

7513 **Mann, David D.** Stevenson's revisions of Treasure island; 'writing down the whole particulars'. Text 3:377–92 '87.

7514 **Hardesty, William H.** and **D.D. Mann**. Robert Louis Stevenson's art of revision; 'The pavilion on the links' as rehearsal for Treasure island. Pa Bib Soc Am 82no3:271–86 S '88.

7515 **Treglown, Jeremy**. R.L. Stevenson and the authors-publishers debate. TLS 15 Ja '88:58–9; E. Mehew 5 F '88:135. illus.
'Authors and publishers, by Robert Louis Stevenson' (p. 59).

7516 **Veeder, William**. 'The texts in question' *in* Veeder, William and G. Hirsh, *ed.* Dr. Jekyll and mr. Hyde after one hundred years. Chicago, University of Chicago pr., [1988]. p.3–13.

STEWART, DUGALD, 1753–1828

7517 **Crawford, Kenneth C.** The Dugald Stewart collection, Edinburgh university library. Biblioth 10no2:31–4 '80.

STOKER, ABRAHAM, 1847–1912

7518 **Roth, Phyllis A.** 'Selected bibliography [of primary and secondary sources]' *in* Bram Stoker. (Twayne's English authors, 343). Boston, [Mass.], Twayne, [1982]. p.157–63.

7519 **Dalby, Richard**. Bram Stoker; a bibliography of first editions; illustrated. London, Dracula pr., 1983. [vii],81p. facsims. 19cm.

7520 **Finné, Jacques**. Bibliographie de Dracula. [Paris], L'age d'homme, [1986]. 215p. 19cm. (Contemporains).
'Bibliographie' (p.[93]–213).

7521 **Dalby, Richard**. Bram Stoker and Dracula. [Collecting]. Bk & Mag Coll 2:15–22 Ap '84. ports., facsims.
'Complete bibliography of Bram Stoker' (p.22).

STOPES, MARIE CHARLOTTE CARMICHAEL (MRS. HUMPHREY VERDON-ROE), 1880–1958

7522 **Publisher's** and personal copies of books by Marie Stopes and other books from her library, some with ms. notes and alterations, 1877–1956, in BL *see* Gould, Alison, Named special collections, 1981: no.818.

7523 **Eaton, Peter**. Stopesiana. [Collecting]. Antiqu Bk Mnthly R 15no10:382–4 Oc '88. port., facsim.

STOPPARD, TOM, 1937–

7524 **Bratt, David**. Tom Stoppard; a reference guide. Boston, G.K. Hall, [1982]. xxxiv,264p. 25cm. (Reference publication in literature).
'Writings by Tom Stoppard' (p.xxxi–iv).

7525 **Page, Malcolm**. '5. A select bibliography [of primary and secondary sources]' *in* File on Stoppard. (Writer-files). London, Methuen, [1986]. p.91–6.

7526 **Rusinko, Susan**. 'Selected bibliography [of primary and secondary sources]' *in* Tom Stoppard. (Twayne's English authors, 419). Boston, Twayne, [1987]. p.152–60.

STOTHARD, THOMAS, 1755–1834

7527 **Finlay, Nancy**. Thomas Stothard's illustrations of Thomson's Seasons for the Royal engagement pocket atlas. Princeton Univ Libr Chron 42no3:165–77 '80.

7528 —— Thomas Stothard's illustrations for Parnell's Hermit. (New & notable). Princeton Univ Libr Chron 45no2:174–7 '84.

STRACHEY, GILES LYTTON, 1880–1932

7529 **Edmonds, Michael**. Lytton Strachey; a bibliography. New York, Garland, 1981. xvii,157p. 21cm.
Bibliogr. of separately-publ. works with quasi-facsim. TP transcrs., collations, contents, bibliogr. notes, but no notes of copies; contribs. to books and pamphlets; contribs. to periodicals; collected ed.; foreign ed.; mss.; and a brief list of criticism of.
Rev. J.H. Stape Bull Bib 41:102–3 '84.

STRACHEY, WILLIAM, 1575–1621

7530 **Foster, Donald W.** 'A checklist of Strachey's works' *in* Elegy by W.S.; a study in attribution. Newark, University of Delaware pr.; London, Associated U.P., [1989]. p.289–90.

STREATFEILD, NOEL, 1895–1986

7531 **Gunn, Katharine**. Noel Streatfeild & her children's books. [Collecting]. Bk & Mag Coll 21:20–7 N '85. port., facsims.
'Complete bibliography of Noel Streatfeild's children's books' (p.216–7).

STUART, GILBERT, 1742–86

7532 **Zachs, William**. Gilbert Stuart. (Some uncollected authors, 55). Bk Coll 37no4:522–46 '88.
'Gilbert Stuart; a bibliographic checklist' (p.537–46): *quaifacsim. TP transcrs., formats, collations, contents for 10 works and 4 other items.*

STUBBS, JOHN FRANCIS ALEXANDER HEATH-, 1918–

7533 **Van Domelen, John E.** John Heath-Stubbs; a checklist. [Fontwell], Centaur pr., [1988]. x,53p. 21cm.
Checklist of books, poems, short stories, etc., reviews by, and criticism of; not indexed.

SUCKLING, SIR JOHN, 1609–41

7534 **Raylor, Timothy**. Samuel Hartlib's copy of 'Upon sir John Suckling's hundred horse'. N&Q 234no4:445–7 D '89.

SULLY, JAMES, 1842–1923

7535 **Block, Ed.** James Sully, 1842–1923, Victorian psychologist; a bibliography, 1871–1917. Bull Bib 43no1:17–22 Mr '86. port.

SUMMERS, ALPHONSE MONTAGUE JOSEPH-MARY AUGUSTUS, 1880–1948

7536 **Frank, Frederick S.**, *ed.* 'Chronology and annotated bibliography' *in* Montague Summers; a bibliographical portrait. Metuchen, N.J., Scarecrow pr., 1988. p.[155]–246.

7537   **Smith, Timothy d'A**. Montague Summers; a bibliography. 2d ed., rev. Wellingborough, Northants., Aquarian pr., [1983]. (First publ. 1964). 170p. port., facsims. 21cm.
'Addenda to the new edition' (p.157–61).
Rev: H. Ormsby-Lennon Yrbk Eng Stud 16:354–6 '86.

7538   **Frank, Frederick S.** Montague Summers; a bibliographical portrait. Bull Bib 45no3:167–78 S '88.

7539 (7:6182*) **Sewell, Brocard**. The manuscripts of Montague Summers. Antigonish R 1no2:30–6 '70.

7540   **Dobson, Roger**. The mysterious Montague Summers. Antiqu Bk Mnthly R 13no7:248–55 Jl '86; B. Sewell (Letters) 13no8:311 Ag '86. port., facsims.
'A checklist of major works by Montague Summers' (p.255).

7541   **Wickham, D.E.**, *ed.* Letters to an editor; Montague Summers to C.K. Ogden. Edinburgh, Tragara pr., 1986. 28p. 24cm. (Ltd. to 145 no. copies).

7542   **Frank, Frederick S.**, *ed.* Montague Summers; a bibliographical portrait. Metuchen, N.J., Scarecrow pr., 1988. xviii,277p. 21cm. (Great bibliographers, 7).
Includes The reverend Montague Summers, by father Brocard Sewell.–The uses of Montague Summers, a pioneer reconsidered, by Robert D. Hume.–Montague Summers; a Gothic tribute, by Devendra P. Varma.

SWIFT, JONATHAN, 1667–1745

7543   **Vieth, David M.** Swift's poetry, 1900–1980; an annotated bibliography of studies. New York, Garland, 1982. xxvi,185p. 21cm. (Reference library of the humanities, 335).
Rev: A.B. England Analytical & Enum Bibliogr 7:37–40 '83.

7544   **Rogers, J. Patrick W.** The pamphleteers on Swift, 1710–1716; a preliminary checklist. Analytical & Enum Bib 1no1/2:16–30 '83.

7545   **Rodino, Richard H.** Swift studies, 1965–1980; an annotated bibliography. New York, Garland, 1984. xl,252p. 20cm. (Reference library of the humanities, 386).
Rev: D.J. Wormersley N&Q 231:114–15 '86.

7546   ——, **H.J. Real** and **H.J. Vienken**. A supplemental bibliography of Swift studies, 1965–1980. [Suppl. to no.7545]. Swift Stud 2:77–96 '87.

7547 **LeFanu, William R.** A catalogue of books belonging to dr. Jonathan Swift, dean of St. Patrick's, Dublin, Aug. 19. 1715. A facsimile of Swift's autograph, with an introd. and alphabetic catalogue. [Cambridge], Cambridge bibliographical society, 1988. vii,70p. port., facsims. 25cm. (Monogr, 10).
Rev: M.J. Jannetta Library ser6 11:279–80 '89.

7548 **Severino, Françoise Lapraz-.** Jonathan Swift: Gulliver's travels, 1726; bibliographie sélective et critique. Soc d'Étud Anglo-Am Bull 27:25–39 N '88.

7549 **Welcher, Jeanne K.** An annotated list of Gulliveriana, 1721–1800. Delmar, N.Y., Scholars' facsimiles & reprints, 1988. 550p. 21cm. (Gulliveriana, 8).

7550 **Downie, J. Alan.** Editor extraordinaire. [Sir Harold Williams]. Scriblerian 13no1:2–4 '80.

7551 **Guskin, Phyllis J.** Intentional accidentals; typography and audience in Swift's Drapier's letters. Eight Cent Life new ser 6no1:80–101 Oc '80.

7552 **Lena, John F.** Illustrations of Gulliver's travels; an addition and correction. [To BLB 1970–79: 6190]. (Bibliographical notes). Pa Bib Soc Am 74no3:258–9 '80.

7553 **Lock, F.P.** The text of Gulliver's travels. Mod Lang R 76no3:513–33 Jl '81.

7554 **Scouten, Arthur H.** 'Swift's poetry and the gentle reader' *in* Fischer, John I. [and others], *ed.* Contemporary studies of Swift's poetry. Newark, University of Delaware pr.; London, Associated U.P., [1981]. p.46–55.

7555 **Downie, J. Alan** and **D. Woolley.** Swift, Oxford, and the composition of Queen's speeches, 1710–1714. Brit Libr J 8no2:121–46 '82. facsims., tables.

7556 **Treadwell, Michael.** 'Swift's relations with the London book trade to 1714' *in* Myers, Robin and M.R.A. Harris, *ed.* Author/publisher relations during the eighteenth and nineteenth centuries. [Oxford], [1983]. p.[1]–36.

7557 **Ellis, Frank H.** A Swift ghost laid. [Faulkner's 1751 ed., v.5]. N&Q 229no3:393 S '84.

7558 **Pugh, Simon C.** A variant second edition of Jonathan Swift's The conduct of the allies. [Described]. N&Q 229no3:388–9 S '84.

7559   **Real, Hermann J.** and **H.J. Vienken**. 'A pretty mixture'; books from Swift's library at Abbotsford house. John Rylands Libr Bull 67no1:522–43 '84.

7560   **McCann, E.J. Wesley.** Jonathan Swift's library. Bk Coll 34no3:323–41 '85. facsims.

7561   **McMinn, Joseph**. Printing Swift. (Books and authors). Éire 20no1:143–9 '85.

7562   **Peterson, Leland D.** Problems of authenticity and text in three early poems attributed to Swift. ['The problem'; 'A love poem from a physician to his mistress'; 'The discovery']. Harvard Libr Bull 33no4:404–24 '85. facsims.

7563   **Vienken, Heinz J.** and **H.J. Real**, *ed.* Proceedings of the first Münster symposium on Jonathan Swift. München, W. Fink, 1985. 396p. illus. 24cm.
Includes Andrew Carpenter and Alan Harrison, Swift's 'O'Rourke's feast' and Sheridan's 'letter': early transcripts by Anthony Raymond.–Robert Halsband, Eighteenth-century illustrations of Gulliver's travels.–Heinz Kosok, Gulliver's children; a classic transformed for young readers [in German ed.].–Marie-Luise Spieckermann, Swift in Germany in the eighteenth-century; a preliminary sketch.–Michael Treadwell, Benjamin Motte, Andrew Tooke, and Gulliver's travels.–Heinz J. Vienken and H.J. Real, Ex libris J.S.; annotating Swift [using books owned by him].–David Woolley, The authorship of An answer to a scurrilous pamphlet [Temple].–James Woolley, The Intelligencer; its dating and contemporaneity.–Real, Hermann J. and Heinz J. Vienken, A catalogue of an exhibition of imprints from Swift's library....

7564   **LeFanu, William R.** A small Swift archive. [King's college, Cambridge]. (Notes). Swift Stud 1:61–3 '86.

7565   **McCann, E.J. Wesley.** The priced copy of the auction catalogue of Swift's library and some other Dublin catalogues. (Notes). Swift Stud 1:64–6 '86.

7566   —— Swift at Tollymore park. [Libr.]. (Irish booklore). Linen Hall R 3no4:13–15 '86. illus., facsims.

7567   **McMinn, Joseph.** Swift and George Faulkner, 'prince of Dublin printers.' (Irish booklore). Linen Hall R 3no3[i.e. 2]:15–16 '86.

7568   **Probyn, Clive T.** Swift's Verses on the death of dr. Swift: the notes. Stud Bib 39:47–61 '86. facsims., table.

7569   **Real, Hermann J.** and **H.J. Vienken**. Books from Stella's library. (Notes). Swift Stud 1:68–72 '86.

7570   **Woolley, David**. The stemma of Gulliver's travels; a first note. Swift Stud 1:51–4 '86. diagr.

7571 **Elias, A.C.** A manuscript of Constantia Grierson's. Swift Stud 2:33–56 '87.
'Appendix: Summary of contents...' (p.54–6).

7572 **Welcher, Jeanne K.** 'Eighteenth-century views of Gulliver; some contrasts between illustrations and prints' *in* Möller, Joachim, *ed.* Imagination on a long rein; English literature illustrated. [Marburg], [1988]. p.82–93. facsims.

7573 **Woolley, David.** The canon of Swift's prose pamphleteering, 1710–1714, and The new way of selling places at court. [Attrib. Swift; 1712]. Swift Stud 3:96–123 '88. facsims.

7574 **Fischer, John I.** 'The legal response to Swift's The public spirit of the whigs [and publ.]' *in* Fischer, John I. [and others], *ed.* Swift and his contexts. New York, AMS pr., [1989]. p.[21]–38.

7575 **Freeman, Arthur.** William Street, 1746, revisited; thirty-two new books from the library of Jonathan Swift. Bk Coll 38no1:68–78 '89.
'Manuscript list of "extra lots" in Swift's sale catalogue, p.16' (p.74–8).

7576 **Woolley, David.** The dean's library and the interlopers. Swift Stud 4:2–12 '89. facsim.

7577 **Woolley, James.** 'Stella's manuscript of Swift's poems' *in* Fischer, John I. [and others], *ed.* Swift and his contexts. New York, AMS pr., [1989]. p.115–32. facsims.

SWINBURNE, ALGERNON CHARLES, 1837–1909

7578 **Beetz, Kirk H.** Algernon Charles Swinburne; a bibliography of secondary works, 1861–1980. Metuchen, N.J., Scarecrow pr., 1982. viii,227p. 21cm. (Scarecrow Author Bibs, 61).
Rev: Choice 20:405 '82; T.L. Meyers Lit Res Newsl 8:84–7 '83; A.H. Harrison Mod Philol 81:89–91 '83.

7579 **Mayfield, John S.** A Swinburne collector in Calydon. Q J Libr Congress 37no1:25–34 '80. port., facsims.

7580 **Preston, Claire.** Swinburne's Poems and ballads, third series, 1889. (Note 440). Bk Coll 31no1:101–3 '82.

7581 **Rooksby, Rikky.** The Swinburne collection at Balliol. Vict Inst J 17:171–9 '89.

SYMONDS, JOHN ADDINGTON, 1840–93

7582   **Markgraf, Carl**. John Addington Symonds; update of a bibliography of writings about him. Eng Lit Transit 28no1:59–78 '85.

SYMONS, ALPHONSE JAMES ALBERT, 1900–41

7583   **Egerton, Diane**. A.J.A. Symons, bibliophile. Devil's Artisan 2:3–9 '80. facsims.

7584   **Sims, George F.** The First edition club. (A.J.A. Symons, I). Antiqu Bk Mnthly R 8no10:372–81 Oc '81; D. Weeks (Letters) 8no11:435 N '81. illus., ports., facsims.

7585   —— 'A.J.A. Symons' *in* The rare book game. Philadelphia, 1985. p.67–80.

7586   **Symons, Julian**. A.J.A. Symons; brother speculator. Bk Coll 34no3:293–308 '85. port., illus., facsims.

7587   **Sims, George F.** Brother speculator: Mandy Gregory, André Simon and the 'sette of odd volumes...'. (A.J.A. Symons, 3). Antiqu Bk Mnthly R 8no11:418–23 N '81; Christina Foyle (Letters) 9no1:21 Ja '82. ports., facsims.

SYMONS, ARTHUR WILLIAM, 1865–1945

7588   **Beckson, Karl**. 'Select bibliography of Symons's works, in chronological order' *in* Arthur Symons; a life. Oxford, Clarendon pr., 1987. p.383–4.

7589   **Morris, Bruce**. Symons, Yeats, and the Knave of hearts. [Yeats as proofreader in 1913]. N&Q 229no4:509–11 D '84.

SYNGE, JOHN MILLINGTON, 1871–1909

7590   **Grene, Nicholas**. Synge's The well of the saints; the problems of a dramatic text. Long Room 22/3:25–7 '81.

7591   **Carpenter, Andrew**. J.M. Synge. [Reissue of 1962–8 Collected works]. (To the editor). TLS 29 Ap '83:433; C.S. Smythe 20 My '83:516.

SYRETT, JANET ('NETTA'), 1865–1943

7592 **Owens, Jill T.** Netta Syrett, a chronological annotated bibliography of her works, 1890–1940. Bull Bib 45no1:8–14 Mr '88.

TAYLOR, ALAN JOHN PERCIVALE, 1906–

7593 **Wrigley, Chris.** A.J.P. Taylor; a complete annotated bibliography and guide to his historical and other writings. [Brighton], Sussex, Harvester pr.; New York, Barnes & Noble, [1980]. ix,607p. 21cm.
Rev: S. Koss TLS 12 D '80:1405.

TAYLOR, ISAAC, ONGAR, 1759–1829

7594 **Collection** of books by Isaac Taylor and members of his family, in BL *see* Gould, Alison, Named special collections, 1981: no.818.

TAYLOR, JOHN, 1578–1653

7595 **McCann, E.J. Wesley.** An unrecorded Belfast edition of John Taylor's Verbum sempiternum. (Irish booklore). Linen Hall R 6no2:14–15 '89. facsim.

TEMPLE, SIR WILLIAM, 1628–99

7596 **Woolley, David.** 'The authorship of An answer to a scurrilous pamphlet, 1693' *in* Vienken, Heinz J. and H.J. Real, *ed.* Proceedings of the first Münster symposium on Jonathan Swift. München, W. Fink, 1985. p.[321]–35. facsims., table.

TENNYSON, ALFRED, 1ST BARON TENNYSON, 1809–92

7597 **Shatto, Susan** and **Marion Shaw.** 'Appendix A: Descriptions of the manuscripts and printed texts' *in* Tennyson, In memoriam. Oxford, Clarendon pr., 1982. p.[305]–26.

7598 **Beetz, Kirk H.** Tennnyson; a bibliography, 1827–1982. Metuchen, N.J., Scarecrow pr., 1984. vi,528p. 21cm. (Scarecrow author bibs, 68).
Rev: Bull Bib 43:263 '86; P.G. Scott Review 8:101–17 '86; Susan Shatto N&Q 232:102–3 '87; C.deL. Ryals Yrbk Eng Stud 18:343–4 '88.

7599 **Lavabre, Simone.** Bibliographie de Tennyson, In memoriam. Cahiers Vict & Edouardiens 24:148–52 Oc '86.

7600 **Shaw, Marion**. An annotated critical bibliography of Alfred, lord Tennyson. With the assistance of Clifton U. Snaith. [Hemel Hempstead, Herts.], Harvester wheatsheaf; [New York], St. Martin's pr., [1989]. xvi,134p. 21cm. (Harvester annotated critical bibs).

7601 (5:13961d) **Campbell, Nancie**. R.H. Shepherd and The lover's tale. [Forgery]. Tennyson Res Bull 2:item C2a N '68.

7602 (5:13964f) **Ray, Gordon N.** Tennyson reads Maud. Vancouver, Publications centre, University of British Columbia, 1968. 47p. facsims. 21cm.
Repr. in Elledge, W. Paul and R.L. Hoffman, *ed.* Romantic and Victorian studies in memory of William H. Marshall. Rutherford, N.J., Fairleigh Dickinson U.P., 1971. p.290–317; Ray, Gordon N. Books as a way of life; essays.... New York, 1988. p.209–32.

7603 (5:13964c) **Tyree, Donald W.** Tennyson's use of Malory; an example. [Revision]. Tennyson Res Bull 2:item C3 '68.

7604 (7:6264) **Hagen, June S.** Tennyson and his publishers, [1979].
Rev: G.P. Landow Analytical & Enum Bib 5:69–71 '81; D. Tomlinson Arnoldian 8:75–6 '81; Rosemary Mundhenk Am Bk Coll new ser 2:48–51 '81; J.J. McGann Review 4:219–53 '82.

7605 **Carroll, R.A.** The Tennyson sales. [From Tennyson research centre, with lists]. Tennyson Res Bull 3no4:141–6 N '80.

7606 **Day, Aidan**. Two unrecorded stages in the revision of Tennyson's Oenone for Poems, 1842. Library ser6 2no3:315–25 S '80. facsims.

7607 **Shatto, Susan**. The Sotheby's sale of Tennyson papers. [July 22, 1980, from Tennyson research centre]. (Brief articles and notes). Vict Poet 18no3:309–12 '80.

7608 —— Tennyson's In memoriam; section 123 in the manuscripts. [Text]. Library ser6 2no3:304–14 S '80. facsims.

7609 **Shaw, Marion**. The opening sections of In memoriam; first and second thoughts. [Revision]. N&Q 225no6:522–5 D '80.

7610 **Day, Aidan**. The Lincoln manuscript fragment of Tennyson's The passing of Arthur. (Bibliographical notes). Library ser6 3no4:343–6 D '81.

7611 —— Notable acquisitions by the Tennyson research centre; Tennyson's annotated copy of William Trollope's Pentalogia graeca and an unlisted ms. poem. Tennyson Res Bull 3no5:203–8 N '81. facsim.

7612 **Paden, William D.** Tennyson's The new Timon, R.H. Shepherd, and Harry Buxton Forman. [Fabricated by Forman, 1897–9]. Stud Bib 34:262–7 '81. facsims.

7613 **Shannon, Edgar F.** The publication of Tennyson's Lucretius. Stud Bib 34:146–86 '81. tables.
'Bibliographical note: Descriptions of manuscripts and proofs' (p.174–8); 'Historical collation' (p.178–84); 'Alterations in the manuscripts' (p.184–6).

7614 **Stein, Richard L.** The pre-Raphaelite Tennyson. [Poems, 1857]. Vict Stud 24no3:278–301 '81. facsims.

7615 **Trapp, Joseph B.** Mantua's Tennyson manuscript. ['To Virgil']. TLS 18 S '81:1081. facsim.

7616 **[Day, Aidan].** Letters from Emily Tennyson Jesse to Ellen Hallam and an 1865 Tennyson presentation copy acquired by the Tennyson research centre. Tennyson Res Bull 4no1:29–31 '82.

7617 **Day, Aidan** and **P.G. Scott**. Tennyson's Ode on the death of the duke of Wellington; addenda to Shannon and Ricks. [BLB 1970–79: 6267]. Stud Bib 35:320–3 '82.

7618 **Collinson, Rowland L.** Tennyson manuscripts at the University of Rochester. Tennyson Res Bull 4no3:134 N '84.

7619 —— The texts of 'The vicar of Shiplake'. Tennyson Res Bull 4no3:114–22 N '84.

7620 **Harris, Jack T.** 'I have never seen a naked Lady of Shallot'. [Illus.]. J Pre-Raphaelite Stud 5no1:76–87 N '84.

7621 **Sturman, Christopher**. Annotations by Tennyson in a newly discovered copy of Poems, chiefly lyrical. Tennyson Res Bull 4no3:123–8 N '84. facsims.

7622 **Brodribb, A.C. Conant.** The poet, the printer & the type in the quarry. Albion 9no2:11–13 '85.
Repr. from BLB 70–79: 6261.

7623 **Ricks, Christopher**. 'The baby boy'; an unpublished version. Tennyson Res Bull 4no4:162 N '85.

7624 **Shannon, Edgar F.** and **C. Ricks**. The Change of the Light brigade; the creation of a poem. Stud Bib 38:1–44 '85.
'Bibliographical note; descriptions of manuscripts and proofs in chronological order' (p.32–7); 'The Charge of the Light brigade; authoritative text...' (p.37–8); 'Historical collation' (p.38–43); 'Alterations in the manuscript' (p.43–4).

7625 **University** of Rochester acquires Tennyson collection. [Rowland L. Collins colln.]. Tennyson Res Bull 4no5: 230 N '86.

7626 **Brockman, James R.** In memoriam–Tennyson–single hinge binding. New Bkbndr 6:27–9 '86. illus.

7627   **Lukitsh, Joanne**. Julia Margaret Cameron's photographic illustrations to Alfred Tennyson's The idylls of the king. Arthurian Lit 7:145–57 '87. illus., port.

7628   **Lottes, Wolfgang**. 'The Lady of Shalott; Tennyson's poem and some Victorian illustrations' *in* Höltgen, Karl J., W. Lottes and P.M. Daly, *ed.* Word and visual imagination; studies in the interaction of English literature and the visual arts. Erlangen, Universitätsbibliothek Erlangen-Nürnberg, 1988. p.269–302. facsims.

7629   **Vaughan, William**. 'Incongruous disciples; the pre-Raphaelites and the Moxon Tennyson' *in* Möller, Joachim, *ed.* Imagination on a long rein; English literature illustrated. [Marburg], [1988]. p.148–60. facsims.

7630   **Scott, Patrick G.** Tennyson's Maud and its American publishers; a relationship considered. Pa Bib Soc Am 83n02:153–67 Je '89.

THACKERAY, WILLIAM MAKEPEACE, 1811–63

7631   **Goldfarb, Sheldon**. William Makepeace Thackeray; an annotated bibliography, 1976–1987. New York, Garland, 1989. xxi,175p. 21cm. (Reference library of the humanities, 857).

_____

7632   **Möller, Joachim**. Buchschmuck oder Verständnishilfe: Text und Illustration in Vanity fair am Beispiel des Husband hunting. Lit in Wissenschaft u. Unterricht (Kiel) 13:89–100 '80.

7633   **Shillingsburg, Peter L.** Publisher's records and analytical bibliography; a Thackerayan example. [The history of Samuel Titmarsh & Bradbury and Evans]. Bk Coll 29n03:343–62 '80. facsims., tables.
'Table I: Textual variants [1849]' (p.360–1); 'II: The 1852 reissue' (p.361–2); 'III. The Smith Elder reissue [1872]' (p.362).

7634   **Harden, Edgar F.** The writing and publication of Esmond. Stud Novel 13n01/2:79–92 '81.

7635   **Olmsted, John C.** Richard Doyle's illustrations to The Newcomes. Stud Novel 13n01/2:93–108 '81. facsims.

7636   **Shillingsburg, Peter L.** Final touches and patches in Vanity fair the first edition. Stud Novel 13n01/2:40–50 '81.

7637   —— The printing, proof-reading, and publishing of Thackeray's Vanity Fair. Stud Bib 34:118–45 '81. tables.
'Chart I: Vanity fair printing schedule' (p.128); 'II: Vanity fair schedule of disbursement' (p.129–31); 'III. Variants within the first edition of Vanity fair' (p.132–44); 'IV. Six title-pages of Vanity fair' (p.145).

7638 **Harden, Edgar F.** The writing and publication of Thackeray's English humourists. Pa Soc Am Pa 76no2:197–207 '82.

7639 **Oram, Richard W.** The confederate Thackeray; Evans and Cogswell's The adventures of Philip. [Pirated]. Am Bk Coll new ser 4no4:27–30 Jl/Ag '83. facsims.

7640 **Maynor, Natalie**. Punctuation and style in Vanity fair; Thackeray versus his compositors. Eng Lang N 22no2:48–55 D '84.

7641 **Shillingsburg, Peter L.** Thackeray in Australia; the periodical press. Vict Pers R 18no4:134–7 '85.

7642 **Goldfarb, Sheldon**. Repeated discomposure; a Vanity fair textual problem. Eng Lang N 24no3:34–6 Mr '87.

THEOBALD, LEWIS, 1688–1744

7643 (5:14001*) **Schwartzstein, Leonard**. The text of The double falsehood. [Passages from Sh. imitated]. N&Q 199no11:471–2 '54.

7644 (5:14001*b) **Frazier, Harriet C.** The rifling of beauty's shores: Theobald and Shakespeare. [The Double falsehood a deliberate forgery]. Neuphilol Mitteilungen 69hft2:232–56 '68.

7645 (7:6296*) —— Speculation on the motives of a forger; Theobald's The double falsehood. Neuphilol Mitteilungen 72hft2:287–96 '71.

7646 (7:6296*c) —— '3. Theobald as Shakespearian editor' *in* A babble of ancestral voices: Shakespeare, Cervantes, and Theobald. The Hague, Mouton, 1974. p.[61]–88.

THOMAS, DYLAN MARLAIS, 1914–53

7647 **Bibliographie**. Cahiers [de la compagnie Madeleine] Renaud–[Jean Louis] Barrault 105:99–102 '83.

7648 (5:14010c) **Cox, James Stevens-**, *ed.* Dylan Thomas; judgment in an action by mrs. Caitlin Thomas to recover from the Times book co. ltd. the manuscript of Under Milk wood. St. Peter Port, C.I., Toucan pr., 1967. 7p. 21cm. (Ltd. to 100 copies).

7649 (5:14011b) ——, *ed.* Under Milk wood; account of an action to recover the original manuscript. With an introd. by Douglas Cleverdon. St. Peter Port, Guernsey, Toucan pr., 1969. 17p. port. 18cm. (Ltd. to 250 copies for sale).

7650 **Lazell, David**. Dylan Thomas; a brief introduction to Dylan's life and works with a guide to his most collectable editions. [Collecting]. Bk & Mag Coll 18:26–33 Ag '85. ports., facsims.
'Bibliography of Dylan Thomas 1st editions' (p.33).

THOMAS, PHILIP EDWARD, 1878–1917

7651 **Musty, John**. Edward Thomas and Siegfried Sassoon. (Collecting country writers, 5). Antiqu Bk Mnthly R 12no8:300–7 Ag '85. port., facsims.
'Check lists of first editions: Edward Thomas' (p.306); '...Siegfried Sassoon' (p.307).

7652 **Sims, George F.** 'In pursuit of Edward Thomas' *in* The rare book game. Philadelphia, 1985. p.15–25.

7653 **Prance, Claude A.** 'Edward Thomas's Horae solitariae' *in* Essays of a book collector; reminiscences on some old books and their authors. West Cornwall, Conn., 1989. p.125–30.

THOMPSON, EDWARD PALMER, 1924–

7654 **Anderson, Perry**. 'Bibliography [selected classified checklist]' *in* Arguments within English Marxism. [London], Verso, [1980]. p.[209]–13.

THOMPSON, FRANCIS JOSEPH, 1859–1907

7655 **Taylor, Beverly**. 'Selected bibliography [of primary and secondary sources]' *in* Francis Thompson. (Twayne's English authors, 436). Boston, [Mass.], Twayne, [1987]. p.149–51.

THOMSON, JAMES, 1700–48

7656 **Scott, Mary Jane** and **P.G. Scott**. The manuscript of James Thomson's Scots elegy. [Elegy upon James Therburn in Chatto]. Stud Scott Lit 17:135–44 '82.

7657 **Sambrook, A. James.** The semi-dependent profession of letters; the case of James Thomson. Stud Voltaire & Eight Cent 264:1142–6 '89.

THOMSON, JAMES, 1834–82

7658 **Crawford, Robert**. A little more 'B.V.' [Revs. by, in Cope's tobacco plant]. N&Q 228no4:307–9 Ag '83.

THYNNE, FRANCIS, 1545?–1608

7659 **Carlson, David R.** The writings and manuscript collections of the Elizabethan alchemist, antiquary, and herald, Francis Thynne. Huntington Libr Q 52no2:203–72 '89. facsims.

TICHBORNE, CHIDIOCK, 1558?–86

7660 **Hirsch, Richard S.M.** The text of Tichborne's lament reconsidered. Eng Lit Renaiss 17no3:[2]p. after p.276 '87. facsim.
Revises text printed in Eng Lit Renaiss 16no2:303–18 '86.

TICKELL, THOMAS, 1686–1740

7661 **Leidig, Helgard Stöver-,** *ed.* 'Texte und Textgeschichte' *in* Die Gedichte Thomas Tickells; Eine historisch-kritische Ausgabe mit Kommentar. (European Univ Stud ser 14. Anglo-Saxon Lang & Lit 99). Frankfurt am Main, P. Lang, [1981]. p.111–69.

TOLKIEN, JOHN RONALD REUEL, 1892–1973

7662 **Christopher, Joe R.** An Inklings bibliography. Mythlore 7no1:41–5 Mr '80; 7no2:42–7 '80; 7no3:43–7 '80; 7no4:42–8 '81; 8no1:43–7 '81; 8no2:43–7 '81; 8no3:43–7 '80; 8no4:43–7 '82; 9no1:37–41 '82; 9no2:42–6 '82; 9no3:42–6 '82; 9no4:51–5 '83; 10no1:50–4 '83; 10no2:51–5 '83;10no3:51–5 '84; 10no4:58–63 '84; 12no4:57–9 '86; 13no1:51–4 '86; 13no4:58–62 '87; 14no4:35,44 '88; 15no2:64–6 '88; with Wayne G. Hammond and Patricia A. Hargis 15no3:61–6 '89; 15no4:62–6 '89; 16no1:64–6 '89; 16no2:58–9,66 '89; 16no3:42–5 '90; 16no4:60–5 '90.

7663 **Rogers, Deborah W.** and **I.A. Rogers**. 'Selected bibliography [of primary and secondary sources]' *in* J.R.R. Tolkien. (Twayne's English authors, 304). Boston, [Mass.], Twayne, [1980]. p.151–8.

7664 **West, Richard C.** Tolkien criticism; an annotated checklist. Rev. ed. [Kent, Ohio], Kent state U.P., 1981. (First publ. 1970). xiv,177p. 22cm. (Serif Bibs & Checklists, 39).
Rev: T.D. Clareson Extrapolation 23:208 '82.

7665 **Jönsson, Åke.** Kommenterad bibliografi. [Annotated checklist]. Arda 2:136–54 '81/2.

7666 **Goodknight, Glenn H.** Tolkien in translation. Mythlore 9no2:22–7 '82. table.

7667 **Jönsson, Åke**. Supplement for 1981–1982 to A Tolkien bibliography, with additions and corrections for earlier years. Arda 3:128–73 '82/3.

7668 **Thomson, George H.** Early reviews of books by J.R.R. Tolkien. Mythlore 11no2:56–60 '84; 11no3:59–63 '85; 12no1:5–63 '85; 12no3:61–2 '86; 12no4:59–62 '86; 13no1:54–9 '86.

7669 **Bertenstaum, Åke**. Supplement for 1983–1984 to A Tolkien bibliography, with additions and corrections for earlier years. Arda 5:124–209 '85.

7670 **Johnson, Judith A.** J.R.R. Tolkien; six decades of criticism. Westport, Conn., Greenwood pr., [1986]. viii,266p. 23cm. (Bibs & Indexes to World Lit).
Rev: Åke Bertenstam Arda 6:126–31 '86 [i.e. '90].

7671 **Jönsson, Åke**. En Tolkienbibliografi 1911–1980; verk av och om J.R.R. Tolkien. A Tolkien bibliography, 1911–1980; works by and about J.R.R. Tolkien. 3d ed. Uppsala, [Uppsala universitet, 1986. (First publ. 1983). 146[1]p. 30cm. (Reprod. from typewriting).
In Swedish and English.
1st ed. rev: J. Peterzén Arda 3:116–18 '82/3.

7672 **Thomson, George H.** Early articles, comments, etcetera about J.R.R. Tolkien; a checklist. Mythlore 13no3:58–63 '87.

7673 —— Minor, early references to Tolkien and his works. Mythlore 14no1:41–2,55 '87.

———

7674 **Christopher, Joe R.** Three letters by J.R.R. Tolkien at the University of Texas, noted. Mythlore 7no2:5 '80.

7675 **Hieatt, Constance B.** The text of The hobbit; putting Tolkien's notes in order. Eng Stud Canada 7no2:212–24 '81.

7676 **Thomas, Lewis E.** J.R.R. Tolkien. [Collecting]. Bk & Mag Coll 17:15–22 Jl '85. port., facsims.
'Complete J.R.R. Tolkien UK bibliography (p.22).

7677 **Ryan, J.S.** Textual emendations in The lord of the rings. Amon Hen 81:17–19 S '86.

7678 **Unwin, Rayner**. The Hobbit 50th anniversary. Sci Fict Chron 8no9:48–50 Je '87. port.
Repr. from Bksllr Ja '87.

TOM, JOHN NICHOLS, 1799–1838

7679 **Hudson, Graham**. Mad John Tom. [Collecting]. Antiqu Bk Mnthly R

16n08:302–3 Ag '89. facsims.

TOMLINSON, HENRY MAJOR, 1873–1958

7680 **Crawford, Fred D.** 'Selected bibliography [of primary and secondary sources]' *in* H.M. Tomlinson. (Twayne's English authors, 308). Boston, Twayne, [1981]. p.245–54.

TOYNBEE, ARNOLD JOSEPH, 1889–1975

7681 **Morton, S. Fiona.** A bibliography of Arnold J. Toynbee. Oxford, O.U.P., 1980. xi,316p. 21cm.

TRAHERNE, THOMAS, 1637–74

7682 **Day, Malcolm M.** 'Selected bibliography [of primary and secondary sources]' *in* Thomas Traherne. (Twayne's English authors, 342). Boston, Twayne, [1982]. p.168–72.

7683 **Kelliher, W. Hilton.** The rediscovery of Thomas Traherne. [Commentaries of heaven ms. in BL]. TLS 14 S '84:1038.

TRESSELL, ROBERT, *pseud. of* ROBERT NOONAN, 1870–1911

7684 (5:14087b) **Swinnerton, Frank A.** The adventures of a manuscript; being the story of The ragged trousered philanthropists. London, Richards pr., [1956]. 27p. 22cm. (Ltd. to 1500 copies).

7685 (5:14087c) **Ball, F.C.** The Ragged trousered philanthropists. TLS 29 Mr '57:193.

TREVISA, JOHN DE, 1326–1402

7686 **Greetham, David C.** Models for the textual transmission of translations; the case of John Trevisa. Stud Bib 37:131–55 '84.
'Appendix: Trevisa the translator' (p.154–5).

TROLLOPE, ANTHONY, 1815–82

7687 **Knelman, Judith.** Trollope's journalism. Library ser6 5no2:140–55 Je '83.
'Appendix: A checklist of Trollope's journalism' (p.150–5): *chronol. checklist, 1849–81.*

7688 **Lyons, Anne K.** Anthony Trollope; an annotated bibliography of periodical works by and about him in the United States and Great Britain to 1900. Greenwood, Fla., Penkevill, [1985]. 163p. 21cm.
Rev: Judith Knelman Vict Pers R 18:156–7 '85.

7689 **Tingay, Lance O.** The Trollope collector; a record of writings by and books about Anthony Trolllope. London, Silverbridge pr., [1985]. vi,115p. 20cm. (Reprod. from typewriting).

7690 **MacDonald, Susan P.** 'Selected bibliography [of primary and secondary sources]' *in* Anthony Trollope. (Twayne's English authors, 441). Boston, Mass., Twayne, [1987]. p.129–36.

7691 (7:6352) **Hall, N. John.** Trollope and his illustrators, [1979].
Rev: F.W. Bradbrook N&Q 227:253–4 '82; J.P. Vernier Yrbk Eng Stud 13:334–6 '83.

7692 **Gresty, Hilary**. Millais and Trollope; author and illustrator. Bk Coll 30no1:43–61 '81. facsims.

7693 **Bailey, J.W.** The Duke's children; rediscovering a Trollope manuscript. Yale Univ Libr Gaz 57no1/2:34–8 Oc '82. facsim.

7694 **Srebrnik, Patricia A.T.** Trollope, James Virtue, and Saint Paul's magazine. Ninet Cent Fict 37no3:443–63 D '82.

7695 **Super, Robert H.** Trollope at the Royal literary fund. Ninet Cent Fict 37no3:316–28 D '82.

7696 **Sutherland, John A.** Trollope at work on The way we live now. Ninet Cent Fict 37no3:472–93 D '82.
The contract.–Forecast calculation.–The working calendar.–The dramatis personae plan.–Nonce plans I.–Chapter plans for the second volume.–The manuscript.–Trollope under pressure.–Chronological reckoning.–Nonce plans II.–Proofs and subsequent editions.

7697 **Wright, Andrew**. 'Trollope revises Trollope' *in* Halperin, John, *ed.* Trollope centenary essays. [London], Macmillan; New York, St. Martin's pr., [1982]. p.[109]–33.
Orley farm.–The small house at Allington.–Mr. Scarborough's family.–Summary and conclusion.

7698 **An** Anthony Trollope exhibition. (Library notes). Princeton Univ Libr Chron 44no2:153–4 '83.

7699 **Hall, N. John.** 'Editing and annotating the letters of Anthony Trollope' *in* Brody, Saul N. and H. Schechter, *ed.* CUNY English forum, 1. New York, AMS pr., 1985. p.269–73.
1. Editing.–2. Annotation.

7700 —— Seeing Trollope's An autobiography through the press; the correspondence of William Blackwood and Henry Merivale Trollope. Princeton Univ Libr Chron 47no2:189–223 '86. port., facsims.

7701 **Hamer, Mary**. Writing by numbers; Trollope's serial fiction. Cam-
bridge, C.U.P., [1987]. xiii,199p. 20cm.
Introduction: Serial fiction in the nineteenth century; Trollope and publishing; The
illustrations.–1. Trollope's method.–2. The relation between plots.–3. The manu-
script of Framley parsonage.–4. Orley farm and The small house at Allington.–5.
Planning versus discovery.–6. Trollope bends the form.–Appendix 1: Trollope and
Millais. 2. The initial publication of Trollope's novels in England.
Rev: J. Adlard TLS 19 Je '87:672.

7702 **Sutherland, John A.** Trollope, publishers and the truth. [In Autobi-
ography]. Prose Stud 10no3:239–49 D '87.

TROLLOPE, FRANCES (MILTON), 1780–1863

7703 **Heineman, Helen**. 'Selected bibliography [of primary and secondary sources]' *in* Frances Trollope. (Twayne's English authors, 370).
Boston, [Mass.], Twayne, [1984]. p.154–60.

TUPPER, JOHN LUCAS, 1824–79

7704 **Landow, George P.** A check list of the writings of John Lucas Tupper,
friend of the pre-Raphaelites. J Pre-Raphaelite Stud 7no1:63–8 N '86.

TURNER, DAWSON, 1775–1858

7705 **Price, J.H.** A note on Aspects of fuci (Dawson Turner, 1806–19).
(Bibliographic notes on works concerning the algae, 5). Archiv Nat
Hist 11no3:440–2 Ap '84.

TWEEDY, ETHEL BRILLIANA (HARVEY), 186?–1940

7706 **Brett, Stanley**. A busy woman: mrs. Alex Tweedy. Priv Libr ser3
3no3:124–8 '80.
'List of books' (p.127–8).

TYNAN, KATHARINE, 1861–1931

7707 (7:6356*) **Fallon, Ann C.** 'Selected bibliography [of primary and secondary sources]' *in* Katharine Tynan. (Twayne's English authors, 272).
Boston, Twayne, [1979]. p.182–7.

TYNDALE, WILLIAM, d.1536

7708 **Millus, Donald J.** and **Anne M. O'Donnell.** The Tyndale edition: still underground. Moreana 23no91/2:59–62 N '86.

UNDERHILL, EVELYN, 1875–1941

7709 **Greene, Dana**. Bibliography of works about and by Evelyn Underhill. Bull Bib 45no2:92–107 Je '88. port.

UPWARD, EDWARD FALAISE, 1903–

7710 **Munton, Alan** and **A. Young**, no.700.

USSHER, ARCHBP. JAMES, 1581–1656

7711 **Brown, Barbara**. Ussher and his European contemporaries; some manuscripts at Dublin. Nouvelles de la République des Lettres 1:71–95 '82. port.
1. Ecclesiastical history.–2. Orientalia.–3. Astronomy and contemporary science.–4. Correspondence.–Appendix 1: Trinity college, Dublin: Ussher's manuscripts.

UTLEY, ALISON, 1884–

7712 **Gunn, Katharine**. The children's books of Alison Uttley. [Collecting]. Bk & Mag Coll 25:24–32 Ap '86. port., facsims.
'Complete UK bibliography of Alison Uttley's children's books' (p.31–2).

VANBURGH, SIR JOHN, 1664–1726

7713 **Fluchere, Marie-Louise**. Sir John Vanbrugh; bibliographie sélective et critique. Soc d'Étud Anglo-Am Bull 11:31–54 N '80.

───────────────

7714 **Ross, John C.** The printing of Vanbrugh's The provok'd wife, 1697. [By James Orme]. Library ser6 4no4:397–409 D '82. tables.
'Appendix B: Orme and his books' (p.407–9).

VAUGHAN, HENRY, 1622–95

7715 **Martinet, Marie-Madeleine**. Henry Vaughan, Silex scintillans; bibliographie sélective et critique. Soc d'Étud Anglo-Am Bull 17:7–34 N '83.

───────────────

7716 **Willard, Thomas**. The publisher of Olor iscanus. [Thomas Vaughan]. (Bibliographical notes). Pa Bib Soc Am 75n02:174–9 '81.

VAUGHAN, RICHARD, 1904–83

7717 **Bianchi, Tony**. 'Bibliography [of primary and secondary material]' *in* Richard Vaughan. (Writers of Wales). Cardiff, University of Wales pr. on behalf of the Welsh arts council, 1984. p.83–5.

7718 Cancelled.

VILLIERS, GEORGE, 2D DUKE OF BUCKINGHAM, 1628–87

7719 **O'Neill, John H.** 'Selected bibliography [of primary and critical sources]' *in* George Villiers, second duke of Buckingham. (Twayne's English authors, 394). Boston, Twayne, [1984]. p.137–41.

WADDELL, HELEN JANE, 1889–1965

7720 **Hall, David J.** Helen Waddell. (Some uncollected authors, 52). Bk Coll 29n03:395–405 '80; (Note 439) 31n01:101 '82.
'Check-list' (p.398–405): *quasifacsim. TP transcrs., collations and some bibliogr. notes on 19 books by; and 7 works ed. by or contrib. to.*

7721 **Kelly, Mary T.** The papers of Helen Waddell (MS 18): a calendar. Belfast, The library, Queen's university of Belfast, 1981. 81p. 30cm. (Duplicated typescript).

WAIN, JOHN BARRINGTON, 1925–

7722 **Salwak, Dale**. 'Selected bibliography [of primary and secondary sources]' *in* John Wain ([Twayne's English authors, 316]). Boston, Twayne, [1981]. p.142–51.

7723 **Hall, John T.D.** 'Hurry back down'; John Wain at sixty: a retrospective exhibition held in the Drummond room, Edinburgh university library...April-September 1985. Edinburgh, 1985. 30p. 20cm.

7724 **Gerard, David**. John Wain, a bibliography. [London], Mansell; Westport, Conn., Meckler, [1987]. xxviii,235p. 21cm.
Bibliogr. of books by, contribs to books and periodicals, materials of critical and biogr. interest, reviews of works by, radio, television and sound recordings.

WAITE, ARTHUR EDWARD, 1857–1942

7725 **Gilbert, Robert A.** A.E. Waite; a bibliography. Wellingborough, Northants., Aquarian pr., [1983]. 192p. port. 21cm.
Descriptive bibliogr. of books and poems; books with contribs. by; privately ptd. rituals and related ephemera, and contribs. to periodicals; with appendix of biogr. or critical studies of,; no locations of copies.
Rev: H. Ormsby-Lennon Yrbk Eng Stud 16:354–6 '86.

WALEY, ARTHUR DAVID, 1889–1966

7726 **Johns, Francis A.** A bibliography of Arthur Waley. 2d ed. London, Athlone pr., [1988]. (First publ. 1968). xiii,160p. facsims. 21cm.
Classified bibliogr. of books, with quasifacsims. TP transcrs. & facsims., collations, bibliogr. notes, etc.; first appearances of translations; articles; original poetry and verse; book revs.; miscellaneous; some appearances in anthologies; and material about.

7727 **Johns, Francis A.** Manifestations of Arthur Waley; some bibliographical and other notes. Brit Libr J 9no2:171–84 '83. port., facsims.

WALKER, CLEMENT, d.1651

7728 **Coleridge, Kathleen A.** The printing and publishing of Clement Walker's History of independency, 1647–1661. Bib Soc Aust & N.Z. Bull 8no1:22–61 '84; A corrigenda note 8no4:203–4 '84.
'Bibliography' (p. 34–61): bibliogr. descrs. with locations of copies and bibliogr. notes and discussion.

7729 **Emmerson, John McL.** A further note on the History of independency, 1647–1661. Bib Soc Aust & N.Z. Bull 8no4:204–7 '84.

WALLACE, ALFRED RUSSEL, 1823–1913

7730 **Fichman, Martin.** 'Selected bibliography [of primary and secondary sources]' *in* Alfred Russel Wallace. (Twayne's English authors, 305). Boston, Twayne, [1981]. p.174–82.

WALLACE, RICHARD HORATIO EDGAR, 1875–1932.

7731 **Kiddle, Charles.** A guide to the first editions of Edgar Wallace. Motcombe, Dorset, Ivory head pr., 1981. 88p. illus., facsims. 21cm. (Ltd. and numbered ed.).

7732 **Kiddle, Charles**. Fifty years on. [Collecting]. Antiqu Bk Mnthly R 9no3:84–7 Mr '82. facsims.

7733 **Lofts, William O.G.** and **D.J. Adley**. Rare Edgar Wallace books. [Collecting]. Bk & Mag Coll 5:56–63 Jl '84. ports., facsims.
'Some Edgar Wallace 1st editions' (p.63).

7734 **Hogan, John A.** Real Life crime stories of Edgar Wallace. Antiqu Bk Mnthly R 12no11:422–5 N '85. illus., facsims.
'Bibliography of Real life crime stories by Edgar Wallace' (p.425).

WALLAS, GRAHAM, 1858–1932

7735 **Moran, Michael G., M.E. Rukstelis** and **D.A. Roberts**. Graham Wallas, 1858–1932: a bibliography. Bull Bib 45no3:194–203 S '88.

WALLER, EDMUND, 1606–87

7736 (7:6374e) **Gilbert, Jack G.** 'Selected bibliography [of primary and secondary sources]' *in* Edmund Waller. (Twayne's English authors, 266). Boston, Twayne, [1979]. p.152–6.

WALPOLE, HORACE, 4TH EARL OF ORFORD, 1717–97

7737 **Orleans house gallery,** RICHMOND-UPON-THAMES. Horace Walpole and Strawberry Hill; 20 September to 7 December 1980, Orleans house gallery. Richmond-upon-Thames, [1980]. 72p. illus., ports., facsims. 21cm.
Stephen Calloway, 'Horace Walpole, writer and printer' (p.18–22).

7738 **Martz, Edwine M.,** *comp.* 'Chronological list of letters' *in* Lewis, Wilmarth S., *ed.* Horace Walpole's correspondence. (The Yale edition of Horace Walpole's correspondence, 43). New Haven, Yale U.P.; Oxford, O.U.P., 1983. p.443–648.

7739 **Sabor, Peter**. Horace Walpole; a reference guide. Boston, Mass., G.K. Hall, [1984]. xxvii,270p. 25cm. (Reference guide to literature).
Rev: J. Black N&Q 231:241–2 '86; J.P.W. Rogers Brit J Eight Cent Stud 11:91 '88.

———————————

7740 (5:14195) **Lewis, Wilmarth S.** Collector's progress, 1951. (Repr. Westport, Conn., Greenwood pr, [1974]).

7741 **Waldegrave, Mary**. 'Lefty' Wilmarth Sheldon Lewis. Bk Coll 29no2:239–50 '80.

7742 **Cauchi, Simon**. Two books from Horace Walpole's library held by the Turnbull. Turnbull Libr Rec 15no1:5–8 My '82. illus., facsim.

7743 **Peltier, Karen V.** Additions and corrections to Hazen's A catalogue of Horace Walpole's library. (Bibliographical note). Pa Bib Soc Am 78no4:473–88 '84.

7744 **Clarke, Stephen P.** Horace Walpole, the Miscellaneous antiquities, and W.S. Lewis. Antiqu Bk Mnthly R 16no2:48–54 F '89. port., illus.
'The Miscellaneous antiquities; a checklist' (p.54).

WALPOLE, SIR HUGH SEYMOUR, 1884–1941

7745 (1:5008bk) **Davis, sir Rupert Hart-**. 'List of books by Hugh Walpole' *in* Hugh Walpole; a biography. London, Macmillan, 1952; New York, Harcourt, Brace & World, [1952]. p.481–3; p.445–7.

WALTON, IZAAK, 1593–1683

7746 **Coigeny, Rodolphe L.** Izaak Walton; a new bibliography, 1653–1987. New York, J. Cummins, 1989. xx,434p. facsims. 26cm.
Bibliogr. catalogue of 460 ed. of The complete angler, *to 1988, with bibliogr. notes*; 'Appendix C: Walton's Lives' (p.[386]–92).
Rev: Jonquil Bevan Bk Coll 39:572–3 '90.

7747 **Bevan, Jonquil.** Some books from Izaak Walton's library. [With list]. Library ser6 2no3:259–63 S '80. facsims.

7748 **Grangvist, Raoul.** Izaak Walton's Lives in the nineteenth and the early twentieth century; a study of a cult object. [Ed. by Thomas Zouch, etc.]. Stud Neophilol 54no2:247–61 '82.
'Appendix [List of Zouch, "major", and "turn of the century editions"]' (p.259–61).

7749 **Bevan, Jonquil,** *ed.* 'IV. The early editions, 1653–1676' *in* The compleat angler, 1653–1676. Oxford, Clarendon pr.; New York, O.U.P., 1983. p.33–51. facsims.
Printing and publication.–Description of editions.

7750 —— Izaak Walton's collections for Fulman's life of John Hales; the Walker part. Bodleian Libr Rec 13no2:160–71 Ap '89.

7751 **Prance, Claude A.** 'A copy of The complete angler' *in* Essays of a book collector; reminiscences on some old books and their authors. West Cornwall, Conn., 1989. p.119–21.

WALTON, WILLIAM, 1902–

7752 **Smith, Carolyn J.** William Walton; a bio-bibliography. New York, Greenwood pr., [1988]. x,246p. 23cm. (Bio-bibliogr. in music, 18).

WARBURTON, BP. WILLIAM, 1698–1779

7753 **Ryley, Robert M.** Warburton's copy of Theobald's Shakespeare. [In Trinity college, Cambr.]. Cambridge Bib Soc Trans 7pt4:449–56 '80.

WARD, MARY AUGUSTA (ARNOLD), MRS. HUMPHRY WARD, 1851–1920

7754 **Thesing, William B.** and **S. Pulsford.** Mrs. Humphry Ward, 1851–1920; a bibliography. [St. Lucia], Dept. of English, University of Queensland, [1987]. iv,71p. port., facsim. 19cm. (Vict Fict Res Guides 13). (Reprod. from typewriting).
Classified checklist of novels, non-fiction books and pamphlets, translations, plays, collections, prefaces, introductions and contributions to periodicals, manuscript material, and ana.

———

7755 **Sutherland, John A.** Macmillans and Robert Elsmere. N&Q 232no1:47–2 Mr '87.

WARNER, REGINALD ('REX') ERNEST, 1905–

7756 **Munton, Alan** and **A. Young,** no.700.

WARREN, JOHN BYRNE LEICESTER, 3D BARON DE TABLEY AND 7TH BARONET, 1835–95

7757 **Uden, B.G. Grant.** Trochees & tetradrachms or bookplates & brambles. Antiqu Bk Mnthly R 14no2:50–7 F '87. port., facsims., illus.
'Check list' (p.57).

WARTON, JOSEPH, 1722–1800

7758 **Vance, John A.** Joseph and Thomas Warton; an annotated bibliography. New York, Garland, 1983. 152p. port. 23cm. (Reference library of the humanities, 359).

7759 —— 'Select bibliography [of primary and secondary sources' *in* Joseph and Thomas Warton. (Twayne's English authors, 380). Boston, Twayne, [1983]. p.136–44.

WARTON, THOMAS, 1728–90 *see under* WARTON, JOSEPH, 1722–1800.

WATSON, THOMAS, 1557?–92

7760 **Williams, Franklin B.** Thomas Watson and Henry VIII. [Woodcut in Amyntas, 1585]. (Bibliographical notes). Library ser6 2n04:445–6 D '80.

WATTS, ALARIC ALEXANDER, 1797–1864

7761 **Hunnisett, Basil**. Alaric Watts and The literary souvenir. Antiqu Bk Mnthly R 13n04:132–5 Ap '86. port., facsims.

WAUGH, EVELYN ARTHUR ST.JOHN, 1903–66

7762 **Edwards, Anthony S.G.** Evelyn Waugh and the New statesman; addenda. (Note 428). Bk Coll 29n02:278 '80.

7763 **Morriss, Margaret**. Evelyn Waugh, a supplementary bibliography, IV. Evelyn Waugh Newsl 14n01:6–8 '80.

7764 **Wölk, Gerhard**. Evelyn Waugh, a supplmentary checklist of criticism. Evelyn Waugh Newsl 14n02:4–5 '80; 15n03: 4–6 '81; 16n03:7–9 '82; 17n02:5–6 '83; 18n02:6–8 '84; 19n03:8–9 '85; 20n02:7–9 '86; 21n02:6–7 '87; 22n02:6–8 '88; 23n02:6–7 '89.

7765 **Davis, Robert M.** A catalogue of the Evelyn Waugh collection at the Humanities research center, the University of Texas at Austin. Troy, N.Y., Whitston, 1981. 369p. 23cm.
Rev: P.A. Doyle Evelyn Waugh Newsl 15:5–6 '81; P. Miles Library ser7 4:460–3 '82; A. Rosenheim N&Q 227:47 '82; C.E. Linck Analytical & Enum Bib 6:47–8 '82; M. Stannard Mod Lang R 80:136–7 '85.

7766 **Lane, Calvin W.** 'Selected bibliography [of primary and secondary sources]' *in* Evelyn Waugh. (Twayne's English authors, 301). Boston, [Mass.], Twayne, [1981]. p.176–85.

7767 **Wise, Brian**. Paperback editions of Waugh published in the U.K. as of December 1980. Evelyn Waugh Newsl 15n02:5 '81; 15n03:4 '81.

7768 **Gallagher, Donat**. New discoveries in Waugh bibliography; primary material. Evelyn Waugh Newsl 16n01:7–9 '82; 16n02:8–9 '82; 17n01:8–9 '83.

7769 **Masin, Anton C.** Catalogue of an exhibit: Evelyn Waugh, 1903–1966, novelist and satirist, May–August 1982. Introd. by Thomas Jemelity. South Bend, Ind., Publ. for University libraries of the University of Notre Dame by And books, [1982]. xiii,38p. port. 22cm. Covertitle.

7770 **McGarva, Duncan**. Evelyn Waugh in Penguins. Penguin Coll Soc Newsl 21:10–11 N '83.

7771 **Wise, Brian [and] Alan M. Cohn.** Additional bibliography.... Evelyn Waugh Newsl 17no3:8 '83.

7772 **Edwards, Anthony S.G.** Evelyn Waugh; unrecorded periodical contributions. (Note 457). Bk Coll 33no3:375 '84.

7773 **Morriss, Margaret** and **D.J. Dooley**. Evelyn Waugh; a reference guide. Boston, Mass., G.K. Hall, [1984]. xx,242p. 23cm. (Reference guide to literature).
       Rev: C.E. Linck Evelyn Waugh Newsl 18:5–6 '84; R.M. Davis Pa Lang & Lit 22:218–20 '86.

7774 **Wise, Brian**. Additional Waugh bibliography, part 1. Evelyn Waugh Newsl 22no1:5 '88; 22no2:8 '88; 23no1:8 '89.

7775 **Davis, Robert M.** 'Brideshead in type [Revision]' *in* Evelyn Waugh, writer. Norman, Okla., Pilgrim books, [1981]. p.167–85.
       Rev: R.L. Montgomery TLS 9 Jl '82:746.

7776 **Montgomery, Robert L.** The case of Black mischief; Evelyn Waugh vs. The tablet. Libr Chron Univ Texas new ser 16:42–61 '81. ports., facsim.

7777 **Sims, George F.** Evelyn Waugh's early writings. [The world to come, 1916]. (To the editor). TLS 27 Ag '82:924.

7778 —— Evelyn Waugh's first book. [The world to come, 1916]. (Letters). Antiqu Bk Mnthly R 9no10:391 Oc '82.

7779 **Davis, Robert M.** Towards a maturer style; the manuscript of Waugh's Remote people. [Revision]. Analytical & Enum Bib 7no1/2:3–15 '83.

7780 —— Waugh memorabilia in Austin. Evelyn Waugh Newsl 17no1:3–5 '83.

7781 **Gallagher, Donat**. New discoveries in Waugh bibliography, 2 & 3. Evelyn Waugh Newsl 16no2:8–9 '83; 17no1:8–9 '83.

7782 **Wright, Stuart**. A note on Evelyn Waugh's Basil Seal rides again. [Unsigned 'signed' copy]. Evelyn Waugh Newsl 17no2:6–7 '83.

7783 **Gallagher, Donat**. Limited editions and 'misprints' unlimited; Evelyn Waugh's The defence of the holy places. Analytical & Enum Bib 8no1:18–31 '84. facsim.

7784 **Thomas, Lewis E.** Evelyn Waugh. [Collecting]. Bk & Mag Coll 7:4–10 S '84. port., facsims.
       'Complete Waugh bibliography' (p.10).

7785 **Gallagher, Donat**. Bibliographical and diary notes. Evelyn Waugh Newsl 19no2:8 '85.

7786 **Davis, Robert M.** Grace beyond the reach of sullen art; Waugh edits Merton. J Mod Lit 13no1:163–6 Mr '86.

7787 **Doyle, Paul A.** Large print editions of Waugh's books. Evelyn Waugh Newsl 21no2:8 '87.

WEBB, GLADYS MARY (MEREDITH), 1881–1927

7788 **Dickins, Gordon**. Mary Webb; a narrative bibliography of her life and works. [Shrewsbury], Shropshire libraries, 1981. 33p. illus. 20cm.

WEBSTER, JOHN, 1580?–1625?

7789 **Moore, Don D.** Recent studies in Webster, 1972–1980. (Recent studies in the English renaissance). Eng Lit Renaiss 12no3:369–75 '82.

7790 **Schuman, Samuel**. 'John Webster on stage; a selected annotated bibliography' *in* Hogg, James, *ed.* Jacobean miscellany 4. Salzburg, Institut für Anglistik und Amerikanistik, Universität Salzburg, 1984. p.99–128.

7791 ——John Webster; a reference guide. Boston, Mass., G.K. Hall, [1985]. xxi,280p. 23cm. (Reference guide to literature).

—————

7792 **Jackson, MacDonald P.** John Webster and Thomas Heywood in Appius and Virginia; a bibliographical approach to the problem. Stud Bib 38:217–35 '85. table.
Introduction.–The quarto of 1654; printer and compositors.–The manuscript copy of Q.–Linguistic discriminators between Webster and Heywood.–Linguistic evidence in Appius and Virginia, 1654.–Conclusion.

7793 **Hammond, Antony**. The White devil in Nicholas Okes's shop. Stud Bib 39:135–76 '86. tables.
Preamble.–1. The type-line.–2. The compositors.–3. Type-study.–Conclusion.–Appendix: Recurrent types.

7794 **Proudfoot, G. Richard.** A Jacobean dramatic fragment. [Foul papers of The duke of Florence]. TLS 13 Je '86:651.

7795 **Shapiro, Isaac A.** The Melbourne manuscript. [The Duke of Florence]. (Letters). TLS 4 Jl '86:735–6; F. Pryor 18 Jl '86:787; I.A. Shapiro 8 Ag '86:865; G.R. Proudfoot 22 Ag '86:913–14; F. Pryor 29 Ag '86:939.

7796 **Pryor, Felix**. John Webster: the Melbourne manuscript. [Duke of Florence]. Dict Lit Biogr Yrbk 1986:138–9 '87. facsims.

7797 **Hammond, Antony** and **Doreen Delvecchio.** The Melbourne manuscript and John Webster; a reproduction and transcript. [The Duke of Florence]. Stud Bib 41:1–32 '88. table, facsims.
The manuscript.–Authorship.–Palaeography.–Vocabulary and spelling.–Linguistic tests.–Subject-matter and style.–Conclusion.–Appendix: The Melbourne manuscript; a diplomatic transcript.

WELLS, HERBERT GEORGE, 1866–1946

7798 **Costa, Richard H.** 'Selected bibliography [of primary and secondary sources]' *in* H.G. Wells. Rev. ed. (Twayne's English authors, 43). Boston, Twayne, [1985]. (First publ. 1967). p.162–70.

7799 **Cain, Melissa**, *comp.* 'H.G. Wells; a selected bibliography' *in* Mullin, Michael, *ed.* H.G. Wells; reality and beyond a collection of critical essays.... Champaign, Ill., Champaign public library and information center, 1986. p.79–90.

7800 **Scheick, William J.** and **J.R. Cox**. H.G. Wells; a reference guide. Boston, Mass., G.K. Hall, [1988]. xxxiii,430p. 25cm. (Reference guide to literature).

7801 **Parrinder, Patrick**. Accueil de Wells en France: Bibliographie. Cahiers Vict & Edouardiens 30:151–7 Oc '89.

7802 —— A list of contemporary reviews on Wells. Wellsian new ser 12:36–43 '89.

———

7803 **Macleod, Helen**. H.G. Wells; his life & works. [Collecting]. Bk & Mag Coll 19:4–16 S '85; 20:28–36 Oc '85. ports., facsims.
'Complete bibliography of H.G. Wells first editions' (p.15–16; 35–6).

7804 **Whiteman, Bruce**. Canadian issues of Anglo-American fiction; the example of H.G. Wells. Pa Bib Soc Am 80no1:75–81 '86.

7805 **Eaton, Peter**. Wellsiana. (Trade tales). Antiqu Bk Mnthly R 15no8:312–14 Ag '88.

7806 **Lake, David**. The current texts of Wells's early SF novels; situation unsatisfactory. Wellsian new ser 11:3–12 '88; 12:21–36 '89.

7807 **Hughes, David Y.** The revisions of The war of the worlds. Cahiers Vict & Edouardiens 30:141–9 Oc '89.

7808 **Philmus, Robert M.** Revisions of Moreau. Cahiers Vict & Edouardiens 30:117–40 Oc '89.

WESKER, ARNOLD, 1932–

7809 **Leeming, Glenda.** 'A select bibliography [of primary and secondary sources]' *in* Wesker on file. London, Methuen, [1985]. p.62–7.

WESLEY, CHARLES, 1707–88 *see under* WESLEY, JOHN, 1703–91.

WESLEY, JOHN, 1703–91

7810 (1:5068b) **Swift, Wesley F.** Portraits and biographies of Charles Wesley. Wesley Hist Soc Proc 31pt4:86–92 D '57. port.

7811 (1:5068c) —— The works of John Wesley. Wesley Hist Soc Proc 31pt8:173–7 D '58. facsims.

7812 **Rogal, Samuel J.** 'Selected bibliography [of primary and secondary works]' *in* John and Charles Wesley. (Twayne's English authors, 368). Boston, Twayne, [1983]. p.162–72.

7813 **Jarboe, Betty M.** John and Charles Wesley; a bibliography. Metuchen, N.J., American theological library association and the Scarecrow pr., 1987. xv,404p. 21cm. (ATLA Bib ser, 22).

7814 **Baker, Frank.** John Wesley's publishing apprenticeship. John Rylands Univ Libr Manchester Bull 70no1:71–80 '88.

WEST, DAME REBECCA, *pseud. of* **CICILY ISABEL (FAIRFIELD) ANDREWS, 1892–1983**

7815 **Deakin, Motley F.** 'Selected bibliography [of primary and secondary sources]' *in* Rebecca West. (Twayne's English authors, 296). Boston, Twayne, 1980. p.178–80.

7816 —— Rebecca West; a supplement to Hutchinson's preliminary list. Bull Bib 39no2:52–8 Je '82.

7817 **Sissons, Michael.** This real night. [The fountain overflows and Macmillans]. (Letters). TLS 23 N '84:1343; L. Dickson 14 D '84:??1984.

WEST, JOHN ALEXANDER ('ALICK'), 1895–1972

7818 **Munton, Alan** and **A. Young**, no.700.

WEST, VICTORIA MARY SACKVILLE-, LADY NICOLSON, 1892–1962

7819 **Gretton, John R.** 'Collecting V. Sackville-West' *in* Essays in book-collecting. [Dereham, Norf.], 1985. p.48–57. port. after p.40.
'Appendix 1: A checklist of the English first editions of V. Sackville-West' (p.54–6): *55 items, 1909–74*; '2. The American first editions…' (p.56): *33 items, 1919–61; and ana.*

7820 —— V. Sackville-West? [A democrat's chapbook, 1942]. (Letters). Antiqu Bk Mnthly R 8no12:474–5 D '81.

7821 **Pomeroy, Elizabeth W.** Within living memory; Vita Sackville-West's poems of land and garden. [Revision of The Land and The garden]. Twent Cent Lit 28no3:269–89 '82.

WHATELY, ARCHBP. RICHARD, 1787–1863

7822 **Akenson, Donald H.** 'Bibliographic comments [i.e. checklist, 1810–77]' *in* Protestant in purgatory; Richard Whately, archbishop of Dublin. (Conference Brit Stud Biogr new ser 2). Hamden, Conn., Archon books, 1981. p.253–69.

WHEATLEY, DENNIS YATES, 1897–1977

7823 **Butler, W.E.** Dennis Yates Wheatley. (Portrait of a bookplate, 8). Bkplate J 4no2:92–4 S '86. facsim.

WHETSTONE, GEORGE, 1544?–87?

7824 **Brown, Barbara.** A note on Thomas Churchyard's bibliography. [G. Whetstone's Censure of a loyal subject ed. by T. Cadman, not Churchyard]. N&Q 225no2:137–8 Ap '80.

WHISTLER, JAMES ABBOTT McNEILL, 1905–44

7825 **Getscher, Robert H.** and **P.G. Marks.** James McNeill Whistler and John Singer Sargent; two annotated bibliographies. New York, Garland, 1986. 520p. 21cm. (Reference library of the humanities, 467).
Classified annotated checklists of works and ana.

7826 **Weintraub, Stanley**. 'Collecting the quarrels; Whistler and The gentle art of making enemies' *in* Brack, O M, *ed.* Twilight of dawn; studies in English literature in transition. Tucson, Publ. for the Arizona state university centennial by the University of Arizona pr., [1987]. p.34–44. facsim.

WHITE, HENRY KIRKE, 1785–1806

7827 **Nottingham. University. Library. Manuscripts department.** The papers of Henry Kirke White, 1785–1806. [Nottingham], 1981. 31p. 30cm. (Duplicated typescript).

WHITE, TERENCE HANBURY, 1906–64

7828 **Gallix, François.** T.H. White; an annotated bibliography. New York, Garland, 1986. xlix,148p. port., facsims. 21cm. (Reference library of the humanities, 655).
Classified annotated checklist of works and ana.

WHITE, THOMAS, 1593–1676

7829 **Southgate, B.C.** Thomas White's Grounds of obedience and government; a note on the dating of the first edition. [1655]. N&Q 226no3:208–9 Je '81.

WHITEHEAD, WILLIAM, 1715–85

7830 **Forster, Harold**. William Whitehead. (Some uncollected authors, 53). Bk Coll 29no4:521–41 '80. facsims.
'Check-list: First editions of William Whitehead' (p.529–41): *TP transcrs., format and some bibliogr. notes for copies in compiler's colln., BL or Bodley.*

WILDE, OSCAR O'FLAHERTIE WILLS, 1856–1900

7831 **Hyde, H. Montgomery.** The riddle of De profundis; who owns the manuscript? Antigonish R 54:106–27 '83. port.

7832 **Schroeder, Horst**. Oscar Wilde: The portrait of mr. W.H.; its composition, publication and reception. Braunschweig, Technische Universität Carolo-Wilhelmina, Seminar für Anglistik und Amerikanistik, 1984. 62p. 19cm.
Introduction.–1. The date of composition of the magazine edition.–2. The publication of....–3. The reception of....–4. The date of composition of the book edition.–5. The publishing agreement with the Bodley head.–6. The history of the 'lost' manuscript.–7. The publication and reception of the book editions.

7833 **Thomas, David A.** Oscar Wilde. [Collecting]. Bk & Mag Coll 8:34–40 Oc '84. port., facsims.
'Complete bibliography of Oscar Wilde first editions' (p.40).

7834 **Lich, Glen E.** 'Anything but a misprint'; comments on an Oscar Wilde typescript. [Revision of An ideal husband]. Sth Central R 3no2:46–54 '86.

7835 **Glavin, John**. Deadly Earnest and Earnest revived; Wilde's four-act play. Ninet Cent Stud 1:13–24 '87.

7836 **Jackson, Russell** and **I. Small**. Some new drafts of a Wilde play. [Typescript of A woman of no importance in Univ. of Bristol theatre colln.]. Eng Lit Transit 30no1:6–15 '87. port.

7837 **Bessler, Gabriele**. Heinrich Vogeler als Illustrator der Märchen von Oscar Wilde. (Buchillustration). Aus dem Antiquariat 4:A165–71 '88. facsims.

7838 **Lawler, Donald**. An inquiry into Oscar Wilde's revisions of The picture of Dorian Gray. New York, Garland, [1988]. 155p. 24cm. (Publs Am & Eng Lit). (Not seen).

7839 **Setz, Wolfram**. Zur Textgestalt des Teleny. [Censorship of Teleny or the reverse of the medal, 1893]. Forum Homosexualität & Lit 5:69–76 '88. facsim.

WILKINS, BP. JOHN, 1614–72

7840 **Schnitker, Brigitte Asbach-**, *ed.* 'The works of John Wilkins' *in* Mercury, or the secret and swift messenger...together with An abstract of dr. Wilkins's Essay.... (Foundations of semiotics). Amsterdam, Benjamins, 1984. p.lxxxi–cix.
Adapted from H.M. Lord (1957): BBLB2 5110.

WILLIAMS, CHARLES, *pseud. of* CHARLES WALTER STANSBY, 1886–1945

7841 **Sibley, Agnes**. 'Selected bibliography [of primary and secondary sources]' *in* Charles Williams. (Twayne's English authors, 322). Boston, Twayne, [1982]. p.155–8.

WILLIAMS, DAVID, 1738–1816

7842 **France, Peter**, *ed.* 'The writings of David Williams' *in* Williams, David. Incidents in my own life.... [Brighton] Sussex, University of Sussex library, 1980. p.89–128.
Checklist, extensively annotated.

WILLIAMS, Ella Gwendolen Rees, 1894–1979 *see* RHYS, JEAN,
pseud.

WILLIAMS, RALPH VAUGHAN, 1872–1958

7843 **Kennedy, Michael.** A catalogue of the works of Ralph Vaughan Williams.
Rev. ed. London, O.U.P., 1982. (First publ. 1964). 329p. music. 22cm.
'Bibliography of the literary writings of Ralph Vaughan Williams' *by* Peter Starbuck
(p.296–310).

WILLIAMS, WILLIAM ('PANTYCELYN'), 1717–91

7844 **Hughes, Glynn T.** 'Select bibliography' *in* Williams Pantycelyn.
(Writers of Wales). Cardiff, University of Wales pr. on behalf of the
Welsh arts council, 1983. p.131–6.

WILLIAMSON, HENRY, 1895–1977

7845 **Gretton, John R.** 'Collecting Henry Williamson' *in* Essays in book-
collecting. [Dereham, Norf.], 1985. p.58–64.
'Appendix I: A checklist of the English first and subsequent editions of Henry Williamson' (p.62–4): *57 items, 1921–83*; 'Books edited or with substantial contributions
by...' (p.64): *14 items, 1929–66; and ana.*

───────────────

7846 **Gretton, John R.** Collecting Henry Williamson. Antiqu Bk Mnthly R
8no3:84–9 Mr '81. ports., illus., facsims.
'Henry Williamson checklist' (p.89).

WILMOT, JOHN, 2D EARL OF ROCHESTER, 1647–80

7847 **Vieth, David M.** Rochester studies, 1925–1982; an annotated bibliography. New York, Garland, 1984. xix,174p. 21cm. (Reference library of the humanities, 457).

7848 **Wasserman, George,** 1986. *no.*4948.

───────────────

7849 **Patterson, John D.** Another text of Rochester's 'To the post boy.'
Restor 4no1:14–16 '80.

7850 **Brooks, David.** A conjectural emendation for Rochester's The mistress. Bib Soc Aust & N.Z. Bull 5no2:75–8 '81.

7851 **Fisher, Nicholas** and **K. Robinson.** The postulated mixed '1680' edition of Rochester's poetry. (Bibliographical notes). Pa Bib Soc Am
75no3:313–15 '81. diagr.

7852 **Robinson, Ken**. A new text of the first song in Rochester's Valentinian. (Bibliographical notes). Pa Bib Soc Am 75no3:311–12 '81.

7853 **Love, Harold H.R.** The text of Rochester's 'Upon nothing'. [Clayton, Vic.], Centre for bibliographical and textual studies, Monash university, [1985]. 46p. facsims., tables. 23cm. (Occas Pa, 1).

7854 **Johnson, J.W.** Did lord Rochester write Sodom? [Yes]. Pa Bib Soc Am 81no2:119–53 '87.
1. The early history of Sodom.–2. The manuscripts.–3. Evidence by Rochester's contemporaries.–4. Internal evidence.

7855 **Carver, Larry**. Rochester's Valentinian. [Revision]. Restor & 18th Cent Theat Res 4no1:25–38 '89.

WILSON, ANDREW ('SNOO'), 1948–

7856 **Trussler, Simon, M. Page** and **Elaine Turner.** Snoo Wilson. (NTQ checklist, no.4). New Theat Q 5no17:86–96,104 F '89.

WILSON, SIR ANGUS FRANK JOHNSTONE, 1913–

7857 **Stape, John H.** Angus Wilson; a supplementary bibliography, 1976–1981. Twent Cent Lit 29no2:249–66 '83.

7858 **Stape, John H.** and **Anne N. Thomas.** Angus Wilson; a bibliography, 1947–1987. London, Mansell, [1988]. xvi,327p. port. 21cm.
Classified checklist of works by and about.
Rev: L. Wood Library ser6 11:174–5 '89; B.C. Bloomfield Bk Coll 38: 416–17 '89; S. Monod Étud Angl 43:236 '90.

WILSON, COLIN, 1931–

7859 **Drost, Jerome**. Colin Wilson; checklist of American editions, articles and selected reference material, 1956–1982. Bull Bib 44no1:3–9 Mr '87.

WILSON, THOMAS, 1525?–81

7860 **Medine, Peter E.** 'Selected bibliography [of primary and secondary sources]' *in* Thomas Wilson. (Twayne's English authors, 431). Boston, Twayne, [1986]. p.190–3.

WINCHILSEA, ANN FINCH, COUNTESS OF, 1661–1720 *see*
FINCH, ANN, COUNTESS OF WINCHILSEA, 1661–1720.

WINKWORTH, CATHERINE, 1827–78

7861 **Miller, David C.** John Leighton, binding designer and the Lyra Germanica. [1855]. Bib Soc Aust & N.Z. Bull 7no1:15–26 '83. facsims.

7862 **Carnie, Robert H.** John Leighton and the Lyra Germanica again. [Bibliogr. descr.]. Bib Soc Aust & N.Z. Bull 8no4:181–90 '84. illus., facsims.

WISE, THOMAS JAMES, 1859–1937

7863 **Barker, Nicolas J.** and **J. Collins**. 'List of forgeries and suspect works sold at auction, 1888–1920' *in* A sequel to An enquiry into the nature of certain nineteenth century pamphlets by John Carter and Graham Pollard; the forgeries of H. Buxton Forman & T.J. Wise re-examined. London, [1983]. p.[303]–33.
See also 'List of works' (p.[368]–75).

7864 **California. University at Los Angeles. William Andrews Clark memorial library.** Shady practices & warm regards; an exhibit of Wise forgeries for the international association of bibliophiles, 1 October–16 December, 1985. Los Angeles, 1985. 12p. 27cm. Covertitle. (Reprod. from typewriting).
'A checklist of the foregeries of T.J. Wise and H. Buxton Forman in the William Andrews Clark library' (p.11–12).

7865 **Myers, Robin**. Top edge gilt: John Carter and Graham Pollard: An enquiry into the nature of certain nineteenth century pamphlets, 1934. (Key works in bibliography, no.10). Antiqu Bk Mnthly R 8no1:4–9 Ja '81; 8no2:52–7 F '81. facsims., ports.
'A selection of bibliographies by Thomas J. Wise, 1854–1937' (p.9); 'Select bibliography' (p.57).

7866 **[Barker, Nicolas J.]**. The new Enquiry; a preview. Bk Coll 31no4:463–80 '82. illus., facsim.
Introduction and ch. 11, 12, 13 of A sequel to An enquiry (no.7869).

7867 **Freeman, Arthur**. The workshop of T.J. Wise. [His colln. of loose leaves of plays]. TLS 17 S '82:990; sir A.M. Fraser 19 N '82:1273.

7868 **Barker, Nicolas J.** 'La contrefaçon littéraire au XIXe siècle et la bibliographie matérielle' *in* Laufer, Roger, *ed*. La bibliographie matérielle. Paris, 1983. p.43–52.

7869 **Barker, Nicolas J.** and **J. Collins**. A sequel to An enquiry into the nature of certain nineteenth century pamphlets by John Carter and Graham Pollard; the forgeries of H. Buxton Forman & T.J. Wise re-examined. London, Scolar pr., [1983]. (Repr. New Castle, Del., Oak Knoll books, 1992). 394p. ports., facsims. 21cm.

Also issued in deluxe ed. ltd. to 80 copies, with repr. of J. Carter and G. Pollard's An enquiry, 1983, [*see*BBTC 14387], *R. and E.B. Browning's*Two poems, 1852, *and anr. essay by N.J. Barker.* Part I: Lives of the forgers. 1. Harry Buxton Forman. 2. Thomas James Wise.–II. The typographical enquiry. 3. The typographical argument. 4. The scope for further typographical analysis. 5. A critique of the typographical argument. 6. The typefounders. 7. The printers. 8. Typography and layout as evidence of forgery and of the forgers' practice. 9. Summary.–III. The course of the crime. 10. Introduction. 11. Sowing the seed. 12. The harvest grows. 13. Reaping the whirlwind. 14. The process of partnership.– Epilogue: Maurice Buxton Forman.–Dossiers.–Appendices: 1. Paper evidence. 2. Note on line blocks. 3. Omitted pamphlets. 4. The correspondence of Forman and Wise. 5. List of forgeries and suspect works sold at auction, 1888–1920. 6. List of types. 7. List of works.–Stop-press [on Wise's thefts from copies of pre–1700 plays].
Rev. T.A.J. Burnett TLS 16 Mr '84:286; A. Freeman Library ser6 6:415–18 '84; D.J. McKitterick Bk Coll 33:105–8 '84; C. Ricks N.Y. R Bks 32:34–6 '85; Janet Ing Fine Print 11:44–5 '85; W.E. Fredeman Review 7:259–96 '85; J.H.P. Pafford N&Q 235:123–4 '90.

7870 **Carter, John W.** and **H.G. Pollard**. An enquiry into the nature of certain nineteenth century pamphlets. [2d ed.] London, Scolar pr., [1983]. (First publ. 1934). xii,444p. 21cm.
Included in deluxe ed. ltd. to 80 copies, of N.J. Barker and J. Collins's A sequel to An enquiry…, *with R. and E.B. Browning's* Two poems, 1852, *and anr. essay by N.J. Barker.*
Rev. T.A.J. Burnett TLS 16 Mr '84:286; A. Freeman Library ser6 6:415–18 '84; D.J. McKitterick Bk Coll 33: 105–8 '84; C. Ricks N.Y. R Bks 32:34–6 '85; Janet Ing Fine Print 11:44–5 '85; W.E. Fredeman Review 7:259–96 '85.

7871 **Watson, John H.,** *pseud. of* L. Toppman and S. Garland. The affair of the unprincipled publisher, by John H. Watson, M.D. as discovered by Lawrence Garland. New Castle, Del., Oak knoll books, 1983. 21p. 24cm. (Ltd. to 325 copies).

7872 **Gallup, Donald C.** The Carter and Pollard Enquiry fifty years after. (Review essay). Pa Bib Soc Am 78no4:447–60 '84.

7873 **Fredeman, William E.** The story of a lie; a sequel to A sequel. [Rev. art. on Carter and Pollard: 7870, and Barker and Collins: 7869]. Review 7:259–96 '85. table.
'Master list of indicted works [belonging to the Wise–Forman canon' (p.280–7).

7874 **Lewis, Roger C.** Thomas J. Wise and the trial books of Rossetti's Poems, 1870. J Pre-Raphaelite & Aesthet Stud 2no1:73–87 '89.
'Appendix: the proof states of Rossetti's Poems (1870) [Listed]' (p.85–7).

WITHER, GEORGE, 1588–1667

7875 **Creigh, Jocelyn C.** George Wither and the Stationers; facts and fiction. (Bibliographical notes). Pa Bib Soc Am 74no1:49–57 '80; A. Pritchard; Jocelyn C. Creigh (Correspondence 76no4: 478–9 '82.

WITTGENSTEIN, LUDWIG JOSEF JOHANN, 1889–1951

7876 **Lapointe, François H.** Ludwig Wittgenstein; a comprehensive bibliography. Westport, Conn., Greenwood pr., 1980. ix,297p. 25cm. (Reprod. from typewriting).

WODEHOUSE, SIR PELHAM GRENVILLE, 1881–1975

7877 (7:6518g) **Usborne, Richard**. 'Books, plays, films' *in* Wodehouse at work to the end. [Rev. ed.] [London], Barrie & Jenkins, [1976]. (Anr. ed. Harmondsworth, Penguin books, 1978). p.[237]–42.

7878 **McIlvaine, Eileen**, *comp*. 'A bibliography of P.G. Wodehouse' *in* Pierpont Morgan library, New York. P.G. Wodehouse; a centenary celebration. Ed. by James R. Heinemann and Donald R. Bensen. New York, Pierpont Morgan library; London, O.U.P., [1981]. p.[89]–197.
> *Classified bibliogr. of novels and semi-autobiogr. works, omnibus ed., publ. plays, Tauchnitz ed., autograph ed., anthologies with Wodehouse contribs., introds. and prefaces, translations of, the dramatic Wodehouse: stage and screen, and works about; with quasifacsim. TP transcrs., collations and bibliogr. notes; not indexed.*

7879 **Jasen, David A.** A bibliography and reader's guide to the first editions of P.G. Wodehouse. 2d ed. [London], Greenhill books, [1986]. (First publ. 1970). 306p. 22cm.

7880 **Pierpont Morgan library,** NEW YORK. P.G. Wodehouse; a centenary celebration. Ed. by James H. Heinemann and Donald R. Bensen. New York, Pierpont Morgan library; London, O.U.P., [1981]. xxi,197p. illus., ports., facsims. 30cm.
> *Includes* How I write my books, P.G. Wodehouse.–Wodehouse's editor: A painless job, Peter Schwed.–Uncollected PGW, David A. Jasen.–On collecting P.G. Wodehouse, Charles E. Gould.–Wodehouse's American illustrators, Walt Reed.–Wodehouse's English illustrators, Bevis Hillier.–Bibliography, Eileen McIlvaine.
> *Rev.* R. Davies Bk World 29 N '81:1–2; C. McGrath N.Y. Times Bk R 27 D '81:4,11; R. Usborne TLS 13 N '81:1328.

7881 **Phelps, Barry**. 'To the critics, these pearls'; P.G. Wodehouse dedications. Antiqu Bk Mnthly R 10no4:120–3 Ap '83. illus., facsims.

7882 **Thomas, Lewis E.** P.G. Wodehouse. [Collecting]. Bk & Mag Coll 6:4–12 Ag '84. port., facsims.
> 'Bibliography of P.G. Wodehouse 1st editions' (p.11–12).

WOOD, ELLEN (PRICE), MRS. HENRY WOOD, 1814–87

7883 **Wanford, Arthur.** Mrs. Henry Wood and the Argosy. Antiqu Bk Mnthly R 16no5:182–3 My '89. port.
> 'Argosy serials, 1866–1892: Mrs. Henry Wood; other authors' (p.183).

WOOLF, ADELINE VIRGINIA (STEPHEN), 1882–1941 *see also*
BOOK PRODUCTION AND DISTRIBUTION—Printers, etc.–Hogarth press, est.1917.

7884 **Kirkpatrick, Brownlee J.** A bibliography of Virginia Woolf. 3d ed. Oxford, Clarendon pr., 1980. (First publ. 1957). xiii,268p. facsims. 21cm. (Soho Bibs, 9).

The standard bibliogr. of books and pamphlets, contribs. to books and books trans. by, contribs. to periodicals, trans. of, foreign ed., parody, works announced but not publ., large print ed. for the blind, communications and the press, books and arts containing single letters or extracts from letters, and mss.
Rev: TLS 24 Ap '81:471; J.H. Stape Bull Bib 41:103–4 '84.

7885 **Rice, Thomas J.** Virginia Woolf; a guide to research. New York, Garland, 1984. xix,258p. 22cm. (Reference library of the humanities, 432).

7886 **Gottlieb, Laura M.** Woolf scholarship in 1983 and 1984. Virginia Woolf Misc Suppl 23:1–10 '85.

7887 **Steele, Elizabeth**. Virginia Woolf's rediscovered essays; sources and allusions. New York, Garland, 1987. xv,238p. 21cm. (Reference library of the humanities, 686).

7888 **DeSalvo, Louise A.** Virginia Woolf's first voyage; a novel in the making. [London], Macmillan, [1980]. xiii,202p. 22cm.
1. Introduction.–2. The beginnings: Melymbrosia, 1908–1909.–3. From Melymbrosia to The voyage out, 1909–1913.–4. The Voyage out, 1911–1915.–5. Revisions for the first American and second English editions, 1919–1920.–6. The death of Rachel.–7. Fiction of masquerade.–Appendix: Location of the drafts.

7889 —— The Granada edition of The voyage out; a corrupt text. [1978]. Virginia Woolf Misc 19:3–4 '82.

7890 **Haule, James M.** 'Le temps passe' and the original typescript; an early version of the Time passes section of To the lighthouse. [Revision]. Twent Cent Lit 29no3:267–311 '83.

7891 **Pellan, Françoise**. Virginia Woolf's posthumous poem. [From Orlando, ed. by V. Sackville-West]. Mod Fict Stud 29no4:695–700 '83.

7892 **Blissinger, Mildred**. From a printer's point of view. [Woolf libr. at Washington S.U.]. Virginia Woolf Misc 22:8 '84.

7893 **Elwood, John**. Early history of the Woolf library. [Washington S.U.]. Virginia Woolf Misc 22:3 '84.

7894 **Hyman, Virginia R.** Hours in their library. Virginia Woolf Misc 22:3 '84. facsim.

7895 **Luedeking, Leila**. Contents of the Woolf library. Virginia Woolf Misc 22:2 '84.

7896 **Steele, Elizabeth**. The value of the Virginia Woolf collection. [Washington S.U.]. Virginia Woolf Misc 22:5 '84.

7897 **Bateman, Judith**. Virginia Woolf. [And Hogarth pr.]. Bk & Mag Coll
20:4–10 Oc '85; 21:36–42 N '85. port., facsim.
'Complete Virginia Woolf bibliography' (p.10, 42).

7898 **Wright, Glenn P.** The Raverat proofs of Mrs. Dalloway. [At UCLA].
Stud Bib 39:241–61 '86. table.
Appendix I: Raverat proofs of Mrs. Dalloway: list of alterations.–II. Transcript of
typescript inserted in Raveret proofs (225.1–17).

7899 **Bell, Anne O.** Editing Virginia Woolf's diary. [Oxford], Perpetua pr.,
1989. 25p. 25cm. (Ltd. to 200 no. and signed copies).

WOOLF, LEONARD SIDNEY, 1880–1969 *see also* BOOK PRODUCTION
AND DISTRIBUTION—Printers, etc.–Hogarth press, est.1917.

7900 **Meyerowitz, Selma S.** 'Selected bibliography [of primary and secondary sources]' *in* Leonard Woolf. (Twayne's English authors, 352).
Boston, Twayne, [1982]. p.221–8.

7901 **Gooneratne, Yasmine**. A novelist at work; the manuscript of Leonard
Woolf's The village in the jungle. J Commonwealth Lit 18no1:91–
104 '83.

WORDSWORTH, DOROTHY, 1771–1855

7902 **Taylor, Elisabeth R.** Dorothy Wordsworth; primary and secondary
sources. Bull Bib 40no4:252–5 D '83.

7903 **Woof, Pamela**. Dorothy Wordsworth's Grasmere journals; readings
in a familiar text. [Deletions]. Wordsworth & Circ 20no1:37–42 '89.

WORDSWORTH, WILLIAM, 1770–1850

7904 **Brown, David M.** Wordsworth scholarship, an annual register. Wordsworth Circ 11no4:218–21 '80.

7905 **Bennet, James R.** The comparative criticism of Blake and Wordsworth;
a bibliography. Wordsworth Circ 14no2:99–106 '83.

7906 **Isnard, Marcel**. Wordsworth and Coleridge; Lyrical Ballads, 1798;
bibliographie sélective et critique. Soc d'Étud Anglo-Am Bull 17:65–
105 N '83.

7907 **Jones, Mark** and **K. Kroeber**. Wordsworth scholarship and criticism, 1973–1984; an annotated bibliography, with selected criticism, 1809–1972. New York, Garland, 1985. xvi,316p. 21cm. (Reference library of the humanities, 536).

7908 **Jordan, Frank**, *ed.*, 1985: no.4375.

7909 **Jones, Mark**. Wordsworth scholarship and criticism; 1984–85 update. Wordsworth Circ 18no4:190–208 '87; ...1986 update. 19no4:220–30 '88.

7910 **Curtis, Jared R.** The Wellesley copy of Wordsworth's Poetical works, 1832. [Containing revisions]. Harvard Libr Bull 27no1:5–15 Ja '80.

7911 **Maccagno, D.** William Wordsworth. [Did he operate a press in Kendal?]. (Readers' queries). N&Q 22no6:536 D '80.

7912 **Roe, Micholas**. Leigh Hunt and Wordsworth's Poems, 1815. [Presentation copy]. Wordsworth Circ 12no1:89–91 '81.

7913 **Ross, Donald J.** Poems 'bound each to each' in the 1815 edition of Wordsworth. Wordsworth Circ 12no2:133–40 '81. table.

7914 **Butler, James A.** Wordsworth's Descriptive sketches; the Huntington and Cornell copies. [Presented to Coleridge]. (Notes and documents). Huntington Libr Q 46no2:175–80 '83. facsims.

7915 **Gill, Stephen C.** Wordsworth's poems; the question of text. R Eng Stud new ser 34no134:172–90 My '83.

7916 **Parrish, Stephen M.** The editor as archæologist. [Editing Wordsworth]. Kentucky R 4no3:3–14 '83.

7917 **Clubbe, John**. The W. Hugh Peal collection at the University of Kentucky. Wordsworth Circ 15no2:73–4 '84.

7918 **Gleckner, Robert F.** Coleridge and Wordsworth together in America. [1st publ. in Christian disciple]. Wordsworth & Circ 15no1:17–19 '84.

7919 **Priestman, Donald G.** Lyrical ballads and variant Ashley 2250. [Ptg.]. Eng Lang N 21no4:41–8 Je '84.

7920 **Grady, Kelley** and **Martha Michael.** A new manuscript of Wordsworth's 'To M.H.'. [Text]. Wordsworth & Circ 16no1:38–40 '85. diagr.

7921 **Moss, Carolyn J.** Wordsworth's marginalia in John Davis's Travels...in the United States.... [In BL]. (Bibliographical notes). Pa Bib Soc Am 79no4:539–41 '85.

7922   **Jump, Harriet**. 'That other eye'; Wordsworth's 1794 revisions of An evening walk. Wordsworth & Circ 17no3:156–73 '86.

7923   **Walker, Eric C.** Wordsworth's 'Third volume' and the collected editions, 1815–20. Pa Bib Soc Am 80no4:437–53 '86.

7924   **Little, Geoffrey.** John Woolley and the Cranbrook Wordworth. [Presentation copy of Poetical works now at Cranbrook school, Sydney]. Sydney Stud Eng 12:117–18 '86/7.

7925   **Brinkley, Robert**. Writing Mont Blanc. [Revision]. Wordsworth & Circ 18no3:108–14 '87.

7926   **Hayden, John O.** William Wordsworth's letter to John Wilson, 1802; a corrected version. Wordsworth & Circ 18no1:33–8 '87.

7927   **Reed, Mark L.** Wordsworth on Wordsworth and much else; new conversational memoranda. [Charles Wordsworth's mss., 1844]. (Bibliographical notes). Pa Bib Soc Am 81no4:451–8 '87.

7928   **Curtis, Jared R.** The making of a reputation; John Carter's correction to the proofs of Wordsworth's Poetical works, 1857. Texte (Toronto) 7:61–80 '88.
    'Appendix [bibliogr. descr. of The poetical works, 1857].

7929   **Parrish, Stephen M.** The whig interpretation of literature. [Editing Wordsworth]. Text 4:343–50 '88.

7930   **Hayden, John O.** The dating of the '1794' version of Wordsworth's An evening walk. [Revision]. Stud Bib 42:265–71 '89.

7931   —— Substantive errors in the standard edition of Wordsworth's prose. (Bibliographical notes). [Ed. by W.J.B. Owen and J.W. Smyser, 1974]. Library ser6 4no1:58–9 Mr '89.

7932   **Stillinger, Jack**. Textual primitivism and the editing of Wordsworth. [Principally The prelude]. Stud Romanticism 28no1:3–28 '89.

WOTTON, SIR HENRY, 1568–1639

7933   **Pebworth, Ted-Larry**. Sir Henry Wotton's O faithless world; the transmission of a coterie poem and a critical old-spelling edition. Analytical & Enum Bib 5no4:205–31 '81. facsim., tables.

WRANGHAM, FRANCIS, 1769–1842

7934   **Lister, Anthony**. Archdeacon Francis Wrangham, 1769–1842. (Collectors & their catalogues). Antiqu Bk Mnthly R 13no8:288–93 Ag '86. facsims.

WRIGHT, GEORGE, fl.1775–87

7935 **Pitcher, Edward W.** New facts on George Wright's eighteenth-century miscellaneous publications. (Bibliographical notes). Pa Bib Soc Am 80no2:237–40 '86.

7936 —— The periodical and miscellaneous publications of George Wright ('Bob Short, junior'). (Bibliographical notes). Pa Bib Soc Am 74no4:379–83 '80.

WROTH, LADY MARY (SIDNEY), fl.1586–1640

7937 **Roberts, Josephine A.** The Huntington manuscript of lady Mary Wroth's play, Loves victorie. Huntington Libr Q 46no2:156–74 '83. facims., table.

WYATT, SIR THOMAS, 1503?–42

7938 **Jentoft, Clyde W.** Sir Thomas Wyatt and Henry Howard, earl of Surrey; a reference guide. Boston, Mass., G.K. Hall, [1980]. xxxvi,192p. 24cm. (Reference guide to literature).
Rev: D.C. Kay N&Q 228:457–8 '83; S.M. Foley Yrbk Eng Stud 13:301–2 '83.

7939 **Caldwell, Ellen C.** Recent studies in sir Thomas Wyatt, 1970–1987. (Recent studies in the English renaissance). Eng Lit Renaiss 19no2:226–46 '89.

———

7940 **Prince, F.T.** Thomas Wyatt. [Text of Epigram 241]. (To the editor). TLS 29 Jl '83:809.

7941 **Daalder, Joost**. Wyatt manuscripts and The court of Venus. Bib Soc Aust & N.Z. Bull 8no2:82–7 '84.

7942 —— Recovering the text of Wyatt's 'Disdain me not without desert'. Stud Neophilol 58no1:59–66 '86.

7943 —— Text and meaning of Wyatt's 'Like as the byrde in the cage enclosed'. Eng Lang N 24no2:24–33 D '86.

7944 —— The significance of the 'Tho' signs in Wyatt's Egerton manuscript. Stud Bib 40:86–100 '87.

7945 —— Are Wyatt's poems in Egerton MS 2711 in chronological order? [Yes]. Eng Stud 69no3:205–23 Je '88; R. Harrier, R.A. Rebholz, H.A. Mason, Replies to Joost Daalder. Am N&Q new ser 1no4:146–52 Oc '88.

7946 ——Wyatt's 'I lead a life unpleasant'; text and interpretation. N&Q 233no1:29–33 Mr '88.

7947 ——Seneca and the text of Marvell's 'Climb at court for me that will.' Pargeron new ser 7:107–10 '89.

WYCHERLEY, WILLIAM, 1640?–1716

7948 **Hume, Robert D.** William Wycherley: text, life, interpretation. (Review article). Mod Philol 78no4:399–415 My '81.
On A. Friedman's The plays.... Oxford, 1979 (1. Text. p.399–405).

WYCLIFFE, JOHN, d.1384

7949 **Oxford. University. Bodleian library.** Wyclif & his followers; an exhibition to mark the 600th anniversary of the death of John Wyclif, December 1984 to April 1985. [Oxford], [1984]. 64p. facsims. 19cm.

WYNDHAM, JOHN, *pseud. of* JOHN WYNDHAM PARKES LUCAS BENYON HARRIS, 1903–69

7950 **Payne, Philip Stephensen-** and **G. Benson**. John Wyndham Parkes Lucas Benyon Harris (10/7/03–10/3/69, Knowle, Warwickshire); a bibliography. Leeds, Stephenson-Payne, [1985]. 18l. facsim. 29cm. (Galactic Central Publ). (Duplicated typescript).

YATES, DORNFORD, *pseud. of* CECIL WILLIAM MERCER, 1885–1960

7951 **Walker, Antony**. Dornford Yates. [Collecting]. Bk & Mag Coll 7:20–4 S '84. port., facsims.
'Complete Dornford Yates bibliography' (p.24).

7952 **Snelling, O. Fred.** Dornford Yates. (Unappreciated authors, 6). Antiqu Bk Mnthly R 12no6:218–25 Je '85. port., facsims.

YATES, EDMUND, 1831–94

7953 **Edwards, Peter D.** Edmund Yates, 1831–1894; a bibliography. [St. Lucia], Dept. of English, University of Queensland, [1980]. 73p. + 73–7p. addenda. ports. 19cm. (Vict Fict Res Guides, 3). (Reprod. from typewriting).
Classified checklist of 291 works and ana.
Rev: Joanne Shattuck Mod Lang R 79:682–3 '84.

YEATS, WILLIAM BUTLER, 1865–1939

7954 **Masin, Anton C.** Catalogue of an exhibit of selections on William Butler Yeats, 1865–1939, poet of the Gael; and the Yeats family contribution to literature and the art of the book, May–September, 1980. With a preface on Yeats at Notre Dame by Rufus William Rauch. [South Bend, Ind.], Memorial library, University of Notre Dame, [1980]. xvii,44p. illus., port., facsims. 21cm.

7955 **Davies, Alastair**, [1982]: no.704.

7956 **Peterson, Richard F.** 'Selected bibliography [of primary and secondary sources]' *in* William Butler Yeats. (Twayne's English authors, 328). Boston, Twayne, [1982]. p.219–21.

7957 **Jochum, Klaus P.S.** A Yeats bibliography for 1981 [–8/9]. Yeats 1:155–73 '83; 2:233–57 '84; 3:175–205 '85; 4:143–76 '86; 5:151–98 '87; 6:175–217 '88; 7:177–206 '89; 8:272–309 '90.

7958 **Gould, Warwick** and **Olympia Sitwell.** 'Gasping on the strand'; a Yeats bibliography, 1981–83. Yeats Ann 3:304–23 '85.

7959 **Sutton, David C.** Location register of twentieth-century English literary manuscripts and letters: current Yeats listings. Yeats Ann 3:295–303 '85; A supplementary list of Yeats holdings. 4:291–6 '86; A cumulative Yeats listing to autumn 1985. 5:289–319 '87.

7960 **Gould, Warwick** and **Olympia Sitwell.** A recent Yeats bibliography, 1983–84. Yeats Ann 4:323–35 '86; ...1984–85. 5: 320–40 '87; ...1985–86. 6:299–317 '88; ...1986–7. 7:293–313 '89.

7961 **Jochum, Klaus P.S.** Preliminary checklist of unpublished European doctoral dissertations on Yeats, 1969–80. [Recent postgraduate research]. Yeats Ann 4:297–9 '86.

7962 **Jochum, Klaus P.S., Olympia Sitwell** and **W. Gould**. Recent postgraduate research. [Dissertations, etc. and diss. abstrs., 1969+]. Yeats Ann 4:297–322 '86.

7963 **O'Shea, Edward**. The 1920s catalogue of W.B. Yeats's library. [Listed]. Yeats Ann 4:279–90 '86.

7964 **Sutton, David C.** Location register of twentieth-century English literary manuscripts and letters; a supplementary listing of Yeats holdings. Yeats Ann 4:291–6 '86.

7965 **Gilbert, R.A.** Magical manuscripts; an introduction to the archives of the Hermetic order of the golden dawn. Yeats Ann 5:163–77 '87. ports., facsims.
The manuscript collections.–The documents.

7966 **Sutton, David C.** Location register of twentieth-century English literary manuscripts and letters; a cumulative Yeats listing to autumn, 1985. Yeats Ann 5:289–319 '87.

7967 **Chapman, Wayne K.** A Descriptive catalog of W.B. Yeats's library; notes supplementary. [To O'Shea, no.7963]. Yeats Ann 6:234–45 '88.

7968 **Osteen, Mark**. Ellmann's Yeats; a bibliography. [His writings about Yeats]. Yeats Ann 7:137–44 '89.

7969 **Clark, David R.** 'That black day'; the manuscripts of 'Crazy Jane on the day of judgement'. [Mountrath], Dolmen pr.; [Atlantic Highlands, N.J.], Humanities pr., [1980]. 55p. facsims. 25cm. (New Yeats papers, 18).
Rev: Margaret Stanley-Vaughan Étud irlandaises 6:249 '81.

7970 **Kelly, John S.** 'Books and numberless dreams; Yeats's relations with his early publishers' *in* Jeffares, A. Norman, *ed*. Yeats, Sligo and Ireland; essays to mark the 21st Yeats international summer school. (Irish literary studies, 6). Totowa, N.J., Barnes & Noble, [1980]. p.232–53.

7971 **Finneran, Richard J.** The composition and final text of W.B. Yeat's 'Crazy Jane on the King'. ICarbs 4no2:67–74 '81. facsim.

7972 **Kenner, Hugh**. 'The most beautiful book'. [Ptg.]. Eng Lit Hist 48no3:594–605 '81.

7973 **Holdsworth, Carolyn**, *ed*. Dissertation abstracts. [From DAI]. Yeats Ann 1:207–20 '82; 2:96–106 '83.

7974 **Allen, James L.** The Yeats tapes. [Microfilm, etc. archives]. Yeats Broadside (Irish Lit Suppl Suppl) 2no2:17,19 '83.

7975 **Finneran, Richard J.** Editing Yeats's poems. [London, Macmillan]; New York, St. Martin's pr., 1983. (Rev. ed. 1990). x,114p. 21cm.
Prolegomena: The myth of the definitive edition.–1. The edition de luxe.–2. The Winding stair and other poems and The collected poems.–3. Collaborative revision: Thomas Mark and George Yeats, 1939–49.–4. A Full moon in March and New poems.–5. Last Poems.–6. Other poems.–Conclusion: Towards the next edition.–Appendix A: Poems by 'Y' in Hibernia, 1882–83. B. Some sources for the poems in Yeats's plays.
Rev: W. Gould TLS 29 Je '84:731; D. Albright N.Y. R Bks 32:29–32 '85; S. Heaney Yeats 3:265–6 '85; Elizabeth Mackenzie N&Q 231:566 '86; G. Bornstein Mod Lang Stud 16:82–7 '86; J.P. Frayne J Eng & Germ Philol 86:139–44 '87.

7976 **Donoghue, Denis**. Editing Yeats. [R.J. Finneran's Poems]. (Letters). TLS 20 Jl '84:811; R.J. Finneran 3 Ag '84; 868–9; A.N. Jeffares; W. Gould 10 Ag '84:893; R.J. Finneran 31 Ag '84:969; W. Gould 21 S '84:1055.

7977 **Finneran, Richard J.** A note on the Scribner archive at the Humanities research center. [Yeats' publ.]. Yeats 2:227–32 '84.

7978 —— The order of Yeats' poems. Irish Univ R 14no2:165–76 '84.
1.The edition de luxe proofs.–2. The collected poems.–3. The order of the plays.–4. The Scribner edition.–5. Mrs. Yeats as a textual editor.

7979 —— The manuscripts of W.B. Yeats's 'Reprisals'. [With texts]. Text 2:269–77 '85.

7980 **Gould, Warwick**. How Ferencz Renyi spoke up, part 2. [Text]. Yeats Ann 3:199–205 '85.

7981 —— Two omissions from The secret rose; stories by W.B. Yeats: a variorum edition. [Text]. Yeats Ann 3:198 '85.

7982 **James, Elizabeth I.** The University of Reading collections. Yeats Ann 3:167–72 '85.

7983 **Masterson, Donald** and **E. O'Shea**. Code breaking and myth making; the Ellis–Yeats edition of Blake's Works. [1893]. Yeats Ann 3:53–80 '85. illus., ports., facsims., table.
Placing Blake in the theosophical tradition: Ellis and Yeats's reading of Swedenborg and Boehme.–The annotations to the Hotten facsimile of The marriage of heaven and hell.–The making of the Blake edition and Yeats's own poetry: 'The two trees' as an example.

7984 **O'Shea, Edward**. A descriptive catalog of W.B. Yeats's library. New York, Garland, 1985. xxiii,390p. 21cm. (Reference library of the humanities, 470).
Rev: R.E. Ward Éire–Ireland 20:154–6 '85; G. Bornstein Yeats 4:219–21 '86; R.J. Finneran Review 9:209–12 '87.

7985 **Schuhard, Ronald**. The lady Gregory–Yeats collection at Emory University. Yeats Ann 3:153–66 '85. facsims.

7986 **Sidnell, Michael J.** Unacceptable hypotheses; the new edition of Yeats's poems and its making. [R.J. Finneran's Editing Yeats's Poems and The poems; a new edition]. Yeats Ann 3:225–43 '85.

7987 **Smythe Colin S.** The Countess Kathleen; a note. [Publ.]. Yeats Ann 3:193–7 '85.

7988 **Baker, Pamela M.** and **Helen M. Young**. W.B. Yeats material in the University of London library. Yeats Ann 4:175–80 '86.

7989 **Balliet, Conrad A.** Yeats manuscript sought. [Correspondence]. Pa Bib Soc Am 80no2:241 '86.

7990   **Kamp, Peter O.W. van de.** Some notes on the literary estate of Pamela Hinkson. [Katharine Tynan's Yeats materials]. Yeats Ann 4:181–6 '86.

7991   **Finneran, Richard J.** W.B. Yeats: early letters and his library. [Rev. article on John Kelley's The collected letters, 1986 and O'Shea, no.7984]. Review 9:205–14 '87.

7992   **Marcus, Philip L.** Yeats's Last poems; a reconsideration. [Text]. Yeats Ann 5:3–14 '87.

7993   **Silver, Jeremy.** Yeats material in the Radio telefis Eireann archives. Yeats Ann 5:186–8 '87.

7994   **Chapman, Wayne K.** The annotated Responsibilities; errors in the Variorum edition and a new reading of the genesis of two poems, 'On those that hated The playboy of the western world' and 'The new faces'. Yeats Ann 6:108–33 '88.

7995   **Gilbert, R.A.** Mss. in a black box; the Golden dawn papers of dr. William Wynn Westcott. Yeats Ann 6:227–33 '88.

7996   **Harper, George M.** 'An old man's frenzy'; editing Yeat's occult papers. Sth Atlantic R 53no2:3–9 My '88.

7997   **Pethica, James**. 'Our Kathleen'; Yeats's collaboration with lady Gregory in the writing of Cathleen ni Houlihan. Yeats Ann (London) 6:3–31 '88.

7998   **Brandes, Rand P.** and **E.G. Wilson**. The Yeats and Ireland collection at Wake Forest university. Yeats Ann 7:213–17 '89.

7999   **Rude, Donald W.** Some new light on W.B. Yeats' Eight poems. Analytical & Enum Bib new ser 3no1:11–15 '89.

YOUNG, ARTHUR, 1741–1820

8000   **Bataille, Robert R.** Arthur Young and the Universal museum of 1762. (Bibliographical notes). Library ser6 6no3:279–85 S '84.

YOUNG, EDWARD, 1683–1765

8001   **Oxford. University. Bodleian library.** Edward Young, poet of the Night-thoughts, 1683–1765; an exhibition.... [Oxford], 1983. [10]p. 21cm. Covertitle.

8002   **May, James E.** A bibliography of secondary materials for the study of Edward Young, 1683–1765. Bull Bib 46no4:230–48 D '89.

8003 —— The Henry Pettit Edward Young collection at the University of Colorado at Boulder libraries; a bibliography. With the assistance of Nora J. Quinlan. Boulder, Col., [Dept. of special collections, University of Colorado at Boulder], 1989. 86p. port. 22cm.

8004 **Bentley, Gerald E., jr.** Young's Night thoughts, a new unillustrated state. [London: R. Edwards, 1797]. Blake 14:34–5 '80.

8005 **Forster, Harold.** The sea-pieces of Edward Young. (Features). Factotum 9:8–10 Ag '80.

8006 **Mills, Trevor.** An unpublished subscription edition of Edward Young's works. [Prospectus, 1726]. (Bibliographical notes). Library ser6 2no4:460–5 D '80. facsim.

8007 **Lange, Thomas V.** A rediscovered colored copy of Young's Night thoughts. Blake 15no3:134–6 '81/2.

8008 **Forster, Harold.** Night-thoughts; an eighteenth century best-seller. Antiqu Bk Mnthly R 10no6:214–17 Je '83. facsims., illus.

8009 —— Rarities and oddities in the works of Edward Young. Bk Coll 32no4:425–38 '83.

8010 **May, James E.** The authority of accidental variants in the Tonson second edition of Edward Young's Love of fame. [1728]. Stud Bib 37:187–97 '84. tables.

8011 —— Hidden editions in Satires I and II of Edward Young's The universal passion. [1728]. Stud Bib 37:181–7 '84.

8012 **McCord, James.** An unrecorded colored copy of Young's Night thoughts. [At Washington univ.]. (Minute particulars). Blake 18no2:116–18 '84.

8013 **May, James E.** Determining final authorial intention in revised satires; the case of Edward Young. [Love of fame and Two epistles in 1757 Works]. Stud Bib 38:276–89 '85.

8014 **Mulhallen, Karen G.** The crying of lot 318 or Young's Night thoughts colored once more. [By Blake]. (Minute particulars). Blake 19no2:71–2 '85.

8015 **May, James E.** Hidden Dublin editions of Edward Young's poetry and other additions and corrections to Forster's list of Irish editions. Long Room 33:6–16 '88.

INDEX

The Index to this volume will be amalgamated with the indexes of previous volumes of the *Index to British Literary Bibliography* in order to provide a cumulative index for the series. Consequently, it is divided into two sequences. The first records the names of authors, editors, compilers, and publishers of items entered in the Bibliography. Full names of persons given shorter forms in the sequence of entries are supplied when the information has come readily to hand: no special search was made in order to expand initials. When I was not sure of the identity of authors writing under different forms of their names, I did not conflate the index entries. However, entries for names when the individual was merely the editor of a collection in which a bibliographical paper was published are distinguished by being placed between parentheses: 'Myers, Robin' gives an example, showing how this practice by comparison distinguishes the author's substantive works.

For consistency with earlier volumes I have mainly ignored the effect of the revision of the Anglo-American cataloguing rules in the index as in the bibliography itself. However, references amongst alternative forms of entry are given to compensate for the difficulties readers experience when familiar cataloguing conventions are altered. I was obliged to abandon the practice of supplying for entries added to earlier volumes compound index references that consisted of the item number in this volume and a reference to the volume in which the item was (or should have been) published earlier.

The second sequence of the index gives access to the specific subjects of the publications that were listed in the bibliography under very broad subject classifications. Numerous references amongst subject headings and the repetition of references under inverted forms of headings, designedly import a large measure of redundancy into this index, so that users may expect usually to satisfy their enquiries at the first point of reference. The structure of the subject index and the application of the subject heading subdividers (e.g., – Bndng., – Collns., – Paper.) are described in *British Literary Bibliography and Textual Criticism, 1890-1969: an Index* [*IBLB*, vol. VI], pp.x-xvi.

Bick, W. 5378
Bick-Janicki, Patricia *see* Janicki, Patricia Bick-.
Bicknell, Peter. 795 2980
Bidwell, John. 1307 2193 2266 2699–700 2735 3084 3267
Bies, Werner. 5822 5971
Bigelow, Charles. 2399 3241 3266 4844
Biggs, Julia. 3483 (3484) (3486–7) (3509) (5694)
Bignes, Richard. 3052
Bill, Eric Geoffrey W. 1712 1715
Billingsley, Dale B. 6620
Billington, Louis. 4124
Bilton, Peter. (7185)
Bindman, David. (4736–7) 4794
Bindoff, Stanley Thomas. (954)
Bingham, Jane. 3428
Binns, James W. 2767 7100
Binns, Norman Evan. 46
Birch, Victor A. 2526
Bird, D.T. 4034
Bird, Sally. 2334
Birley, sir Robert. 1307
Birmingham. Public library. 3063 6067
────── Shakespeare library. 7022
Birmingham bibliographical society. 1019
Birrell, Thomas Anthony. 193 1522–3 3108 4945
Bishko, C. Julian. 438
Bishop, Diana. 2623
Bishop, James. 4262
Bishop, Morchard. 5852
Bishop, Paul. 780–1
Bishop, Thomas. 4668
Bishop, William John. 1840
Black, David H.L. 3841
Black, George. 4468
Black, Hester Mary. 3643
Black, Jeremy. 623 1039 1044 1311 3109 4124 4165 4183 (4211) 4216 4221 4225 4311 4315 6680 6871
Black, Judith M. 4173
Black, Michael H. 2258–9 6317 6338
Black, R.D. Collinson. 87
Black, Stephen A. 7078
Blackburn. Museum and art gallery. 1675
Blackwell, B.H., bksllrs., Oxford. 5560
Blackwell, Kenneth. 69 6911 6914 6920 6923–4 6927–30 6933
Blagden, Cyprian. 2706
Blair, Rhonda L. 4942
Blake, Norman Francis. 440 444 1115 2269–

70 2277 2280 2781 5051–2 5059 5063 5069 6422 6591
Blakiston, Jack M.G. 1651
Blamires, David Malcolm. 6102
Blanch, Robert J. 437 (5071)
Blanchard, Lydia. 6307
Blanchard, Robert G. 4893
Blanchon, Marie-Thérèse. 3764
Blatchly, John M. 1801–2
Blau, Peter E. 5474
Blaydes, Sophia B. 5300
Blayney, Peter William Main. 7231 7240 7457
Blewett, David. 3969 5330 5335
Blewett, Philip. 2106
Bliss, Anthony. 2346
Bliss, Carey S. 2766
Bliss, Lee. 4651
Bliss, Trudy. 4810
Blissett, William. (60) (3072) (3904) (4745)
Blissinger, Mildred. 7892
Block, Ed. 7535
Blodgett, James E. 5062
Blogie, Jeanne. 2032
Blom, Joannes Maria. 4404 4430
Blond, Anthony. 3187
Blondel, Madeleine. 3731 4533
Bloomfield, Barry Cambray. 222 1354 1380 1718 1871 3843 4599 4601 6290
Bloomfield, Mark Ambrose. 950
Bloxom, Marguerite D. 6689
Bloy, Colin H. 2998
Blum, Abbe. 6582
Blum, Rudolf. 119–20
Blumberg, Jane. 822
Blutim, Robin. 809
Boardman, Phillip C. 4585
Boase, Thomas S.R. 3322
Bode, Christoph. 5698
Böker, Uwe. (3730)
Boffey, Julia. 1115 4351
Bogan, James. (4728)
Bogardus, Ralph F. 6034
Boitani, Piero. (5033)
Boll, Theophilus E.M. 1132 6857
Bolton, Claire. 2086 2911 3251–2
Bolton, H.C. 3134
Boltz, Ingeborg. 6981
Bomans, Godfried. 5369
Bompiani, Valentino. 3148
Bond, Peter A. 4286
Bond, William Henry. 59 1500

Hargreaves, Henry. 454
Haring-Smith, Tori *see* Smith, Tori Haring-.
Harker, Jean. 1761
Harland, Elizabeth. 3692
Harley, David. 6915 6931
Harley, J.B. 4008
Harley, Jane. 2636
Harling, Robert. 2394
Harmer, Michael. 175
Harmon, Maurice. 928 5136
Harmon, Robert Bartlett. 52 6893
Harmsworth, Geoffrey. 4280
Harner, James L. 7 50 2510 3713–4 5289
    6424 7399
Harper, George Mills. 7996
Harrier, Richard. 7945
Harrington, Frank G. 5806
Harris, Brian E. 794
Harris, Elizabeth M. 3043
Harris, Frances. 585 602 1123 1543 1556
    2720 6441–2 6460
Harris, Greg. 6471
Harris, Jack T. 7620
Harris, James Rendel. 2239
Harris, Jennifer. 6630
Harris, John. 213 1441 1456 2950
Harris, John B. 6497
Harris, Kate. 1115 5717 5910
Harris, Kevin. 5016 5403
Harris, Michael Ronald Anthony. 90 (116)
    (193–4) (197) (217) (220) 613 (966)
    (973) (991) 1007 1064 1071 1074 1080
    1093 1103 1116 (1120) (1125) (1137)
    (1172) (1280) (1322) (1340) (1346)
    (1509) (1513) (1518) 2044 (2039–40)
    (2183) (2218) (2245) (2289) (2312)
    (2548) (2573) 2651 (2710–12) (2715)
    (2782) (2878) (2882) (2922) (3101)
    (3111) (3163) (3239) 3278 (3736) 3278
    3351 (3828) (3942) (4010) 4124 (4153)
    4166 4203 4209 4211 4264 (4437)
    (4488) 4528 (5688) (5927) (6516)
    (6958) (7556)
Harris, P.R. 829 834
Harris, Richard H. 3622
Harris, Richard L. 3512
Harris, Styron. 6242
Harris, Sylvia. 5306
Harris, William O. 4830
Harrison, Alan. 7563
Harrison, James. 6246
Harrison, John. 6458
Harrison, Phillipa. 4921

Harrop, Dorothy A. 42 1157 1201 1205 1207
    1213 1238 1240 1248–50 1255 2435
    2437–8 2660 2730 3063 3227
Harst, Marie-Theres. 2784
Hart, Clive. 6181 6195 6204
Hart, Thomas Copeland. 6801
Härtel, Helmut. (457) (1062) (5715)
Harthan, John Plant. 1157
Hartley, Christopher. 1490
Hartley, Jean. 6294
Hartley, Robert A. 4503
Harvard university. Dept. of English and
    American literature and language. 4
—— Houghton library. 399 5578 5593 6071
—— Libraries. 4961
Harvey, A.D. 5779 6760
Harvey, Anthony P. 4105
Harvey, D.R. 4077
Harvey, Nancy Lenz. 7256
Harvey, R.A. 1432
Haskell, Grace Clark. 2663
Haslewood, Joseph. 2696
Hassall, Joan. 3946
Hassall, W.O. 856 1481
Hastings, Paul. 1371
Hatley, Victor A. 1938 1947
Hatton, Reginald. (695)
Haule, James M. 7890
Hauswedell, Ernst. 2542
Havighurst, Alfred Freeman. 13
Havlice, Patricia Pate. 3507
Hawes, Donald. 2644 3382
Hawkes, Nicolas. 228
Hawkes, Terence. 7110
Haworth-Booth, Mark *see* Booth, Mark
    Haworth-.
Hawthorn, Jeremy. 5240
Hay, Denys. 82
Hay, John. 406
Hay, Louis. 132 351
Hay, Malcolm. 4820
Hayashi, Tetsumaro. 6407
Hayden, John O. 7926 7930–1
Hayes, Deborah. 5749
Hayley, Barbara. 4145 4965–6
Hayman, David. 6163 6177 6181 6205
Hayman, John. 6910
Haymon, Sylvia. 5851
Hays, Michael L. 3538
Haythornthwaite, Jo Ann. 1741 6682–3
Haywood, Ian. 3824–6 5030
Hazell, Ralph C. 2794
Hazen, Allen Tracy. 6069

Jordan, Gerald. 4048
Jordan, R.J. 7453
Josef Weinberger, ltd. 3162
Joseph, Richard. 3166
Jowett, John. 6129 7123 7192–3 7200–1 7219
    7302 7322 7346
Joyce, Beverly A. 3348
Joyce, Stephen J. 6195
Joyce, Steven. 7362
Joyce, William L. (967)
Joye, Gill. 4021
Judkins, David C. 6112
Jump, Harriet. 7922

Kahn, Coppélia. (6989)
Kahn, E. 1717
Kahrl, George M. 3563
Kaimowitz, Jeffrey H. 6592
Kain, Richard M. 6181 6187 6206
Kainen, Jacob. 3019 3889
Kaiser, John R. 5842
Kallendorf, Craig. 746
Kalnins, Mara. (6338)
Kaminski, Thomas. 206
Kamowski, William. 5078
Kamp, Peter O.W. van de. 7990
Kamps, Ivo. 7025
Kane, George. 342 380 5060 5062 5097
    6281 6286
Kansas. University. Kenneth Spencer re-
    search library. 486 663 3831 5706
Kaplan, Joel H. 6526 6529
Kapstein, Matthew. 4707
Karel, Thomas A. 6688
Kastan, David Scott. 123
Kaufman, Paul. 1300 1669 1928 4911
Kavanagh, Peter. 6217
Kay, Dennis. (7402)
Kay, Wallace G. 6342
Kaye, Barbara, *pseud. of* Mary A. (mrs. P.H.)
    Muir. 2544
Keane, Robert N. 6882
Kearney, Anthony. 5178
Kearney, Patrick John. 3696 3702
Keating, Peter. 4374
Keeble, N.H. 1042 4646 (4917)
Keegan, Timothy. 6075
Keeling, Denis F. 1349–50
Keen, Michael E. 3515
Keen, Ralph. 6619
Kehr, Wolfgang. 2391
Keiser, George R. 1698 4421
Keith, Sara. 3743 3745

Keitt, Diane. 5411
Kelleher, D. 1186
Kelley, Maurice. 6580
Kelley, Philip. 4874 4876 4881 4884
Kelley, Theresa M. 4774
Kelliher, William Hilton. 421 2071 2158
    5185 5350 6446 7196 7416 7683
Kellogg, Robert L. 438
Kelly, Alexander Garfield. 6012
Kelly, C.M. 3856 3891
Kelly, Dawn P. 3969 5415
Kelly, Gary. 6959
Kelly, John S. 7970
Kelly, Joseph. 6113
Kelly, Lionel. 4564
Kelly, Mary T. 7721
Kelly, Richard. 5509
Kelly, Thomas. 1355
Kelly, William Ashford. 731 1532 6971
Kelvin, Norman 6635
Kemnitz, Charles. 6142
Kemp, D. Alasdair. 1843–4
Kempson, E.G.H. 1825
Kennedy, Brian P. 1545
Kennedy, Campbell. 4009
Kennedy, Edward Donald. 481 (6288)
    (6456)
Kennedy, Michael. 7843
Kennedy, Richard. 2464 3225
Kennedy, Veronica M.S. 6734
Kenner, Hugh. 6164 6196 7972
Kenneth Ritchie Wimbledon library *see*
    Wimbledon lawn tennis museum, Lon-
    don. Kenneth Ritchie Wimbledon li-
    brary.
Kenney, E.J. (747)
Kenny, Shirley Strum. 369 3097
Kent, Christopher A. 3602 3608 4261 4274
Kenyon, John R. 1460 4100
Kenyon, ld. 1307
Ker, Neil Ripley. 430 (493) 1079 1357 1471
    1582 1756–7 1763 1796
Kernan, Alvin Bernard. 6097
Kerr, ld. John. 2036
Kerrigan, John. 7118 7238 7259–61 7263
Kerrigan, Philip P. 1094 3059–62 3064
Kessler, Alfred R. 5112
Ketchell, Christopher. 877–8
Kevan, D. Keith E. 4099
Key, Neil. 6966
Keynes, sir Geoffrey Langdon. 255 2550
    4744 4750 4760–1 4794 5661 5846 5854
    6396

Lister, W.B.C. 4540

Literary and historical editing. 65

Litster, John. 4511

Little, Geoffrey. 5154 5158 7924

Little, Monte. 1376 1827

Litvak, Leon. 6657

Litzinger, Boyd. 5944

Liu Houling. 6997

Liverpool bibliographical society. 1000–1

Livingston, Carole Rose. 3399

Llasera, Margaret. 5431

Lloyd, Henry. 4049

Lloyd, Leslie John. 1610

Lloyd-Roberts, Thomas *see* Roberts, Thomas Lloyd-.

Loades, David M. 1030

Loasby, B.J. 2689

Location register of twentieth-century English literary manuscripts and letters. 710

Lock, F.P. 7553

Locke, George. 3041 3792

Lockwood, Thomas. 3599 5594

Loewenstein, Joseph. 2740 6130 7176

Lofts, William Oliver Guillmont. 3364 3380 3426 3435 3466 3470 5029 5637 7733

Logan, Maureen F. 7313

Lohf, Kenneth A. 2752 4621

Lohrli, Anne. 3288 4270 5181–2 5623

London. Arts council *see* Arts council of Great Britain, London.

—— Guildhall library. 811 814

—— University. Library resources co-ordinating committee. History of art subject sub-committee. 3301

—— —— University college. Bentham committee. 4703

Long, Douglas. 4703

Long, Patricia M. 1363

Long, William B. 3556 7346

Longbotham, J. 1853

Longfield, Ada K. 2150

Longford, Elizabeth. 1414

Longrie, Michael. 5611

Lonoff, Sue. 5179

Lonsdale, Roger. 6080

Looney, J. Anna. 905

Lopez, Tony. 5722

Lottes, Wolfgang. (2672) (6814) (7476) (7478) 7628

Loudon, James Hamilton. 2678

Loudon, Jean. (4035)

Lough, J. 4535

Love, Harold H.R. 318–9 558 975 3120 4363 7853

Low, D.M. (2292)

Low, David. 2007 5771

Low, sir David Alexander Cecil. 2542

Lowe, Rachel. 5347–8

Lowens, Peter J. 5232

Lowery, Robert G. 6664 (6669)

Lowry, Martin J.C. 82 986 2283

Lubasz, H.M. 1025

Lubett, Denise Y. 1260

Luborsky, Ruth Samson. 7469

Lucas, G.R. 1926

Lucas, Mary. 1663

Lucas, Peter J. 2165 4349

Lucas, R. Valerie. 4455

Luciano, Juan V. Martinez *see* Martinez Luciano, Juan V.

Luck, James. 4050

Lucow, Ben. 7395

Ludgrove, Michael. 1547

Ludlum, Charles. 5072

Luedeking, Leila. 7895

Lukitsh, Joanne. 7627

Lull, Janis. 5887

Lulofs, Timothy J. 5992

Lumiansky, R.M. 6453–4 6456

Lund, Michael. 3780

Lund, Roger D. 548

Lunsford, Andrea A. 4459

Luria, Maxwell. 2021

Lusardi, James P. 6615

Lusty, sir Robert. 2264 3141

Lutman, Stephen. 5385

Lyall, Roderick J. 1115

Lyle, E.B. 3414

Lyman, Philip. 6248

Lyon, Thomas E. 4386

Lyons, Anne K. 7688

Lytle, Guy Fitch. 2164 (2163) (5437) (6819)

Maas, Henry. 5953

Macalister, John. 6791

MacAree, David. 5322 5328

McAulay, Alexander. 3129

McAvoy, William C. 68 7338

McBain, Ed. 3148

McBrien, William. 7444

McCabe, Richard A. 4355 5832

Maccagno, D. 7911

McCall, Robin H. 4686

McCann, E.J. Wesley. 102 1051 7560 7565–6 7595

McCann, Timothy John. 866 2387 2928–9

Winnington, G. Peter. 6727–9 6731
Winship, Michael. 3829
Winstanley, F.H. 4549 6060
Winston, Robert P. 7084
Winton, Calhoun. 1032
Wirtjes, Hanneke. (331) (3108)
Wisconsin. University. Library. 2318
Wise, Brian. 7767 7771 7774
Wise, R.D. 6361
Wishart, David. 3037 3236
Wishart, Eric. 4348
Wittmann, Reinhard. (1023)
Wittreich, Joseph Anthony. 4417
Witworth, Charles W. 7319
Wodehouse, sir Pelham Grenville. 7880
Wölfle, Lotte Roth. 2542
Wölk, Gerhard. 7764
Wolf, Edwin. 1268
Wolf, Richard B. 5257
Wolf, William D. 5186
Wolfe, Christine M. 1988
Wolfe, Peter. (5770)
Wolff, Dorothy. 6519
Wolff, Michael. (3416) (6902)
Wolff, Robert Lee. 3752
Wolfshohl, Clarence. 2486
Wolfson, John. 1307
Wolpe, Berthold. 3237
Wolpers, Theodor. 7027
Wood, Alberta Auringer. 4007
Wood, Anthony. 1452
Wood, G.A.M. 271
Wood, H.H. 901
Wood, J. Laurence. 587 599 608 639 649 1215 2013 3022 3213 3974 5327
Wood, Michael Boyd. 6459
Wood, Naomi Caldwell-. 29
Wood, Nigel. (5659)
Wood, P.B. 1838 1864 6832
Wood, Paul. 3030
Wood, Peter W. 29
Wood, Roma. 1131 7359
Wood, Sally. 2051 2593 2644 3362 7485
Woodbridge, Linda. 7001
Wooden, Warren W. 3472 5634–5
Woodfield, Bryan. 2898
Woodfine, Philip. 1046
Woodman, Thomas M. 6718
Woodmansee, Martha. 1141
Woodnutt, Roma. 6202
Woodring, Carl Ray. 5164
Woods, C.J. 4539

Woods, Oliver. 4262
Woods, Samuel H. 5699
Woodson, William C. 7076
Woodward, David A. 249 2071
Woodward, G.R. 3015 5966
Woodworth, David P. 4276
Woof, Pamela. 7903
Woof, Robert S. 5351
Woolf, Cecil. 7452
Woolf, Daniel R. 520 4819 5017
Woolhouse, Roger. 6400
Woolley, David. 7555 7563 7570 7573 7576 7596
Woolley, James. 1626 4215 7563 7577
Woolmer, J. Howard. 222 2461 (2467) 2652–3 2900 4566 6134
Woolnough, Charles W. 2126
Woolrich, A.P. 2829
Woolrych, Austin. 1686
Wordsworth, Jonathan. 4384
Wormald, C.P. 1954
Wormell, Deborah. 6976
Worth, George John. 5375
Worthen, John. 6310 6313 6340 6348
Worthington-Williams, Michael see Williams, Michael Worthington-.
Wortman, William A. 19
Woudhuysen, Henry R. 408 1388 1685–6 1719 5446 7409 7412
Wright, Andrew. 7697
Wright, C.J. 3844
Wright, Constance S. 5083–4 5102
Wright, Deborah Kemp. 7417
Wright, Glenn P. 7898
Wright, H. Bunker 6807
Wright, J.E. 1847
Wright, Mark. 4837
Wright, Nancy E. 5467
Wright, Norman. 4291 4299
Wright, Ruth C. 137
Wright, Stephen K. 3576
Wright, Stuart. 7782
Wright, Thomas F. 1368
Wright, William C. 5255
Wrigley, Chris. 7593
Wuttke, Dieter. 1489
Wyatt, C.M. 5674
Wyatt, Diana. 3558
Wyatt, R.J. 4545
Wyllie, John Cook. 59 2949
Wynne, Marjorie G. 6157
Wynne-Tyson, Jon see Tyson, Jon Wynne-.

INDEX OF SUBJECTS

Subject headings are sorted letter by letter to the first stop (a space is not treated as a stop) but prefixes like 'bp., archbp., sir, ld.' and county identifiers are ignored in sorting. British places precede the identical names of localities elsewhere. Headings between single quotation marks like 'BLUE PENCIL' are technical terms of which the meaning is discussed in the items referred to. Item numbers printed in **bold** face refer to the entries under the same subject heading in the main arrangement of the Bibliography.

—— Text. 5132

CLARE, Robert, fl.1692–1705. 4195

CLARENDON, Edward Hyde, earl of, 1609–74 *see* HYDE, Edward, earl of Clarendon, 1609–74.

CLARENDON GALLERY, London–Collns. 3929

CLARK LIBRARY, Calif. *see* CALIFORNIA. UNIVERSITY AT LOS ANGELES. WILLIAM ANDREWS CLARK MEMORIAL LIBRARY.

CLARKE, Arthur Charles, 1917– . **5135**

—— Bibs. 5135

—— *Childhood's end.* 5135

CLARKE, Austin, 1896–1974. **5136**

—— *Sword of the west.* 5136

—— Text. 5136

CLARKE, Charles Cowden-, 1787–1877–Shakespeare's *Plays.* 7080

CLARKE, Henry Patrick, 1889–1931. 3937 3949

—— Bibs. 3949

CLARKE, Marcus Andrew Hislop, 1846–81. **5137**

—— *His natural life.* 5137

—— Publ. 5137

CLASSICAL LITERATURE *see* FOREIGN BOOKS PUBLISHED IN BRITAIN–Classical.

CLASSICAL TRADITION–Bibs. 743 746

CLAVELL, Robert, d.1711. 2050

CLAY, Charles John, Cambridge, 1827– . 2258–9

CLAY, John, Daventry, 1713–75. 2030 **2301–2** 4217

CLAY, Samuel, Warwick, 1744–1800. 1820

CLELAND, Charles, Edinburgh, fl.1784–92. 1226

CLELAND, John, 1709–89. **5138–42**

—— Bibs. 5138–9

—— *Fanny Hill* see *Memoirs of a woman of pleasure.*

—— *Memoirs of a woman of pleasure.* 1034 5138–41

—— Publ. 5142

—— Text. 5141

CLEMENTS, Jeff, fl.1963–86. 1267

CLENELL, Luke, Newcastle-upon-Tyne, 1781–1817. 2216

—— Bibs. 2216

CLERICAL DIRECTORIES *see* DIRECTORIES, CLERICAL.

CLERIHEWS. 4395

—— Bibs. 4395

CLERK, Alexander, fl.1547–91–*Book of common order.* 3357

CLERKENWELL, London *see* LONDON. CLERKENWELL.

CLEVELAND, John, 1613–58. **5143**

—— *A dialogue.* 5143

—— Mss. 5143

—— *The rebel Scot.* 5143

CLEVELAND, Yorks.–Bibs. 876

CLEVERDON, Thomas Douglas James, 1903–87. 2000 **2303–4**

CLIFFORD, Margaret (Russell), countess of Cumberland, 1560?–1616. 7472

CLOISTER PRESS, Heaton Mersey, est.1921–Bibs. 2842

CLOTH BOOKBINDINGS *see* BOOKBINDING/S, CLOTH.

CLOUGH, Arthur Hugh, 1819–61. **5144**

—— *Adam and Eve.* 5144

—— Text. 5144

CLYMER, George E., 1754–1834. 3019

COATES, John William, 1853–1925. 2996

COATES BROTHERS, ltd., est.1877. 2996

COATS OF ARMS. 3843

COBBETT, William, 1762–1835. 4261

—— Paper. 2132

COBHAM FAMILY–Libr. 1810

COCHRAN, Alexander Smith, 1874–1929. 515

COCK, Christopher, fl.1720–53. 2039

COCKERELL, Douglas Bennett, 1870–1945. 2308

COCKERELL, Patience Scott, 1878– . 2309

—— Bibs. 2309

COCKERELL, sir Sydney Carlyle, 1867–1962–Libr. 1526 6634

COCKERELL, Sydney Morris, 1906–87. 2305–7 2310 2660 6634

—— Bibs. 2305

COCKERELL FAMILY, bookbinders, fl.1890–1962. **2305–10**

COEFFIN, Martin, Exeter, fl.1505–38. 3132

COIGENY, Rodolphe L., fl.1945–89–Libr. 7746

COINAGE–1701–1800. 3496

COKE, vice–chamberlain, fl.1705–15–Mss. 3596

COKE, Desmond F.T., 1879–1931. **5145**

—— Bibs. 5145

COKE, sir Edward, 1552–1634–Libr. 1481

CORNWALL–Librs. **1603**

—— Literacy. 1953

—— Newspapers. **4131**

—— —— Bibs. 4131

CORRECTORS OF THE PRESS *see also* FLEMING, Abraham, 1552?–1607; GRIERSON, Constantia (Crawley), 1705–32.

CORRY, John, 1760?–1825. **5260**

—— Bibs. 5260

CORSON, James Clarkson, 1905–88. 199

—— Libr. 6952

COTSWOLD OLIMPICKS–Collns. 3658

COTTON, Charles, 1630–87. **5261–2**

—— *Contentation of anglers.* 5262

—— Mss. 5261–2

COTTON, sir Robert Bruce, 1571–1631. 1386

—— Libr. 825 1427

COULTER, Samuel, 1755–1803–Libr. 1725

COUNTERFEIT NEWSPAPERS *see* NEWSPAPERS, COUNTERFEIT.

COUNTRY HOUSES *see* HOUSES, COUNTRY.

COUNTY LIBRARIES *see* LIBRARIES, COUNTY.

COURSE DESCRIPTIONS *see* BIBLIOGRAPHICAL DESCRIPTION–Course descriptions.

COURT BOOKSHOP. 3450

COURT OF VENUS, The. 7941

COURTENAY, sir William Percy Honeywood, 1799–1838 *see* TOM, John Nichols, 1799–1838.

COURTESY BOOKS. **3505**

—— Bibs. 3505

—— 1475–1640–Bibs. 3505

—— 1801–1900–Bibs. 3849

—— 1901–2000–Bibs. 3849

COUTTS, Angela Georgina Burdett-, baroness Burdett-Coutts, 1814–1906. **5263**

—— Bibs. 5263

—— *Common things.* 5396

—— Publ. 5396

COVENANTERS, SCOTTISH–Ptg. 2915

COVENT GARDEN JOURNAL. 5584

COVENT GARDEN THEATRE, London *see* LONDON. COVENT GARDEN THEATRE.

COVERS, BOOK *see* BOOK COVERS.

——, PAPER *see* PAPER COVERS.

COWARD, sir Nöel Pierce, 1899–1973. **5264**

—— Bibs. 5264

COWDEN-CLARKE, Charles, 1787–1877 *see* CLARKE, Charles Cowden-, 1787–1877.

COWELLS, W.S., ltd., Ipswich. 2921

COWLEY, Abraham, 1618–67. **5265**

—— Text. 5265

—— *The civil war.* 5265

COWPER, Sarah, 1643–1720–Libr. 5265

COWPER, William, 1731–1800. **5266–7**

—— Mss. 5267

—— *Ode on reading Richardson's History.* 5267

—— Text. 4224

COWTAN, Mawer, Oxford, fl.1840. 2149

COWTEM, Mawer, Oxford, fl.1840 *see* COWTAN, Mawer, Oxford, fl.1840

COX, Edward William, 1809–79. 4418

COX AND WYMAN, est.1777. 2858

COXE, Henry Octavius, 1811–81. 854

CRACE, sir John Gregory, 1887–1968. 2149

CRAFTS STUDY CENTRE, London–Collns. 2476

CRAFTSMAN, The. 587 4202 5586

—— Ptg. 4202

CRAFTSMEN IN LITERATURE–Bibs. 3489

CRAIG, Edward Gordon, 1872–1966. **5268–71**

—— Letters. 5271

—— *On the art of the theatre.* 5271

—— Ptg. 5270

—— Publ. 5269 5271

—— Shakespeare's *Hamlet.* 5270 7178

—— *The mask.* 5269

CRAIK, Dinah Maria (Mulock), 1826–87. **5272**

—— Bibs. 5272

CRAKANTHORPE, Richard, 1567–1624. **5273**

—— *Logic.* 5273

CRANACH PRESS, Weimar, est.1913–Shakespeare's *Hamlet.* 5270 7178

CRANE, Ralph, fl.1575–1632. **5274** 7321–2

—— Middleton's *The witch.* 6524

—— Shakespeare's *The tempest.* 7321–2

CRANE, Walter, 1845–1915. **2314–15** 3675

CRANFORD SERIES (Macmillans)–Bibs. 3365

CRANMER, archbp. Thomas, 1489–1556. **5275**

—— Bibs. 5275

CRASHAW, Richard, 1612?–49. **5276–8**

—— Bibs. 5276–7

CRAVAN, Arthur, fl.1887–1919?. 3820 3822

CRAVEN CHAPEL BOOK SOCIETY, Bayswater, London. 1707

DELIUS TRUST, London–Collns. 5346 5348
DE MACHLINIA, William, fl.1482–90 *see* MACHLINIA, William de, fl.1482–90.
DEMOCRAT'S CHAPBOOK, A, 1942. 7820
DENBIGHSHIRE–Ptg. **2807**
DENHAM, sir John, 1615–69. **5350**
—— Letters. 5350
—— Mss. 5350
DENMARK *see* BRITISH BOOKS PUBLISHED ABROAD–Denmark.
DENT, J.M. AND SONS, est.1888–*Mediaeval towns series.* 3376
—— —— Bibs. 3376
DENT, Joseph Mallaby, 1849–1926. 2336
—— Mss. 2336
DEQUINCEY, Thomas, 1785–1859. **5351-3**
—— Bibs. 5351
—— Collns. 5351
—— *Confessions of an opium eater.* 5353
—— Mss. 5353
DERBY, Derbys. DERBY PHILOSOPHICAL SOCIETY. LIBRARY. 1608
—— Librs. 1608 2808
—— Ptg. 2808
—— PUBLIC LIBRARY–Collns. 5261
DERBY, Alice Spencer, countess of, 1559–1637 *see* SPENCER, Alice, countess of Derby, 1559–1637.
DERBYSHIRE. **796-7**
—— Bakewell–Bibs. 797
—— Bibs. 796–7 3521
—— Bksllng. **1994**
—— Collns. 796
—— Directories. **3521**
—— Librs. **1607-8**
—— Newspapers. **4133-5**
—— —— Bibs. 4133–4
—— Ptg. **2808**
DERBYSHIRE ARCHÆOLOGICAL AND NATURAL HISTORY SOCIETY. LIBRARY–Collns. 796
DERING, sir Edward, 1598–1644–Libr. 1461 1507 7186
DERRY–Paper. 2077
DERRY AND RAPHOE DIOCESAN LIBRARY–Collns. 4307
DESIGNER BOOKBINDERS, est.1968. 1154 1174 1255–6
DESIGNER BOOKBINDERS NEWLETTER. 1276
DESIGNERS, BOOKBINDING *see* BOOKBINDING DESIGNERS.

DETECTIVE FICTION *see* FICTION, DETECTIVE.
DEUTSCHE LESE-BIBLIOTHEK, London. 1723
DEVAL, Laurie, 1923–81. 2014
DE VERE, Edward, 17th earl of Oxford, 1550–1604–Letters. 7143
DEVEREUX, Robert, 2d earl of Essex, 1566–1601. **5354**
—— Handwr. 5354
DEVICES, PRINTERS' *see* TYPE AND TYPOGRAPHY–Devices.
DEVONSHIRE. 624
—— Booktrade. **991**
—— Librs. **1609-13**
—— Literacy. 1945–6 1949
—— Paper. **2082**
—— Ptg. **2809-12**
—— —— Bibs. 2809
—— Publ. **3132**
—— 1801–1900–Literacy. 1945
DE WILDE, Samuel, 1751?–1832–Bell's *British theatre.* 2203
DEXTER, John Furber, 1847–1927–Libr. 5390
DIALOGUES OF CREATURES MORALISED. 5845
DIARIES. **3506-9**
—— Bibs. 3506–8
—— Collns. 3508–9
—— 1475–1700–Bibs. 3506
——, CHILDREN'S. 3509
DIBDIN, Thomas Frognall, 1776–1847. 162 1509 **5355-61**
—— *Bibliomania.* 5360
—— Bibs. 5359
—— Collns. 5359
—— *Horae bibliographicae Cantabrigienses.* 5361
—— *Lincoln nosegay.* 4679
—— Mss. 5360–1
—— *Typographical antiquities.* 5355–6
DICEY, William, Northampton, fl.1713–54. 3418
DICKENS, Arthur Geoffrey, 1910– –Bibs. 485
DICKENS, Charles John Huffam, 1817–70 *see also* ALL THE YEAR ROUND; HOUSEHOLD WORDS. 1127 **5362-419**
—— *American Notes.* 5405
—— *Barnaby Rudge*–Bibs. 5376
—— *Battle of life.* 5413

—— 1701–1800. 3663 3666
—— —— Bibs. 3841
—— —— Collns. 3662
—— 1801–1900. 3649 3667 3675 3686
—— —— Bibs. 3841
—— —— Collns. 3652 3660 3662 3692
—— 1801–1901. 7679
—— 1901–2000. 3651 653 3655 3672–3 3676 3678–83 3687 3689
—— —— Collns. 3649 3658 4090
EPITAPH FOR RICHARD, DUKE OF YORK– Text. 480
EPWORTH, Lincs.–Newspapers. 4158
EPWORTH BELLS. 4158
ERASMUS, Desiderius, 1466–1536. 769
—— Libr. 1719
ERGHOME, John, fl.1372–Libr. 1459
ERNEST BENN, ltd., est.1923. 3145 4698
EROTICA. **3696–702**
—— Bibs. 3696
—— Collns. 3696 3701–2
—— 1701–1800–Illus. 3698
—— 1801–1900. 3699
—— —— Mss. 3700
—— 1901–2000. 3701
ERSKINE, Robert, 1677–1718. 1464
—— Libr. 1453
ESDAILE, Arundell James Kennedy, 1880–1956. 157
ESHER, Surrey–Paper. 2119
ESHTON HALL, Yorks.–Libr. 1496
ESPARTO. 2073 2083
ESPIONAGE FICTION *see* FICTION, ESPIO-NAGE.
ESSAYS AND REVIEWS, 1860. 673
ESSEX. **799**
—— Bibs. 799
—— Librs. **1636–40**
—— —— Bibs. 799
—— Maps–Bibs. 799
—— Ptg. **2816–22**
ESSEX, Robert Devereux, 2d earl, 1566–1601 *see* DEVEREUX, Robert, 2d earl of Essex, 1566–1601.
ESSEX HOUSE PRESS, Chipping Camden, Glos., 1898–1909. **2359–61**
—— Bibs. 2359 2361
ESSEX LITERARY AND SCIENTIFIC INSTI-TUTE, Saffron Waldon, est.1832. LIB-RARY. 1637
ESTC NORTH AMERICA. 579 584 588 597 600 610 619–20

ETCHELLS, Frederick, 1876–1973. 3177
ETCHING/S. 2970
ETHEREGE, sir George, 1636–91/2. **5557–9**
—— Bibs. 5558
—— Libr. 5559
—— *Man of mode*–Bibs. 5558
ETON, Bucks. COLLEGE. LIBRARY–Collns. 2576
—— Ptg. 2785
ETTINGTON, Warws.–Libr. 1328
EUGENE, prince of Savoie-Carignan, 1663–1736. 641
EUROPA PRESS, Belfast, 1935–9. 2880
—— Bibs. 2880
EUROPEAN MAGAZINE. 4210 5266 6830
EUSDEN, Laurence, 1688–1730–Libr. 1562
EVANION, Henry Evans, *pseud. of* Henry Evans, 1832?–1905–Libr. 3612 3692
EVANS, Carodoc, 1879–1945–Bibs. 881
EVANS, Edmund, 1826–1905. 2252 3474
EVANS, Evan, 1731–89–*De bardis dissertatio.* 3050
—— *Some specimens of the poetry of the ancient Welsh bards.* 3050
EVANS, Harold, 1911–83. 4247
EVANS, Henry, 1832?–1905 *see* EVANION, Henry Evans, *pseud.*
EVANS, John Gwenogvryn, 1852–1930. 2803
EVELYN, John, 1655–99. 2143 **5560–3**
—— Bibs. 5560
—— Collns. 5562
—— *Fumifugium.* 5561
—— Libr. 1307 5560 5562–3
—— Publ. 5561
EVENING ADVERTISER. 4225
EVENING CHRONICLE. 5393
EVENING OFFICE OF THE CHURCH–Bibs. 4404
EVERYMAN–Ptg. 3547
EWEN, Cecil Henry L'Estrange, fl.1929–49–Libr. 4305
EWING, Juliana Horatia (Gatty), 1841–85–Illus. 2316
EX LIBRIS *see* BOOKPLATES.
——, MANUSCRIPT. 1397
EXAMINER, The. 5856
EXCHANGE RATE CURRENTS. 3494
EXCISE–Advertisements. 4192
—— Newspapers *see* NEWSPAPER STAMPS.
EXETER, Devon. 616
—— Librs. 1610

FELL AND ROCK CLIMBING CLUB OF THE ENGLISH LAKE DISTRICT. LIBRARY–Collns. 4501

FELLTHAM, Owen, 1602?–68. **5568–9**

—— *A form of prayer.* 5568

—— *Resolves.* 5569

—— Text. 5568–9

FEMALE READER, The, 1789. 5691

FENN, George Manville, 1831–1909. **5570**

—— Bibs. 5570

FENNELL, John, Edinburgh, fl.1619. 1234

FERGUSON, James, 1710–76. **5571**

—— Bibs. 5571

FERN BOOKS. 3394

—— Collns. 3394

FERRABY FAMILY, Hull, fl.1706–1848. 1021

FERRIER, Susan Edmonstone, 1782–1854. **5572–3**

—— Bibs. 5572–3

FICTION. **3703–816**

—— Bibs. 851 3703–11

—— 1475–1700. 3419 **3713–16**

—— —— Bibs. 3713–14

—— 1701–1800. 3420 3452 **3717–41** 5329

—— —— Bibs. 3452 3717–30

—— —— —— Bibs. 3732

—— —— Bksllng. 3734

—— —— Collns. 3719

—— —— Publ. 3735 3740–1

—— 1801–1900. 3742–60 **3762–91** 3794 7883

—— —— Bibs. 3718 3720 3725–6 3729 3742–67 3776 3779 3794

—— —— Collns. 3752 3754 3763 3773–4 3787

—— —— Illus. 3790 3964

—— —— Ptg. 3775

—— —— Publ. 3740 3779 3781–3 3785 3788 3791

—— —— Scotland. 3784

—— —— Text. 3777 3786 3789

—— 1901–2000. **3792–816**

—— —— Bibs. 2428 3361 3366–7 3749 3753 3761 3792–809 3814–5

—— —— Bksllng. 3811

—— —— Collns. 3792 3813–4

—— —— Ireland–Bibs. 928

—— —— Publ. 2428 3286 3812

—— —— Text. 3812

——, BRITISH MUSEUM–Bibs. 823

——, CATASTROPHE–Bibs. 3755

——, CRIME–Bibs. 2428 3367 3708 3710

3798 3804

——, DETECTIVE. 3815

—— Bibs. 3704 3803 3807 3815

——, ESPIONAGE–Bibs. 3366 3798

——, GOTHIC–Bibs. 570 3705 3720–1 3725 3728–9 3764 3794

——, MYSTERY–Bibs. 3803–4 3806

—— Collns. 3813

——, PERIODICAL–Bibs. 3748 3750–1 3757–8 3762 3765 3767 3795 3802

——, SCIENCE *see* SCIENCE FICTION.

——, SERIAL. 3739 3771 5327 7883

—— Bibs. 3723 3732 3759

FICTION HOUSE, ltd., fl.1935–50. 3361

FIELD, Michael, *pseud.* of Katherine Harris Bradley, 1846–1913 and Edith Emma Cooper, 1862–1914. 6850

FIELDING, Henry, 1707–54. **5574–95**

—— *Amelia.* 5585 5589

—— Bibs. 5575–8 5582 5587

—— Collns. 5578 5593

—— *Essay on eating.* 5592

—— *Institute of the pleas of the crown.* 5593

—— *Joseph Andrews.* 5588

—— *Juvenal.* 5591

—— Letters. 5581 5595

—— Libr. 5584

—— *Miscellanies.* 5579

—— *Norfolk lanthorn.* 5586

—— *On hunters and politicians.* 5586

—— *On the benefit of laughing.* 5586

—— *Physiogonomist's academy.* 5592

—— Ptg. 2524

—— Publ. 5587

—— Text. 292 5579–80 5585 5588–9 5591 5593

—— *The physiognomist.* 5586

—— *Tom Jones.* 5580 5582

—— —— Bibs. 5575

—— *Works.* 2524 5583 5585

FIFESHIRE–Ptg. **2823**

—— Publ. **3134**

FILDES, sir Samuel Luke, 1844–1927–Dickens's *Mystery of Edwin Drood.* 5384

—— Dickens's *Our mutual friend.* 5384

FILLINHAM, fl.1860?–Libr. 3662

FINANCIAL NEWS. 4266

FINCH, Ann, countess of Winchilsea, 1661–1720. **5596**

—— *Miscellany poems.* 5596

—— Publ. 5596

FINE PAPER *see* PAPER AND PAPERMAK-

ING, FINE.

FINGERPRINTS, BIBLIOGRAPHICAL. 243–4 246

FINZI, Gerald Raphael, 1901–56–Libr. 1524 4063

FIRBANK, Arthur Annesley Ronald, 1886–1926. **5597–8**

—— Bibs. 5597–8

FIREBRAND, The. 4139

FIREWORKS. **3817**

—— Bibs. 3817

FIRST BOOKS *see* BOOKS, FIRST.

FIRST EDITION CLUB, 1922–31. 7584

FIRST EDITIONS *see* EDITIONS, FIRST.

FISHER, mr., fl.1782–*Beauties of administration.* 639

FISHER, George, 1879– . 2442

FISHER, bp. John, 1459–1535. 6616

—— Publ. 6616

FISHER, Roy, 1930– . **5599**

—— Bibs. 5599

FISHER, Thomas, Rochester, fl.1764–86. 3282

FITZ PARK MUSEUM, Keswick–Collns. 7458

FITZGERALD, Edward, 1809–83. **5600**

FITZGERALD, Francis Scott Key, 1896–1940. 775

—— Bibs. 781

FITZMAURICE, George, 1878–1963. **5601**

FITZSIMON, Henry, 1566–1641–*Catalogus praecipuorum sanctorum Hiberniae.* 4432

—— Mss. 4432

FIVE SEASONS PRESS. 3075

FLAXMAN, John, 1755–1835–Illus. 4769

—— *The casket.* 4769

FLEECE PRESS, Wakefield, est.1984. 2946 3089

—— Bibs. 2946

FLEETWOOD, bp. William, 1656–1723–Ptg. 3036

—— *Sermon on the fast day.* 1045

—— *Sermons.* 3036

—— Text. 1045

FLEMING, Abraham, 1552?–1607. 3042

FLEMING, Albert, fl.1887. 6910

FLEMING, Ian Lancaster, 1908–64. **5602**

—— Bibs. 5602

—— Collns. 5602

FLETCHER, John, 1579–1625 *see also* BEAUMONT, Francis, 1584–1616 and John FLETCHER, 1579–1625. **5603–6**

—— Bibs. 5603

—— *Bloody brother.* 5604

—— *Sir John van Olden Barnavelt.* 5606

—— Text. 5604–6

—— *Wife for a month.* 5605

FLETCHER, John, 1729–85. **5607**

—— Collns. 5607

FLEURON, The. 3219

FLEURONS *see* TYPE AND TYPOGRAPHY–Flowers.

FLICHERE, Jean Guillaume de la, 1729–85 *see* FLETCHER, John, 1729–85.

FLINT, F.S., fl.1915–*Cadences.* 4566

FLINTHAM HALL, Notts.–Libr. 1751

FLINTSHIRE–Librs. **1641**

—— Paper. **2085**

FLODDEN FIELD. 4354

FLORIDA. STATE UNIVERSITY, Talahassee. LIBRARY–Collns. 686 4391

—— UNIVERSITY. BALDWIN LIBRARY–Collns. 3429 3453

FLOWER, Francis, fl.1560–96. 7414

FLOWER BOOKS. **3818**

FLYING STATIONERS *see* BOOKSELLERS, ITINERANT.

FOGES, Wolfgang, 1910–86. 3248

FOG'S WEEKLY JOURNAL. 5586

FOLEY, Samuel, 1655–95–Libr. 4307

FOLGER SHAKESPEARE LIBRARY, Washington, D.C. 7020 7026

—— Collns. 499 3552 4198 7007 7013

FOLIATION. 3017

FOLIO SOCIETY, est.1947. **2369–70**

—— Bibs. 2369 3923

—— Illus. 3923

FOLKLORE. **3819**

—— Bibs. 3819

—— AND LITERATURE–Bibs. 3819

FOOT, Isaac, 1888–1960–Libr. 1447

FOOTBALL–Collns. 4511

FOOTBALL PROGRAMMES *see* PROGRAMMES, FOOTBALL.

FOOTE, Charles Benjamin, fl.1894–Libr. 5886

FOOTE, Samuel, 1720–77. **5608**

—— Bibs. 5608

—— Publ. 2365

FOOTNOTES. 3014

FORBES, Edward, 1815–54. 4107

FORBES, J.D., 1809–68–Libr. 4471

FORD, Ford Madox (formerly Hueffer), 1873–1939. **5609–14**

—— Bibs. 697 701 5194 5609–11

tions with Carlyle. 4983
FROXFIELD, Wilts.–Bndng. 2657–60
FRYE, Bartholomew, Manchester, fl.1816–24. 1187 1222
FRYE, Gerhard Bartholomaüs, fl.1783. 1222
FULLER, S. AND J., fl.1810. 3485
FULTON, Robert (Am. engr. 18–19th cent.). 2700
FURNESS, Horace Howard, 1833–1912. 7087
FURNISS, Harry, 1854–1925. 3878
—— Bibs. 3878
FURNIVAL BOOKS (Joiner and Steele)–Bibs. 3379
FURNIVALL, Frederick James, 1825–1910–Chaucer's *Canterbury tales.* 5062
FUSELI, Henry (Johann Heinrich Fuessli), 1741–1825–Pope's *Rape of the lock.* 6771
FUTURISM–Bibs. 696 705 709

G., R., fl.1600–*Albion's queen.* 3715
GABLER, Hans Walter, 1931–Joyce's *Ulysses.* 6149 6176 6194 6196–7
GAELIC BOOKS. 3046
—— Collns. 1473
GAELIC NEWSPAPERS *see* NEWSPAPERS, GAELIC.
GAINSBOROUGH, Lincs.–Bksllng. 2002
—— Librs. 1697
—— Ptg. 2849
GAISFORD, Thomas, 1779–1855–Libr. 1553
GALEN, 129–99?–*Questionary of surgeons.* 4043
GALLEY CLUB, London. 3216
GALLEY PROOFS *see* PROOFS, GALLEY.
GALSWORTHY, John, 1867–1933. **5638–40**
—— Bibs. 701 5638
—— Collns. 5639–40
—— Text. 3629
GALT, John, 1779–1839. **5641–2**
—— Publ. 5641
—— *Ringan Gilhaize.* 5642
—— Text. 5642
GALWAY–Bksllng. **1998**
—— Librs. **1642**
GANT, William, Bristol, 1734–81. 1999
GAOL LITERATURE–Exeter. 616
—— 1701–1800. 616
GARDEMAU, Balthazar, 1656?–1739–Libr. 1416

GARDENER'S PASSETAUNCE, The, c.1512. 513
GARDENING AND GARDENS. **3830–7**
—— Bibs. 3830–2
—— Collns. 1881 3831 3833–5
—— Ireland–Bibs. 3391
—— 1801–1900. 3836
GARDINER, sir Alan Henderson, 1879–1963–*Egyptian grammar.* 3236
GARDINER, Alfred George, 1866–1946. 4284
GARDINER, Charles Wrey, 1901–81. 2821
GARDNER, Anthony, Chiddingfold, 1887– . 1235
GARDNER, dame Helen Louise, 1908–86. **5643**
—— Bibs. 5643
GARDNER, Thomas, fl.1735–47. 3152
GARDNER, Willoughby, 1860–1953–Libr. 1460
GARIOCH, Robert, *pseud. of* Robert Garioch Sutherland, 1909– . **4387**
—— Bibs. 4387
—— Publ. 3180
GARLAND OF RACHEL, 1881. 671
GARNER, William, Kent, fl.1749?–1827. 1660
GARNETT, David, 1892–1981. **5644**
—— Bibs. 5644
—— Libr. 5644
GARNETT, Edward, 1868–1937–Lawrence's *Sons and lovers.* 6330
—— Libr. 5226
GARNETT, Jeremiah, Manchester, 1793–1870. 4151
GARNETT, Rachel ('Ray') Alice (Marshall), 1891–1940. 3924
GARNETT, Richard, 1835–1906. **5645**
GARNETT FAMILY–Bibs. 5644
GARRARD, Apsley Cherry-, 1886–1959. 1448
GARRATT, John Geoffrey, 1914–87. 189
GARRICK, David, 1717–79. **5646–7**
—— Bibs. 5646–7
—— Collns. 7030
—— Libr. 3563 3567
—— Text. 4226
GARROW, Joseph, 1789–1857–Dante's *Vita nuova.* 766
GARTH, sir Samuel, 1661–1719. **5648**
—— Bibs. 5648
GARWOOD, Tirzah, 1908–51. 3957
GASCOYNE, David Emery, 1916– . **5649**

BURG.
GUTHRIE, James Joshua, 1874–1952. 2577
GUTHRIE, William Tyrone, 1900– –Libr. 1527
GWATKIN, Henry Melvill, 1844–1916–Libr. 1462
GWENT–Islwyn–Bibs. 897
—— Torfaen–Bibs. 898
GWERNHAYLOD, Flint.–Paper. 2147
GWYNN, John, 1811–89. 1208
GWYNN FAMILY, est.1842. 1208
GYBBE, William, fl.1443–94. 4349

HABERLY, Lloyd, 1896–1981. 2437
HACKET, bp. John, 1592–1670. 792
HADDINGTON, East Lothian–Librs. 1411
HADDO HOUSE, Ellen, Aber.–Libr. 1490
HADDON, Alfred Cort, 1855–1940–Libr. 1551
HAEGHEN, Ferdinand van der, 1830–1913. 150
HAGADOT–Bibs. 3981
HAGGARD, sir Henry Rider, 1856–1925. **5788–93**
—— *Allan Quatermain.* 5793
—— Bibs. 5788–91 5793
—— Collns. 5791
—— *King Solomon's mines.* 5792
HAGLEY HALL, Worcs.–Libr. 1810
HAGUE, Louis, 1806–85. 1160
HAGUE, The, Netherlands–Publ. 3579
HAGUE AND GILL, Speen, Berks., 1905–80–1. 2386 2401
HAKLUYT, Richard, 1552?–1616. **5794**
—— Bibs. 5794
HALES, Stephen, 1677–1761. **5795**
—— Bibs. 5795
—— *Friendly admonition to the drinkers.* 5795
HALIFAX, George Savile, marquis of, 1633–95 see SAVILE, George, marquis of Halifax, 1633–95.
HALIFAX, Yorks.–Bksllng. 4779
—— Bndng. 1239
—— Librs. 1837
HALL, Anna Maria (Fielding), 1800–81. **5796**
—— Collns. 5796
HALL, John Vine, Maidstone, 1774–1860. 2001
HALL, bp. Joseph, 1574–1656. **5797–8**

—— *Mundus alter idem.* 5797
—— Ptg. 5797
HALL, Thomas, 1610–65–Libr. 1813
HALLAM, Arthur Henry, 1811–33. **5799**
—— *Materials for a life of A.T.* 5799
—— Publ. 5799
HALL HARDING, pprmkrs., est.1853. 2099
HAMILTON, ltd., Stafford, fl.1945. 3361
HAMILTON, Charles Harod St. John, 1876–1961–*Adventures of Herlock Sholmes.* 5476
—— —— Bibs. 5476
HAMILTON, HAMISH, ltd., est.1931 see HAMISH HAMILTON, ltd., est.1931.
HAMILTON, Hamish, 1900–88. 3148
HAMILTON, John Arthur, 1845–1924–*Manuscript in a red box.* 3286
HAMILTON, Patrick, 1904–62. **5800**
—— Publ. 5800
HAMILTON, Robert, Edinburgh, fl.1809–30. 1227
HAMILTON, William, 1751–1801. 4787
HAMISH HAMILTON, ltd., est.1931. 3148
HAMMETT, Dashiell, 1894–1961–Bibs. 782
HAMPDEN PRESS, 1929–45. 2871
—— Bibs. 2871
HAMPSHIRE. **801**
—— Bibs. 801
—— Librs. **1651–3**
—— New forest–Bibs. 801
—— Paper. **2086**
—— Ptg. **2834**
—— COUNTY LIBRARY. SOUTHAMPTON REFERENCE LIBRARY–Collns. 4021
HAMPSHIRE BOOK CLUB. 1653
HANBOROUGH PUBLISHING COMPANY, ltd., est.1942. 3361
HAND AND FLOWER PRESS, 1940–64. 2859
HANDBOOKS–Bibs. 2581
HAND COLOURING see COLOURING, HAND.
HANDEL, George Frederick, 1685–1759. **5801–4**
—— Bibs. 5801
—— Mss. 5802
—— Ptg. 5804
—— Text. 5803
—— *Works.* 3210
HANDMADE PAPER see PAPER AND PAPER-MAKING, HAND.
HAND PRESSES see PRESSES (AS MACHINES), HAND.

HANDWRITING. 46
——, FORGED *see* FORGERIES, HAND-
WRITING.
HANK JANSON *see* FRANCIS, Stephen
Daniel, 1917– .
HANKEY, Frederick, fl.1828?–78. 3700
HANLEY, James, 1901–85. **5805–6**
—— Bibs. 5805
—— Collns. 5806
HANOVER SQUARE CHAPEL, London.
LIBRARY. 1855
HANSARD, Thomas Curzon, 1776–1833.
2874
HARBINGER. 4747
HARDING, Denys Wyatt, 1906– . **5807**
—— Bibs. 5807
HARDWICKE, Robert, 1822–1875. 3165
3175
HARDWICKE'S SCIENCE–GOSSIP. 4472
HARDY, J.C., fl.1982–Libr. 3719
HARDY, Thomas, 1840–1928. **5808–31**
—— Bibs. 701 5808–13 5823 5826
—— Collns. 5811 5823
—— *Complete poems.* 5822
—— *Far from the madding crowd.* 5818
—— Illus. 5815
—— *Jude the obscure.* 5825 5828
—— Libr. 5814
—— Map of Wessex. 5819
—— Mss. 5822
—— *Pair of blue eyes.* 5820
—— Publ. 5817 5821 5826–7
—— *Return of the native.* 5825
—— *Spectre of the real.* 5830
—— *Tess of the D'Urbervilles.* 3785 5816 5821
5825
—— Text. 5816 5818–20 5822 5824–5
5829–31
—— *The trumpet-major.* 5825 5831
—— *Two on a tower.* 5825
—— *Under the greenwood tree.* 5825
HARE, Henry, 2d baron Coleraine, 1636–
1708. **5832**
HARE, Julian Charles, 1795–1855–Libr.
1538
HARINGTON, John, baron Harington of
Exton, d.1613–Libr. 1779
HARINGTON, sir John, 1561–1612. 2173
5833–9 7408 7418
—— Ariosto's *Orlando furioso.* 5835 5837
—— Bibs. 5833
—— Handwr. 5839

—— Mss. 5834 5836 5838
—— *Of the death of master Devereaux.* 5834
—— Ptg. 5837
—— Sidney's *Arcadia.* 7409
—— *Supply or addition.* 5836
—— Virgil's *Aeneid.* 5839
HARLEY, Robert, 1st earl of Oxford, 1661–
1724. **5840** 7555
—— Libr. 206 3311
—— Mss. 5840
HARMONDSWORTH, Middlesex–Publ.
2596–644
—— —— Bibs. 2578–95
HARMSWORTH, Alfred, 1st viscount North-
cliffe, 1865–1922. 4280 4282
HARMSWORTH, Cecil, 1st baron Harm-
sworth, 1869–1948. 4282
HARMSWORTH, Harold, 1st viscount Ro-
thermere, 1868–1940. 4282
HARMSWORTH, sir Hildebrand, 1872–
1929. 4282
HARMSWORTH, sir Robert Leicester,
1870–1937. 4282
—— Libr. 4914
HARMSWORTH MAGAZINE–Bibs. 3802
HARNEY, George Julian, 1817–97–Libr.
3636
HARP OF ZION–Publ. 4386
HARPER, Robert, fl.1701–67?–Libr. 4328
HARPER AND BROS, N.Y.–James's *The Amer-
ican.* 6031
HARRIS, sir Augustus Henry Glossop, 1852–
96–Libr. 4338
HARRIS, John, 1756–1846. **2447–9** 3454
3460
—— Bibs. 2447–9
HARRIS, John Wyndham Parkes Lucas
Benyon, 1903–69 *see* WYNDHAM, John,
pseud.
HARRIS, Thomas, fl.1741–53. 5325
HARRISON, Frederic, 1831–1923. **5841**
—— Bibs. 5841
HARRISON, Tony, 1937– . **5842**
—— Bibs. 5842
*HARRIS'S LIST OF COVENT GARDEN LA-
DIES.* 645 649
HARRY RANSOM HUMANITIES RE-
SEARCH CENTER *see* TEXAS. UNIVER-
SITY AT AUSTIN. HARRY RANSOM
HUMANITIES RESEARCH CENTER.
HART, Thomas Copeman, fl.1920–84. 6801
HART, William Matthew, 1830–1908. 3355

HEINEMANN, William, 1863–1920. **2451–2**
—— Letters. 2451
HEINEMANN EDUCATIONAL BOOKS, est.1961. 2452
HELDMANN, Richard Bernard, 1857–1915 *see* MARSH, Richard, *pseud.*
HELEN'S TOWER, Clandeboy. 1328
HELLESDON, Norf.–Paper. 2113
HELLIER, sir Samuel, 1736–84–Libr. 1897
HELPSTON, Cambs.–Paper. 2069
HELSHAM, Samuel, Dublin, fl.1681–9. 992
HELSINKI. UNIVERSITY. LIBRARY–Collns. 1464
HELVÉTIUS, Claude Adrien, 1715–71–*De l'homme.* 3176
—— Publ. 3176
HEMERDON HOUSE, Plymton–Libr. 1609
HEMINGE, John, fl.1556–1630. 7048
HENDERSON, Archibal, fl.1911–*Life of Shaw.* 7366
HENLEY, Berks.–Librs. 1577
HENNIKER, Florence, *pseud. of* Florence Ellen Hungerford (Milnes) Major, 1855–1923. 5830
HENREY, Blanche Elizabeth Edith, 1906–83. 171
HENRY V, king of England, 1387–1422–Libr. 1546
HENRY ALLNUTT AND SON, pprmkrs., Maidstone, Kent. 2069
HENRY E. HUNTINGTON LIBRARY AND ART GALLERY, San Marino, Calif.–Collns. 441 3572 4369 4733 4799 6073 6523 7914 7937
HENRYSON, Robert, 1430?–1506? **5870–1**
—— Bibs. 905 5870
—— *Testament of Cresseid.* 5871
—— Text. 5871
HENSLOWE, Philip, d.1616–*Diary.* 5027
HENTY, George Alfred, 1832–1902. **5872–3**
—— Bibs. 5872–3
—— Collns. 5872
HEPTINSTALL, W., fl.1795–*Bible.* 3325
HERALDRY. **3842–5**
—— Bibs. 3842
—— Collns. 3842
—— Libr. 1879
—— Mss.–Bibs. 3842
HERBALS. **3846**
HERBERT, sir Alan Patrick, 1890–1971. **5874**
—— Bibs. 5874

—— Collns. 5874
HERBERT, Edward, 1st baron Herbert of Cherbury, 1583–1648. **5875–6**
—— Bibs. 5876
—— Libr. 5875
HERBERT, George, 1593–1633. 1149 **5877–88**
—— Bibs. 5877–80
—— Collns. 5886
—— Mss. 5883–5
—— *Outlandish recreations.* 5888
—— Publ. 3108
—— Text. 5881–2 5884 5887
—— *The temple.* 3108 5881–3 5886
—— *To the lord chancellor.* 5885
HERBERT, Mary (Sidney), countess of Pembroke, 1561–1621. 2172 **5889–91**
—— Bibs. 5889
—— *Psalms.* 5890
—— Text. 5890
HEREFORD, Herefs.–Bndng. 1185
—— Librs. 1654–5 2943
—— CATHEDRAL. LIBRARY. 1654–5
—— —— —— Collns. 506 1656
HEREFORDSHIRE. **802**
—— Bibs. 802
—— Bndng. **1185**
—— Collns. 802
—— Librs. **1654–6**
—— COUNTY LIBRARIES–Collns. 802
HERING, Charles Ernst Christian, 1764–1815. 1198
HERMETIC ORDER OF THE GOLDEN DAWN–Bibs. 7965
—— Mss. 7995
HERRICK, Robert, 1591–1674. **5892–6**
—— Bibs. 5892–5
—— Illus. 5896
—— Publ. 2362
—— Text. 4224
HERRINGMAN, Henry, 1627–8–1704–Davenant's *Law against lovers.* 5301
HERTFORD, Herts.–Paper. 2087
HERTFORDSHIRE. **803**
—— Albury–Bibs. 803
—— Bibs. 803
—— Newspapers. **4142**
—— Paper. **2087**
—— Ptg. **2835–6**
HEWETT, Christopher, 1938–1983. 3161 3164
HEWETT, Thomas, d.1773–Libr. 1802

JULIAN, John, 1839–1913–Libr. 3853
JUNIUS, Franciscus, 1589–1677–*Cædmonis monachi paraphrasis*. 1494
JUNIUS, *pseud.* **6211–15**
—— Bibs. 6211–12
JUSTIFICATION. 226
JUVENILE LIBRARY. 3456

KAIN, Richard M., fl.1934–84–Libr. 6187
KANSAS. UNIVERSITY. KENNETH SPENCER RESEARCH LIBRARY–Collns. 486 663 3831 5706 6153
KARSLAKE, Frank, 1851–1920. 2446
KAUFFER, Edward McKnight, 1890–1954– Bibs. 3858
KAVANAGH, Patrick Joseph Gregory, 1931– . **6216–17**
KEANE, Charles, 1823–91. 3941
KEATLEY TRUST. LIBRARY. 1248
KEATS, John, 1795–1821. **6218–27**
—— Bibs. 650 4375 6218–21
—— *Endymion*. 6224
—— Letters–Bibs. 6221
—— Libr. 6222
—— *Ode on indolence*. 6227
—— *Poems*. 6225
—— Ptg. 6225
—— Publ. 6226
—— Text. 6223–7
KEBELL, Thomas, 1439?–1500–Libr. 1421
KEEPSAKE PRESS, Richmond, Surrey, est.1951. 2925 3071
KEEPSAKES. 3694–5
KELE, John, fl.1552–71. 2866
KELE, Richard, fl.1546–52. 2866
KELLY, Hugh, 1739–77. 4213 **6228**
—— Bibs. 6228
KELMSCOTT MANOR, Oxon.–Collns. 2483
KELMSCOTT PRESS, Hammersmith, 1891– 8. **2477–90** 3080
—— Bibs. 2477 2490
—— Chaucer's *Canterbury tales*. 2485
—— Collns. 2477 2490
—— Type. 2487
KEMPE, Margery, fl.1373–1440–Ptg. 2747
—— *Short treatise of contemplation*. 2747
KEMPE, William, fl.1580–93. 7040
KEMPLAY, Christopher, Leeds, fl.1804–72. 4192
KEMSLEY, James Gomer Berry, 1st viscount,

1883–1968 *see* BERRY, James Gomer, 1st viscount Kemsley, 1883–1968.
KENDAL, Westm.–Librs. 1822
—— Newspapers. 4189
—— Paper. 1083
—— Ptg. 7911
—— GRAMMAR SCHOOL. SANDES LIBRARY–Collns. 1822
KENDAL CHRONICLE. 4189
KENDREW, James, York, 1772–1841. **2492– 3**
—— Bibs. 2492
KENNEDY, Richard, 1911?–89. 2464 2469
KENNETH RITCHIE WIMBLEDON LIBRARY *see* WIMBLEDON LAWN TENNIS MUSEUM, London. KENNETH RITCHIE WIMBLEDON LIBRARY.
KENNETT, bp. White, 1660–1728. 405 3512
KENRICK, John Arthur, West Bromwich, 1830–1926. 2919
KENRICK, William, 1725?–79. 7434
KENRICK AND JEFFERSON, West Bromwich, est.1878. 2919
KENSINGTON, London *see* LONDON. KENSINGTON.
KENSINGTON BOOK SOCIETY, London, fl.1826 *see* LONDON. KENSINGTON BOOK SOCIETY, fl.1826.
KENT. **804**
—— Bibs. 804
—— Bksllng. **2001**
—— Booktrade. **998–9** 1070 1083
—— Librs. **1660–6** 1840
—— Newspapers. **4147–8**
—— —— Bibs. 4147
—— Paper. **2088–91**
—— Ptg. **2837–41**
—— ARCHIVE OFFICE, Canterbury–Collns. 4630
—— UNIVERSITY. LIBRARY–Collns. 3610
KENT, William, 1684?–1748. 3968
KENTUCKY. UNIVERSITY. LIBRARY–Collns. 672 682 6264
—— —— MARGARET I. KING LIBRARY– Collns. 654 6546 6565 6887 7917
KENYON, sir Frederick George, 1863–1952. 1651
KER, John, 3d duke of Roxburgh, 1714– 1804–Libr. 3311
KER, Neil Ripley, 1908–82. 174 176–8
—— Bibs. 493
KERRICH, Thomas, 1748–1828–Libr. 791

NOVER SQUARE CHAPEL, London.
—— HARMONDSWORTH *see* HARMONDSWORTH, Middlesex.
—— HEYTHROP COLLEGE *see* HEYTHROP COLLEGE, London. LIBRARY.
—— KENSINGTON–Librs. 1705 1713 1722
—— KENSINGTON BOOK SOCIETY, fl.1826. 1705
—— LAMBETH–Librs. 1712 1715 1724
—— —— PUBLIC LIBRARY. 4619
—— LAMBETH PALACE. LIBRARY. 1712 1724
—— —— —— Collns. 1715 3892
—— LEIGHTON HOUSE. 1255–6
—— LIBRARIES–Collns. 810
—— LINCOLN'S INN. LIBRARY–Collns. 4307
—— LINNEAN SOCIETY *see* LINNEAN SOCIETY OF LONDON.
—— LIVERY COMPANIES–Bibs. 811 814
—— LONDON BRIDGE. 1005
—— MEDICAL SOCIETY *see* MEDICAL SOCIETY OF LONDON, est.1773.
—— MUSEUM OF LONDON–Collns. 3648
—— NATIONAL MARITIME MUSEUM *see* NATIONAL MARITIME MUSEUM, Greenwich.
—— NEW ELTHAM–Ptg. 2876
—— OSLER CLUB *see* OSLER CLUB, London, est.1928.
—— PADDINGTON–Librs. 1710
—— PATERNOSTER ROW. 1006
—— POETRY SOCIETY *see* POETRY SOCIETY, London.
—— POULTRY–Bksllng. 2866
—— PRIMROSE HILL–Ptg. 2862
—— —— Ptg.–Bibs. 2850
—— RICHMOND *see* RICHMOND, Surrey.
—— ROYAL COLLEGE OF OBSTETRICIANS AND GYNÆCOLOGISTS *see* ROYAL COLLEGE OF OBSTETRICIANS AND GYNÆCOLOGISTS, London.
—— ROYAL COMMONWEALTH SOCIETY *see* ROYAL COMMONWEALTH SOCIETY, London.
—— ROYAL INSTITUTE OF BRITISH ARCHITECTS *see* ROYAL INSTITUTE OF BRITISH ARCHITECTS, London.
—— SAINT PANCRAS–Collns. 815
—— SAINT PAUL'S CROSS–Bibs. 4481
—— SAINT PAUL'S SCHOOL. LIBRARY–Collns. 5109
—— —— Collns. 1719
—— SCHOOL OF PHOTOENGRAVING AND LITHOGRAPHY. 2873
—— SCIENCE MUSEUM–Collns. 3005 3023
—— SOUTHWARK. SAINT SAVIOUR'S CHURCH–Collns. 816
—— SYDENHAM–Librs. 1840
—— SYDENHAM DISTRICT MEDICAL SOCIETY BOOK CLUB. 1840
—— THAMES RIVER *see* RIVER THAMES.
—— TWICKENHAM. 7737
—— —— Librs. 1721
—— UNIVERSITY. IMPERIAL COLLEGE OF SCIENCE AND TECHNOLOGY–Collns. 4516
—— —— JEWS' COLLEGE. LIBRARY. 1717
—— —— LIBRARIES–Collns. 3301 7988
—— —— SCHOOL OF SLAVONIC AND EAST EUROPEAN STUDIES. LIBRARY–Collns. 1455
—— —— UNIVERSITY COLLEGE. JAMES JOYCE CENTRE–Collns. 6143
—— —— —— LIBRARY–Collns. 4703 5844 6140 6728
—— —— —— MOCATTA LIBRARY. 1706
—— —— —— SCHOOL OF LIBRARY, ARCHIVE AND INFORMATION STUDIES. 275
—— —— WYE COLLEGE, Ashford. LIBRARY–Collns. 1663
—— WANDSWORTH–Paper. 2119
—— WELLCOME INSTITUTE FOR THE HISTORY OF MEDICINE *see* WELLCOME INSTITUTE FOR THE HISTORY OF MEDICINE, London.
—— WESTMINSTER–Ptg.–Bibs. 2681
—— —— WESTMINSTER LIBRARY, fl.1789-1822. 1720
—— WESTMINSTER ABBEY. CHAPEL ROYAL–Collns. 4078
—— —— LIBRARY–Collns. 513 1242 2180
—— WOOLWICH–Librs. 1840
LONDON AND WESTMINSTER MAGAZINE. 4261
LONDON COURANT. 4160
LONDON GAZETTE. 4161 4163 7489
—— Ptg. 4165
LONDON LIBRARY. 4978–9 5298
LONDON LIBRARY SOCIETY, fl.1785-1801. 1716 1720
LONDON MAGAZINE–Bibs. 3802
—— *Essays on various subjects*–Bibs. 3723

—— Yeats. 7975

REYNOLDES, Richard, fl.1563–71–*Chronicle of all the noble emperors.* 508

—— Ptg. 508

REYNOLDS, George William Macarthur, 1814–79. 4261 **6833–4**

—— Bibs. 6833

—— Mss. 6834

REYNOLDS, John, fl.1694–1743. 2162

—— Mela's *De situ orbis.* 2162

REYNOLDS, Paul Revere, 1904–88. 7365

RHETORIC. **4449–59**

—— Bibs. 4449–59

—— Scotland–Bibs. 4449–50

—— 1475–1640–Bibs. 4451 4455

—— 1475–1700–Bibs. 4456–7

—— 1641–1700–Bibs. 4452 4454

—— 1701–1800–Bibs. 4449–50 4452

—— 1801–1900–Bibs. 4449–50 4453

RHODE ISLAND. SCHOOL OF DESIGN. MUSEUM OF ART–Collns. 3882 3893

RHYS, Ernest Percival, 1859–1946. **6835**

—— Bibs. 6835

RHYS, Jean, *pseud. of* Ella Gwendolen Rees Williams, 1890–1979. **6836–41**

—— Bibs. 6836–9

—— Collns. 6839

—— Mss. 6841

—— *Rapunzel Rapunzel.* 6840

—— Text. 6840

—— *Wide Sargasso sea.* 6841

RHYS, John David, 1534–1609–*Cambro-brytannicae Cymraecaeve linguae institutiones et rudimenta.* 3051

RICE, Samuel James, 1843–82–Publ. 4713

RICHARD, Edward, 1714–77–Librs. 1458

RICHARD DE BURY, bp., 1287–1342? 1465

RICHARDS, Thomas Franklin Grant, 1872–1948. **2669**

—— Mss. 2668 3124

RICHARDS, William Urmston Searle, 1856–96?. 3844

RICHARDSON, Samuel, 1689–1761. 2366 **6842–9**

—— Bibs. 6842–3

—— *Clarissa.* 6844 6846–7 6849

—— Collns. 6849

—— Libr. 6848

—— Mss. 6845

—— Text. 6844 6846–7

RICHMOND, JOHN, ltd., 1912–29 *see* JOHN RICHMOND, ltd., 1912–29.

RICHMOND, Surrey. LIBRARIES–Collns. 6765

—— Ptg. 2925 3071

RICKETTS, Charles de Sousy, 1866–1931. 2729 **6850**

—— Letters. 6850

RICKWOOD, John Edgell, 1898– . **6851**

—— Bibs. 700 6851

RIDDELL, Maria, 1776–1818. **6852**

—— Libr. 6852

RIDGWAY'S MILITANT WEEKLY (U.S.). 5211

RIDLER, William, 1909–80. 154

—— Libr. 3063 3227

RIGHTS OF WAY–Collns. 4524

RING, BOOKSELLERS' *see* BOOKSELLERS' RING.

RIPPEY, Arthur Gordon, 1907– –Libr. 6094–5

RITCHIE, Anne Isabella (Thackeray), lady, 1837–1919. **6853–5**

—— Bibs. 6853–4

—— Collns. 6855

RIVER THAMES–Bibs. 786

—— Ptg. 3695

ROBERTS, sir Charles George Douglas, 1860–1945–Shelley's *Adonais and Alastor.* 7385

ROBERTS, John, Clerkenwell, est.1898. 2856

ROBERTS, John, Clerkenwell, 1898–1982. 2872 3073

ROBERTS, Katherine ('Kate'), 1891– –Bibs. 881

ROBERTS, Michael, 1902–48. **6856**

—— Bibs. 6856

ROBERTS, Michael, fl.1935–88–Libr. 1554

ROBERTS, Morley, 1857–1942. **6857**

—— Bibs. 6857

ROBERTS, sir Sydney Castle, 1889–1966. 2259

ROBERTS, Warren Everett, 1924– –Libr. 6339

ROBERTSON, George, 1860–1930. 2293

ROBERTSON, J. AND M., bksllrs., Glasgow, fl.1798. 3310

ROBERTSON, John McKinnon, 1856–1933. **6858**

—— Bibs. 6858

ROBERTSON, Thomas William, 1829–71. **6859–60**

—— Bibs. 6859–60

SPORTS AND RECREATIONS. **4492–514**
—— Bibs. 4492–7 4499–503
—— Illus.–Bibs. 4500
SPOTSWOOD, William, Dublin, fl.1774–84. 3135
SPRANGE, Jasper, Tunbridge Wells, fl.1780–1814. 2837
SPRIGG, Christopher St.John, 1907–37 *see* CAUDWELL, Christopher, *pseud.*
SPRINGFIELD MILL, Totnes, Devon. 2060
SPY, The. 5919
SQUIBB, Lawrence, 1604–74–*Book of all the several officers.* 621
SQUIRE, William, 1809–90–Cromwell's *Letters.* 4985
SQUIRE, William Barclay, 1855–1927–Libr. 4335
STABLES, William Gordon, 1840–1910. **7479**
—— Bibs. 7479
STAFFORD, Staffs.–Bksllng. 1984
—— Publ. 3361
STAFFORDSHIRE–Librs. **1795–8**
—— Ptg. **2919–20**
STAGE-DIRECTIONS *see* EDITING–Stage-directions.
STAGING–Bibs. 3533
STAINFORTH, Francis John, fl.1861–Libr. 589
STAMFORD, Lincs.–Newspapers. 4155 4157
—— —— Bibs. 4143
STAMPS, COPYRIGHT *see* COPYRIGHT STAMPS.
——, POSTAGE. 5397
—— Newspapers. 3683
STANBROOK ABBEY PRESS, Callow End, Worcs., est.1876. **2697**
STANDARDISATION *see* EDITING–Standardisation.
STANFIELD, Clarkson, 1793–1867–Dickens's Christmas books. 5384
STANFORD, Edward, 1827–1904. 2854
STANFORD HALL, Leics.–Libr. 1439
STANFORD UNIVERSITY. LIBRARY–Collns. 5680
STANHOPE, Charles, 3d earl Stanhope, 1753–1816. **2698–700**
STANHOPE, Philip Dormer, 4th earl of Chesterfield, 1694–1773. **7480**
STANHOPE, Philip Henry, 5th earl Stanhope, 1805–75. 4615
STANHOPE, sir Edward, 1546?–1608. 1583

STANLEY, John, 1713–86–*Teraminta.* 4092
—— Text. 4092
STANLEY MORISON ROOM *see* CAMBRIDGE, Cambs. UNIVERSITY. LIBRARY. STANLEY MORISON ROOM.
STANNFORD, Henry, fl.1570–1616–Libr. 1522
STANSBY, William, fl.1597–1639. **2701–3**
—— Jonson's *Works.* 2703
STANTON, Blair Hughes-, 1902–81. 2437 2535 3919
—— Bibs. 3919
STAPLEDON, William Olaf, 1886–1950. **7481–3**
—— Bibs. 7481–2
—— *Last and first men.* 7483
—— Mss. 7483
STAPLES, John Alexander, fl.1758–1814–*Tour in Ireland.* 4539
STAR, The. 4160
STARK, dame Freya Madeline (mrs. S.H. Perowne), 1893–1993. **7484**
—— Bibs. 7484
—— Collns. 7484
STATIONERS, RUNNING *see* BOOKSELLERS, ITINERANT.
STATIONERS' COMPANIES. 955
STATIONERS' COMPANY, London, est.1557. 197 955 992 1076 1126 2196 2259 **2704–13** 2758 7875
—— Almanacs. 3281 3283–4
—— Bibs. 2707 2711
—— Mss. 2711 2713
—— *Registers, etc.* 549 2707
STATUTES–Bibs. 961
—— Ptg. 3999
—— 1475–1640. 3999
—— —— Bibs. 3999
STAUNTON, Howard, 1810–74–Shakespeare's *Plays.* 7080
STAVELEY, Ronald, fl.1936–80. 139
STEAD, William Thomas, 1849–1912. **7485–7**
—— Bibs. 7485
—— *Masterpiece library.* 7486
STEELE, sir Richard, 1672–1729. **7488–90**
—— Bibs. 7488
—— *Poetical miscellanies.* 7490
—— Ptg. 7490
STEEL ENGRAVING/S *see* ENGRAVING/S, STEEL.
STEEPLE ASHTON, Wilts.–Librs. 1828

TEXAS. TECHNOLOGICAL UNIVERSITY, Lubbock. LIBRARY–Collns. 5233 5244 5444 5450
—— UNIVERSITY AT AUSTIN. HARRY RANSOM HUMANITIES RESEARCH CENTER–Collns. 4830 4995
—— —— HUMANITIES RESEARCH CENTER–Collns. 700 1200 1429 2389–90 3787 4370 4667 4958 5939 6144 6156 6160 6163 6174 6339 6379 6393 6855 6882 7021 7028 7674 7765 7780 7977
'TEXT'. 123 125 130 132
TEXT. 97 115
TEXTBOOKS–Publ. 3115
TEXTUAL AUTHORITY *see* AUTHORITY, TEXTUAL.
—— COLLATON *see* COLLATION, TEXTUAL.
TEXTUAL CRITICISM AND EDITING. 47 51 54 **276–388**
—— Aids and devices. 389–93
—— Bibs. 28 276–7
—— Collating machines. 397–8
—— Copy-text. 376
—— Intention. 4798
—— Manuals. 344 350 354
—— Stemmatics. 317–8
—— 1801–1900. 325 372
THACKERAY, William, fl.1664–92. 3419
—— Publ. 2686
THACKERAY, William Makepeace, 1811–63. 4261 **7631–42**
—— *Adventures of Philip.* 7639
—— Bibs. 7631
—— *English humourists.* 7638
—— *Esmond.* 7634
—— *Henry Esmond.* 3785
—— *History of Samuel Titmarsh.* 7633
—— Illus. 7632 7635
—— Ptg. 7637 7640
—— Publ. 7633–4 7637–9
—— Text. 296 7633–4 7636–7 7640 7642
—— *The Newcomes.* 7635
—— *Vanity fair.* 7632 7636–7 7640 7642
—— AS ILLUSTRATOR. 5384
THAMES RIVER *see* RIVER THAMES.
THAXTED, Essex.–Ptg. 2817–8 2820 2822 3088 3255 3262
THEATRE–Collns. 3612
—— 1475–1700–Bibs. 3564
—— 1641–1700–Bibs. 3593
—— —— Collns. 3574

—— 1701–1800–Bibs. 3593
—— —— Collns. 3574
—— 1801–1900–Bibs. 3603
—— —— Collns. 3574
—— 1901–2000–Bibs. 3623 3626
—, PRIVATE–Collns. 4337
—— PROGRAMMES *see* PROGRAMMES, THEATRE.
THEATRICAL BIOGRAPHIES *see* BIOGRAPHIES AND AUTOBIOGRAPHIES, THEATRICAL.
—— COMPANIES, TOURING–Bibs. 3537
THEATRICAL MAGAZINE–Bibs. 3586
—— NEWSPAPERS AND PERIODICALS *see* NEWSPAPERS AND PERIODICALS, THEATRICAL.
THEOBALD, Lewis, 1688–1744. **7643–6**
—— Shakespeare's *Plays.* 7073 7644–5 7753
—— Text. 7073 7643
—— *The double falsehood.* 7643–5
THEOLOGICAL LIBRARIES *see* LIBRARIES, THEOLOGICAL.
THESES–Bibs. 6305 6918 6923
—— Bndng. 1226
THETFORD, Norf.–Paper. 2113
THIEVES, BOOK *see* BOOK THIEVES.
THOMAS, Alan G., d.1992. 1307
THOMAS, Dylan Marlais, 1914–53. **7647–50**
—— Bibs. 7647 7650
—— Collns. 7650
—— Mss. 7648–9
—— *Under Milk wood.* 7648–9
THOMAS, J. AND E., AND GREEN, Wooburn Green, Bucks. *see* J. AND E. THOMAS AND GREEN, pprmkrs., Wooburn Green, Bucks.
THOMAS, Owen, 1812–91–Libr. 1463
THOMAS, sir Percy, 1883–1969–Bibs. 3294
THOMAS, Philip Edward, 1878–1917. **7651–3**
—— Bibs. 7651
—— Collns. 7652
—— *Horae solitariae.* 7653
THOMAS, Robert Stuart, 1913– –Bibs. 881
THOMAS, STEPHENS AND GREEN, pprmkrs., Maidstone, est.1860. 2433
THOMAS, Thomas, Cambridge, 1553–88. 2259
THOMAS, William, Maidstone, d.1874. 2433
THOMAS, sir William Beach, 1868–1957– Bibs. 6494
THOMAS AND GREEN, pprmkrs., Wooburn

—— Bibs. 700 7710

URRY, John, 1666–1715–Chaucer's *Canterbury tales.* 5062

—— Chaucer's *Works.* 5046 5084–5 5095

URSWICK, Christopher, fl.1440–1522–Libr. 1539

USSHER, archbp. James, 1581–1656. **7711**

—— —— Collns. 7711

—— —— Mss. 1626 7711

UTLEY, Alison, 1884– . **7712**

—— Bibs. 7712

—— Collns. 7712

UTOPIAS–Bibs. 3707 3711

UXBRIDGE, Middlesex–Bibs. 4434

—— Ptg. 2884

VALE PRESS, 1896–1904. **2729**

VAMBERY, Arminius, 1832–1913. 763

VANBURGH, sir John, 1664–1726. **7713–14**

—— Bibs. 7713

—— Ptg. 7714

—— *The provoked wife.* 7714

VANDERBILT UNIVERSITY. LIBRARY–Collns. 1479 3636

VAN DER NOOT, Jan Baptista, 1539–40–90 *see* NOOT, Jan Baptista van der, 1539–40–90.

VANITY FAIR–Bibs. 3868

—— Illus. 3868

VAN VOORST, John, 1804–98. 3174

VAUGHAN, Frank, Windsor, 1873–1960. 1178

VAUGHAN, Henry, 1622–95. **7715–16**

—— Bibs. 7715

—— *Olor iscanus.* 7716

—— *Silex scintillans*–Bibs. 7715

VAUGHAN, Richard, 1904–83. **7717**

—— Bibs. 7717

VAUGHAN, Thomas, 17th cent. 7716

VENNARD, Richard, d.1615?–*True testimony.* 6043

VEPERY PRESS, Madras. 4401

VERMONT. UNIVERSITY. BAILEY-HOWE LIBRARY–Collns. 2295

VERNOR, HOOD AND SHARPE, 1806–12. 5927

VERPLANCK, Gulian Cromelin, 1786–1870. 7084

—— *Shakespeare.* 7080

VERSIFICATION–Bibs. 4406–7

'VERSIONING'. 84 361

VERTICAL TITLEPAGES *see* TITLEPAGES, VERTICAL.

VETERINARY SCIENCE–Collns. 1845

VICTOR GOLLANCZ, ltd., est.1927. 2430

VICTORIA, Aust. STATE LIBRARY, Melbourne–Collns. 487 551 1179 5158

VICTORIA, B.C. UNIVERSITY. LIBRARY–Collns. 5737 5739 5741 5748

VICTORIA AND ALBERT MUSEUM, South Kensington, London. LIBRARY. 1713

—— —— Collns. 2351 2490 3433 3476 3870 6794

VIDEO SPECTRAL COMPARATOR. 392

VIKING BOOKS (Viking press)–Bibs. 3361

VILLAGE LIBRARIES *see* LIBRARIES, VILLAGE.

VILLIERS, George, 2d duke of Buckingham, 1628–87. **7719**

—— Bibs. 7719

—— *Works.* 6747

VINDICATION OF THE INTENDED ALTERATIONS, 1729. 1282

VIRGIL (Publius Vergilius Maro), 70–19–*Æneid.* 5839

VIRTUE, James Sprent, 1829–92–Trollope. 7694

VLACQ, Adrian, The Hague, 1600?–66? 6588

VODREY, Joseph Kelly, fl.1983–Libr. 2414

VOGELER, Heinrich Johann, 1872–1942. 7837

VOX STELLARUM–Ptg. 3281

VOYAGES *see* TRAVEL BOOKS.

VOYSEY, Charles Francis Annesley, 1857–1941. 2149

WADDELL, Helen Jane, 1889–1965. **7720–1**

—— Bibs. 7720–1

—— Collns. 7721

WADDIE AND COMPANY, Edinburgh, est.1860. 2889

WADE, Arthur Edward, fl.1970–*Flora Dubliniensis.* 3392

—— —— Publ. 3392

WADE, Arthur Sarsfield Wade, 1883–1959 *see* ROHMER, Sax, *pseud.*

WADE, Josiah, 1842–1908. 3029

WADSWORTH, Alfred Powell, Manchester,